FPGEE®
REVIEW

A COMPANION GUIDE TO
NAPLEX®: STRATEGIES, PRACTICE & REVIEW

JOHN A. KRIAK
PharmD

KAPLAN
PUBLISHING
New York

FPGEE® is a federally registered trademark and service mark owned by the National Association of Boards of Pharmacy (NABP), which neither sponsors nor endorses this product.

Published by Kaplan Publishing, a division of Kaplan, Inc.
750 Third Avenue
New York, NY 10017

978-1-5062-2978-2

10 9 8 7 6 5 4 3 2 1

Contents

About the Author

John A. Kriak, PharmD is an educational consultant for Kaplan Medical. He began working with Kaplan Medical in 1995 when we wrote the first version of the PCAT (Pharmacy College Admission Test) review book. Since then Dr. Kriak has worked as a content developer and question bank item writer for both NAPLEX and USMLE Step 1 and 2 programs. He received his Doctor of Pharmacy degree from the Duquesne University.

The author would like to acknowledge the outstanding Kaplan's *NAPLEX® Strategies, Practice, and Review* book authors: Amie D. Brooks, PharmD, FCCP, BCPS, BCACP; Cynthia Sanoski, BS, PharmD, FCCP, BCPS; Emily R. Hajjar, PharmD, BCPS, BCACP, CGP; Brian R. Overholser, PharmD, FCCP.

The author would also like to acknowledge the contributions of Dr. Alexander Stone Macnow, MD, and the Kaplan Editorial Team.

For My Children: Christopher, Alexander, Madison, Mackenzie & Camden...
You are my world... You are the future!

Unit I

Overview of Kaplan FPGEE Preparation

How to Use This Book

Congratulations! You are now on your way to prepare for the Foreign Pharmacy Graduate Equivalency Examination (FPGEE®). The content within this book contains the high-yield information needed for you to perform well on exam day.

Note: This book is designed to be used in conjunction with **Kaplan's *NAPLEX® Strategies, Practice, and Review* book**, which covers foundational and clinical pharmacy. Using both books in combination will provide you with the necessary information to do your best on exam day.

Note that NOT all the information contained in the NAPLEX book is required for the FPGEE. Therefore, we have included a "User's Guide" to help guide you through your study.

1. Review the table of contents for both the NAPLEX and FPGEE books to get a basic understanding of the layout for each book.
2. Review each section found within the Complete NAPLEX Review Book User's Guide in Unit II to fully understand how both review texts are integrated.
3. Choose the method of study that works best for you: either review both texts side-by-side OR review the FPGEE text first and then the NAPLEX text, paying close attention to the independent FPGEE-focused review of the *NAPLEX Strategies, Practice, and Review* text to focus on only the highest-yield NAPLEX concepts.
4. Begin your review!

Review Structure

The content of this book is designed to provide a focused and succinct review of each competency area tested on the FPGEE. It is not intended to replace a standard pharmacy textbook and/or reference source. However, along with Kaplan's NAPLEX book, these two texts should be your primary review materials prior to exam day.

Kaplan recommends that you begin your FPGEE review process in "non-strength" areas. Therefore you can devote additional time to review these more difficult concepts.

Since this book is used in conjunction with the NAPLEX review text, here is a brief overview of the layout of that text. The NAPLEX review is arranged by disease states, focusing on the following:

- Definitions of the disease
- Diagnosis
- Signs and symptoms
- Guidelines
- Guidelines summary
- Medication charts
- Storage & administration pearls
- Patient education pearls

At the end of each chapter there are a few practice questions. These questions can help you review and apply the content that you have just reviewed.

FPGEE Introduction and Test-Taking Strategies

FPGEE OVERVIEW

The Foreign Pharmacy Graduate Equivalency Examination, or FPGEE, is delivered by the National Association of Boards of Pharmacy (NABP®) and used by the Foreign Pharmacy Graduate Examination Committee™ (FPGEC) and individual state boards of pharmacy as part of their assessment of competence to practice pharmacy in the United States.

To take the FPGEE, you must meet the eligibility requirements of the FPGEC. A detailed description of the requirements can be found on the NABP website at **nabp.net.**

The FPGEC is also responsible for the candidate certification process and operates under the direction of the NABP. The committee will determine your eligibility in accordance with their policies, which include providing documents on your educational background and foreign licensure as well as passing the FPGEE and the Test of English as a Foreign Language™ (TOEFL®) Internet-based Test (iBT).

FPGEC certification permits foreign graduates to partially fulfill eligibility requirements for licensure in the particular states that require the certification. Thus, FPGEC certification is not a license to practice pharmacy. In order to practice in the United States, you must be licensed in the state you wish to practice.

FPGEE Content and Structure

The FPGEE is a computer-adaptive test, consisting of 250 multiple-choice questions administered over 5 1/2 hours. The exam is administered 2x/year at over 200 Pearson VUE testing centers in the United States. The questions represent most of the topics covered in pharmacy school, with a focus on the clinical and practical content.

In the past, only multiple-choice and K-type questions appeared on the FPGEE. However, today there are a variety of question types on the exam. The newer question formats include:

- Multiple choice
- Multiple response
- Constructed response
- Ordered response
- Hot spot

Each type of question is described with examples in the following section. These example are designed ONLY to represent the question structure rather than to highlight actual FPGEE content.

Multiple Choice

Multiple choice is the most common type of question on the exam.

Which of the following is the most likely serious complication of gentamicin toxicity?

(A) Drowsiness
(B) Hepatotoxicity
(C) Hypotension
(D) Nephrotoxicity
(E) Pulmonary fibrosis

Multiple Response

Multiple response questions have replaced the K-style questions on the FPGEE. The approach is to view each answer choice as a True or False answer/statement.

A patient who is prescribed enalapril should be counseled on the potential development of which of the following? (Select **ALL** that apply.)

(A) Corneal opacities
(B) Chronic cough
(C) Hypercalcemia
(D) Hyperkalemia
(E) Pulmonary fibrosis

Constructed Response

Constructed response questions are basically “fill-in-the-blank.” These often appear in calculation-type questions where you are asked to provide an answer to the nearest whole number. The NABP provided examples where the units of the final answer have been stated in the question. Thus, provide only numeric responses.

The “Sig” for a lactulose prescription for a patient with severe constipation is “15 mL bid × 7 days with 2 refill.” How many total mL will be dispensed if the patient gets all of the refills filled? (Answer must be numeric; round the final answer to the nearest **WHOLE** number.)

Ordered Response

Ordered response questions ask the candidate to assign ranks to an unordered list of options. The NABP has listed a sample question in this format to rank topical corticosteroids from highest to lowest potencies. We have provided an example using the potencies of the opioid analgesics.

Rank the following opioid analgesics from highest to lowest potency. (**ALL** options must be used.)

Unordered Options	Ordered Response
Codeine	
Fentanyl	
Morphine	
Oxycodone	

Hot Spot

Hot spot questions ask you to identify a part of a diagram, such as identifying within an HIV life cycle diagram the correct portion during which maraviroc exerts its mechanism of action. We have provided an example using the site of action for diuretics in the nephron.

> Using the diagram below, identify where on the nephron hydrochlorothiazide would exert the greatest effect. (Select the TEXT response, and left-click the mouse. To change your answer, move the cursor, select an alternate TEXT response and click.)

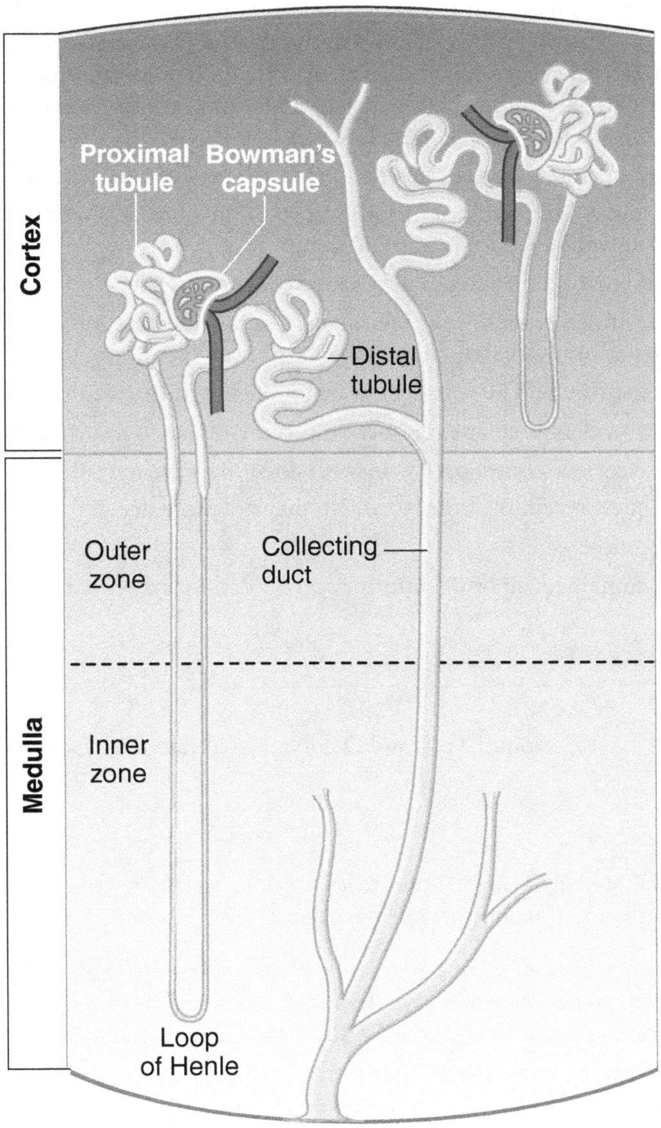

How Is the FPGEE Scored?

Your FPGEE score is a scaled score. It is not a percentile or number-correct score. The scale is 0–150, with a **minimum passing score of 75.** The algorithms for determining your scaled score are highly confidential and are not released to the public.

Your FPGEE score will be released on a secure website approximately 8 weeks after the exam.

CAT Format

The computer-adaptive test (CAT) nature of the exam organizes questions based on the accuracy of your response to the previous question. This type of testing ensures that the questions are organized based on your skill level. For example, one question may be easier, then the next is more difficult. If you miss a question, the following question may be easier. Using this format, the computer is able to calculate your overall level of competence. Additional information about the FPGEE exam format include the following:

- Focus on answering the questions correctly and not on the apparent ease or difficulty of a given series of questions.
- The exam is 5 hours and 30 minutes, not including a 30 minute break. That means there is approximately 1 minute 19 seconds to complete each of the 250 questions.
- There is a timer at the top of the screen to help gauge your progress.
- You will be provided with an erasable note board and pen during the exam. Use the board to help you eliminate answer choices, perform calculations, etc.
- On the computer screen, you will be able to activate an on-screen calculator.
- You are not permitted to change an answer once you have confirmed it as an answer choice.
- You cannot go back to review a question (or answer) once you have moved on to the next question.
- You must answer all questions in the order in which they are presented.
- You cannot skip a question.
- Each question is self-contained; all of the information needed to answer a question is presented on the computer screen.

FPGEE Registration

The FPGEE is administered 2x/year, around April and October. Go to **nabp.net** for more information.

FPGEE BLUEPRINT

The questions on the FPGEE are based on U.S. pharmacy school curriculum, which includes the basic biomedical sciences as well as both clinical and nonclinical pharmacy content.

The FPGEE Competency Statements provide a blueprint of the topics covered on the exam. In 2015, the NABP revised the blueprint and competency statements for the FPGEE to reflect the expanded role of today's clinical pharmacist. The layout of this book parallels the current FPGEE competency statements:

- **Each chapter is based on the competency statement categories.**
- **The objectives for each chapter are based on the FPGEE competency statements.**

The major competence areas are as follows:

- **Competence Area 1:** Basic Biomedical Sciences (10% of exam)
- **Competence Area 2:** Pharmaceutical Sciences (33% of exam)
- **Competence Area 3:** Social/Behavioral/Administrative Sciences (22% of exam)
- **Competence Area 4:** Clinical Sciences (35% of exam)

For specific competency statements under each competence area, go to **nabp.net**.

TEST-TAKING STRATEGIES

As you review each chapter in this book, it is imperative that you focus on personal areas of weakness.

Maximizing Your Study Results

- Determine your strengths and weaknesses. This can be accomplished by briefly reviewing the content in both the FPGEE and NAPLEX review texts as well as taking the Pre-FPGEE (see nabp.net for more information).
- Review your weakest subjects first, then review all other areas, and then come back to your weak areas.
- Design a study schedule and make adjustments according to your progress. Your schedule should include time for family, work, and leisure activities. Be sure to schedule extra time before exam day to revisit your weaker areas.
- When reviewing the content, try to imagine possible exam question scenarios. For example, when reviewing a table in the FPGEE review text, ask yourself, "What types of questions could be derived from this content?"
- In the NAPLEX review text, focus heavily on the Top 200 drugs identified with a star (☆) in the tables throughout.
- When reviewing a practice question, make sure you understand why your correct answers were correct and why your incorrect answer choices were incorrect.

General Test-Taking Strategies

- If you find yourself unable to answer a question, guess. There is no penalty for guessing wrong.
- Do not spend too much time analyzing a question; remember you have about 1 minute 19 seconds per question, so you must keep moving. Simply guess.
- There are experimental questions on the exam that aren't calculated into your final score, so if you miss one of these, it will not be counted.
- Try to quickly narrow down the answer choices before selecting an answer. Eliminate the obviously wrong answers. This will make your chances of getting a "guess" correct.
- Keep a positive attitude in your studying and on exam day. If you have a bad day or get a tough question, don't let it bother you. Once you choose an answer, forget about it and move on.

RELEVANCE OF NAPLEX TO THE FPGEE

The NAPLEX is designed to evaluate knowledge of pharmacy practice in the United States. Specifically, it evaluates whether a prospective pharmacist is able to:

- Recognize current practice standards for safe and effective pharmacotherapy
- Recognize safe and effective procedures of preparing and dispensing medications
- Optimize therapeutic outcomes in individual patients
- Deliver health-related information to both patients and other healthcare professionals to promote optimal patient outcomes

The NAPLEX assesses whether a pharmacy school graduate is able to safely and effectively practice pharmacy in the United States.

Relevance of NAPLEX to FPGEE

Like the NAPLEX, the FPGEE also evaluates whether a foreign pharmacy school graduate is able to safely and effectively practice pharmacy in the United States. The main difference between both examinations is that the NAPLEX primarily focuses on the general pharmacy and clinical aspects of pharmacy school curriculum, whereas the FPGEE evaluates knowledge of the "entire" pharmacy school curriculum. More specifically:

The NAPLEX and FPGEE require proficiency in **pharmaceutical sciences** and **clinical sciences**.

The FPGEE also requires proficiency in **basic biomedical sciences** and **social/behavioral/administrative pharmacy sciences.** (Note: Some social/behavioral/administrative principles are starting to appear on the NAPLEX.)

Kaplan's *NAPLEX Strategies, Practice, and Review* book primarily focuses on the pharmaceutical and clinical science requirements of the NAPLEX. Many of the concepts covered in this review book are **directly** applicable to the FPGEE. However, the FPGEE Focused Review of the NAPLEX Text section will help identify high-yield topics (tested on the FPGEE) and streamline the review process.

Unit II

FPGEE-Focused Review of the NAPLEX Text

Complete NAPLEX Review Book User's Guide

USING KAPLAN'S NAPLEX REVIEW BOOK IN CONJUNCTION WITH FPGEE REVIEW BOOK

The NAPLEX and FPGEE share many similarities in the general and clinical pharmacy competency requirements. However, the basic biomedical sciences and social/behavioral/administrative sciences are also covered on the FPGEE. Thus, only the highest-yield general and clinical pharmacy concepts (required for the NAPLEX) will appear on the FPGEE. Likewise only the highest-yield topics found in Kaplan's *NAPLEX Strategies, Practice, and Review* book will be tested on the FPGEE.

The FPGEE-focused review of the NAPLEX text is designed to help you outline and easily access high-yield topics in Kaplan's *NAPLEX Strategies, Practice, and Review* book. This "User's Guide" outlines 2 options to accommodate different learning styles.

Option 1: FPGEE Book Chapter Guide to NAPLEX Content

Provides a Kaplan NAPLEX text content roadmap that follows the Kaplan *FPGEE Review* book chapter (and chapter section) organization found in Unit III of this text.

- This first option has been designed to help you review one topic at a time in its entirety. For example, the Pharmacogenomics and Genetics chapter in Unit III (FPGEE Comprehensive Review) discusses selected FPGEE specific concepts and also references material in the NAPLEX text.
- This method of study requires the simultaneous use of both textbooks.

Option 2: Independent FPGEE-focused review of the *NAPLEX Strategies, Practice, and Review* Text

Provides a FPGEE-focused review of the entire *NAPLEX Strategies, Practice, and Review* book starting on page 1 and ending on the last page of content review.

- This second option has been provided for candidates who may want to review one textbook at a time. For example, you may want to first review the "general" medicinal chemistry concepts discussed in Unit III (of this text) and then at a later date review the "clinical" concepts discussed in the NAPLEX text.
- This review ALSO provides detailed chapter-specific tables that outline the high-yield FPGEE-specific concepts in the NAPLEX text.
- This method of study allows for independent use of each textbook.
- **It is strongly recommended that you reference these tables when reviewing the NAPLEX content from any reference source in this book.**

Option 3 would be to review ALL the concepts in both textbooks. However, our recommendation is that you first become proficient in the high-yield NAPLEX topics and then (if time permits) begin to review additional concepts in the NAPLEX text.

Now let's begin!

FPGEE BOOK CHAPTER GUIDE TO NAPLEX CONTENT

The FPGEE Book Chapter Guide to NAPLEX Content provides a high-yield outline of essential concepts from Kaplan's *NAPLEX Strategies, Practice, and Review* book. Each bullet point briefly outlines the high-yield content in the NAPLEX text (in the appropriate section) that you should review when studying that particular chapter.

Here are some key points to consider when using this Kaplan FPGEE Book chapter guide to NAPLEX content:

- Kaplan's *NAPLEX Strategies, Practice, and Review* book only provides information on selected FPGEE concepts—hence, the need for two separate textbooks (FPGEE Review and NAPLEX Review).
- The FPGEE exam evaluates the *entire* pharmacy curriculum; hence, only the highest-yield therapeutic and pharmacy practice concepts in the *NAPLEX Strategies, Practice, and Review* book are likely to be tested on the FPGEE.
- When reviewing this chapter guide, there may be additional concepts related to a competency statement NOT covered in the NAPLEX book (see below).
- Unit III of this text provides a comprehensive review of the subject matter associated with each FPGEE competency statement as well as the references provided in this chapter guide.

The recommended FPGEE concepts in the NAPLEX book may vary between chapters and/or drug classes. For example, a bullet point may indicate that adverse effects should be known for one drug class but not another. Also, while MOST adverse effects are important for the NAPLEX, only the highest-yield adverse effects are relevant for the FGPEE.

- These same concepts can be applied to other NAPLEX/FPGEE topics.

There are instances where you will see duplicate NAPLEX text references. For example, the NAPLEX text reference is the same for the FPGEE pharmacokinetics and FPGEE clinical pharmacokinetics chapters (9 and 24, respectively).

Finally, before you get started, remember that Unit III (FPGEE Comprehensive Review) is your recommended primary study source.

FPGEE Book Chapter Guide to NAPLEX Content

Part 1 – Basic Biomedical Sciences

Chapter 2: Biochemistry

Enzymology and coenzymes and kinetics

- NAPLEX Reference: **Over-the-Counter Medications chapter** (Vitamins)
- Know both vitamin designations (i.e. B1 and thiamine) as well as deficiency manifestation.

Part 2 – Pharmaceutical Sciences

Chapter 5: Medicinal Chemistry

Physicochemical drug properties related to ADME and therapeutics effects

- NAPLEX Reference: **Pharmaceutics chapter** (Physical Pharmacy)
- Review all of the content on these pages with a focus on Solubility and Lipophilicity, Ionization Behavior, as well as Rate and Half-Life Equations.

Impact of drug chemistry and drug metabolism on therapeutic decisions

- NAPLEX Reference: **Biopharmaceutics and Drug Disposition chapter** (Drug Metabolism)
- All of the concepts are important; however, memorization of common drugs for each metabolism pathway is lower yield.

Chapter 6: Pharmacology and Toxicology

Drug development

- NAPLEX Reference: **Health Policy chapter** (FDA regulatory process)
- Basic knowledge of New Drug Application (NDA) process, Investigational New Drugs, and clinical trial phases and objectives is needed.

Drug toxicology

- NAPLEX Reference: **Antidotes chapter** (Antidotes, General Antidotes)
- Knowledge of antidote definitions, acute poisoning principles, and general antidotes is needed. From tables, know toxic/overdose substance along with generic and brand name of antidote. The rest of the content is lower yield.

Chapter 7: Pharmacognosy and Dietary Supplements

Natural product principles and drug classes

- NAPLEX Reference: **Over-the-Counter Medications chapter** (Top 10 Herbals and Supplements)
- Focus on the brand and the generic drug names, uses, indications, and primary side effects.

Dietary Supplements

- NAPLEX Reference: **Over-the-Counter Medications chapter** (Vitamins)
- Know vitamin designations (i.e. B1 and thiamine) as well as deficiency manifestation.

Chapter 8: Pharmaceutics/Biopharmaceutics

Principles of drug delivery and dosage forms

- NAPLEX Reference: **Pharmaceutics chapter** (Pharmaceutical Dosage Forms) **and Biopharmaceutics and Drug Disposition chapter**
- All of the pharmaceutics concepts covered on these pages are important. For biopharmaceutics and drug disposition, focus on absorption, volume of distribution, plasma protein binding, phase I and II reactions, enzyme inhibition, drugs involved in inhibition and induction of metabolic enzymes, genetic variability, and common drugs metabolized by pathway.

Chapter 9: Pharmacokinetics

Principles of pharmacokinetics

- NAPLEX Reference: **Pharmacokinetics chapter** and **Biopharmaceutics and Drug Disposition chapter**
- All of the pharmacokinetics concepts covered in this chapter are high-yield topics. For biopharmaceutics and drug disposition focus on absorption, volume of distribution, plasma protein binding, phase I and II reactions, enzyme inhibition, drugs involved in inhibition and induction of metabolic enzymes, genetic variability, and common drugs metabolized by pathway.

Chapter 10: Pharmacogenomics and Genetics

Clinical pharmacogenomics and genetic principles

- NAPLEX Reference: **Pharmacogenomics chapter** and **Biopharmaceutics and Drug Disposition chapter** (focus on Drug Metabolism)
- All of the pharmacogenomics concepts covered in the Pharmacogenomics chapter and Drug Metabolism section of the Biopharmaceutics chapter are high-yield topics. For biopharmaceutics and drug disposition,

focus on absorption, volume of distribution, and plasma protein. You should be able to apply these principles to clinical scenarios on the FPGEE.

Chapter 11: Sterile and Nonsterile Compounding

Extemporaneous prescription preparation and dosage form calculations

- NAPLEX Reference: **Calculation chapter**
- Be familiar with all of the calculations in this chapter. You should be able to perform the basic pharmacy calculations depicted on these pages.

Part 3 – Social/Behavioral/Administrative Sciences

Chapter 17: Biostatistics and Research Study Design

Introduction to research study design

- NAPLEX Reference: **Biostatistics chapter**
- Be familiar with all of concepts in this chapter. You should be able to answer questions on descriptive and inferential statistics, as well as be able to answer questions on central tendency, variability, distributions, and standard deviations. You should also be proficient in statistical test selection and clinical trial design.

Chapter 20: Social and Behavioral Aspects of Pharmacy Practice

Death and dying

- NAPLEX Reference: **Pain Management chapter**
- Pain management is a high-yield topic for the FPGEE. You should be familiar with all of the information covered on these pages with a focus on the drugs, mechanism of action (MOA), Contraindications, Primary Side Effects, Drug Interactions, and Med Pearls.

Part 4 – Clinical Sciences

Chapter 22: Evidence-Based Pharmacy Practice

Interpretation and evaluation of drug information

- NAPLEX Reference: **Drug Information chapter**
- You should be knowledgeable about each of the most commonly used references in pharmacy, including an understanding of the clinical content found in each reference.

Medication therapy management

- NAPLEX Reference: **Health Policy chapter** (Medication Therapy management)
- You should be knowledgeable about the principles of medication therapy management including goal, objective, and types of services provided.

Chapter 23: Clinical Pathophysiology

Clinical application of pathophysiological principles

- NAPLEX Reference: **Cardiovascular, Endocrine, and Respiratory chapters** (Hypertension, Dyslipidemia, Heart Failure, Diabetes, and Asthma)
- High-yield disease states for the FPGEE include hypertension, dyslipidemia, heart failure, diabetes mellitus, and asthma. You should be familiar with the pathophysiology of these conditions.

Chapter 24: Clinical Pharmacokinetics

Clinical application of pharmacokinetic data

- NAPLEX Reference: **Pharmacokinetics chapters**
- All of the pharmacokinetics concepts covered in this chapter are high-yield topics. You should be able to apply these principles to clinical scenarios on the FPGEE.

Chapter 25: Pharmacogenomics

Application of pharmacogenomic data to drug therapy

- NAPLEX Reference: **Pharmacogenomics chapter** and **Biopharmaceutics and Drug Disposition chapter** (focus on Drug Metabolism)
- All of the pharmacogenomics concepts covered in the Pharmacogenomics chapter and Drug Metabolism section of the Biopharmaceutics chapter are high-yield topics. You should be able to apply these principles to clinical scenarios on the FPGEE.

Chapter 26: Disease Prevention and U.S. Population Health

Health, wellness, and disease prevention with pharmacological and nonpharmacological therapies

- NAPLEX Reference: **Preventative Medicine chapter** (Weight Loss, Smoking Cessation) **Over-the-Counter Medications chapter**
- Focus on the general principles of weight loss and smoking cessation as well as the medications used to treat these conditions. For the over-the-counter medications, know how to diagnose and apply guideline recommendations to these conditions as well as know the medication tables.

Immunizations

- NAPLEX Reference: **Preventative Medicine chapter** (Immunizations)
- Focus on the live vs. attenuated vaccines as well as brand and generic names, route of administration, and target population for each vaccine.

Chapter 27: Patient Assessment

Clinical laboratory and diagnostic tests

- NAPLEX Reference: **Clinical Lab Tests chapter**
- Be familiar with normal laboratory test values. You should also be able to recognize both normal and abnormal laboratory values.

Chapter 28: Therapeutic Decision Making

Introduction to therapeutic decision making

- NAPLEX Reference: **Therapeutics chapters**
- See Independent FPGEE-focused review of the *NAPLEX Strategies, Practice, and Review* text for specific recommendations.
- **The tables in the Independent FPGEE-focused review of the *NAPLEX Strategies, Practice, and Review* text should be reviewed prior to studying this content. These tables outline the highest-yield concepts for the FPGEE.**

Therapeutic drug concentrations

- NAPLEX Reference: **Clinical Lab Tests chapter** (Therapeutic Drug Levels)
- You should know the normal therapeutic values for the drugs listed in this table.

Individualized, evidence-based pharmacotherapeutic drug regimens and treatment plans: from diagnosis to follow-up

- NAPLEX Reference: **Therapeutics chapters**
- **See the Complete NAPLEX Review Book User's Guide in Unit II of this text for guidance on high-yield topics.**
- **The tables in the Independent FPGEE-focused review of the *NAPLEX Strategies, Practice, and Review* text should be reviewed prior to studying this content. These tables outline the highest-yield concepts for the FPGEE.**

Promotion of nonprescription and natural products

- NAPLEX Reference: **Over-the-Counter Medications chapter**
- For the nonprescription and natural products, know how to diagnose and apply guideline recommendations to these conditions as well as know the medication tables.

Management of drug toxicity and drug-induced diseases

- NAPLEX Reference: **Antidotes chapter**
- Basic knowledge of antidote definitions, acute poisoning principles, and general antidotes is needed. From the tables, focus on toxic/overdose substance along with generic and brand name of antidote. The rest of content is lower yield.

INDEPENDENT FPGEE-FOCUSED REVIEW OF THE *NAPLEX STRATEGIES, PRACTICE, AND REVIEW* TEXT

This section provides a FPGEE-focused review of the entire *NAPLEX Strategies, Practice, and Review* book, starting on page 1 and ending the last page of content review. Whereas the FPGEE Book Chapter Guide to NAPLEX Content follows the chapter/section arrangement of Unit III in this book, this User's Guide follows the chapter outline of the NAPLEX book.

When reviewing the material presented in this chapter, you should understand the following:

- The information provided in this chapter is designed to highlight the high-yield concepts and principles covered in Kaplan's *NAPLEX Strategies, Practice, and Review* book. Additional concepts not mentioned in this review guide (and provided in the NAPLEX text) may appear on the FPGEE. Ideally, you should review and become proficient in ALL of the concepts discussed in the NAPLEX review text. For example, the highest-yield clinical chapters in the NAPLEX text are cardiovascular, infectious disease, endocrinology, gastrointestinal, pain management, psychiatric disorders, bone and joint disorders, and dermatologic disorders. However, there may be some questions from the oncology and antidotes chapters.
- The page numbers in the NAPLEX text and FPGEE competency statements corresponding to each NAPLEX chapter have been provided.
- The guidance section in each chapter review will provide a list of the highest-yield sections in each NAPLEX chapter followed by a table that provides a detailed review of concepts covered throughout the entire chapter.
- The questions at the end of each NAPLEX text chapter cover only high-yield topics; hence, you should know the concepts covered in these questions.

Under the highest-yield concepts section of each topic (i.e. hypertension) there is a recommendation to know various components of each drug table, such as mechanism of action (MOA), primary side effect, etc. You should have a general understanding of each of these components.

- For example, the MOA for ACE inhibitors is listed as follows: inhibit angiotensin-converting enzyme and prevent the conversion of angiotensin I to angiotensin II → vasodilation, ↓ aldosterone production; also inhibit degradation of bradykinin.

- You should know that enalapril (ACE inhibitor) inhibits the conversion of angiotensin I to angiotensin II and inhibits bradykinin degradation. You do NOT need to know the formal mechanism but should be able to make an association.
- As for side effects and contraindications, do NOT memorize a laundry list of each, but be familiar with different side effects, i.e. do not memorize nausea, vomiting, and dizziness, since these are commonly seen with many medications.

High-Yield Chapter Topics

Cardiovascular Disorders Chapter

FPGEE competency statements discussed in chapter

- 4.2.1 Clinical application of pathophysiological principles
- 4.7.3 Individualized assessment of pharmacotherapeutic drug regimens
- 4.7.5 Patient-centered, culturally-relevant treatment plans

Guidance

- Highest-yield sections: Hypertension, Dyslipidemia, Heart Failure, Antithrombotic Drugs

Topic	Highest-Yield Concepts
Hypertension	• Guidelines summary for hypertension diagnosis and treatment in different patient populations • Diuretics – Know mechanism of action (MOA), contraindications, differing side effects, Med Pearls • Beta-Blockers – Know B1 vs B1B2, contraindication, side effects, Med Pearls • ACE inhibitors and ARBS – Know MOA, contraindications, primary side effects, drug interactions • Calcium Channel Blockers – DHPs vs non-DHPs, contraindications, side effects, Med Pearls • Alpha 1 antagonists, A2 agonists, direct vasodilators – MOA, contraindications, side effects, Med Pearls • Patient education pearls
Dyslipidemia	• Factors that need to be considered when evaluating whether or not a patient is a candidate for statin therapy • Guidelines summary for diagnosis and treatment • Bile Acid Resins, Niacin, Fibric Acid Derivatives, Omea-2, Statins – MOA, contraindications, primary side effects, key monitoring • Patient education pearls
Heart failure	• Medications worsening CHF, signs and symptoms, guideline summary • Loop diuretics, ACE inhibitors, ARBs and Beta Blockers, Digoxin, Aldosterone Receptor Antagonists, Hydralazine - MOA, contraindications, primary side effects, drug interactions, Med Pearls • Patient education pearls
Antiarrhythmic drugs	• Antiarrhythmics – Know drug class (1A, III, etc), primary side effects. • Extra: Amiodarone – Know Med Pearls

(Continued)

Topic	Highest-Yield Concepts
Antithrombotic drugs	• Vitamin K antagonist (Warfarin) – MOA, contraindications, primary side effects, Drug interactions, Med Pearls, antidotes • Direct thrombin inhibitor, Factor Xa inhibitor – MOA, contraindications, Med Pearls
Ischemic heart disease	• Definition of ischemic heart disease
Acute pharmacologic management of UA/NSTEMI and STEMI	• Anti-Ischemic and Analgesic Therapy + Antiplatelet therapy (know theory; dosing is lower yield)
Secondary prevention of MI	• Theory on drugs of choice • Anticoagulants, fibrinolytics - MOA, contraindications, primary side effects, drug interactions, Med Pearls, antidotes (if available)
Learning points	• Understand the principles surrounding each of the learning points.

Infectious Diseases Chapter

FPGEE competency statements discussed in chapter

- 1.3.2 Pathogenic microorganisms
- 4.7.3 Individualized assessment of pharmacotherapeutic drug regimens
- 4.7.5 Patient-centered, culturally-relevant treatment plans

Guidance

- Highest-yield sections: Urinary Tract Infections, Pneumonia, Sexually Transmitted Diseases, Human Immunodeficiency Virus, Medication Charts: Antibacterial, Antifungal, and Antiviral Agents.

Topic	Highest-Yield Concepts
Principles of antibiotic therapy	• Factors to consider when selecting antibiotic therapy
Urinary tract infections	• Common organisms for UTI • Treatments for acute cystitis and pyelonephritis (outpatient and inpatient)
Pneumonia	• Differentiate organisms between community-acquired and hospital-acquired pneumonia. • Treatments of choice for each type of pneumonia
Meningitis	• Organisms by age group • Empiric treatment by age group
Otitis media	• Common organisms • Recommended antibiotic therapy for management of uncomplicated AOM • Duration of therapy
Sexually transmitted diseases	• Causative organisms • Guidelines summary

(Continued)

Topic	Highest-Yield Concepts
Skin and soft tissue infections	• Common organisms • Guidelines summary
Invasive fungal infections	• Drugs of choice for selected invasive fungal infections
Medication Charts: Antibacterial agents	• For ALL antibacterials – For each agent, know drug class contraindications, primary side effects, and Med Pearls. • NOTE: Spectrum of activity is important, but do NOT memorize each of the bacteria listed. However, knowing the drugs used in Pseudomonas, MRSA, and atypical bacteria is important.
Medication Charts: Antifungal agents	• For ALL antifungals – For each agent, know drug class contraindications, primary side effects, and Med Pearls. • Azole antifungals – Know drug interactions.
Medication Charts: Antiviral agents	• For ALL antivirals – Know spectrum of activity, contraindications, primary side effects, and Med Pearls.
Human immunodeficiency virus	• Guidelines summary • Know drugs of choice for prophylaxis and treatment of opportunistic infections in patients with HIV. • For ALL HIV medications – Know drug class.
Tuberculosis	• Guidelines summary • For ALL tuberculosis medications – Know primary side effects and Med Pearls.
Learning Points	• Understand the principles surrounding each of the learning points.

Pulmonary Disorders Chapter

FPGEE competency statements discussed in chapter

- 4.2.1 Clinical application of pathophysiological principles
- 4.7.3 Individualized assessment of pharmacotherapeutic drug regimens
- 4.7.5 Patient-centered, culturally-relevant treatment plans

Guidance

- Highest-yield sections: Asthma and COPD

Topic	Highest-Yield Concepts
Asthma	• Diagnosis • Signs and symptoms • Guidelines summary • Asthma treatment summary • For ALL asthma medications – Know MOA, contraindications, primary side effects, and Med Pearls.

(Continued)

Topic	Highest-Yield Concepts
Chronic obstructive pulmonary disease	• Guidelines summary • COPD treatment summary • For ALL COPD medications – Know MOA, contraindications, primary side effects, and Med Pearls.
Learning Points	• Understand the principles surrounding each of the learning points.

Endocrine Disorders Chapter

FPGEE competency statements discussed in chapter

- 4.2.1 Clinical application of pathophysiological principles
- 4.7.3 Individualized assessment of pharmacotherapeutic drug regimens
- 4.7.5 Patient-centered, culturally-relevant treatment plans

Guidance

- Highest-yield section: Diabetes Mellitus

Topic	Highest-Yield Concepts
Diabetes mellitus	• Type 1 vs Type 2 definitions • Diagnosis • Signs and symptoms • Diabetes complications • Treatment algorithm • Insulin – Know classification, onset, peak, duration, and comments. • For ALL type 2 diabetes medications – Know MOA, drug classes, contraindications, primary side effects, and Med Pearls. • Patient education pearls
Hypothyroidism	• Drugs for hypothyroidism – Know T4 vs T3 component, contraindications, and Med Pearls
Hyperthyroidism	• Drugs for hyperthyroidism – Know MOA, primary side effects, and Med Pearls.
Polycystic ovarian syndrome	• Guidelines summary
Learning Points	• Understand the principles surrounding each of the learning points.

Neurological Disorders Chapter

FPGEE competency statements discussed in chapter

- 4.7.3 Individualized assessment of pharmacotherapeutic drug regimens
- 4.7.5 Patient-centered, culturally-relevant treatment plans

Guidance

- Highest-yield sections: Epilepsy, Parkinson's Disease, Migraine Headache

Topic	Highest-Yield Concepts
Multiple sclerosis	• Guidelines summary • Disease-modifying drugs – indications and Med Pearls • Patient education pearls
Epilepsy	• Definitions • Signs and symptoms • Guidelines summary • ALL anti-epileptic drugs – Know indications and Med Pearls. • For Carbamazepine, valproic acid, phenytoin – Know primary side effects. • Selected AED drug interactions – Know AED comment (i.e. Carbamazepine strong CYP3A4 inducer) • Patient education pearls
Parkinson's disease	• Signs and symptoms • Summary of treatment recommendations • ALL drugs for Parkinson's disease – MOA, Med Pearls • Patient education pearls
Migraine headache	• Summary of treatment recommendations • ALL drugs for migraine – MOA, primary side effects, Med Pearls • Patient education pearls
Alzheimer's disease	• Guidelines summary • ALL drugs for Alzheimer's Disease – MOA, primary side effects, Med Pearls • Patient education pearls
Learning Points	• Understand the principles surrounding each of the learning points.

Gastrointestinal Disorders Chapter

FPGEE competency statements discussed in chapter

- 4.7.3 Individualized assessment of pharmacotherapeutic drug regimens
- 4.7.5 Patient-centered, culturally-relevant treatment plans

Guidance

- Highest-yield sections: Gastroesophageal reflux disease/peptic ulcer disease

Topic	Highest-Yield Concepts
Gastroesophageal reflux disease/peptic ulcer disease	• Definitions • Signs and symptoms • Guidelines summary • ALL GERD/PUD drugs – MOA, drug interactions, Med Pearls • Side effects for metoclopramide • Patient education pearls

(Continued)

Topic	Highest-Yield Concepts
Inflammatory bowel disease	• Signs and symptoms • Guidelines summary • ALL IBD drugs – General MOA, Med Pearls
Learning Points	• Understand the principles surrounding each of the learning points.

Viral Hepatitis Chapter

FPGEE competency statements discussed in chapter

- 4.7.3 Individualized assessment of pharmacotherapeutic drug regimens
- 4.7.5 Patient-centered, culturally-relevant treatment plans

Guidance

- Highest-yield sections: General review of sections only

Topic	Highest-Yield Concepts
Hepatitis B	• Guidelines summary • Recognize indications for ALL hepatitis B drugs
Hepatitis C	• Guidelines summary • Recognize indications for ALL hepatitis C drugs

Renal Disorders Chapter

FPGEE competency statements discussed in chapter

- 4.7.3 Individualized assessment of pharmacotherapeutic drug regimens
- 4.7.5 Patient-centered, culturally-relevant treatment plans

Guidance

- Highest-yield sections: Renal Disorders

Topic	Highest-Yield Concepts
Renal disorders	• Guidelines summary • Estimating renal clearance (Know equation.) • Be familiar with medications requiring dose adjustment in renal disease. (Do NOT memorize the entire list.) • ALL renal drugs – Indications, primary side effects, Med Pearls

Oncology Chapter

FPGEE competency statements discussed in chapter

- 4.7.3 Individualized assessment of pharmacotherapeutic drug regimens
- 4.7.5 Patient-centered, culturally-relevant treatment plans

Guidance

- Highest-yield sections: Cancer Drugs and Supportive Care

Topic	Highest-Yield Concepts
Lymphoma	• Briefly review
Leukemia	• Briefly review
Lung cancer	• Briefly review
Colorectal cancer	• Briefly review
Breast cancer	• Briefly review
Prostate cancer	• Briefly review
Ovarian cancer	• Briefly review
Cancer drugs	• ALL cancer drugs – Recognize drug class and primary side effects. • Chemotherapy agents: Common adverse effects
Supportive care	• Nausea and vomiting • Management of neutropenia and anemia • Antiemetic drugs – MOA, primary side effect, Med Pearls • Colony-stimulating factors – MOA, primary side effects, key monitoring, Med Pearls
Learning Points	• Understand the principles surrounding each of the learning points.

Psychiatric Disorders Chapter

FPGEE competency statements discussed in chapter

- 4.7.3 Individualized assessment of pharmacotherapeutic drug regimens
- 4.7.5 Patient-centered, culturally-relevant treatment plans

Guidance

- Highest-yield sections: Depression, Anxiety, Bipolar Disorder, Schizophrenia, Insomnia, ADHD

Topic	Highest-Yield Concepts
Depression	• Diagnosis (Recognize symptoms) • Guidelines summary • ALL antidepressants – MOA, contraindications, primary side effects, Med Pearls
Anxiety	• Signs and symptoms • Summary of treatment recommendations • ALL anxiolytics – MOA, contraindications, primary side effects, Med Pearls • Lorazepam, temazepam, and oxazepam are metabolized outside of the liver. • Patient education pearls

(Continued)

Topic	Highest-Yield Concepts
Bipolar disorder	• Definition • Signs and symptoms • Guidelines summary • Mood stabilizers – MOA, contraindications, primary side effects, Med Pearls
Schizophrenia	• Signs and symptoms • Guidelines summary • ALL antipsychotics – MOA, contraindications, primary side effects, Med Pearls • Patient education pearls
Insomnia	• Guidelines summary • Treatment algorithm • ALL drugs for insomnia – MOA, contraindications, primary side effects, Med Pearls • Patient education pearls
ADHD	• Be familiar with signs and symptoms • Guidelines summary • ALL drugs for insomnia – Contraindications, primary side effects, Med Pearls • Patient education pearls
Learning Points	• Understand the principles surrounding each of the learning points.

Pain Management Chapter

FPGEE competency statements discussed in chapter

- 3.9.5 Death and dying
- 4.7.3 Individualized assessment of pharmacotherapeutic drug regimens
- 4.7.5 Patient-centered, culturally-relevant treatment plans

Guidance

- Highest-yield sections: Nonsteroidal Anti-inflammatory Drugs (NSAIDs), Nonopioid Pain Management, Opioid Pain Management

Topic	Highest-Yield Concepts
Pain management	• Definitions • Guidelines summary
Nonsteroidal anti-inflammatory drugs (NSAIDs)	• ALL NSAIDs – MOA, contraindications, primary side effects, drug interactions, Med Pearls
Nonopioid pain management	• ALL Nonopioids – MOA, contraindications, primary side effects, drug interactions, Med Pearls
Opioid pain management	• ALL opioids – MOA, contraindications, primary side effects, drug interactions, Med Pearls
Learning Points	• Understand the principles surrounding each of the learning points.

Bone and Joint Disorders Chapter

FPGEE competency statements discussed in chapter

- 4.7.3 Individualized assessment of pharmacotherapeutic drug regimens
- 4.7.5 Patient-centered, culturally-relevant treatment plans

Guidance

- Highest-yield sections: Osteoarthritis, Osteoporosis, Gout

Topic	Highest Yield Concepts
Osteoarthritis	• Signs and symptoms • Guidelines summary • Treatment algorithm • ALL drugs for osteoarthritis – MOA, contraindications, primary side effects, drug interactions, Med Pearls • Patient education pearls
Rheumatoid arthritis	• Signs and symptoms • Guidelines summary • Treatment algorithm • ALL drugs for rheumatoid arthritis – Contraindications, primary side effects • Patient education pearls
Osteoporosis	• Signs and symptoms • Guidelines summary • Treatment algorithm • ALL drugs for osteoporosis – Contraindications, primary side effects, Med Pearls • Patient education pearls
Gout	• Signs and symptoms • Guidelines summary • Treatment algorithm • ALL drugs for gout – MOA, contraindications, primary side effects, Med Pearls • Patient education pearls
Learning Points	• Understand the principles surrounding each of the learning points.

Ophthalmologic and Otic Disorders Chapter

FPGEE competency statements discussed in chapter

- 4.7.3 Individualized assessment of pharmacotherapeutic drug regimens
- 4.7.5 Patient-centered, culturally-relevant treatment plans

Guidance

- Highest-yield section: Glaucoma

Topic	Highest-Yield Concepts
Glaucoma	• Overview of treatment • ALL glaucoma medications – MOA, contraindications, Med Pearls • Beta-Blockers – Know Betaxolol is B1 specific. • Patient education pearls
Impacted cerumen, water-clogged ears, and otitis externa	• Overview of treatment • Patient education pearls
Learning Points	• Understand the principles surrounding each of the learning points.

Hematologic Disorders Chapter

FPGEE competency statements discussed in chapter

- 4.7.3 Individualized assessment of pharmacotherapeutic drug regimens
- 4.7.5 Patient-centered, culturally-relevant treatment plans

Guidance

- Highest-yield sections: General review of sections only

Topic	Highest-Yield Concepts
Iron deficiency anemia	• Guidelines summary • Drugs for iron deficiency anemia – Primary side effects, Med Pearls • Patient education pearls
Anemia of chronic kidney disease and dialysis	• Guidelines summary • Drugs for anemia of CKD – Contraindications, primary side effects, Med Pearls • Patient education pearls
Pernicious anemia	• Treatment summary • Drugs for pernicious anemia – Med Pearls • Patient education pearls
Learning Points	• Understand the principles surrounding each of the learning points.

Dermatologic Disorders Chapter

FPGEE competency statements discussed in chapter

- 4.7.3 Individualized assessment of pharmacotherapeutic drug regimens
- 4.7.5 Patient-centered, culturally-relevant treatment plans

Guidance

- Highest-yield sections: Acne, Psoriasis

Topic	Highest-Yield Concepts
Acne	• Guidelines summary • Drugs for acne – Contraindications, primary side effects, Med Pearls • Patient education pearls
Psoriasis	• Summary of treatment recommendations • Drugs for Psoriasis – Route of administration, contraindications, primary side effects, Med Pearls • Patient education pearls
Learning Points	• Understand the principles surrounding each of the learning points.

Antidotes Chapter

FPGEE competency statements discussed in chapter

- 2.2.6 Drug toxicology
- 4.7.3 Individualized assessment of pharmacotherapeutic drug regimens
- 4.7.5 Patient-centered, culturally-relevant treatment plans

Guidance

- Highest-yield section: General Antidotes

Topic	Highest-Yield Concepts
Antidotes	• Review activated charcoal and gastric lavage. Know their benefits and limitations.
General antidotes	• Know the antidote and its indication as well as Med Pearls.
Learning Points	• Understand the principles surrounding each of the learning points.

Reproductive Health and Urologic Disorders Chapter

FPGEE competency statements discussed in chapter

- 4.7.3 Individualized assessment of pharmacotherapeutic drug regimens
- 4.7.5 Patient-centered, culturally-relevant treatment plans

Guidance

- Highest-yield sections: Erectile Dysfunction, Benign Prostatic Hyperplasia

Topic	Highest-Yield Concepts
Pregnancy/lactation	• Principles of drug use during pregnancy and lactation • Pregnancy categories • Sample known teratogens

(Continued)

Topic	Highest-Yield Concepts
Contraception	• Therapy selection • Advantages and disadvantages of contraception • Adverse effects associated with hormonal imbalance • Do NOT memorize the individual contraceptives. • Patient education pearls
Hormone replacement therapy	• Guidelines summary • Drugs for hormone replacement therapy – Contraindications, primary side effects, Med Pearls • Patient education pearls
Erectile dysfunction	• Guidelines summary • Erectile dysfunction treatment summary • Drugs for erectile dysfunction – MOA, route of administration, contraindications, primary side effects, drug interactions, Med Pearls • Patient education pearls
Benign prostatic hyperplasia	• Guidelines summary • BPH treatment summary • Drugs for erectile dysfunction – MOA, contraindications, primary side effects, drug interactions, Med Pearls • Patient education pearls
Urinary incontinence	• Summary of treatment recommendations • Drugs for urinary incontinence – MOA, contraindications, primary side effects, drug interactions, Med Pearls • Patient education pearls

Solid Organ Transplant/Immunosuppression Chapter

FPGEE competency statements discussed in chapter

- 4.7.3 Individualized assessment of pharmacotherapeutic drug regimens
- 4.7.5 Patient-centered, culturally-relevant treatment plans

Guidance

- Highest-yield sections: General review of sections only

Topic	Highest-Yield Concepts
Solid organ transplant/ immunosuppression	• ALL immunosuppressants – MOA, primary side effects, Med Pearls
Learning Points	• Understand the principles surrounding each of the learning points.

Special Populations Chapter

FPGEE competency statements discussed in chapter

- 4.7.3 Individualized assessment of pharmacotherapeutic drug regimens
- 4.7.5 Patient-centered, culturally-relevant treatment plans

Guidance

- Highest-yield sections: Whole chapter

Topic	Highest-Yield Concepts
Pediatrics	• Physiological changes (with focus on pharmacokinetics) • Principles of drug use
Geriatrics	• Physiological changes (with focus on pharmacokinetics) • Principles of drug use
Pregnancy and Lactation	• Physiological changes (with focus on pharmacokinetics) • Principles of drug use • Teratogens (Know these!)

Preventive Medicine Chapter

FPGEE competency statements discussed in chapter

- 4.5.2 Health, wellness, and disease prevention
- 4.5.3 Immunizations

Guidance

- Highest-yield sections: Immunizations, Smoking Cessation

Topic	Highest-Yield Concepts
Immunization	• Immunizations – Live vs inactivated vaccines, route of administration, indications, Med Pearls
Weight loss	• Definitions • Drugs for weight loss – MOA, primary side effects, contraindications
Smoking cessation	• Guidelines summary • Drugs for smoking cessation – MOA, primary side effects, contraindications
Learning Points	• Understand the principles surrounding each of the learning points.

Clinical Lab Tests Chapter

FPGEE competency statements discussed in chapter

- 4.6.4 Clinical laboratory and diagnostic tests
- 4.7.2 Therapeutic drug concentrations
- 4.7.4 Triage and patient referral principles

Guidance

- Highest-yield sections: Therapeutic Drug Levels

Topic	Highest-Yield Concepts
Electrolytes and minerals	• Be familiar with normal range of electrolytes and minerals.
Renal	• Be familiar with normal range of renal function tests.

(Continued)

Topic	Highest-Yield Concepts
Hepatic	• Be familiar with normal range of hepatic function tests.
Endocrine	• Be familiar with normal range of endocrine values. • Know A1C reference table values.
Cardiology	• Be familiar with normal range of cardiac test values.
Hematology	• Be familiar with normal range of hematology test values.
Therapeutic drug levels	• Know normal therapeutic drug levels.

Over-the-Counter Medications Chapter

FPGEE competency statements discussed in chapter

- 1.2.2 Enzymology and coenzymes and kinetics
- 2.3.1 Natural product principles
- 2.3.2 Natural product drug classes
- 2.3.3 Dietary supplements
- 4.7.7 Promotion of nonprescription and natural products

Guidance

- Highest-yield sections: ALL sections in this chapter are high yield

Topic	Highest-Yield Concepts
Vitamins	• Know both vitamin designations (i.e. B1 and thiamine) as well as deficiency manifestation.
Common herbals and supplements	• Common usage • Drug tables – Primary side effects
Decongestants	• Signs and symptoms • Guidelines summary • Decongestant table – MOA, contraindications, primary side effects, drug interactions, Med Pearls
Antihistamines	• Signs and symptoms • Adverse effects • Guidelines summary • Antihistamine table – MOA, contraindications, primary side effects, drug interactions, Med Pearls
Cough suppressants and expectorants	• Diagnosis • Signs and symptoms • Guidelines summary • Cough suppressant and expectorant tables – MOA, contraindications, primary side effects, drug interactions, Med Pearls

(Continued)

Topic	Highest-Yield Concepts
Antidiarrheals	• Diagnosis • Signs and symptoms • Guidelines summary • Antidiarrheal table – MOA, contraindications, primary side effects, drug interactions, Med Pearls
Laxatives	• Diagnosis • Signs and symptoms • Guidelines summary • Drugs for constipation table – MOA, contraindications, primary side effects, drug interactions, Med Pearls
Antifungals	• Diagnosis • Signs and symptoms • Guidelines summary • Topical Antifungal Medications to Treat Tinea Table – MOA, contraindications, primary side effects, drug interactions, Med Pearls
Pediculocides	• Diagnosis • Signs and symptoms • Guideline summary • Pediculocides medications table – MOA, contraindications, primary side effects, drug interactions, Med Pearls
Atopic dermatitis medications	• Diagnosis • Signs and symptoms • Guideline summary • Atopic dermatitis medication table – MOA, contraindications, primary side effects, drug interactions, Med Pearls
Poison ivy medications	• Diagnosis • Signs and symptoms • Guideline summary • Poison Ivy medication table – MOA, contraindications, primary side effects, drug interactions, Med Pearls
Sunscreens	• Diagnosis • Signs and symptoms • Guideline summary
Learning Points	• Understand the principles surrounding each of the learning points.

Pharmaceutics Chapter

FPGEE competency statements discussed in chapter

- 2.1.1 Physicochemical drug properties related to ADME
- 2.1.2 Chemical basis for therapeutics effects
- 2.4.1 Drug delivery and dosage forms

- 2.4.2 Methods of drug preparation
- 2.4.3 Physicochemical properties of drugs and dosage forms
- 2.4.4 Principles of drug and dosage form stability

Guidance

- Highest-yield sections: All sections in this chapter are high yield

Topic	Highest-Yield Concepts
Physical pharmacy	• Solubility and lipophilicity • Ionization behavior • Rate and half-life equations
Pharmaceutical dosage forms	• Know whole section
Learning Points	• Understand the principles surrounding each of the learning points.

Biopharmaceutics and Drug Disposition Chapter

FPGEE competency statements discussed in chapter

- 2.1.5 Drug metabolism pathways
- 2.1.6 Chemistry and therapeutic decisions
- 2.6.1 Molecular genetics and pharmacogenomics principles
- 2.6.2 Impact of genetic variation and drug effects
- 4.4.1 Application of pharmacogenomic data to drug therapy

Guidance

- Highest-yield sections: All sections in this chapter are high yield

Topic	Highest-Yield Concepts
Drug liberation and absorption	• Barriers to drug absorption
Drug distribution	• Volume of distribution • Plasma protein binding
Drug metabolism	• Phase I and II reactions • Enzyme inhibition • Drugs involved in inhibition of metabolic enzymes • Enzyme induction • Drugs involved in Induction of metabolic enzymes • Genetic variability (See Pharmacogenomics Chapter) • Common drugs metabolized by pathway (be familiar with these)
Drug excretion	• Review entire section • Know Cockroft-Gault equation
Learning Points	• Understand the principles surrounding each of the learning points.

Pharmacokinetics Chapter

FPGEE competency statements discussed in chapter

- 2.5.1 Linear and nonlinear drug kinetics
- 2.5.2 Bioavailability and bioequivalence
- 2.5.3 Determinates of drug onset and duration
- 4.3.1 Application of pharmacokinetic data to drug therapy
- 4.3.2 Importance of pharmacokinetics with low-therapeutic-index drugs

Guidance

- Highest-yield sections: Plasma Drug Concentration Profiles, Basic Pharmacokinetic Parameters, Oral Dosing, Multiple Dosing Factor and Accumulation Factor, Nonlinear Pharmacokinetics

Topic	Highest-Yield Concepts
Plasma drug concentration profiles	• Plasma concentration vs time curves for intravenous and oral drug administration
Theoretical compartments	• One-compartment model
Basic pharmacokinetic parameters	• Bioavailable fraction • Elimination rate constant • Half-life • Clearance • Volume of distribution • Area under the curve
Oral dosing	• Be familiar with whole section.
Multiple drug dosing	• Be familiar with whole section.
Multiple dosing factor and accumulation factor	• Peak-to-trough ratio • Loading doses • Constant and intermittent IV infusion
Nonlinear pharmacokinetics	• Peak-to-trough ratio
Learning Points	• Understand the principles surrounding each of the learning points.

Calculations Chapter

FPGEE competency statements discussed in chapter

- 2.7.2 Extemporaneous prescription preparation
- 2.7.3 Dosage form calculations

Guidance

- Highest-yield sections: Problem-solving Techniques, Fundamentals of Units and Measurement, Density, Specific Gravity, and Specific Volume, Reducing and Enlarging Formulas, Dosage Calculations, Dilution, Concentration, and Alligation, Compounding Calculations

Topic	Highest-Yield Concepts
Plasma drug concentration profiles	• Plasma concentration vs time curves for intravenous and oral drug administration
Theoretical compartments	• One-compartment model
Basic pharmacokinetic parameters	• Bioavailable fraction • Elimination rate constant • Half-life • Clearance • Volume of distribution • Area under the curve
Oral dosing	• Be familiar with whole section.
Multiple drug dosing	• Be familiar with whole section.
Multiple dosing factor and accumulation factor	• Peak-to-trough ratio • Loading doses • Constant and intermittent IV infusion
Nonlinear pharmacokinetics	• Peak-to-trough ratio
Learning Points	• Understand the principles surrounding each of the learning points.

Biostatistics Chapter

FPGEE competency statements discussed in chapter

- 3.6.1 Introduction to research study design
- 3.6.2 Application of statistical and research findings

Guidance

- Highest-yield sections: All sections in this chapter are high yield

Topic	Highest-Yield Concepts
Descriptive statistics: Summarizing the data	• Differentiate between descriptive and inferential statistics. • Be able to answer questions on central tendency, variability, distributions, and standard deviations.
Statistical test selection	• Know the general statistical definitions. • Be able to answer questions on confidence intervals, relative risk, odds ratio, p-value, statistical significance, statistical significance vs clinical significance, types of error, statistical power, and correlation.
Clinical trial design	• When given a scenario, be able to choose the appropriate statistical test. • Know characteristics of each statistical test. • Differentiate between ordinal and nominal data. • Outline the characteristics of each type of clinical trial as well as the data obtained and benefits/limitations of each clinical trial.
Learning Points	• Understand the principles surrounding each of the learning points.

Pharmacogenomics Chapter

FPGEE competency statements discussed in chapter

- 2.6.1 Molecular genetics and pharmacogenomics principles
- 2.6.2 Impact of genetic variation and drug effects
- 4.4.1 Application of pharmacogenomics data to drug therapy
- 4.7.3 Individualized assessment of pharmacotherapeutic drug regimens
- 4.7.5 Patient-centered, culturally-relevant treatment plans

Guidance

- Highest-yield sections: Whole chapter

Topic	Highest-Yield Concepts
Definitions	• Be familiar with concepts.
Phase I Metabolism	• Know cytochrome p450 concepts and impact of polymorphisms. • Know common drug metabolized by pathway (table). • Be familiar with Glucose-6-phosphate dehydrogenase AND drugs to avoid.
Phase II Metabolism	• Differentiate between Glucuronidation and Acetylation. • Know VKORC1.
Learning Points	• Know these concepts.

Drug Information Chapter

FPGEE competency statement discussed in chapter

- 4.7.1 Introduction to therapeutic decision-making

Guidance

- Highest-yield sections: All sections in this chapter are high yield

Topic	Highest-Yield Concepts
General drug information resources	• You should be able to answer questions pertaining to the clinical content found in each reference.
Pharmacotherapy resources	• You should be able to answer questions pertaining to the clinical content found in this reference.
Internal medicine resources	• You should be able to answer questions pertaining to the clinical content found in this reference.
Drug interaction resources	• You should be able to answer questions pertaining to the clinical content found in this reference.
Adverse drug reaction resources	• You should be able to answer questions pertaining to the clinical content found in this reference.
Parenteral drug compatibility/ stability resources	• You should be able to answer questions pertaining to the clinical content found in this reference.
Pharmacology resources	• You should be able to answer questions pertaining to the clinical content found in this reference.

(Continued)

Topic	Highest-Yield Concepts
Compounding and pharmaceutics resources	• You should be able to answer questions pertaining to the clinical content found in this reference.
Drug identification resources	• You should be able to answer questions pertaining to the clinical content found in this reference.
Foreign drug information resources	• You should be able to answer questions pertaining to the clinical content found in this reference.
Pediatric drug information resources	• You should be able to answer questions pertaining to the clinical content found in this reference.
Pregnancy and lactation resources	• You should be able to answer questions pertaining to the clinical content found in this reference.
OTC drug resources	• You should be able to answer questions pertaining to the clinical content found in this reference.
Natural products resources	• You should be able to answer questions pertaining to the clinical content found in this reference.
Comparison charts	• You should be able to answer questions pertaining to the clinical content found in this reference.
Learning Points	• Understand the principles surrounding each of the learning points.

Health Policy Chapter

FPGEE competency statements discussed in chapter

- 2.2.5 Drug development
- 4.7.8 Management of drug toxicity and drug-induced diseases

Guidance

- Highest-yield sections: All sections in this chapter are high yield

Topic	Highest-Yield Concepts
HIPAA	• Definition of HIPAA • Types of protected health information
FDA regulatory process	• New Drug Application (NDA) process • Components of the Investigational New Drug (IND) application • Types of IND • Clinical trial phases and objectives of each phase
The Joint Commission accreditation process	• Joint Commission's responsibility
Medication therapy management (MTM)	• Goals and objectives of MTM • Types of MTM services provided
Learning Points	• Understand the principles surrounding each of the learning points.

Unit III

FPGEE Comprehensive Review

Human Anatomy and Physiology 1

Learning Objectives

- ❑ Illustrate the anatomy and physiology of each major body system
- ❑ Discuss normal human physiology at both the organ and system level

Knowledge of the structure and function of the human body is the foundation on which medicine and medical practices are built. Understanding normal human anatomy and physiology helps clinicians identify pathological conditions and recognize adverse drug events, and establishes a baseline to which to a patient should be returned following a therapeutic intervention.

CELL STRUCTURE AND PHYSIOLOGY

The human body contains ~37 trillion cells which create tissue from which organs form. Each cell serves a purpose, communicating and carrying out the reactions that make life possible. Interestingly, bacteria outnumber the eukaryotic cells in our bodies about 10:1.

The number of cells from which the human body is created is not nearly as impressive, however, as the numerous functions those cells can perform; the functions range from conduction of impulses through the nervous system to allowing for memory and learning, to the simultaneous contraction of cardiac myocytes to allow for the pumping of blood through the entire human body. To understand the human organism as a whole and how the human body reacts to various pathogens, an understanding of cell biology is required.

Cell Theory

The original form of the cell theory consisted of 3 basic tenets:

- All living things are composed of cells.
- The cell is the basic functional unit of life.
- Cells arise only from preexisting cells.

Through advances of molecular biology, a 4th tenet has been added:

- Cells carry genetic information in the form of deoxyribonucleic acid (DNA). This genetic material is passed on from parent to daughter cell.

Eukaryotic Cells

The first major distinction between living organisms is whether they are composed of prokaryotic or eukaryotic cells. Eukaryotic organisms can be unicellular or multicellular. Whereas **eukaryotic cells** contain a true nucleus enclosed in a membrane, **prokaryotic cells** do not contain a nucleus.

The major organelles are identified below.

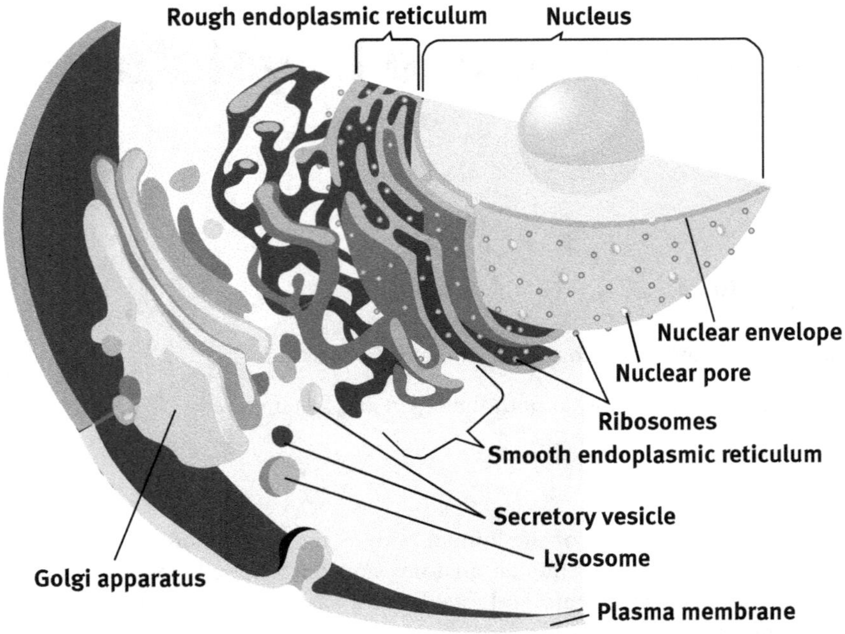

Figure 1-1. Eukaryotic Cell
Numerous membrane-bound organelles are found in the cytoplasm of a eukaryotic cell.

Membrane-Bound Organelles

Each cell has a cell membrane enclosing a semifluid cytosol in which the **organelles** are suspended. In eukaryotic cells, most organelles are membrane-bound, allowing for compartmentalization of functions.

- Membranes of eukaryotic cells consist of a phospholipid bilayer. This membrane is unique in that its surfaces are hydrophilic, electrostatically interacting with the aqueous environments inside and outside of the cell, while its inner portion is hydrophobic, which helps to provide a highly selective barrier between the interior of the cell and the external environment.
- The **cytosol** allows for the diffusion of molecules throughout the cell.
- Within the **nucleus**, genetic material is encoded in **deoxyribonucleic acid** (**DNA**), which is organized into **chromosomes**.
- Eukaryotic cells reproduce by **mitosis**, allowing for the formation of 2 identical daughter cells.

Nucleus

As the control center of the cell, the **nucleus** contains all of the genetic material necessary for replication of the cell. The nucleus is surrounded by the **nuclear membrane** or **envelope**, a double membrane that maintains a nuclear environment separate and distinct from the cytoplasm. **Nuclear pores** in the nuclear membrane allow for selective 2-way exchange of material between the cytoplasm and the nucleus.

Key Concept

The nuclear envelope creates 2 distinct environments within the cell because it separates the nucleus from the cytoplasm. This allows for compartmentalization of transcription (the formation of hnRNA from DNA, which is subsequently processed to form mRNA) and translation (the formation of a peptide from mRNA).

The genetic material (DNA) contains coding regions called **genes.**

- Linear DNA is wound around organizing proteins known as **histones**, and is then further wound into linear strands called **chromosomes.**
- The location of DNA in the nucleus allows for the compartmentalization of DNA transcription separate from RNA translation.

Finally, there is a subsection of the nucleus known as the **nucleolus**, where the **ribosomal RNA (rRNA)** is synthesized. The nucleolus actually takes up approximately 25 percent of the volume of the entire nucleus and can often be identified as a darker spot in the nucleus.

Mitochondria

Mitochondria are often called *the power plants of the cell*, in reference to their important metabolic functions. The mitochondrion contains 2 layers: the outer and inner membranes.

- The **outer membrane** serves as a barrier between the cytosol and the inner environment of the mitochondrion.
- The **inner membrane**, which is thrown into numerous infoldings called **cristae**, contains the molecules and enzymes necessary for the electron transport chain.

The cristae are highly convoluted structures that increase the surface area available for electron transport chain enzymes. The space between the inner and outer membranes is called the **intermembrane space**; the space inside the inner membrane is called the mitochondrial **matrix.** The pumping of protons from the mitochondrial matrix to the intermembrane space establishes the proton-motive force. Ultimately, these protons flow through *ATP synthase* to generate ATP during oxidative phosphorylation.

Mitochondria are different from other parts of the cell in that they are semi-autonomous.

- Contain some of their own genes and replicate independently of the nucleus via binary fission
- Are paradigmatic examples of **cytoplasmic** or **extranuclear inheritance**—the transmission of genetic material independent of the nucleus
- Are thought to have evolved from an anaerobic prokaryote engulfing an aerobic prokaryote and establishing a symbiotic relationship

In addition to keeping the cell alive by providing energy, the mitochondria are also capable of killing the cell by release of enzymes from the electron transport chain. This release kickstarts a process known as **apoptosis**, or programmed cell death.

Lysosomes

Lysosomes are membrane-bound structures containing hydrolytic enzymes that are capable of breaking down many different substrates, including substances ingested by endocytosis and cellular waste products. The lysosomal membrane sequesters these enzymes to prevent damage to the cell. However, release of these enzymes can occur in a process known as **autolysis.** Like mitochondria, when lysosomes release their hydrolytic enzymes, it results in apoptosis. In this case, the released enzymes directly lead to the degradation of cellular components.

Endoplasmic Reticulum

The **endoplasmic reticulum (ER)** is a series of interconnected membranes that are actually contiguous with the nuclear envelope. The double membrane of the endoplasmic reticulum is folded into numerous invaginations, creating complex structures with a central lumen.

There are 2 varieties of ER: rough and smooth.

- **Rough ER** (**RER**) is studded with **ribosomes** that permit the translation of proteins destined for secretion directly into its lumen.
- **Smooth ER** (**SER**) lacks ribosomes, and is utilized primarily for lipid synthesis (e.g., phospholipids in cell membrane) and the detoxification of certain drugs and poisons.
- The SER also transports proteins from the RER to the Golgi apparatus.

Golgi Apparatus

Key Concept

Not all cells have the same relative distribution of organelles. Form will follow function. Cells that require a lot of energy for locomotion (e.g., sperm cells) have high concentrations of mitochondria. Cells involved in secretion (e.g., pancreatic islet cells and other endocrine tissues) have high concentrations of RER and Golgi apparatus. Other cells, e.g., red blood cells which primarily serve a transport function, have no organelles at all.

The **Golgi apparatus** consists of stacked membrane-bound sacs. Materials from the ER are transferred to the Golgi apparatus in vesicles. Once in the Golgi apparatus, these cellular products may be modified by the addition of various groups, including carbohydrates, phosphates, and sulfates.

The Golgi apparatus may also modify cellular products through the introduction of signal sequences, which direct the delivery of the product to a specific cellular location. After modification and sorting in the Golgi apparatus, cellular products are repackaged in vesicles, which are subsequently transferred to the correct cellular location. If the product is destined for secretion, then the secretory vesicle merges with the cell membrane and its contents are released via **exocytosis**.

Peroxisomes

Peroxisomes contain hydrogen peroxide. One of the primary functions of peroxisomes is the breakdown of very long chain fatty acids via β-oxidation. Peroxisomes participate in the synthesis of phospholipids and contain some of the enzymes involved in the pentose phosphate pathway.

Cytoskeleton

The **cytoskeleton** provides structure to the cell and helps it to maintain its shape. In addition, the cytoskeleton provides a conduit for the transport of materials around the cell. There are 3 components of the cytoskeleton: microfilaments, microtubules, and intermediate filaments.

Microfilaments

Microfilaments are made up of solid polymerized rods of **actin**.

- The actin filaments are organized into bundles and networks and are resistant to both compression and fracture, providing protection for the cell.
- Actin filaments can also use ATP to generate force for movement by interacting with **myosin**, such as in muscle contraction.

Microfilaments also play a role in **cytokinesis**, or the division of materials between daughter cells. During mitosis, the **cleavage furrow** is formed from microfilaments, which organize as a ring at the site of division between the 2 new daughter cells. As the actin filaments within this ring contract, the ring becomes smaller, eventually pinching off the connection between the two daughter cells.

Microtubules

Key Concept

Motor proteins like kinesin and dynein are classic examples of nonenzymatic protein function, along with binding proteins, cell adhesion molecules, immunoglobulins, and ion channels. Motor proteins often travel along cytoskeletal structures to accomplish their functions.

Unlike microfilaments, **microtubules** are hollow polymers of **tubulin** proteins. Microtubules radiate throughout the cell, providing the primary pathways along which motor proteins like **kinesin** and **dynein** carry vesicles.

Cilia and flagella are motile structures composed of microtubules.

- **Cilia** are projections from a cell that are primarily involved in movement of materials along the surface of the cell; for example, cilia line the respiratory tract and are involved in movement of mucus.
- **Flagella** are structures involved in movement of the cell itself, such as the movement of sperm cells through the reproductive tract.

Cilia and flagella share the same structure, composed of 9 pairs of microtubules forming an outer ring, with 2 microtubules in the center. This is known as a **9 + 2 structure** and is seen only in eukaryotic organelles of motility. Bacterial flagella have a different structure with a different chemical composition.

Centrioles are found in a region of the cell called the **centrosome.** They are the organizing centers for microtubules and are structured as 9 triplets of microtubules with a hollow center. During mitosis, the centrioles migrate to opposite poles of the dividing cell and organize the mitotic spindle. The microtubules emanating from the centrioles attach to the chromosomes via complexes called **kinetochores** and can exert force on the sister chromatids, pulling them apart.

Intermediate Filaments

Intermediate filaments are a diverse group of filamentous proteins, including keratin, desmin, vimentin, and lamins. Many intermediate filaments are involved in cell–cell adhesion or maintenance of the overall integrity of the cytoskeleton. Intermediate filaments are able to withstand a tremendous amount of tension, making the cell structure more rigid. In addition, intermediate filaments help anchor other organelles, including the nucleus. The identity of the intermediate filament proteins within a cell is specific to the cell and tissue type.

INTEGUMENTARY SYSTEM

By both weight and size, the **skin** (**integument**) is the largest organ in the body. It makes up on average about 16% of total body weight. Skin is one of the major components of nonspecific immune defense, protecting us from exposure to the elements and invasion by pathogens.

The skin has several layers. Starting from the deepest layer and working outward, these layers are the **hypodermis** (**subcutaneous** layer), **dermis**, and **epidermis**. Skin is derived from the ectoderm.

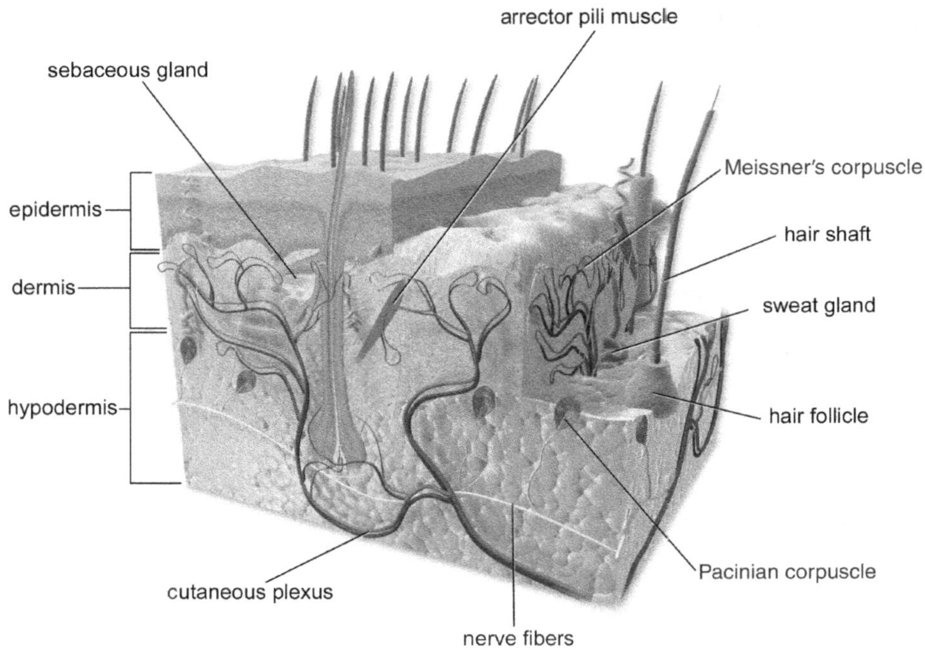

Figure 1-2. Anatomy of the Skin and Subcutaneous Tissue

Epidermis

The **epidermis** is also subdivided into layers called **strata**. From the deepest layer outward, these layers are as follows:

- Stratum basale
- Stratum spinosum
- Stratum granulosum
- Stratum lucidum
- Stratum corneum

The **stratum basale** contains stem cells and is responsible for proliferation of **keratinocytes**, the predominant cells of the skin that produce **keratin.**

In the **stratum spinosum**, these cells become connected to each other; this layer is also the site of Langerhans cells (described below).

In the **stratum granulosum**, the keratinocytes die and lose their nuclei.

The **stratum lucidum** is only present in thick, hairless skin, such as the skin on the sole of the foot or the palms, and is nearly transparent.

Finally, the **stratum corneum** contains up to several dozen layers of flattened keratinocytes, forming a barrier that prevents invasion by pathogens and that helps to prevent loss of fluids and salt. Hair projects above the skin, and there are openings for sweat and sebaceous glands.

Mnemonic

Layers of the skin (superficial to deep): **C**ome, **L**et's **G**et **S**un **B**urned

- Stratum **c**orneum
- Stratum **l**ucidum
- Stratum **g**ranulosum
- Stratum **s**pinosum
- Stratum **b**asale

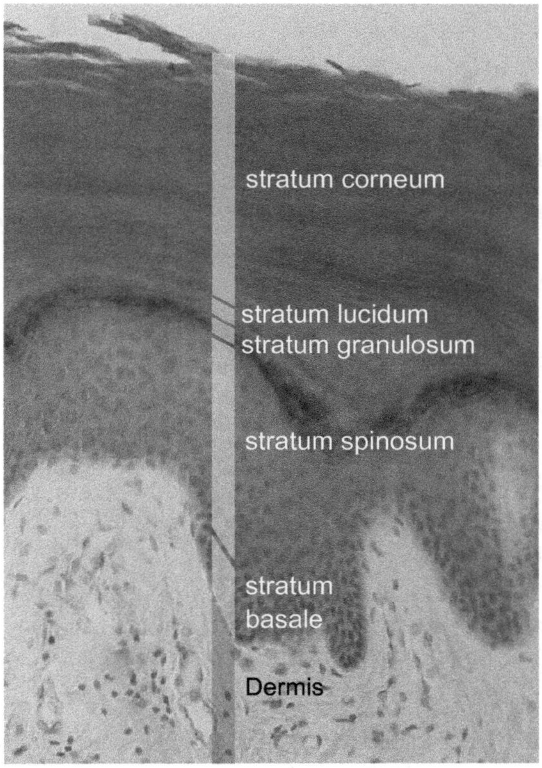

Figure 1-3. Layers of the Epidermis

Other Cells of the Epidermis

In the epidermis, the main cells are keratinocytes. Keratin is resistant to damage and provides protection against injury, water, and pathogens. **Calluses** form from excessive keratin deposition in areas of repeated strain due to friction; they provide protection to avoid damage in the future. **Fingernails** and **hair** are also formed from keratin and are produced by specialized cells in the skin.

Bridge to Pathology

People with albinism suffer from a genetic metabolic disorder characterized by the inability to synthesize melanin. Typically, albinism is inherited in an autosomal recessive fashion. Patients are extremely sensitive to the harmful effects of the sun. Depigmentation can also occur.

Melanocytes are derived from neural crest cells and found in the stratum basale. They produce **melanin**, a pigment that serves to protect the skin from DNA damage caused by ultraviolet radiation. Once produced, the pigment is passed to the keratinocytes. All humans actually have comparable numbers of melanocytes; skin color is caused by varying levels of activity of the melanocytes. More active melanocytes result in darker skin tones. Upon exposure to ultraviolet radiation, melanocytes increase activity, resulting in a darker skin color.

Langerhans cells are actually special macrophages that reside within stratum spinosum. These cells are capable of presenting antigens to T-cells in order to activate the immune system.

Dermis

The dermis also consists of multiple layers.

- **Papillary layer:** upper layer (right below epidermis) consisting of loose connective tissue
- **Reticular layer:** denser, sits below papillary layer
- Sweat glands, blood vessels, and hair follicles originate in dermis

Most sensory receptors are also located in the dermis. **Merkel cells (discs)**, for example, are sensory receptors present at the epidermal–dermal junction. These cells are connected to sensory neurons and are responsible for deep pressure and texture sensation within the skin. Other sensory organs in the skin include free nerve endings, which respond to pain; **Meissner's corpuscles**, which respond to light touch; **Ruffini endings**, which respond to stretch; and **Pacinian corpuscles**, which respond to deep pressure and vibration.

Hypodermis

Finally, the **hypodermis** is a layer of connective tissue that connects the skin to the rest of the body. This layer contains fat and fibrous tissue.

CARDIOVASCULAR SYSTEM

Systolic Performance of the Ventricle

Systolic performance actually means the overall force generated by the ventricular muscle during systole. The heart does 2 things in systole: pressurizes and ejects blood. An important factor influencing this systolic performance is the number of cross-bridges cycling during contraction. The greater the number of cross-bridges cycling, the greater the force of contraction.

Systolic performance is determined by 3 variables: preload, contractility, and afterload. Together, these factors determine the overall systolic performance of the ventricle. Recent work has demonstrated that they are not completely independent, but the generalizations made here will apply to the physiologic and clinical setting.

Preload

As in skeletal muscle, preload is the load on the muscle in the relaxed state, i.e., it is the load or prestretch on ventricular muscle at the end of diastole. On ventricular muscle preload is not measured directly; rather, indices are utilized. The best indices of preload on ventricular muscle are those measured directly in the ventricles. Indices of left ventricular preload:

- Left ventricular end-diastolic volume (LVEDV)
- Left ventricular end-diastolic pressure (LVEDP)

Possibly somewhat less reliable indices of left ventricular preload are those measured in the venous system:

- Central venous pressure (CVP)
- Pulmonary capillary wedge pressure (PCWP)
- Right atrial pressure (RAP)

Pulmonary wedge pressure, sometimes called pulmonary capillary wedge pressure, is measured from the tip of a Swan-Ganz catheter, which, after passing through the right heart, has been wedged in a small pulmonary artery. The tip is pointing downstream toward the pulmonary capillaries, and the pressure measured at the tip is probably very close to pulmonary capillary pressure. Since the vessel is occluded and assuming minimal flow, the pressure is probably also very close to left atrial pressure, as well. A rise in pulmonary capillary wedge pressure is evidence of an increase in preload on the left ventricle. In some cases, such as in mitral stenosis, it is not a good index of left ventricular preload. Measurement of systemic central venous pressure is used as an index of preload.

Preload Factor in Systolic Performance (Frank-Starling Mechanism)

The preload effect can be explained by observing change in sarcomere length.

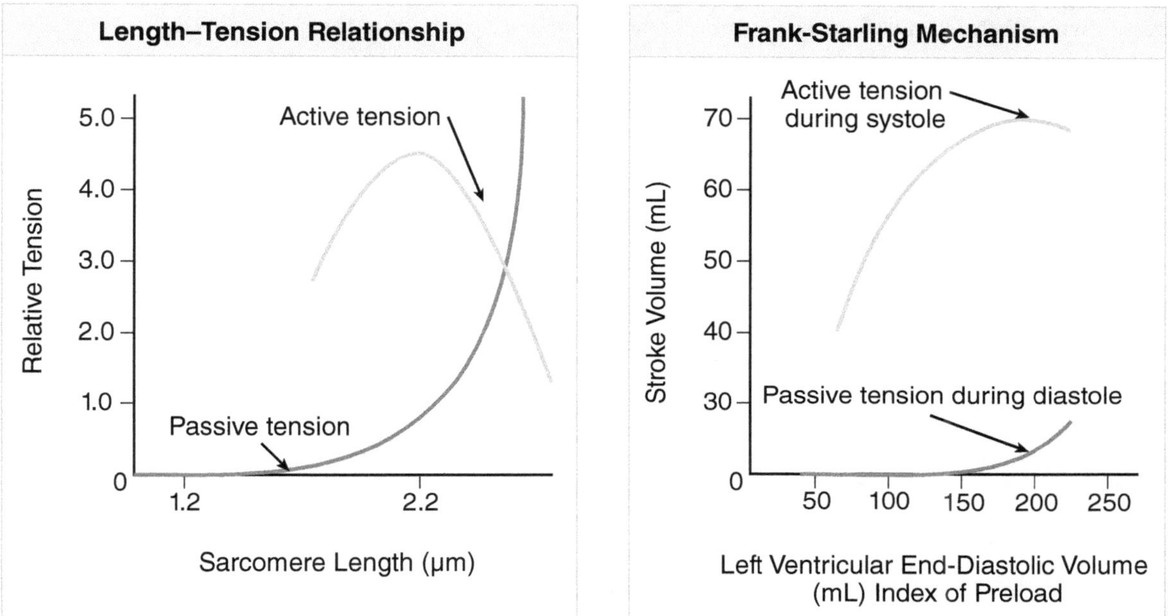

Figure 1-4. Length–Tension Relationships in Skeletal and Cardiac Muscle

The resting length of skeletal muscle *in vivo* is at a sarcomere length close to the optimum for maximal cross-bridge linking between actin and myosin during contraction (L_o).

Heart muscle at the end of diastole is below this point. Thus, in a normal heart, increased preload increases sarcomere length toward the optimum actin-myosin overlap. This results in more cross-linking and a more forceful contraction during systole.

Contractility (Inotropic State)

Contractility can be defined as a change in performance at a given preload and afterload. Thus, contractility is a change in the force of contraction at any given sarcomere length.

- Acute changes in contractility are due to changes in the intracellular dynamics of calcium.
- Drugs that increase contractility usually provide more calcium and at a faster rate to the contractile machinery.
- More calcium increases the availability of cross-link sites on the actin, increasing cross-linking and the force of contraction during systole.
- Calcium dynamics do not explain chronic losses in contractility, which in most cases are due to overall myocyte dysfunction.

Indices of Contractility

Increased *dp/dt* (change in pressure vs. change in time) is rate of pressure development during isovolumetric contraction. Contractility affects the rate at which the ventricular muscle develops active tension, which is expressed as pressure in the ventricle during isovolumetric contraction.

Increased ejection fraction (stroke volume/end-diastolic volume). Ejection fraction can now be estimated fairly easily by a noninvasive technique and is currently a common clinical index of contractility. There is no ideal index of contractility. Ejection fraction is influenced by afterload, but in most cases an increase in contractility is accompanied by an increase in ejection fraction. Note that ejection fraction simply indicates the percentage of blood ejected from the ventricle; it does not by itself give information about preload or stroke volume.

When contractility increases, there are changes in addition to an increased force of contraction. The solid line in the following figure represents left ventricular pressure before (and the dashed line after) an increase in contractility via increased sympathetic stimulation. The numbers refer to the descriptions after the figure.

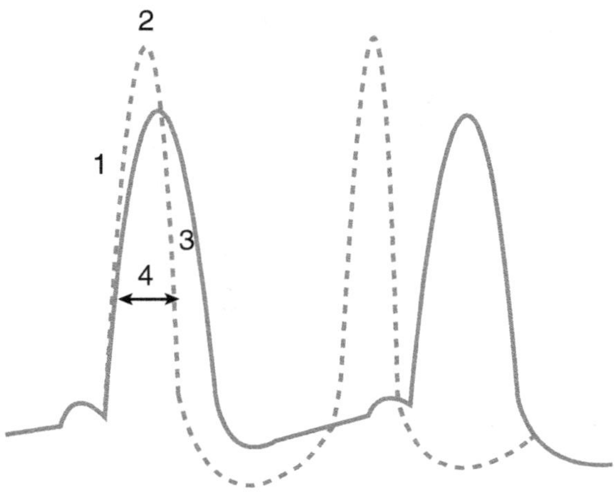

Figure 1-5. Effects of Increased Contractility

The overall changes induced by increased contractility can be summarized as follows:

1. Increased *dp/dt*: increased slope, thus increased rate of pressure development
2. Increased peak left ventricular pressure due to a more forceful contraction
3. Increased rate of relaxation due to increased rate of calcium sequestration
4. Decreased systolic interval due to effects #1 and #3

Both an increased preload and an increased contractility are accompanied by an increased peak left ventricular pressure, but only with an increase in contractility is there a decrease in the systolic interval.

Whereas contractility affects systolic interval, heart rate determines diastolic interval. Thus, increased sympathetic activity to the heart produces the following:

- Systolic interval decreased: contractility effect
- Diastolic interval decreased: heart rate effect

A high heart rate (pacemaker-induced) produces a small increase in contractility (Bowditch effect). Because Ca^{2+} enters the cell more rapidly than it is sequestered by the sarcoplasmic reticulum, intracellular Ca^{2+} increases. The increased contractility helps compensate for the reduced filling time associated with high heart rates.

Afterload

Afterload is defined as the "load" against which the heart must eject blood. Exactly what constitutes afterload to the heart is the subject of much debate. Probably the best marker of afterload is **systemic vascular resistance** (SVR), also called **total peripheral resistance** (TPR). However, TPR is not routinely calculated clinically and thus arterial pressure (diastolic, mean, or systolic) is often used as the index of afterload.

Afterload is increased in 3 main situations:

- When aortic pressure is increased (elevated mean arterial pressure); for example, when hypertension increases the afterload, the left ventricle has to work harder to overcome the elevated arterial pressures.
- When systemic vascular resistance is increased, resulting in increased resistance and decreased compliance.
- In aortic stenosis, resulting in pressure overload of the left ventricle.

In general, when afterload increases, there is an initial fall in stroke volume.

Organization of the Cardiovascular System

The following figure illustrates the general organization of the cardiovascular system.

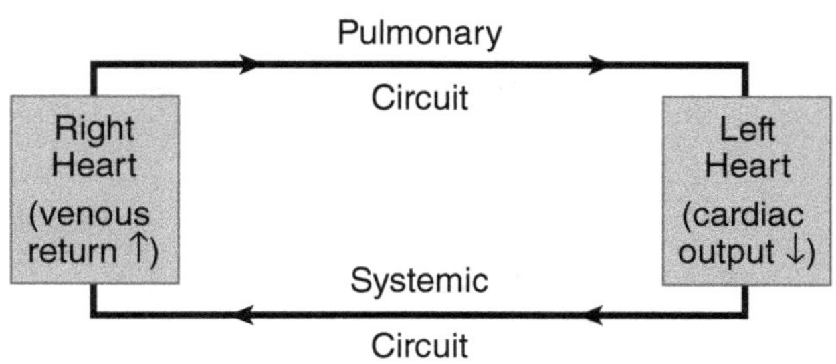

Figure 1-6. Overview of Circulatory System

In a Nutshell

The function of the heart is to transport blood and deliver oxygen in order to maintain adequate tissue perfusion. It also removes waste products, e.g., CO_2 created by tissue metabolism.

Because the heart is a "demand pump" that pumps out whatever blood comes back into it from the venous system, it is effectively the amount of blood returning to the heart that determines how much blood the heart pumps out.

The cardiovascular system consists of 2 pumps (left and right ventricles) and 2 circuits (pulmonary and systemic) connected in series.

- When circuits are connected in series, flow must be equal in the 2 circuits.
- Cardiac output is the output of either the left or right ventricle, and because of the series system, they are equal.
- The chemical composition of pulmonary venous blood is very close to the chemical composition of systemic arterial blood.
- Systemic mixed venous blood entering the right atrium has the same composition as pulmonary arterial blood.

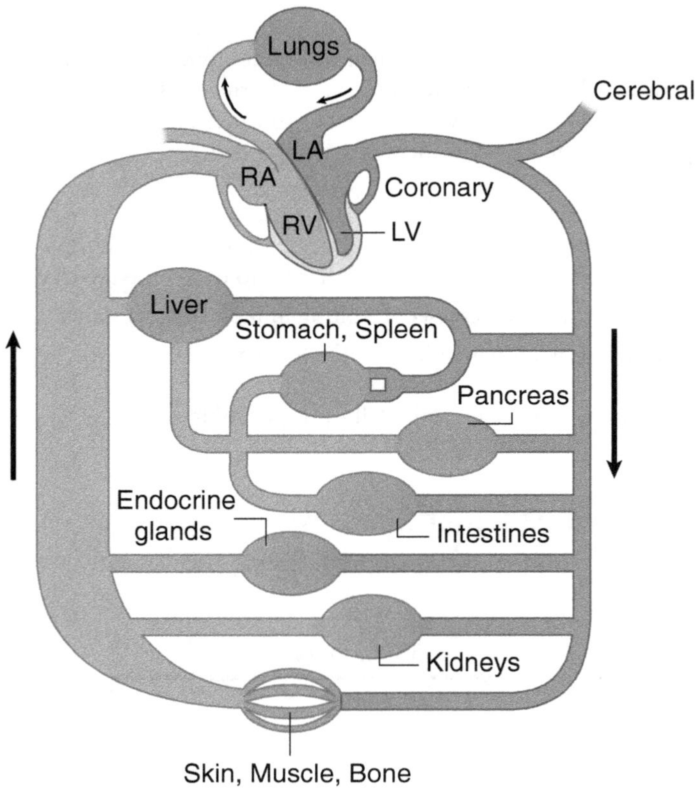

Figure 1-7. Systemic Circuit

Bridge to Pharmacology

Drugs that mimic norepinephrine (NE) cause the same cardiovascular effects that NE produces. These include alpha-1 agonists, NE releasers, and NE reuptake inhibitors.

Bridge to Pharmacology

Drugs that block NE's vascular effects (alpha blockers) prevent NE release, liberate NO, activate beta-2 receptors, block calcium entry into smooth muscle cells, and/or open smooth muscle potassium channels that mimic the vasodilatory effects indicated.

Bridge to Pathology

Sepsis, anaphylaxis, and neurogenic shock are examples of uncontrolled vasodilation in the periphery, leading to diminished mean arterial pressure (MAP).

ENDOCRINE SYSTEM

The endocrine system includes a variety of glands that produce hormones that regulate the body systems involved in metabolism, growth, development, and tissue function, as well as many others.

Hypothalamic–Anterior Pituitary Axis

The hormones in this system are all water-soluble. The hypothalamic hormones are synthesized in the neuron cell body, packaged in vesicles, and transported down the axon to be stored and released from the nerve terminals.

- The pituitary is located in the bony sella turcica at the base of the skull. It hangs from the hypothalamus by a stalk (the infundibulum) and is controlled by the hypothalamus. The dura membrane (diaphragm sellae) separates it from and prevents cerebrospinal fluid from entering the sella turcica.
- The optic chiasm is 5–10 mm above this diaphragm.
- In the hypothalamic–anterior pituitary system, hormonal release is mainly pulsatile. A possible exception is the thyroid system.
- The pulsatile release of GnRH prevents downregulation of its receptors on the gonadotrophs of the anterior pituitary. A constant infusion of GnRH will cause a decrease in the release of both LH and FSH.

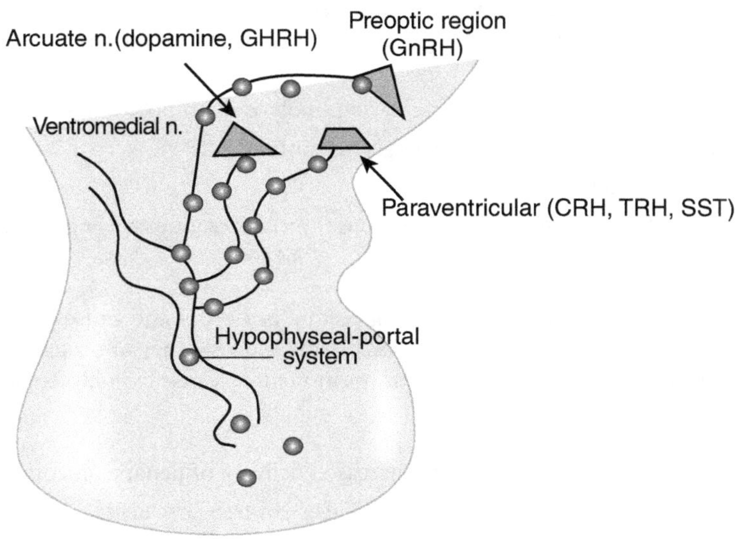

Figure 1-8. Hypothalamic–Anterior Pituitary Axis

- The hypothalamic hormones, thyrotropin-releasing hormone (TRH), corticotropin-releasing hormone (CRH), growth hormone–releasing hormone (GHRH), somatostatin (SST), and dopamine are synthesized in neuronal cell bodies in the arcuate and paraventricular nuclei; gonadotropin-releasing hormone (GnRH) is synthesized in the preoptic nucleus.
- The nerve endings all come together in the median eminence region of the hypothalamus. The hormones are then secreted into the hypophyseal-portal system and transported to the anterior pituitary.
- Hypothalamic hormones bind to receptors on cells of the anterior pituitary and modify the secretion of thyroid-stimulating hormone (TSH) (thyrotropin), corticotropin (ACTH), luteinizing hormone (LH), follicle-stimulating hormone (FSH), growth hormone (GH), and prolactin.

Hormones of the Posterior Pituitary

The hormones of the posterior pituitary are made up of distal neuron terminals.

- Secreted hormones; arginine vasopressin (ADH), oxytocin—both are peptide hormones.
- Cell bodies located in the supraoptic nucleus and paraventricular nucleus of the hypothalamus.
- ADH is a major controller of water excretion and regulator of extracellular osmolarity.
- The osmoreceptor neurons in the hypothalamus are extremely sensitive and are able to maintain ECF osmolarity within a very narrow range.
- There is a downward shift in plasma osmolarity regulation in pregnancy, the menstrual cycle, and with volume depletion. In the latter case osmoregulation is secondary to volume regulation; a return of circulating volume occurs even though osmolarity decreases.
- Volume receptors are less sensitive than osmoreceptors and a change of 10–15% in volume is required to produce a measurable change in ADH.
- Angiotensin II and CRH can stimulate the release of ADH.

Physiologic Actions of Glucocorticoids

Stress includes states such as trauma, exposure to cold, illness, starvation, and exercise. The capacity to withstand stress is dependent on adequate secretion of the glucocorticoids. Stress hormones usually act to mobilize energy stores.

- **Growth hormone** mobilizes fatty acids by increasing lipolysis in adipose tissue
- **Glucagon** mobilizes glucose by increasing liver glycogenolysis
- **Cortisol** mobilizes fat, protein, carbohydrate
- **Epinephrine** (in some forms of stress such as exercise) mobilizes glucose via glycogenolysis and fat via lipolysis

All stress hormones raise plasma glucose. Severe hypoglycemia is a crisis and causes a rapid increase in all stress hormones. By definition, because these hormones raise plasma glucose, they are referred to as counterregulatory hormones (opposite to insulin). A deficiency in a stress hormone may cause hypoglycemia.

Cortisol promotes the mobilization of energy stores.

- **Proteins:** Cortisol promotes degradation and increased delivery of hepatic gluconeogenic precursors.
- **Lipids:** Cortisol promotes lipolysis and increased delivery of free fatty acids and glycerol.
- **Carbohydrates:** Cortisol raises blood glucose, making more glucose available for nervous tissue. Two mechanisms are involved:
  - Cortisol counteracts insulin's action in most tissues (muscle, lymphoid, and fat).
  - Cortisol increases hepatic output of glucose by regulating the enzymes involved in gluconeogenesis, particularly phosphoenolpyruvate carboxykinase (PEPCK) (not from liver glycogenolysis).

Physiologic Actions of Aldosterone

The primary target tissue for aldosterone is the kidney, where it increases Na^+ reabsorption by the principal cells of the kidney's collecting ducts. Because water is reabsorbed along with the Na^+, aldosterone can be considered to control the amount of Na^+ rather than the concentration of Na^+ in the ECF.

Aldosterone also promotes the secretion of H^+ by the intercalated cells of the collecting duct, and K^+ secretion by the principal cells. The Na^+-conserving action of aldosterone is also seen in salivary ducts, sweat glands, and the distal colon.

The following figure shows the overall effects of aldosterone. This is a generalized representation of the effect of aldosterone on the renal distal tubule/collecting duct region.

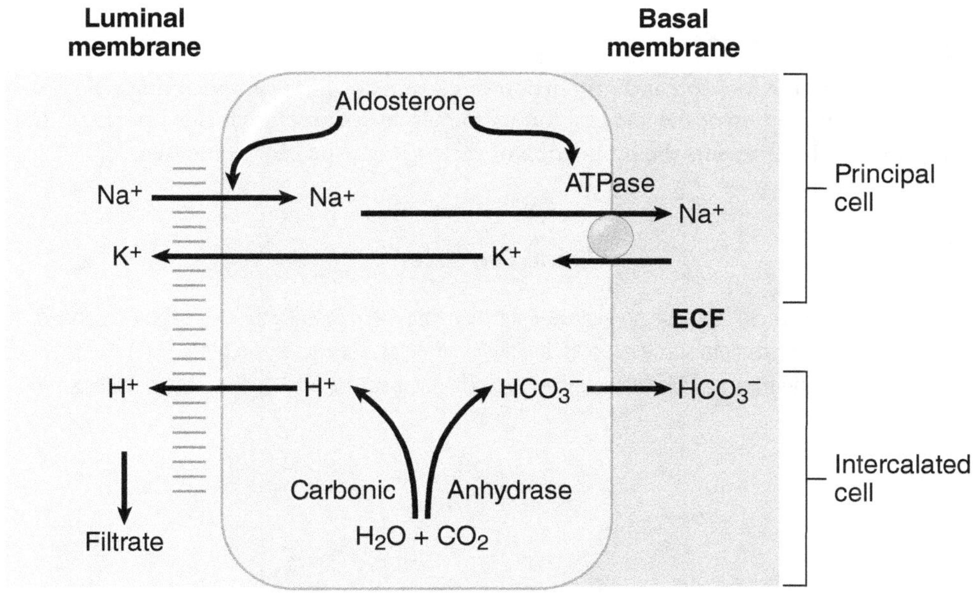

Figure 1-9. Late Distal Tubule and Collecting Duct

Hormones of the Adrenal Medulla

- Secretion of the adrenal medulla is 20% norepinephrine and 80% epinephrine.
- Phenylethanolamine-N-methyltransferase (PMNT) converts norepinephrine into epinephrine.
- Half-life of the catecholamines is only about 2 minutes. Metabolic end products include metanephrines and vanillylmandelic acid (VMA) both of which can be measured in plasma and urine.
- Removal of the adrenal medulla reduces plasma epinephrine to very low levels but does not alter plasma norepinephrine. Most circulating norepinephrine arises from postganglionic sympathetic neurons.
- Because many of the actions of epinephrine are also mediated by norepinephrine, the adrenal medulla is not essential for life.
- The vasoconstrictive action of norepinephrine is essential for the maintenance of normal blood pressure, especially when an individual is standing. Plasma norepinephrine levels double when one goes from a lying to a standing position. People with inadequate production of norepinephrine suffer from orthostatic hypotension.
- Epinephrine is a stress hormone and rapidly increases in response to exercise, exposure to cold, emergencies, and hypoglycemia.

Major Metabolic Actions of Epinephrine

- **Liver:** Epinephrine increases the activity of liver and muscle phosphorylase, promoting glycogenolysis. This increases glucose output by the liver.
- **Skeletal muscle:** Epinephrine promotes glycogenolysis but because muscle lacks glucose-6-phosphatase, glucose cannot be released by skeletal muscle; instead, it must be metabolized at least to lactate before being released into the circulation.

- **Adipose tissue:** Epinephrine increases lipolysis in adipose tissue by increasing the activity of hormone-sensitive lipase. Glycerol from TG breakdown is a minor substrate for gluconeogenesis.
- Epinephrine increases the **metabolic rate.** This will not occur without thyroid hormones or the adrenal cortex.

Hormones of the Islets of Langerhans

The following figure shows the location and proportion of each major hormone-secreting cell type of the islets of Langerhans. Dashed arrows represent the local inhibitory paracrine action of each islet hormone, and the diameter of each circle approximately represents the proportion of each cell type present in the islets.

Clinical Correlate

For years C-peptide was considered to have no biological function, but more recently this has been questioned. Studies suggest that C-peptide receptors exist on cells. In addition, C-peptide may serve a protective role, helping to prevent the renal, neural, and microvascular pathologies seen when it is absent, i.e., type I diabetes mellitus.

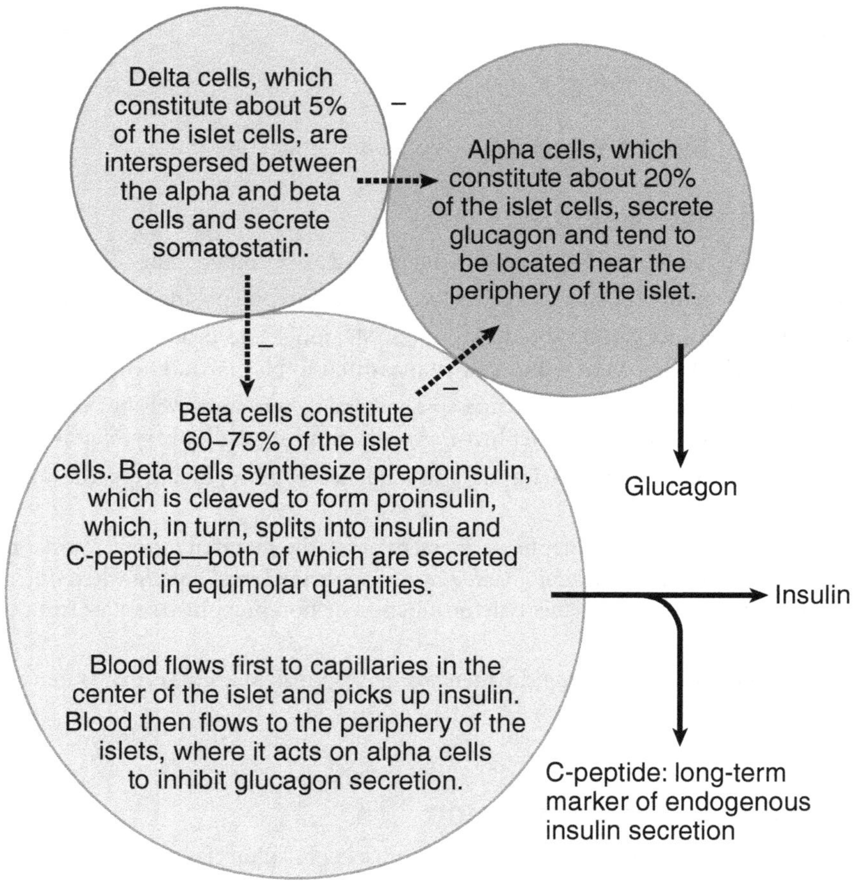

Figure 1-10. Hormones of the Pancreatic Islets

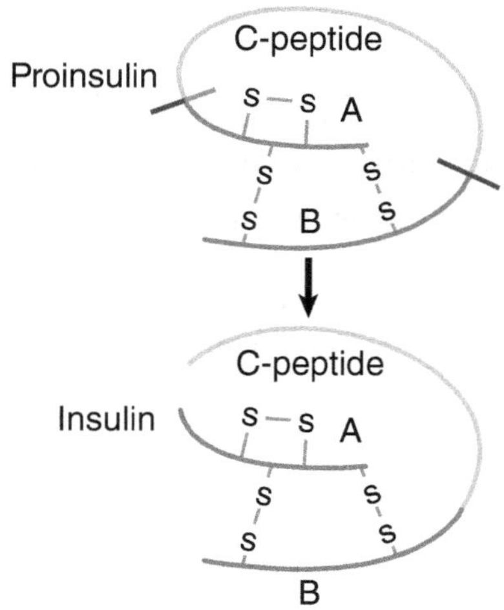

Figure 1-11. Insulin

Actions of Insulin

The portion of the insulin receptor that faces **externally** has the hormone-binding domain. The portion of the insulin receptor that faces the **cytosol** has tyrosine kinase activity. When occupied by insulin, the receptor phosphorylates itself and other proteins.

Glucose is taken up by peripheral tissues by facilitated diffusion. Insulin facilitates this uptake in some tissues. Typically the insulin receptor causes the insertion of glucose transporters in the membrane.

The tissues which **require insulin** for effective uptake of glucose are adipose tissue, resting skeletal muscle (although glucose can enter working muscle without the aid of insulin), and liver (because of glucokinase stimulation).

The tissues in which glucose uptake is **not affected by insulin** are nervous tissue, kidney tubules, intestinal mucosa, red blood cells, and β-cells of pancreas.

Metabolic Actions of Insulin

Insulin is a major anabolic hormone which secretes in response to a carbohydrate-and/or protein-containing meal. Anabolic hormones promote protein synthesis (increase lean body mass). Other anabolic hormones include thyroid hormones, growth hormone/IGF-1, and sex steroids (androgens).

Effects of Insulin on Carbohydrate Metabolism

By increasing glucose uptake in muscle, its metabolism in muscle and fat increases, i.e., its conversion to carbon dioxide and water is increased.

Insulin increases glycogen synthesis in liver and muscle. The activity of enzymes that promote glycogen synthesis (glucokinase and glycogen synthetase) is increased, and the activity of those enzymes that promote glycogen breakdown (phosphorylase and glucose-6-phosphatase) is decreased.

Glucokinase and glucose-6-phosphatase are expressed by the liver but not by muscle.

Effects of Insulin on Protein Metabolism

- Insulin increases amino acid uptake by muscle cells.
- Insulin increases protein synthesis.
- Insulin decreases protein breakdown (deficiency of insulin results in a breakdown of protein).

Effects of Insulin on Fat Metabolism

Insulin increases:

- Glucose uptake by fat cells (increases membrane transporters); by increasing glucose uptake, insulin also makes triose phosphates available for triglyceride synthesis in adipose tissue.
- Triglyceride uptake by fat cells; it increases the activity of lipoprotein lipase. Lipoprotein lipase is located on the endothelium of capillaries, and it catalyzes the release of free fatty acids from triglycerides.
- Triglyceride synthesis (lipogenesis) in adipose tissue and liver by stimulating the rate-limiting step, namely the carboxylation of acetyl CoA to malonyl CoA. In other words, insulin stimulates the conversion of carbohydrate into fat.

Summary

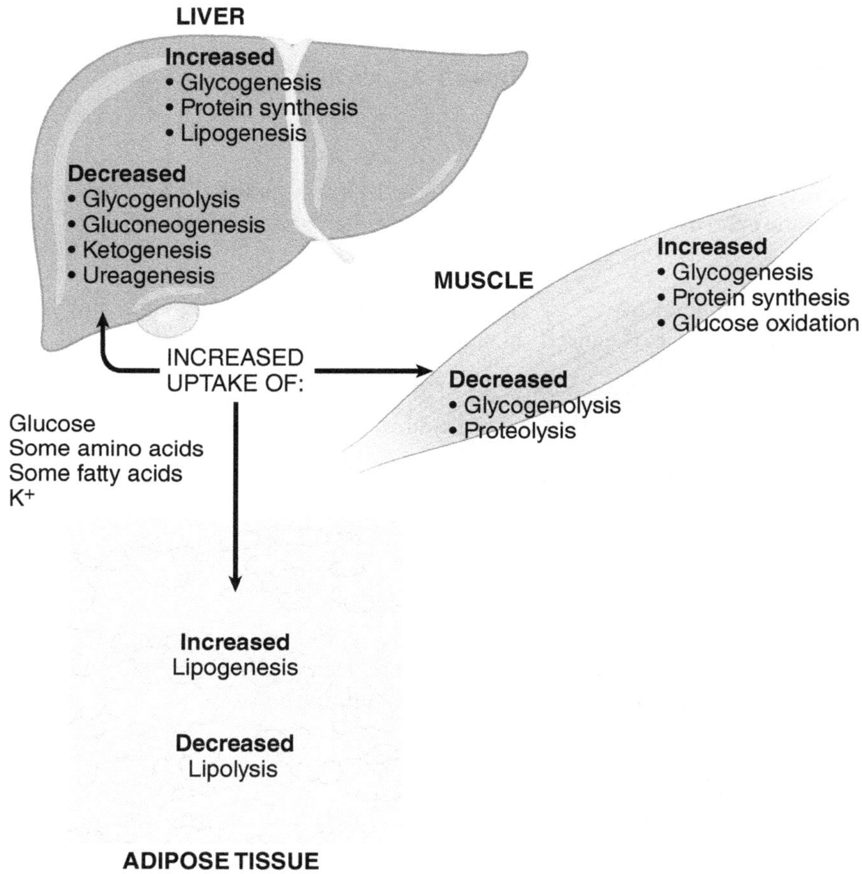

Figure 1-12. Major Actions of Insulin

Parathyroid Hormone (PTH)

A decrease in the free calcium is the signal to increase PTH secretion and the function of PTH is to raise free calcium, which it does by several mechanisms.

- Increases Ca^{2+} reabsorption in distal tubule of the kidney.
- Inhibits phosphate (Pi) reabsorption in proximal tubule of the kidney.

- Stimulates the 1-alpha-hydroxylase enzyme in kidney, converting inactive vitamin D to its active form.
- Causes bone resorption, releasing Ca^{2+} and Pi into the blood.

Bone Resorption

The mechanisms of PTH-induced bone resorption are complex and not fully understood. However, the following generalizations do apply.

- Osteoblasts express receptors for PTH. Binding of PTH stimulates the osteoblast to release RANK-L. This, in turn, increases osteoclastic activity resulting in bone resorption and the release of calcium and phosphate into the blood.
- Although counterintuitive, intermittent spikes in PTH (e.g. intravenous or subcutaneous injection) stimulate osteoblastic activity, resulting in bone deposition. Thus, PTH can be useful in treating osteoporosis in the clinical setting.

Regulation of PTH Secretion

PTH is a peptide hormone released from the parathyroid glands in response to lowered plasma free Ca^{2+}.

- Free Ca^{2+} in the plasma is the primary regulator of PTH.
- The negative feedback relationship between plasma calcium and PTH secretion is highly sigmoidal, with the steep portion of the curve representing the normal range of plasma free calcium.
- To sense the free calcium, the parathyroid cell depends upon high levels of expression of the calcium-sensing receptor (CaSR).
- In most cells, exocytosis depends on a rise in intracellular free calcium. In the parathyroid gland, a fall in intracellular free calcium causes release.
- Depletion of magnesium stores can create a reversible hypoparathyroidism.

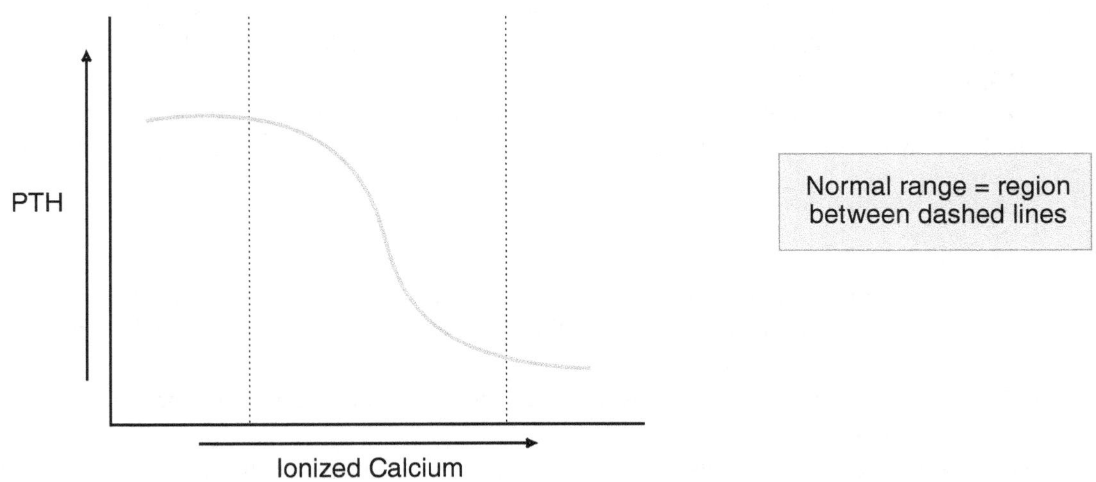

Figure 1-13. Relationship between Plasma Calcium and PTH

Calcitonin

Calcitonin (CT) is a peptide hormone secreted by the parafollicular cells (C cells) of the thyroid gland. It is released in response to elevated free calcium.

- Calcitonin lowers plasma calcium by decreasing the activity of osteoclasts, thus decreasing bone resorption. Calcitonin is useful in the treatment of Paget's disease, severe hypercalcemia, and osteoporosis.

- Calcitonin is not a major controller of Ca^{2+} in humans. Removing the thyroid (with the C cells) or excess of calcitonin via a C cell tumor (medullary carcinoma of the thyroid) has little impact on plasma calcium.
- No deficiency or excess disease has been described.

Thyroid Hormones

In mammals, thyroid hormones are essential for normal growth and maturation. Therefore, thyroid hormones are major anabolic hormones.

Dietary intake of about 500 µg per day is typical, mainly in the form of iodide (I^-) or iodine (I). To maintain normal thyroid hormone secretion, 150 µg is the minimal intake necessary. I^- is the form absorbed from the small intestine.

- The functional unit of the thyroid gland is the follicle.
- The lumen is filled with thyroglobulin, which contains large numbers of thyroid hormone molecules.
- Surrounding the lumen are the follicle cells, which function to both synthesize and release thyroid hormones.

Physiologic Actions of Thyroid Hormones

In many tissues, thyroid hormones are not the prime indicators or the major inhibitors of specific cellular processes. Rather, a multitude of processes function properly only when optimal amounts of thyroid hormones are present. This underscores the permissive nature of thyroid hormones.

Metabolic Rate

- Thyroid hormones increase metabolic rate, as evidenced by increased O_2 consumption and heat production.
- Thyroid hormones increase the activity of the membrane-bound Na^+/K^-ATPase in many tissues; it can be argued that it is the increased pumping of Na^+ that accounts for most of the increase in metabolic rate.
- The increase in metabolic rate produced by a single dose of T_4 occurs only after a latency of several hours but may last 6 days or more.
- Thyroid hormones are absolutely necessary for normal brain maturation and essential for normal menstrual cycles. Hypothyroidism leads to menstrual irregularities (menorrhagia) and infertility (anovulatory cycles).

Growth and Maturation (T4 and T3 Anabolic Hormones)

Fetal growth rates appear normal in the absence of thyroid hormone production (i.e., if the fetus is hypothyroid). However, without adequate thyroid hormones during the perinatal period, abnormalities rapidly develop in nervous system maturation.

- Synapses develop abnormally and there is decreased dendritic branching and myelination. These abnormalities lead to mental retardation.
- These neural changes are irreversible and lead to cretinism unless replacement therapy is started soon after birth.

Lipid Metabolism

- Thyroid hormone accelerates cholesterol clearance from the plasma.
- Thyroid hormones are required for conversion of carotene to vitamin A; as a consequence, hypothyroid individuals can suffer from night blindness and yellowing of the skin.

CHO Metabolism

- Thyroid hormone increases the rate of glucose absorption from the small intestine.

Cardiovascular Effects

- Thyroid hormones have positive inotropic and chronotropic effects on the heart.
- The increased contractility is partly direct and partly indirect: they increase the number and affinity of β-adrenergic receptors in the heart, thereby increasing the sensitivity to catecholamines.
- Acting on the SA node, they directly increase heart rate.
- Cardiac output is increased, and both heart rate and stroke volume are elevated.
- Systolic pressure increases are due to increased stroke volume, and diastolic pressure decreases are due to decreased peripheral resistance.
- Thyroid hormones in the normal range are required for optimum cardiac performance.

Physiologic Actions of Growth Hormone

All anabolic hormones (i.e., growth hormone, insulin, thyroid hormones, and androgens) are required for normal growth. Most of the direct actions of these hormones are consistent with their actions as a stress hormone. A direct anabolic action of these hormones is the promotion of amino acid entry into cells, thus making these amino acids more available for protein synthesis. However, most of the anabolic actions of growth hormone are indirect via the production of growth factors.

Physiological effects of growth hormone include mobilization of fatty acids by increasing lipolysis in adipose tissue. This increases muscle mass and calcium retention, stimulates the immune system and has other physiological effects.

NEUROLOGY

The autonomic nervous system (ANS) is responsible for the motor innervation of smooth muscle, cardiac muscle, and glands of the body. The ANS is composed of 2 divisions: sympathetic and parasympathetic. In both divisions there are 2 neurons in the peripheral distribution of the motor innervation.

- Preganglionic neuron with cell body in CNS
- Postganglionic neuron with cell body in a ganglion in PNS

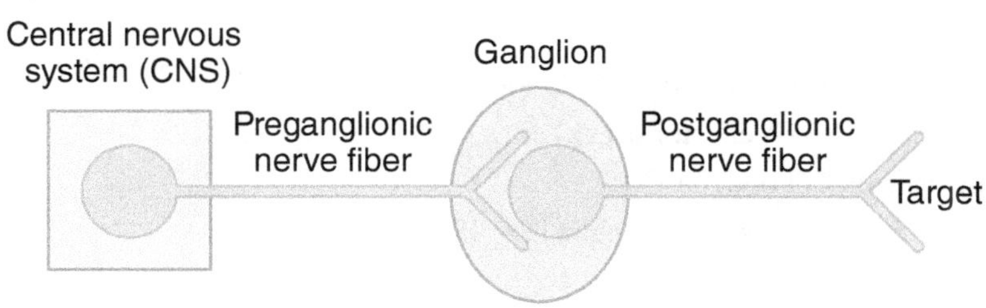

Figure 1-14. Autonomic Nervous System

Peripheral Nervous System

N_N: neuronal nicotinic receptor

N_M: muscle nicotinic receptor

NE: norepinephrine

M: muscarinic receptor

ACh: acetylcholine

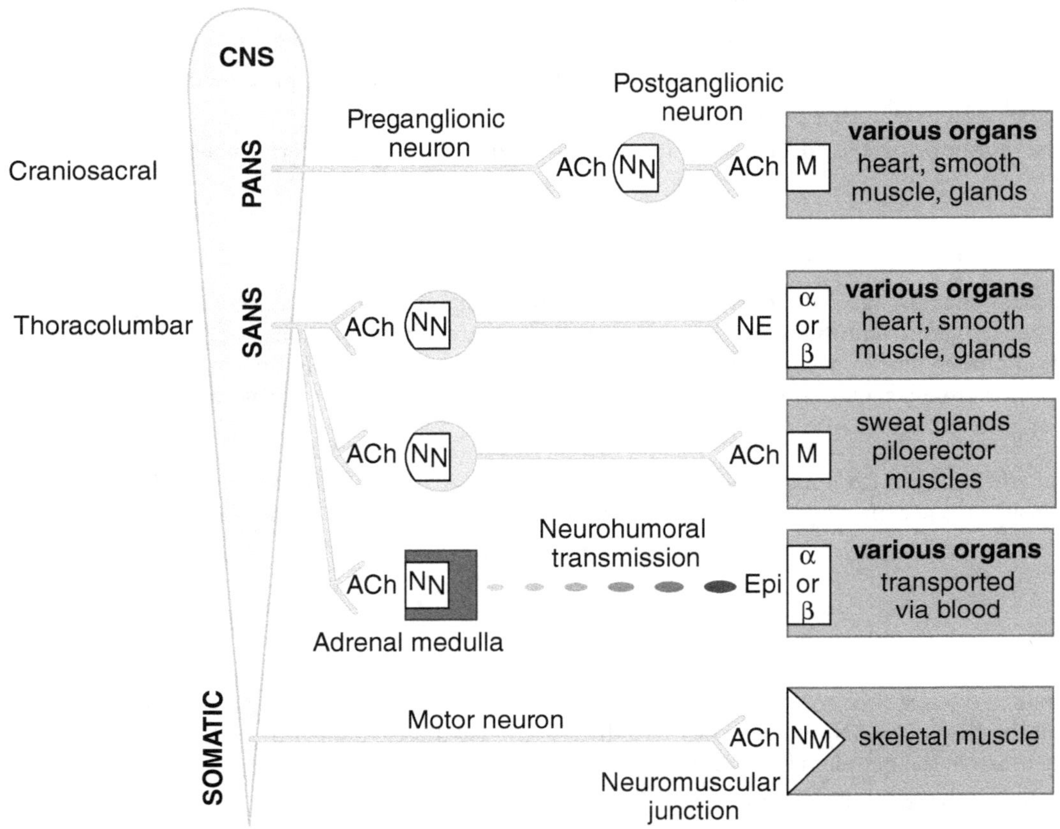

Figure 1-15. Autonomic and Somatic Nervous System Neurotransmitters/Receptors

- **Somatic nervous system:** 1 neuron (from CNS → effector organ)
- **ANS:** 2 neurons (from CNS → effector organ)
  - **Preganglionic** neuron: cell body in CNS
  - **Postganglionic** neuron: cell body in ganglia in PNS
  - **Parasympathetic:** long preganglionic, short postganglionic
  - **Sympathetic:** short preganglionic, long postganglionic (except adrenal medulla)

Parasympathetic Nervous System

Clinical Correlate

Hirschsprung's disease results from missing terminal ganglia in wall of rectum. Infant cannot pass meconium.

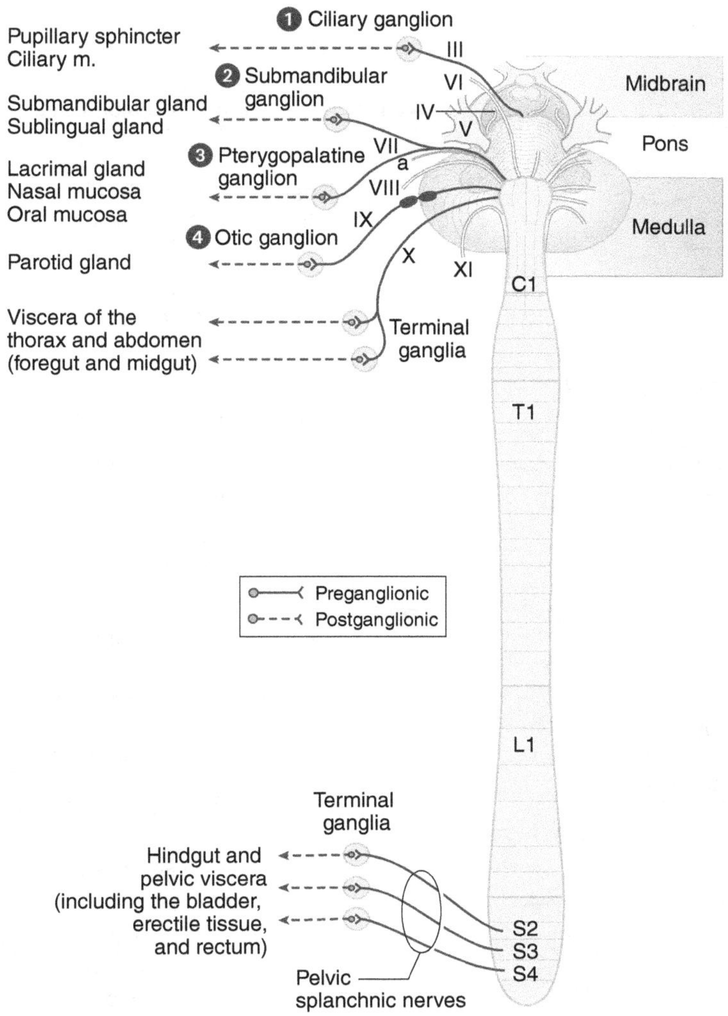

Figure 1-16. Overview of Parasympathetic Outflow

Table 1-1. Parasympathetic = Craniosacral Outflow

Origin	Site of Synapse	Innervation
Cranial nerves III, VII, IX	Four cranial ganglia	Glands and smooth muscle of the head
Cranial nerve X	Terminal ganglia (in or near the walls of viscera)	Viscera of the neck, thorax, foregut, and midgut
Pelvic splanchnic nerves (S2, S3, S4)	Terminal ganglia (in or near the walls of viscera)	Hindgut and pelvic viscera (including bladder and erectile tissue)

Note

Horner's syndrome results in *ipsilateral* ptosis, miosis, anhydrosis

Sympathetic Nervous System

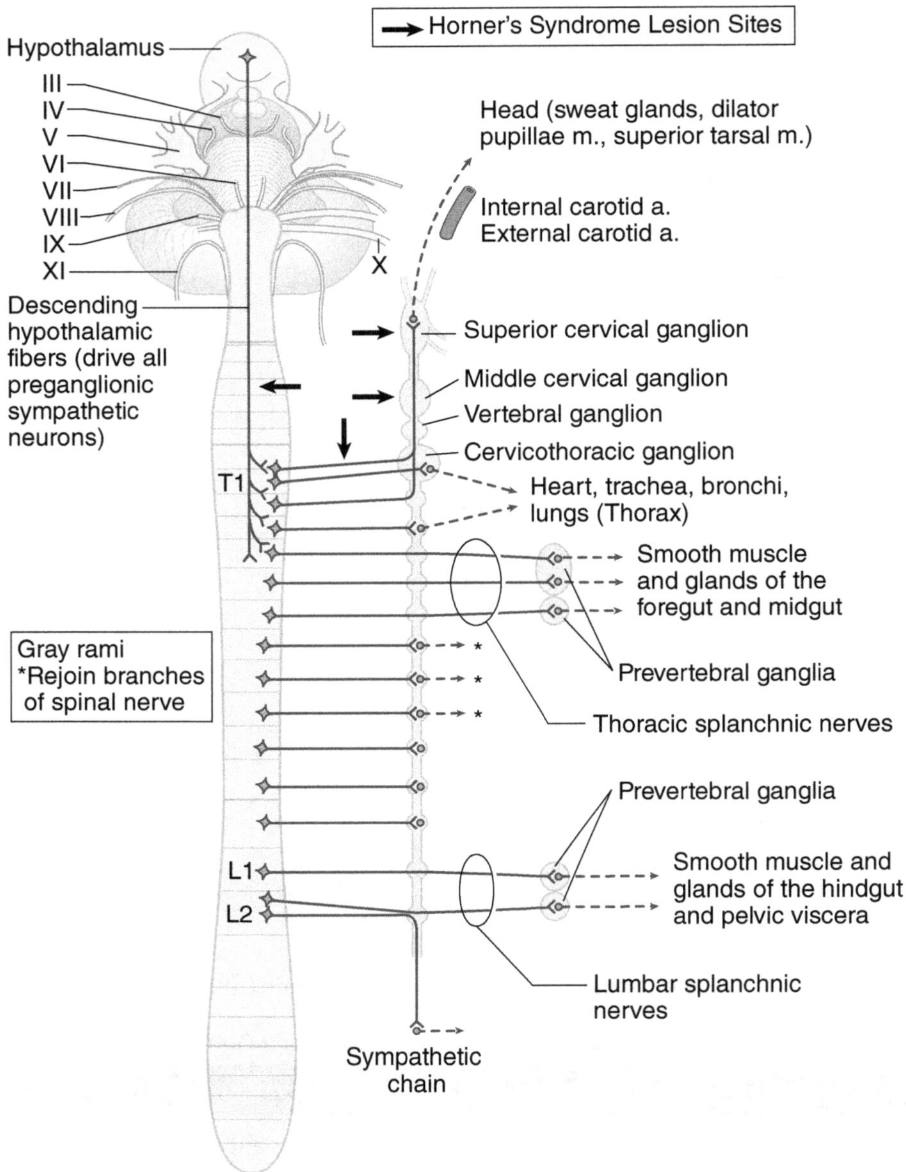

Figure 1-17. Overview of Sympathetic Outflow

Neurons

Neurons are cells that are morphologically and functionally polarized so information can pass from one end of the cell to the other. They are classified by the form and number of their processes as bipolar, unipolar, or multipolar. The cell body of the neuron contains the nucleus and membrane-bound cytoplasmic organelles typical of a eukaryotic cell, including endoplasmic reticulum (ER), Golgi apparatus, mitochondria, and lysosomes. The nucleus and nucleolus are prominent in neurons.

The cytoplasm contains Nissl substance, clumps of rough ER with bound polysomes. The cytoplasm also contains free polysomes; free and bound polysomes in the Nissl substance are sites of protein synthesis.

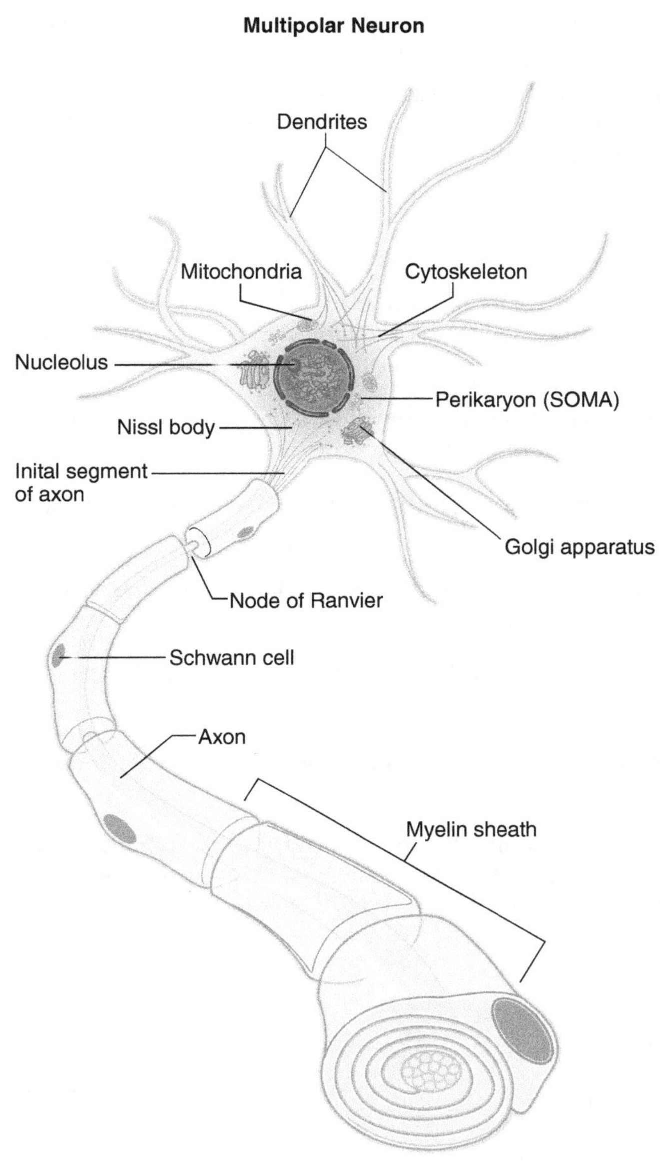

Figure 1-18. Neuron Structure

The following are key points related to neurons:

- **Neurons** are composed of a cell body, dendrites, and an axon. They contain pigments such as melanin and lipofuscin.
- The **cell body** (soma or perikaryon) contains a nucleus, other cellular components, and rough endoplasmic reticulum (ER). Microtubules and neurofilaments form the cytoskeleton. They are important for axonal transport.
- **Dendrites** receive and transmit information to the cell body.
- **Axons** arise from the perikaryon or proximal dendrite. They contain microtubules and neurofilaments. Rapid axonal transport utilizes microtubules. Kinesins promote anterograde transport, whereas dynein promotes retrograde transport.
- **Myelin** is the covering of axons and is composed of phospholipids and cholesterol. Axons may be myelinated or nonmyelinated. Schwann cells myelinate a single peripheral nervous system (PNS) axon.

- Neurons may also associate with several axons (unmyelinated) without forming myelin. **Oligodendrocytes** form myelin in the central nervous system (CNS). One oligodendrocyte myelinates many axons.
- The **node of Ranvier** is a collar of naked axon between a proximal and distal bundle of myelin that has myelinated the axon. Its purpose is to allow rapid signal transport by rapidly moving from one node to the next, which is called saltatory conduction.

Spinal Cord

The spinal cord is housed in the vertebral canal. It is continuous with the medulla below the pyramidal decussation and terminates as the conus medullaris at the second lumbar vertebra of the adult. The roots of 31 pairs of spinal nerves arise segmentally from the spinal cord.

There are **8 cervical pairs** of spinal nerves (C1 through C8). The cervical enlargement (C5 through T1) gives rise to the rootlets that form the brachial plexus, which innervates the upper limbs.

There are **12 thoracic pairs** of spinal nerves (T1 through T12). Spinal nerves emanating from thoracic levels innervate most of the trunk.

There are **5 lumbar pairs** of spinal nerves (L1 through L5). The lumbar enlargement (L1 through S2) gives rise to rootlets that form the lumbar and sacral plexuses, which innervate the lower limbs.

There are **5 sacral pairs** of spinal nerves (S1 through S5). Spinal nerves at the sacral level innervate part of the lower limbs and the pelvis.

There is **one coccygeal pair** of spinal nerves. The cauda equina consists of the dorsal and ventral roots of the lumbar, sacral, and coccygeal spinal nerves.

Inside the spinal cord, gray matter is centrally located and shaped like a butterfly. It contains neuronal cell bodies, their dendrites, and the proximal parts of axons. White matter that surrounds the gray matter on all sides contains bundles of functionally similar axons called tracts or fasciculi, which ascend or descend in the spinal cord.

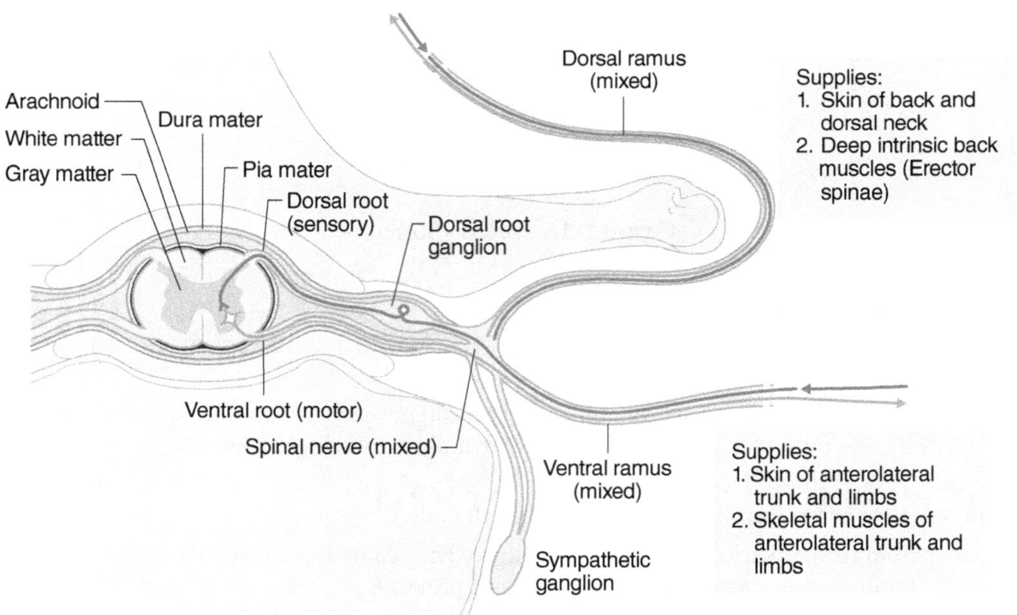

Figure 1-19. Cross Section of Spinal Cord and Parts of Spinal Nerve

Cranial Nerves

Twelve pairs of cranial nerves (CN) emerge from the brain and lead to various parts of the head, neck, and trunk.

Table 1-2. Cranial Nerves: Functional Features

CN	Name	Type	Function	Results of Lesions
I	Olfactory	Sensory	Smells	Anosmia
II	Optic	Sensory	Sees	Visual field deficits (anopsia) Loss of light reflex with III Only nerve to be affected by MS
III	Oculomotor	Motor	Innervates SR, IR, MR, IO extraocular muscles: adduction (MR) most important action Raises eyelid (levator palpebrae superioris) Constricts pupil (sphincter pupillae) Accommodates (ciliary muscle)	Diplopia, external strabismus Loss of parallel gaze Ptosis Dilated pupil, loss of light reflex with II Loss of near response
IV	Trochlear	Motor	Superior oblique—depresses and abducts eyeball (makes eyeball look down and out) Intorts	Weakness looking down with adducted eye Trouble going down stairs Head tilts away from lesioned side
V	Trigeminal Ophthalmic (V1) Maxillary (V2) Mandibular (V3)	Mixed	General sensation (touch, pain, temperature) of forehead/scalp/cornea General sensation of palate, nasal cavity, maxillary face, maxillary teeth General sensation of anterior $^2/_3$ of tongue, mandibular face, mandibular teeth Motor to muscles of mastication (temporalis, masseter, medial and lateral pterygoids) and anterior belly of digastric, mylohyoid, tensor tympani, tensor palati	V1—loss of general sensation in skin of forehead/scalp Loss of blink reflex with VII V2—loss of general sensation in skin over maxilla, maxillary teeth V3—loss of general sensation in skin over mandible, mandibular teeth, tongue, weakness in chewing Jaw deviation toward weak side Trigeminal neuralgia—intractable pain in V2 or V3 territory
VI	Abducens	Motor	Lateral rectus—abducts eyeball	Diplopia, internal strabismus Loss of parallel gaze, "pseudoptosis"

(Continued)

CN	Name	Type	Function	Results of Lesions
VII	Facial	Mixed	To muscles of facial expression, posterior belly of digastric, stylohyoid, stapedius Salivation (submandibular, sublingual glands) Skin behind ear Taste in anterior $\frac{2}{3}$ of tongue/palate Tears (lacrimal gland)	Corner of mouth droops, cannot close eye, cannot wrinkle forehead, loss of blink reflex, hyperacusis; Bell palsy—lesion of nerve in facial canal Pain behind ear Alteration or loss of taste (ageusia) Eye dry and red
VIII	Vestibulocochlear	Sensory	Hearing Angular acceleration (head turning) Linear acceleration (gravity)	Sensorineural hearing loss Loss of balance, nystagmus
IX	Glossopharyngeal	Mixed	Oropharynx sensation, carotid sinus/body Salivation (parotid gland) All sensation of posterior $\frac{1}{3}$ of tongue Motor to one muscle—stylopharyngeus	Loss of gag reflex with X
X	Vagus	Mixed	To muscles of palate and pharynx for swallowing except tensor palati (V) and stylopharyngeus (IX) To all muscles of larynx (phonates) Sensory of larynx and laryngopharynx Sensory of GI tract To GI tract smooth muscle and glands in foregut and midgut	Nasal speech, nasal regurgitation Dysphagia, palate droop Uvula pointing away from affected side Hoarseness/fixed vocal cord Loss of gag reflex with IX Loss of cough reflex
XI	Accessory	Motor	Head rotation to opposite side (sternocleidomastoid) Elevates and rotates scapula (trapezius)	Weakness turning chin to opposite side Shoulder droop
XII	Hypoglossal	Motor	Tongue movement (styloglossus, hyoglossus, genioglossus, and intrinsic tongue muscles—palatoglossus is by X)	Tongue pointing toward same (affected) side on protrusion

Abbreviations: IO, inferior oblique; IR, inferior rectus; MR, medial rectus; MS, multiple sclerosis; SR, superior rectus

RESPIRATORY SYSTEM

Lung Volume and Capacity Definitions

Tidal volume (VT): amount of air that enters or leaves the lung in a single respiratory cycle (500 mL)

Functional residual capacity (FRC): amount of gas in the lungs at the end of a passive expiration; the neutral or equilibrium point for the respiratory system (2,700 mL); it is a marker for lung compliance

Inspiratory capacity (IC): maximal volume of gas that can be inspired from FRC (4,000 mL)

Inspiratory reserve volume (IRV): additional amount of air that can be inhaled after a normal inspiration (3,500 mL)

Expiratory reserve volume (ERV): additional volume that can be expired after a passive expiration (1,500 mL)

Residual volume (RV): amount of air in the lung after a maximal expiration (1,200 mL)

Vital capacity (VC): maximal volume that can be expired after a maximal inspiration (5,500 mL)

Total lung capacity (TLC): amount of air in the lung after a maximal inspiration (6,700 mL)

The purpose of understanding lung mechanics is to view them in the larger clinical picture of pulmonary function test (PFT) interpretation. The PFT is the key diagnostic test for the pulmonologist, just as the EKG is to the cardiologist. PFTs consist of 3 individual tests:

- Measurements of static lung compartments (meaning lung volumes)
- Airflow used to evaluate dynamic compliance using a spirometer
- Alveolar membrane permeability using carbon monoxide as a marker of diffusion

Lung Volumes and Capacities

The following figure graphs the relationships among the various lung volumes and capacities. Clinical measurements of specific volumes and capacities provide insights into lung function and the origin of disease processes. Those that provide the greatest information display an *.

The values for the volumes and capacities given below are typical for a 70 kg male.

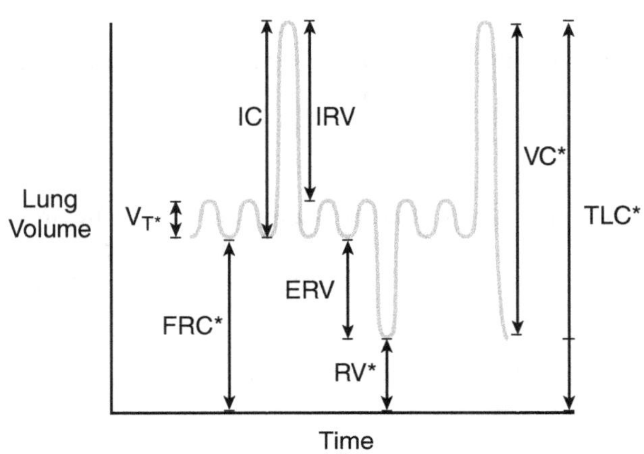

Figure 1-20. Lung Volumes and Capacities

A spirometer can measure only changes in lung volume. As such, it cannot measure the residual volume (RV) or any capacity containing RV. Thus, TLC and FRC cannot be measured using simple spirometry; an indirect method must be used. Three common indirect methods are helium dilution, nitrogen washout, and plethysmography.

Ventilation

Total ventilation is also referred to as minute volume or minute ventilation. It is the total volume of air moved in or out (usually the volume expired) of the lungs per minute.

$$\dot{V}_E = V_T \times f$$

$\dot{V}_E$ = total ventilation
V_T = tidal volume
f = respiratory rate

Normal resting values would be:

V_T = 500 mL
f = 15
500 mL × 15/min = 7,500 mL/min

Dead Space

In a Nutshell

What is the function of functional residual capacity (FRC)?

Answer: Breathing is cyclic, while blood flow through the pulmonary capillary bed is continuous. During the respiratory cycle, there are short periods of apneas at the end of inspiration and expiration when there is no ventilation but there is continuous blood flow. Without the FRC acting as a buffer for continued gas exchange during apneic periods, these conditions would in effect create an intrapulmonary shunt, inducing deoxygenated blood from the pulmonary capillaries to empty into the pulmonary veins.

Regions of the respiratory system that contain air but are not exchanging O_2 and CO_2 with blood are considered dead space.

Anatomic Dead Space

Anatomic dead space consists of airway regions that, because of inherent structure, are not capable of O_2 and CO_2 exchange with the blood. Anatomic dead space (anatV_D) includes the conducting zone, which ends at the level of the terminal bronchioles. Significant gas exchange (O_2 uptake and CO_2 removal) with the blood occurs only in the alveoli.

The size of the anatV_D in mL is approximately equal to a person's weight in pounds. Thus a 150-lb individual has an anatomic dead space of 150 mL.

Composition of the Anatomic Dead Space and the Respiratory Zone

The respiratory zone is a very constant environment. Under resting conditions, rhythmic ventilation introduces a small volume into a much larger respiratory zone. Thus, the partial pressure of gases in the alveolar compartment changes very little during normal rhythmic ventilation.

Composition at the end of expiration (before inspiration)

At the end of an expiration, the anatV_D is filled with air that originated in the alveoli or respiratory zone. Thus, the composition of the air in the entire respiratory system is the same at this static point in the respiratory cycle. This also means that a sample of expired gas taken near the end of expiration (end tidal air) is representative of the respiratory zone.

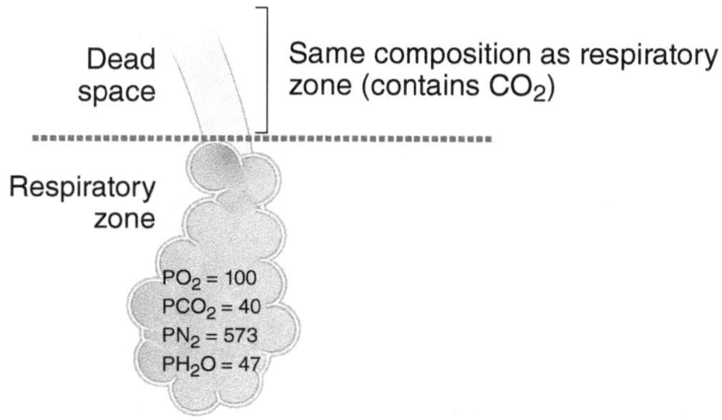

Figure 1-21. End of Expiration

Composition at the end of inspiration (before expiration)

- The first 150 mL of air to reach the alveoli comes from the anatV_D.
- It is air that remained in the dead space at the end of the previous expiration and has the same composition as alveolar gas.
- After the first 150 mL enters the alveoli, room air is added to the respiratory zone.
- At the end of inspiration the anatV_D is filled with room air.
- The presence of the anatV_D implies the following: in order to get fresh air into the alveoli, one must always take a tidal volume larger than the volume of the anatV_D.

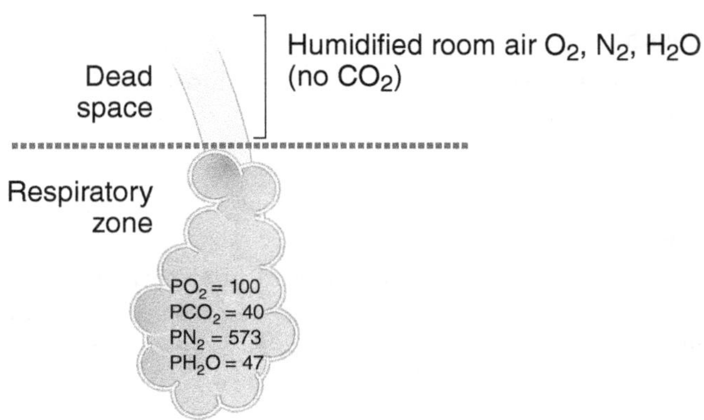

Figure 1-22. End of Inspiration

Alveolar Dead Space

Alveolar dead space (alvV_D) refers to alveoli containing air but without blood flow in the surrounding capillaries. An example is a pulmonary embolus.

Physiologic Dead Space

Physiologic dead space (physiolV_D) refers to the total dead space in the lung system (anatV_D + alvV_D). When the physiol V_D is greater than the anatV_D, it implies the presence of alvV_D, i.e., somewhere in the lung, alveoli are being ventilated but not perfused.

Total Ventilation

$$\dot{V} = VT\ (f)$$
$$= 500\ (15)$$
$$= 7{,}500\ \text{mL/min}$$

Minute ventilation ($\dot{V}$) is the total volume of air entering the lungs per minute.

Alveolar Ventilation

Alveolar ventilation $\dot{V}_A$ represents the room air delivered to the respiratory zone per breath.

- The first 150 mL of each inspiration comes from the anatomic dead space and does not contribute to alveolar ventilation.
- However, every additional mL beyond 150 does contribute to alveolar ventilation.

$\dot{V}_A$ = alveolar ventilation
V_T = tidal volume
V_D = dead space
f = respiratory rate

$$\dot{V}_A = (V_T - V_D)\ f$$
$$= (500\ \text{mL} - 150\ \text{mL})\ 15 = 5250\ \text{mL/min}$$

The alveolar ventilation per inspiration is 350 mL. This equation implies that the volume of fresh air that enters the respiratory zone per minute depends on the pattern of breathing (how large a V_T and the rate of breathing).

Increases in the Depth of Breathing

There are equal increases in total and alveolar ventilation per breath, since dead space volume is constant. If the depth of breathing increases from a depth of 500 mL to a depth of 700 mL, the increase in total and alveolar ventilation is 200 mL per breath.

Increases in the Rate of Breathing

There is a greater increase in total ventilation per minute than in alveolar ventilation per minute, because the increased rate causes increased ventilation of dead space and alveoli. For every additional inspiration with a tidal volume of 500 mL, total ventilation increases 500 mL, but alveolar ventilation only increases by 350 mL (assuming dead space is 150 mL).

For example, given the following, which person has the greater alveolar ventilation?

	Tidal Volume	Rate	Total Ventilation
Person A	600 mL	10/min	6,000 mL/min
Person B	300 mL	20/min	6,000 mL/min

Answer: Person A. Person B has rapid, shallow breathing. This person has a large component of dead-space ventilation (first 150 mL of each inspiration). Even though total ventilation may be normal, alveolar ventilation is decreased. Therefore, the individual is hypoventilating.

In rapid, shallow breathing, total ventilation may be above normal, but alveolar ventilation may be below normal.

MUSCULAR AND SKELETAL SYSTEMS

The skeletal and muscular systems work together to allow for movement and provide a framework for the human body.

Skeletal Muscle Structure–Function Relationships

A myofibril is an elongated contractile muscle tread found in human striated muscle cells.

Ultrastructure of a Myofibril

- A muscle is made up of individual cells called muscle fibers.
- Longitudinally within the muscle fibers, there are bundles of myofibrils. A magnified portion is shown in the figure below.
- A myofibril can be subdivided into individual sarcomeres. A sarcomere is demarked by a Z line.
- Sarcomeres are composed of filaments creating bands as illustrated below.
- Contraction causes no change in the length of the A band, a shortening of the I band, and a shortening in the H zone (band).
- Titin anchors myosin and is an important component of striated muscle's elasticity.

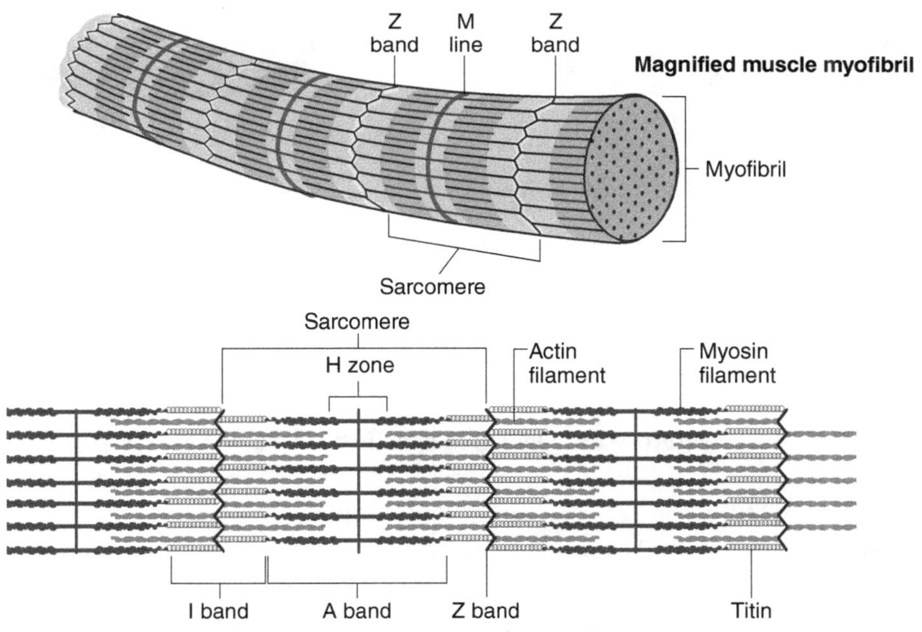

Figure 1-23. Organization of Sarcomeres

Ultrastructure of the Sarcoplasmic Reticulum

The external and internal membrane system of a skeletal muscle cell is displayed here.

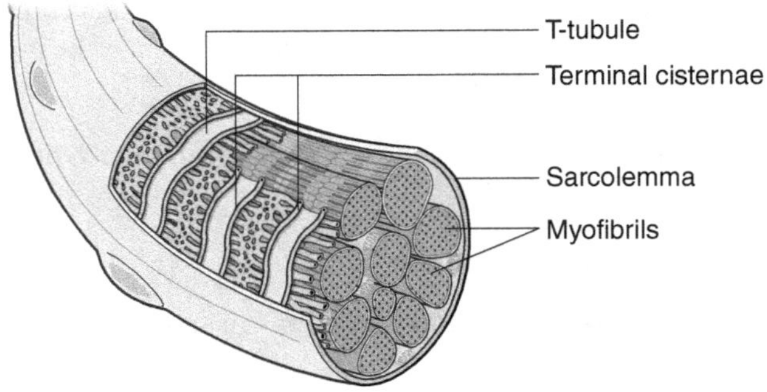

Figure 1-24. Skeletal Muscle Cell Membranes

T-tubule membranes are extensions of the surface membrane; therefore, the interiors of the T-tubules are part of the extracellular compartment.

Terminal cisternae: The sarcoplasmic reticulum is part of the internal membrane system, one function of which is to store calcium. In skeletal muscle, most of the calcium is stored in the terminal cisternae close to the T-tubule system.

Functional Proteins of the Sarcomere

The following figure shows the relationships among the various proteins that make up the thin and thick filaments in striated muscle (skeletal and cardiac) and the changes that occur with contraction.

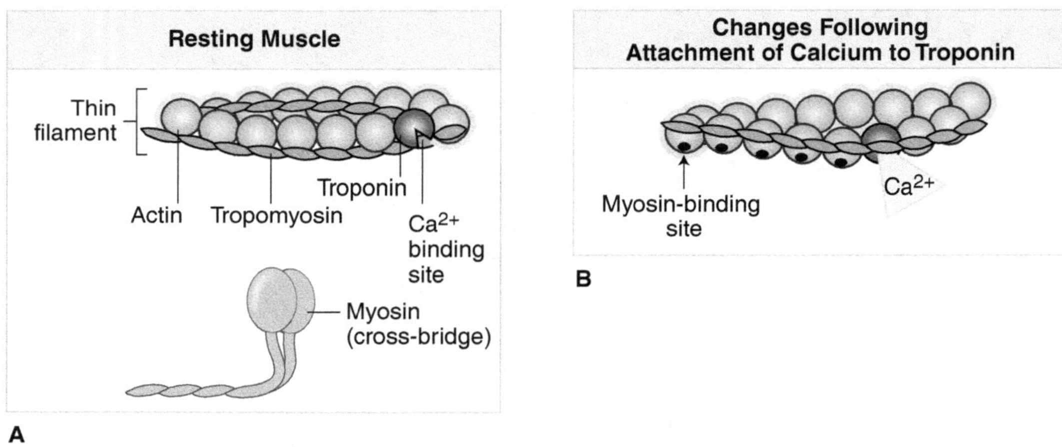

Figure 1-25. Regulation of Actin by Troponin

Proteins of the Thin Filaments

- **Actin** is the structural protein of the thin filament. It possesses attachment sites for myosin.
- **Tropomyosin** blocks myosin binding sites on actin.
- **Troponin** is composed of 3 subunits: **troponin-T** (binds to tropomyosin), **troponin-I** (binds to actin and inhibits contraction), and **troponin-C** (binds to calcium).
  - Under resting conditions, no calcium is bound to the troponin, preventing actin and myosin from interacting.
  - When calcium binds to troponin-C, the troponin-tropomyosin complex moves, exposing actin's binding site for myosin.

Proteins of the Thick Filaments

Myosin has ATPase activity. The splitting of ATP puts myosin in a "high energy" state; it also increases myosin's affinity for actin.

- Once myosin binds to actin, the chemical energy is transferred to mechanical energy, causing myosin to pull the actin filament. This generates active tension in the muscle and is commonly referred to as "the power stroke."
- If the force generated by the power stroke is sufficient to move the load, then the muscle shortens (isotonic contraction).
- If the force generated is not sufficient to move the load, then the muscle doesn't shorten (isometric contraction).

Cross-Bridge Interactions (Chemical-Mechanical Transduction)

Cross-bridge cycling starts when free calcium is available and attaches to troponin, which in turn moves tropomyosin so that myosin binds to actin. There are several steps involved for cross-bridge cycling in a contracting muscle.

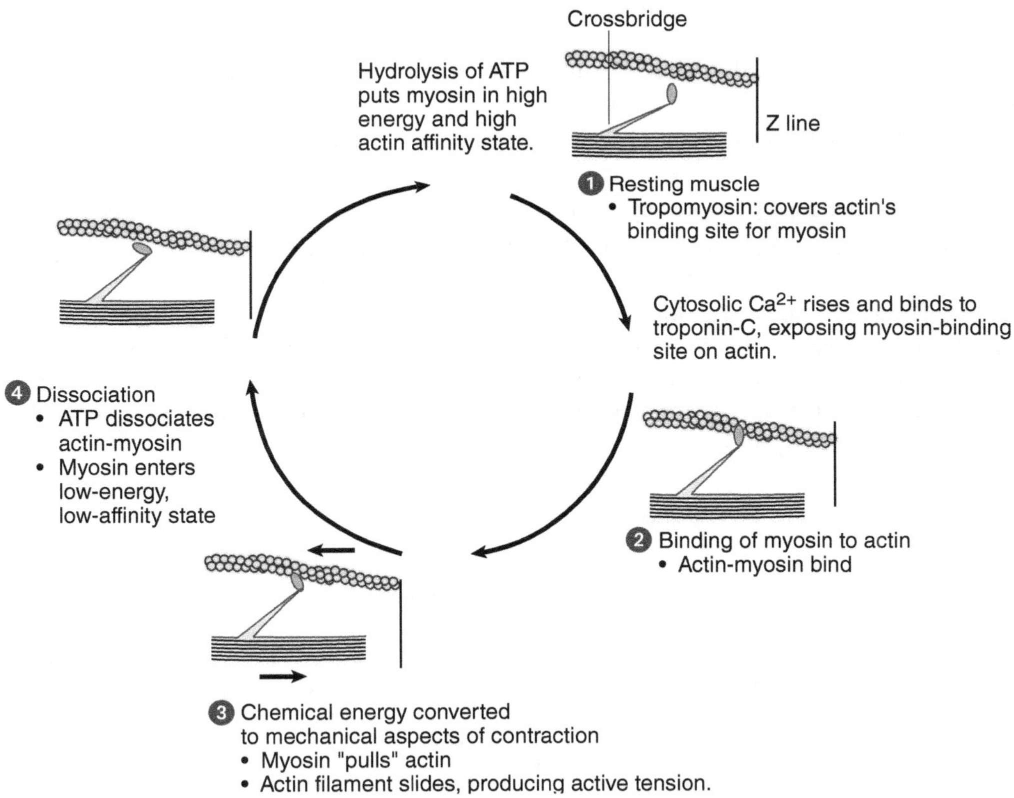

Figure 1-26. Crossbridge Cycling During Contraction

Contraction is the continuous cycling of cross-bridges. ATP is not required to form the cross-bridge linking to actin but is required to break the link with actin. Cross-bridge cycling (contraction) continues until either of the following occurs:

- Withdrawal of Ca^{2+}: cycling stops at position 1 (normal resting muscle)
- ATP is depleted: cycling stops at position 3 (rigor mortis; this would not occur under physiologic conditions)

Comparison of Striated Muscles (Skeletal vs. Cardiac)

Skeletal and cardiac muscle are both striated muscle and share many similarities. Nevertheless, there are important differences.

Similarities

- Both have the same functional proteins, i.e., actin, tropomyosin, troponin, myosin, and titin.
- A rise in cytosolic Ca^{2+} initiates cross-bridge cycling thereby producing active tension.
- ATP plays the same role.
- Both have SERCA.
- Both have RyR receptors on the SR and thus show calcium-induced calcium release.

Bridge to Pathology

Dysfunction in the titin protein has been associated with dilated and restrictive cardiomyopathies (see next section).

Differences

- Extracellular Ca^{2+} is involved in cardiac contractions, but not skeletal muscle. This extracellular Ca^{2+} causes calcium-induced calcium release in cardiac cells.
- Magnitude of SR Ca^{2+} release can be altered in cardiac (see section on cardiac mechanics), but not skeletal muscle.
- Cardiac cells are electrically coupled by gap junctions, which do not exist in skeletal muscle.
- Cardiac myocytes remove cytosolic Ca^{2+} by 2 mechanisms: SERCA and a Na^+—Ca^{2+} exchanger (3 Na^+ in, 1 Ca^{2+} out) on the sarcolemmal membrane. Skeletal muscle only utilizes SERCA.
- Cardiac cells have a prolonged action potential. The figure below illustrates that the twitch tension is already falling (muscle starting to relax) while the action potential is still in the absolute refractory period. Thus, a second action potential cannot be evoked before the mechanical event is almost completed. This approximately equal mechanical and electrical event prevents summation of the force and if the muscle can't summate, it can't tetanize.

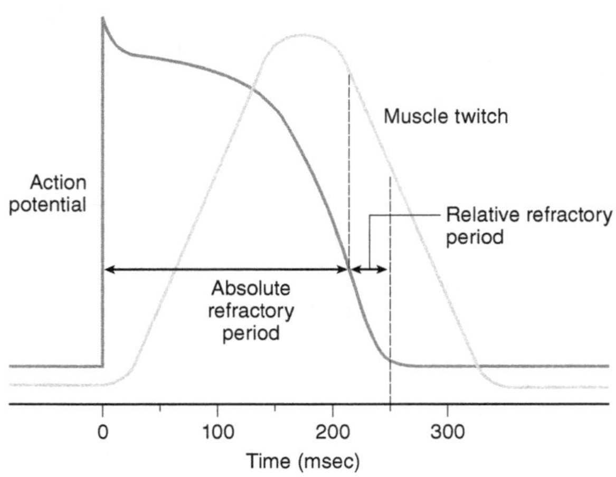

Figure 1-27. Force and Refractory Periods

Comparison of Muscle Types

Table 1-3. Histologic Features of Skeletal, Cardiac, and Smooth Muscle

Skeletal	Cardiac	Smooth
Striated	Striated	Nonstriated
Actin and myosin form sarcomeres	Actin and myosin form sarcomeres	Actin and myosin not organized into sarcomeres
Sarcolemma lacks junctional complexes between fibers	Junctional complexes between fibers including gap junctions	Gap junctions
Each fiber innervated	Electrical syncytium	Electrical syncytium
Troponin to bind calcium	Troponin to bind calcium	Calmodulin to bind calcium
High ATPase activity (fast muscle)	Intermediate ATPase activity	Low ATPase activity (slow muscle)
Extensive sarcoplasmic reticulum	Intermediate sarcoplasmic reticulum	Limited sarcoplasmic reticulum
T-tubules form triadic contacts with reticulum at A-I junctions	T-tubules form dyadic contact with reticulum near Z lines	Lack T-tubules, SR controlled by second messengers
Surface membrane lacks calcium channels	Voltage-gated calcium channels	Voltage-gated calcium channels

Skeletal System

The skeletal system is comprised of bones, cartilage, and joints. Together they form the human skeleton, the solid framework around which all of the organs, connective tissue, and neural networks are built.

- **Bones**: weight bearing structure of human body; responsible for maintaining the strength and framework of human skeleton
- **Cartilage**: form of connective tissue less tough/rigid than bone; connects the joints between bones, rib cage, ear, nose, bronchial tubes, and intervertebral discs
- **Joints**: joints occur between "2 or more bones," "bone and cartilage" and "cartilage and cartilage"; permit mobility in the human skeleton

The primary functions of the human skeletal are:

- Strength, support, and shape of the human body
- Protection of organs
- Initiation and leverage of movement in conjunction with skeletal muscle
- Production of red blood cells in the bone marrow

Bone Remodeling

Bone undergoes continual remodeling throughout life, although the turnover is faster in younger individuals. As many as 300,000 bone-remodeling sites are active in a normal person. Bone remodeling involves the interplay between bone-building cells (osteoblasts) and cells that break down bone (osteoclasts).

- Osteoblasts cause bone deposition and they secrete 2 proteins:
  - **RANK-L (Receptor Activator of Nuclear KappaB Ligand)** binds to the RANK receptor, which is expressed on precursor cells resulting in their differentiation into active osteoclasts. Active osteoclasts also express the RANK receptor, which, when stimulated, activates osteoclastic activity.
  - **OPG (osteoprotegerin)** binds RANK-L, thereby preventing it from binding onto precursor or osteoclast cells. This reduces differentiation and overall osteoclastic activity. Thus, OPG acts as a "decoy" for RANK-L.

LYMPHATIC SYSTEM

The **lymphatics** play a pivotal role in maintaining a low interstitial fluid volume and protein content. Lymphatic flow is directly proportional to interstitial fluid pressure, thus a rise in this pressure promotes fluid movement out of the interstitium via the lymphatics.

The lymphatics also remove proteins from the interstitium. Recall that the lymphatics return their fluid and protein content to the general circulation by coalescing into the lymphatic ducts, which in turn empty into to the subclavian veins.

DIGESTIVE SYSTEM

The human gastrointestinal (GI) tract is responsible for transporting, digesting, and absorbing nutrients, as well as expelling waste. High-yield concepts pertaining to the intestinal tract include:

- Sympathetic activity slows processes in the GI tract, whereas parasympathetic does the opposite.
- Secretin is required for releasing pancreatic bicarbonate, which neutralizes stomach acid entering the duodenum.
- CCK is required to release pancreatic enzymes and for the release of bile into the duodenum.
- Gastric stomach activity and its secretion is inhibited by stomach acid.
- Because of regional pacemaker activity, there is always some basal motor activity in the GI tract.
- Swallowing and defecation are reflexes requiring the central nervous system.
- Relaxation of the lower esophageal sphincter is due to the release of VIP.
- Following a meal, local distension and parasympathetic activity increase stomach motility. An overload of the duodenum decreases stomach motility.
- There are mixing and propulsive movements in the small intestine and colon.
- Salivary secretions are regulated via parasympathetic input. The reabsorption of sodium chloride produces a fluid that is hypotonic.
- Gastric acid secretion via a hydrogen/potassium-ATPase pump is stimulated by acetylcholine, histamine, and gastrin. A low stomach pH and a duodenal overload inhibit acid secretion.
- Pancreatic enzymes are required for the digestion of carbohydrate, protein, and lipids.
- Pancreatic fluid high in bicarbonate is required to neutralize acid entering the duodenum.
- Bile salts form micelles that are required for the digestion and absorption of lipids. Only in the distal ileum can they be actively reabsorbed. They must be recycled because the liver has a limited ability for their synthesis.
- Bile pigments are water-soluble compounds excreted via the bile and intestine.
- Electrolytes and water, but not bile pigments or bile salts, can be absorbed from the gall bladder lumen.
- Digestion of lipid requires bile micelles and pancreatic lipases. End products absorbed include 2-monoglycerides and fatty acids.
- Digestion of carbohydrate requires pancreatic amylases and the small intestinal brush border enzymes. End products absorbed will be the monosaccharides. Disaccharides cannot be absorbed from the small intestine.

- Digestion of protein requires the pancreatic proteases, which must be initially activated by enterokinase/ enteropeptidase and the intestinal brush border enzymes.
- End products absorbed include amino acids and very small peptides.
- Absorption of carbohydrate, amino acids, and small peptides is mainly by secondary active transport at the luminal membrane in the small intestine.
- Lipids are absorbed by diffusion via micelles; the chylomicrons formed in mucosal cells enter the lymphatics.
- Most of the water and electrolytes are reabsorbed in the small intestine. The distal ileum reabsorbs the bile salts and intrinsic factor–vitamin B12 complex.
- The colon does not have digestive enzymes or the transporters to absorb the end products of digestion.
- The colon has a net absorption of water and electrolytes, which is influenced by aldosterone but has a net secretion of bicarbonate and potassium.
- Diarrhea is the loss of isotonic fluid, which is high in bicarbonate and potassium.

Structure

The GI tract consists of a muscular tube starting from the oral cavity and extends to the rectum and anus.

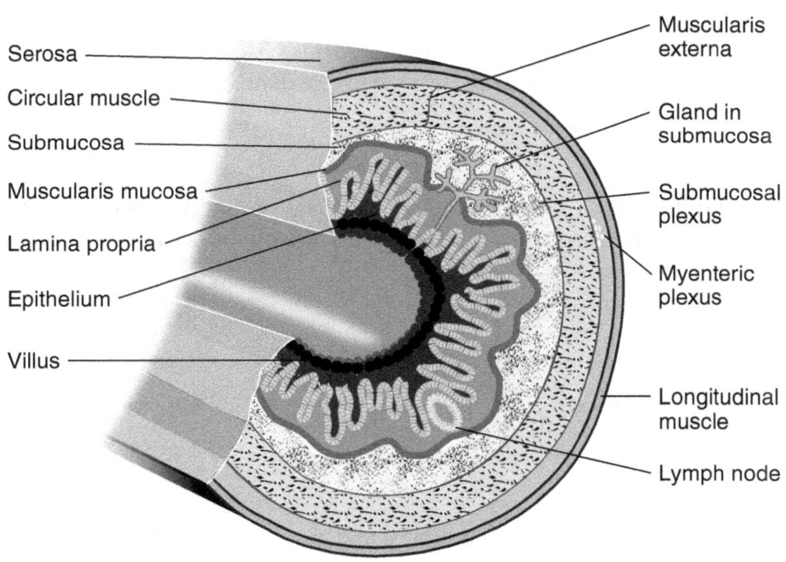

Figure 1-28. Gastrointestinal Tract

Mucosa

- Epithelium: single layer of specialized cells; some are involved in secretions and some release hormones
- Lamina propria: layer of connective tissue containing glands, hormone-containing cells, lymph nodes, and capillaries
- Muscularis mucosa: thin layer of muscle, the contraction of which causes folding and ridges in the mucosal layers

Submucosa

- Layer of connective tissue containing glands, large blood vessels, and lymphatics
- Outermost region has a nerve net called the submucosal (Meissner's) plexus
- Meissner's plexus is part of the enteric nervous system and is involved in secretory activity

Muscularis Externa

- Inner layer of circular muscle
- Outer layer of longitudinal muscle
- Myenteric nerve plexus is involved in motor activity in between the muscle layers

Serosa

- Outermost layer of GI tract containing connective tissue and a layer of epithelial cells
- Within this layer, autonomic nerve fibers run and eventually synapse on target cells and the enteric nerve plexus

Note

Sympathetic regulation of the splanchnic circulation does not involve the enteric nervous system.

Nervous Control

Residing in the GI tract is a vast neural network called the enteric nervous system (Meissner's and myenteric plexi), upon which normal GI function is dependent. The enteric nervous system is innervated by the autonomic nervous system and serves as the final mediator for virtually all neurally mediated changes.

Sympathetic

The diagram below illustrates how the synaptic junction at the end of a nerve fiber secretes norepinephrine (NE), which then induces responses in the GI system. An increase in sympathetic activity slows processes.

Transmitter	Response
NE	↓ motility ↓ secretions ↑ constriction of sphincters

Parasympathetic

An increase in parasympathetic activity promotes digestive and absorptive processes.

Transmitter	Target	Response
ACh		↑ motility ↑ secretions
VIP		↓ constriction of sphincters
GRP	G cell	↑ gastrin

VIP: vasoactive intestinal peptide, an inhibitory parasympathetic transmitter

GRP: gastrin-releasing peptide; stimulates the release of gastrin from G cells

Endocrine Control

A variety of endocrine hormones control the GI tract.

Table 1-4. Endocrine Control of the GI System

Hormone**	Source	Stimulus	Stomach Motility and Secretion	Pancreas	Gallbladder
Secretin	S cells lining duodenum	Acid entering duodenum	Inhibits	Stimulates fluid secretion (HCO_3^-)	
CCK	Cells lining duodenum	Fat and amino acids entering duodenum	Inhibits emptying	Stimulates enzyme secretion	1. Contraction 2. Relaxation sphincter (Oddi)
Gastrin	G cells of stomach	Stomach distension	Stimulates		
	Antrum	Parasym (GRP) Peptides			
	Duodenum	Stomach acid inhibits*			
GIP **GLP**	Duodenum	Fat, CHO, amino acids	Inhibits		Increases insulin Decreases glucagon

CCK = cholecystokinin; GIP = gastric inhibitory peptide (glucose insulinotropic peptide), GLP = glucagon-like peptide

*Note: In a non–acid-producing stomach (e.g., chronic gastritis), the reduced negative feedback increases circulating gastrin.

**All 5 hormones stimulate insulin release.

Motility

The GI tract produces motility using smooth muscle subunits linked by gap junctions.

Characteristics of Smooth Muscle

Electrical Activity

Electrical activity, gastric motility and methods of stimulation are important characteristics of smooth muscle that impact the functioning of the intestinal tract.

- Resting membrane potential −40 to −65 mV. Close to depolarization.
- Oscillation of membrane potential is generated by interstitial cells (interstitial cells of Cajal) that act as pacemakers. This is referred to as slow waves or basic electrical rhythm, and if threshold is reached it generates action potentials.

Note

Anticholinergic medications such as atropine or tricyclic antidepressants slow GI motility.

Gastric Motility

The primary factors and additional aspects are illustrated here.

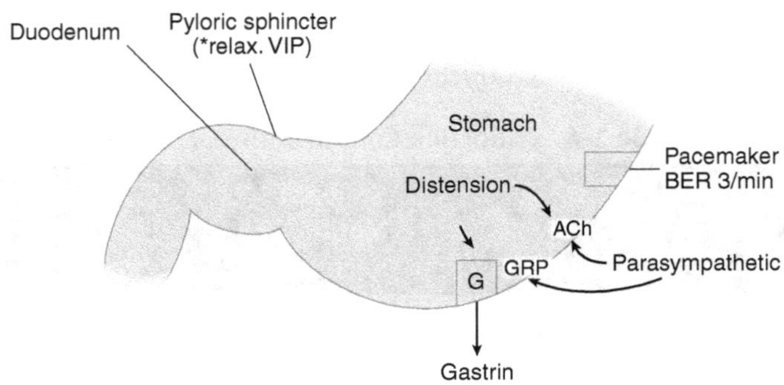

Figure 1-29. Endocrine and Neural Control of the Stomach

ACh: acetylcholine

BER: basic electrical rhythm

GRP: gastrin-releasing peptide

VIP: vasoactive intestinal polypeptide

Stimulation

- Acetylcholine released in response to activation of parasympathetics
- Local distension

Inhibition

- Low pH of stomach contents inhibits the release of gastrin
- Feedback from duodenal release of hormones (CCK, secretin, and GIP)

URINARY SYSTEM, BODY FLUIDS, AND ELECTROLYTES

The function of the kidney is to do the following:

- Excrete waste products: urea, uric acid, creatinine
- Water and electrolyte balance
- Acid/base balance
- Secrete the hormone erythropoietin and the enzyme renin into the circulation
- Hydroxylate 25-hydroxy-Vit D to form active form of vitamin D (1,25 dihydroxy-Vit D)

Organization of the Kidney

Nephrons (the functioning unit of the kidney) with glomeruli in the outer cortex have short loops of Henle (cortical nephrons). Those with glomeruli in the inner cortex have long loops of Henle that penetrate the medullary region (juxtamedullary nephrons).

- $\frac{7}{8}$ of all nephrons are cortical nephrons
- $\frac{1}{8}$ of all nephrons are juxtamedullary nephrons

Nephron structures in the medulla consist of the long loops of Henle and the terminal regions of the collecting ducts. All other structures, including the first section of the collecting ducts, are in the cortex.

- In the cortex, the proximal and distal tubules, as well as the initial segment of the collecting duct, are surrounded by a capillary network, and the interstitium is close to an isotonic environment (300 mOsm/kg).
- The medullary region has capillary loops organized similar to the loops of Henle, known as the vasa recta.

- The slow flow through these capillary loops preserves the osmolar gradient of the interstitium.
- However, this slow flow also keeps the PO_2 of the medulla lower than that in the cortex and even though the metabolic rate of the medulla is lower than in the cortex, it is more susceptible to ischemic damage.

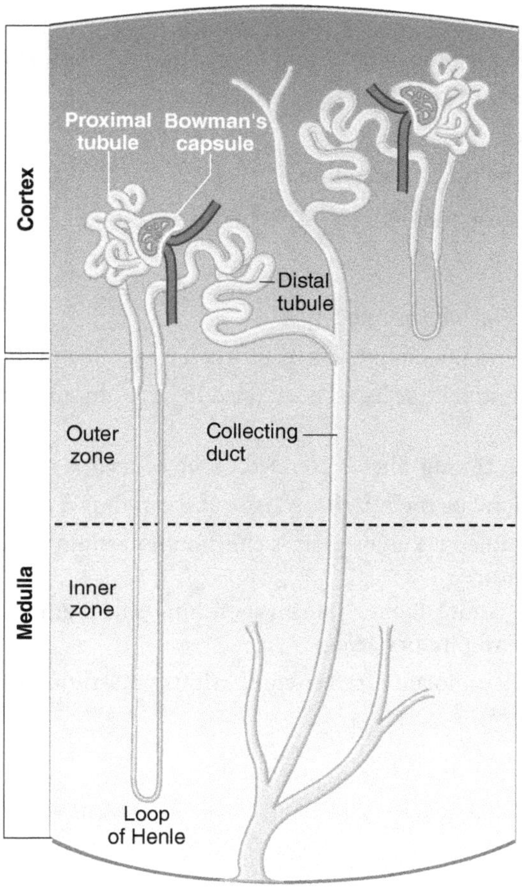

Figure 1-30. Nephron Structures

Function of the Nephron

There are 4 basic renal processes: filtration, reabsorption, secretion, and excretion.

Filtration

- Blood is filtered by nephrons, the functional units of the kidney.
- Each nephron begins in a renal corpuscle (site of filtration), which is composed of a glomerulus enclosed in a Bowman's capsule.
- An ultrafiltrate resembling plasma enters Bowman's space.
- Filtration is driven by Starling forces.
- The ultrafiltrate is passed through, in turn, the proximal convoluted tubule, the loop of Henle, the distal convoluted tubule, and a series of collecting ducts to form urine.
- Filtration rate or filtered load is the amount of a substance (in mg) that is filtered at the glomeruli in a minute (mg/min).

Reabsorption

- Tubular reabsorption is the process by which solutes and water are removed from the tubular fluid that was formed in Bowman's space and transported into the blood.
- Reabsorption rate is the amount (in mg) that is reabsorbed from the ultrafiltrate in a minute (mg/min).

Secretion

- Tubular secretion is the transfer of materials from peritubular capillaries to the renal tubular lumen.
- Tubular secretion is primarily the result of active transport.
- Usually only a few substances are secreted.
- Many drugs are eliminated by tubular secretion.
- Secretion rate is the amount (in mg) that is secreted into the ultrafiltrate in a minute (mg/min).

Excretion

- Substances that are in the urine are excreted.
- A substance that is filtered and not completely reabsorbed is excreted in the urine.
- A substance that is filtered and then secreted is excreted in large amounts in the urine because it comes from 2 places in the nephron.
- Excretion rate is the amount (in mg) that is excreted in the urine in a minute (mg/min).
- Insulin and epinephrine stimulate the Na^+/K^+-ATPase and can thus reduce plasma potassium.
- Long term balance is maintained via aldosterone's effect on potassium secretion in the distal tubule and collecting ducts of the nephrons.
- Acidosis and increased ECF osmolality (cell shrinkage) shifts potassium from the ICF to the ECF. Inorganic fixed acid > organic acids > respiratory acidosis
- Alkalosis and decreased ECF osmolality (cell swelling) shifts potassium from the ECF to the ICF. Metabolic alkalosis > respiratory alkalosis

Potassium Secretion and Excretion by the Kidney

Potassium secretion is determined mainly by 2 factors: filtrate flow and sodium reabsorption (creates negative potential of the lumen).

- Increased flow and/or aldosterone increases potassium secretion and excretion.
- Decreased flow and/or aldosterone decreases potassium secretion and excretion.

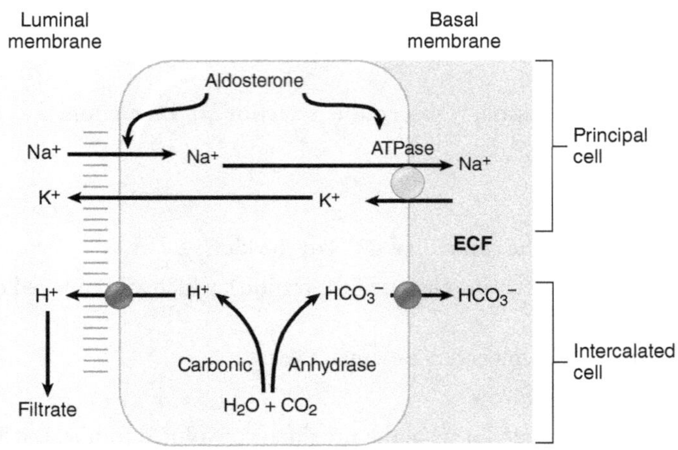

Figure 1-31. Late Distal Tubule and Collecting Duct

Acid–Base Disorders

Acidosis: shifts potassium from the ICF to ECF. Decreased intracellular potassium reduces the potassium gradient, thus potassium secretion falls. (both promote hyperkalemia). However, this negative potassium balance in acidosis is not typically sustained because hyperkalemia stimulates aldosterone.

Alkalosis: shifts potassium from ECF to ICF. Increased intracellular potassium increases potassium secretion (both promote hypokalemia).

Clinical Correlate

A 55-year-old woman with a history of end-stage renal failure presents with confusion after missing a dialysis session. Her potassium is elevated. While waiting for the nurse to set up the dialysis, the patient is treated with an injection of bicarbonate and insulin with dextrose.

Giving bicarbonate gives the patient an alkalosis. This causes protons to leave the intracellular space down its concentration gradient. To maintain electroneutrality, potassium shifts into cells. This decreases the extracellular potassium concentration. Insulin activates the sodium/potassium ATPase and that increases the shift of potassium into the cell also.

Potassium Balance

Promoters of Hyperkalemia

- Transcellular shifts: metabolic acidosis, hyperglycemia, insulin deficiency or resistance, muscle trauma
- GI: excessive intake (on rare occasions)
- Kidney: acute oliguric kidney disease, chronic kidney disease where GFR decreases dramatically from normal, hypoaldosteronism

Consequences of Hyperkalemia

- Neuromuscular function: muscle weakness, general fatigue if chronic
- Cardiac: high T wave, eventually in severe hyperkalemia ventricular fibrillation
- Metabolic: metabolic acidosis

Promoters of Hypokalemia

- Transcellular shifts: metabolic alkalosis, sudden increases in insulin and catecholamines
- GI: diarrhea, vomiting, low potassium diet (rarely has an effect on its own)
- Kidney: diuretics due to increased flow (thiazides, loop diuretics, osmotic diuresis), hyperaldosteronism (adrenal adenoma, renal arterial stenosis), increased excretion of negative ions (bicarbonate, ketone bodies), renal tubular acidosis types I and II.

Consequences of Hypokalemia

- Neuromuscular function: muscle weakness, general fatigue
- Cardiac: hyperpolarization affects excitability and delays repolarization.
- EKG effects: low T wave, high U wave
- Metabolic: decreased insulin response to carbohydrate load, decrease growth rate in children, nephrogenic diabetes insipidus, metabolic alkalosis

REPRODUCTIVE SYSTEM

Male Reproductive System

The male reproductive system is responsible for the production of both sperm and male sex hormones.

Hypothalamic-Pituitary-Gonadal (HPG) Axis in Males

Note

LH, FSH, TSH, and human chorionic gonadotropin (hCG) are glycoproteins with identical alpha subunits. The beta subunits differ and thus confer specificity.

The following figure summarizes factors involved in the overall control of adult male hormone secretion.

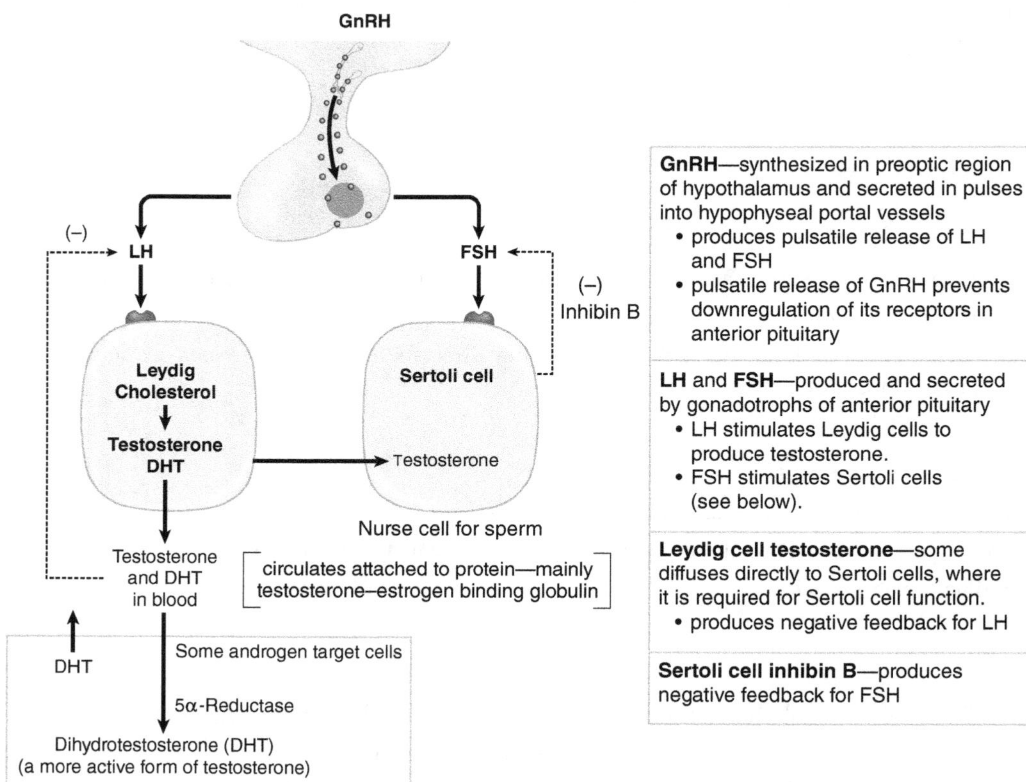

Figure 1-32. Control of Testes

LH/Leydig Cells

Leydig cells express receptors for LH, a peptide hormone which activates Gs—cAMP (which in turn initiates testosterone production by activating steroidogenic acute regulatory protein [StAR]).

- Testosterone diffuses into Sertoli cells (high concentration) and into the blood.
- Circulating testosterone provides negative feedback to regulate LH secretion at the level of the hypothalamus and anterior pituitary.

5α-Reductase

Some target tissues express this enzyme, which converts testosterone into the more potent dihydrotestosterone. Some important physiologic effects primarily mediated by dihydrotestosterone are as follows:

- Sexual differentiation: differentiation to form male external genitalia
- Growth of the prostate
- Male-pattern baldness
- Increased activity of sebaceous glands
- Synthesis of NO synthase in penile tissue

FSH/Sertoli Cells

FSH binds to Sertoli cells and activates a Gs-cAMP pathway. Sertoli cells release inhibin B, which has negative feedback on FSH secretion.

Female Reproductive System

Females of reproductive age experience cycles of hormonal activity that repeat at approximately once a month.

Menstrual Cycle

The menstrual cycle (approximately 28 days) can be divided into the following phases or events. By convention, the first day of bleeding (menses) is called day 1 of the menstrual cycle.

- The **follicular phase** (first 2 weeks) is also called the proliferative or preovulatory phase. This phase is dominated by the peripheral effects of estrogen, which include the replacement of the endometrial cells lost during menses.
- **Ovulation** (~day 14) is preceded by the LH surge, which induces ovulation.
- The luteal phase (~2 weeks) is dominated by the elevated plasma levels of progesterone, and along with lower levels of secreted estrogen, creates a secretory quiescent endometrium that prepares the uterus for implantation.
- **Menses**: Withdrawal of hormonal support of the endometrium at this time causes necrosis and menstruation.

Follicular Phase (~days 1 to 14)

- By convention, the first day of bleeding (menses) is called day 1 of the menstrual cycle.
- During the follicular phase, FSH secretion is slightly elevated, causing proliferation of granulosa cells and increased estrogen secretion within a cohort of follicles.
- One follicle has greater cellular growth and secretes more estradiol (dominant follicle), which promotes growth and increased sensitivity to FSH; thus the follicle continues to develop. The remaining follicles, lacking sufficient FSH, synthesize only androgen and become atretic (die).

Figures 1-33 through 1-36 illustrate the hormonal regulation of the menstrual cycle. The graphs represent the plasma hormonal levels throughout the cycle. The length of the menstrual cycle varies, but an average length is 28 days. Each of the plasma hormone concentrations is plotted relative to the day on which its concentration is lowest, i.e., just prior to menses (day 28). The accompanying diagram illustrates specific aspects of the phase under consideration.

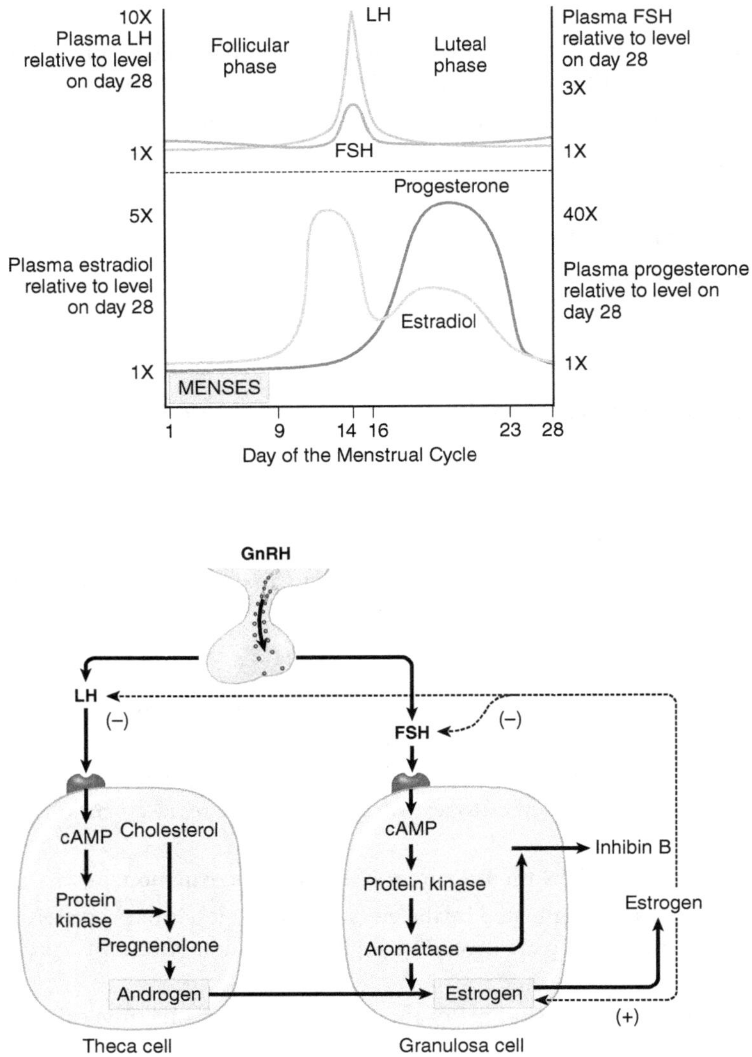

Figure 1-33. Follicular Phase Relationships Approximately Days 1 to 14

Theca Cells: Under LH stimulation, which acts intracellularly via cAMP, cholesterol is transported into the mitochondria (StAR is activated). The pathway continues through intermediates to androgens. Little androgen is secreted into the blood; most of the androgen enters the adjacent granulosa cells.

Granulosa Cells: Possess the follicle's only FSH receptors. When coupled to FSH, these act via cAMP to increase the activity of aromatase; aromatase converts the androgens to estrogens (mainly estradiol).

Estrogen: Some of the estrogen produced by the granulosa cells is released into the blood and inhibits the release of LH and FSH from the anterior pituitary. However, another fraction of the estrogen acts locally on granulosa cells, increasing their proliferation and sensitivity to FSH.

- This local positive effect of estrogens causes a rising level of circulating estrogens during the follicular phase, but at the same time FSH is decreasing because of the inhibitory effect of estrogen on FSH release.
- Granulosa cells also release inhibin B.
- Inhibin B inhibits the secretion of FSH by the pituitary but its role in the menstrual cycle is poorly understood.

Peripheral effects of estrogen produced by the granulosa cells during the follicular phase include:

- Circulating estrogens stimulate the female sex accessory organs and secondary sex characteristics.
- Rising levels of estrogens cause the endometrial cells of the uterine mucosal layers to increase their rate of mitotic division (proliferate).
- Circulating estrogens cause the cervical mucus to be thin and watery, making the cervix easy for sperm to traverse.

Ovulation

Ovulation takes place ~day 14. Since ovulation is always 14 days before the end of the cycle, you can subtract 14 from the cycle length to find the day of ovulation.

Cycle length – 14 = ovulation day

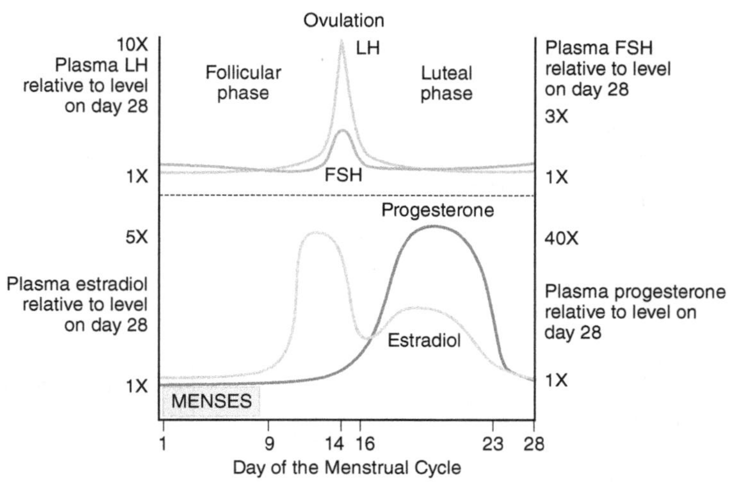

Ovulation occurs approximately day 14

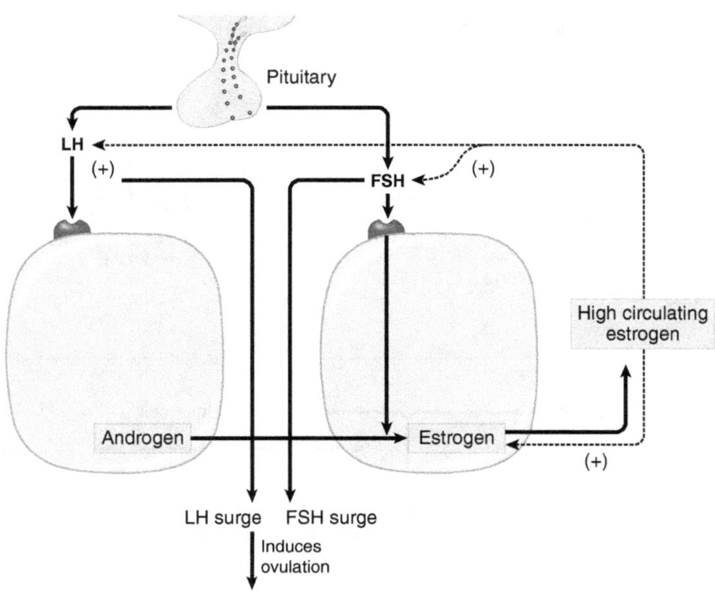

Figure 1-34. Pituitary-Ovarian Relationships at Ovulation

Estrogen Levels

Near the end of the follicular phase there is a dramatic rise in circulating estrogen. When estrogens rise above a certain level, they no longer inhibit the release of LH and FSH. Instead, they stimulate the release of LH and FSH (negative feedback loop to positive feedback loop). This causes a surge in the release of LH and FSH. Only the LH surge is essential for the induction of ovulation and formation of the corpus luteum. Notice from the figure that the LH surge and ovulation occur after estrogen peaks. Therefore, if estrogens are still rising, ovulation has not occurred.

Follicular rupture occurs 24–36 hours after the onset of the LH surge. During this time interval, LH removes the restraint upon meiosis, which has been arrested in prophase for years. The first meiotic division is completed, and the first polar body is extruded.

Positive feedback loops are rare in the body. Only ovulation with estrogen and parturition with oxytocin represent positive feedback loops.

Luteal Phase (~days 14–28)

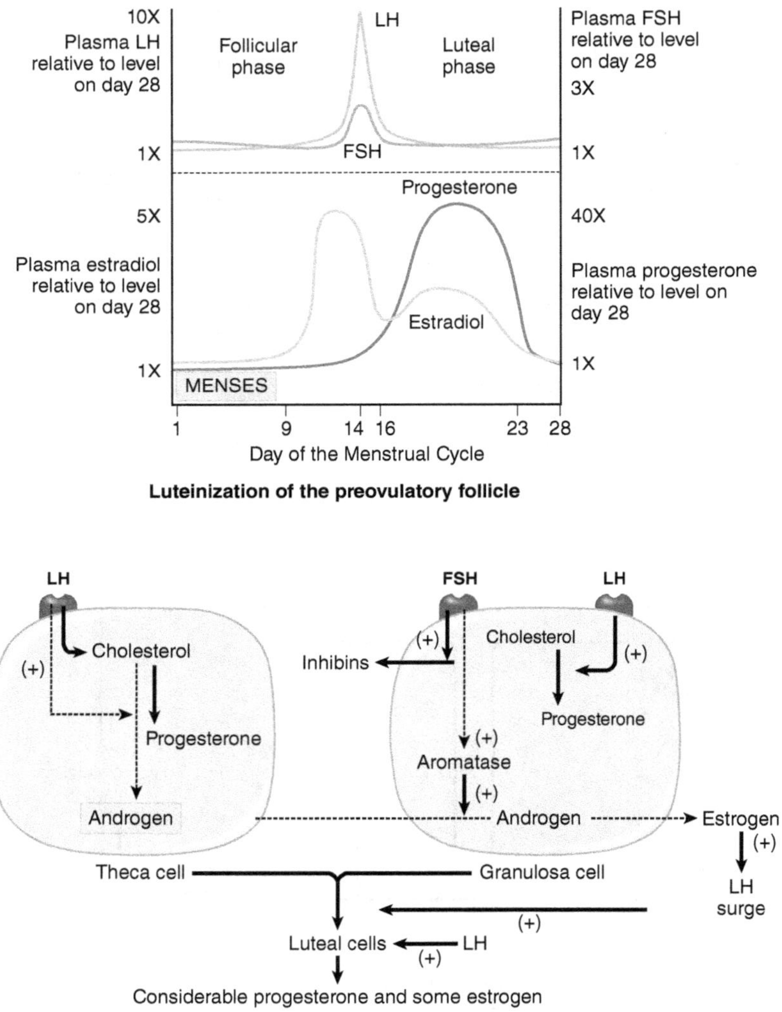

Figure 1-35. The Luteal Phase Reactions

Preovulatory Follicle

In the latter stages of the follicular phase, intracellular changes within the granulosa and theca cells occur in preparation for their conversion into luteal cells.

- Estradiol, in conjunction with FSH, causes the granulosa cells to produce LH receptors.
- The metabolic pathways are then altered to favor the production of progesterone.
- This would include a decrease in the activity of aromatase and a drop in estrogen production.

LH Surge

Induced by the elevated estrogens, it causes the granulosa cells and theca cells to be transformed into luteal cells and increases the secretion of progesterone.

Corpus Luteum

The process of luteinization occurs following the exit of the oocyte from the follicle. The corpus luteum is made up of the remaining granulosa cells, thecal cells, and supportive tissue. Once formed, the luteal cells are stimulated by LH to secrete considerable progesterone and some estrogen. Progesterone inhibits LH secretion (negative feedback). The corpus luteum secretes inhibin A, which has negative feedback on FSH.

The increased plasma level of progesterone has several actions:

- Causes the uterine endometrium to become secretory, providing a source of nutrients for the blastocyst
- Causes the cervical mucus to become thick, sealing off the uterus from further entry of sperm or bacteria
- Has thermogenic properties, causing the basal body temperature to increase by 0.5–1.0° F

Menses

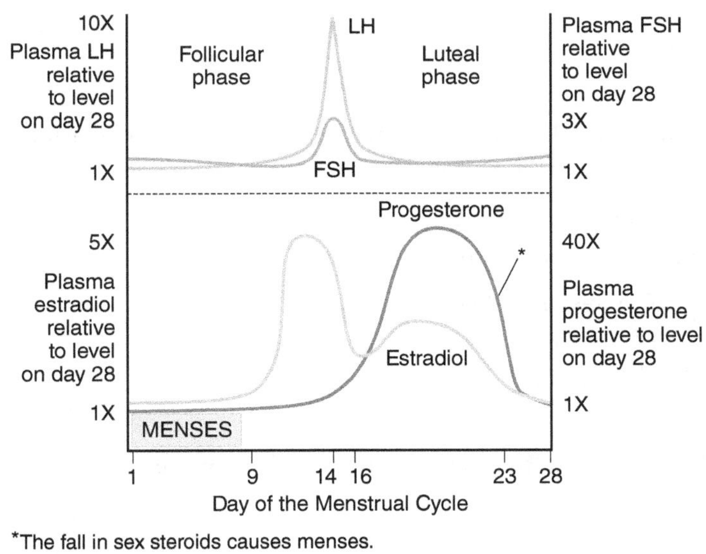

Figure 1-36. Onset of Menses

- The life of the corpus luteum is finite, hence the luteal phase is only 14 days.
- Initially, the corpus luteum is very responsive to LH. Over time however, as the corpus luteum becomes less functional, it becomes less responsive to LH.

- Progesterone exerts negative feedback on LH, which contributes to the demise of the corpus luteum.
- With the demise of the corpus luteum, progesterone and estradiol fall to levels that are unable to support the endometrial changes, and menses begins.

Menstruation is due to a lack of gonadal sex steroids.

New Cycle

During the 3 days prior to and during menses, plasma levels of progesterone and estradiol are at their low point; negative feedback restraint for gonadotropin secretion is removed. FSH secretion rises slightly and initiates the next cycle of follicular growth.

The length of the follicular phase of the menstrual cycle is more variable than the length of the luteal phase. Long cycles are usually due to a prolonged follicular phase and short cycles to a short follicular phase. Once ovulation has occurred, menses generally follows in about 14 days. The length of the menstrual cycle in days minus 14 gives the most likely day of ovulation.

PRACTICE QUESTIONS

1. A patient with type 1 diabetes injects insulin subcutaneously 4 times daily. For each injection, the insulin needle will pass through which of the following first?

   A. Stratum basale
   B. Stratum corneum
   C. Stratum granulosum
   D. Stratum lucidum
   E. Stratum spinosum

2. A pharmacist takes a patient's blood pressure and obtains a systolic and diastolic value. Which of the following is also a measure of afterload in the same patient?

   A. Central venous pressure
   B. Left ventricular end-diastolic pressure
   C. Pulmonary capillary wedge pressure
   D. Right atrial pressure
   E. Total peripheral resistance

3. Oxidation of acetyl-CoA derived from carbohydrates, fats and proteins occurs in which of the following?

   A. Lysosomes
   B. Mitochondria
   C. Peroxisomes
   D. Rough endoplasmic reticulum
   E. Smooth endoplasmic reticulum

4. A patient with trigeminal neuralgia is prescribed carbamazepine. This condition is caused by a sensory disruption of which cranial nerve?

   A. III
   B. IV
   C. V
   D. VIII
   E. IX

5. Which of the following has the largest volume in mL?

   A. Functional residual capacity
   B. Inspiratory capacity
   C. Residual volume
   D. Tidal volume
   E. Vital capacity

6. Which of the following is a characteristic of skeletal muscle but NOT cardiac muscle?

   A. Actin and myosin form sarcomeres in skeletal muscle
   B. Neither contains a sarcoplasmic reticulum
   C. Skeletal muscle is striated
   D. Surface membrane lacks calcium channels
   E. Troponin binds to calcium in skeletal muscle

7. Which of the following are true statements about the intestinal tract?

   A. An increase in sympathetic activity increases gastrointestinal processes.
   B. Norepinephrine is responsible for increasing gastrointestinal processes.
   C. Parasympathetic stimulation has no impact on gastrointestinal processes.
   D. Sympathetic stimulation has no impact on gastrointestinal processes.
   E. The gastrointestinal tract is primarily under parasympathetic control.

8. Which of the following has no impact on potassium blood levels?

   A. Acidosis
   B. Alkalosis
   C. Epinephrine
   D. Growth hormone
   E. Insulin

9. Finasteride acts by inhibiting the activity of 5-alpha-reductase. In patients taking this medication, researchers would expect to see decreased levels of which of the following?

   A. Dihydrotestosterone
   B. Estradiol
   C. Estrogen
   D. Estrone
   E. Testosterone

10. A patient with type 2 diabetes is mistakenly given a larger than prescribed dose of Humalog® and they become hypoglycemic. Which of the following stress hormones will most rapidly increase the patient's glucose levels back towards normal?

    A. Aldosterone

    B. Calcitonin

    C. Epinephrine

    D. Insulin

    E. Parathyroid hormone

Answers and Explanations

1. **The correct answer is B.** You're being asked, "what is the top layer of skin?" The stratum corneum (top skin layer) contains up to several dozen layers of flattened keratinocytes, forming a barrier that prevents invasion by pathogens and that helps to prevent loss of fluids and salt. Hair projects above the skin, and there are openings for sweat and sebaceous glands. The order of layers of the skin (superficial to deep) can be remembered with the mnemonic: Come, Let's Get Sun Burned." They are: Stratum corneum (choice B), Stratum lucidum (choice D), Stratum granulosum (choice C), Stratum spinosum (choice E) and Stratum basale (choice A).

2. **The correct answer is E.** Afterload is considered the "load" that the heart must eject blood against. One of the best indicators of afterload is systemic vascular resistance (SVR), also known as total peripheral resistance (TPR). TPR is not routinely calculated clinically and thus arterial pressure (diastolic, mean, or systolic) is often used as the index of afterload. Preload is defined as the load or pre-stretch on ventricular muscle at the end of diastole. Preload is not measured directly; however, the best indices of preload on ventricular muscle are those measured directly in the ventricles. Indices of left ventricular preload include left ventricular end-diastolic volume (LVEDV) and left ventricular end-diastolic pressure (LVEDP). Choices A, C and D are somewhat less reliable indices of left ventricular preload.

3. **The correct answer is B.** Mitochondria are often called the power plants of the cell. They are responsible for the oxidation of acetyl-CoA derived from carbohydrates, fats and proteins into carbon dioxide and biochemical energy in the form of adenosine triphosphate (ATP). Lysosomes (choice A) contain hydrolytic enzymes that break down substances ingested by endocytosis and cellular waste products. One of the primary functions of peroxisomes (choice C) is the breakdown of very long chain fatty acids via β-oxidation. The rough endoplasmic reticulum (ER) (choice D) is studded with ribosomes that permit the translation of proteins destined for secretion directly into its lumen. The smooth ER (choice E) lacks ribosomes and is utilized primarily for lipid synthesis (such as the phospholipids in the cell membrane) and the detoxification of certain drugs and poisons.

4. **The correct answer is C.** Trigeminal neuralgia is a facial pain syndrome characterized by unilateral pain following the sensory distribution of cranial nerve V. It is often accompanied by a brief facial spasm or tic. A high level overview of the cranial nerves are as follows:

    1. Olfactory: Smell
    2. Optic: Sight
    3. Oculomotor: Ocular movement, pupil constriction
    4. Trochlear: depresses and abducts eyeball
    5. Trigeminal: General sensation (touch, pain, temperature) of forehead, face, scalp and cornea
    6. Abducens: abducts eyeball
    7. Facial: Facial muscles, salivation, taste in anterior $\frac{2}{3}$ of tongue, tears
    8. Vestibulocochlear: hearing, angular and linear acceleration
    9. Glossopharyngeal: oropharyngeal sensations, salivation, sensation of posterior $\frac{1}{3}$ of tongue

10. Vagus: swallowing, muscle of larynx, sensory GI tract
11. Accessory: Head rotation, elevate and rotate scapula
12. Hypoglossal: Tongue movement

5. **The correct answer is E.** The vital capacity (VC) is the maximal volume that can be expired after a maximal inspiration (5,500 mL). Functional residual capacity (FRC; choice A) is a marker for lung compliance and the amount of gas in the lungs at the end of a passive expiration (2,700 mL). Inspiratory capacity (IC; choice B) is the maximal volume of gas that can be inspired from FRC (4,000 mL). Residual volume (RV; choice C) is the amount of air in the lung after a maximal expiration (1,200 mL). Tidal volume (VT; choice D) is the amount of air that enters or leaves the lung in a single respiratory cycle (500 mL).

6. **The correct answer is D.** One of the primary differences between skeletal and cardiac muscle is that the skeletal muscle surface membrane lacks calcium channels. From a pharmacy perspective, this is important since the administration of a calcium channel blocker will NOT affect the activity of skeletal muscles. Choices A, C and E are characteristics of both skeletal and cardiac muscles. Choice B is incorrect since both skeletal and cardiac muscles have a sarcoplasmic reticulum.

7. **The correct answer is E.** Normal GI function is dependent on the enteric nervous system, which is innervated by the autonomic nervous system and serves as the final mediator for virtually all neurally mediated changes. The gastrointestinal tract is primarily under parasympathetic control (choice E is correct and C is incorrect). An increase in acetylcholine release in response to parasympathetic activity promotes digestive and absorptive processes (choice B). Conversely, an increase in sympathetic activity slows gastrointestinal processes (choice A and D).

8. **The correct answer is D.** Growth hormone stimulates growth, cell reproduction, and cell regeneration in humans. Acidosis (choice A) and increased extracellular fluid (ECF) osmolality (cell shrinkage) shifts potassium from the intracellular fluid (ICF) to the ECF ultimately leading to hyperkalemia. Alkalosis (choice B) and decreased ECF osmolality (cell swelling) shifts potassium from the ECF to the ICF ultimately leading to hypokalemia. Epinephrine (choice C) and insulin (choice E) stimulate the Na^+/K^+ ATPase in the nephron and can reduce plasma potassium.

9. **The correct answer is A.** The enzyme 5-alpha-reductase is responsible for the conversion of testosterone into the more potent dihydrotestosterone (choice A). Thus when this enzyme's activity is inhibited by finasteride, one would expect to see decreased blood levels of dihydrotestosterone (not testosterone – choice E). The enzyme aromatase catalyzes the last steps of estrogen (choice C) synthesis by transforming androstenedione to estrone (choice D) and testosterone to estradiol (choice B).

10. **The correct answer is C.** Stress includes states such as trauma, illness, exercise and even hypoglycemia caused by inappropriate Humalog (aspartate insulin [choice D] injections). Stress hormones act to mobilize energy stores. The stress hormones are:

    - Growth hormone: mobilizes fatty acids by increasing lipolysis in adipose tissue
    - Glucagon: mobilizes glucose by increasing liver glycogenolysis
    - Cortisol: mobilizes fat, protein, carbohydrate
    - Epinephrine, in some forms of stress such as exercise: mobilizes glucose via glycogenolysis and fat via lipolysis

    All stress hormones raise plasma glucose with epinephrine providing the most rapid response. Severe hypoglycemia is a crisis and causes a rapid increase in all stress hormones. Aldosterone (choice A) increases sodium reabsorption by the principal cells of the kidney's collecting ducts. Calcitonin (choice B) lowers plasma calcium by decreasing the activity of osteoclasts, thus decreasing bone resorption. Parathyroid hormone (choice E) raises free calcium levels.

Biochemistry 2

Learning Objectives

- ❑ Explain biomacromolecule chemistry concepts
- ❑ Demonstrate understanding of enzymology and coenzymes and kinetics
- ❑ Discuss principles of cell chemistry
- ❑ Elaborate on cellular transport and mobility principles
- ❑ Answer questions on recombinant DNA biotechnology
- ❑ Summarize principles of protein synthesis

Biochemistry explores the chemical reactions within and relating to living organisms. It focuses on the complex processes happening at a molecular level.

The science of biochemistry encompasses a wide range of scientific disciplines, including genetics, microbiology, forensics, plant science, and medicine.

BIOMACROMOLECULE CHEMISTRY CONCEPTS

Biomacromolecules are large "biological" molecules, such as amino acids, that are composed of hundreds or thousands of atoms.

Amino Acids

All amino acids have a central carbon atom attached to a carboxyl group, an amino group, and a hydrogen atom. The amino acids differ from one another only in the chemical nature of the side chain (R). There are hundreds of amino acids in nature, but only 20 are used as building blocks of proteins in humans.

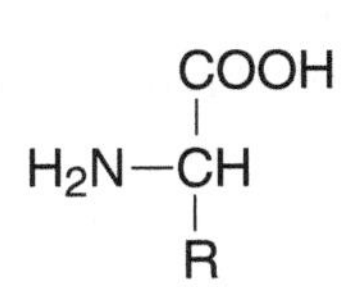

Figure 2-1. Generalized Structure of Amino Acids

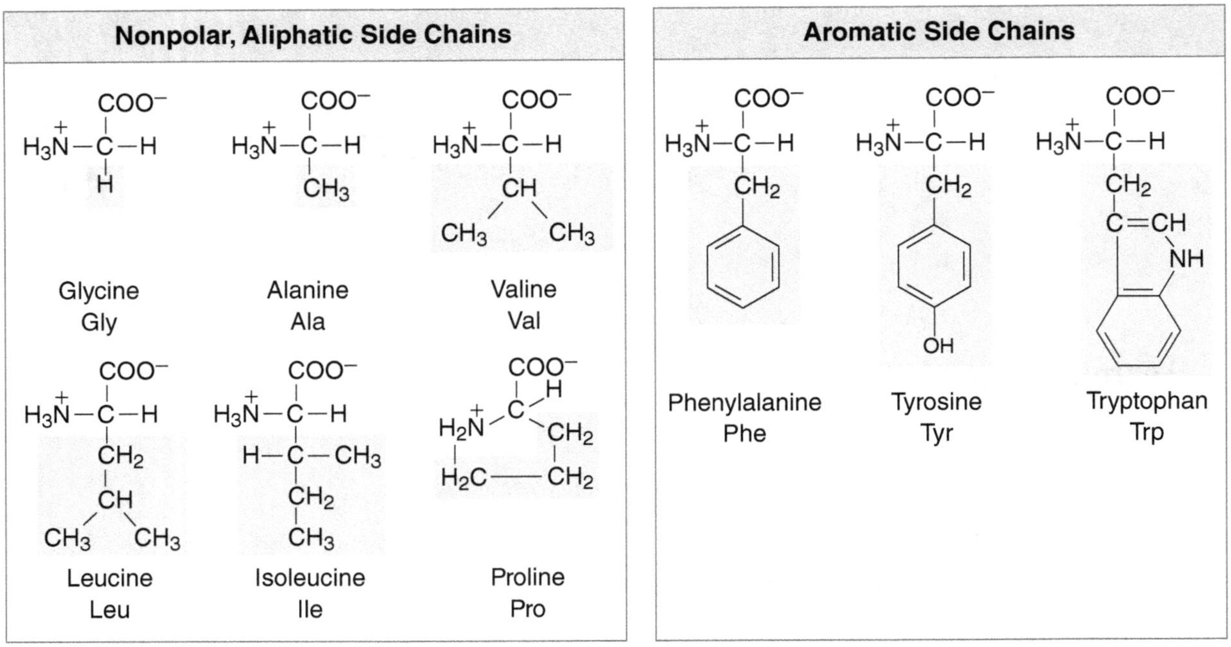

Figure 2-2. Hydrophobic Amino Acids

Classification

The amino acids can be classified as either hydrophobic or hydrophilic, depending on the ease with which their side chains interact with water. In general, proteins fold so that amino acids with hydrophobic side chains are in the interior of the molecule where they are protected from water and those with hydrophilic side chains are on the surface.

Hydrophobic amino acids are shown in Figure 2-2. Additional points about some of these amino acids include:

- Phenylalanine and tyrosine are precursors for catecholamines.
- Tryptophan can form serotonin and niacin.
- Valine, leucine, and isoleucine are branched-chain amino acids whose metabolism is abnormal in maple syrup urine disease.
- Proline is a secondary amine whose presence in a protein disrupts normal secondary structure.

Hydrophilic amino acids have side chains that contain O or N atoms. Some of the hydrophilic side chains are charged at physiologic pH. The acidic amino acids (aspartic and glutamic acids) have carboxyl groups that are negatively charged, whereas the basic amino acids (lysine, arginine, and histidine) have nitrogen atoms that are positively charged. The structures of the hydrophilic amino acids are shown in Figure 2-3. Additional points about some of these amino acids include:

- Serine and threonine are sites for O-linked glycosylation of proteins, a posttranslational modification that should be associated with the Golgi apparatus.
- Asparagine is a site for N-linked glycosylation of proteins, a posttranslational modification that should be associated with the endoplasmic reticulum.
- Cysteine contains sulfur and can form disulfide bonds to stabilize the shape (tertiary structure) of proteins. Destroying disulfide bonds denatures proteins.
- Methionine, another sulfur-containing amino acid, is part of S-adenosylmethionine (SAM), a methyl donor in biochemical pathways.

Tyrosine can be considered either nonpolar or polar because of the ability of the -OH group to form a hydrogen bond.

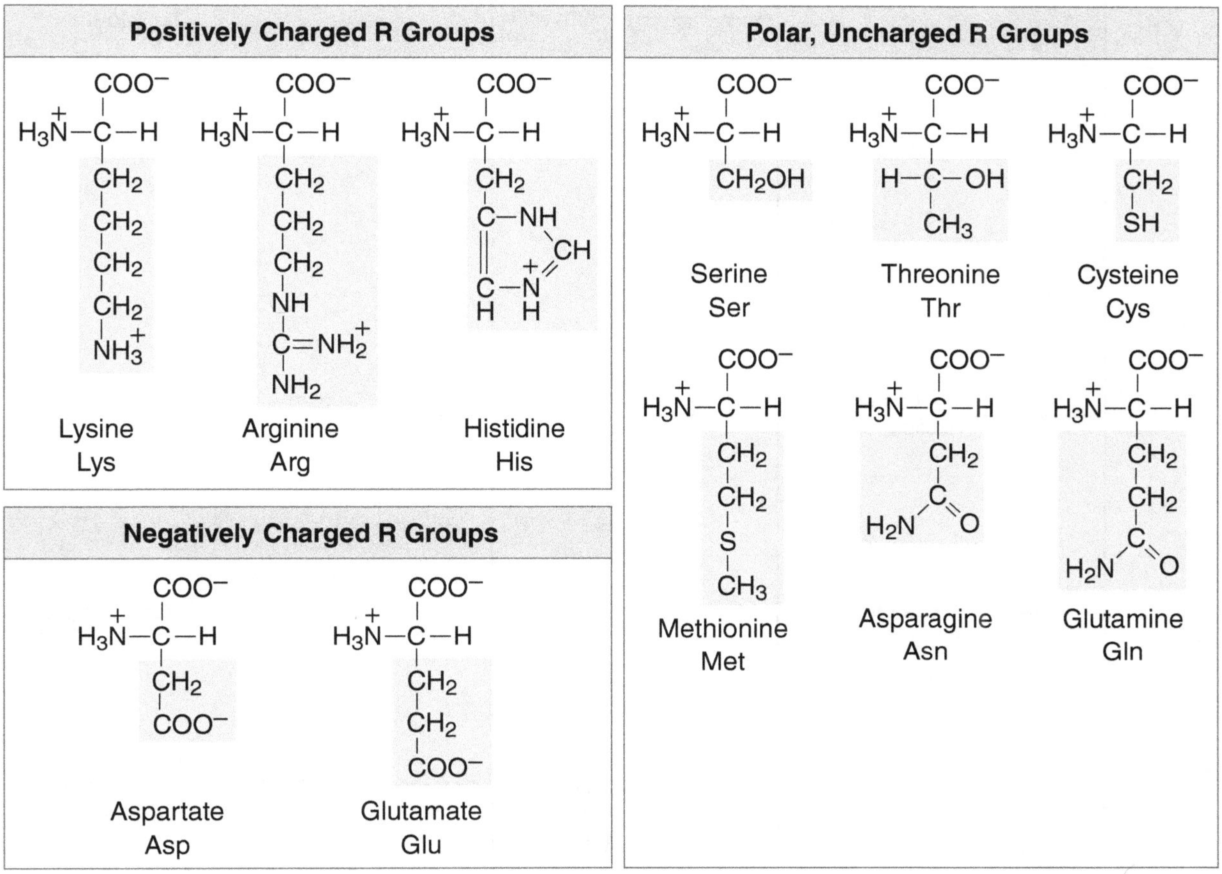

Figure 2-3. Hydrophilic Amino Acids

Methionine can be considered nonpolar or polar because it has a sulfur in it.

DIGESTION

Figure 2-4 summarizes the regional entry of the major digestive enzymes proceeding from the mouth, stomach, and through the small intestine.

Digestive Enzymes and End Products

Triglycerides

Stomach: Fatty materials are pulverized to decrease particle size and increase surface area.

Small intestine: Bile micelles emulsify the fat, and pancreatic lipases digest it. Micelles and pancreatic lipase are required for triglyceride digestion. The major end products are 2-monoglycerides and fatty acids.

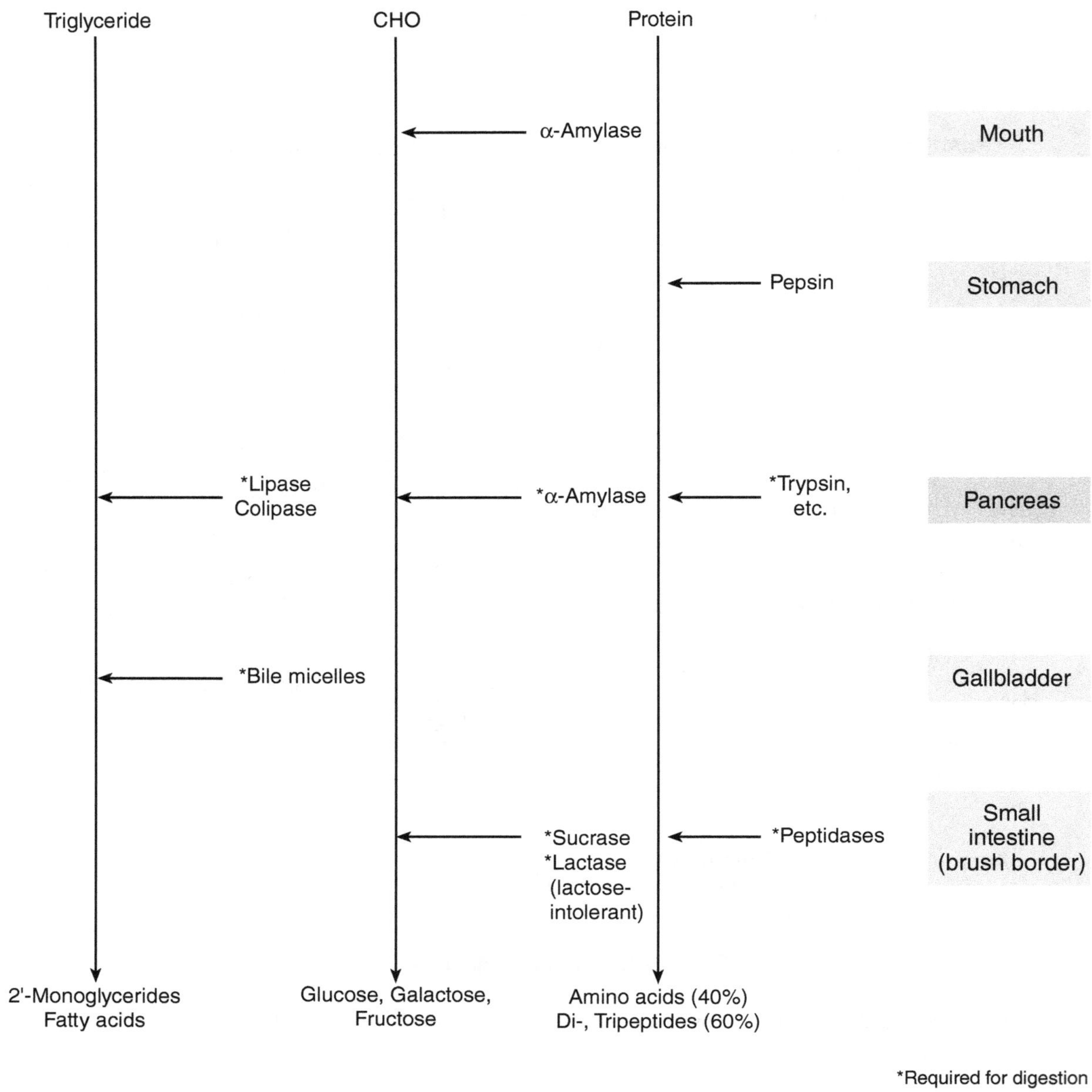

Figure 2-4. Summary of Digestive Processes

Carbohydrates

Mouth: Salivary α-amylase begins the digestion, and its activity continues in the stomach until acid penetrates the bolus; however, it is not a required enzyme.

Small intestine: Pancreatic α-amylase, a required enzyme for CHO digestion, continues the process. Hydrolysis of starch by α-amylase goes on in solution in the lumen of the small intestine, mostly in the duodenum. Further processing or splitting of these trisaccharides, disaccharides, and oligosaccharides is necessary but does not take place in solution; rather, it occurs on the brush border. The enzymes—α-dextrinase (or α-glucoamylase), isomaltase, and maltase—are all bound to the brush border (apical membrane of enterocytes). Brush border enzymes have their highest activity in the jejunum (upper). These brush border enzymes are required for digestion mainly because disaccharides—e.g., sucrose, lactose—are not absorbed from the gut.

- The α-dextrinase cleaves terminal α-1,4 bonds, producing free glucose.
- Lactase hydrolyzes lactose into glucose and galactose. Lactase deficiency (lactose intolerance) leads to osmotic diarrhea.
- Sucrase splits sucrose into glucose and fructose.
- Maltase (also a brush border enzyme) breaks down the maltose and maltotriose to form 2 and 3 glucose units, respectively.
- The monosaccharide end products—glucose, galactose, and fructose—are readily absorbed from the small intestine, also mainly in the jejunum.

Proteins

Stomach: Pepsin begins the digestion of protein in the acid medium of the stomach; however, it is not an essential enzyme.

Small intestine: Digestion continues with the pancreatic proteases (trypsin, chymotrypsin, elastase, and carboxypeptidases A and B), which are essential enzymes.

Protein digestion is completed by the small intestinal brush border enzymes, dipeptidases, and an aminopeptidase. The main end products are amino acids (40%) and dipeptides and tripeptides (60%).

Pancreatic enzymes are required for triglyceride, CHO, and protein digestion. Circulating CCK is almost totally responsible for their secretion following a meal.

ABSORPTION

Carbohydrates, proteins, lipids, vitamins and minerals are all absorbed from the intestinal tract.

Bridge to Pathology

Celiac disease is an immune reaction to gluten (protein found in wheat) that damages intestinal cells; the end result is diminished absorptive capacity of the small intestine.

Bridge to Pathology

Many amino acid transporters are selective for specific amino acids. Hartnup's disease is a genetic deficiency in the transporter for tryptophan.

Carbohydrate and Protein

The following figure illustrates the major transport processes carrying sugars and amino acids across the luminal and basal membranes of cells lining the small intestine.

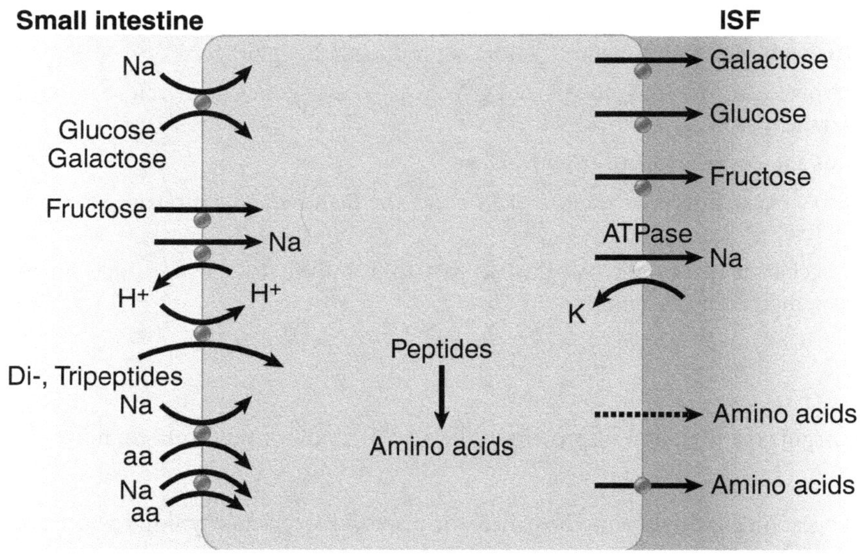

Figure 2-5. Absorption of Carbohydrates and Proteins

Carbohydrate

- **Luminal membrane:** Glucose and galactose are actively absorbed (secondary active transport linked to sodium) via the sodium-glucose linked transporter 1 (SGLT-1). Fructose is absorbed independently by facilitated diffusion.
- **Basal membrane:** The monosaccharides are absorbed passively mainly via facilitated diffusion.

Protein

- **Luminal membrane:** amino acids are transported by secondary active transport linked to sodium. Small peptides uptake powered by a Na-H antiporter.
- **Basal membrane:** simple diffusion of amino acids, although it is now known some protein-mediated transport also occurs.

Lipids

Figure 2-6 summarizes the digestion and absorption of lipid substances. The end products of triglyceride digestion, 2-monoglycerides and fatty acids, remain as lipid-soluble substances that are then taken up by the micelles.

Digestive products of fats found in the micelles and absorbed from the intestinal lumen may include:

- Fatty acids (long chain)
- 2-Monoglyceride
- Cholesterol
- Lysolecithin
- Vitamins A, D, E, K
- Bile salts, which stabilize the micelles

Micelles diffuse to the brush border of the intestine. The diffusion through the unstirred layer is the rate-limiting step of fat absorption.

The digested lipids then diffuse across the brush border in the lipid matrix. In the mucosal cell, triglyceride is resynthesized and forms lipid droplets (chylomicrons). These leave the intestine via the lymphatic circulation (lacteals). They then enter the bloodstream via the thoracic duct. The more water-soluble short-chain fatty acids can be absorbed by simple diffusion directly into the bloodstream. The bile salts are actively reabsorbed in the distal ileum.

Bridge to Biochemistry

Chylomicrons contain apolipoprotein B-48. Once in the systemic circulation, chylomicrons are converted to VLDL (very low-density lipoprotein) and they incorporate apoproteins C-II and E from HDL (high-density liproprotein).

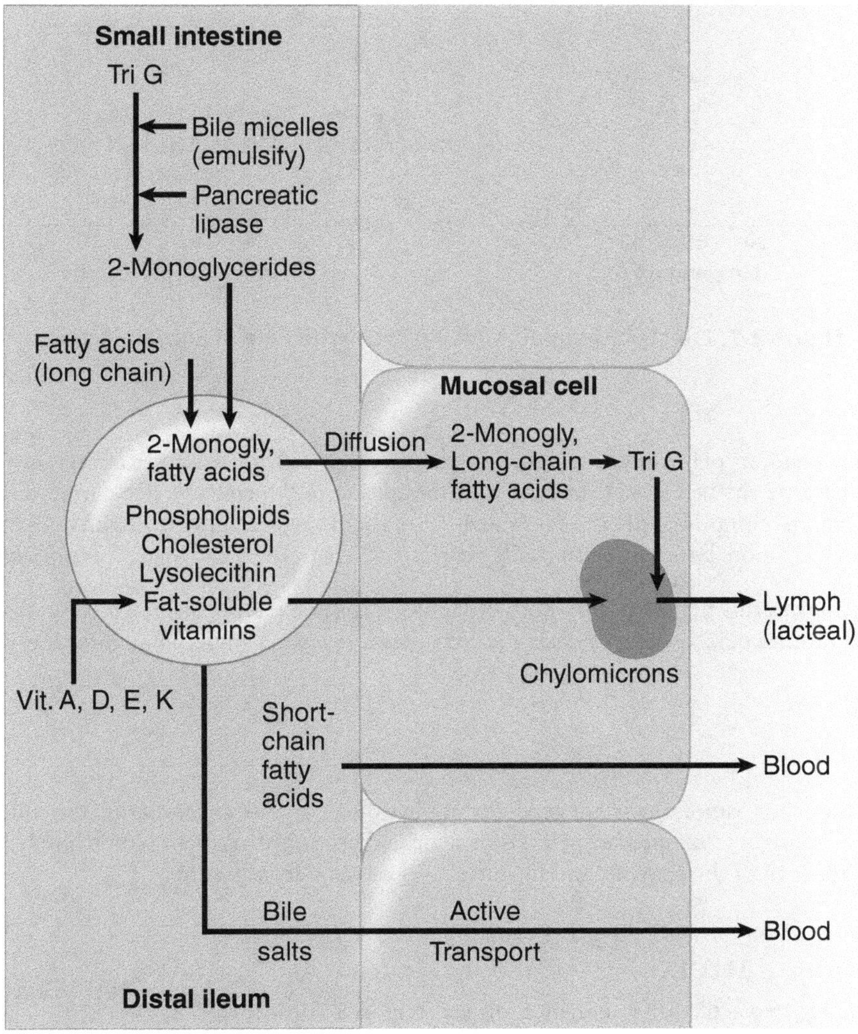

Figure 2-6. Absorption of Lipids

ENZYMOLOGY AND COENZYMES AND KINETICS

The activity of an enzyme is heavily influenced by its environment; in particular, temperature, acidity or alkalinity (pH), and high salinity have significant effects on the ability of an enzyme to carry out its function. Enzyme activity may also be influenced by the presence of a coenzyme.

Temperature

Enzyme-catalyzed reactions tend to double in velocity for every 10°C increase in temperature until the optimum temperature is reached; for the human body, this is 37°C (98.6°F or 310 K). After this, activity falls off sharply, as the enzyme will denature at higher temperatures. Some enzymes that are overheated may regain their function if cooled.

A real-life example of temperature dependence occurs in Siamese cats. Siamese cats are dark on their faces, ears, tails, and feet but white elsewhere. Why? The enzyme responsible for pigmentation, *tyrosinase*, is mutated. It is ineffective at body temperature but at cooler temperatures becomes active. Thus, only the tail, feet, ears, and face (cooled by air passing through the nose and mouth) have an active form of the enzyme and are dark.

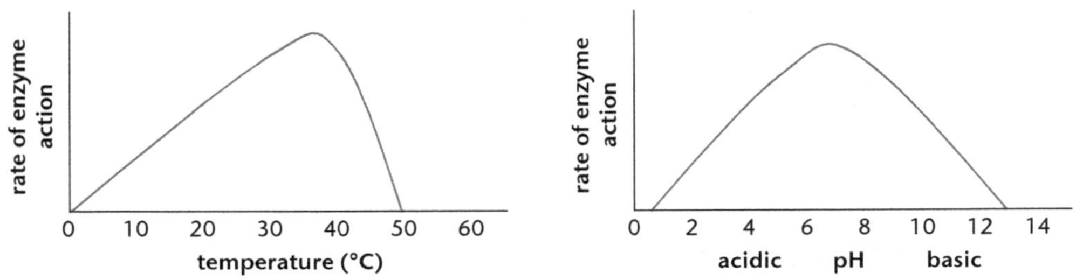

Figure 2-7. Effects of Temperature and pH on the Rate of Enzyme Action

pH

Most enzymes also depend on pH in order to function properly, not only because pH affects the ionization of the active site, but also because changes in pH can lead to denaturation of the enzyme. For enzymes that circulate and function in human blood, this optimal pH is 7.4, as shown in the above figure. A pH < 7.35 in human blood is termed acidemia. Even though it's more basic than *chemically* neutral 7.0, it is more acidic than *physiologically* neutral 7.4.

Where might exceptions to this pH 7.4 occur? Both are in our digestive tract. Pepsin, which works in the stomach, has maximal activity around pH 2, whereas pancreatic enzymes, which work in the small intestine, work best around pH 8.5.

Salinity

While the effect of salinity or osmolarity is not generally of physiologic significance, altering the concentration of salt can change enzyme activity *in vitro*. Increasing levels of salt can disrupt hydrogen and ionic bonds, causing a partial change in the conformation of the enzyme, and in some cases causing denaturation.

Coenzymes and Cofactors

Coenzymes are organic molecules that enhance or are required for the enzyme to express its activity. They are generally small molecules that provide a transfer site for an enzyme. The B vitamins are classic examples of coenzymes.

NAPLEX Reference

Over-the-Counter Medications chapter: "Vitamins"

Cofactors are non-protein compounds that enhance enzyme function by increasing the rate of catalysis. They are generally metal ions, such as iron, copper, zinc, magnesium, cobalt, and molybdenum.

Regulation of Enzyme Activity

Although enzymes are useful, the body must be able to control when they work; for example, enzymes involved in mitosis should be shut off when cells are no longer dividing (in the G_0 phase). This may be accomplished in a variety of ways, as described below.

Feedback Regulation

Enzymes are often subject to regulation by products further down a given metabolic pathway, a process called **feedback regulation.** Less often, enzymes may be regulated by intermediates that precede the enzyme in the pathway, also called **feed-forward regulation.** This is clearly evident in the study of metabolism. While there are some examples of feedback activation, feedback inhibition is far more common. Feedback inhibition, or **negative feedback**, helps maintain homeostasis: once we have enough of a given product, we want to turn off the pathway that creates that product, rather than creating more. In feedback inhibition, the product may bind to the active site of an enzyme or multiple enzymes that acted earlier in its biosynthetic pathway, thereby competitively inhibiting these enzymes and making them unavailable for use. This is schematically represented in the following figure, as we see product D feeding back to inhibit the first enzyme in the pathway.

Bridge to Physiology

Negative feedback is an important topic in both enzymology and the endocrine system. Remember, most hormonal feedback loops are also inhibited by negative feedback.

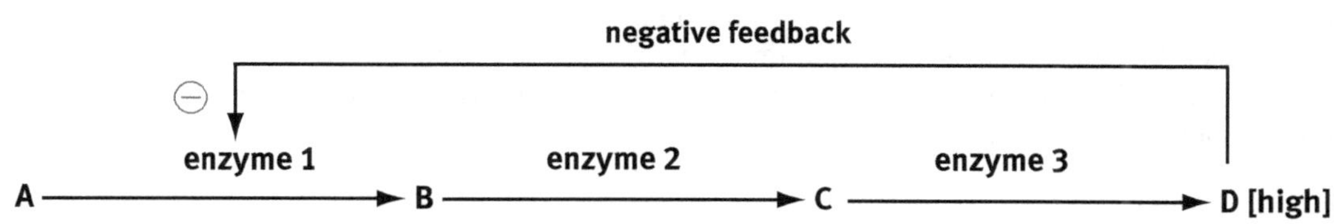

Figure 2-8. Feedback Inhibition by the Product of a Metabolic Pathway
A high concentration of the product, D, inhibits enzyme 1, slowing the entire pathway.

Reversible Inhibition

There are 4 types of reversible inhibition: competitive, noncompetitive, mixed, and uncompetitive. On the exam you will most often encounter competitive and noncompetitive inhibition, but be aware of how all the types are different. Table 2-1 at the end of this section summarizes the features of each type of reversible inhibition.

Bridge to Pharmacology

The concept of competitive inhibition has relevance in the clinical setting. For example, methanol (wood alcohol), if ingested, is enzymatically converted to toxic metabolites, which can cause blindness and even death. Administration of intravenous ethanol is the treatment of choice for a patient suffering from methanol poisoning. Ethanol works by competing with methanol for the active sites of the enzymes involved.

Competitive inhibition simply involves occupancy of the active site. Substrates cannot access enzymatic binding sites if there is an inhibitor in the way. Competitive inhibition can be overcome by adding more substrate so that the substrate-to-inhibitor ratio is higher. If more molecules of substrate are available than molecules of inhibitor, then the enzyme will be more likely to bind substrate than inhibitor (assuming the enzyme has equal affinity for both molecules). Adding a competitive inhibitor does not alter the value of v_{max} because if enough substrate is added, it will outcompete the inhibitor and be able to run the reaction at maximum velocity. A competitive inhibitor does increase the measured value of K_m. This is because the substrate concentration has to be higher to reach half the maximum velocity in the presence of the inhibitor. A Lineweaver–Burk plot compares an enzyme with and without a competitive inhibitor.

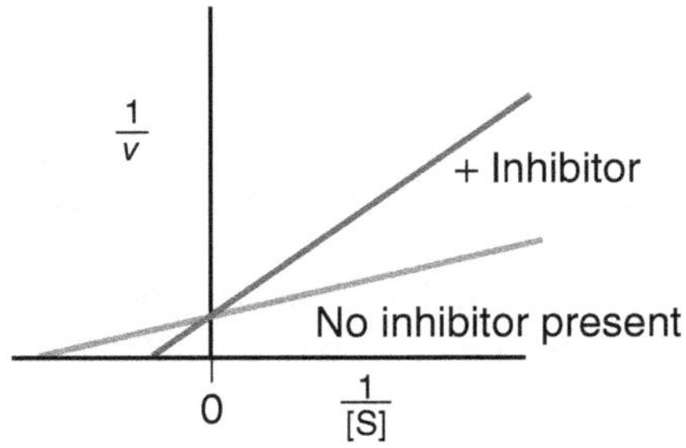

Figure 2-9. Lineweaver–Burk Plot of Competitive Inhibition

Noncompetitive inhibitors bind to an allosteric site instead of the active site, which induces a change in enzyme conformation. Allosteric sites are non-catalytic regions of the enzyme that bind regulators. Because the 2 molecules do not compete for the same site, inhibition is considered noncompetitive and cannot be overcome by adding more substrate. Noncompetitive inhibitors bind equally well to the enzyme and the enzyme–substrate complex, unlike mixed inhibitors. Once the enzyme's conformation is altered, no amount of extra substrate will be conducive to forming an enzyme–substrate complex. Adding a noncompetitive inhibitor decreases the measured value of v_{max} because there is less enzyme available to react; it does not, however, alter the value of K_m because any copies of the enzyme that are still active maintain the same affinity for their substrate. A Lineweaver–Burk plot of an enzyme with and without a noncompetitive inhibitor is shown here:

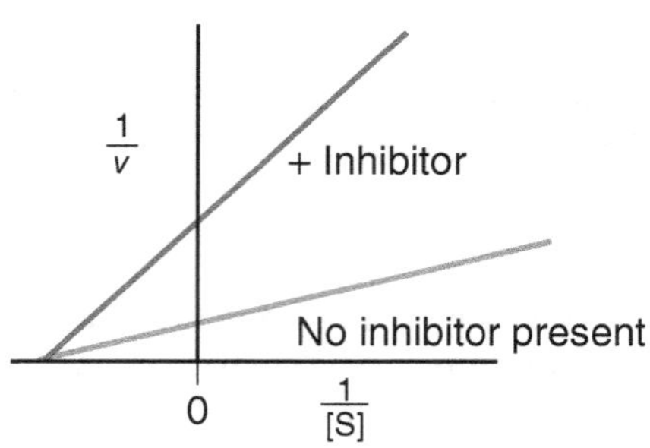

Figure 2-10. Lineweaver–Burk Plot of Noncompetitive Inhibition

Mixed inhibition results when an inhibitor can bind to either the enzyme or the enzyme–substrate complex, but has different affinity for each. If the inhibitor had the same affinity for both, it would be a noncompetitive inhibitor. Mixed inhibitors do not bind at the active site, but at an allosteric site. Mixed inhibition alters the experimental value of K_m depending on the preference of the inhibitor for the enzyme *vs.* the enzyme–substrate complex. If the inhibitor preferentially binds to the enzyme, it increases the K_m value (lowers affinity); if the inhibitor binds to the enzyme–substrate complex, it lowers the K_m value (increases affinity). In either case, v_{max} is decreased. On a Lineweaver–Burk plot, the curves for the activity with and without the inhibitor intersect at a point that is not on either axis.

Uncompetitive inhibitors bind only to the enzyme–substrate complex and essentially lock the substrate in the enzyme, preventing its release. This can be interpreted as increasing affinity between the enzyme and substrate. Because the enzyme–substrate complex has already formed upon binding, uncompetitive inhibitors must bind at an allosteric site; in fact, it is the formation of the enzyme–substrate complex that creates a conformational change allowing an uncompetitive inhibitor to bind. Thus, uncompetitive inhibitors lower K_m and v_{max}. On a Lineweaver–Burk plot, the curves for activity with and without an uncompetitive inhibitor are parallel.

Table 2-1. Comparison of Reversible Inhibitors

	Competitive	Noncompetitive	Mixed	Uncompetitive
Binding Site	Active site	Allosteric site	Allosteric site	Allosteric site
Impact on K_m	Increases	Unchanged	Increases or Decreases	Decreases
Impact on v_{max}	Unchanged	Decreases	Decreases	Decreases

In **irreversible inhibition**, the active site is made unavailable for a prolonged period of time, or the enzyme is permanently altered; this type of inhibition is not easily overcome or reversed. A pharmacology example is aspirin. Acetylsalicylic acid (aspirin) irreversibly modifies *cyclooxygenase-1*. The enzyme can no longer bind its substrate (*arachidonic acid*) to make its products (*prostaglandins*), which are involved in modulating pain and inflammatory responses. To make more prostaglandins, new cyclooxygenase-1 will have to be synthesized through transcription and translation. Irreversible inhibition is a prime drug mechanism, and something that you will come across often in pharmacy school.

Enzymes that are allosteric have multiple binding sites. The active site is present, as well as at least one other site that can regulate the availability of the active site. These are known as **allosteric sites. Allosteric enzymes** alternate between an active and an inactive form. The inactive form cannot carry out the enzymatic reaction.

Molecules that bind to the allosteric site may be either **allosteric activators** or **allosteric inhibitors.** Binding of either causes a conformational shift in the protein; however, the effect differs. An activator will result in a shift that makes the active site more available for binding to the substrate, whereas an inhibitor will make it less available. In addition to being able to alter the conformation of the protein, binding of activators or inhibitors may alter the activity of the enzyme. Michaelis–Menten plots of cooperative allosteric enzyme kinetics often have a sigmoidal (S-shaped) curve.

In addition to transient interactions, enzymes are often subject to covalent modification. Enzymes can be activated or deactivated by **phosphorylation** or **dephosphorylation.** One cannot predict whether phosphorylation or dephosphorylation will activate an enzyme without experimental determination. **Glycosylation**, the covalent attachment of sugar moieties, is another covalent enzyme modification. Glycosylation can tag an enzyme for transport within the cell, or can modify protein activity and selectivity. Specific mechanisms for the modification of enzymes by glycosylation are still being studied, and are beyond the scope of the FPGEE.

Certain enzymes are particularly dangerous if they are not tightly controlled. These include the digestive enzymes like *trypsin*, which, if released from the pancreas in an uncontrolled manner, would digest the organ itself. To avoid this danger, these enzymes and many others are secreted as inactive **zymogens** like *trypsinogen*. Zymogens contain a catalytic (active) domain and regulatory domain. The regulatory domain must be either removed or altered to expose the active site. Apoptotic enzymes (*caspases*) exhibit similar regulation. Most zymogens have the suffix ***–ogen.***

CELL CHEMISTRY

Hormones are responsible for initiating numerous cellular processes.

Hormones and Signal Transduction

A hormone is any compound produced by a cell, which by binding to its cognate receptor alters the metabolism of the cell bearing the hormone-receptor complex. Although a few hormones bind to receptors on the cell that produces them (autoregulation or autocrine function), hormones are more commonly thought of as acting on some other cell, either close by (paracrine) or at a distant site (telecrine).

Paracrine hormones are secreted into the interstitial space and generally have a very short half-life. These include the prostaglandins and the neurotransmitters. Telecrine hormones are secreted into the bloodstream, generally have a longer half-life, and include the endocrine and gastrointestinal (GI) hormones. It is sometimes implied that reference is being made to endocrine hormones when the word "hormones" is used in a general sense.

The GI and endocrine hormones are discussed in detail in Chapter 1 of this book. Although there is some overlap, the chapter you are reading (Chapter 2) presents basic mechanistic concepts applicable to all hormones, whereas coverage in Human Anatomy and Physiology (Chapter 1) emphasizes the physiologic consequences of hormonal action.

Hormones are divided into 2 categories: water soluble (hydrophilic) and lipid soluble (lipophilic or hydrophobic).

Table 2-2. Two Classes of Hormones

Water Soluble	Lipid Soluble
Receptor in cell membrane	Receptor inside cell
Second messengers often involved. Protein kinases activated	Hormone–receptor complex binds hormone response elements (HRE) of enhancer regions in DNA
Protein phosphorylation to modify activity of enzymes (requires minutes)	––
Control of gene expression through proteins such as cAMP response element binding (CREB) protein (requires hours)	Control of gene expression (requires hours)
Examples: insulin, glucagon, catecholamines	Examples: steroids, calcitriol, thyroxines, retinoic acid

Mechanism of Water-soluble Hormones

Water-soluble hormones must transmit signals to affect metabolism and gene expression without themselves entering the cytoplasm. They often do so via second messenger systems that activate protein kinases.

A **protein kinase** is an enzyme that phosphorylates other proteins, changing their activity (e.g., phosphorylation of acetyl CoA carboxylase inhibits it). Examples of protein kinases are listed in the following table along with the second messengers that activate them.

Table 2-3. Summary of Signal Transduction by Water-Soluble Hormones

Pathway	G Protein	Enzyme	Second Messenger(s)	Protein Kinase	Examples
cAMP	G_s (G_i)	Adenyl cyclase	cAMP	Protein kinase A	Glucagon Epinephrine (β, α-2) Vasopressin (V2, ADH) kidney
PIP_2	G_q	Phospholipase C	DAG, IP_3, Ca^{2+}	Protein kinase C	Vasopressin (V1, V3) vascular smooth muscle Epinephrine (α_1)
cGMP	None	Guanyl cyclase	cGMP	Protein kinase G	Atrial natriuretic factor (ANF) Nitric oxide (NO)
Insulin, growth factors	Monomeric $p21^{ras}$	––	––	Tyrosine kinase activity of receptor	Insulin Insulin-like growth factor (IGF) Platelet-derived growth factor (PDGF) Epidermal growth factor (EGF)

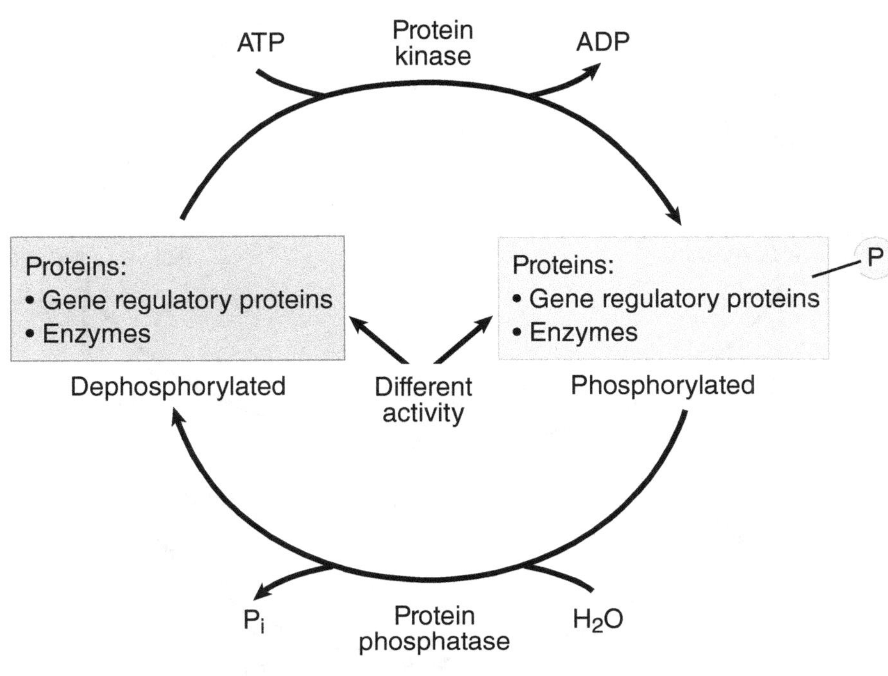

Figure 2-11. Protein Kinases and Phosphatase

Some water-soluble hormones bind to receptors with intrinsic protein kinase activity (often tyrosine kinases). In this case, no second messenger is required for protein kinase activation. The insulin receptor is an example of a tyrosine kinase receptor.

Activation of a protein kinase causes:

- Phosphorylation of enzymes to rapidly increase or decrease their activity.
- Phosphorylation of gene regulatory proteins such as CREB to control gene expression, usually over several hours. The typical result is to add more enzyme to the cell. CREB induces the phosphoenolpyruvate carboxykinase (PEPCK) gene. Kinetically, an increase in the number of enzymes means an increase in V_{max} for that reaction.

Both represent strategies to control metabolism. The action of protein kinases is reversed by protein phosphatases.

Sequence of Events From Receptor to Protein Kinase

There are a number of events that occur after a hormone binds to a receptor.

Receptors in these pathways are coupled through trimetric **G proteins** in the membrane. The 3 subunits in this type of G protein are α, β, and γ. In its inactive form, the α subunit binds GDP and is in complex with the β and γ subunits. When a hormone binds to its receptor, the receptor becomes activated and, in turn, engages the corresponding G protein (step 1 in the below figure). The GDP is replaced with GTP, enabling the α subunit to dissociate from the β and γ subunits (step 2). The activated α subunit alters the activity of adenylate cyclase. If the α subunit is α_s, then the enzyme is activated; if the α subunit is α_i, then the enzyme is inhibited. The GTP in the activated α subunit will be dephosphorylated to GDP (step 3) and will rebind to the β and γ subunits (step 4), rendering the G protein inactive.

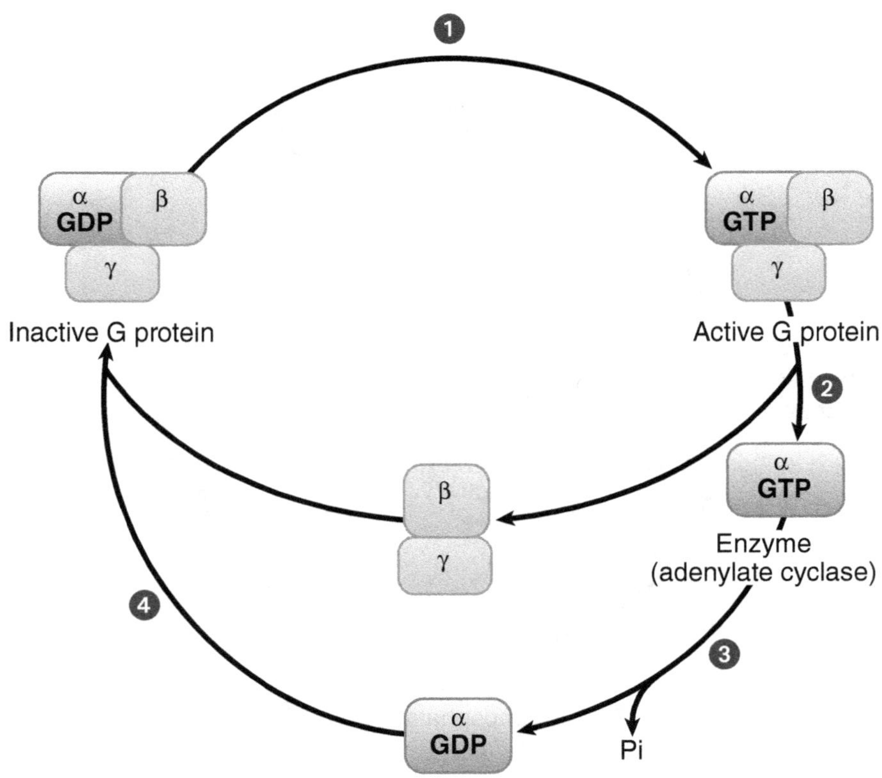

Figure 2-12. Trimeric G Protein Cycle

The receptors all have characteristic 7-helix membrane-spanning domains. The sequence of events leading from receptor to activation of the protein kinase via the **cAMP** and **PIP$_2$** second messenger systems is as follows:

- Hormone binds receptor
- Trimeric G protein in membrane is engaged
- Enzyme (adenylate cyclase or phospholipase) activated
- Second messenger generated
- Protein kinase activated
- Protein phosphorylation (minutes) and gene expression (hours)

An example of inhibition of adenylate cyclase via G_i is epinephrine inhibition (through its binding to α_2 adrenergic receptor) of insulin release from β cells of the pancreas.

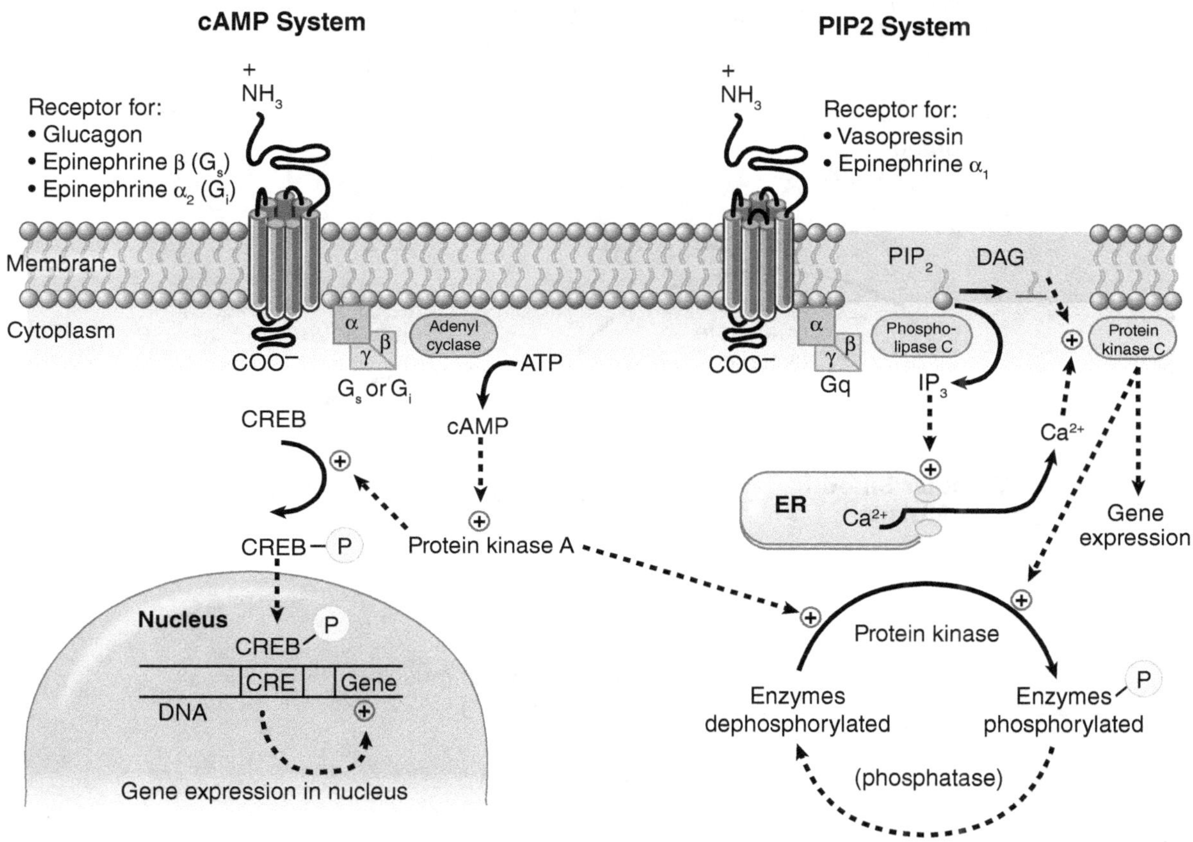

Figure 2-13. Cyclic AMP and Phosphatidylinositol Bisphosphate (PIP$_2$)

cGMP

> **Note**
>
> Once generated, the second messengers cAMP and cGMP are slowly degraded by a class of enzymes called phosphodiesterases (PDEs).

Atrial natriuretic factor (ANF), produced by cells in the atrium of the heart in response to distension, binds the ANF receptor in vascular smooth muscle and in the kidney. The ANF receptor spans the membrane and has guanylate cyclase activity associated with the cytoplasmic domain. It causes relaxation of vascular smooth muscle, resulting in vasodilation, and in the kidney it promotes sodium and water excretion.

Nitric oxide (NO) is synthesized by vascular endothelium in response to vasodilators. It diffuses into the surrounding vascular smooth muscle, where it directly binds the heme group of soluble guanylate cyclase, activating the enzyme.

Both the ANF receptor and the soluble guanylate cyclase are associated with the same vascular smooth muscle cells.

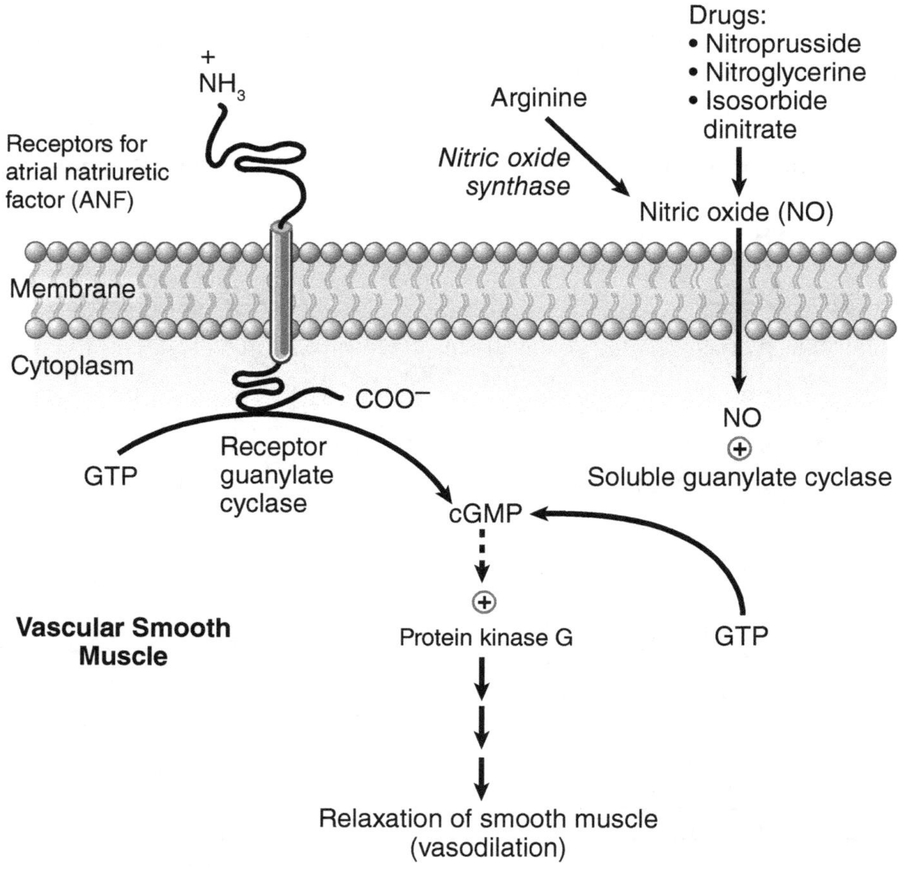

Figure 2-14. Cyclic GMP

The sequence from receptor to protein kinase is quite similar to the one above for cAMP with 2 important variations:

Bridge to Microbiology

E. coli heat stable toxin (STa)

A similar guanylate cyclase receptor in enterocytes is the target of *E. coli* heat-stable toxin (STa). The toxin binds to, and stimulates, the guanylate cyclase increasing cGMP. This causes increased activity of CFTR and diarrhea.

- The ANF receptor has intrinsic guanylate cyclase activity. Because no G protein is required in the membrane, the receptor lacks the 7-helix membrane-spanning domain.
- Nitric oxide diffuses into the cell and directly activates a soluble, cytoplasmic guanylate cyclase, so no receptor or G protein is required.

Insulin binding activates the **tyrosine kinase** activity associated with the cytoplasmic domain of its receptor. There is no trimeric G protein, enzyme, or second messenger required to activate this protein tyrosine kinase activity:

- Hormone binds receptor
- Receptor tyrosine kinase (protein kinase) is activated
- Protein phosphorylation (autophosphorylation and activation of other proteins)

Once autophosphorylation begins, a complex of other events ensues. An insulin receptor substrate (IRS-1) binds the receptor and is phosphorylated on tyrosine residues, allowing proteins with SH2 (*src* homology) domains to bind to the phosphotyrosine residues on IRS-1 and become active. In this way, the receptor activates several enzyme cascades, which involve:

- Activation of phosphatidylinositol-3 kinase (PI-3 kinase), one of whose effects in adipose and muscle tissues is to increase GLUT-4 in the membrane
- Activation of protein phosphatases. Paradoxically, insulin stimulation via its tyrosine kinase receptor ultimately may lead to dephosphorylating enzymes
- Stimulation of the monomeric G protein ($p21^{ras}$) encoded by the normal *ras* gene

All these mechanisms can be involved in controlling gene expression, although the pathways by which this occurs have not yet been completely characterized.

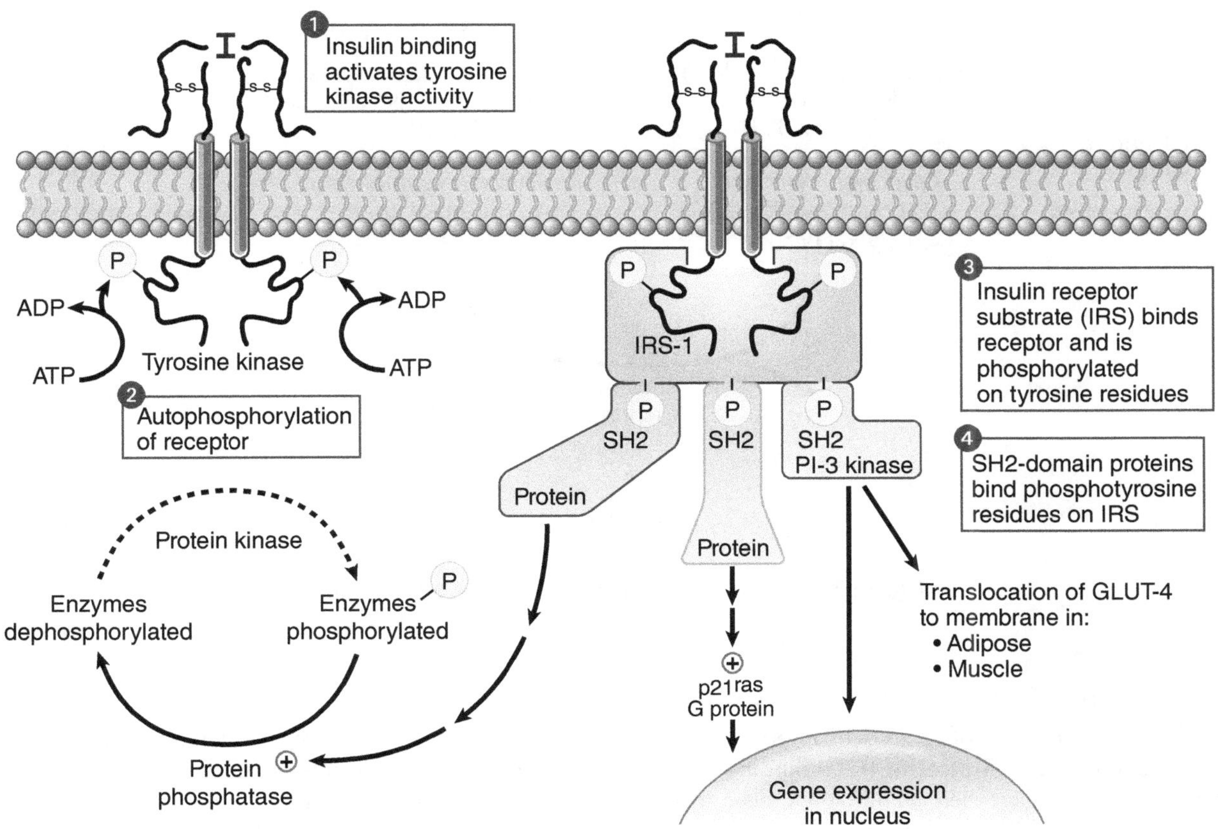

Figure 2-15. Insulin Receptor

Tyrosine kinase receptors are also involved in signaling by several growth factors including platelet-derived growth factor (PDGF) and epidermal growth factor (EGF).

Insulin and **glucagon** have a functional relationship. Insulin, associated with well-fed and absorptive metabolism, and glucagon, associated with fasting and postabsorptive metabolism, usually oppose each other with respect to pathways of energy metabolism. Glucagon works through the cAMP system to activate protein kinase A, favoring phosphorylation of rate-limiting enzymes, whereas insulin often activates protein phosphatases that dephosphorylate many of the same enzymes.

An example of this opposition in glycogen metabolism is shown in Figure 2-16. Glucagon promotes phosphorylation of both rate-limiting enzymes (glycogen phosphorylase for glycogenolysis and glycogen synthase for glycogen synthesis). The result is twofold in that synthesis slows and degradation increases, but both effects contribute to the same physiologic outcome, release of glucose from the liver during hypoglycemia. Insulin reverses this pattern, promoting glucose storage after a meal. The reciprocal relationship between glucagon and insulin is manifested in other metabolic pathways, such as triglyceride synthesis and degradation.

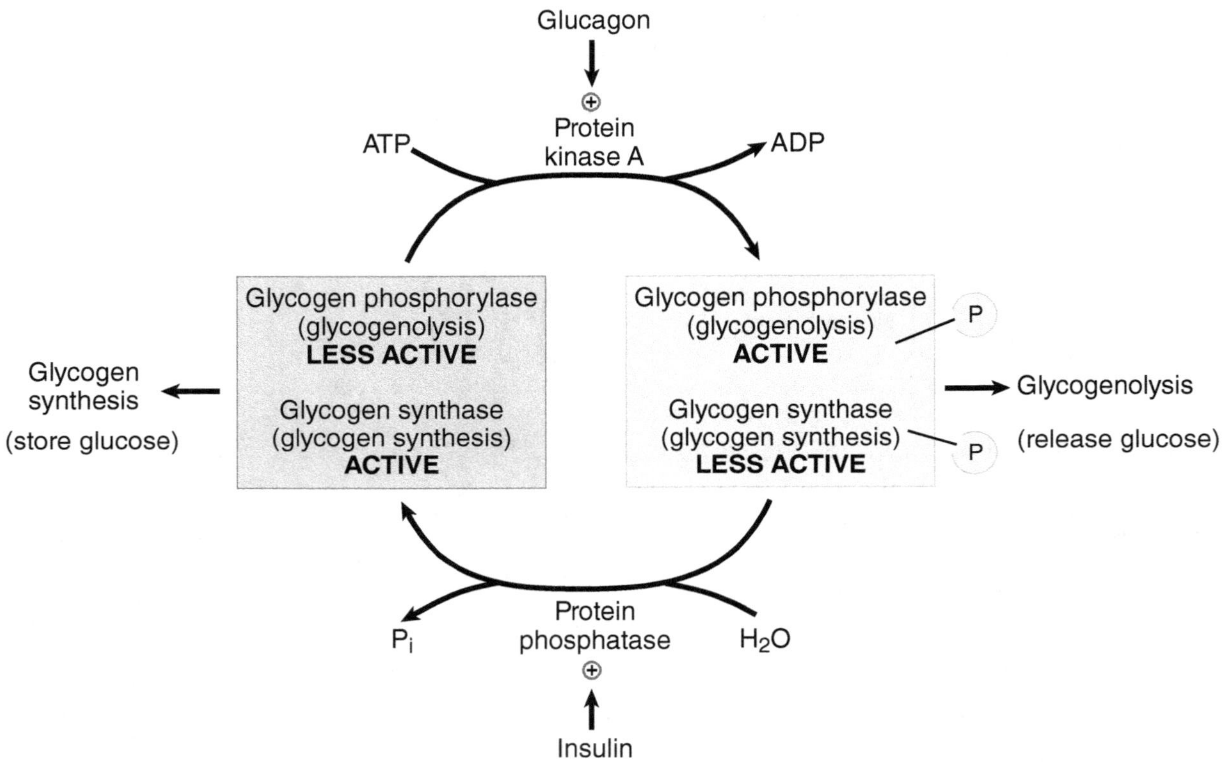

Figure 2-16. Opposing Activities of Insulin and Glucagon

G Proteins in Signal Transduction

Table 2-2 is a summary of the major components of water-soluble hormone pathways reviewed in this section. There are several different G proteins (GTP-binding) involved. Trimeric G proteins include G_s, G_i, G_q, G_t (transducin). Receptors that engage these all have the 7-helix membrane-spanning structure. Receptor stimulation causes the Gα subunit to bind GTP and become active. The Gα subunit subsequently hydrolyzes the GTP to GDP, terminating the signal. The p21^{ras} G protein is monomeric.

G-protein defects can cause disease in several ways, some of which are summarized in the following table.

Table 2-4. Abnormal G Proteins and Disease

Defect	Example	Disease
ADP-ribosylation by:	$G_s\alpha$	Diarrhea of cholera
• *Cholera* toxin	$G_s\alpha$	Traveler's diarrhea
• *E. coli* toxin	$G_i\alpha$	Pertussis (whooping cough)
• *Pertussis* toxin		
Oncogenic mutations	$p21^{ras}$ (*ras*)	Colon, lung, breast, bladder tumors

Certain bacterial exotoxins are enzymes that attach the adenosine diphosphate (ADP)-ribose residue of NAD to Gα subunits, an activity known as **ADP-ribosylation**. In humans, some ADP-ribosylation is physiological, but it may also be pathological:

- *Vibrio cholerae* exotoxin ADP-ribosylates $G_s\alpha$, leading to an increase in cAMP and subsequently chloride secretion from intestinal mucosal cells, and causing the diarrhea of cholera.
- Certain strains of *Escherichia coli* release toxins (heat labile or LT) similar to cholera toxin, producing traveler's diarrhea.
- *Bordetella pertussis* exotoxin ADP-ribosylates $G_i\alpha$, dramatically reducing its responsiveness to the receptor, thus increasing cAMP. It is not known how this relates to the persistent paroxysmal coughing symptomatic of pertussis (whooping cough).

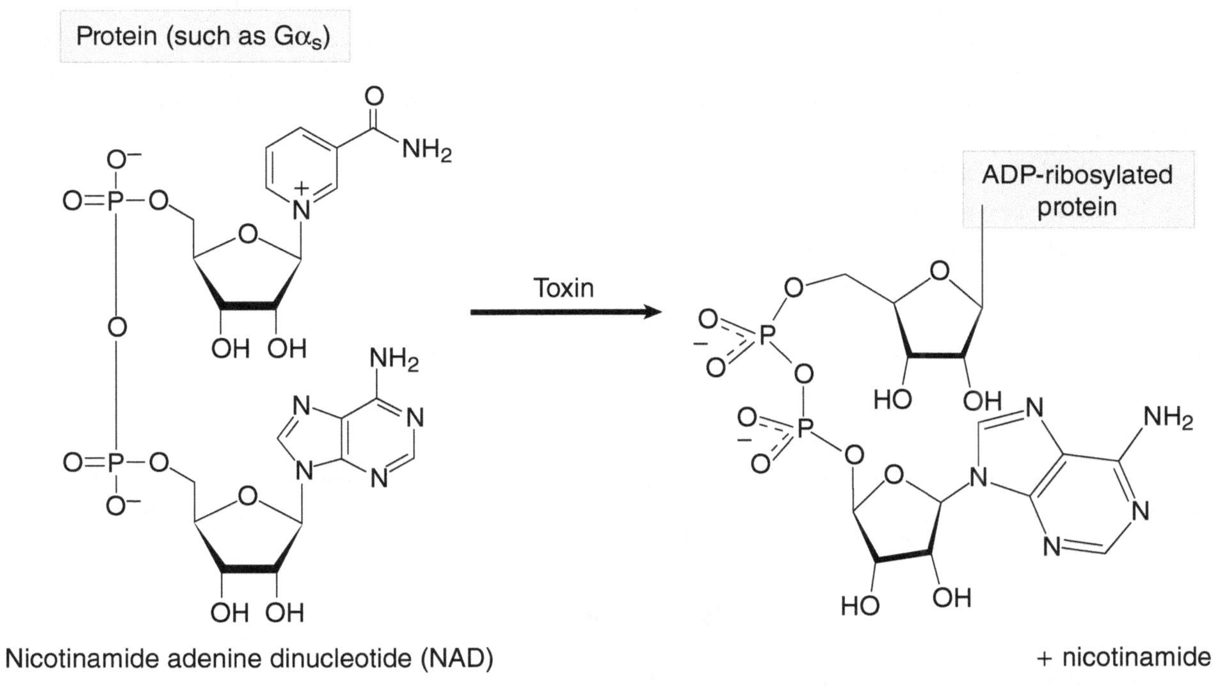

Figure 2-17. ADP-Ribosylation of a Protein

Lipid-Soluble Hormones

Lipid-soluble hormones diffuse through the cell membrane, where they bind to their respective receptors inside the cell. The receptors have a DNA-binding domain (usually Zn-fingers) and interact with specific response elements in enhancer (or possibly silencer) regions associated with certain genes. For example, the cortisol receptor binds to its response element in the enhancer region of the phosphoenolpyruvate carboxykinase (PEPCK) gene. By increasing the amount of PEPCK in the hepatocyte, cortisol can increase the capacity for gluconeogenesis, one of its mechanisms for responding to chronic stress often associated with injury.

CELLULAR TRANSPORT AND MOBILITY PRINCIPLES

The K_m and V_{max} parameters that apply to enzymes are also applicable to transporters in membranes. The kinetics of transport can be derived from the Michaelis-Menten and Lineweaver-Burk equations, where K_m refers to the solute concentration at which the transporter is functioning at half its maximum activity. The importance of K_m values for membrane transporters is exemplified with the variety of glucose transporters (GLUT) and their respective physiologic roles.

Glycolysis

All cells can carry out glycolysis. In a few tissues, most importantly red blood cells, glycolysis represents the only energy-yielding pathway available. Glucose is the major monosaccharide that enters the pathway, but others such as galactose and fructose can also be used. The first steps in glucose metabolism in any cell are transport across the membrane and phosphorylation by kinase enzymes inside the cell to prevent it from leaving via the transporter.

Carbohydrate Digestion

Only a very small amount of the total carbohydrates ingested are monosaccharides. Most of the carbohydrates in foods are in complex forms, such as starch (amylose and amylopectin) and the disaccharides sucrose and lactose. In the mouth, secreted salivary amylase randomly hydrolyzes the starch polymers to dextrins (<8–10 glucoses). Upon entry of food into the stomach, the acid pH destroys the salivary amylase. In the intestine, the dextrins are hydrolyzed to the disaccharides maltose and isomaltose. Disaccharides in the intestinal brush border complete the digestion process:

- Maltase cleaves maltose to 2 glucoses
- Isomaltase cleaves isomaltose to 2 glucoses
- Lactase cleaves lactose to glucose and galactose
- Sucrase cleaves sucrose to glucose and fructose

Uptake of glucose into the mucosal cells is performed by the sodium/glucose transporter, an active transport system.

Glucose Transport

Glucose entry into most cells is concentration-driven and independent of sodium. Four glucose transporters (GLUT) are listed in Table 2-5. They have different affinities for glucose coinciding with their respective physiologic roles. Normal glucose concentration in peripheral blood is 4–6 mM (70–110 mg/dL).

Bridge to Physiology

GLUT 4 translocation to the cell membrane in skeletal muscle is stimulated by exercise. This effect, which is independent of insulin, involves a 5′ AMP-activated kinase.

- GLUT 1 and GLUT 3 mediate basal glucose uptake in most tissues, including brain, nerves, and red blood cells. Their high affinities for glucose ensure glucose entry even during periods of relative hypoglycemia. At normal glucose concentration, GLUT 1 and GLUT 3 are at V_{max}.

- GLUT 2, a low-affinity transporter, is in hepatocytes. After a meal, portal blood from the intestine is rich in glucose. GLUT 2 captures the excess glucose primarily for storage. When the glucose concentration drops below the K_m for the transporter, much of the remainder leaves the liver and enters the peripheral circulation. In the β-islet cells of the pancreas. GLUT-2, along with glucokinase, serves as the glucose sensor for insulin release.
- GLUT 4 is in adipose tissue and muscle and responds to the glucose concentration in peripheral blood. The rate of glucose transport in these 2 tissues is increased by insulin, which stimulates the movement of additional GLUT 4 transporters to the membrane by a mechanism involving exocytosis.

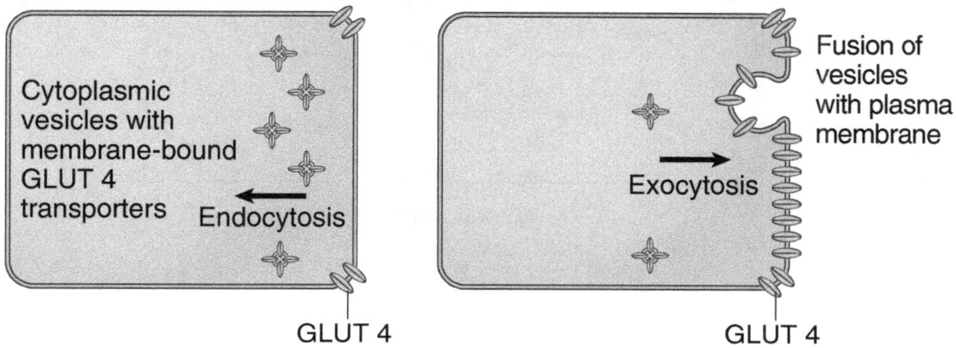

Figure 2-18. Insulin Regulation of Glucose Transport in Muscle and Adipose Cells

Although basal transport occurs in all cells independently of insulin, the transport rate increases in adipose tissue and muscle when insulin levels rise. Muscle stores excess glucose as glycogen, and adipose tissue requires glucose to form dihydroxyacetone phosphate (DHAP), which is converted to glycerol phosphate used to store incoming fatty acids as triglyceride (TGL, 3 fatty acids attached to glycerol).

Table 2-5. Major Glucose Transporters in Human Cells

Name	Tissues	K_m, Glucose	Functions
GLUT 1	Most tissues (brain, red cells)	~1 mM	Basal uptake of glucose
GLUT 2	Liver Pancreatic β-cells	~15 mM	Uptake and release of glucose by the liver β-cell glucose sensor
GLUT 3	Most tissues	~1 mM	Basal uptake
GLUT 4	Skeletal muscle Adipose tissue	~5 mM	Insulin-stimulated glucose uptake; stimulated by exercise in skeletal muscle

Normal blood glucose concentration is 4–6 mM (72–110 mg/dL).

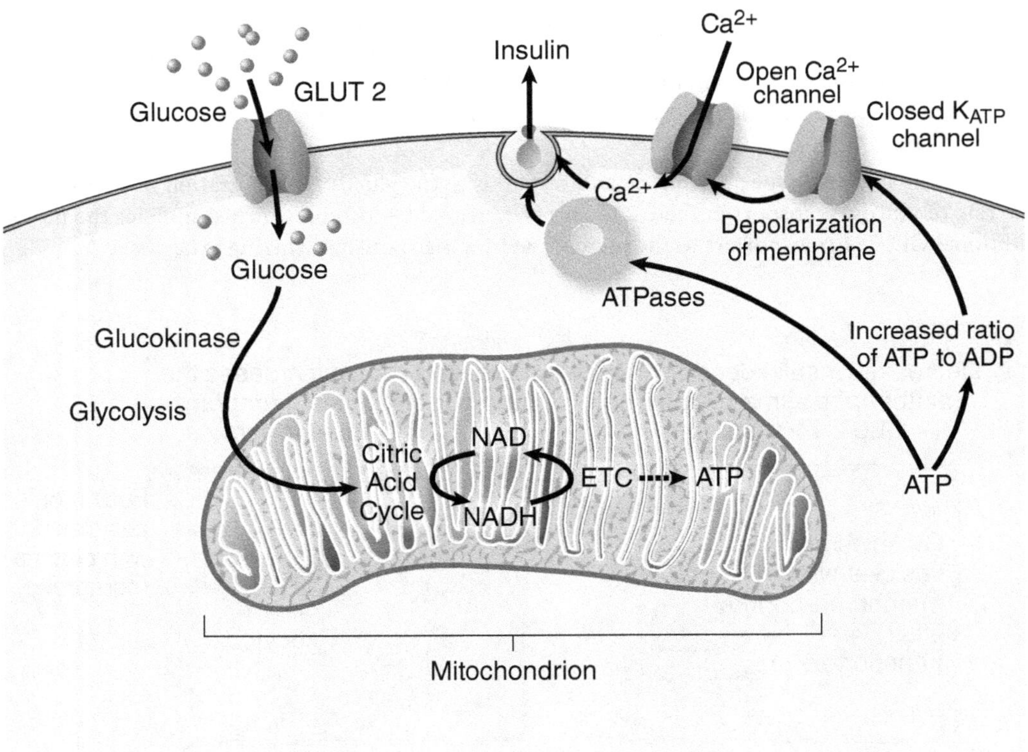

Figure 2-19. GLUT 2 and Glucokinase Together Function as the Glucose Sensor in Pancreatic β-Islet Cells

> **Note**
>
> Glucose induces genetic expression of the insulin gene. Insulin secretion by the pancreatic β-cells is biphasic. Glucose stimulates the first phase (within 15 minutes) with release of preformed insulin. The second phase (several hours) involves insulin synthesis at the gene level.

Glycolysis

Glycolysis is a cytoplasmic pathway that converts glucose into 2 pyruvates, releasing a modest amount of energy captured in 2 substrate-level phosphorylations and one oxidation reaction. If a cell has mitochondria and oxygen, glycolysis is aerobic. If either mitochondria or oxygen is lacking, glycolysis may occur anaerobically (erythrocytes, exercising skeletal muscle), although some of the available energy is lost.

RECOMBINANT DNA BIOTECHNOLOGY

Recombinant DNA technology allows a DNA fragment from any source to be joined *in vitro* with a nucleic acid vector that can replicate autonomously in microorganisms. This provides a means of analyzing and altering genes and proteins. It also provides the reagents necessary for genetic testing for carrier detection and prenatal diagnosis of genetic diseases and for gene therapy. Additionally, this technology can provide a source of a specific protein, such as recombinant human insulin, in almost unlimited quantities.

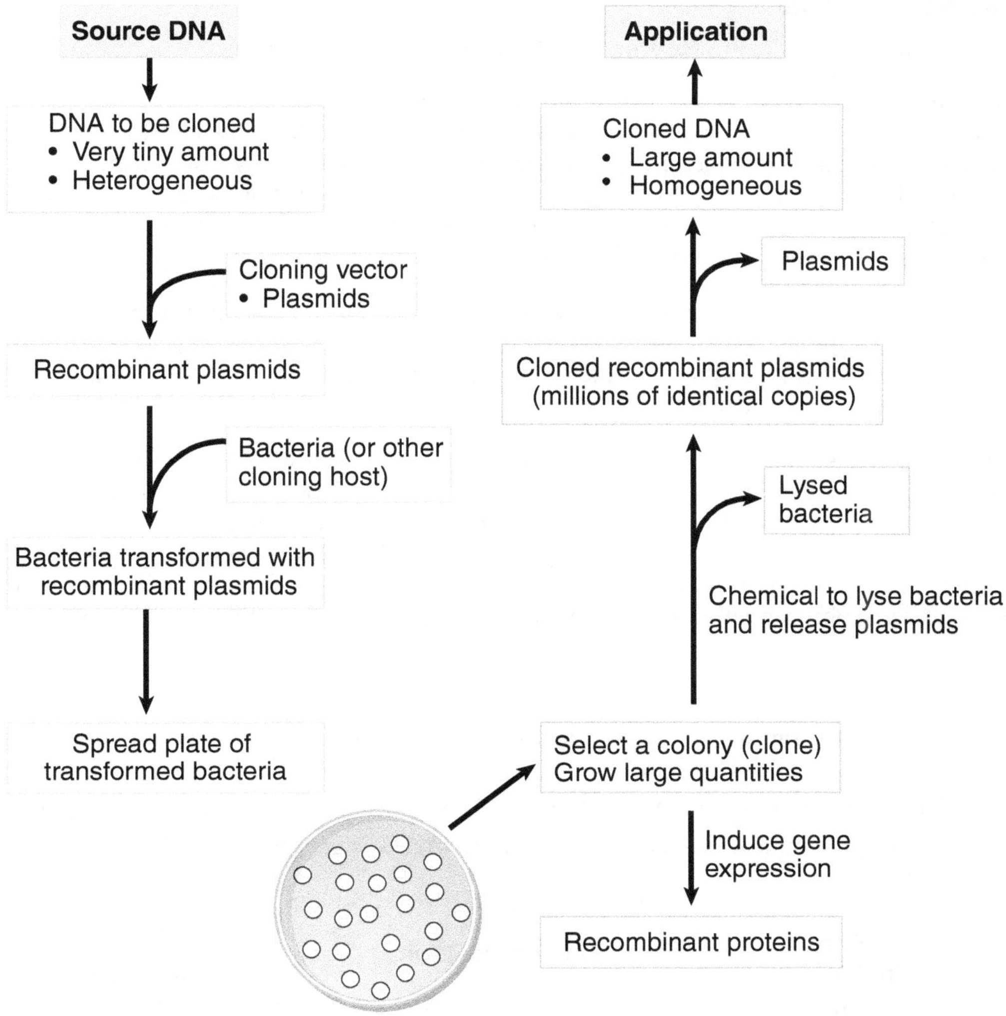

Figure 2-20. Cloning Recombinant DNA

The DNA to be cloned is usually present in a small quantity and is part of a heterogeneous mixture containing other DNA sequences. The goal is to produce a large quantity of homogeneous DNA for one of the above applications. The steps of cloning DNA and isolating the cloned material are as follows:

- Ligate the DNA into a piece of nucleic acid (the vector) that can be autonomously replicated in a living organism. The vector containing the new DNA is referred to as a recombinant vector.
- Transfer the recombinant vectors into host cells.
- Grow the host cells in isolated colonies so that each colony contains only one recombinant vector.
- Each cultured colony is a clone; all members are genetically identical.
- Select a colony for study.
- Grow a large quantity of that colony.
- Lyse the host cells and re-isolate the replicated recombinant vectors.
- Remove (by restriction enzyme cutting) the cloned DNA from the vector.

PROTEIN SYNTHESIS

Protein synthesis involves a series of steps where human cells generate new proteins.

The first stage in the expression of genetic information is **transcription** of the information in the base sequence of a double-stranded DNA molecule to form the base sequence of a single-stranded molecule of RNA. For any particular gene, only one strand of the DNA molecule, called the template strand, is copied by RNA polymerase as it synthesizes RNA in the 5′ to 3′ direction. Because RNA polymerase moves in the 3′ to 5′ direction along the template strand of DNA, the RNA product is antiparallel and complementary to the template. RNA polymerase recognizes start signals (promoters) and stop signals (terminators) for each of the thousands of transcription units in the genome of an organism.

The second stage in gene expression is **translation** of the nucleotide sequence of a messenger RNA molecule into the amino acid sequence of a protein. The genetic code is defined as the relationship between the sequence of nucleotides in DNA (or its RNA transcripts) and the sequence of amino acids in a protein. Each amino acid is specified by one or more nucleotide triplets (codons) in the DNA.

During translation, mRNA acts as a working copy of the gene in which the codons for each amino acid in the protein have been transcribed from DNA to mRNA. tRNAs serve as adapter molecules that couple the codons in mRNA with the amino acids they each specify, thus aligning them in the appropriate sequence before peptide bond formation. Translation takes place on ribosomes, complexes of protein and rRNA that serve as the molecular machines coordinating the interactions between mRNA, tRNA, the enzymes, and the protein factors required for protein synthesis. Many proteins undergo posttranslational modifications as they prepare to assume their ultimate roles in the cell.

Genetic Code

Most genetic code tables designate the codons for amino acids as mRNA sequences. Important features of the genetic code include:

- Each codon consists of 3 bases (triplet). There are 64 codons, all written in the 5′ to 3′ direction.
- 61 codons code for amino acids. The other 3 (UAA, UGA, UAG) are stop codons (or nonsense codons) that terminate translation.

First Position (5' End)	Second Position: U	C	A	G	Third Position (3' End)
U	UUU UUC } Phe UUA UUG } Leu	UCU UCC UCA UCG } Ser	UAU UAC } Tyr UAA UAG } Stop	UGU UGC } Cys UGA Stop UGG Trp	U C A G
C	CUU CUC CUA CUG } Leu	CCU CCC CCA CCG } Pro	CAU CAC } His CAA CAG } Gln	CGU CGC CGA CGG } Arg	U C A G
A	AUU AUC AUA } Ile AUG Met	ACU ACC ACA ACG } Thr	AAU AAC } Asn AAA AAG } Lys	AGU AGC } Ser AGA AGG } Arg	U C A G
G	GUU GUC GUA GUG } Val	GCU GCC GCA GCG } Ala	GAU GAC } Asp GAA GAG } Glu	GGU GGC GGA GGG } Gly	U C A G

Figure 2-21. The Genetic Code

- There is 1 start codon (initiation codon), AUG, coding for methionine. Protein synthesis begins with methionine (Met) in eukaryotes, and formylmethionine (fmet) in prokaryotes.
- The code is unambiguous. Each codon specifies no more than one amino acid.
- The code is degenerate. More than one codon can specify a single amino acid. All amino acids, except Met and tryptophan (Trp), have more than one codon.
- For those amino acids having more than one codon, the first 2 bases in the codon are usually the same. The base in the third position often varies.
- The code is universal (the same in all organisms). Some minor exceptions to this occur in mitochondria.
- The code is commaless (contiguous). There are no spacers or "commas" between codons on an mRNA.
- Neighboring codons on a message are nonoverlapping.

Translation (Protein Synthesis)

Protein synthesis occurs by peptide bond formation between successive amino acids whose order is specified by a gene and thus by an mRNA. The formation of a peptide bond between the carboxyl group on one amino acid and the amino group of another is illustrated in the following figure.

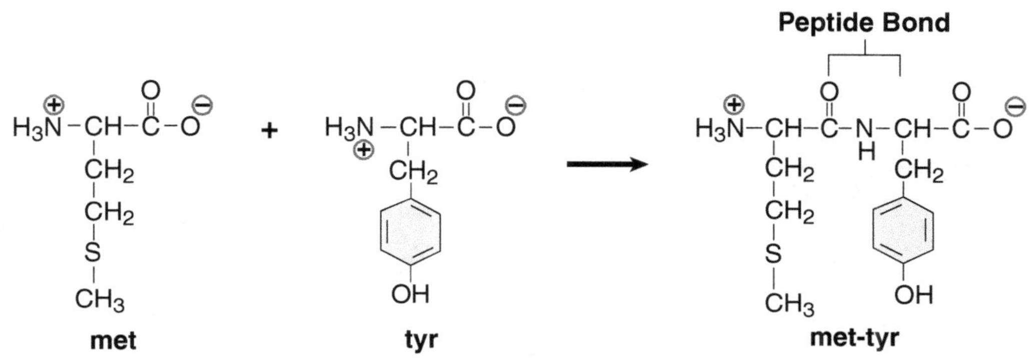

Figure 2-22. Peptide Bond Formation

During translation, the amino acids are attached to the 3′ ends of their respective tRNAs. The aminoacyl–tRNAs are situated in the P and A sites of the ribosome. Notice that the peptide bond forms between the carboxyl group of the amino acid (or growing peptide) in the P site and the amino group of the next amino acid in the A site. Proteins are synthesized from the amino to the carboxyl terminus.

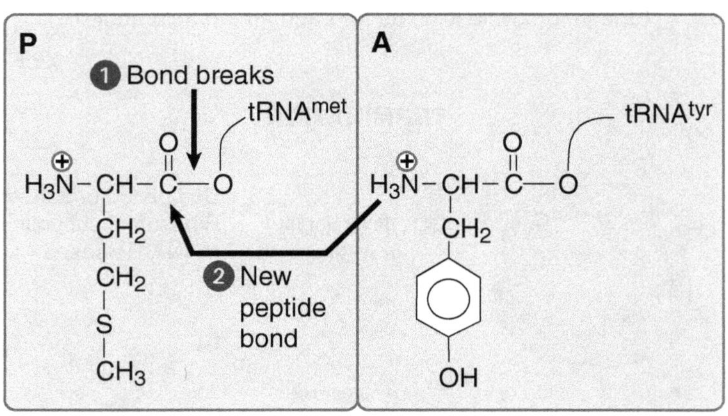

Figure 2-23. Formation of a Peptide Bond by a Ribosome During Translation

Translation occurs in the cytoplasm of both prokaryotic (Pr) and eukaryotic (Eu) cells. In prokaryotes, ribosomes can begin translating the mRNA even before RNA polymerase completes its transcription. In eukaryotes, translation and transcription are completely separated in time and space with transcription in the nucleus and translation in the cytoplasm. The process of protein synthesis occurs in 3 stages: initiation, elongation, and termination. Special protein factors for initiation (IF), elongation (EF), and termination (release factors), as well as GTP, are required for each of these stages.

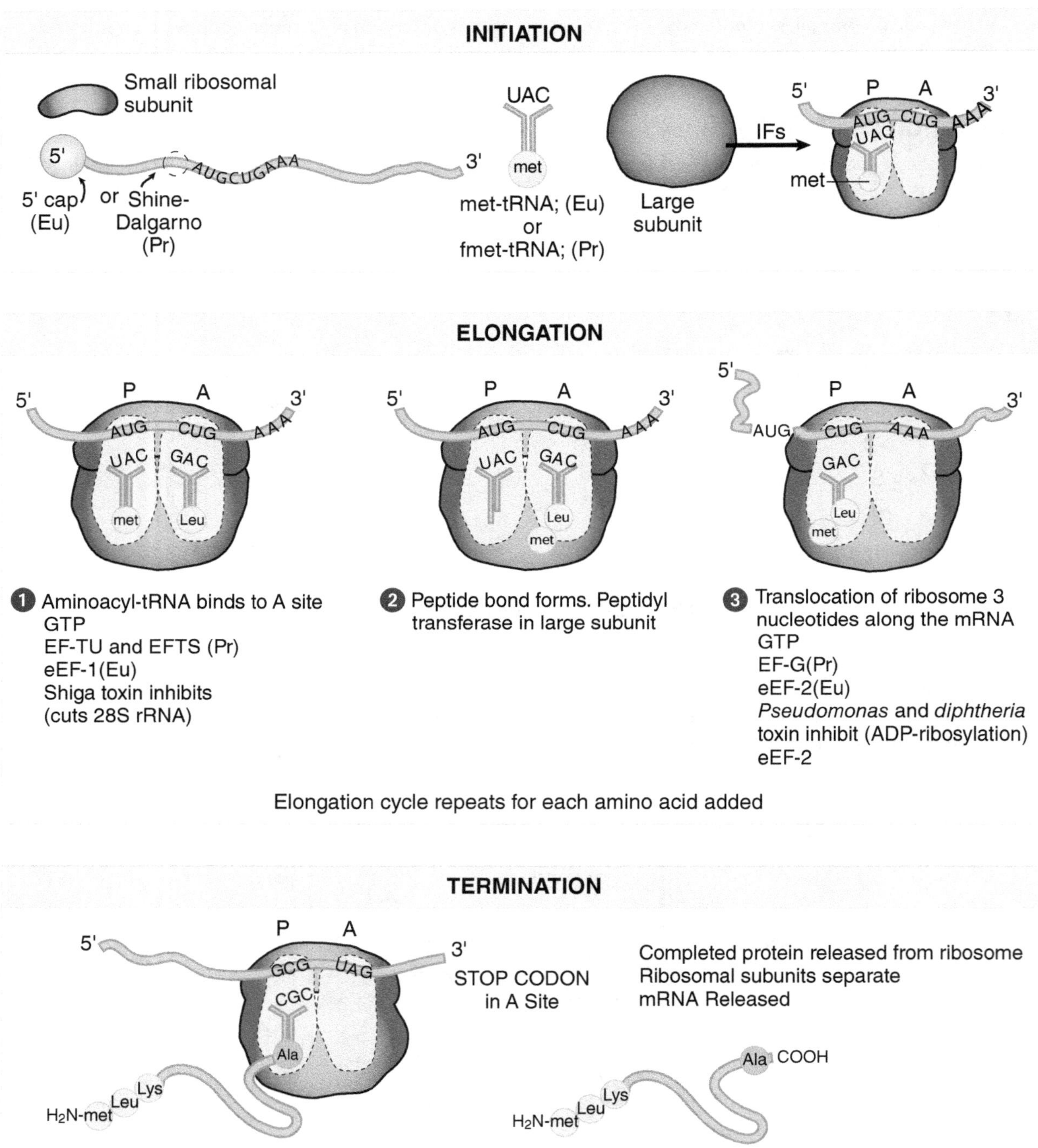

Figure 2-24. Steps in Translation

In **initiation**, the small ribosomal subunit binds to the mRNA. In prokaryotes, the 16S rRNA of the small subunit binds to the Shine-Dalgarno sequence in the 5′ untranslated region of the mRNA. In eukaryotes, the small subunit binds to the 5′ cap structure and slides down the message to the first AUG.

The charged initiator tRNA becomes bound to the AUG start codon on the message through base pairing with its anticodon. The initiator tRNA in prokaryotes carries fmet, whereas the initiator tRNA in eukaryotes carries Met.

The large subunit binds to the small subunit, forming the completed initiation complex.

There are 2 important binding sites on the ribosome called the P site and the A site.

- The peptidyl site (P site) is the site on the ribosome where (f)met–$tRNA_i$ initially binds. After formation of the first peptide bond, the P site is a binding site for the growing peptide chain.
- The aminoacyl site (A site) binds each new incoming tRNA molecule carrying an activated amino acid.

Elongation is a 3-step cycle that is repeated for each amino acid added to the protein after the initiator methionine. Each cycle uses 4 high-energy bonds (2 from the ATP used in amino acid activation to charge the tRNA, and 2 from GTP). During elongation, the ribosome moves in the 5′ to 3′ direction along the mRNA, synthesizing the protein from amino to carboxyl terminus. The 3 steps are:

- A charged tRNA binds in the A site. The particular aminoacyl–tRNA is determined by the mRNA codon aligned with the A site.
- Peptidyl transferase, an enzyme that is part of the large subunit, forms the peptide bond between the new amino acid and the carboxyl end of the growing polypeptide chain. The bond linking the growing peptide to the tRNA in the P site is broken, and the growing peptide attaches to the tRNA located in the A site.
- In the translocation step, the ribosome moves exactly 3 nucleotides (one codon) along the message. This moves the growing peptidyl–tRNA into the P site and aligns the next codon to be translated with the empty A site.

In eukaryotic cells, elongation factor-2 (eEF-2) used in translocation is inactivated through ADP-ribosylation by *Pseudomonas* and *Diphtheria* toxins. Shiga and Shiga-like toxins clip an adenine residue from the 28S rRNA in the 60S subunit stopping protein synthesis in eukaryotic cells.

When any of the 3 stop (**termination** or nonsense) codons moves into the A site, peptidyl transferase (with the help of release factor) hydrolyzes the completed protein from the final tRNA in the P site. The mRNA, ribosome, tRNA, and other factors can all be reused for additional protein synthesis.

PRACTICE QUESTIONS

1. Phenelzine is an antidepressant that acts by increasing norepinephrine levels in the CNS. Food products high in which of the following amino acids are contraindicated for use with this drug since it is a norepinephrine precursor?

   A. Proline

   B. Serine

   C. Threonine

   D. Tryptophan

   E. Tyrosine

2. Which of the following amino acids must be supplemented through food?
   - A. Aspartic acid
   - B. Cysteine
   - C. Glutamic acid
   - D. Glutamine
   - E. Histidine

3. Which of the following enzymes has maximal activity in a highly acidic environment?
   - A. Acetylcholinesterase
   - B. Pancreatic lipase
   - C. Pepsin
   - D. Phosphodiesterase
   - E. Trypsinogen

4. A patient is said to be deficient in an essential coenzyme. Which of the following is most likely deficient in this patient?
   - A. Carbonic anhydrase
   - B. Sodium
   - C. Testosterone
   - D. Thiamine
   - E. Zinc

5. A patient is taking a medication that binds to an allosteric site on an enzyme instead of the active site, which induces a change in enzyme conformation. The drug is best described as which of the following?
   - A. Competitive inhibitor
   - B. Mixed inhibitor
   - C. Irreversible inhibitor
   - D. Noncompetitive inhibitor
   - E. Uncompetitive inhibitor

6. Which of the following is classified as a hydrophilic hormone?
   - A. Calcitriol
   - B. Cortisol
   - C. T3
   - D. Insulin
   - E. Retinoic Acid

7. Which of the following are most likely involved in recombinant DNA technology?
   - A. Bacteria
   - B. Fungi
   - C. Helminths
   - D. Parasites
   - E. Viruses

8. Which of the following is a true statement regarding the human genetic code?

   A. All amino acids have more than 1 codon that specifies it.
   B. Codons are written in the 3′ to 5′ direction.
   C. Each codon consists of 3 bases.
   D. Each codon specifies more than one amino acid.
   E. There are 64 codons that code for amino acids.

9. Which of the following is the immediate precursor of norepinephrine?

   A. DOPA
   B. Dopamine
   C. Epinephrine
   D. Tyrosine
   E. Vanillylmandelic acid

10. In patients with type 2 diabetes, it is recommended that they exercise regularly to decrease insulin resistance and facilitate glucose transport into muscle. This effect is likely mediated through which of the following?

    A. GLUT 1
    B. GLUT 2
    C. GLUT 3
    D. GLUT 4
    E. GLUT 5

Answers and Explanations

1. **The correct answer is E.** Phenelzine non-selectively inhibits monoamine oxidase leading to decreased norepinephrine metabolism. Phenylalanine and tyrosine are precursors for catecholamines, such as norepinephrine and dopamine. Proline (choice A) is a secondary amine whose presence in a protein disrupts normal secondary structure. Serine (choice B) and threonine (choice C) are sites for O-linked glycosylation of proteins, a posttranslational modification that should be associated with the Golgi apparatus. Tryptophan (choice D) can form serotonin and niacin.

2. **The correct answer is E.** Humans can produce 10 of the required 20 amino acids (AA). The other AAs must be supplied in food. Failure to obtain any of the essential AAs (those humans cannot make) results in degradation of the body's proteins and loss of selected essential functions. The 10 amino acids that humans can produce are alanine, asparagine, aspartic acid (choice A), cysteine (choice B), glutamic acid (choice C), glutamine (choice D), glycine, proline, serine and tyrosine. Tyrosine is produced directly from phenylalanine; hence, if one's diet is deficient in phenylalanine, tyrosine will be required. The essential amino acids are arginine (required only for the young), histidine (choice E is correct), isoleucine, leucine, lysine, methionine, phenylalanine, threonine, tryptophan, and valine.

3. **The correct answer is C.** Most enzymes depend on pH in order to function properly, not only because pH affects the ionization of the active site, but also because changes in pH can lead to denaturation of the enzyme. For enzymes that circulate and function in human blood, such as acetylcholinesterase (choice A) and phosphodiesterase (choice D), this optimal pH is 7.4. Pepsin, which works in the stomach, has maximal

activity around pH 2 (choice C is correct). Digestive enzymes, such as pancreatic lipase (choice B) and trypsinogen (choice E), are found in the small intestine and are most effective when the pH is 8.5.

4. **The correct answer is D.** Coenzymes are organic molecules that enhance or are required for an enzyme to express its activity. They are generally small molecules that provide a transfer site for an enzyme. The B vitamins, such as thiamine, are classic examples of coenzymes. Cofactors are non-protein compounds that enhance enzyme function by increasing the rate of catalysis. They are generally metal ions, such as iron, copper, magnesium, cobalt, and zinc (choice E). Zinc is a cofactor for both carbonic anhydrase (choice A). Sodium (choice B) is a common electrolyte that helps to maintain plasma tonicity. Testosterone (choice C) is a hormone responsible for male reproductive function and increasing muscle and bone mass.

5. **The correct answer is D.** There are 4 types of reversible inhibition (choice C): competitive, noncompetitive, mixed, and uncompetitive. Noncompetitive inhibitors (choice D is correct) bind to an allosteric site instead of the active site, which induces a change in enzyme conformation. Allosteric sites are non-catalytic regions of the enzyme that bind regulators. Because the 2 molecules do not compete for the same site, inhibition is considered noncompetitive and cannot be overcome by adding more substrate. Competitive inhibition (choice A) involves occupancy of the active site thus inhibiting the substrate from binding to the active site. Mixed inhibition (choice B) results when an inhibitor can bind to either the enzyme or the enzyme–substrate complex, but has different affinity for each. Uncompetitive inhibitors (choice E) bind only to the enzyme–substrate complex and essentially lock the substrate in the enzyme, preventing its release.

6. **The correct answer is D.** Hormones are divided into 2 categories: water soluble (hydrophilic) and lipid soluble (lipophilic, also known as hydrophobic). Water-soluble hormones (i.e. insulin, glucagon, norepinephrine) act via second messenger systems that activate protein kinases. They do not enter the cytoplasm. All the other answer choices are lipophilic and diffuse through the cell membrane, where they bind to their respective receptors inside the cell.

7. **The correct answer is A.** Recombinant DNA (rDNA) technology permits a DNA fragment from any source to be joined in vitro with a nucleic acid vector that can replicate autonomously in microorganisms, such as bacteria. In other words, rDNA joins together DNA molecules from 2 different species and inserts them into the host organism (usually a bacteria) to produce new genetic combinations or reproduce a protein, such as insulin.

8. **The correct answer is C.** Regarding the genetic code, each codon consists of 3 bases (triplet). There are 64 codons, each of which is written in the 5′ to 3′ direction (choice B). Of these 64 codons, 61 codons code for amino acids (choice E). The other 3 (UAA, UGA, UAG) are stop codons (or nonsense codons) that terminate translation. Each codon specifies no more than one amino acid (choice D); however, all amino acids, except Met and tryptophan (Trp), have more than one codon (choice A).

9. **The correct answer is B.** Physiologically, the amino acid tyrosine (choice D) is transported into the sympathetic nerve axon. It is then converted to DOPA (choice A) by tyrosine hydroxylase (rate-limiting step for NE synthesis). DOPA is further converted to dopamine by DOPA decarboxylase. Dopamine (choice B) is transported into vesicles then converted to norepinephrine (NE) by dopamine β-hydroxylase (DBH). Epinephrine (choice C) is synthesized from norepinephrine within the adrenal medulla. NE and epinephrine are metabolized by both catechol-O-methytransferase (COMT) and monoamine oxidase (MAO). The final metabolite of these pathways is vanillylmandelic acid (choice E).

10. **The correct answer is D.** Glucose entry into most cells is concentration driven and independent of sodium. There are 4 primary glucose transporters (GLUT) each of which has different affinities for glucose corresponding to their respective physiologic roles. GLUT 4 is found in adipose tissues as well as cardiac and skeletal muscle. GLUT 4, the insulin-regulated glucose transporter, is stimulated by exercise. GLUT 1 (choice A) is found in the brain and red blood cells. GLUT 2 (choice B) is found in the liver and pancreatic beta cells. GLUT 3 (choice C) is found mostly in neurons. GLUT 5 (choice E) is a fructose transporter in enterocytes.

Clinical Microbiology 3

Learning Objectives

- ❑ Explain the general characteristics of microorganisms
- ❑ Demonstrate understanding of clinically-relevant pathogenic microorganisms

Infectious diseases are caused by a variety of organisms, including bacteria, viruses, fungi, and parasites. Collectively, these microorganisms are a significant cause of morbidity and mortality in the United States and the rest of the world. Understanding the general characteristics of these organisms is essential for all health care providers.

CHARACTERISTICS OF MICROORGANISMS

Bacterial Cell Envelope

The bacterial cell envelope is a multilayered structure that protects microorganisms from the outside environment.

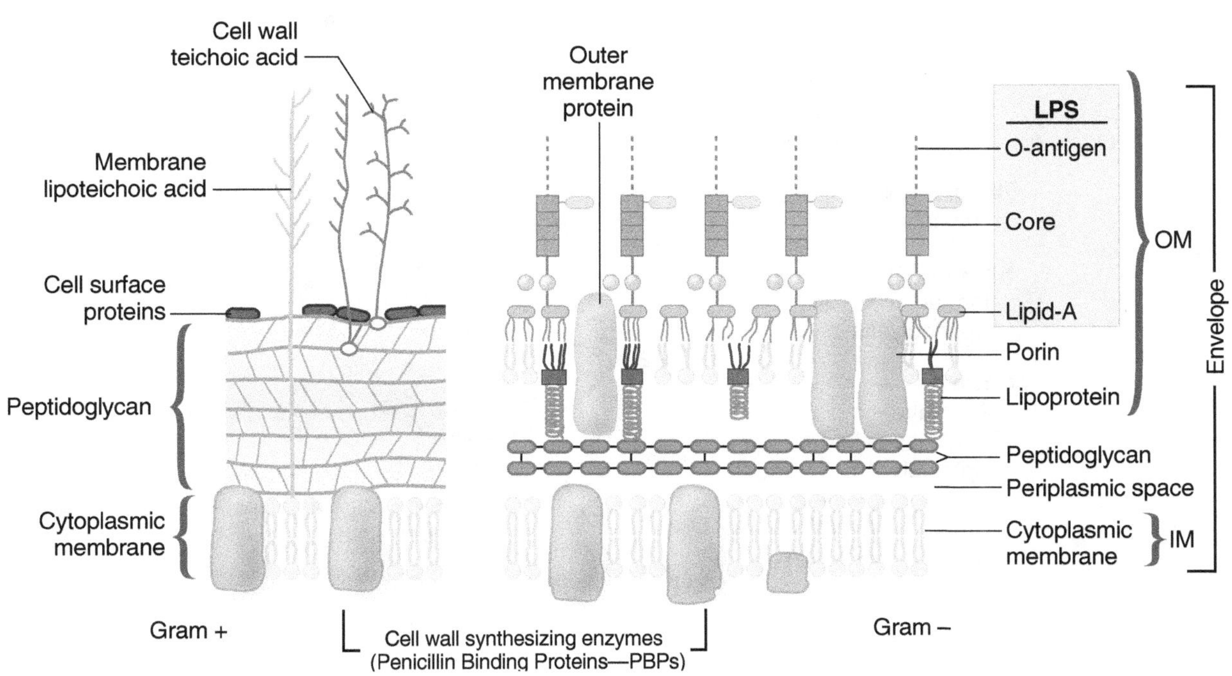

Figure 3-1. Bacterial Cell Envelope

Note

Nomenclature

Genus and species names are **italicized** and **abbreviated**, e.g., *Enterobacter aerogenes* = *E. aerogenes*.

Endospores

Bacterial endospores are defined as non-reproductive structures found in certain bacteria, such as Bacillus and Clostridium.

Organisms: Bacillus and Clostridium

Function

- Survival not reproductive (1 bacterium → 1 spore)
- Resistance to chemicals, dessiccation, radiation, freezing, and heat

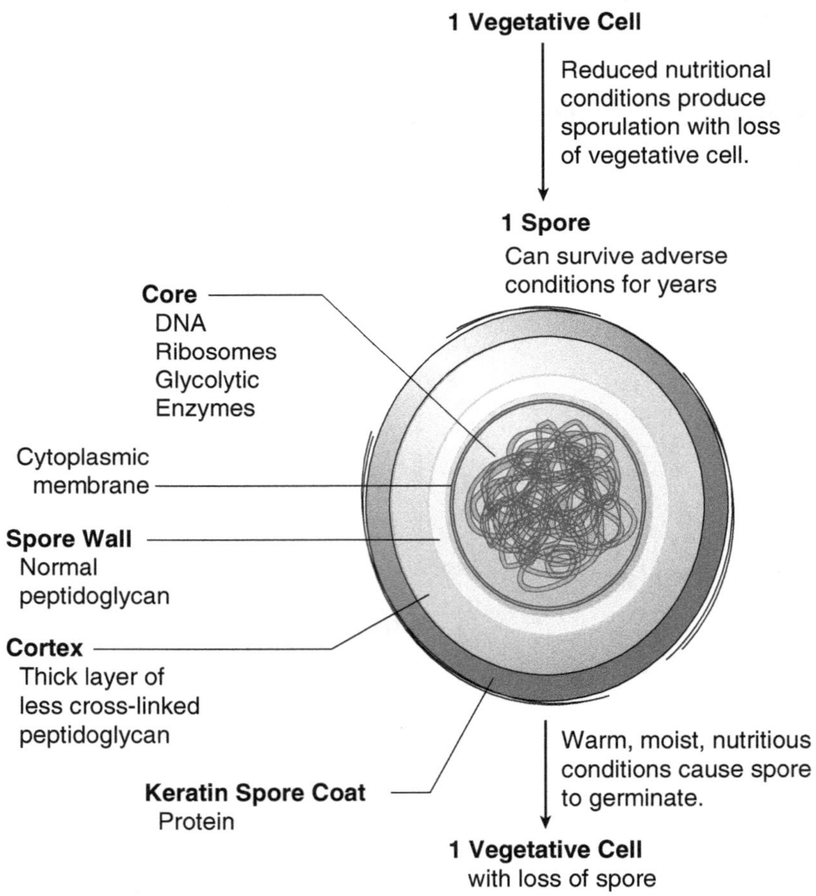

Figure 3-2. Endospore

Mechanism of Resistance

- New enzymes (i.e., dipicolinic acid synthetase, heat-resistant catalase)
- Increases or decreases in other enzymes
- Dehydration: calcium dipicolinate in core
- Keratin spore coat

Note

Spores of fungi have a reproductive role.

Bacterial Growth and Death

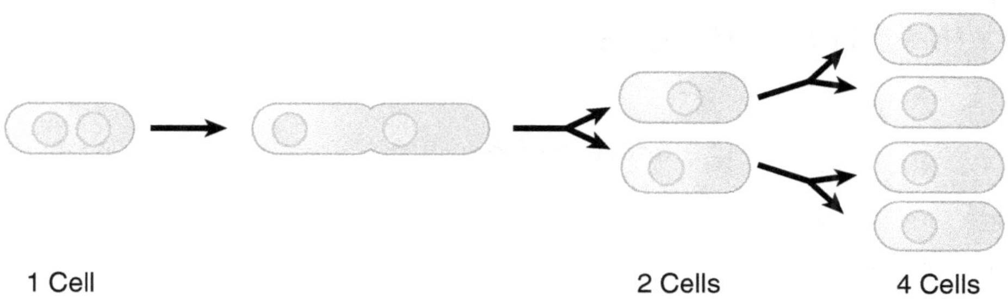

Figure 3-3. Exponential Growth by Binary Fission

In a Nutshell

Lag Phase

- Initial Phase (only 1 lag phase)
- Detoxifying medium
- Turning on enzymes to utilize medium
- For exam, number of cells at beginning equals number of cells at end of lag phase.

Log Phase

- Rapid exponential growth
- Generation time = time it takes 1 cell to divide into 2. This is determined during log phase.

Stationary Phase

- Nutrients used up
- Toxic products like acids and alkali begin to accumulate.
- Number of new cells equals the number of dying cells.

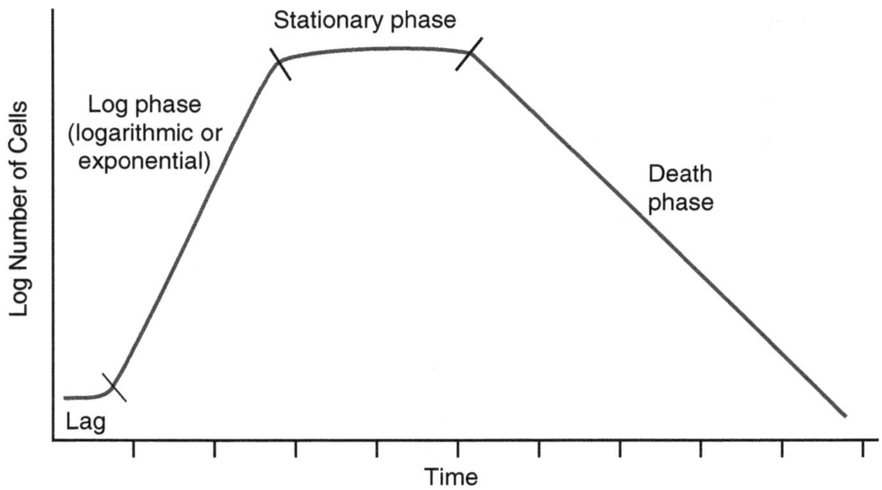

Figure 3-4. Bacterial Growth Curve

MEDICALLY IMPORTANT VIRUSES

Bridge to Biochemistry

Positive-sense = coding strand

Negative-sense = template strand

Structure and Morphology

DNA or RNA* + Structural proteins (capsomers, etc.) = Nucleocapsid = Naked capsid virus

Enzymes, e.g., polymerase

Nucleocapsid + Host membrane with viral-specified glycoproteins (critical for infectiousness of viral progeny) = Enveloped virus

Figure 3-5. The Basic Virion

*Positive-sense RNA = (+)RNA (can be used itself as mRNA)
ss = Single stranded
ds = Double stranded
*Negative-sense RNA = (–)RNA

- Complementary to mRNA
- Cannot be used as mRNA
- Requires virion-associated, RNA-dependent RNA polymerase (as part of the mature virus)

Viral Structure

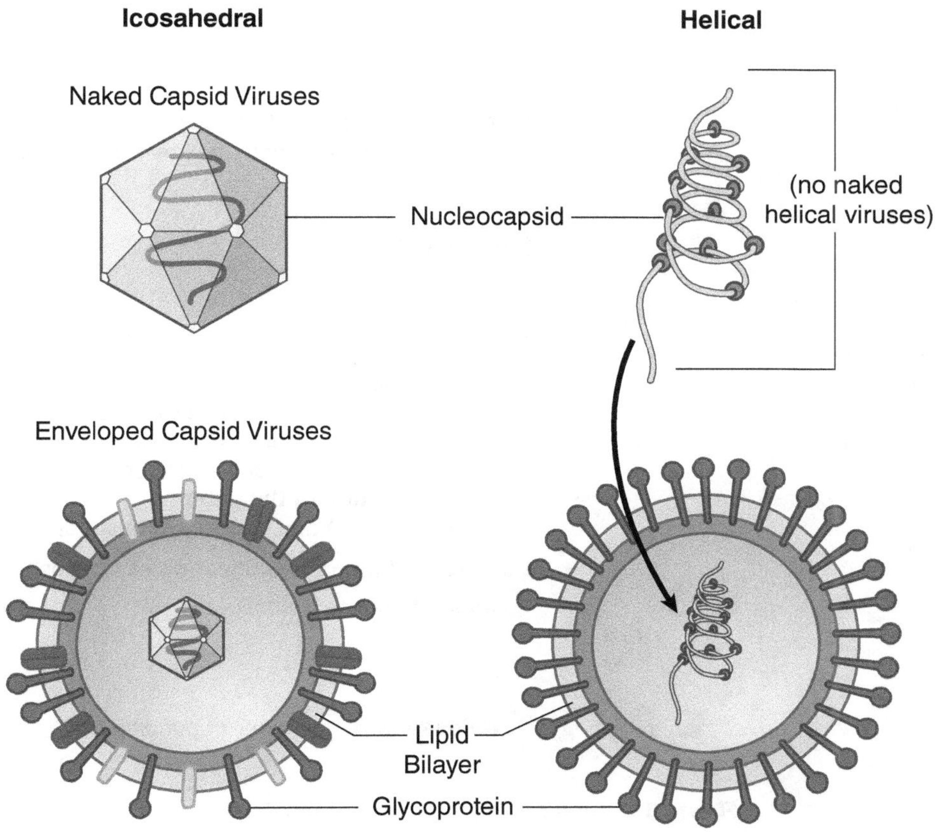

Figure 3-6. Morphology of Viruses

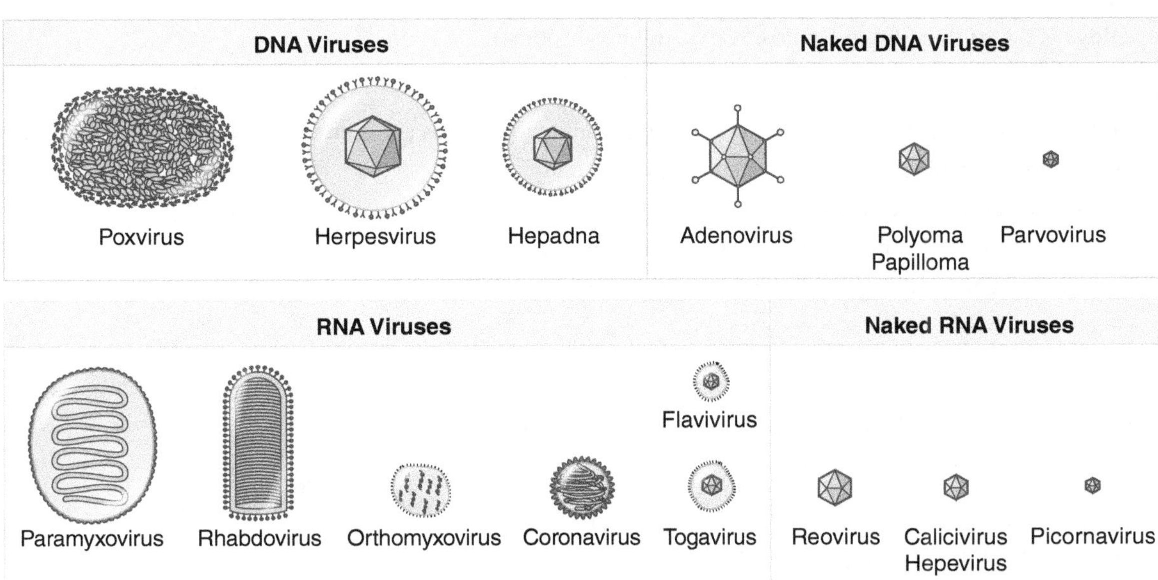

Figure 3-7. Relative Sizes and Shapes of Different Viruses

Viral Replication

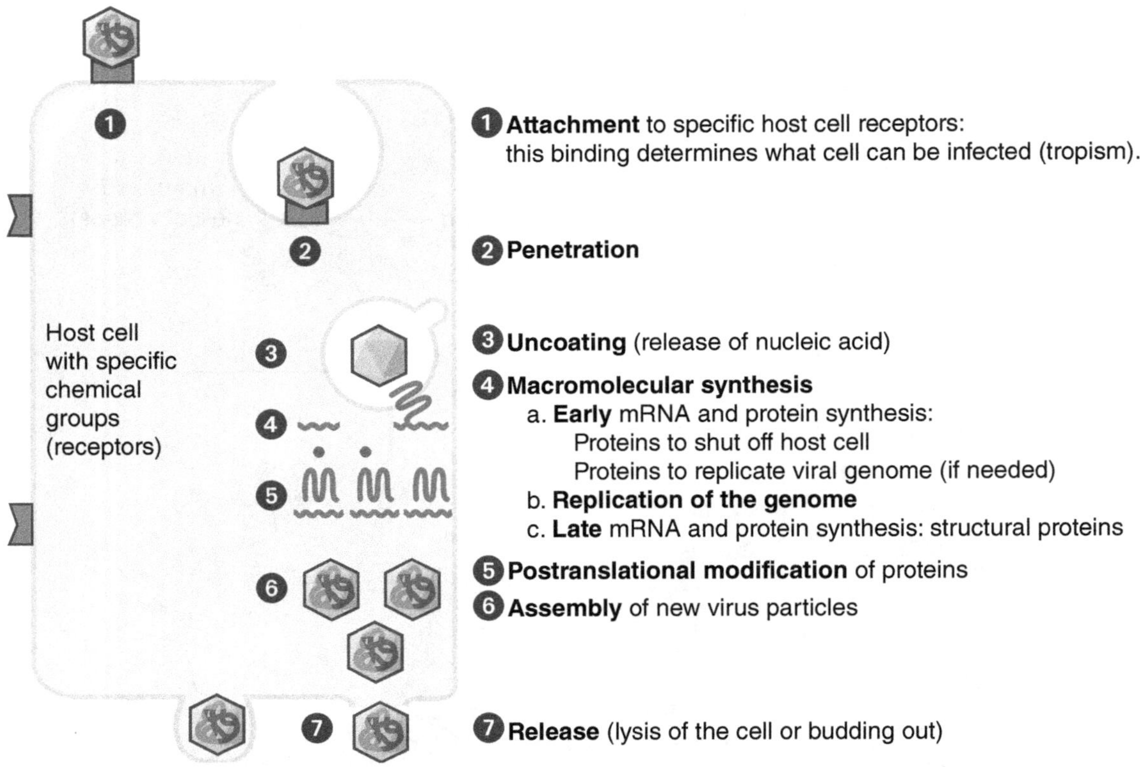

Figure 3-8. Generalized Viral Replication Scheme

MEDICALLY IMPORTANT FUNGI

Mycology

Mycology is the study of fungi (molds, yeasts, and mushrooms).

All fungi are

- **Eukaryotic** (e.g., true nucleus, 80S ribosomes, mitochondria, as are humans).
- Complex carbohydrate cell walls: chitin, glucan, and mannan.
- **Ergosterol** = Major membrane sterol

  Imidazole antifungals inhibit synthesis of ergosterol.

  Polyene antifungals bind more tightly to ergosterol than cholesterol.

Fungal Morphology

Hyphae = filamentous cellular units of molds and mushrooms

Nonseptate Hyphae

- No cross walls
- Broad hyphae with irregular width
- Broad angle of branching

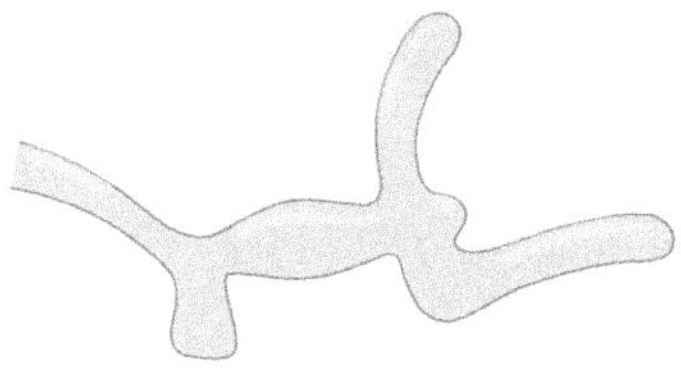

Figure 3-9. Nonseptate Hyphae

Septate Hyphae

- With cross walls
- Width is fairly regular (tube-like).

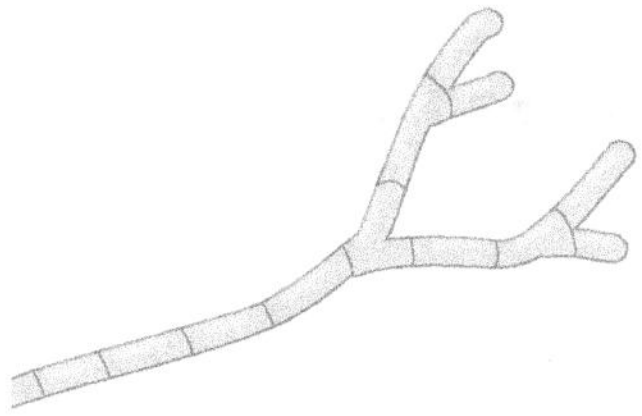

Figure 3-10. Septate Hyphae

Hyphal Coloration

- Dematiaceous: dark colored (gray, olive)
- Hyaline: clear

Mat of hyphae = mycelium

Yeasts = single celled (round to oval) fungi

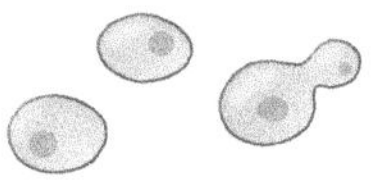

Figure 3-11. Yeasts

Dimorphic Fungi

- Fungi able to convert from hyphal to yeast or yeast-like forms.
- Thermally dimorphic: in the "cold" are the mold form.

Key Dimorphic Fungi

Histoplasma
Blastomyces
Coccidioides
Sporothrix

Note

Mnemonic

Body **H**eat **C**hanges **S**hape for the dimorphic fungi.

- *Blastomyces*
- *Histoplasma*
- *Coccidioides*
- *Sporothrix*

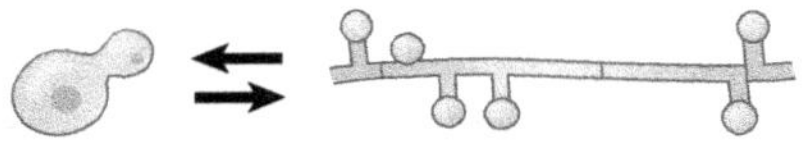

Figure 3-12. Dimorphic Fungi

Pseudohyphae (Candida Albicans)

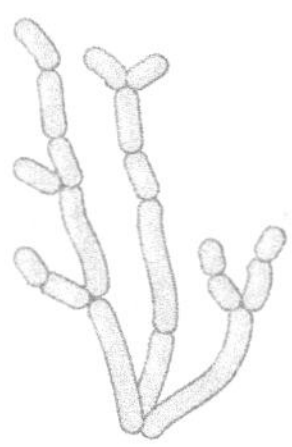

Figure 3-13. Candida Pseudohyphae

Hyphae with constrictions at each septum

Spore Types

Conidia

- **Asexual spores**
- Formed off of hyphae
- Common
- Airborne

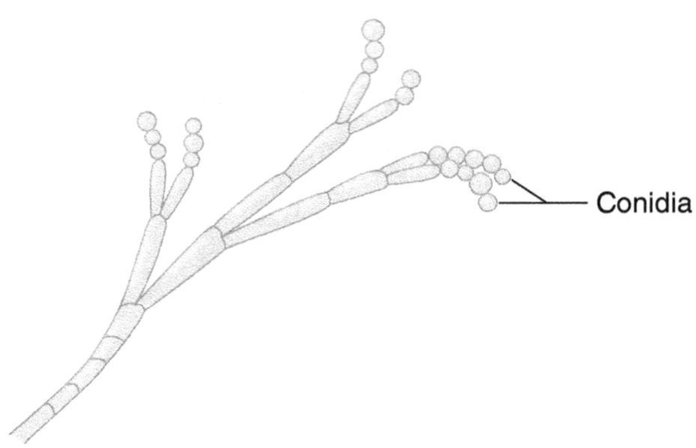

Figure 3-14. Conidia

Blastoconidia: "Buds" on yeasts (asexual budding daughter yeast cells)

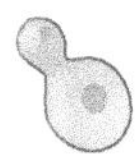

Figure 3-15. Blastoconidia

Arthroconidia: Asexual spores formed by a **"joint"**

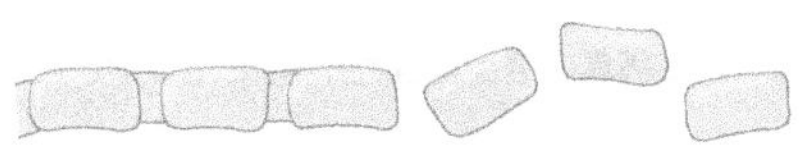

Figure 3-16. Arthroconidia

Spherules and Endospores ***(Coccidioides)***: Spores inside the spherules in tissues

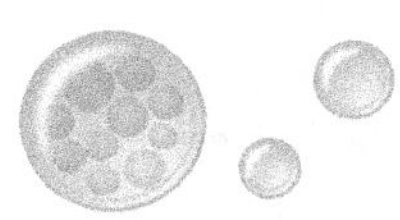

Figure 3-17. Endospores and Spherules

THE BACTERIAL GENETIC MATERIAL

Three different types of DNA may be found in a bacterial cell: bacterial chromosomal DNA, plasmid DNA, or bacteriophage DNA.

Bacterial Chromosome (Genome)

Bridge to Pharmacology

Fluoroquinolones

Exert their mechanism of action by inhibiting DNA gyrase and topoisomerase enzymes

- Most bacteria have only **one chromosome but often multiple copies** of it in the cell.
- Most bacterial chromosomes are a **large, covalently closed, circular DNA molecule** (about 1,000 times the diameter of the cell).
- The chromosome is **organized into loops** around a proteinaceous center. A single-stranded topoisomerase (1 nick) will relax only the nicked loop, allowing DNA synthesis or transcription.
- Most have **around 2,000 genes**. (*E. coli* has about 4,500 kbases.)
- All **essential genes** are on the bacterial chromosome.

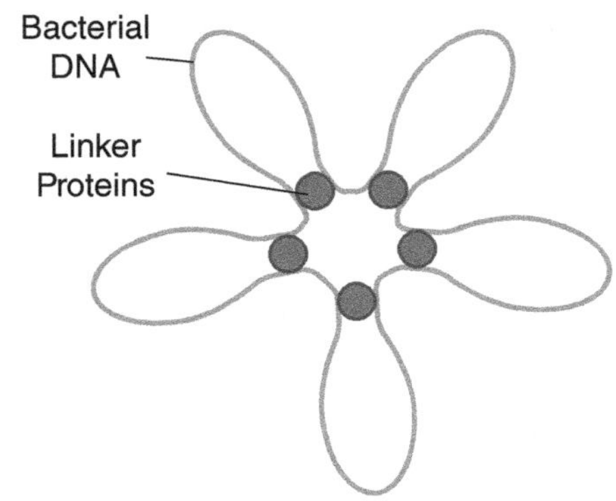

Figure 3-18. The Bacterial Chromosome

Plasmids

- Are **extrachromosomal genetic elements** found in bacteria (and eukaryotes)
- Are generally covalently closed, **circular DNA**
- Are **small** (1.5–400 kB)
- Can **replicate autonomously** in bacterial cells
- One subclass of plasmids, called **episomes**, may be integrated into the bacterial DNA. Episomes have insertion sequences matching those on the bacterial chromosome.
- Plasmids carry the genetic material for a variety of genes, e.g., the **fertility genes** directing conjugation (*tra* operon), many of the genes for **antibiotic resistance**, and most **bacterial exotoxins.**
- They contain genes that are **nonessential** for bacterial life.

Bacteriophage (= Phage = Bacterial Virus) Genome

- **Stable pieces of bacteriophage DNA** may be present in the bacterial cell.
- These are **generally repressed temperate phage (called prophage)** inserted into the bacterial chromosome.
- Besides the repressor protein, prophage DNA may also direct synthesis of other proteins. Most notable are gene products that make bacteria more pathogenic. This enhanced virulence is called **lysogenic conversion.**

HOST RESISTANCE TO VIRAL INFECTION

The human body is able to defend against a viral infection using both primary and immune defenses.

Primary Defenses

- Skin barrier (dead keratinized cells impervious to viruses)
- Skin has acids and other inhibitors produced by normal bacterial flora
- Mucociliary elevator

Immune Defense

Innate immune response

- Interferon
- Complement
- Natural killer cells

Adaptive immune response

- Antibody
- Cytotoxic T lymphocytes

Interferon Production

Bridge to Biochemistry

Production of IFN and most immunologic cytokines is under the control of the transcription factor NFκB.

Interferons (IFNs) are a family of eukaryotic cell proteins classified according to the cell of origin. IFN-alpha and IFN-beta are produced by a variety of virus-infected cells.

- Act on target cells to **inhibit viral replication**.
- Do not act directly on the virus.
- Are **not virus-specific**.
- Are **species-specific** (e.g., mouse IFN versus human IFN).

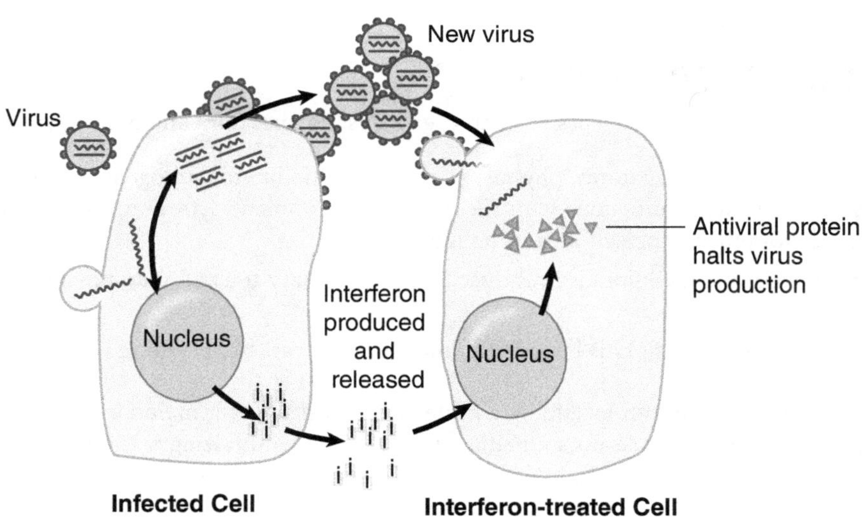

Figure 3-19. Interferon Production

Clinical Correlate

Therapeutic Use of Interferons

Since the first description of interferons almost 50 years ago, a multitude of dramatic immunomodulatory roles have been discovered for this group of proteins. As a group, interferons induce increases in the expression of class I and II MHC molecules and augment NK cell activity. They increase the efficiency of presentation of antigens to both cytotoxic and helper cell populations. Cloning of the genes that encode α, β, and γ interferons has made it possible to produce amounts of these products which makes their use clinically practical.

Interferon-α has well-known antiviral activity and has been used in the treatment of hepatitis B and C infections. Within cancer therapy, IFN-α has shown promise in treatment of hairy B-cell leukemia, chronic myelogenous leukemia, and Kaposi sarcoma.

Interferon-β was the first drug shown to have a positive effect on young adults with multiple sclerosis. Patients treated with IFN-β enjoy longer periods of remission and reduced severity of relapses.

Interferon-γ is being used in the treatment of chronic granulomatous disease (CGD). This molecule is a potent inducer of macrophage activation and a promoter of inflammatory responses. Its application appears to significantly reverse the CGD patient's inability to generate toxic oxygen metabolites inside phagocytic cells.

The side effects of IFN therapy are fortunately mild and can be managed with acetaminophen. They include headache, fever, chills, and fatigue and diminish with continued treatment.

Interferon inhibits viral protein synthesis

- Through activation of an RNA endonuclease, which digests viral RNA.
- By activation (by phosphorylation) of protein kinase that inactivates eIF2, inhibiting viral protein synthesis.

Exogenous human IFN (produced by recombinant DNA technology) may be used in antiviral therapy for chronic, active HBV and HCV infections.

PATHOGENIC MICROORGANISMS

In the human body, there are 2 primary types of microorganisms: **normal flora** and **pathogenic microorganisms.**

Normal flora influences a person's anatomy, physiology, and susceptibility to pathogenic microorganisms. **Normal flora is found on body surfaces** contiguous with the outside environment. However, **these organisms can cause infection** if misplaced from their "normal" area in/on the body.

- Example 1: If the normal fecal flora is introduced into the urinary tract or abdominal cavity, then infection can result.
- Example 2: The normal skin flora is introduced into a urinary catheter resulting in infection.

Normal flora also contributes to health by adding a protective host defense; it maintains conditions such as pH so other organisms may not grow. It also serves a nutritional function by synthesizing K and B vitamins and competing for space (in the intestinal tract, for example) to prohibit the growth of pathogenic organisms.

Colonization

(Important unless organism is traumatically implanted.)

Adherence to cell surfaces involves

- **Pili/fimbriae:** primary mechanism in most gram-negative cells.
- **Teichoic acids:** primary mechanism of gram-positive cells.

- **Adhesins:** colonizing factor adhesins, pertussis toxin, and hemagglutinins.
- **IgA proteases:** make it easier for pathogens to colonize.
- **Partial adherence** to inert materials, **biofilms**: *Staph. epidermidis, Streptococcus mutans, Pseudomonas aeruginosa*

Note

Mnemonic

Streptococcus pneumoniae

Klebsiella pneumoniae

Haemophilus influenzae

Pseudomonas aeruginosa

Neisseria meningitidis

Cryptococcus neoformans

(**S**ome **K**illers **H**ave **P**retty **N**ice **C**apsules)

Avoiding Immediate Destruction by Host Defense System

- **Anti-phagocytic surface components** (inhibit phagocytic uptake):
  - **Capsules**/slime layers:
    - ***Streptococcus pyogenes* M protein**
    - ***Neisseria gonorrhoeae* pili**
    - ***Staphylococcus aureus* A protein**
- **IgA proteases,** destruction of mucosal IgA: *Neisseria, Haemophilus, S. pneumoniae*

"Hunting and Gathering" Needed Nutrients

Siderophores steal (chelate) and import iron.

Antigenic Variation

Note

Intracellular Organisms

- Elicit different immune responses
- Different pathology
- Different antibiotics
- Different culture techniques

- Changing surface antigens to avoid immune destruction
- *N. gonorrhoeae*—pili and outer membrane proteins
- *Trypanosoma brucei rhodesiense* and *T. b. gambiense*—phase variation
- Enterobacteriaceae: capsular and flagellar antigens may or may not be expressed
- HIV, influenza—antigenic drift

Ability to Survive Intracellularly

- **Evading intracellular killing by professional phagocytic cells** allows intracellular growth:
  - *M. tuberculosis* survives by inhibiting phagosome-lysosome fusion.
  - *Listeria* quickly escapes the phagosome into the cytoplasm **before** phagosome-lysosome fusion.
- **Invasins**: surface proteins that allow an organism to bind to and invade normally non-phagocytic human cells, escaping the immune system. Best studied invasin is on *YersiniaYersinia pseudotuberculosis* (an organism causing diarrhea).
- Damage from viruses is largely from intracellular replication, which either kills cells, transforms them or, in the case of latent viruses, may do no noticeable damage.

Type III Secretion Systems

- Tunnel from the bacteria to the host cell (macrophage) that delivers bacterial toxins directly to the host cell
- Have been demonstrated in many pathogens: *E. coli, Salmonella* species, *Yersinia* species, *P. aeruginosa*, and *Chlamydia*

Inflammation or Immune-Mediated Damage

- **Cross-reaction of bacteria-induced antibodies with tissue antigens** causes disease. Rheumatic fever is one example.
- **Delayed hypersensitivity and the granulomatous response** stimulated by the presence of intracellular bacteria is responsible for neurological damage in leprosy, cavitation in tuberculosis, and fallopian tube blockage resulting in infertility from *Chlamydia* PID (pelvic inflammatory disease).
- **Immune complexes** damage the kidney in poststreptococcal acute glomerulonephritis.
- **Peptidoglycan-teichoic acid** (large fragments) of gram-positive cells:
  - Serves as a structural toxin released when cells die
  - Chemotactic for neutrophils

Physical Damage

- Swelling from infection in a fixed space damages tissues; examples: meningitis and cysticercosis.
- Large physical size of organism may cause problems; example: *Ascaris lumbricoides* blocking bile duct.
- Aggressive tissue invasion from *Entamoeba histolytica* causes intestinal ulceration and releases intestinal bacteria, compounding problems.

Toxins

Toxins may aid in invasiveness, damage cells, inhibit cellular processes, or trigger immune response and damage.

Structural Toxins

- **Endotoxin** (Lipopolysaccharide = LPS)
  - LPS is part of the **gram-negative outer membrane.**
  - **Toxic portion is lipid A**: generally not released (and toxic) until death of cell. Exception: *N. meningitidis,* which over-produces outer membrane fragments.
  - **LPS is heat stable** and not strongly immunogenic so it **cannot be converted to a toxoid.**
  - Mechanism
    - **LPS activates macrophages,** leading to release of TNF-alpha, IL-1, and IL-6.
    - IL-1 is a major mediator of fever.

  - Macrophage activation and products lead to tissue damage.
  - Damage to the endothelium from **bradykinin-induced vasodilation leads to shock.**
  - **Coagulation** (DIC) is mediated through the **activation of Hageman factor.**
- **Peptidoglycan, Teichoic Acids**

Exotoxins

- Are **protein toxins,** generally **quite toxic** and **secreted by** bacterial **cells** (some gram +, some gram –)
- **Can be modified** by chemicals or heat to produce a **toxoid** that still is **immunogenic, but no longer toxic** so can be used as a vaccine
- **A-B** (or "2") **component** protein toxins
  - **B** component **binds** to specific cell receptors to facilitate the internalization of A.
  - **A** component is the **active (toxic) component** (often an enzyme such as an ADP ribosyl transferase).
  - Exotoxins may be subclassed as enterotoxins, neurotoxins, or cytotoxins.
- **Cytolysins**: lyse cells from outside by damaging membrane.
  - **C.** *perfringens* **alphatoxin** is a **lecithinase.**
  - ***Staphylococcus aureus*** **alpha toxin** inserts itself to form **pores** in the membrane.

Gram-Negative and Gram-Positive Bacteria

You should be able to recognize the most common gram-positive and gram-negative bacteria.

Table 3-1. Important Gram-Positive Bacteria

Gram Positive Bacteria	
Cocci	• *Staphylococcus* • *Streptococcus*
Rods	
Aerobic or facultative anaerobic	• *Bacillus* • *Listeria* • *Corynebacterium* • *Nocardia* • *Mycobacterium*
Anaerobic	• *Clostridium* • *Actinomyces* • *Eubacterium* • *Propionibacterium* • *Lactobacillus*

Note: Spore formers are *Bacillus* and *Clostridium*.

Table 3-2. Important Gram-Negative Bacteria

Aerobic	
Cocci	• *Neisseria* • *Moraxella*
Rods	
• *Pseudomonas* • *Legionella* • *Brucella* • *Bordetella*† • *Francisella*	• *Eikenella* • *Kingella*
Helical or curved (and microaerophilic)	• *Campylobacter* • *Helicobacter*
Facultative Anaerobic Rods	
Enterobacteriaceae†	• *Escherichia* • *Shigella* • *Salmonella* • *Citrobacter* • *Klebsiella* • *Enterobacter* • *Serratia* • *Proteus* • *Yersinia*
Vibrionaceae	• *Vibrio*
Pasteurellaceae	• *Pasteurella* • *Haemophilus*
Anaerobic straight to helical rods	• *Bacteroides/Prevotella* • *Fusobacterium*
Spirochetes	• *Treponema* • *Borrelia* • *Leptospira*
Rickettsiaceae and relatives	• *Rickettsia* • *Bartonella* • *Ehrlichia*
Chlamydiaceae	• *Chlamydia* • *Chlamydophila*

Pulmonary Infections

Bacterial pneumonia, acute inflammation, and consolidation (solidification) of the lungs are all generally caused by a bacterial agent.

Clinical signs and symptoms of pulmonary infections include fever and chills; productive cough with yellow-green (pus) or rusty (bloody) sputum; tachypnea; pleuritic chest pain; and decreased breath sounds, rales, and dullness to percussion.

Table 3-3. Selected Organisms Found in Respiratory Infections and Individual Characteristics

Organism	Gram Stain	Common Clinical Etiology	Common Treatment Measures
Staphylococcus Aureus	Plump gram-positive cocci in clumps	Nosocomial, influenzae, long-term care	Nafcillin or cefazolin for MSSA; MRSA is treated with linezolid or vancomycin
Streptococcus Pneumonia	Gram-positive diplococci	COPD, following URI	Macrolide or cephalosporin
Escherichia coli	Gram-negative rods	Primarily nosocomial	Amoxicillin/clavulanate; ampicillin-sulbactam; third generation cephalosporin – Aminoglycoside can be added for severe infections
Haemophilus Influenzae	Pleomorphic gram-negative coccobacilli	Nosocomial, COPD, following URI	Second or third generation cephalosporin, azithromycin
Klebsiella pneumonia	Gram-negative encapsulated rods	Nosocomial, diabetes, alcohol abuse	Amoxicillin/clavulanate; ampicillin-sulbactam; third generation cephalosporin – Aminoglycoside can be added for severe infections
Pseudomonas aeruginosa	Gram-negative rods	Nosocomial, cystic fibrosis, ventilators	Antipseudomonal beta-lactam (or fluoroquinolone) +/– aminoglycoside
Moraxella Catarrhalis	Gram-negative diplococci	Nosocomial, COPD, elderly	Second or third generation cephalosporin, azithromycin, Amoxicillin/clavulanate; ampicillin-sulbactam
Mycobacteria pneumoniae	N/A	Community acquired	Macrolide; tetracycline
Legionella species	N/A	Community acquired	Macrolide or Fluoroquinolone
Anaerobes	Mixed	Aspiration, periodontal disease, immunocompromised	Beta-lactam with acceptable coverage
Pneumocystis jiroveci	N/A	HIV, immunocompromised	SMX-TMP; pentamidine; Prednisone is often added

NOTE: Common treatment measures are listed; however, other acceptable treatment measures are also employed

Laboratory studies typically show elevated white blood cell counts with a left shift (an increase in immature leukocytes). Chest x-ray for lobar pneumonia typically shows lobar or segmental consolidation (opacification), and for bronchopneumonia typically shows patchy opacification.

Pleural effusion may also be picked up on chest x-ray. For all of these different infections, the key to an effective treatment regimen includes identification of the causative organism and early treatment with antibiotics.

You should be familiar with the most commonly seen organisms in respiratory infections, their Gram stain characteristics, common clinical settings where these bacteria are found, and the most commonly used antibiotics to treat these infections. See table 3.3.

Ear, Nose, Throat, Upper Respiratory System Infections

Table 3-4. Ear, Nose, Throat, Upper Respiratory System Infections

Type Infection	Case Vignette/Key Clues	Common Causal Agents
Acute otitis media	Red, bulging tympanic membrane, fever (102–103°F); pain goes away if drum ruptures or if ear tubes are patent.	*Streptococcus pneumoniae* *H. influenzae* (often nontypeable, recurs) *Moraxella catarrhalis* RSV Rhinovirus
Otitis externa	Ear pain—list of organisms	Normal flora (NF) often involved Often mixed infections: *Staph aureus,* (from NF)* *Candida albicans,* (from NF)* *Proteus* (water organism) *Pseudomonas* (water)
Malignant otitis externa	Severe ear pain in diabetic; life threatening	*Pseudomonas aeruginosa*
Sinusitis	Sinus pain; low-grade fever	Same as for acute otitis media
Oral cavitary disease	Painful mouth—overgrowth of spirochetes and fusiform bacteria	*Fusobacterium* and treponemes (normal oral spirochetes)
	Sore mouth with thick white coating (painful red base under); increased risk: premature infants, AIDS, IC pts, pts on antibiotics, vitamin C deficiency	*Candida*
Sore throat	Inflamed tonsils/pharynx, which may be purulent and may develop abscesses; cervical lymphadenopathy, fever, stomach upset; sandpaper rash	*Streptococcus pyogenes* (group A strep) Rash indicates presence of erythrogenic exotoxin A
	Throat looking like strep with severe fatigue, lymphadenopathy, fever, rash; heterophile (+); Downey type II cells	Epstein-Barr virus

(*Continued*)

Type Infection	Case Vignette/Key Clues	Common Causal Agents
	Low-grade fever with a 1–2 day gradual onset of membranous nasopharyngitis or obstructive laryngotracheitis; bull neck from lymphadenopathy; elevated BUN; abnormal ECG; little change in WBC (toxin). Exudate bleeds profusely when dislodged	*Corynebacterium diphtheriae* (diphtheria)
Common cold	Rhinitis, sneezing, coughing; list CA with seasonal peaks	Rhinoviruses (summer–fall) Coronaviruses (winter–spring) Human metapneumovirus Adenovirus, many others

Infections of the CNS

Infections of the central nervous system (CNS) in non-immunocompromised individuals can be caused by almost any infectious agent, including bacteria, mycobacteria, fungi, protozoa, and viruses.

It is essential to have a good understanding of the most common etiological bacteria in a given patient with meningitis.

- You should assess the importance of the patient's age, community setting, certain medical conditions, and recent travel.
- For example, the most common organisms in bacterial meningitis can vary widely depending on the patient's age; hence, the treatment of choice also varies.

Table 3-5. Most Common Causes of Bacterial Meningitis by Age

Age Group	Most Common Bacteria Causing the Meningitis
Newborn	*Group B Streptococci, Streptococcus pneumoniae, Escherichia coli, Listeria monocytogenes*
Infants and Children	*Streptococcus pneumoniae, Neisseria meningitidis, Haemophilus influenzae type b (Hib), Group B Streptococcus*
Adolescents and young adults	*Neisseria meningitidis, Streptococcus pneumonia*
Adult	*Streptococcus pneumoniae, Neisseria meningitidis, Haemophilus influenzae type b (Hib), Group B Streptococcus, Listeria monocyto-genes*

Table was derived from the Centers for Disease Control and Prevention website (http://www.cdc.gov/meningitis/bacterial.html) in May 2016.

One of the most effective ways to protect a child (or adult) from contracting certain types of bacterial meningitis is to administer a vaccine per the CDC's recommended vaccine schedule. Available vaccines to prevent bacterial meningitis include protection against:

- *Neisseria meningitidis*
- *Streptococcus pneumoniae*
- *Haemophilus influenzae type b (Hib)*

Cystitis

Cystitis is an infection of the urinary bladder that predominantly occurs in women. Initial presentation commonly includes dysuria, frequency, urgency, and suprapubic pain.

- Hematuria, low-grade fever; foul-smelling and cloudy urine are less common. On exam, suprapubic tenderness is generally present with no flank tenderness.
- *E. coli* are found in >80% of cystitis cases. Other gram-negative bacilli (*Proteus*, *Klebsiella*, *Enterobacter*, etc) comprise the remaining 15–20% with occasional cases of *Staphylococcus saprophyticus.*
- Urinalysis (WBCs, RBCs, protein, and bacteria) is the most common diagnostic tool. The appearance of WBCs is the most important diagnostic finding.
- For uncomplicated cystitis, 3 days of trimethoprim/sulfamethoxazole, nitrofurantoin, or any quinolone is adequate for treatment. Fluoroquinolones should not be used to treat cystitis in pregnant women.

Sexually Transmitted Diseases

Sexually transmitted diseases (STDs) are a common occurrence in both men and women despite aggressive educational efforts encouraging safe sexual practice. Although STDs are most commonly associated with their anogenital manifestations, most infections also result in infections outside of the anogenital region (skin, eyes, oral cavity, or other locations).

Table 3-6. Most Common STDs and Their High-Yield Characteristics

Disease (Definition)	Etiology	Findings/Diagnosis	Treatment
Urethritis (Inflammation of the urethra)	Gonococcal urethritis caused by *Neisseria gonorrhoeae*; Nongonococcal urethritis caused by either *Chlamydia trachomatis* (50%), *Ureaplasma urealyticum* (20%), Other (10%)	Purulent urethral discharge; dysuria, urgency, and frequency in urination.	Single-dose IM ceftriaxone and single-dose azithromycin orally is the treatment of choice. An alternative regimen with doxycycline for 7 days can also be used.
Pelvic Inflammatory Disease (Infections involving the fallopian tubes, uterus or ovaries)	*N. gonorrhoeae*, *Chlamydia*, Mycoplasma, anaerobic bacteria, or gram-negative bacteria; intrauterine devices predispose to PID.	Lower abdominal and pelvic pain on palpation of the cervix, uterus, or adnexa; fever, leukocytosis, and discharge are common.	Doxycycline and cefoxitin (or cefotetan) for inpatient therapy. Outpatient therapy is with single-dose ceftriaxone intramuscularly and doxycycline orally for 2 weeks.
Chancroid (painful genital ulcers and suppuration of the inguinal lymph nodes)	*Haemophilus ducreyi* (Gram-negative bacillus)	Small, soft, painful papules that become shallow ulcers with ragged edges. They vary in size and coalesce. Inguinal lymph nodes become very tender and enlarged.	Azithromycin single dose or ceftriaxone intramuscularly (single dose).
Lymphogranuloma Venereum (transitory primary lesion followed by suppurative lymphangitis)	*Chlamydia trachomatis*	Small, transient, nonindurated lesion that ulcerates and heals quickly; unilateral enlargement of inguinal lymph nodes (tender)	Doxycycline (or erythromycin as an alternative).

(*Continued*)

Disease (Definition)	Etiology	Findings/Diagnosis	Treatment
Genital Herpes (painful genital ulcerations)	Herpes virus, Type II	Vesicles develop on the skin or mucous membranes; they become eroded and painful and present with circular ulcers with a red areola. Itching and soreness usually precede them.	Oral acyclovir, famciclovir, or valacyclovir. Must explain to the patient the relapsing nature of the disease.
Genital Warts (condylomata acuminata or venereal warts)	Papilloma virus	Appear as soft, moist, minute, pink, or red swellings that grow rapidly and become pedunculated. Their cauliflower appearance makes them unique in appearance.	Destruction (curettage, sclerotherapy, trichloroacetic acid); Cryotherapy; Podophyllin; Imiquimod (an immune stimulant)
Syphilis (occurs in stages)	*Treponema pallidum*	Early infectious syphilis: Primary stage (Chancre that appears within the third week and disappears); Secondary stage (Cutaneous rashes, lymphadenopathy, alopecia); Tertiary (neurological)	Penicillin is the drug of choice for all stages of syphilis. Penicillin allergic patients can be treated with doxycycline for primary and secondary syphilis, but must be desensitized in tertiary syphilis.

Opportunistic Infections

The clinical manifestations of HIV infection vary over time:

- The acute phase is characterized by viremia with a reduction in CD4 count, mononucleosis-like viral symptoms and lymphadenopathy as well as seroconversion.
- The latent phase is characterized by asymptomatic or persistent generalized lymphadenopathy with continued viral replication in the lymph nodes and spleen, low level of virus in the blood, and minor opportunistic infections including oral thrush (candidiasis) and herpes zoster. The average duration of latent phase is 10 years.
- Progression to AIDS (third phase) occurs with reduction of CD4 count to <200 cells/mL, which is accompanied by reemergence of viremia and development of AIDS-defining diseases, possibly to eventual death.

Table 3-7. Opportunistic Infection and Common Sites of Infection in AIDS Patients

Opportunistic Infection	Common Sites of Infection
Pneumocystis jirovecii	Lung (pneumonia), bone marrow
Mycobacterium tuberculosis	Lung, disseminated
Mycobacterium avium-intracellulare	Lung, GI tract, disseminated
Coccidioidomycosis	Lung, disseminated
Histoplasmosis	Lung, disseminated

(*Continued*)

Opportunistic Infection	Common Sites of Infection
Cytomegalovirus	Lung, retina, adrenals, and GI tract
Giardia lamblia	GI tract
Cryptosporidium	GI tract
Herpes simplex virus	Esophagus and CNS (encephalitis)
Candida	Oral pharynx and esophagus
Aspergillus	CNS, lungs, blood vessels
Toxoplasmosis	CNS
Cryptococcus	CNS (meningitis)
JC virus	CNS (progressive multifocal leukoencephalopathy)
Bartonella spp.	Skin, mucosa, bone (bacillary angiomatosis)

PRACTICE QUESTIONS

1. Respiratory secretions from a patient show catalase-positive, gram-positive cocci that are able to grow on mannitol salt agar. The most likely organism is which of the following?

   A. *Haemophilus Influenzae*
   B. *Klebsiella pneumonia*
   C. *Legionella pneumophila*
   D. *Staphylococcus aureus*
   E. *Streptococcus pyogenes*

2. If a patient is identified as having an infection caused by a bacteria that adheres to cell surfaces with teichoic acid, the infection is most likely caused by which of the following?

   A. *Haemophilus Influenzae*
   B. *Klebsiella pneumonia*
   C. *Legionella pneumophila*
   D. *Pseudomonas aeruginosa*
   E. *Streptococcus pneumoniae*

3. A patient in the hospital is diagnosed with a spore-forming organism. The infection is likely caused by which of the following?

   A. *Clostridium difficile*
   B. *Klebsiella pneumonia*
   C. *Legionella pneumophila*
   D. *Moraxella Catarrhalis*
   E. *Streptococcus pneumonia*

4. Parvovirus is described as a naked DNA virus. Which of the following is also a naked DNA virus?

   A. Adenovirus
   B. Coronavirus
   C. Hepadna
   D. Hepevirus
   E. Herpesvirus

5. A 25-year-old HIV infected female develops a non-dimorphic fungal infection. If a germ tube test demonstrates pseudohyphae and hyphae, her infection is most likely caused by:

   A. *Blastomyces dermatitidis*
   B. *Candida albicans*
   C. *Coccidioides immitis*
   D. *Histoplasma capsulatum*
   E. *Sporothrix schenckii*

6. If the normal flora in the intestinal tract were eliminated, a patient would mostly likely become deficient in which of the following vitamins?

   A. A
   B. B12
   C. C
   D. D
   E. E

7. The most common cause of cystitis in females is which of the following?

   A. Enterobacter spp.
   B. *Escherichia coli*
   C. *Klebsiella pneumoniae*
   D. *Proteus mirabilis*
   E. *Staphylococcus saprophyticus*

8. Which of the following bacteria are NOT encapsulated?

   A. *Escherichia coli*
   B. *Klebsiella pneumoniae*
   C. *Haemophilus influenza*
   D. *Neisseria meningitidis*
   E. *Streptococcus pneumoniae*

9. If a patient is prescribed an antibiotic that prevents bacterial DNA synthesis by inhibiting the enzyme topoisomerase, they were most likely prescribed which of the following?

   A. Azithromycin
   B. Cephalexin
   C. Ciprofloxacin
   D. Gentamicin
   E. Vancomycin

10. A patient with community acquired pneumonia fails therapy with amoxicillin and clavulanic acid; however, is successfully treated with azithromycin. Which of the following organisms is most likely the cause of the patient's pneumonia?

   A. *Haemophilus Influenzae*
   B. *Klebsiella pneumonia*
   C. *Legionella pneumophila*
   D. *Moraxella Catarrhalis*
   E. *Streptococcus pneumonia*

Answers and Explanations

1. **The correct answer is D.** The organism described is most likely *Staphylococcus aureus*, which are catalase-positive, gram-positive cocci that can grow on a mannitol salt agar. *Haemophilus Influenzae* (choice A) are pleomorphic gram-negative coccobacilli. *Klebsiella pneumonia* (choice B) are gram-negative encapsulated rods. *Legionella pneumophila* (choice C) are weakly gram-negative, pleomorphic rods requiring cysteine and iron. They grow on charcoal-yeast extract agar (CYE agar). *Streptococcus pyogenes* (choice E) is a beta-hemolytic, coagulase (−), catalase (−), gram-positive coccus that grows in chains.

2. **The correct answer is E.** *Streptococcus pneumoniae* is a gram (+), catalase (−), α hemolytic, soluble in bile, optochin sensitive bacteria. Pathogenic features of the bacteria include a polysaccharide capsule (major virulence factor), IgA protease and Teichoic acid. Teichoic acids are the primary mechanism by which this (and many other gram positive) bacteria adhere to cell surfaces. Teichoic acids are only seen in gram (+) bacteria. Choices A, B and D are gram (−)organisms and choice C is an atypical bacteria.

3. **The correct answer is A.** Endospores occur with certain gram-positive bacteria (i.e. Bacillus and Clostridium) and serve as a form of survival (1 bacterium has 1 spore). These spores are resistant to chemicals, desiccation, radiation, freezing, and heat. Of the organisms listed, *Clostridium difficile* is an anaerobic, spore-forming gram-positive rod. None of the other organisms are spore-forming.

4. **The correct answer is A.** Viruses can be classified as being DNA or RNA viruses. They can be further classified as being enveloped or non-enveloped (naked). Examples of naked DNA viruses include Papillomavirus, Polyomavirus and Parvovirus as well as Adenovirus, which causes acute respiratory disease, pharyngoconjunctivitis, epidemic keratoconjunctivitis and pediatric gastroenteritis. Coronavirus (choice C) is an enveloped RNA virus. Hepadna (choice C) and Herpesvirus (choice E) are enveloped DNA viruses. Hepevirus (choice D) is a naked RNA virus.

5. **The correct answer is B.** *Candida albicans* forms pseudohyphae and true hyphae when it invades tissues (nonpathogenic Candida do not). The key here is the appearance of pseudohyphae (hyphae with constrictions at each septum), which are seen in Candida. Dimorphic fungi are able to convert from hyphal to yeast or yeast-like forms in different temperatures; they are thermally dimorphic (in the "cold" they are in the "mold" form). *Blastomyces dermatitidis* (choice A), *Coccidioides immitis* (choice C), *Histoplasma capsulatum* (choice D), and *Sporothrix schenckii* (choice E) are all dimorphic fungi.

6. **The correct answer is B.** The normal flora contributes to health by helping to maintain conditions such as intestinal pH so that other organisms cannot grow. They also serve a nutritional function by synthesizing K and B vitamins (i.e. Vitamin B12) as well as compete for space (in the intestinal tract for example) to prohibit the growth of pathogenic organisms. Vitamin B12 deficiency is associated with the development of pernicious anemia. All of the other answer choices are commonly found in dietary sources. Vitamin D can also be available through exposure to sunlight.

7. **The correct answer is B.** Cystitis is an infection of the urinary bladder that predominantly occurs in women. The most common initial presenting symptoms include dysuria, frequency, and suprapubic pain. *E. coli* are found in >80% of cystitis cases. Other gram-negative bacilli (*Proteus mirabilis* [choice D], *Klebsiella pneumoniae* [choice C], *Enterobacter spp* [choice A], etc) comprise the remaining 15–20% of cases with occasional infections caused by *Staphylococcus saprophyticus* (choice E).

8. **The correct answer is A.** The bacterial capsule is a virulence factor since it augments the ability of bacteria to cause disease by preventing phagocytosis. *Escherichia coli* is the only answer choice without a capsule. *Escherichia coli* is a gram-negative, facultative anaerobic, oxidase negative rod. The encapsulated organisms can be remembered with the following mnemonic: **S**ome **K**illers **H**ave **P**retty **N**ice **C**apsules. These organisms are ***S**treptococcus pneumoniae,* ***K**lebsiella pneumoniae,* ***H**aemophilus influenzae,* ***P**seudomonas aeruginosa,* ***N**eisseria meningitidis* and ***C**ryptococcus neoformans.*

9. **The correct answer is C.** Ciprofloxacin is a fluoroquinolone antibiotic that acts by inhibiting bacterial DNA gyrase and topoisomerase IV. Azithromycin (choice A) binds to the bacterial 50S ribosomal subunit and inhibits protein synthesis. Cephalexin (choice B) inhibits cell wall mucopeptide synthesis. Gentamicin (choice D) binds to the bacterial 30S ribosomal subunit and inhibits protein synthesis. Vancomycin (choice E) inhibits bacterial cell wall and RNA synthesis.

10. **The correct answer is C.** The atypical bacteria, such as Legionella pneumophila and Mycobacteria pneumoniae are unresponsive to beta-lactam therapy. The treatments of choice for these organisms include the macrolides (azithromycin, erythromycin), fluoroquinolones (levofloxacin, ciprofloxacin) and doxycycline.

Immunology 4

Learning Objectives

- ❑ Differentiate between innate and adaptive immunity
- ❑ Demonstrate understanding of antibodies
- ❑ Show proficiency on the different types of hypersensitivity reactions

Numerous times each day, the human body is exposed to several types of bacteria, viruses, fungi, and parasites. It is generally able to defend against a serious infection. Even when people get sick (common cold, sinus infection), the immune system is usually able to contain and eliminate the infection.

Immunology is a branch of biomedical science that focuses on the response of an organism (i.e. human) to an antigenic challenge. It also deals with a human's ability to recognize and combat pathogenic microorganisms (Chapter 3), tissues (organ transplantation), and other foreign materials.

INNATE AND ADAPTIVE IMMUNITY

The immune system is designed to recognize and respond to non-self antigen in a coordinated manner. Additionally, cells that are diseased, damaged, distressed or dying are recognized and eliminated by the immune system.

The immune system is divided into 2 complementary arms: the **innate** and the **adaptive** immune systems.

Innate Immunity

Innate immunity provides the body's first line of defense against infectious agents. It involves several defensive barriers:

- Anatomic and physical (skin, mucous membranes and normal flora)
- Physiologic (temperature, pH, anti-microbials and cytokines)
- Complement
- Cellular: phagocytes and granulocytes
- Inflammation

Innate immune defenses have the following characteristics in common:

- Are **present intrinsically** with or without previous stimulation
- Have **limited specificity** for shared microbe and cellular structures (pathogen-associated molecular patterns [PAMPs] and damage-associated molecular patterns [DAMPs])
- Have **limited diversity** as reflected by a limited number of pattern recognition receptors
- Are not enhanced in activity upon subsequent exposure—**no memory**

Adaptive Immunity

The components of the adaptive immune response are B and T lymphocytes and their effector cells. Adaptive immune defenses have the following characteristics in common:

- Each B and T lymphocyte is **specific** for a particular antigen
- As a population, lymphocytes have extensive diversity
- Are enhanced with each repeat exposure—**immunologic memory**
- Are capable of **distinguishing self** from **non-self**
- Are **self-limiting**

The features of adaptive immunity are designed to give the individual the best possible defense against disease.

- **Specificity** is required, along with **immunologic memory,** to protect against persistent or recurrent challenge.
- **Diversity** is required to protect against the maximum number of potential pathogens.
- **Specialization** of effector function is necessary so that the most effective defense can be mounted against diverse challenges.
- The ability to **distinguish between self** (host cells) **and non-self** (pathogens) is vital in inhibiting an auto-immune response.
- **Self-limitation** allows the system to return to a basal resting state after a challenge to conserve energy and resources and to avoid uncontrolled cell proliferation resulting in leukemia or lymphoma.

Table 4-1. Innate versus Adaptive Immunity

Characteristics	Innate	Adaptive
Specificity	For pathogen-associated molecular patterns (PAMPs)	For specific antigens of microbial and nonmicrobial agents
Diversity	Limited	High
Memory	No	Yes
Self-reactivity	No	No
Components		
Anatomic and physiologic barriers	Skin, mucosa, normal flora, temperature, pH, antimicrobials, and cytokines	Lymph nodes, spleen, mucosal-associated lymphoid tissues
Blood proteins	Complement	Antibodies
Cells	Phagocytes, granulocytes and natural killer (NK) cells	B lymphocytes and T lymphocytes

The innate and adaptive arms of the immune response work in collaboration to stop an infection. Once a pathogen has broken through the anatomic and physiologic barriers, the innate immune response is immediately activated. Oftentimes it is able to contain and eliminate the infection.

When the innate immune response is unable to control the replication of a pathogen, the adaptive immune response is engaged and activated by the innate immune response in an antigen-specific manner. Typically, it takes 1–2 weeks after the primary infection for the adaptive immune response to begin clearance of the infection through the action of effector cells and antibodies.

Once an infection has been cleared, both the innate and adaptive immune responses cease. Antibodies and residual effector cells continue to provide protective immunity, while memory cells provide long-term immunologic protection from subsequent infection.

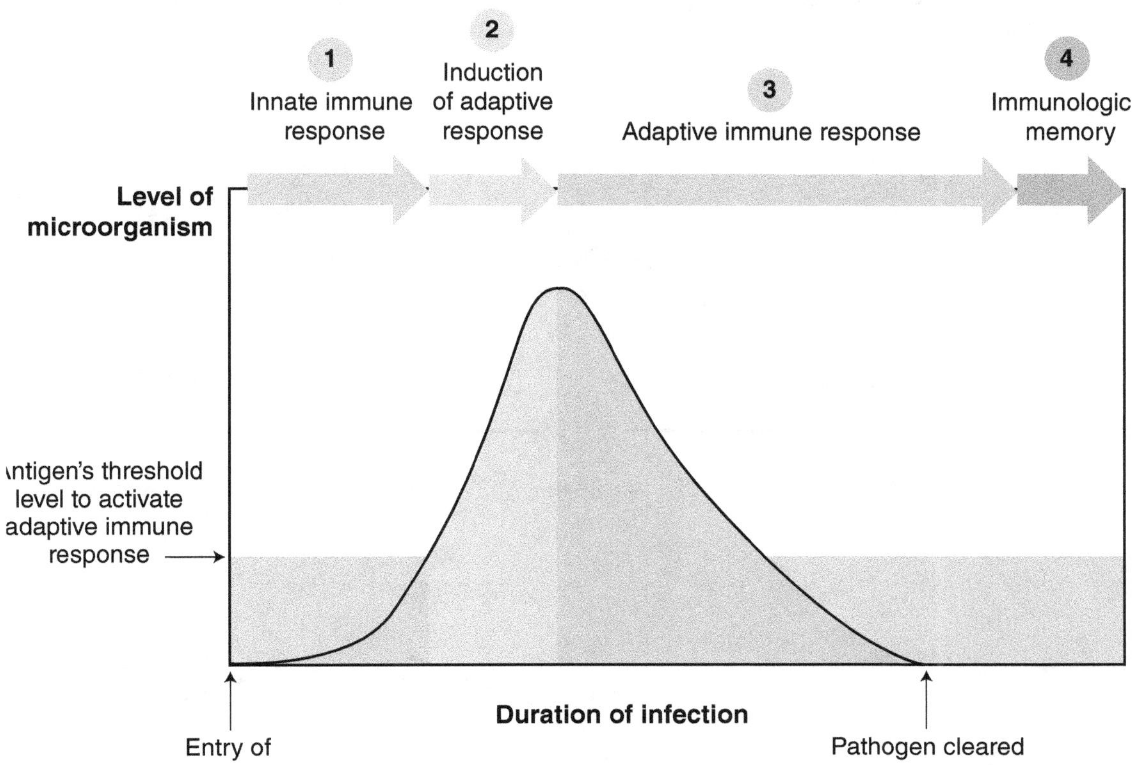

Figure 4-1. Timeline of the Immune Response to an Acute Infection

The innate and adaptive immune responses do not act independently of one another; rather, they work by a positive feedback mechanism.

- Phagocytic cells recognize pathogens by binding PAMPs through various pattern-recognition receptors leading to phagocytosis.
- Phagocytic cells process and present antigen to facilitate stimulation of specific T lymphocytes with subsequent release of cytokines that trigger initiation of specific immune responses.
- T lymphocytes produce cytokines that enhance microbicidal activities of phagocytes.
- Cytokines released by phagocytes and T lymphocytes will drive differentiation of B lymphocytes into plasma cells and isotype switching.
- Antibodies will aid in the destruction of pathogen through opsonization, complement activation and antibody-dependent cellular cytotoxicity.

Origin of the Immune System

Hematopoiesis involves the production, development, differentiation, and maturation of the blood cells (erythrocytes, megakaryocytes and leukocytes) from **multipotent stem cells.** The site of hematopoiesis changes during development.

During embryogenesis and early fetal development, the yolk sac is the site of hematopoiesis. Once organogenesis begins, hematopoiesis shifts to the liver and spleen, and finally, to the bone marrow where it will remain throughout adulthood.

These **multipotent stem cells** found in the bone marrow have the ability to undergo asymmetric division. One of the 2 daughter cells will serve to renew the population of stem cells (**self-renewal**), while the other can give rise to either a common lymphoid progenitor cell or a common myeloid progenitor cell (**potency**). The multipotent stem cells will differentiate into the various lymphoid and myeloid cells in response to various cytokines and growth factors.

- The **common lymphoid progenitor cell** gives rise to B lymphocytes, T lymphocytes and natural killer (NK) cells.
- The **common myeloid progenitor cell** gives rise to erythrocytes, megakaryocytes/thrombocytes, mast cells, eosinophils, basophils, neutrophils, monocytes/macrophages and dendritic cells.

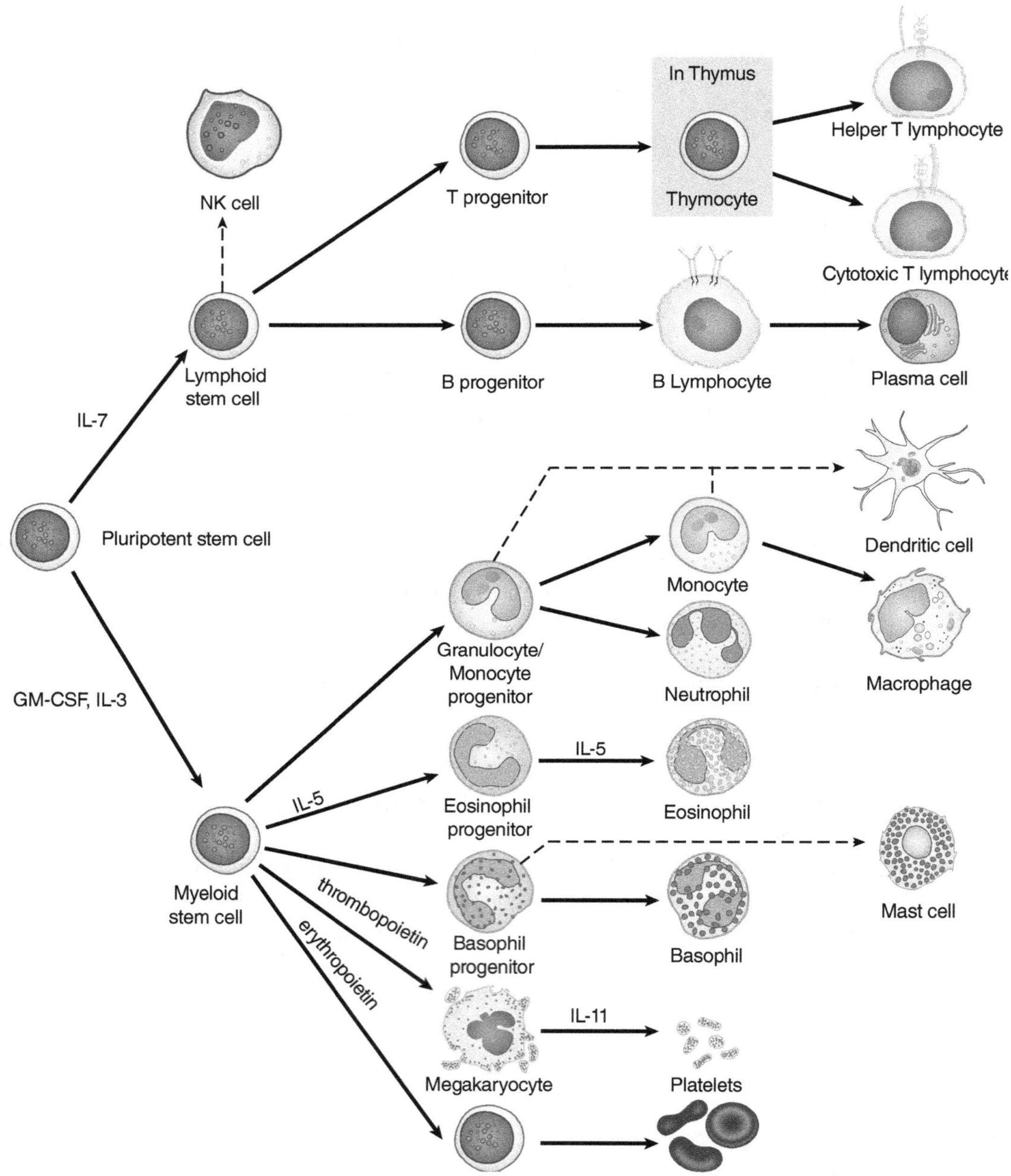

Figure 4-2. Ontogeny of Immune Cells

Function of the Immune System

The white blood cells of both the myeloid and lymphoid stem cells have specialized functions in the body once their differentiation in the bone marrow is complete. Cells of the myeloid lineage, except erythrocytes and megakaryocytes, perform non-specific, stereotypic responses and are members of the innate branch of the immune response. B lymphocytes and T lymphocytes of the lymphoid lineage perform focused, antigen-specific roles in immunity. Natural killer cells are also from the lymphoid lineage but participate in innate immunity.

Although B lymphocytes and T lymphocytes in the bloodstream are almost morphologically indistinguishable at the light microscopic level, they represent 2 interdependent cell lineages.

- **B lymphocytes** remain within the **bone marrow** to complete their development.
- **T lymphocytes** leave the bone marrow and undergo development within the **thymus.**

Table 4-2. White Blood Cells

Myeloid Cell	Tissue Location	Physical Description	Function
Neutrophil or polymorpho-nuclear (PMN) cell 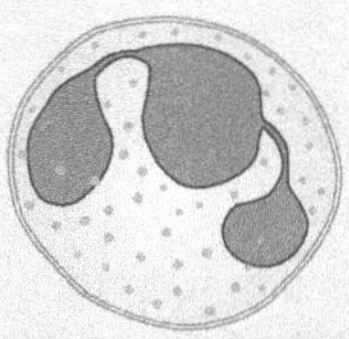	Most abundant circulating blood cell	Granulocyte with a segmented, lobular nuclei (3–5 lobes) and small pink cytoplasmic granules	Phagocytic activity aimed at killing extracellular pathogens
Lymphoid Cell	**Tissue Location**	**Physical Description**	**Function**
Lymphocyte 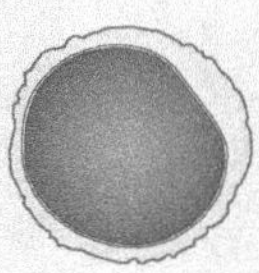	Bloodstream, second-ary lymphoid tissues	Large, dark-staining nucleus with a thin rim of cytoplasm Surface markers: B lymphocytes — CD19, 20, 21 T lymphocytes — CD3 Helper T cells — CD4 CTLs — CD8	No function until activated in the secondary lymphoid tissues
Plasma cell 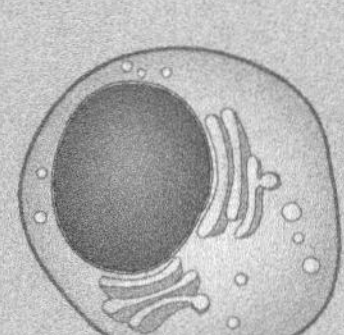	Bloodstream, second-ary lymphoid tissue and bone marrow	Small eccentric nucleus, intensely staining Golgi apparatus	Terminally differentiated B lymphocyte that secretes antibodies
Natural killer cell 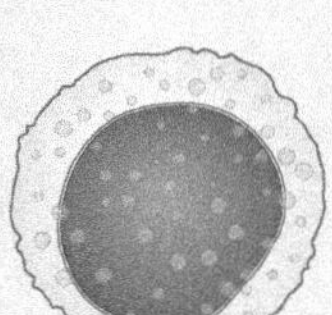	Bloodstream	Lymphocyte with large cytoplasmic granules Surface markers: CD16, 56	Kills virally infected cells and tumor cells

(Continued)

Myeloid Cell	Tissue Location	Physical Description	Function
Monocyte 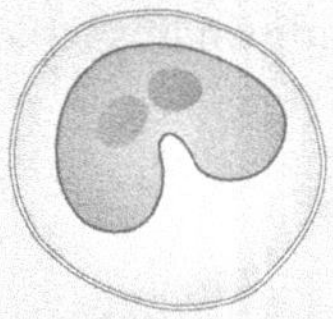	Circulating blood cell	Agranulocyte with a bean or kidney-shaped nucleus	Precursor of tissue macrophage
Macrophage 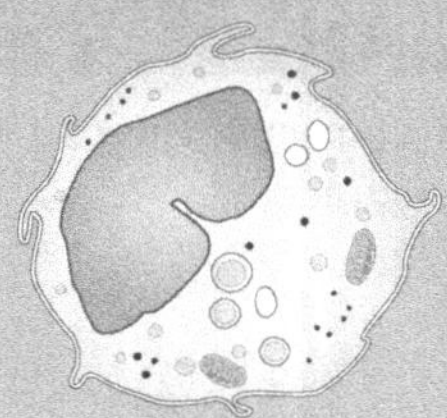	Resident in all tissues	Agranulocyte with a ruffled cytoplasmic membrane and cytoplasmic vacuoles and vesicles	• Phagocyte • Professional antigen-presenting cell • T-cell activator
Dendritic cell 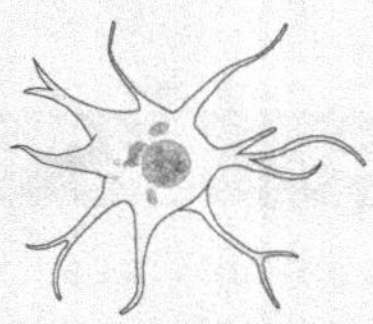	Resident in epithelial and lymphoid tissue	Agranulocyte with thin, stellate cytoplasmic projections	• Phagocyte • Professional antigen-presenting cell • T-cell activator
Eosinophil 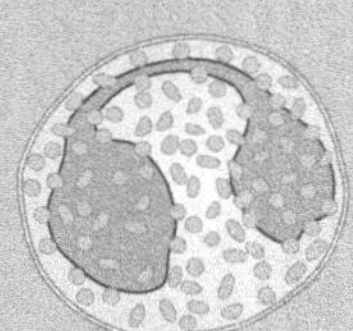	Circulating blood cell recruited into loose connective tissue of the respiratory and GI tracts	Granulocyte with bilobed nucleus and large pink cytoplasmic granules	• Elimination of large extracellular parasites • Type I hypersensitivity
Mast cell 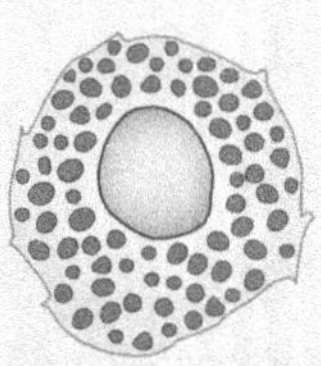	Reside in most tissues adjacent to blood vessels	Granulocyte with small nucleus and large blue cytoplasmic granule	• Elimination of large extracellular parasites • Type I hypersensitivity
Basophil 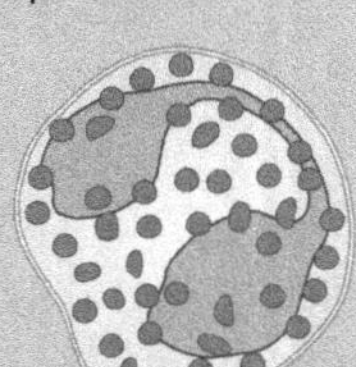	Low frequency circulating blood cell	Granulocyte with bilobed nucleus and large blue cytoplasmic granules	• Elimination of large extracellular parasites • Type I hypersensitivity

Both B and T lymphocytes have surface membrane receptors designed to bind to specific antigens.

- The **natural killer (NK) cell** (the third type of lymphocyte) is a large granular lymphocyte that recognizes tumor and virally infected cells through non-specific binding.

Laboratory evaluation of patients commonly involves assessment of white blood cell morphology and relative counts by examination of a blood sample. Changes in the morphology and proportions of white blood cells indicate the presence of some pathologic state. A standard white blood cell differential includes neutrophils, band cells, lymphocytes (B lymphocytes, T lymphocytes, and NK cells), monocytes, eosinophils and basophils.

ANTIBODIES

An antibody (Ab), otherwise known as an immunoglobulin (Ig), is an immune system protein that identifies and neutralizes pathogens (i.e. bacteria, virus, fungus, etc.).

Antigen Recognition Molecules of Lymphocytes

Each cell of the lymphoid lineage is clinically identified by the characteristic surface molecules it possesses.

- The mature, naïve **B lymphocyte**, in its mature ready-to-respond form, **expresses 2 isotypes of antibody or immunoglobulin called IgM and IgD** within its surface membrane.
- The mature, naïve **T cell** expresses a single genetically related molecule, called the **T-cell receptor (TCR)**, on its surface.

Both of these types of antigen receptors are encoded within the immunoglobulin superfamily of genes and are expressed in literally millions of variations in different lymphocytes as a result of complex and random rearrangements of the cells' DNA.

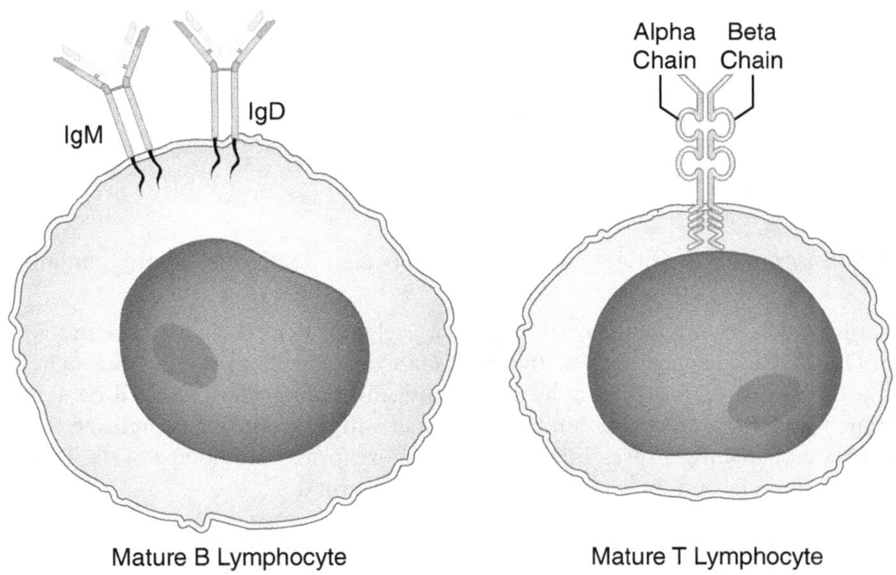

Figure 4-3. Antigen Receptors of Mature Lymphocytes

The antigen receptor of the B lymphocyte, or **membrane-bound immunoglobulin**, is a 4-chain glycoprotein molecule that serves as the basic monomeric unit for each of the **distinct antibody molecules** destined to circulate freely in the serum. This monomer has 2 identical halves, each composed of a **heavy chain** and a **light chain.** A cytoplasmic tail on the carboxy-terminus of each heavy chain extends through the plasma membrane and anchors the molecule to the cell surface. The 2 halves are held together by disulfide bonds into a shape resembling a "Y." Some flexibility of movement is permitted between the halves by disulfide bonds forming a **hinge region.**

On the N-terminal end of the molecule where the heavy and light chains lie side by side, an antigen binding site is formed whose 3-dimensional shape will accommodate the noncovalent binding of one, or a very small number, of related antigens. The unique structure of the antigen binding site is called the **idiotype** of the molecule. Although 2 classes **(isotypes)** of membrane immunoglobulin (IgM and IgD) are coexpressed on the surface of a mature, naïve B lymphocyte, only one idiotype or **antigenic specificity** is expressed per cell (although in multiple copies). Each individual is capable of producing hundreds of millions of unique idiotypes.

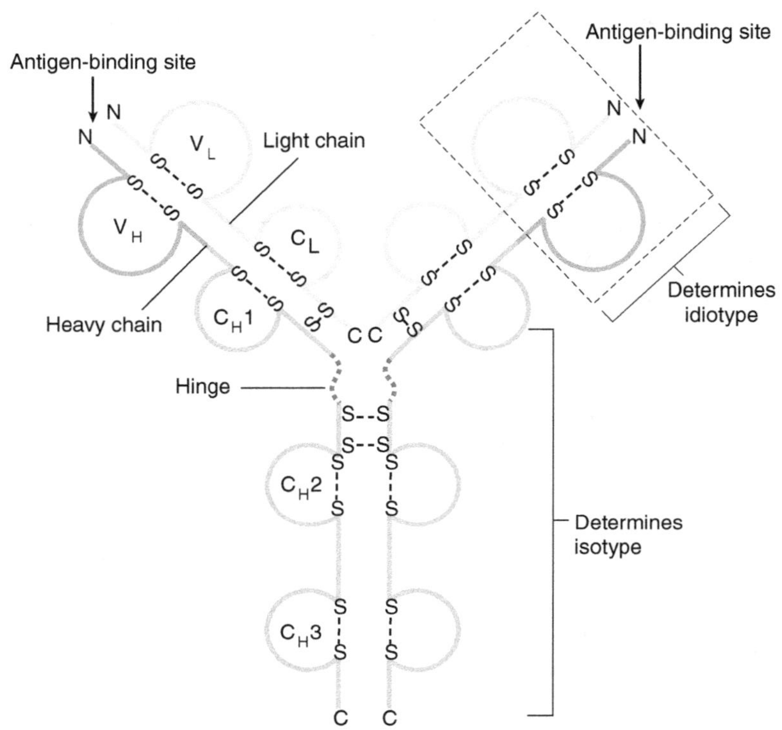

Figure 4-4. B-Lymphocyte Antigen Recognition Molecule (Membrane-Bound Immunoglobulin)

The antigen receptor of the T lymphocyte is composed of 2 glycoprotein chains: a beta and alpha chain that are similar in length. On the carboxy-terminus of the chains, a cytoplasmic tail extends through the membrane for anchorage. On the N-terminal end of the molecule, an antigen-binding site is formed between the 2 chains; its 3-dimensional shape will accommodate the binding of a small antigenic **peptide complexed to an MHC molecule** presented on the surface of an antigen-presenting cell. This groove forms the idiotype of the TCR. There is no hinge region present in this molecule, and thus its conformation is quite rigid.

The membrane receptors of B lymphocytes are designed to bind **unprocessed antigens** of almost any chemical composition (i.e., polysaccharides, proteins, and lipids), whereas the TCR is designed to bind only **peptides complexed to MHC.** Also, although the B-cell receptor is ultimately modified to the secreted **antibody**, the TCR is never released from its membrane-bound location.

In association with these unique antigen-recognition molecules on the surface of B and T cells, accessory molecules are intimately associated with the receptors that function in signal transduction. Thus, when a lymphocyte binds to an antigen complementary to its idiotype, a cascade of messages transferred through its **signal transduction complex** will culminate in intracytoplasmic phosphorylation events leading to activation of the cell.

- In the B cell, this signal transduction complex is composed of 2 invariant chains, Ig-alpha and Ig-beta, and a B-cell co-receptor consisting of CD19, CD21 and CD81.
- The B-cell co-receptor is implicated in the attachment of several infectious agents. CD21 is the receptor for EBV, and CD81 is the receptor for hepatitis C and *Plasmodium vivax.*
- In the T cell, the signal transduction complex is a multichain structure called CD3.

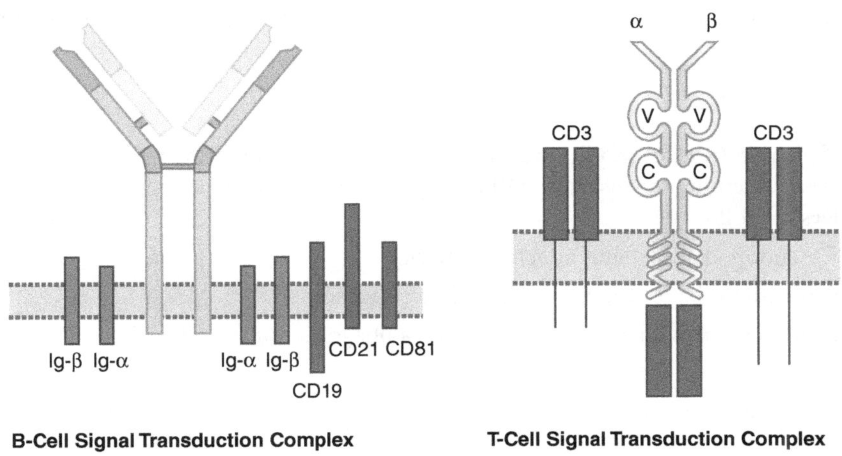

Figure 4-5. Lymphocyte Signal Transduction

Table 4-3. B- versus T-Lymphocyte Antigen Receptors

Property	B-Cell Antigen Receptor	T-Cell Antigen Receptor
Molecules/Lymphocyte	100,000	100,000
Idiotypes/Lymphocyte	1	1
Isotypes/Lymphocyte	2 (IgM and IgD)	1 (α/β)
Is secretion possible?	Yes	No
Number of combining sites/molecule	2	1
Mobility	Flexible (hinge region)	Rigid
Signal-transduction molecules	Ig-α, Ig-β, CD19, CD21	CD3

Acute Inflammatory Response

Antigens are normally introduced into the body across the mucosa or the epithelia. The acute inflammatory response is often the first response to this invasion and represents a response of the innate immune system to block the challenge.

The first step in the acute inflammatory response is activation of the vascular endothelium in the breached epithelial barrier. Cytokines and other inflammatory mediators released in the area as a result of tissue damage induce expression of selectin-type adhesion molecules on the endothelial cells. Neutrophils are the first cells to bind to the inflamed endothelium and extravasate into the tissues, peaking within 6 hours. Monocytes, macrophages, and even eosinophils may arrive 5-6 hours later in response to neutrophil-released mediators.

The extravasation of phagocytes into the area requires 4 sequential, overlapping steps:

- Rolling
- Activation by chemo-attractants
- Arrest and adhesion
- Transendothelial migration

Once in the tissues, **neutrophils express increased levels of receptors for chemoattractants** and exhibit chemotaxis migrating up a concentration gradient toward the attractant. **Neutrophils release chemoattractive factors that call in other phagocytes.**

Phagocytosis

Once chemotaxis of phagocytic cells into the area of antigen entry is accomplished, these cells ingest and digest particulate debris, such as microorganisms, host cellular debris, and activated clotting factors. This process, called phagocytosis, involves the following:

- Extension of pseudopodia to engulf attached material
- Fusion of the pseudopodia to trap the material in a phagosome
- Fusion of the phagosome with a lysosome to create a phagolysosome
- Digestion
- Exocytosis of digested contents

Neutrophils release granule contents into extracellular milieu during phagocytosis and inflammation in which the neutrophils die, forming what is known as pus. They extrude nuclear contents, histones, neutrophil extracellular traps (NETs) which function to:

- Trap and kill pathogens
- May damage tissues when enzymes, ROS, get released into tissues

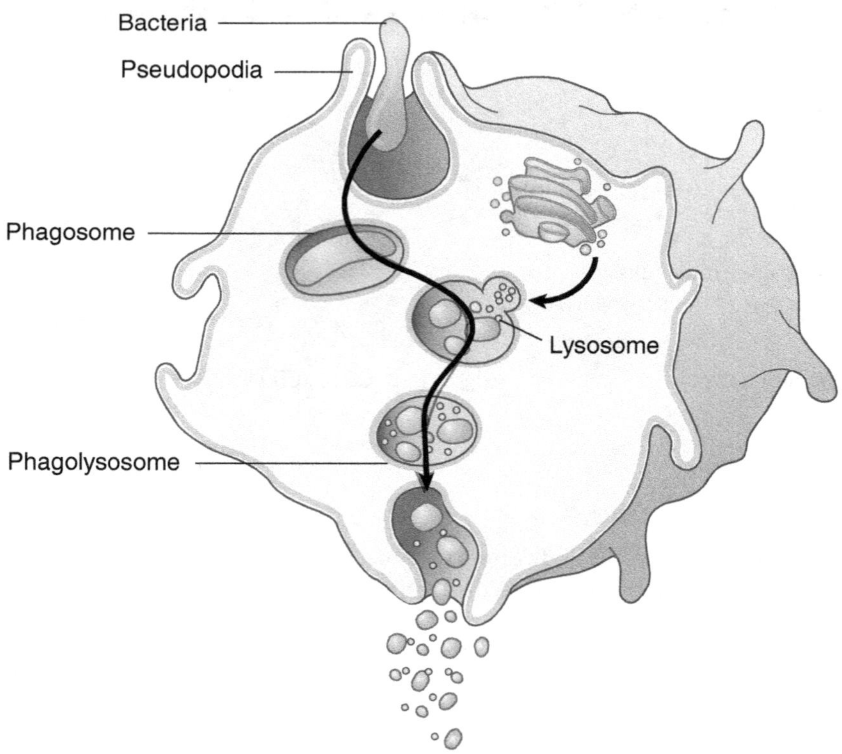

Figure 4-6. Phagocytosis

Opsonization

Both macrophages and neutrophils have membrane receptors for certain types of antibodies (IgG) and certain complement components (C3b). If an antigen is coated with either of these materials, adherence and phagocytosis may be enhanced by up to 4,000-fold. Thus, antibody and complement are called **opsonins**, and the means by which they enhance phagocytosis is called opsonization.

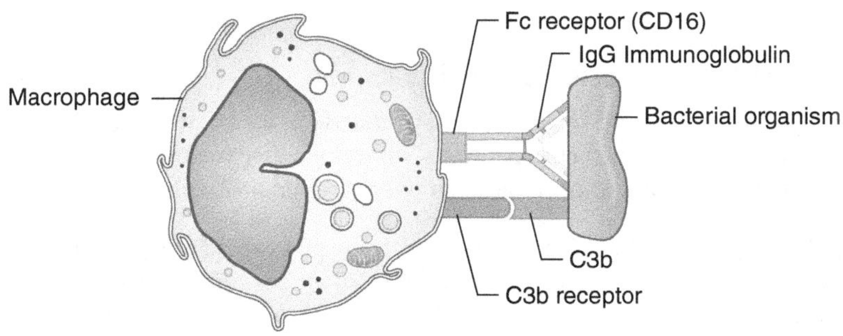

Figure 4-7. Opsonization of Bacteria with Antibody and Complement C3b

Intracellular Killing

During phagocytosis, a metabolic process known as the respiratory burst activates a membrane-bound oxidase that generates oxygen metabolites, which are toxic to ingested microorganisms. Two oxygen-dependent mechanisms of intracellular digestion are activated as a result of this process.

- NADPH oxidase reduces oxygen to superoxide anion, which generates hydroxyl radicals and hydrogen peroxide, which are microbicidal.
- Myeloperoxidase in the lysosomes acts on hydrogen peroxide and chloride ions to produce hypochlorite (the active ingredient in household bleach), which is microbicidal.

Additionally, reactive nitrogen intermediates play an important role. Inducible nitric oxide synthase converts arginine to nitric oxide, which has potent antimicrobial properties.

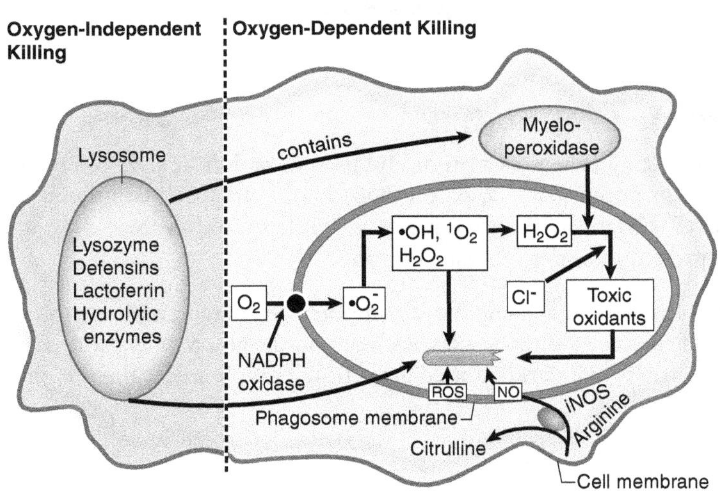

Figure 4-8. Metabolic Stimulation and Killing Within the Phagocyte

The lysosomal contents of phagocytes contain oxygen-independent degradative materials:

- Lysozyme digests bacterial cell walls by cleaving peptidoglycan
- Defensins form channels in bacterial cell membranes
- Lactoferrin chelates iron
- Hydrolytic enzymes

Enzyme-linked Immunosorbent Assay (ELISA)

The ELISA is an extremely sensitive test (as little as 10^{-9} g of material can be detected). It can be used to **detect the presence of hormones, drugs, antibiotics, serum proteins, infectious disease antigens, and tumor markers**. It does so by utilizing a chromogenic substrate that undergoes an enzyme-mediated color change.

In the **screening test for HIV infection, the ELISA is used with the p24 capsid antigen** coated onto microtiter plates. The serum from the patient is then added, followed by addition of an enzyme-labeled antihuman immunoglobulin. Finally, the chromogenic substrate is added, and the production of a color change in the well can be observed.

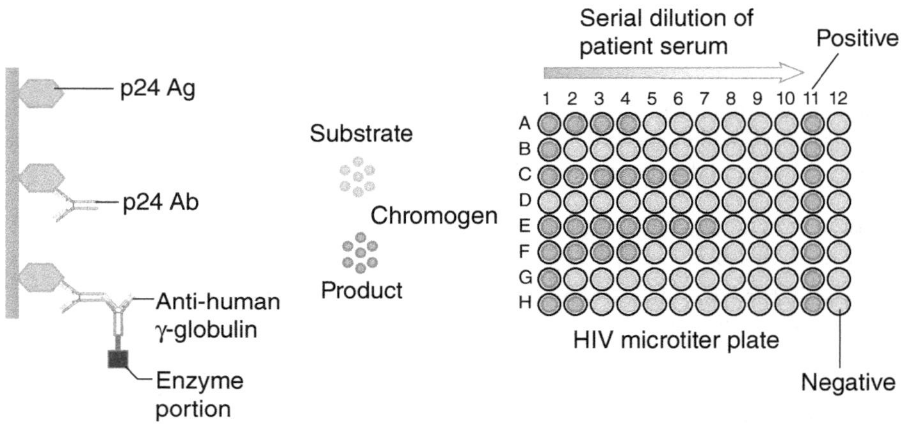

Figure 4-9. ELISA Test

Fluorescence-Activated Cell Sorting

Fluorescence-activated cell sorting (FACS) is a procedure used to rapidly analyze cell types in a complex mixture by sorting the cells into different populations based on their binding to specific fluorescently labelled antibodies. By using antibodies against cell-surface markers conjugated to different fluorescent dyes, it is possible to analyze the relative numbers of cells present in a specific tissue location.

As cells pass through the apparatus in a single file, a computer-generated graph is produced, plotting the intensity and color of fluorescence of each cell along the axes. Each dot on the graph reflects the passage of a cell with a certain level and color of fluorescence, so the darkly dotted areas of the graph reflect the presence of many cells of similar attributes.

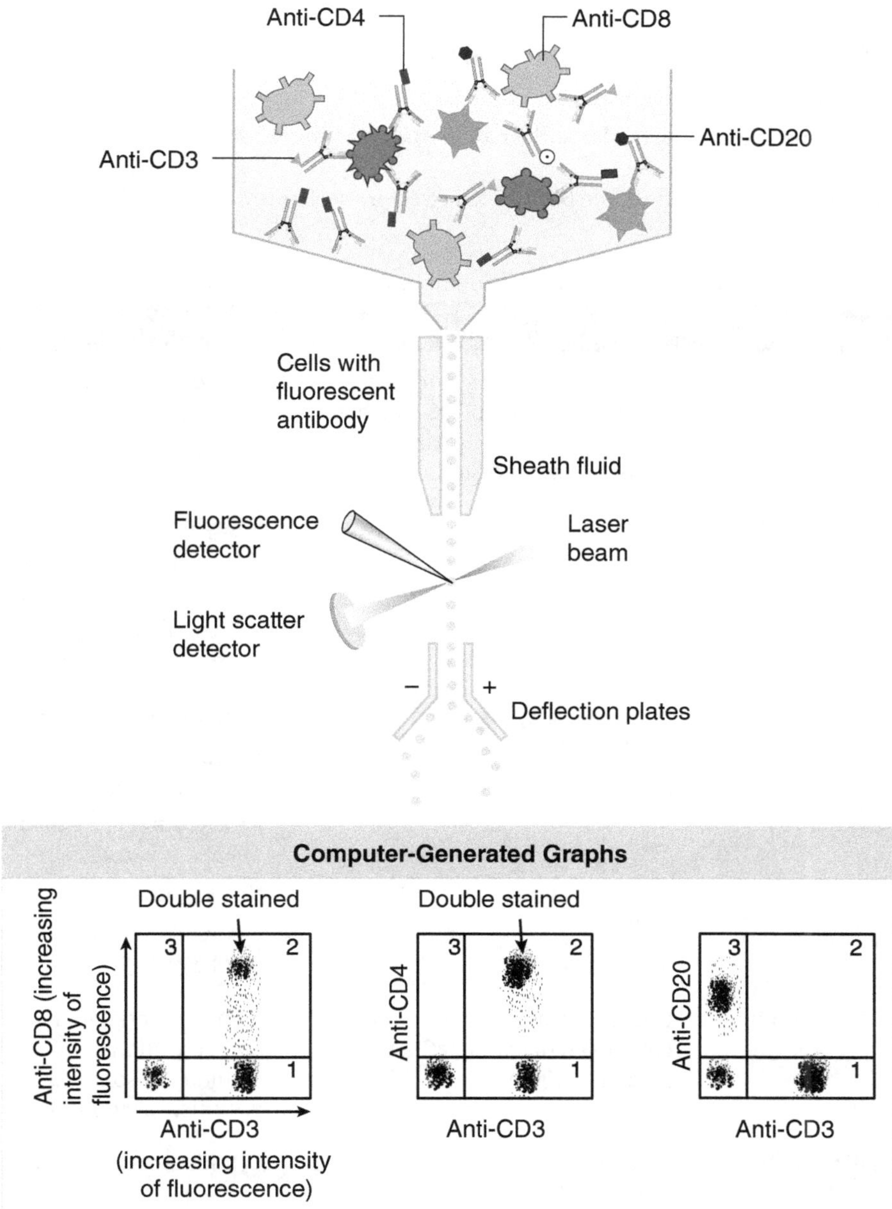

Figure 4-10. Flow Cytometric Analysis

HYPERSENSITIVITY REACTIONS

Hypersensitivity diseases are conditions in which immune responses cause tissue damage. They may result from uncontrolled or excessive responses against **foreign antigens** or from a **failure of self-tolerance**, in which case they are called **autoimmune diseases**.

The 2 principal factors which determine the clinical and pathologic consequences of such conditions are the **type of immune response** elicited and the **nature and location of the inciting antigen**.

What the hypersensitivity reactions have in common:

- The first exposure to the antigen "sensitizes" lymphocytes.
- Subsequent exposures elicit a damaging reaction.
- The response is specific to a particular antigen or a cross-reacting substance.

Hypersensitivity diseases are classified on the basis of the effector mechanism responsible for tissue injury.

Table 4-4. Classification of Immunologic Diseases

Type of Hypersensitivity	Immune Mechanisms	Mechanisms of Tissue Injury
Immediate (type I)	Activation of Th2 cells resulting in the production of IgE which in turn binds to FcεR on mast cells, basophils and eosinophils	**Immediate reaction** • Degranulation and release of vasoactive amines (ie. histamine) and proteases **Late-phase reaction** • Synthesis and secretion of prostaglandins and leukotrienes • Cytokine-induced inflammation and leukocyte recruitment
Antibody-mediated (type II)	IgM and IgG against surface (cell surface or extracellular matrix)	**Complement-mediated (cytotoxic)** • Opsonization and enhances phagocytosis • Recruitment and activation of inflammatory cells **Non-cytotoxic** • Change in physiologic behavior of a cell
Immune complex–mediated (type III)	Deposition of immune complexes comprised of IgM or IgG and soluble antigen	Complement-mediated recruitment and activation of inflammatory cells resulting in some combination of arthritis, vasculitis and/or nephritis.
Delayed-type hypersensitivity (type IV)	Inflammatory cytokines, IFN-γ and IL-17, produced by CD4+ Th1 and Th17 cells, respectively.	**Cytokine-mediated tissue damage** • IFN-γ activation of macrophage • IL-17 recruitment and activation of neutrophil **Direct killing** • CTL-mediated cellular death
		CD8+ CTLs (T-cell-mediated cytolysis) Direct target cell killing, cytokine-mediated inflammation

PRACTICE QUESTIONS

1. Shortly after being administered the second dose of a new amoxicillin prescription, a child develops shortness of breath and both the tongue and lips begin to swell. This reaction is best characterized as what type of hypersensitivity?

   A. I
   B. II (cytotoxic)
   C. II (noncytotoxic)
   D. III
   E. IV

2. Components of the adaptive immune response include which of the following?

   A. B lymphocytes
   B. Complement
   C. Granulocytes
   D. Phagocytes
   E. Skin

3. During phagocytosis intracellular "killing" mechanisms involve which of the following?

   A. B lymphocytes
   B. Complement
   C. Granulocytes
   D. Hydrogen peroxide
   E. T lymphocytes

4. In the diagnosis of HIV, ELISA is used to detect which of the following?

   A. Ingegrase
   B. gp120 surface protein
   C. gp41 transmembrane protein
   D. p24 capsid antigen
   E. Reverse transcriptase

5. Which of the following is derived from a lymphoid stem cell?

   A. Erythrocytes
   B. Mast cell
   C. Monocyte
   D. Natural Killer Cell
   E. Neutrophil

6. Elevated levels of which of the following would be seen first in a child diagnosed with a viral infection?
   A. IgA
   B. IgD
   C. IgE
   D. IgG
   E. IgM

7. Which of the following is the immediate precursor of plasma cells?
   A. B lymphocyte
   B. Macrophage
   C. Megakaryocyte
   D. Monocyte
   E. Thymocyte

8. Two days after coming home from a camping trip, a child develops a rash on his forearms and calfves. If the rash is believed to be caused by poison ivy, it would best be classified as what type of hypersensitivity?
   A. I
   B. II (cytotoxic)
   C. II (noncytotoxic)
   D. III
   E. IV

9. Which of the following is a FALSE statement about the human immune system?
   A. Anatomical barriers are considered the first line of defense.
   B. Immunological memory is a characteristic of adaptive immunity.
   C. It generally takes <24 hours after the primary infection for the adaptive immune response to begin clearance of the infection.
   D. The ability to distinguish between self (host cells) and non-self (pathogens) is a function of adaptive immunity.
   E. The complement cascade is part of the innate immune system.

10. The mast cell stabilizer, cromolyn, antagonizes the effects of which of the following?
    A. IgA
    B. IgD
    C. IgE
    D. IgG
    E. IgM

Answers and Explanations

1. **The correct answer is A.** The child is having an immediate type I hypersensitivity (anaphylactic) reaction to amoxicillin. This type of hypersensitivity occurs within a few minutes following the reintroduction of an allergen, such as beta-lactam antibiotics, macrolides, sulfonamides and aspirin. It is caused by the degranulation and release of vasoactive amines (i.e. histamine) and proteases. Type II reactions, cytotoxic (i.e. rheumatic fever - choice B) and noncytotoxic (Graves disease - choice C), are antibody-mediated reactions where antibodies against cell surface or extracellular matrix antigens cause diseases that are specific to the tissues where those antigens are present. Type III (choice D) or immune complex hypersensitivity (i.e. serum sickness, SLE) occurs when an immune complex causes systemic-wide complement activation. Type IV (choice E) or T-cell mediated hypersensitivity is a delayed-type reaction and can be seen with the tuberculin skin test, contact dermatitis and Hashimoto thyroiditis.

2. **The correct answer is A.** The immune system is divided into 2 complementary components: innate and adaptive immune systems. Innate immunity provides the body's first line of defense against infectious agents and includes physical barriers, such as skin (choice E) and normal flora; physiological barriers (i.e. temperature, pH); complement (choice B); inflammation and immune system cells, such as granulocytes (choice C); and phagocytes (choice D). The components of the adaptive immune response are B and T lymphocytes and their effector cells.

3. **The correct answer is D.** Phagocytosis is part of human innate immunity. During phagocytosis, a metabolic process activates a membrane-bound oxidase that generates oxygen metabolites (i.e. hydrogen peroxide) which are toxic to ingested microorganisms. Complement (choice B) and granulocytes (choice C); are also part of the innate immune response. B lymphocytes (choice A) and T lymphocytes (choice E) are part of adaptive immunity.

4. **The correct answer is D.** The ELISA is an extremely sensitive test that can be used to detect the presence of hormones, drugs, serum proteins, and tumor markers. ELISA uses a chromogenic substrate that undergoes an enzyme-mediated color change. In the screening test for HIV infection, the ELISA is used with the p24 capsid antigen coated onto microtiter plates. All of the other answer choices are components of HIV but not detected by ELISA.

5. **The correct answer is D.** Multipotent stem cells, found in the bone marrow, will differentiate into the various lymphoid and myeloid cells in response to various cytokines and growth factors. The common lymphoid progenitor cell gives rise to B lymphocytes, T lymphocytes, and natural killer (NK) cells. The common myeloid progenitor cell gives rise to erythrocytes (choice A), megakaryocytes/thrombocytes, mast cells (choice B), eosinophils, basophils, monocytes/macrophages (choice C), neutrophils (choice E) and dendritic cells.

6. **The correct answer is E.** IgM would be the first immunoglobin (Ig) produced in response to a viral infection. IgG (choice D) is found in blood, would be expected to increase shortly after IgM levels increase and is the only Ig whose Fc region can be recognized by phagocytes and natural killer cells. IgG levels could be expected to rapidly increase after the second antigenic challenge. IgA (choice A) is an immunoglobulin that is primarily found in external body secretions, such as saliva, tear, and colostrum. IgD (choice B) mainly functions as an antigen receptor on B cells that have not been exposed to antigens. IgE (choice C) binds to allergens and triggers histamine release from mast cells and basophils.

7. **The correct answer is A.** The pluripotent stem cells found in the bone marrow differentiate into lymphoid and myeloid stem cells. The common lymphoid progenitor cell gives rise to B lymphocytes, T lymphocytes, and natural killer (NK) cells. The B lymphocytes give rise to plasma cells which secrete antibodies. Monocytes (choice D) are the precursor cells for macrophages (choice B). Megakaryocyte (choice C) are the precursors of platelets. Thymocytes (choice E) give rise to both Helper T and Cytotoxic T lymphocytes.

8. **The correct answer is E.** Hypersensitivity reactions are conditions where tissue damage is caused by immune responses. Type IV or T-cell mediated hypersensitivity, for example, is a delayed-type reaction and can be seen with the tuberculin skin test, contact dermatitis and Hashimoto thyroiditis. Type I hypersensitivity (choice A - anaphylactic) reactions occur within a few minutes following the reintroduction of an allergen (i.e. antibiotics, aspirin, etc) as a result of degranulation and release of vasoactive amines (i.e. histamine) and proteases. Type II reactions, cytotoxic (i.e. autoimmune hemolytic anemia - choice B) and noncytotoxic (Myasthenia gravis - choice C), are antibody-mediated reactions where antibodies against cell surface or extracellular matrix antigens cause diseases that are specific to the tissues where those antigens are present. Type III (choice D) or immune complex hypersensitivity (i.e. Arthus reaction, poststreptococcal glomerulonephritis, SLE), occurs when an immune complex causes systemic-wide complement activation.

9. **The correct answer is C.** Innate immunity is the first line of defense against pathogens. When this response is unable to control the replication of a pathogen, the adaptive immune response is engaged and activated by the innate immune response in an antigen-specific manner. Generally, it takes 1-2 weeks after the primary infection for the adaptive immune response to begin clearance of the infection through the action of effector cells and antibodies. All of the other answer choices are true statements.

10. **The correct answer is C.** Cromolyn is a mast cell stabilizer that has traditionally been used for the treatment of allergic asthma since it inhibits mast cell degranulation. Physiologically, IgE binds to allergens and triggers histamine release from both mast cells and basophils; hence, cromolyn antagonizes the effects of IgE. IgA (choice A) is an immunoglobulin that is primarily found in external body secretions, such as saliva, tear, and colostrum. IgD (choice B) mainly functions as an antigen receptor on B cells that have not been exposed to antigens. IgM (choice E) would be the first immunoglobin (Ig) produced in response to an antigen, such as a bacterial or viral infection. IgG (choice D) is found in blood, would be expected to increase shortly after IgM levels increase, and is the only Ig whose Fc region can be recognized by phagocytes and natural killer cells. IgG levels could be expected to rapidly increase after the second antigenic challenge.

Medicinal Chemistry 5

Learning Objectives

- ❑ Demonstrate an understanding of the physicochemical drug properties related to ADME
- ❑ Discuss the chemical basis for therapeutics effects
- ❑ Explain the principles of pharmacophores
- ❑ Discuss principles of drug-target interactions
- ❑ Answer questions on drug metabolism pathways
- ❑ Show proficiency in chemistry and therapeutic decisions

Medicinal chemistry combines the sciences of general chemistry, organic chemistry, biochemistry, and pharmacology to aid in the design of new medications. It also helps researchers and clinicians understand how a drug's physicochemical properties affect its ADME (absorption, distribution, metabolism and elimination) profile, drug-target interactions, and therapeutic effects.

PHYSICOCHEMICAL DRUG PROPERTIES RELATED TO ADME AND THERAPEUTICS EFFECTS

As the name implies, the physicochemical properties of a medication include both the physical and chemical properties of a drug. These properties include molecular weight, polar surface area, ionization behavior, lipophilicity, etc. The physical and chemical properties of a medication affect its ADME (absorption, distribution, metabolism, excretion) profile and ultimately its therapeutic impact. For example, if a medication's absorption is altered, it will not fully exert the desired therapeutic effect.

Kaplan's *NAPLEX Strategies, Practice, and Review* book provides a high-yield overview of physical pharmacy concepts specifically relating to physiochemical drug properties in the Pharmaceutics chapter.

> **NAPLEX Reference**
>
> **Pharmaceutics chapter:**
> "Physical Pharmacy"

Stereochemistry

Optical isomers, also called **stereoisomers**, are compounds that have the same chemical formula; these molecules differ from one another only in terms of the spatial arrangement of their component atoms. A special type of isomerism exists between stereoisomers that are nonidentical, nonsuperimposable mirror images of each other. These molecules are called **enantiomers**. A chiral carbon atom is one that has 4 different groups attached to it; any molecule that contains chiral carbons and no internal planes of symmetry has an enantiomer.

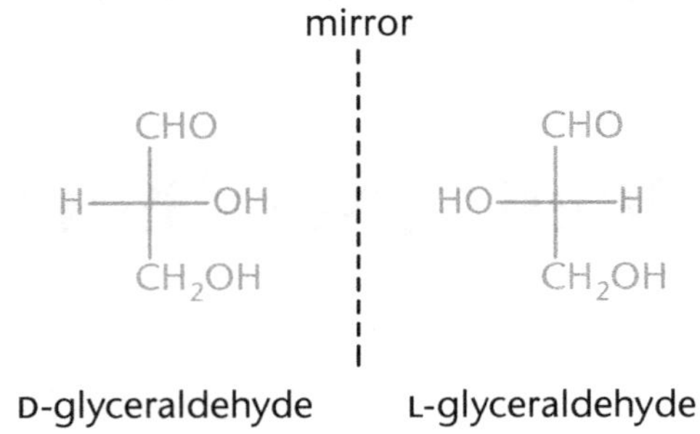

Figure 5-1. Enantiomers of Glyceraldehyde

This figure illustrates the 2 enantiomers of glyceraldehyde: D- and L-glyceraldehyde. The particular 3-dimensional arrangement of the groups attached to the chiral carbon determines the compound's **absolute configuration.** While organic chemists use the newer (*R*) and (*S*) system when denoting absolute configuration, biochemists use the older D and L system. Notice in the figure above that D-glyceraldehyde and L-glyceraldehyde are mirror images of one another—this makes them enantiomers because they *must* have opposite absolute configurations. Because there is only 1 chiral carbon present, these are the only 2 stereoisomers that exist for glyceraldehyde. As the number of chiral carbons increases, so does the number of possible stereoisomers because 1 compound may have many diastereomers. The number of possible stereoisomers of a compound can be calculated by:

$$\text{Number of stereoisomers with common backbone} = 2^n$$

where n is the number of chiral carbons in the molecule.

Key Concept

The 2 systems for naming chiral carbons are not interchangeable! While some D-isomers are equivalent with *(R)*, others are *(S)*. When dealing with biomolecules like sugars, anticipate using the biochemists' method of nomenclature: D and L.

Key Concept

When trying to figure out how many possible stereoisomers can exist for a multi-carbon compound, identify the number of chiral carbons (n) and plug into the formula 2^n. For example, $2^1 = 2$ stereoisomers and $2^2 = 4$ stereoisomers.

Early in the twentieth century, scientists used glyceraldehyde to learn about the optical rotation of sugars. The results of this early study led to the D and L naming convention. D-Glyceraldehyde was later determined to exhibit a positive rotation (designated as D-(+)-glyceraldehyde), and L-glyceraldehyde a negative rotation (designated as L-(–)-glyceraldehyde). Note that the direction of rotation, (+) or (–), must be determined experimentally and cannot be determined from the D or L designation for the sugar.

Key Concept

D and L are based on the stereochemistry of glyceraldehyde. These are NOT directly related to the (+) and (–) designations denoting optical rotation.

On the FPGEE, all monosaccharides are assigned the D or L configuration based on their relationship to glyceraldehyde. The **Fischer projection** is a simple 2-dimensional drawing of stereoisomers. Recall that in a Fischer projection, the horizontal lines are wedges (out of the page), while vertical lines are dashes (into the page).

Figure 5-2. Fisher Projection
Horizontal lines are wedges (out of the page); vertical lines are dashes (into the page).

Fischer projections allow scientists to identify different enantiomers. Using this system of structural representation, all D-sugars have the hydroxide of their highest-numbered chiral center on the right, and all L-sugars have that hydroxide on the left. Because D-glucose and L-glucose are enantiomers, this means that *every* chiral center in D-glucose has the opposite configuration of L-glucose.

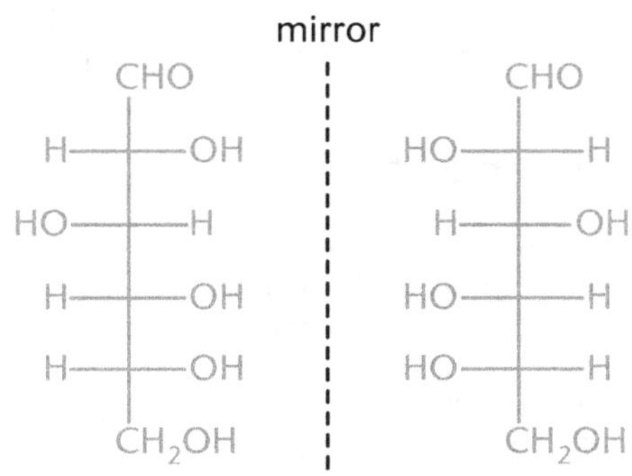

D-glucose L-glucose

Figure 5-3. Enantiomers of Glucose

Make sure that you are familiar with these 3 types of stereoisomers:

1. The same sugars, in different optical families, are **enantiomers** (such as D-glucose and L-glucose).
2. Two sugars that are in the same family (both are either ketoses or aldoses, and have the same number of carbons) that are not identical and are not mirror images of each other are **diastereomers.**
3. A special subtype of diastereomers are those that differ in configuration at exactly one chiral center. These are defined as **epimers** (such as D-*ribose* and D-*arabinose*, which only differ at C-2).

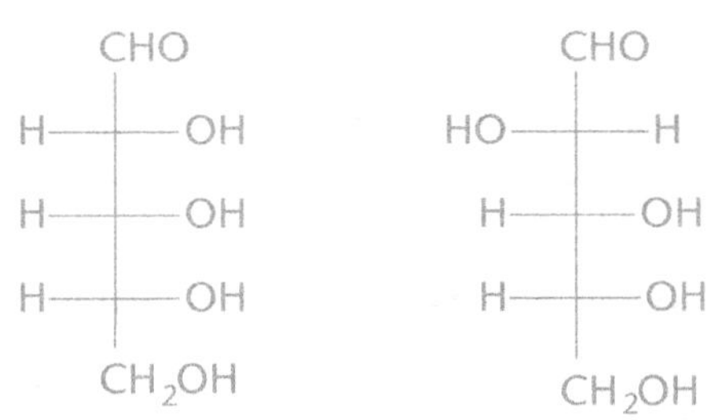

D-ribose D-arabinose

Figure 5-4. D-Ribose and D-Arabinose Are C-2 Epimers

There are 4 different stereoisomers of an aldotetrose, which includes 2 optical forms of *erythrose* and 2 optical forms of *threose*.

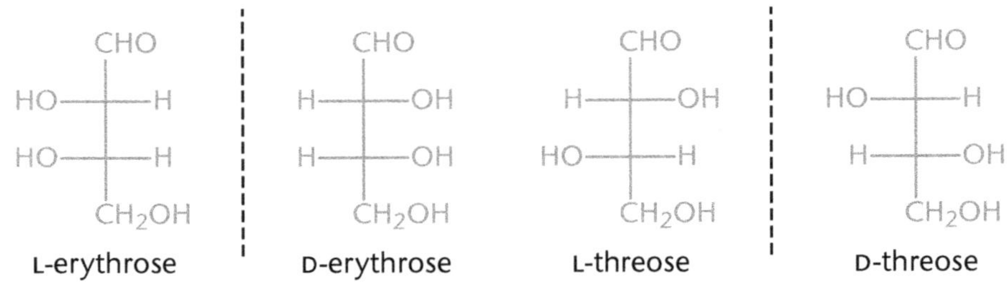

Figure 5-5. Four Stereoisomers of an Aldotetrose

Because D-erythrose and L-erythrose are nonsuperimposable mirror images of one another, they are enantiomers. On the other hand, while D-erythrose and D-threose are *not* mirror images of one another, they are still nonsuperimposable, which makes them diastereomers. Similarly, L-erythrose and D-threose are diastereomers. Because they differ in configuration at only one chiral center, they can also be defined as epimers of one another. Remember, a compound can have only one enantiomer (the left hand to its right hand, or vice-versa), but may have multiple diastereomers, depending on how many (and which) chiral carbons are inverted between the 2 molecules.

PRINCIPLES OF PHARMACOPHORES

The concept of a pharmacophore was originally introduced in 1909 and initially defined "a molecular framework that carries (phoros) the essential features responsible for a drug's (pharmacon) biological activity." This same concept still remains largely unchanged today; however, its range of application has been vastly expanded.

According to a recent definition by IUPAC, a pharmacophore model is "an ensemble of steric and electronic features that are necessary to ensure the optimal supramolecular interactions with a specific biological target and to trigger (or block) its biological response." In short, a pharmacophore can be defined as the drug's molecular framework responsible for its biological activity.

A pharmacophore can be developed by scientists to determine the precise complementarities between a ligand and its binding site. For example, only drugs with a specific molecular framework will bind to the 5-HT2C receptor. An image of 5-HT2C best fit mapped with the 4 features of the agonist pharmacophore is provided:

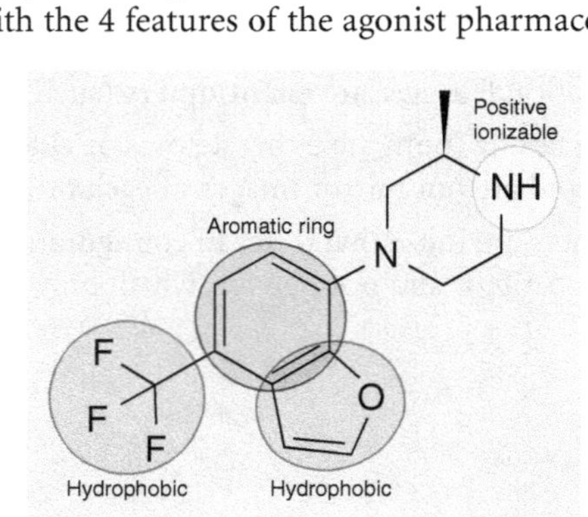

Figure 5-6. Pharmacophore-5-HT2C

The same concepts can be applied to ALL medications currently used today. For example, only medications with specific steric and electronic features bind to the Beta-1 receptor, inhibit the activity of Angiotensin Converting Enzyme, or inhibit bacterial cell wall synthesis.

DRUG-TARGET INTERACTIONS

A more in-depth discussion of pharmacodynamics can be found in Chapter 6; however, here are some key concepts surrounding drug structure-activity relationships and their impact on drug-target interactions.

Pharmacophores are regarded as an ensemble of steric and electronic features necessary to ensure the optimal supramolecular interactions with a specific biological target structure and to trigger (or to block) its biological response.

- See Figure 5-6, which is best fit mapped with the 4 features of the agonist pharmacophore.
- This definition accentuates the abstraction of steric and electronic interactions of drug compounds exhibiting similar biological effects (as their physiological counterparts) within the same binding site in an equivalent situation, such as a cell receptor.

With respect to drug design and development, a pharmacophore model must provide accurate and effective data for drug manufacturers investigating structure-activity (SAR) relationships.

- A classic example of different SARs for drugs in the same class can be seen with opioids where 200 mg codeine = 30 mg hydrocodone = 15–20 mg oxycodone. The difference in drug potency is directly related to the SAR between each opioid and the mu receptor.

The chemical nature of the functional groups ultimately affects the SAR involved in ligand-target interactions leading to varying degrees of affinity and potency.

IMPACT OF DRUG CHEMISTRY AND DRUG METABOLISM ON THERAPEUTIC DECISIONS

Pharmacokinetic characteristics of drug molecules concern the processes of ADME (absorption, distribution, metabolism, and excretion) with medications being eliminated from the body through various metabolism and excretion pathways.

Drug metabolism (biotransformation) can result in the chemical conversion of a prodrug (i.e. codeine) into an active compound. It can also convert the parent compound into active or inactive metabolites, which are further metabolized or eliminated renally.

The ability of the patient to metabolize a given drug can have a dramatic impact on the prescriber's decision to use one medication or another therapeutically. Thus, it is essential you have an understanding of the types of drug metabolism and the applicability of drug chemistry and metabolism on therapeutic decisions.

Kaplan's *NAPLEX Strategies, Practice, and Review* book (Biopharmaceutics and Drug Disposition chapter: "Drug Metabolism") provides a high-yield review of drug metabolism principles and factors affecting biotransformation.

NAPLEX Reference

Biopharmaceutics and Drug Disposition chapter:

"Drug Metabolism"

Biotransformation

Clinical Correlate

Active Metabolites

Biotransformation of the benzodiazepine diazepam results in formation of nordiazepam, a metabolite with sedative-hypnotic activity and a long duration of action.

- The general principle of biotransformation is the metabolic conversion of drug molecules to more water-soluble metabolites that are more readily excreted.
- In many cases, metabolism of a drug results in its conversion to compounds that have little or no pharmacologic activity.
- In other cases, biotransformation of an active compound may lead to the formation of metabolites that also have pharmacologic actions.
- A few compounds (**prodrugs**) have no activity until they undergo metabolic activation.

Drug	→	Inactive metabolite(s)
Drug	→	Active metabolite(s)
Prodrug	→	Drug

Figure 5-7. *Biotransformation of Drugs*

Biotransformation Classification

Clinical Correlate

Grapefruit Juice

Active components in grapefruit juice include furanocoumarins capable of inhibiting the metabolism of many drugs, including alprazolam, midazolam, atorvastatin, and cyclosporine. Such compounds may also enhance oral bioavailability by decreasing first-pass metabolism and inhibiting drug transporters in the GI tract responsible for intestinal efflux of drugs.

There are 2 broad types of biotransformation: phase I and phase II.

Phase I

Definition: modification of the drug molecule via oxidation, reduction, or hydrolysis.

- Microsomal metabolism

  Cytochrome P450 isozymes

  - These are major enzyme systems involved in phase I reactions. Localized in the smooth endoplastic reticulum (microsomal fraction) of cells (especially liver, but including GI tract, lungs, and kidney).
  - P450s have an absolute requirement for molecular oxygen and NADPH.
  - Oxidations include hydroxylations and dealkylations.
  - Multiple CYP families differing by amino acid (AA) composition, by substrate specificity, and by sensitivity to inhibitors and to inducing agents.

Table 5-1. Cytochrome P450 Isozymes

CYP450	Substrate Example	Inducers	Inhibitors	Genetic Polymorphisms
1A2	Theophylline Acetaminophen	Aromatic hydrocarbons (smoke) Cruciferous vegetables	Quinolones Macrolides	No
2C9	Phenytoin Warfarin	General inducers*	—	Yes
2D6	Many cardiovascular and CNS drugs	None known	Haloperidol Quinidine	Yes
3A4	60% of drugs in PDR	General inducers*	General inhibitors† Grapefruit juice	No

*General inducers: anticonvulsants (barbiturates, phenytoin, carbamazepine), antibiotics (rifampin), chronic alcohol, St. John's Wort.
†General inhibitors: antiulcer medications (cimetidine, omeprazole), antimicrobials (chloramphenicol, macrolides, ritonavir, ketoconazole), acute alcohol.

- Nonmicrosomal metabolism

  Hydrolysis
  - Phase I reaction involving addition of a water molecule with subsequent bond breakage
  - Includes esterases and amidases
  - Genetic polymorphism exists with pseudocholinesterases
  - Example: local anesthetics and succinylcholine

  Monoamine oxidases
  - Metabolism of endogenous amine neurotransmitters (dopamine, norepinephrine, and serotonin)
  - Metabolism of exogenous compounds (tyramine)

  Alcohol metabolism
  - Alcohols are metabolized to aldehydes and then to acids by dehydrogenases
  - Genetic polymorphisms exist

Phase II

Definition: Conjugation with endogenous compounds via the activity of transferases

- May follow phase I or occur directly
- Types of conjugation:

  Glucuronidation
  - Inducible
  - May undergo enterohepatic cycling (Drug: Glucuronide → intestinal bacterial glucuronidases → free drug)
  - Reduced activity in neonates
  - Examples: morphine and chloramphenicol

  Acetylation
  - Genotypic variations (fast and slow metabolizers)
  - Drug-induced SLE by slow acetylators with hydralazine > procainamide > isoniazid (INH)

  Glutathione (GSH) conjugation
  - Depletion of GSH in the liver is associated with acetaminophen hepatotoxicity

PRACTICE QUESTIONS

NAPLEX Question Reference

Pharmaceutics End of Chapter Questions

1. Which of the following best represents the principle of a pharmacophore for atenolol?

   A. The 3-dimensional shape of atenolol that makes it bind to and antagonize beta receptors

   B. The chemical cascade produced after atenolol binds to the beta-1 receptor

   C. The effect produced on the heart rate after atenolol binds to the beta-1 receptor

   D. The molecular configuration of the beta receptor

   E. Atenolol does not have a pharmacophore model since it is an antagonist

2. Codeine is best classified as which of the following?
   A. Benzodiazepine
   B. Mu receptor agonist
   C. Mu receptor antagonist
   D. Prodrug
   E. Respiratory stimulant

3. A medication that affects which of the following cytochrome enzymes will impact phenytoin blood levels?
   A. CYP1A1
   B. CYP2C9
   C. CYP2D6
   D. CYP3A4
   E. CYP3A5

4. Which of the following forms of metabolism is classified as a phase I reaction?
   A. Acetylation
   B. Amino acid conjugation
   C. Glucuronidation
   D. Methylation
   E. Oxidation

5. Hydralazine-induced systemic lupus erythematous is more likely to be seen in patients that have a:
   A. Decreased rate of acetylation
   B. Decreased rate of glucuronidation
   C. Increased rate of acetylation
   D. Increased rate of glucuronidation
   E. Increased rate of methylation

6. The enantiomer of D-Ribose is which of the following?
   A. D-Arabinose
   B. D-Glucose
   C. D-Ribose
   D. L-Arabinose
   E. L-Ribose

Answers and Explanations

1. **The correct answer is A.** A pharmacophore, according to the IUPAC is "an ensemble of steric and electronic features that is necessary to ensure the optimal supramolecular interactions with a specific biological target and to trigger (or block) its biological response" (choice E is incorrect). A pharmacophore can be defined as the drug's 3-dimensional molecular framework responsible for its biological activity.

2. **The correct answer is D.** Codeine is defined as a prodrug, itself inactive (choices B and C are incorrect), but demethylated to the active opioid (choice A is incorrect) morphine by the liver enzyme CYP2D6. The analgesic, respiratory depressant (choice E) and other pharmacological effects of codeine have been speculated to come from its conversion to morphine. Morphine is an agonist (choices B and C) at the mu, kappa and delta receptors.

3. **The correct answer is B.** Phenytoin acts by modulating neuronal voltage-dependent sodium and calcium channels. It is a substrate for both CYP2C9 and CYP2C19. Thus a medication inhibiting or inducing CYP2C9 will increase or decrease phenytoin blood levels, respectively.

4. **The correct answer is E.** There are 2 general types of drug hepatic biotransformation: Phase I and Phase II. Phase II metabolism involves a modification of the drug molecule via oxidation, reduction, or hydrolysis. Oxidations include hydroxylation and dealkylation reactions. All of the other answer choices are Phase II metabolism reactions.

5. **The correct answer is A.** Phase II drug metabolism reactions involve conjugation with endogenous compounds via the activity of transferases. Types of phase II reactions include acetylation, glucuronidation and methylation. With respect to drug-induced systemic lupus erythematous (DISLE), predisposing factors to the development of DISLE include a slow drug-acetylator phenotype and advancing patient age. Medications associated with the DISLE include hydralazine, procainamide and isoniazid. Chloramphenicol, meprobamate and morphine undergo glucuronidation. Catecholamines, niacinamide and thiouracil undergo methylation.

6. **The correct answer is E.** Enantiomers are the same sugars, but in different optical families. Thus the enantiomer of D-Ribose (choice C is incorrect) is L-Ribose (choice E is correct). Two sugars that are in the same family (both are either ketoses or aldoses, and have the same number of carbons) that are not identical and are not mirror images of each other are diastereomers. Examples of diasteromers are D-Threose and D-Erythrose. Epimers are a subtype of diastereomers and differ in configuration at exactly one chiral center. Examples include d-ribose and d-arabinose, which only differ at C-2. Pharmacologically, the antineoplastics doxorubicin and epirubicin are epimers.

Pharmacology and Toxicology 6

Learning Objectives

- ❑ Answer questions on drug mechanisms of action
- ❑ Demonstrate understanding of pharmacodynamics principles
- ❑ Discuss principles of adverse drug effects
- ❑ Categorize drug-drug interactions
- ❑ Describe drug development processes
- ❑ Show proficiency in drug toxicology

The science of pharmacology is concerned with the indications, physiologic effects, and mechanisms of drug action. A branch of pharmacology is toxicology, which examines the adverse, sometimes deadly, effects caused by drugs and other chemicals.

DRUG MECHANISMS OF ACTION

The mechanism of action (MOA) of a drug compound refers to the precise interaction by which it produces its pharmacological effect. The MOA involves the molecular targets to which the medication binds, the effect produced upon binding, and the resultant effect at a tissue and/or body system level.

> **NAPLEX Reference**
>
> **Therapeutics chapters:**
> "Mechanism of Action" portion of Drug Tables

The Review of Therapeutics section of Kaplan's *NAPLEX Strategies, Practice, and Review* book (Therapeutics chapters) covers the required high-yield drug classes. The **MOA** for each drug and/or drug class including biologics is **listed at the top of each drug table**.

A review of cellular mechanisms of action can be found in the Pharmacodynamics and Drug Interactions section of this chapter.

PHARMACODYNAMICS AND DRUG INTERACTIONS

Pharmacokinetics describes what the body does to a drug after it is administered, while **pharmacodynamics** describes what the drug does to the body (or body component) once it binds to its intended target (e.g., quantitative and qualitative drug dosing, signaling mechanisms, and steady state). Drug-drug interactions are significant in that one medication can impact the pharmacodynamics or pharmacokinetics of another medication.

Pharmacodynamic and Drug Interaction Definitions

Bridge to Biochemistry

Definitions

Affinity: how well a drug and a receptor recognize each other. Affinity is inversely related to the K_d of the drug. Notice the analogy to the K_m value used in enzyme kinetic studies.

Potency: the quantity of drug required to achieve a desired effect. In D-R measurements, the chosen effect is usually 50% of the maximal effect, but clinically, *any* size response can be sought.

Efficacy: the maximal effect an agonist can achieve at the highest practical concentration. Notice the analogy with the V_{max} used in enzyme kinetic studies.

Pharmacodynamics relates to drugs binding to receptors and their effects.

- **Agonist:** A drug is called an agonist when binding to the receptor results in a response.
- **Antagonist:** A drug is called an antagonist when binding to the receptor is *not* associated with a response. The drug has an effect only by preventing an agonist from binding to the receptor.
- **Affinity**: ability of drug to bind to receptor, shown by the proximity of the curve to the *y* axis (if the curves are parallel); the nearer the *y* axis, the greater the affinity
- **Potency**: shows relative doses of 2 or more agonists to produce the same magnitude of effect, again shown by the proximity of the respective curves to the *y* axis (if the curves do not cross)
- **Efficacy**: a measure of how well a drug produces a response (effectiveness), shown by the maximal height reached by the curve

Graded (Quantitative) Dose-Response (D-R) Curves

Plots of dose (or **log dose**) vs. response for drugs (**agonists**) that activate receptors can reveal information about affinity, potency, and efficacy of these agonists.

Parallel and Nonparallel D-R Curves

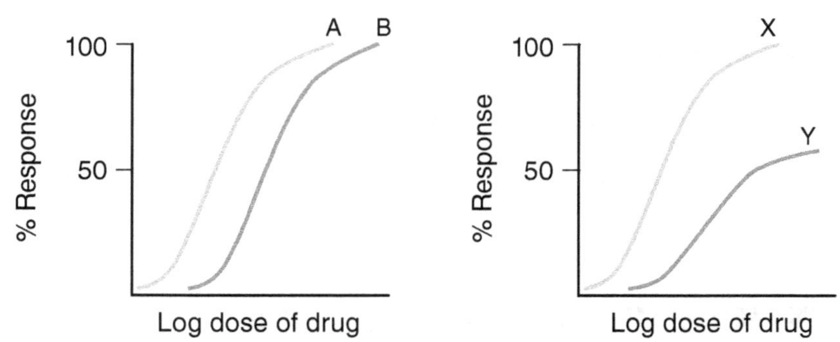

Figure 6-1. D-R Curves for 2 Drugs Acting on the Same (left) and Different (right) Receptors

It may be seen from the log dose-response curves that:

- When 2 drugs interact with the same receptor (same pharmacologic mechanism), the D-R curves will have parallel slopes. Drugs A and B have the same mechanism; drugs X and Y do not.

- Affinity can be compared only when 2 drugs bind to the same receptor. Drug A has a greater affinity than drug B.
- In terms of potency, drug A has greater potency than drug B, and X is more potent than Y.
- In terms of efficacy, drugs A and B are equivalent. Drug X has greater efficacy than drug Y.

Full and Partial Agonists

Full agonists produce a maximal response—they have maximal efficacy. **Partial agonists** are incapable of eliciting a maximal response and are less effective than full agonists. In the figure below, drug B is a full agonist, and drugs A and C are partial agonists. Drug A is more potent than drug C, and drug B is more potent than drug C.

Note that no general comparisons can be made between drugs A and B in terms of potency because the former is a partial agonist and the latter is a full agonist. At low responses, A is more potent than B, but at high responses, the reverse is true.

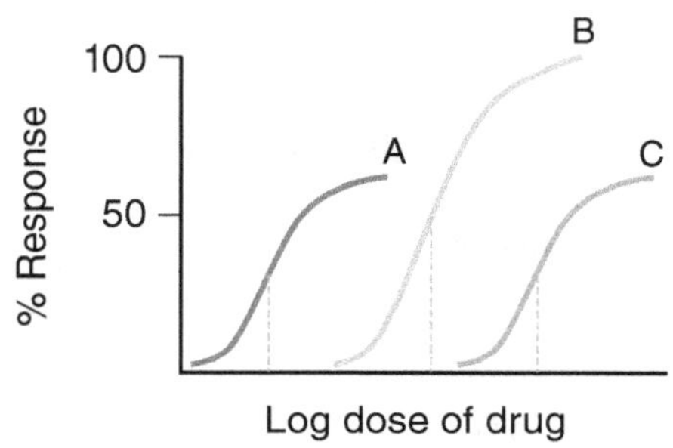

Figure 6-2. Efficacy and Potency of Full and Partial Agonists

Duality of Partial Agonists

In the figure below, the lower curve represents effects of a partial agonist when used alone—its ceiling effect = 50% of maximal in this example.

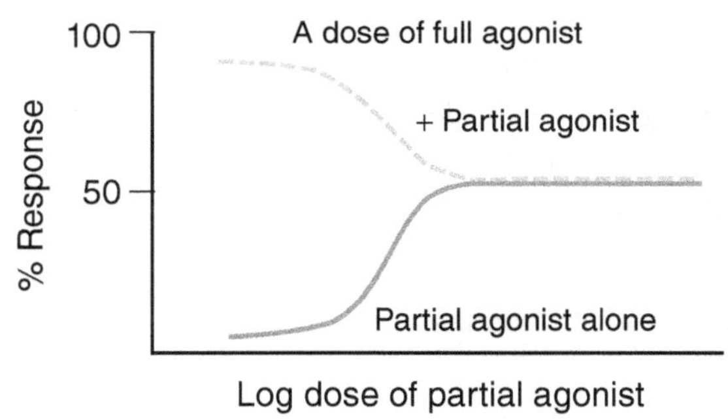

Figure 6-3. Duality of Partial Agonists

- The upper curve shows the effect of increasing doses of the partial agonist on the maximal response (100%) achieved in the presence of or by pretreatment with a full agonist.
- As the partial agonist displaces the full agonist from the receptor, the response is reduced—the partial agonist is acting as an **antagonist**.

Antagonism and Potentiation

- Graded dose-response curves also provide information about antagonists—drugs that interact with receptors to interfere with their activation by agonists.

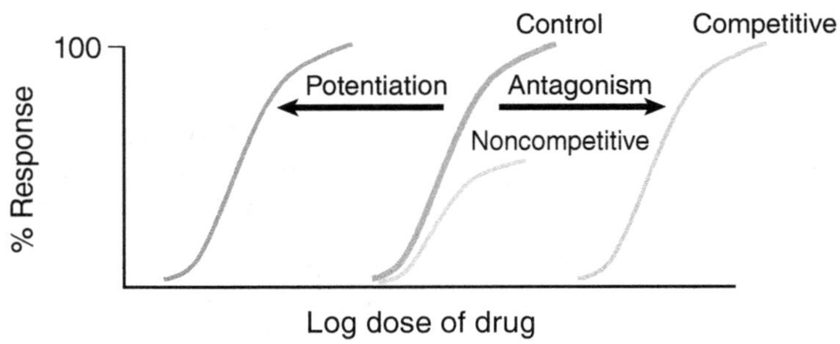

Figure 6-4. D-R Curves of Antagonists and Potentiators

Bridge to Biochemistry

Parallels between Receptor Antagonists and Enzyme Inhibitors

Competitive antagonists are analogous to competitive inhibitors; they decrease affinity (↑ K_m) but not maximal response (V_{max} remains the same).

Noncompetitive antagonists decrease V_{max} but do not change the K_m.

- Pharmacologic antagonism (same receptor)
  - Competitive antagonists:
    - Cause a parallel shift to the right in the D-R curve for agonists
    - Can be reversed by ↑ the dose of the agonist drug
    - Appears to ↓ the potency of the agonist
  - Noncompetitive antagonists:
    - Cause a nonparallel shift to the right
    - Can be only partially reversed by ↑ the dose of the agonist
    - Appear to ↓ the efficacy of the agonist
- Physiologic antagonism (different receptor)
  - Two agonists with opposing action antagonize each other
  - Example: a vasoconstrictor with a vasodilator
- Chemical antagonism:
  - Formation of a complex between effector drug and another compound
  - Example: protamine binds to heparin to reverse its actions
- Potentiation
  - Causes a parallel shift to the left to the D-R curve
  - Appears to ↑ the potency of the agonist

Quantal (Cumulative) D-R Curves

Quantal D-R curves plot the percentage of a population responding to a specified drug effect versus dose or log dose. They permit estimations of the median effective dose, or effective dose in 50% of a population—ED50. Quantal curves can reveal the range of intersubject variability in drug response. Steep D-R curves reflect little variability; flat D-R curves indicate great variability in patient sensitivity to the effects of a drug.

Toxicity and the Therapeutic Index (TI)

Comparisons between ED50 and TD50 values permit evaluation of the relative safety of a drug (the therapeutic index), as would comparison between ED50 and the lethal median dose (LD50) if the latter is known.

$$TI = \frac{TD50}{ED50} \text{ or } \frac{LD50}{ED50}$$

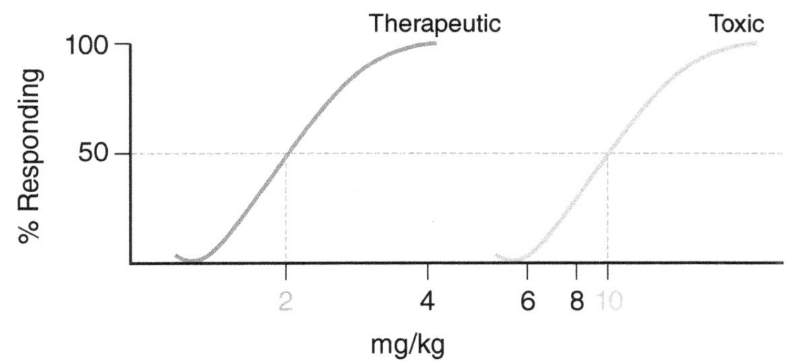

Figure 6-5. Quantal D-R Curves of Therapeutic and Toxic Effects of a Drug

D-R curves can also show the relationship between dose and toxic effects of a drug. The median toxic dose of a drug (TD50) is the dose which causes toxicity in 50% of a population. From the data shown, $TI = \frac{10}{2} = 5$. Such indices are of most value when toxicity represents an extension of the pharmacologic actions of a drug. They do not predict idiosyncratic reactions or drug hypersensitivity.

Signaling Mechanisms: Types of Drug-Responsive Signaling Mechanisms

Binding of an agonist drug to its receptor activates an effector or signaling mechanism. Several types of drug-responsive signaling mechanisms are known.

Intracellular Receptors

- These include receptors for steroids. Binding of hormones or drugs to such receptors releases regulatory proteins that permit activation and in some cases dimerization of the hormone-receptor complex. Such complexes translocate to the nucleus, where they interact with response elements in spacer DNA. This interaction leads to changes in gene expression. For example, drugs interacting with glucocorticoid receptors lead to gene expression of proteins that inhibit the production of inflammatory mediators.
- Other examples include intracellular receptors for thyroid hormones, gonadal steroids, and vitamin D.
- Pharmacologic responses elicited via modification of gene expression are usually slower in onset but longer in duration than many other drugs.

Membrane Receptors Directly Coupled to Ion Channels

- Many drugs act by mimicking or antagonizing the actions of endogenous ligands that regulate flow of ions through excitable membranes via their activation of receptors that are directly coupled (no second messengers) to ion channels.
- For example, the nicotinic receptor for ACh (present in autonomic nervous system [ANS] ganglia, the skeletal myoneural junction, and the central nervous system [CNS]) is coupled to a Na^+/K^+ ion channel.

The receptor is a target for many drugs, including nicotine, choline esters, ganglion blockers, and skeletal muscle relaxants.

- Similarly, the GABAA receptor in the CNS, which is coupled to a chloride ion channel, can be modulated by anticonvulsants, benzodiazepines, and barbiturates.

Receptors Linked Via Coupling Proteins to Intracellular Effectors

- Many receptor systems are coupled via GTP-binding proteins (G-proteins) to adenylyl cyclase, the enzyme that converts ATP to cAMP, a second messenger that promotes protein phosphorylation by activating protein kinase A. These receptors are typically "serpentine," with 7 transmembrane spanning domains, the third of which is coupled to the G-protein effector mechanism.
- Protein kinase A serves to phosphorylate a set of tissue-specific substrate enzymes or transcription factors (CREB), thereby affecting their activity.

In a Nutshell

Key ANS Receptors

M_1, M_3, α_1: G_q activation of phospholipase C

M_2, α_2, D_2: G_i inhibition of adenylyl cyclase

β_1, β_2, D_1: G_s activation of adenylyl cyclase

G_s Proteins

- Binding of agonists to receptors linked to G_s proteins increases cAMP production.
- Such receptors include those for catecholamines (beta), dopamine (D_1), glucagon, histamine (H_2), prostacyclin, and some serotonin subtypes.

G_i Proteins

- Binding of agonists to receptors linked to G_i proteins decreases cAMP production.
- Such receptors include adrenoreceptors ($alpha_2$), ACh (M_2), dopamine (D_2 subtypes), and several opioid and serotonin subtypes.

G_q Proteins

- Other receptor systems are coupled via GTP-binding proteins (G_q), which activate phospholipase C. Activation of this enzyme releases the second messengers inositol triphosphate (IP_3) and diacylglycerol (DAG) from the membrane phospholipid phosphatidylinositol bisphosphate (PIP_2). The IP_3 induces release of Ca^{2+} from the sarcoplasmic reticulum (SR), which, together with DAG, activates protein kinase C. The protein kinase C serves then to phosphorylate a set of tissue-specific substrate enzymes, usually not phosphorylated by protein kinase A, and thereby affects their activity.
- These signaling mechanisms are invoked following activation of receptors for ACh (M_1 and M_3), norepinephrine ($alpha_1$), angiotensin II, and several serotonin subtypes.

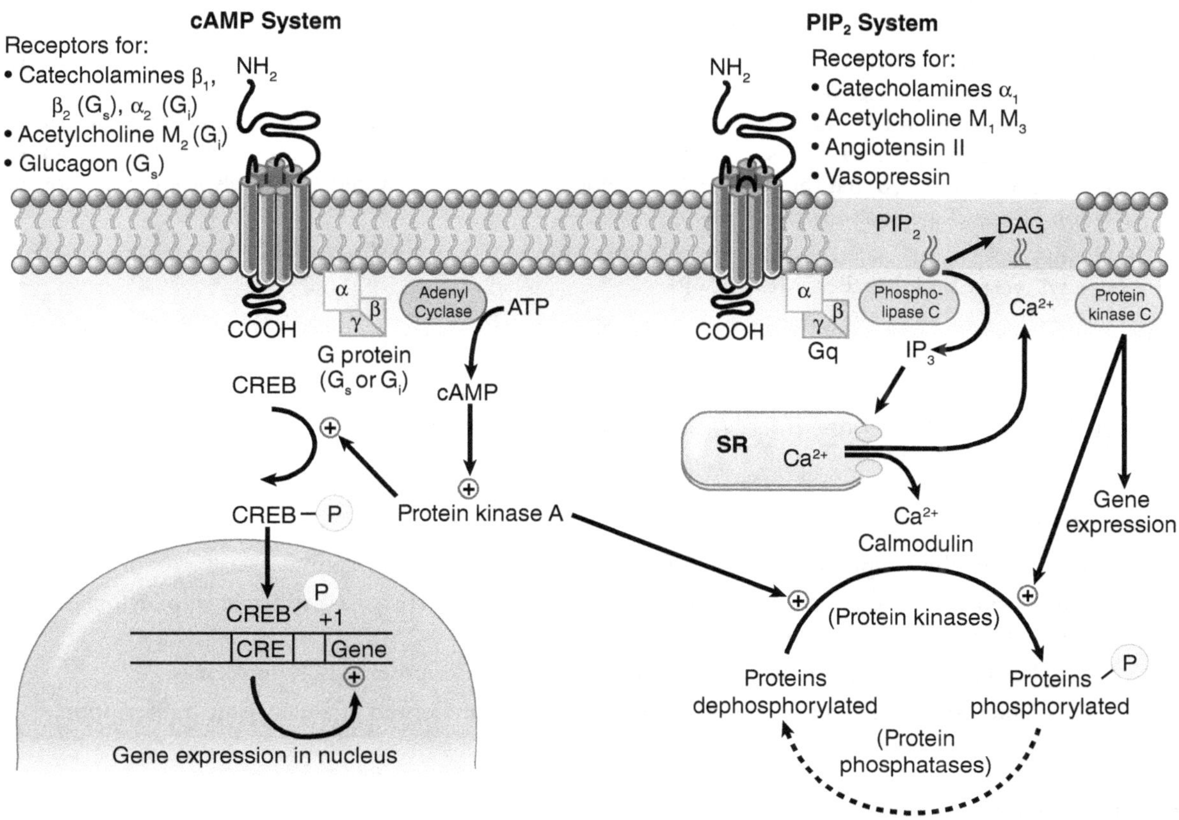

Figure 6-6. Receptors Using Cyclic AMP and IP_3, DAG, Ca^{2+} as Second Messengers

Cyclic GMP and Nitric Oxide Signaling

- cGMP is a second messenger in vascular smooth muscle that facilitates dephosphorylation of myosin light chains, preventing their interaction with actin and thus causing vasodilation.
- Nitric oxide (NO) is synthesized in endothelial cells and diffuses into smooth muscle.
- NO activates guanylyl cyclase, thus increasing cGMP in smooth muscle.
- Vasodilators ↑ synthesis of NO by endothelial cells.

Clinical Correlate

Drugs acting via NO include nitrates (e.g., nitroglycerin) and M-receptor agonists (e.g., bethanechol). Endogenous compounds acting via NO include bradykinin and histamine.

Receptors That Function as Enzymes or Transporters

- There are multiple examples of drug action that depend on enzyme inhibition, including inhibitors of acetylcholinesterase, angiotensin-converting enzyme, aspartate protease, carbonic anhydrase, cyclooxygenases, dihydrofolate reductase, DNA/RNA polymerases, monoamine oxidases, Na^+/K^+-ATPase, neuraminidase, and reverse transcriptase.
- Examples of drug action on transporter systems include the inhibitors of reuptake of several neurotransmitters, including dopamine, GABA, norepinephrine, and serotonin.

Receptors That Function as Transmembrane Enzymes

- These receptors mediate the first steps in signaling by insulin and growth factors, including epidermal growth factor (EGF) and platelet-derived growth factor (PDGF). They are membrane-spanning macromolecules with recognition sites for the binding of insulin and growth factors located externally and a cytoplasmic domain that usually functions as a tyrosine kinase. Binding of the ligand causes conformational changes (e.g., dimerization) so that the tyrosine kinase domains become activated, ultimately leading to phosphorylation of tissue-specific substrate proteins.
- Guanyl cyclase–associated receptors: stimulation of receptors to atrial natriuretic peptide activates the guanyl cyclase and ↑ cyclic GMP (cGMP)

Clinical Correlate

Imatinib is a specific tyrosine-kinase (TK) inhibitor, while sorafenib is a non-specific TK inhibitor.

Receptors for Cytokines

- These include the receptors for erythropoietin, somatotropin, and interferons.
- Their receptors are membrane spanning and on activation can activate a distinctive set of cytoplasmic tyrosine kinases (Janus kinases [JAKs]).
- JAKs phosphorylate signal transducers and activators of transcription (STAT) molecules.
- STATs dimerize and then dissociate, cross the nuclear membrane, and modulate gene transcription.

Steady State

- Steady state is reached either when **rate in** = **rate out** or when values associated with a dosing interval are the same as those in the succeeding interval.

Plateau Principle

Note

$$MD = \frac{C^{ss} \times Cl \times \tau}{f}$$

See legend on page 16.

Classic Clues

Time and Steady State

50% = 1 × half-life

90% = 3.3 × half-life

95% = 4–5 × half-life

"100"% = >7 × half-life

The time to reach steady state is dependent only on the elimination half-life of a drug and is independent of dose size and frequency of administration, assuming the drug is eliminated by first-order kinetics.

The following figure shows plasma levels (solid lines) achieved following the IV bolus administration of 100 units of a drug at intervals equivalent to every **half-life $t_{1/2}$= 4 h (τ)**. With such intermittent dosing, plasma levels oscillate through peaks and troughs, with averages shown in the diagram by the dashed line.

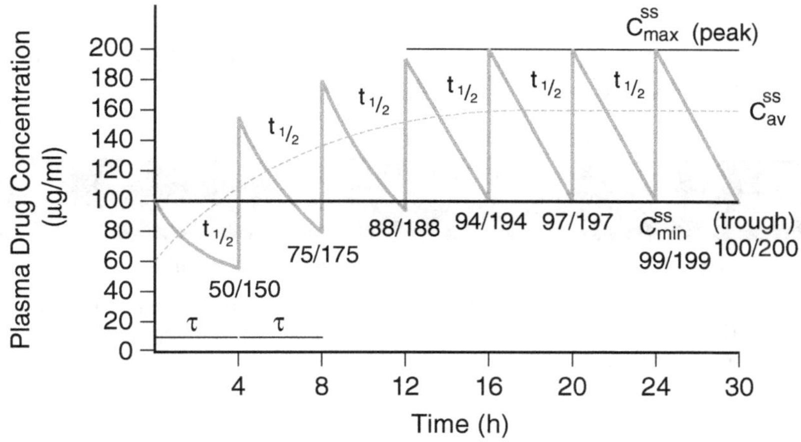

Figure 6-7. Oscillations in Plasma Levels following IV Bolus Administration at Intervals Equal to Drug Half-Life

Note: Although it takes >7 $t_{1/2}$ to reach **mathematical** steady state, by convention **clinical** steady state is accepted to be reached at 4–5 $t_{1/2}$.

Introduction to Drug-Drug Interactions

A drug-drug interaction occurs when one medication affects the pharmacodynamic or pharmacokinetic properties of another medication. More simply stated, a drug-drug interaction affects the adverse effect profile or therapeutic impact of one or more medications.

Drug interactions can be described as:

- Pharmacokinetic: Resulting in alterations in the absorption, distribution, metabolism, and excretion (ADME) of a drug.
- Pharmacodynamic: Resulting in an extension or antagonism of a drug's therapeutic effect. For example, the co-administration of a receptor antagonist and an agonist for the same receptor.
- Synergistic: The interaction causes an increase in the effects of one or both of the drugs. The resulting therapeutic effects are much greater than the sum of the 2 individual effects produced by each agent.
- Antagonistic: The interaction causes a decrease in the therapeutic effect of one or both of the drugs.

The Review of Therapeutics Section of the Kaplan's *NAPLEX Strategies, Practice, and Review* book (Therapeutics chapters) covers the required high-yield drug classes. High-yield **drug-drug interactions** for each individual drug and/or drug class including biologics are **listed in each drug table**.

NAPLEX Reference

Therapeutics chapters:

"Drug-Drug Interactions" portion of Drug Tables

ADVERSE DRUG EFFECTS

Adverse drug effects (ADEs) are defined as any injury (injuries) resulting from medication use and include varying degrees of physical harm, mental harm, or loss of physiological function. ADEs encompass the largest single category of ALL adverse events experienced by hospitalized patients, for example. The appearance of ADEs is associated with increased morbidity and mortality, prolonged hospitalizations, decreased medication adherence, and overall higher costs of patient care.

Drug reactions can be categorized into immunologic and nonimmunologic reactions with the majority (75 to 80 percent) of all ADEs being classified as predictable, nonimmunologic reactions. The remaining 20 to 25 percent of ADEs are classified as unpredictable effects that may or may not be immune mediated. Immune-mediated ADEs account for 5 to 10 percent of all drug reactions. Immunologic AEDs are also known as drug hypersensitivity reactions.

You should be familiar with each type of immune-mediated ADE and the proposed mechanism of tissue injury, as well as examples of nonimmunologic predictable and unpredictable ADEs.

Table 6-1. Hypersensitivity Reactions

Type of Hypersensitivity	Immune Mechanisms	Mechanisms of Tissue Injury
Immediate (type I)	Activation of Th2 cells resulting in the production of IgE which in turn binds to FcεR on mast cells, basophils and eosinophils	**Immediate reaction** Degranulation and release of vasoactive amines (i.e. histamine) and proteases. Examples • Anaphylaxis to beta-lactam antibiotics, sulfonamides and salicylates. **Late-phase reaction** Synthesis and secretion of prostaglandins and leukotrienes Cytokine-induced inflammation and leukocyte recruitment
Antibody-mediated (type II)	IgM and IgG against surface (cell surface or extracellular matrix)	**Complement-mediated (cytotoxic)** Opsonization and enhances phagocytosis Recruitment and activation of inflammatory cells Example • Hemolytic anemia from penicillin **Non-cytotoxic** Change in physiologic behavior of a cell
Immune complex–mediated (type III)	Deposition of immune complexes comprised of IgM or IgG and soluble antigen	Complement-mediated recruitment and activation of inflammatory cells resulting in some combination of arthritis, vasculitis or nephritis. Examples: • Lupus-like syndrome (hydralazine, procainamide) • Stevens-Johnson Syndrome (sulfonamides, anticonvulsants) • Serum Sickness (cefaclor)
Delayed-type hypersensitivity (type IV)	Inflammatory cytokines, IFN-g and IL-17, produced by CD4+ Th1 and Th17 cells, respectively.	**Cytokine-mediated tissue damage** IFN-g activation of macrophage IL-17 recruitment and activation of neutrophil **Direct killing** CTL-mediated cellular death

Table 6-2. Nonimmunologic Predictable ADEs

Nonimmunologic Predictable ADEs	
Pharmacologic side effect	Dry mouth from antihistamines; bradycardia from beta blocker
Secondary pharmacologic side effect	Thrush or vaginal candidiasis while taking antibiotics
Drug toxicity	Hepatotoxicity from methotrexate; agranulocytosis with clozapine
Drug-drug interactions	Bleeding from warfarin while taking clarithromycin or ciprofloxacin
Drug overdose	Respiratory depression with opioids or benzodiazepines
Nonimmunologic Unpredictable ADEs	
Pseudoallergic	Anaphylactoid reaction after radiocontrast media
Idiosyncratic	Hemolytic anemia in a patient with G6PD deficiency after primaquine therapy
Intolerance	Tinnitus after a single, small dose of aspirin

The Review of Therapeutics Section of Kaplan's *NAPLEX Strategies, Practice, and Review* book (Therapeutics chapters) covers the required high-yield drug classes. High-yield **adverse effects** for each individual drug and/or drug class including biologics are **listed in each drug table.**

NAPLEX Reference

Therapeutics chapters: "Adverse Reactions" portion of Drug Tables

DRUG DEVELOPMENT

According the U.S. FDA, "American consumers benefit from having access to the safest and most advanced pharmaceutical system in the world." The responsibility of fulfilling this promise to the American public lies on the FDA's Center for Drug Evaluation and Research (CDER).

NAPLEX Reference

Health Policy chapter:

"FDA Regulatory Process"

CDER's most widely known responsibility is to evaluate new drugs (via clinical trials) before they can be administered and later sold to the American consumer. CDER's evaluation not only prevents illegitimate and/or unsubstantiated claims (quackery), but also provides physicians and patients the information needed to safely and effectively prescribe and consume medications. CDER also ensures that ALL FDA-approved medications (brand-name and generic) work as intended and that their health benefits outweigh their known risks. Note: CDER also ensures that these "known risks" are appropriately presented to the American public.

CDER's primary mission is to guarantee that ALL drugs marketed in the United States (prescription and nonprescription) are safe and effective. CDER does not test drugs, although the Center's Office of Testing and Research does conduct limited research in the areas of drug quality, safety, and effectiveness.

Many drug companies submit a new drug application (NDA) to initially introduce a new drug product into the U.S. market. It is the responsibility of the company seeking to market a drug to test it through a series of clinical trial phases (See NAPLEX reference for more information) and submit evidence that it is safe and effective. A team of CDER physicians, statisticians, chemists, pharmacologists, and other scientists reviews the sponsor's NDA containing the data and proposed labeling.

DRUG TOXICOLOGY

Toxicology is defined as the study of drugs, chemicals, and poisons and the effects these compounds have on the performance and health of the

NAPLEX Reference

Antidotes chapter:

"Antidotes"

"General Antidotes"

consumer. There are a number of factors that can contribute to the development of drug toxicity, including drug distribution and quantity ingested.

Drug distribution throughout the body is based upon many factors, including the physical and chemical properties of the drug, drug formulation, method of ingestion (intravenous, inhalation, etc.), and the digestive (for oral ingestion) and circulatory functions of the patient. Normal (therapeutic) doses of drugs are those amounts which are prescribed for an intended therapeutic purpose. Thus, in patients with normal hepatic and renal function, properly calculated medication doses generally result in predictable therapeutic and adverse effects.

Non-therapeutic drug ingestion can occur when medications (for example) are ingested in large amounts, leading to supra-therapeutic concentrations and subsequent toxicity. Conversely, drugs ingested at low doses generally result in subtherapeutic concentrations and produce little to no therapeutic effect.

Non-therapeutic drug ingestion may also include administration in a manner or frequency not prescribed by the physician. This may include multiple drug combinations (drinking alcohol with opiates), repeated or excessive ingestion, and subversion of the formulation. An example of the latter is where a drug (i.e. opiate or amphetamine) formulated for oral, sustained release is used illicitly by crushing, dissolving, "snorting," or injecting it intravenously.

The final form of non-therapeutic drug/compound ingestion occurs unexpectedly when a biological, chemical, or toxin is released into a specified environment. You should be familiar with selected clinical findings related to chemical, toxin and biological agents.

Table 6-3. Common Clinical Findings for Chemicals, Toxins, and Biological Agents

Clinical Characteristic	Biologic Agents	Chemical Agent	Toxins
Timing of symptoms	Delayed (days to weeks)	Often rapid onset (minutes to days)*	Delayed (hours to days)
Multiple simultaneous victims with similar symptoms in a concentrated geographic area	Less likely, dispersion of victims is more likely	Common	Common
Respiratory distress	Common	Common	Common
Rash	Common	No	Rare
Vesicles	Depends on biological agent	Sulfur mustard, Lewisite	T-2 exposure only
Neuromuscular effects (i.e. seizures, weakness)	Generally No	Cyanide or nerve agents	Yes with Botulinum exposure
Fever	Yes	No	No
Failure to respond to typical therapy	Yes (multi-antibiotic resistant organisms)	Depends upon extent and severity of exposure	Depends upon severity of exposure

Irrespective of the etiology of the toxic syndrome, interpretation of toxicological results generally begins with an understanding of which drugs and drug concentrations are therapeutic and which are not.

Forensic (post-mortem) toxicology testing is generally conducted by a laboratory for medico-legal purposes, which may include cause of death and/or criminal investigations. The results, which are often considered evidence, may be subject to use in a court of law. Typical drugs and substances that may undergo toxicology screening for a forensic toxicology report include:

- Volatiles (i.e. ethanol, acetone, methanol, toluene)
- Illicit drugs (i.e. heroin, cocaine, PCP, methamphetamine)
- Prescription drugs (i.e. benzodiazepines, opiates, amphetamines, barbiturates)
- Over-the-counter substances (i.e. dextromethorphan, ibuprofen, acetaminophen)
- Drug metabolites (break-down products of drugs)

Common Toxic Syndromes

Table 6-4. Signs, Symptoms, and Interventions or Antidotes for Common Toxic Syndromes

Compound(s)	Signs and Symptoms	Interventions and Antidotes
AChE inhibitors	Miosis, salivation, sweats, GI cramps, diarrhea, muscle twitches → seizures, coma, respiration failure	Respiratory support; atropine + pralidoxime (for irreversible AChE inhibitors)
Atropine and muscarinic blockers	↑ HR, ↑ BP, hyperthermia (hot, dry skin), delirium, hallucinations, mydriasis	Control cardiovascular symptoms and hyperthermia + physostigmine (crosses blood–brain barrier)
Carbon monoxide (>10% carboxyHb)	Nausea and vomiting, dyspnea with hyperventilation, mydriasis, vertigo; cardiovascular signs prominent, ↓ BP, syncope, ↑ HR, arrhythmias	Hyperbaric O_2 and decontamination (humidified 100% O_2 okay in mild overdose)
CNS stimulants	Anxiety/agitation, hyperthermia (warm, sweaty skin), mydriasis, ↑ HR, ↑ BP, psychosis, seizures	Control cardiovascular symptoms, hyperthermia, and seizures— +/– BZs or antipsychotics
Opioid analgesics	Lethargy, sedation, ↓ HR, ↓ BP, hypoventilation, miosis, coma, respiration failure	Ventilatory support; naloxone at frequent intervals
Salicylates (ASA)*	Confusion, lethargy, hyperventilation, hyperthermia, dehydration, hypokalemia, acidosis, seizures, coma	Correct acidosis and electrolytes—urinary alkalinization, possible hemodialysis
Sedative-hypnotics and ethanol	Disinhibition (initial), lethargy, ataxia, nystagmus, stupor, coma, hypothermia, respiratory failure	Ventilatory support—flumazenil if BZs implicated
SSRIs	Agitation, confusion, hallucination, muscle rigidity, hyperthermia, ↑ HR, ↑ BP, seizures	Control hyperthermia and seizures—possible use of cyproheptadine, antipsychotics, and BZs
Tricyclic antidepressants	Mydriasis, hyperthermia (hot, dry skin), 3 Cs (convulsions, coma, and cardiotoxicity) → arrhythmias	Control seizures and hyperthermia, correct acidosis and possible arrhythmias

*More details in antiinflammatory section

Heavy Metal Poisoning

Signs and symptoms are distinctive, but usually result from inhibition of –SH groups on enzymes and regulatory proteins.

Table 6-5. Signs, Symptoms, and Interventions or Antidotes for Heavy Metal Poisoning

Metals and Source	Signs and Symptoms	Interventions and Antidotes
Arsenic (wood preservatives, pesticides, ant poisons)	*Acute:* gastroenteritis, hypotension, metabolic acidosis, garlic breath, "rice water" stools, torsades, seizures *Chronic:* pallor, skin pigmentation (raindrop pattern), alopecia, stocking glove neuropathy, myelosuppression	Activated charcoal, **dimercaprol** **Penicillamine** or succimer
Iron (medicinal for anemias and prenatal supplements)	*Acute* (mainly children): severe GI distress → necrotizing gastroenteritis with hematemesis and bloody diarrhea, dyspnea, shock, coma	Gastric aspiration + carbonate lavage, **deferoxamine** IV
Lead (tap water, leaded paint chips, herbal remedies, gas sniffing, glazed kitchenware, etc.)	*Acute:* nausea and vomiting, GI distress and pain, malaise, tremor, tinnitus, paresthesias, encephalopathy (red or black feces) *Chronic:* multisystem effects—anemia (↓ heme synthesis), neuropathy (wrist drop), nephropathy (proteinuria, failure), hepatitis, mental retardation (from pica), ↓ fertility and ↑ stillbirths	Decontamination—gastric lavage + **dimercaprol** (severe) or EDTA or succimer (penicillamine if unable to use dimercaprol or succimer) Children: **succimer** PO
Mercury (elemental in instruments); salts used in amalgams, batteries, dyes, electroplating, fireworks, photography	*Acute:* vapor inhalation—chest pain, dyspnea, pneumonitis *Acute:* inorganic salt ingestion—hemorrhagic gastroenteritis, acute tubular necrosis, shock *Chronic:* organic Hg—CNS effects, ataxia, paresthesias, auditory and visual loss, loosening of teeth	**Succimer** PO or **dimercaprol (IM)** Activated charcoal for oral ingestion, then support with succimer PO or dimercaprol (*not* IV)→ causes redistribution of Hg to the CNS →↑ neurotoxicity

Antidotes

Table 6-6. Summary of Antidotes

Antidote	Type of Poisoning
Acetylcysteine	Acetaminophen
Atropine + pralidoxime (for irreversible AChE inhibitors)	AChE inhibitors—physostigmine, neostigmine, and pyridostigmine; organophosphates, including insecticides, such as malathion and parathion
Deferoxamine	Iron and iron salts
Digoxin immune F(ab)	Digoxin
Dimercaprol (BAL)	Arsenic, gold, mercury, lead; oral succimer for milder lead and mercury toxicity
EDTA	Backup in lead poisoning, then for rarer toxicities (Cd, Cr, Co, Mn, Zn)
Esmolol	Theophylline, beta agonists
Ethanol, fomepizole	Methanol or ethylene glycol

(Continued)

Antidote	Type of Poisoning
Flumazenil	Benzodiazepines, zolpidem, zaleplon
Naloxone	Opioid analgesics
Oxygen	Carbon monoxide
Penicillamine	Copper (e.g., Wilson's disease), iron, lead, mercury
Physostigmine	Anticholinergics: atropine, antihistamine, antiparkinsonian—*not* tricyclics
Protamine	Heparins
Vitamin K	Warfarin and coumarin anticoagulants
Activated charcoal	Nonspecific: all oral poisonings except Fe, CN, Li, solvents, mineral acids, or corrosives

PRACTICE QUESTIONS

NAPLEX Question Reference

Health Policy End of Chapter Questions

NAPLEX Question Reference

Antidotes End of Chapter Questions

1. A patient currently receiving morphine is administered buprenorphine; the most likely effect is which of the following?

   A. Additive effects
   B. Competitive antagonism
   C. No impact
   D. Noncompetitive antagonism
   E. Synergy

2. An IV infusion of a drug is started at 200 mg/h. If the drug's clearance = 30 L/h, what is the approximate plasma level at steady state?

   A. 3.34 mg/L
   B. 6.67 mg/L
   C. 13.3 mg/L
   D. 600 mg/L
   E. 6000 mg/L

3. The combination of metolazone and furosemide is best described as which of the following?

   A. Additive effect
   B. Pharmacodynamic antagonism
   C. Pharmacokinetic antagonism
   D. Synergistic
   E. There is no interaction

4. A patient develops hemolytic anemia after being administered penicillin. This reaction is best characterized what type of hypersensitivity?

    A. I
    B. II (cytotoxic)
    C. II (noncytotoxic)
    D. III
    E. IV

5. A 3-year-old child is brought to the emergency department (ED) after eating his mother's ferrous sulfate tablets. In the ED, the child throws up blood. The treatment of choice for this patient is which of the following?

    A. Dimecaprol
    B. Deferoxamine
    C. Naloxone
    D. N-acetylcysteine
    E. Penicillamine

6. With respect to a patient's heart rate, the administration of atropine to a patient currently receiving atenolol would best be termed as which of the following?

    A. Additive effects
    B. Chemical antagonism
    C. No impact
    D. Physiological antagonism
    E. Synergy

7. A 27-year-old female tries to commit suicide by ingesting 45 tablets of Percocet® and 45 tablets of Valium®. Following an attempted gastric lavage, how many antidotes should be administered?

    A. 1
    B. 2
    C. 3
    D. 4
    E. 5

Answers and Explanations

1. **The correct answer is B.** Morphine is a full agonist and buprenorphine is a partial agonist at the mu receptor. Partial agonists (i.e. buprenorphine) bind to and activate a given receptor (i.e. mu receptor), but have only partial efficacy at the receptor relative to a full agonist (i.e. morphine). When a full agonist and partial agonist are administered together, the partial agonist actually acts as a competitive antagonist. The partial agonist is competing with the full agonist for the receptor. The net result is a decrease in the receptor activation normally seen with full agonist alone (choice B is correct and choices A, C and E are incorrect). Noncompetitive antagonists (choice D) decrease the efficacy of the agonist and can only be partially reversed by increasing the dose of the agonist.

2. **The correct answer is B.** We can use the following equation: Maintenance dose (MD) = Clearance (CL) X Concentration at Steady State (Css) X dosing interval (T). Note that since it is a constant IV infusion, you do not need to consider the dosing interval. Thus, Css = MD/CL or Css = 200 mg/hr / 30 L/h = 6.67 mg/L.

3. **The correct answer is D.** Metolazone is a thiazide diuretic that acts in the proximal convoluted tubule and furosemide is a loop diuretic that acts in the loop of Henle. The combination of these 2 diuretics will produce an effect that is greater than the individual effects of both agents combined; hence, the combination of the 2 is best termed synergy (choice D) and not additive (choice A). Pharmacodynamic antagonism (choice B) results in an antagonistic therapeutic effect for the agonist at the same receptor. An example would be administering propranolol and albuterol to an asthmatic patient. Pharmacokinetic antagonism (choice C) affects the ADME characteristics of a drug.

4. **The correct answer is B.** Type II hypersensitivity reactions are classified as being cytotoxic (i.e. Hemolytic anemia from penicillin and rheumatic fever) and noncytotoxic (Grave's disease, myasthenia gravis - choice C). These reactions are antibody-mediated reactions where antibodies against the cell surface or extracellular matrix antigens cause diseases that are specific to the tissues where those antigens are present. Type I (choice C) hypersensitivity (anaphylactic) reactions occur within a few minutes following the reintroduction of an allergen, such as beta-lactam antibiotics, macrolides, sulfonamides and aspirin. It is caused by the degranulation and release of vasoactive amines (i.e. histamine) and proteases. Type III (choice D) or immune complex hypersensitivity (i.e. serum sickness, SLE) occurs when an immune complex causes systemic-wide complement activation. Type IV (choice E) or T-cell mediated hypersensitivity is a delayed-type reaction and can be seen with the tuberculin skin test, contact dermatitis and Hashimoto thyroiditis.

5. **The correct answer is B.** Ferrous sulfate (Iron) is administered to pregnant women. Normally this medication is found in blister packs to prevent poisoning; however, the mother may have removed the tablets from the blister pack. Deferoxamine chelates iron and is the antidote for iron poisoning. Dimercaprol (choice A) is used to treat lead, arsenic, and/or mercury toxicity. Naloxone (choice C) is used in opioid overdoses. N-acetylcysteine (choice D) is used in acetaminophen overdoses. Penicillamine (choice E) is used in copper poisoning and Wilson's disease.

6. **The correct answer is D.** Physiologic antagonism is where 2 drugs act at different receptors and the effects produced antagonize one another. In this case, atropine (a muscarinic antagonist) will increase heart rate in a patient currently receiving atenolol (beta-1 receptor antagonist) to decrease their heart rate. Both medications bind to different receptors; hence, they are termed physiological antagonists (choices A, C and E are incorrect). Chemical antagonists (choice B) impact the pharmacodynamics of one another to decrease the final blood level of the drug (i.e. protamine binds to heparin to reverse its action).

7. **The correct answer is C.** Percocet® is the brand name product that contains the opioid oxycodone and the analgesic acetaminophen. Valium® is the brand name product that contains the benzodiazepine diazepam. Each of these 3 medications has an antidote: oxycodone's antidote is naloxone; acetaminophen's antidote is N-acetylcysteine and diazepam's antidote is flumazenil.

Pharmacognosy and Dietary Supplements 7

Learning Objectives

- ❏ Discuss natural product principles
- ❏ Differentiate the natural product drug classes
- ❏ Demonstrate understanding of dietary supplements

The American Society of Pharmacognosy defines pharmacognosy as "the study of the physical, chemical, biochemical, and biological properties of drugs, drug substances, or potential drugs or drug substances of natural origin as well as the search for new drugs from natural sources." Although this is a relatively recent definition, the use of plant medicine predates written human history. However, since history has been recorded, the medicinal benefits of plants are well documented.

It is known today that many compounds derived from plants produce pharmacological effects through some of the same processes as existing medications. Thus, herbal and natural products can produce beneficial therapeutic effects. However, they also can produce harmful side effects. These same concepts can also be applied to dietary supplements.

With herbal medications and dietary supplements being used more frequently by the general population, it is essential to understand the benefits and risks of these medicinal compounds.

NATURAL PRODUCT PRINCIPLES AND DRUG CLASSES

"Natural" medicinals are available without prescription and are considered to be nutritional supplements rather than drugs. Herbal (botanic) products are marketed without FDA review of safety and efficacy, and there are no requirements governing the purity or the chemical identities of constituents. Evidence supporting the clinical effectiveness of herbal products is commonly incomplete.

The following tables summarize the characteristics of selected herbal medications and the most common purified nutritional supplements.

NAPLEX Reference

There is a more comprehensive review of natural/herbal products in Kaplan's *NAPLEX Strategies, Practice, and Review* book.

Over-the-Counter Medications chapter: "Common Herbals and Supplements"

Table 7-1. Characteristics of Selected Herbals

Name	Medicinal Use(s)	Possible Mechanism(s)	Side Effects
Echinacea	↓ Cold symptoms	↑ ILs and TNF	GI distress, dizziness, headache
Garlic	Hyperlipidemias, cancer (evidence is weak)	Inhibits HMG-CoA reductase and ACE	Allergies, hypotension, antiplatelet actions; use caution when used with anticoagulants
Gingko	Intermittent claudication; Alzheimer's disease (evidence is weak)	Antioxidant, free radical scavenger, ↑ NO	Anxiety, GI distress, insomnia, antiplatelet actions; **use caution when used with anticoagulants**
Ginseng	Possible ↑ in mental and physical performance (evidence is weak)	Unknown	Insomnia, nervousness, hypertension, mastalgia, vaginal bleeding
Saw palmetto	Symptomatic treatment of BPH	5α-reductase inhibitor and androgen receptor antagonist	GI pain, decreased libido, headache, hypertension
St. John's wort	Depressive disorder (variable evidence for clinical efficacy)	May enhance brain 5HT functions	Major drug interactions: **serotonin syndrome** with SSRIs; induces P450, leading to ↓effects of multiple drugs

Table 7-2. Purified Nutritional Supplements

Name	Pharmacology	Side Effects
Dehydroepiandrosterone (DHEA)	Androgen precursor advocated for treatment of AIDS (↑CD4 in females), Alzheimer's disease and "aging," diabetes, hypercholesterolemia, and SLE (↓in symptoms and "flare-ups" in females)	*Females:* androgenization and concern regarding CV disease and breast cancer *Males:* feminization in young and concern in elderly regarding BPH and cancer
Melatonin	Serotonin metabolite used for "jet-lag" and sleep disorders	Drowsiness, sedation, headache. Contraindicated in pregnancy, in women trying to conceive (↓LH), and in nursing mothers (↓prolactin)

DIETARY SUPPLEMENTS

Vitamins are organic substances needed in small quantities for maintenance of body systems and overall health. They are often received through dietary intake, but can be supplemented if a patient does not obtain adequate quantities through diet alone. Water-soluble vitamins (B vitamins and vitamin C) are excreted via the kidneys and thus do not often reach toxic limits within the body. However, fat-soluble vitamins (vitamins A, D, E, and K) can accumulate and are capable of achieving toxic levels. Thus, you should understand the benefits and risks associated with the use of vitamins.

NAPLEX References

Over-the-Counter Medications chapter: "Vitamins"

Clinical Lab Tests chapter: "Electrolytes and Minerals"

A more comprehensive review of vitamins in the "Promotion of Nonprescription and Natural Products" section of FPGEE (Chapter 28). A more comprehensive review of minerals is found in the "Clinical Laboratory and Diagnostic Tests" section of FPGEE (Chapter 27).

PRACTICE QUESTIONS

1. Saw palmetto is believed to have a mechanism of action that is most similar to which of the following?

    A. Alprostadil
    B. Finasteride
    C. Minoxidil
    D. Tadalafil
    E. Terazosin

NAPLEX Question Reference

Over-the-Counter Medications End of Chapter Questions

2. A physician recommends Vitamin B9 for a patient. The pharmacist should recommend which of the following?

    A. Biotin
    B. Folic acid
    C. Niacin
    D. Pyridoxine
    E. Thiamine

3. Which of the following will cause a pharmacodynamic interaction with warfarin?

    A. Echinacea
    B. Gingko
    C. Ginseng
    D. Saw Palmetto
    E. St. John's wort

4. A patient with pernicious anemia should be treated with which of the following vitamins?

    A. Biotin
    B. Cyanocobalamin
    C. Niacin
    D. Pyridoxine
    E. Thiamine

5. A patient with hyponatremia has which of the following?

    A. Potassium < 3.5 mEq/L
    B. Potassium < 135 mEq/L
    C. Sodium < 3.5 mEq/L
    D. Sodium < 8.5 mEq/L
    E. Sodium < 135 mEq/L

6. Melatonin is derived from which of the following essential amino acids?

    A. Isoleucine
    B. Leucine
    C. Lysine
    D. Threonine
    E. Tryptophan

7. A patient comes to the emergency department with altered mental status, tachycardia and muscle rigidity. These symptoms were most likely caused by taking excessive amount of which of the following for an extended period of time?

    A. Echinacea
    B. Garlic
    C. Ginseng
    D. Saw Palmetto
    E. St. John's wort

Answers and Explanations

1. **The correct answer is B.** Saw palmetto is a natural product that has been used for the symptomatic treatment of benign prostatic hypertrophy (BPH). It is believed to work by acting as a 5α-reductase inhibitor and androgen receptor antagonist. Finasteride acts by inhibiting type II 5α-reductase thereby interfering with the conversion of testosterone to 5α-dihydrotestosterone. Alprostadil (choice A), used in the treatment of erectile dysfunction, is a prostaglandin E1 analog that relaxes arterial smooth muscle, produces vasodilation and inhibits platelet aggregation. Minoxidil (choice C) is used orally for severe hypertension and acts by directly dilating peripheral vessels. Tadalafil (choice D), used in the treatment of erectile dysfunction and BPH, acts by inhibiting phosphodiesterase type 5, enhancing effects of nitric oxide-activated increases in cGMP. Terazosin (choice E), used in the treatment of hypertension and BPH, acts by antagonizing peripheral alpha-1 adrenergic receptors.

2. **The correct answer is B.** Pharmacists should know both "classifications" for the B vitamins. They are as follows: Thiamine (B1), Riboflavin (B2), Niacin (B3), Pantothenate (B5), Pyridoxine (B6), Biotin (B7), Folic acid (B9), and Cyanocobalamin (B12).

3. **The correct answer is B.** Warfarin is an anticoagulant that inhibits vitamin K-dependent coagulation factor synthesis (II, VII, IX, X, proteins C and S). Gingko is used for the treatment of intermittent claudication due to its antiplatelet effects. Since this drug affects one "clotting" process and warfarin affects another, there would be a pharmacodynamic interaction between these 2 medications. St. John's wort induces the CYP450 systems and would be expected to decrease warfarin's blood level; hence, there is a pharmacokinetic (affects ADME process) interaction between warfarin and St. John's wort. There are no major interactions between warfarin and the other answer choices.

4. **The correct answer is B.** Pernicious anemia is a type of megaloblastic anemia caused by autoimmune (atrophic) gastritis. This condition is associated with failure of intrinsic factor production that leads to vitamin B12 deficiency. Thus, the treatment of choice is vitamin B12 (cyanocobalamin). Biotin (choice A) is used to treat dermatitis and hair loss. Niacin (choice C) is used to treat pellagra and hypercholesteremia. Pyridoxine (choice D) is used to treat neuropathy and prevent isoniazid-induced neuropathy. Thiamine (choice E) is used to treat Beriberi and Wernicke-Korsakoff syndrome.

5. **The correct answer is E.** Hyponatremia is mostly defined as a serum sodium level <135 mEq/L and is considered severe when the serum sodium level <125 mEq/L. Hypokalemia is mostly defined as a serum potassium level <3.5 mEq/L (choice A) and is considered severe when the serum potassium level <3.0 mEq/L. Hypocalcemia is mostly defined as a serum calcium level <8.5 mg/dL.

6. **The correct answer is E.** Melatonin is a derivative of the essential amino acid tryptophan. It acts by binding to the melatonin receptor type 1A, which then acts on adenylate cyclase and the inhibition of a cAMP signal transduction pathway. It is used for the treatment of "jet-lag" and sleep disorders.

7. **The correct answer is E.** The patient most likely has serotonin syndrome, which generally consists of the triad of altered mental status (confusion, seizures), dysautonomia (diaphoresis, hypertension, mydriasis, tachycardia), and neuromuscular changes (muscle rigidity, hyperreflexia). This condition is most likely seen with St. John's wort since it enhances serotonin activity in the CNS. Echinacea (choice A) causes GI distress, dizziness and headache. Garlic (choice B) has antiplatelet effects and can cause bleeding. Ginseng (choice C) causes insomnia, nervousness and hypertension. Saw Palmetto (choice D) causes GI pain, decreased libido and hypertension.

Pharmaceutics/Biopharmaceutics 8

Learning Objectives

- ❑ Explain drug delivery and dosage forms
- ❑ Describe methods of drug preparation
- ❑ Answer questions on the physicochemical properties of drugs and dosage forms
- ❑ Discuss principles of drug and dosage form stability

In order for a medication to exert its desired therapeutic effect, it must first reach its intended target (receptor, enzyme, etc). Prior to this happening, the drug must be delivered into the human body.

The drug delivery process begins with a patient "taking" a drug dosage form that contains the actual medicinal compound. Effectively getting this compound to the target site in sufficient concentrations to exert a therapeutic effect is the collective focus of pharmaceutics and biopharmaceutics.

Together these sciences incorporate drug physicochemical properties, ADME principles, pharmacokinetics, and drug dosage formulation and design to help get the drug from outside of the body to its intended site of action inside the body.

PRINCIPLES OF DRUG DELIVERY AND DOSAGE FORMS

Drug dosage forms are defined as the physical form (tablet, powder for inhalation, IV solution, etc.) by which a medication will be delivered into the human body. Each of these dosage forms is "delivered" via a specific route of administration (oral, inhalation, intravenous, etc).

There are a number of factors that need to be considered before a pharmaceutical manufacturer designs a dosage form. Primary considerations include:

- Nature of the illness being treated
- Manner in which the illness is most effectively treated
- Age of the patient
- Condition of the patient
- Stability of the drug
- Physiochemical properties of the drug
- Appropriateness of the dosage form

NAPLEX References

Pharmaceutics chapter: "Pharmaceutical Dosage Forms"

Biopharmaceutics and Drug Disposition chapter

- Timeframe and physiological environment where the drug molecule will be liberated from its dosage form
- Drug absorption, distribution, metabolism and elimination (ADME) principles

These concepts (and others) are discussed in the "Pharmaceutical Dosage Forms" section of Kaplan's *NAPLEX Strategies, Practice, and Review* book Pharmaceutics chapter.

Once the medication is delivered into the human body by a dosage form, the biopharmaceutical principles of ADME (absorption, distribution, metabolism and excretion) apply. ADME concepts are discussed in the Biopharmaceutics and Drug Disposition chapter of Kaplan's *NAPLEX Strategies, Practice, and Review* book.

PRACTICE QUESTIONS

NAPLEX Question Reference

Pharmaceutics End of Chapter Questions

1. The main difference between oral emulsions (that contain both water and oil) and topical emulsions is that:

   A. Oral is O/W only
   B. Oral is W/O only
   C. Oral can be both O/W and W/O
   D. Topical is O/W only
   E. Topical is W/O only

NAPLEX Question Reference

Biopharmaceutics and Drug Disposition End of Chapter Questions

2. When making a suspension, which of the following is the primary factor to consider?

   A. Particle color
   B. Particle number
   C. Partical pKa
   D. Particle shape
   E. Particle size

3. Which of the following contains the least amount of alcohol?

   A. Elixir
   B. Fluid extract
   C. Spirits
   D. Syrup
   E. Tincture

4. When designing a drug dosage form, a pharmaceutical manufacturer must consider which of the following?

   A. Medication stability
   B. Most effective way to treat the condition
   C. Patient population
   D. Physiochemical properties of the drug
   E. All of the above

5. A physician calls the pharmacy to recommend a corticosteroid delivery vehicle for a patient with a lesion under an area covered by hair. Which of the following would be most recommended?

   A. Cream
   B. Liquid
   C. Lotion
   D. Ointment
   E. Oleaginous base

Answers and Explanations

1. **The correct answer is A.** Emulsions are described as dispersions that consist of non-miscible liquids. Emulsions contain a dispersed phase (internal phase) and a dispersion medium (external phase). Oral products contain only oil-in-water (O/W) emulsions because the water must be in the external phase to be palatable to the patient. Conversely, topical products are available in both W/O and O/W formulations.

2. **The correct answer is E.** A pharmacist or pharmaceutical manufacturer is primarily concerned with making suspensions that have a particle size small enough to stay suspended in the dispersion medium being used. Furthermore, the particles cannot be so small that they begin to attract one another and begin to clump. Pharmaceutical manufacturers will use 2 techniques to prevent this from occurring: controlled flocculation and structured vehicles.

3. **The correct answer is D.** On the FPGEE, the candidate is required to know the key features of each dosage form, including the different liquid dosage forms. Syrups are the most commonly used liquid dosage forms. They contain sugar or sugar substitutes, little or no alcohol as well as thickeners to improve their ability to mask the taste of the bitter drug products. All of the other answer choices contain varying amounts of alcohol.

4. **The correct answer is E.** There are numerous factors that need to be considered before a pharmaceutical manufacturer designs a dosage form. In addition to the answer choices listed, the following must also be considered: Nature of the illness being treated; appropriateness of the dosage form, timeframe and physiological environment where the drug molecule will be liberated from its dosage form as well as drug ADME properties.

5. **The correct answer is C.** Lotions are creamy emulsions that will not adhere to hair but will adhere to the skin. Lotions are considered to be the best delivery vehicle to treat lesions in an area covered by hair. Creams (choice A) can be considered a more viscous form of lotion AND will adhere to both hair and skin. However, if a lotion is not available as a delivery vehicle for a given medication, creams are the next best choice. Liquids (choice B) will not adhere to either the skin or hair. Ointments are "greasy" products that will strongly adhere to both the skin and hair. As a general rule, ointments are used for "dry" lesions and creams are used for "wet" lesions to dry them out. Oleaginous bases (choice E) are greasy, petroleum-based products used for emollient effects and should not be used to treat lesions covered by hair.

Pharmacokinetics 9

Learning Objectives

- ❑ Show proficiency in linear and nonlinear drug kinetics
- ❑ Differentiate between bioavailability and bioequivalence
- ❑ Explain determinates of drug onset and duration

Pharmacokinetics focuses on drug concentrations in the body and is dependent on the movement of drugs throughout the body, including:

- Drug absorption (for most methods of delivery)
- Drug distribution from one compartment to another
- Drug biotransformation (metabolism)
- Drug elimination

Clinical pharmacokinetics applies these principles to help design individualized drug therapies, dosing regimens, and therapeutic drug monitoring.

PRINCIPLES OF PHARMACOKINETICS

Pharmacokinetics is primarily concerned with "what the body does to the drug" once it is ingested. Pharmacodynamics (Chapter 6) is concerned with "what the drug does to the body (or body component) once it binds to its intended target."

- Pharmacokinetics is covered in Kaplan's *NAPLEX Strategies, Practice, and Review* book.
- Clinical pharmacokinetics is discussed in Chapter 24 of this book.

NAPLEX References

Pharmacokinetics chapter

Biopharmaceutics and Drug Disposition chapter

More specifically, pharmacokinetics can be defined as the branch of pharmacology concerned with the movement of drugs throughout the body with an emphasis on the time course of drug absorption, distribution, metabolism, and excretion. With the development of strong correlations between drug concentrations and their pharmacologic responses (therapeutic window), clinical pharmacokinetics has become an integral part of medicine today.

Clinical pharmacokinetics focuses on the application of these principles for the development of safe and effective drug therapies. Pharmacogenomics (covered in Chapter 10) can be considered a recent addition to the science of clinical pharmacokinetics. One area of pharmacogenomics focuses on how a patient's unique genetic profile impacts their ability to metabolize certain medications.

Primary goals of clinical pharmacokinetics (and pharmacogenomics) include:

- enhancement of medication efficacy;
- decreasing drug toxicity; and
- arriving at the most effective medication dose in the shortest period of time.

Clinically there are numerous "calculations" commonly used to solve pharmacokinetic questions. However, only the basic (less complicated) equations are likely to appear on the FPGEE. With that being said, you should understand the basic pharmacokinetic and biopharmaceutics equations, graphs, and tables covered in Kaplan's *NAPLEX Strategies, Practice, and Review* book.

PRACTICE QUESTIONS

1. A 200-mg dose of a medication has a known therapeutic effect of 4 hours despite having a half-life of 6 hours. How long would a dose of 400 mg be effective? Assume no toxicity at this dose.

    A. 4 hours
    B. 6 hours
    C. 8 hours
    D. 10 hours
    E. 12 hours

NAPLEX Question Reference

Pharmacokinetics End of Chapter Questions

2. Following a 500 mg IV bolus of a medication, it is calculated that 250 mg of the drug remains after 3 hours. Assuming first-order elimination, approximately what amount of the drug will be in the body after 9 more hours?

    A. 15.6 mg
    B. 31.25 mg
    C. 62.5 mg
    D. 93.75 mg
    E. 125 mg

3. Highly plasma protein bound medications have which of the following characteristics?

    A. Are easily filtered at the glomerulus
    B. Are found outside the central compartment
    C. Effectively cross the BBB
    D. Generally do not interact with other highly plasma protein bound medications
    E. Have small Vd

4. Which of the following is NOT required for bioequivalence?

    A. Same AUC
    B. Same bioavailability
    C. Same manufacturer
    D. Same maximum blood concentration
    E. Same Tmax

5. Which of the following is most representative of medications administered via the IV route?
   A. Avoids first pass-metabolism
   B. Bioavailability is dependent on the individual agent
   C. Most rapid form of absorption
   D. Only for medications that cannot be delivered via other routes
   E. Slowest onset time

Answers and Explanations

1. **The correct answer is D.** The therapeutic efficacy of the drug is different than its half-life. This means that the drug is above its minimal effective concentration (MEC) for 4 hours. Thus, doubling the dose (to 200 mg) means that the drug level will be above the MEC for a longer period of time. Since the elimination half-life is 6 h, 200 mg of the drug will remain in the body after the first 6 hours (following a 400 mg dose). Hence, the total duration of effectiveness will be 10 hours: 6 hours + 4 hours (effective duration for a 200 mg dose) = 10 hours.

2. **The correct answer is B.** This is a simple first-order half-life calculation. We are told that ½ of the drug (500 mg/2 = 250 mg) is eliminated in 3 hours. Hence, its elimination half-life equals 3 hours. With the passage of each half-life, the amount of drug in the body (or in the blood) will decrease to 50% of its former level. Thus, another 3 hours (6 hours total) after administration, there will be 125 mg; after another 3 hours (9 hours total) after administration, there will be 62.5 mg; and after another 3 hours (12 hours total) after administration, there will be 31.25 mg.

3. **The correct answer is E.** Most lipid-soluble medications need a "carrier" in the blood. The most common carrier is albumin. A highly plasma protein bound (PPB) medication will remain in the central compartment (choice B) with the albumin; hence, binding to plasma proteins keeps the drug in the plasma. This results in a lower volume of distribution (Vd). Drugs bound to albumin do not get filtered at the glomerulus (choice A) or cross the blood-brain barrier (choice C). Highly PPB medications generally interact (choice D) with other drugs that are also highly bound (i.e. warfarin plus sulfonamides).

4. **The correct answer is C.** The FDA defined bioequivalence as "the absence of a significant difference in the rate and extent to which the active ingredient or active moiety in pharmaceutical equivalents or pharmaceutical alternatives becomes available at the site of drug action when administered at the same molar dose under similar conditions in an appropriately designed study. Thus bioequivalent products will have the same AUC (choice A), bioavailability (choice B), Cmax (choice D) and Tmax (choice E). The medications can be manufactured by different companies (i.e. Original manufacturer and generic manufacturer).

5. **The correct answer is A.** Intravenous administration of medication avoids first-pass metabolism which is common with orally administered medications. Drugs administered via the IV route have 100% bioavailability ($f = 1$) since the entire dose enters systemic circulation (choice B). Intravenous administration does not involve absorption (choice C) since there is no movement from the site of administration into the blood. There are numerous medications that can be administered both via IV, oral and other routes of administration (choice D). IV administration provides an almost instantaneous pharmacological effect (choice E).

Pharmacogenomics and Genetics 10

Learning Objectives

- ❑ Discuss molecular genetics and pharmacogenomics principles
- ❑ Describe the impact of genetic variation and drug effects

Pharmacogenomics is the study of how genes affect a person's response to drugs. This relatively new field of medicine combines pharmacology, pharmacokinetics, biopharmaceutics, and genomics (the study of genes and their functions) to develop safe and effective medications as well as help clinicians design individualized medication regimens (drug and dose) tailored to a person's genetic makeup.

Due to its clinical importance, pharmacogenomics has recently been added to both the FPGEE and NAPLEX.

CLINICAL PHARMACOGENOMIC AND GENETIC PRINCIPLES

According to the FDA, pharmacogenomics can play an important role in identifying responders and non-responders to medications, avoiding adverse events, and optimizing drug dose.

With the knowledge gained from the Human Genome Project, researchers are learning how inherited differences in genes affect the body's response to medications. These genetic differences will be used to predict whether a medication will be effective for a particular person and to help prevent adverse drug reactions.

> **NAPLEX Reference**
>
> **Pharmacogenomics chapter**
> **Biopharmaceutics and Drug Disposition chapter:** Focus on "Drug Metabolism"

According to the National Human Genome Research Institute of the NIH, the following are now widely accepted pharmacogenomic principles:

- Depending on a person's genetic makeup, some drugs may work more or less effectively or may produce more or fewer side effects for one person than they do in other people.
- It is predicted that doctors will be able to routinely use information about one's genetic makeup to choose both drugs and drug doses that offer the greatest chance of a successful therapeutic outcome.
- Pharmacogenomics is likely to help to save time and money. By using information about one's genetic makeup, doctors may be able to avoid the trial-and-error approach of administering various drugs that may not be appropriate based on one's genetic make-up.
- Many drugs (developed by pharmaceutical companies) are available as a "one size fits all" dose; however, clinicians know that these medications don't work the same way for everyone. Hence, it can be difficult to predict who will benefit from a medication, who will not respond at all, and who will experience adverse drug events (ADEs). Remember, ADEs are a significant cause of hospitalizations and deaths in the United States.

> **NAPLEX Reference**
>
> **Biopharmaceutics and Drug Disposition chapter:**
> "Drug Metabolism"

A more in-depth review of pharmacogenomics can be found in Kaplan's *NAPLEX Strategies, Practice, and Review* book. The information pertaining to drug metabolism in the Biopharmaceutics and Drug Disposition chapter in the NAPLEX text can also be extrapolated to pharmacogenomics.

PRACTICE QUESTIONS

1. A patient receiving codeine, who is a CYP2D6 poor metabolizer, is likely to see which of the following as compared to a patient that is a normal CYP2D6 metabolizer?

    A. Decreased blood levels of codeine
    B. Increased therapeutic effects of codeine
    C. Decreased therapeutic effects of morphine
    D. More rapid increase in effect of morphine
    E. Codeine is not metabolized by CYP2D6 so there is no change in its therapeutic effect

NAPLEX Question Reference

Pharmacogenomics End of Chapter Questions + Biopharmaceutics and Drug Disposition End of Chapter Questions

2. Which of the following is the phase II drug metabolism reaction most commonly associated with a genetic polymorphism?

    A. Acetylation
    B. Glucuronidation
    C. Glutathione conjugation
    D. Oxidation
    E. Reduction

3. Which of the following metabolizer status types is NOT correctly matched with its haplotype combination?

    A. Poor metabolizer (PM): 2 non-functional alleles
    B. Intermediate metabolizers (IM): 1 non-functional allele and 1 normally functioning allele
    C. Extensive metabolizer (EM): 2 normally functioning alleles
    D. Ultra-rapid metabolizer (UM): 1 or more alleles duplicated or amplified alleles compared to EM
    E. All of the above are correct

4. General mechanisms by which pharmacogenetic factors can influence the response to medications include all of the following EXCEPT:

    A. Disease pathogenesis
    B. Hepatic metabolism
    C. Idiosyncratic reactions
    D. Pharmacodynamics
    E. Renal elimination

5. Combined together, what percentage of medications available today are metabolized by CYP2C9, CYP2C19, CYP2D6, and CYP3A4?

   A. 10% – 20%

   B. 30% – 40%

   C. 60% – 70%

   D. 80% – 90%

   E. Approximately 100%

Answers and Explanations

1. **The correct answer is C.** Codeine is a prodrug that is inactive (choice B) until it is demethylated to the active opioid morphine by the liver enzyme CYP2D6 (choice E). The analgesic, respiratory depressant and other pharmacological effects of codeine have been speculated to come from its conversion to morphine. Morphine is an agonist at the mu, kappa and delta receptors. Thus, a CYP2D6 poor metabolizer would be expected to see decreased therapeutic effects of morphine (choice C is correct and D is incorrect) and increased codeine blood levels (choice A).

2. **The correct answer is A.** Phase II drug metabolism involves the transfer of chemical groupings (i.e. acetyl [choice A], glucuronide [choice B] and glutathione [choice C]) to drugs or their metabolites via conjugation reactions involving transferase enzymes. Acetylation reactions are associated with a genetic polymorphism (slow acetylator). These individuals are slow to metabolize drugs via acetylation and are particularly susceptible to drug-induced lupus when taking hydralazine, procainamide, or isoniazid. Both oxidation (choice D) and reduction (choice E) are phase I metabolism reactions.

3. **The correct answer is E.** A patient's drug metabolizing status can often be predicted based on the different combinations of haplotypes they express. There are 4 different drug metabolizer status types: poor metabolizers (PM), intermediate metabolizers (IM), extensive/normal metabolizers (EM) and ultra-rapid metabolizers (UM). PM's have 2 non-functional alleles and thus have little enzyme activity. IM's have 1 non-functional allele and 1 normally functioning allele; hence, have decreased enzyme activity. EM's have 2 normally functioning alleles thus have "normal" enzyme activity. NOTE: The dose and dosing schedule for most pharmaceutical medications are based off of EM's status. UM's have 1 or more alleles duplicated or amplified compared to EM; hence, will metabolize drugs more rapidly.

4. **The correct answer is E.** Genetic polymorphisms for many medication metabolizing enzymes and drug targets (i.e. receptors) have been identified and most likely contribute to interpatient variability in drug response. The 4 general mechanisms by which genetic/pharmacogenetic factors can influence the response to pharmacologic agents include disease pathogenesis (specific molecular defects - choice A), hepatic metabolism (CYP polymorphisms – choice B), idiosyncratic reactions (i.e. hypersensitivity reaction probability – choice C) and pharmacodynamics (i.e. modulation of therapeutic target – choice D). Renal elimination is not impacted by pharmacogenomics factors.

5. **The correct answer is C.** The clinically most important polymorphic variations in hepatic cytochromes P450 (CYP) are CYP2C9, CYP2C19, CYP2D6, and CYP3A4 genes, which code for enzymes that are responsible for the phase I metabolism of approximately 60 to 70 percent of all medications used in patients today.

Sterile and Nonsterile Compounding 11

Learning Objectives

- ❑ Explain USP sterile and nonsterile compounding guidelines
- ❑ Solve problems on extemporaneous prescription preparation
- ❑ Demonstrate proficiency in dosage form calculations
- ❑ Describe sterile admixture techniques

Although most medications are available in pre-formulated dosage forms, pharmacists (retail and institutional) may be asked to compound sterile and nonsterile products. Thus, you should be familiar with sterile and nonsterile compounding guidelines and procedures.

USP STERILE AND NONSTERILE COMPOUNDING GUIDELINES

The United States Pharmacopeia (USP) is a compendium of drug information for the United States and is published annually by the United States Pharmacopoeial Convention. The National Formulary (a complete drug formulary) is published in conjunction with the USP as the USP-NF.

In the United States, if a drug (ingredient or product) has an applicable USP quality standard (in the form of a USP-NF monograph), it must conform in order to use the designation "USP" or "NF." Drugs subject to USP standards include both human drugs (prescription, over-the-counter) and animal drugs.

USP-NF standards also have a role in U.S. federal law. A drug (ingredient or product) with a name recognized in USP-NF is considered adulterated if it does not satisfy compendial standards for strength, quality, or purity. USP also sets standards for dietary supplements, food ingredients, and drug compounding (sterile and non-sterile). The USP does not enforce its standards; however, it provides the guidance necessary for the FDA and other government authorities in the United States and elsewhere to enforce these standards.

USP compounding standards, for example, help compounding practitioners (including pharmacists) adhere to widely acknowledged and scientifically accepted procedures and help facilitate the development and delivery of safe and effective compounded medications to patients.

As of June 2016, there are 5 essential compounding chapters in the USP–NF. The pharmacist compounding the sterile or non-sterile product must adhere to the guidance provided in each of these chapters.

- Chapter 797 (Pharmaceutical Compounding–Sterile Preparations): Provides guidance on procedures and requirements for properly compounding sterile preparations and outlines the conditions and practices to prevent patient harm secondary to microbial contamination, variability in intended strength, and other unintended compounding errors.
- Chapter 795 (Pharmaceutical Compounding–Nonsterile Preparations): Provides guidance on procedures and requirements for properly compounding non-sterile preparations for both humans and animals.

- Chapter 1160 (Pharmaceutical Calculations in Prescription Compounding): Provides guidance and assistance on correctly performing the necessary calculations needed to compound a given prescription.
- Chapter 1163 (Quality Assurance in Pharmaceutical Compounding): Defines a quality assurance program for compounding standards which includes sections on testing of dosage units, weight, and volume assessment and disinfecting principles, containers, and outsourcing.
- Chapter 1176 (Prescription Balances and Volumetric Apparatus): Defines acceptable balances and volumetric apparatus (e.g., pipets, cylinders, conical graduates, etc) used to weigh/measure drug and/or excipients used in pharmaceutical compounding.

The USP has designated compounding categories. Note: All information on sterile and non-sterile compounding was derived from USP Chapters 795 and 797.

Table 11-1. Sterile and Nonsterile Compounding

Sterile Compounding	
Low Risk Level Compounding	Compounded with aseptic manipulations entirely within an ISO Class 5 or better air quality device, usually within an ISO Class 7 environment, using sterile products, components, and devices. Compounded products involve not more than 3 commercially manufactured packages of sterile products and not more than 2 entries into any one sterile container or package. Manipulations are limited to aseptically opening ampules, penetrating disinfected stoppers on vials with sterile needles and sterile syringes.
Medium Risk Level Compounding	Compounded with aseptic manipulations entirely within an ISO Class 5 or better air quality device, usually within an ISO Class 7 environment, using sterile products, components, and devices. Compounded products are compounded aseptically for multiple individual doses that are pooled together to prepare one sterile compounded product. Compounding process includes complex aseptic manipulations other than single volumes using 4 or more sterile products.
High Risk Level Compounding	Sterile products are compounded from non-sterile ingredients and/or compounded using any non-sterile devices, containers or equipment. Products are prepared from sterile ingredients, containers, devices or equipment that are exposed to less than ISO Class 5 air. There is more than a 6-hour delay prior to sterilization of the compounded product.
Nonsterile Compounding	
Simple	Making a preparation that has a USP compounding monograph or that appears in a peer-reviewed journal article that contains specific quantities of all components, compounding procedure and equipment and stability date for that formulation with appropriate beyond use date (BUD) or reconstituting or manipulating commercial products that may require the addition of one or more ingredients as directed by the manufacturer.
Moderate	Making a preparation that requires special calculations or procedures (such as calibration of dosage unit mold cavities) to determine quantities of components per preparation or per individualized dosage units; or making a preparation for which stability data for that specific formulation are not available.
Complex	Making a preparation that requires special training, environment, facilities, equipment, and procedures to ensure appropriate therapeutic outcomes.

(Continued)

Hazardous Drug Compounding

The National Institute for Occupational Safety and Health (NIOSH) maintains a list of antineoplastic and other Hazardous Drugs used in healthcare. Compounding a product from this list is categorized as "Hazardous drug compounding".

A sterile compounded product is given a microbial contamination risk level according to the potential for the introduction of contamination during the process of compounding. The assignment of risk level is based on several factors including: type of components used; compounding environment and the complexity of the compounding process.

EXTEMPORANEOUS PRESCRIPTION PREPARATION AND DOSAGE FORM CALCULATIONS

Extemporaneous compounding is the preparation, assembling, packaging, and labeling of a compounded drug product prescribed by a licensed practitioner for use in a patient. The resultant compounded product will be in a form or formulation that the drug is not readily available in from a pharmaceutical manufacturer.

NAPLEX Reference

Calculations chapter

According to the USP-NF, there are 2 types of pharmaceutical compounding (outlined in detail in the previous section):

- Sterile compounds: IV products, ophthalmics, parenteral nutrition, chemotherapy, and others
- Nonsterile compounds: Creams, ointments, oral suspensions, capsules, suppositories, and others

For both sterile and nonsterile compounding, a general workflow should be followed:

1. Interpret the prescription.
2. Verify and correct all missing or confusing information regarding the recipe.
3. Verify the drug dosage regimen, dosage form, and route of administration.
4. Outline the compounding procedure.
5. Choose appropriate compounding equipment.
6. Perform all compounding calculations.
7. Obtain all of the required ingredients (active compound and excipients). Note: The preferred grade for both drug and excipients are USP or NF.
8. Following USP guidelines, prepare the compounded product and perform a visual inspection of the product.
9. Choose an appropriate container for the compounded product.
10. Determine an appropriate beyond use date (BUD).
11. Label the container appropriately.
12. Document the compounding process for refills or future reference.

There are a variety of procedure and calculation examples found in the Calculations chapter of Kaplan's *NAPLEX Strategies, Practice, and Review* book.

STERILE ADMIXTURE TECHNIQUES

USP 797 (Pharmaceutical Compounding-Sterile Preparations) provides guidance on procedures and requirements for properly compounding sterile preparations. It outlines the conditions and practices to prevent patient harm secondary to microbial contamination, excessive bacterial endotoxins, variability in intended strength, and other unintended compounding errors.

- The primary source of information on sterile admixture techniques can be found in the "USP Sterile and Nonsterile Compounding Guidelines" section of this chapter.
- Additional information can be found at www.usp.org.

One of the first ways to ensure USP 797 is followed is with adequate personnel compounding competency. Compounded Sterile Product (CSP) personnel should be able to demonstrate proficiency in:

- Proper aseptic technique
- Proper cleaning, disinfecting, and sterilization procedures
- Competency to perform end-product testing and sterilization
- Proper hand hygiene technique
- Proper gloving and garbing technique
- Competency in the use of sterile devices, such as filter needles, injection port adapters, etc.
- Competency in the use of pharmacy compounding devices
- Competency in identifying ingredients by identity, quality and purity
- Competency in the compounding of hazardous drugs and radiopharmaceuticals
- Competency in the compounding of allergen extracts
- Competency in packaging CSPs
- Competency in assigning CSPs beyond use dates
- Competency in labeling CSPs

It is generally accepted that direct or physical contact of critical sites of compounded sterile products (CSPs) with contaminants, especially microbial sources, poses the greatest probability of risk to patients. Hence, compounding personnel must prevent contact contamination of CSPs both within and outside ISO Class 5 areas.

USP guidelines state that in critical areas, defined as the area in immediate proximity of an exposed sterilized container and filling/closing operations, the particle per cubic meter must be no more than 3520 particles/m^3 in a size of 0.5 micrometers or larger when counted at representative locations normally not more than 1 foot away from the work site, within the airflow, and during filling/closing operations.

You should also know the clean air classifications and ISO designations, as defined in the following table.

Table 11-2. Clean Air Classifications and ISO Designations

Clean Air Classification	ISO Designation	$\geq$ 0.5 µm particles/m^3
100	5	3,520
1,000	6	35,200
10,000	7	352,000
100,000	8	3,520,000

PRACTICE QUESTIONS

NAPLEX Question Reference

Calculations End of Chapter Questions

1. A pharmacist is performing a compounding process that includes complex aseptic manipulations with 5 different aseptic products. According to USP designations, this scenario would best be classified as which of the following?

   A. Moderate Nonsterile Compounding
   B. Complex Nonsterile Compounding
   C. Low Risk Level Sterile Compounding
   D. Medium Risk Level Sterile Compounding
   E. High Risk Level Sterile Compounding

2. A compounding pharmacist is working in an area where no more than 3520 particles/m^3 in a size of 0.5 micrometers or larger are counted at representative locations. This area has an ISO designation of which of the following?

   A. 3
   B. 4
   C. 5
   D. 6
   E. 7

3. Which of the following is true regarding HEPA filters?

   A. HEPA stands for high-efficiency particulate assistance.
   B. High energy ultraviolet light may be incorporated to kill live organisms trapped within it.
   C. It is used only in medical facilities.
   D. It is required to remove nearly 100% of particles that have a size of 0.1 μm or larger.
   E. All of the above are true

4. How many milliliters of a 15% "drug" solution are needed to prepare 240 mL of a 1:350 w/v solution?

   A. 1.8 mL
   B. 4.6 mL
   C. 9.2 mL
   D. 13.4 mL
   E. 16.2 mL

5. A physician requests that a TPN be prepared with a final potassium concentration of 40 mEq/L. If the TPN has a total volume of 1350 mL, how many mL of a 2 mEq/mL solution will be needed to fill the order? (Round to the nearest whole number.)

   A. 13 mL
   B. 18 mL
   C. 27 mL
   D. 52 mL
   E. 66 mL

Answers and Explanations

1. **The correct answer is D.** The USP designated compounding categories are based on whether the compound is being made in a sterile or nonsterile environment, the type of components used, as well as the level of complexity required to make each compound. For example, Medium Risk Level Sterile Compounding involves compounded products that are compounded aseptically for multiple individual doses that are pooled together to prepare one sterile compounded product. The process for this level of compounding includes complex aseptic manipulations other than single volumes using 4 or more sterile products. Medium Risk Level Sterile Compounding requires aseptic manipulations entirely within an ISO Class 5 or better air quality device. Requirements and definitions for each of the other answer choices are found in the Sterile and Nonsterile Compounding tables in the "USP Sterile and Nonsterile Compounding Guidelines" section of this chapter.

2. **The correct answer is C.** USP guidelines state that in critical areas, defined as the area in immediate proximity of an exposed sterilized container and filling/closing operations, the particle per cubic meter must be no more than 3520 particles/m^3 in a size of 0.5 micrometers or larger when counted at representative locations normally not more than 1 foot away from the work site, within the airflow, and during filling/closing operations. This area is classified as an ISO designation of 5 AND a clean air classification of 100.

3. **The correct answer is B.** High-efficiency particulate arrestance (HEPA), otherwise known as high-efficiency particulate arresting (choice A), is a type of air filter commonly used in hospitals, aircraft and even personal homes (choice C). A HEPA filter must remove (from the air that passes through it) 99.97% of particles that have a size of 0.3 μm (or larger) according to federal regulations (choice D). Medical-use HEPA filtration systems generally incorporate high-energy ultra-violet light units to eradicate organisms trapped by the filter media (choice B is correct). The highest-rated HEPA filtration units have an efficiency rating of 99.995%. This type of rating ensures an extremely high level of protection against airborne disease transmission.

4. **The correct answer is B.** The solution can be performed using the following steps:

   - 1 g/350 mL = X g/240 mL = 0.69 g
   - 15 g/100 mL = 0.69 g/x mL = 4.6 mL

5. **The correct answer is C.** The potassium required to fill the TPN prescription can be calculated using the following series of steps: 40 mEq/L X 1350 mL/bag X 1 L/1000 mL X 1 mL/2 mEq = 27 mL

U.S. Health Care and Public Health 12

Learning Objectives

- ❑ Provide a U.S. health care system overview
- ❑ Summarize principles of U.S. health care delivery financing
- ❑ Explain external influences on U.S. health care delivery
- ❑ Demonstrate proficiency in public health and wellness
- ❑ Differentiate U.S. vs. world health care delivery systems

The United States has one of the most complex and diverse health care systems in the world. For example, health care is provided to the American public by many separate governmental and public organizations, each with different rules, regulations, and methods of financing. Also, numerous health care facilities are owned and operated by private sector businesses. In fact, it is estimated that approximately 60% of U.S. community hospitals are non-profit, 20% are government owned, and 20% are for-profit private institutions.

To further complicate the system, there are numerous external forces (social, political, and economic) that impact health care delivery in the United States. Thus, as an integral part of the health care team, pharmacists should understand the complex health care system in the United States, as well as essential public health principles.

U.S. HEALTH CARE SYSTEM

According to the U.S. Centers for Medicare and Medicaid Services (CMS), health care spending in the United States increased 5.3 percent in 2014, following growth of 2.9 percent in 2013, to reach $3.0 trillion (or $9,523 per person). It is believed that the greatest growth experienced in 2014 was primarily due to the major coverage expansions under the Affordable Care Act (Obamacare), particularly for Medicaid and private health insurance. The share of the economy devoted to health care spending was 17.5 percent, up from 17.3 percent in 2013.

General Trends

Recent years have seen a rise in chronic conditions, and a decline in the number of patients with acute conditions.

- Since 1960, the death rate for heart disease has declined, while the rate for cancer has increased.
- People age >65 visit the physician about twice as often as those age <45. This pattern is strongest for men because women see physicians for gynecologic reasons.
- The most common principal diagnosis resulting in an office visit to a physician
  - For men: essential hypertension
  - For women: pregnancy

- The average length of a hospital stay has been declining slowly but steadily since 1970; it is now 4.9 days.
- Average hospital occupancy rate is about 69% nationwide; 50% is the break-even point for a hospital.
- Largest portion of hospital budget is for personnel.
- Whites have 10 times the number of physician visits as blacks.
- More malpractice suits involve breast cancer than any other diagnosis.
- Physicians and pharmacists are regulated by State Medical Boards; hospitals are accredited by the Joint Commission for Accreditation of Healthcare Organizations (JCAHO).

Mental Illness

Over the past 30 years, there has been a decrease in the number of persons who occupy hospital beds for mental illness.

- Admissions have not changed: stays are shorter; more outpatient treatment and serial admissions.
- Reasons for shorter stays: development of medication; movement to deinstitutionalize people.
- Most psychiatric care hospitals are run by states.
- One in 10 persons will be hospitalized at some time in their lives for psychiatric reasons (includes substance-related disorders).

Hospitalization

- Most admissions: psychiatric reasons
- Most days in hospital: diseases of cardiovascular system
- Most days lost from work: diseases of upper respiratory system
- Ambulatory clinics: back pain 30% of cases
- Most work-related disability: muscle/skeletal problems

Health Care Payments

- Capitation: prospective payment system. Payments are made for number of people the provider is responsible for, <u>not</u> care delivered.
- Medicare: federal government program that provides insurance payment for the elderly, the disabled, and dependents of the disabled.
  - Medicare <u>does not</u> generally cover routine physical exams, nursing home care, or prescription drugs.
  - Medicare <u>does</u> cover ambulance transport, dialysis, and speech and occupational therapy.

HIV/AIDS

About 1,000,000 adults and 200,000 children in the U.S. are HIV-positive (male 1:100, female 1:800)

1. One in 5 living with HIV is unaware of their infection.
2. In some inner-city areas, as many as 50% of males are HIV-positive.
3. AIDS is now the *9th* leading cause of death for all men aged 25 to 34.
   a. Better treatments have reduced mortality.
   b. Unintended injuries is #1
4. Most dangerous sexual practice: anal intercourse
5. Recent evidence that HIV can be transmitted by oral sex
6. If the patient has AIDS today, most likely homo/bisexual man
7. If recently became HIV-positive, most likely IV drug user

8. Fastest growing method of HIV transmission: heterosexual contact (especially for blacks and Hispanics)
    a. Heterosexual transmission is easier from men to women than from women to men
    b. Risk of acquiring for men is greater if contact occurs during menses.
    c. Uncircumcised men are more likely to be seropositive and contract HIV during sex.
9. HIV transmission rates
    a. Risk from single sexual encounter with man who is not a member of a risk group: 1 in 5 million
    b. Risk from single encounter with man who is a member of a high risk group: 1 in 20 to 1 in 2
    c. Needle-stick (with HIV-positive blood): 1 in 100 to 1 in 1,000 (average 1 in 250)
    d. Seroconversion from blood transfusion: 2 of 3
    e. If the mother is HIV-positive, 100% of children will test positive at birth
        i. About 20% of these remain HIV-positive after 1 year.
        ii. Breastfeeding increases transmission rate to 50%.
        iii. AZT reduces risk by half (to about 10%). AZT + C-section reduces transmission rate to 5%.

Morbidity and Mortality

For this section, patterns—not specific numbers—are what matter.

Mandatory Reportable Diseases

When mandatory reportable diseases are encountered, they must be reported to the local Public Health Department, who will inform the CDC.

Table 12-1. Selected Mandatory Reportable Diseases

Diagnosis	Rank Order
Chlamydia	1
Gonorrhea	2
Chicken pox	3
AIDS	4
Syphilis	5
Salmonella	6
Hepatitis A	7
Tuberculosis	8
Lyme	9
Hepatitis B	10
Pertussis	11
Hepatitis-Other	12
Legionnaires	13
Mumps	14
Rubella	15
Measles	16

Table 12-2. Top 3 Non-genetic Causes of Death in the U.S.

	% of Total Deaths
Tobacco	19%
Diet/Activity	14%
Alcohol	5%

Cancer Rates

Female lung cancer rates are increasing:

- 5.1 per 100,000 in 1965
- more than 30 per 100,000 in 2008

Most common cancer for either sex

a. Basal cell or squamous cell cancers: 900,000 cases per year
b. Basal cell 90% of skin cancers
c. Melanoma: 42,000 cases per year, more than 7,000 deaths
d. Incidence rate 16 times higher for whites than blacks

Table 12-3. Leading Sites of Cancer Incidence and Death

Types of Cancer	Incidence	Deaths
Males		
Prostate	1	2
Lung	2	1
Colorectal	3	3
Females		
Breast	1	2
Lung	2	1
Colorectal	3	3

Table 12-4. U.S. Mortality Rates per 100,000

Cause of Death	Rate per 100,000
Heart disease	191
Cancer	184
Chronic lower respiratory disease	41.4
Stroke (cerebrovascular diseases)	46.0
Accidents (unintentional injuries)	39.4 (approx. 50% vehicles)
Alzheimer's disease	27.2
Diabetes mellitus	23.5

(Continued)

Cause of Death	Rate per 100,000
Nephritis, nephrotic syndrome, and nephrosis	14.7
Influenza and Pneumonia	17.2
Intentional self-harm (suicide)	12.3

U.S. Deaths and Mortality

- Number of deaths: 2,468,435
- Death rate: 799.5 deaths per 100,000 population
- Life expectancy: 78.7 years
- Infant Mortality rate: 6.15 deaths per 1,000 live births

Number of Deaths for Leading Causes of Death

- Heart disease: 597,689
- Cancer: 574,743
- Chronic lower respiratory diseases: 138,080
- Stroke (cerebrovascular diseases): 129,476
- Accidents (unintentional injuries): 120,859
- Alzheimer's disease: 83,494
- Diabetes: 69,071
- Nephritis, nephrotic syndrome, and nephrosis: 50,476
- Influenza and Pneumonia: 50,097
- Intentional self-harm (suicide): 38,364

Table 12-5. Top 3 Leading Causes of Death by Age Group

Rank	Less than 1	1 to 4	4 to 9	10 to 14	15 to 24	25 to 34	35 to 44	45 to 54	55 to 65	over 65
#1	Congenital anomalies	Unintended injuries	Unintended injuries	Unintended injuries	Unintended injuries	Unintended injuries	Neoplasia	Neoplasia	Neoplasia	Heart disease
#2	Short gestation	Congenital anomalies	Neoplasia	Neoplasia	Homicide	Suicide	Unintended injuries	Heart disease	Heart disease	Neoplasia
#3	SIDS	Neoplasia	Congenital anomalies	Suicide	Suicide	Homicide	Heart disease	Unintended injuries	Bronchitis, asthma, emphysema	Cerebro-vascular

Now that the important health care utilization trends in the United States have been explored, let's review some of the ways that the U.S. health care system is financed.

Nongovernment Methods of Payment for Services

Fee-for-service: payment is rendered after service is delivered. Economic incentive is to do more so more can be billed.

i. Physicians make money when more treatment is provided.

ii. Danger = overtreatment

Standard insurance (indemnity insurance): Insurance company helps patient pay for health care in exchange for a periodic payment by patient (*premium*)

- Patient shares in payment by means of:
- Deductible: patient pays a certain amount before insurance assistance begins
  - Annual deductible: patient pays certain amount each year
  - Per-occurrence deductible: patient pays certain amount each time services are rendered
- Copayment: remainder of bill is divided between patient and insurance company
  - Copayment calculation takes place only after deductible is satisfied
  - Common copayments may be:
    1. Patient 20%/insurance 80% or
    2. Patient 30%/insurance 70%

i. Blue Cross Blue Shield: nonprofit insurance company
  - Blue Cross covers hospital charges
  - Blue Shield covers physician services
  - Coverage comes with deductibles and copayments
  - Premiums intended to cover only:
    - Benefits
    - Administrative costs
    - Catastrophic losses

a. Health maintenance organization (HMO): prepaid group practice
  i. Either hires physicians or contracts with physicians to provide services
  ii. Payment by *capitation*: a fixed payment is made each month
    - Members pay a fixed amount per month.
    - Physicians are paid for the number of patients they are responsible for, not for how much they do for each patient. The same payment is made whether services are used or not.
    - No additional (or only minimal) payment is made when services *are* used.
    - Physicians make money when patients stay well and do not need to use services.
    - Incentives:
      - Under treatment
      - More likely to foster preventive medicine

Table 12-6. Types of HMOs

Type	Payment to Physicians	Who Owns Facilities	Importance of HMO Patients to Practice
Staff Model	Salary	HMO	Only patients
Group Model	Fixed capitation, profit sharing	HMO	Core
Network Model	Negotiated capitation	Practice	Less important
Individual Practice Association (IPA)	Many contracts, negotiated fee schedules	Practice	Secondary

b. Preferred provider organization (PPO): fee-for-service at a discount
  i. Insurance company contracts to provide services at a present price or discount
  ii. Discount is substantial, often 30% below standard fees for primary care and 50% below standard fees for specialists

iii. In exchange for discount, insurer agrees to provide incentives for patient to use contracted providers
iv. Provider makes money on volume, i.e., less money per patient but more patients. Efficiency is rewarded.
v. Provider is limited in ability to raise prices.
vi. Insurance company conducts utilization review to be sure that only appropriate services are delivered and billed.
vii. Providers may "bid for patients," seeking greater volume by offering deeper discounts.

Government Methods of Payment for Services

a. Medicare: Federal government program that makes health care payments to those on Social Security
   i. Program pays health care costs for the:
      - Elderly (age >65)
      - Disabled
      - Dependents of disabled
   ii. Part A pays for hospital care; part B pays for physician services.
   iii. Annual deductibles and copayments are applicable.
   iv. Patient can use up Medicare benefits.
   v. If providers accept "assignment," they must accept Medicare-set fees only.
   vi. Covered services include: hospital stays; laboratory workups; non-self-administered drugs; ambulatory surgery; physical, speech, and occupational therapy; rehabilitation; kidney dialysis; ambulance transport; diabetes testing equipment; pneumococcal and hepatitis B vaccination. Some prescription coverage is available for an added fee.
   vii. Services *not* covered: routine physicals; eye/ear examinations for glasses/hearing aids; immunizations; routine foot care; custodial (nursing home) care; most self-administered drugs.

b. Medicaid: health care payments for those on welfare
   i. Joint state/federal program
   ii. Covers all care, including hospital stays, physician services, medication, and nursing homes. However, Medicaid payments to providers are generally far below standard fees.
   iii. If poor and over age 65, Medicare is first used, then Medicaid
   iv. No deductibles, copayments, or fees
   v. Each state sets eligibility, services covered, and administration, hence wide differences across the United States.

c. Diagnostic-related groups (DRGs)
   DRGs are payment categories used to classify patients (especially Medicare patients) for the purpose of reimbursing hospitals for each case in a given category. There is a fixed fee, regardless of the actual costs incurred, since patients within each category are clinically similar and are expected to use the same level of hospital resources. DRGs have been used in the United States since the early 1980s to determine how much Medicare pays the hospital for services. They are assigned based on diagnosis, procedure, age, sex, discharge status, and presence of complications or comorbidities (see below).
   i. Limits what the government will pay (but does not set prices)
   ii. Prospective payment is set by taking national median cost to treat each of approximately 500 different diagnoses.
   iii. Payment is determined by adding or subtracting from this median cost according to a formula that includes:
      - Principal and up to 4 secondary diagnoses
      - Principal procedures
      - Patient's age
      - Patient's gender

- Patient's discharge status
- Prevailing wage rate in the area
- Extra payments for teaching hospitals
- Extra payments also for "outliers": patients costing far beyond usual expenses

iv. Consequences of DRGs
- More outpatient treatment
- Quicker discharges from hospital
- Serial admissions (new payments after 31 days)
- Inflation in number of diagnoses
- Preferences for certain diagnoses and procedures that pay more
- Upcoding: recording a diagnosis that pays more (which is illegal)

v. DRGs generally do not apply to psychiatric, pediatric, or physical rehabilitation cases.

d. Resource-based relative-value scale (RBRVS)
RBRVS is a program used to determine how much money providers should be compensated. It is used by Medicare and HMOs. This program assigns a relative value to procedures and services performed and is adjusted by geographic region.

i. Sets government payments to physicians (and insurance companies, as well)
ii. Pays fairly well, but takes capacity to set fees away from individual providers
iii. Payments are made using a formula that includes:
- Amount of time, work, skill, and effort required
- Typical costs of physician's practice (including malpractice premiums)
- Typical cost of physician's postgraduate (residency, fellowship) training
- Typical office overhead

iv. Consequences of RBRVS
- Higher payments to primary care; lower payments to procedure-based specialties
- Higher payments for cognitive work (talking with and thinking about the patient)

EXTERNAL INFLUENCE ON U.S. HEALTH CARE DELIVERY

There are a number of external forces (social, political, and economic) on the delivery of healthcare in the United States. These forces can be identified (and described) based on the source of funds and types of spending by each sponsor.

According to the United States Centers for Medicare and Medicaid Services (CMS) there were 4 primary sources of health care funds in 2014.

1. **Medicaid:** Total Medicaid spending increased 11% in 2014 after already increasing 5.9% in 2013. Medicaid expenditures accounted for 16% of total national health expenditures in 2014. It should be noted that State and local Medicaid expenditures only increased 0.9%, while federal Medicaid expenditures increased 18.4% in 2014. The increased spending by the federal government was largely caused by the newly eligible enrollees under the Affordable Care Act (ACA or Obamacare), which were fully financed by the federal government.
2. **Medicare:** Medicare spending increased 5.5% to $618.7 billion in 2014. This is an increase of 3.0% growth in 2013. This increase was primarily attributable to faster growth in spending for prescription drugs, physician and clinical services, and government administration (including the political impact of Obamacare) and the net cost of insurance. Medicare accounted for 20% of total health care spending.
3. **Private health insurance:** Private health insurance expenditures in 2014 increased by 4.4% to $991.0 billion, which accounted for 33% of total health care spending. The 4.4% growth increase in 2014 was much larger than the 1.6% increase in 2013. Once again, the increased rate of growth reflected the impacts of the ACA,

including the introduction of marketplace plans, health insurance premium tax credits, health insurance industry fees, and mandated benefit design changes.

4. **Out-of-pocket:** Out-of-pocket or "cash payment" spending also increased by 1.3% in 2014 to $329.8 billion. This was actually a decrease compared to the 2.1% increase in 2013. The slowdown in 2014 was influenced by the expansion of insurance coverage (through ACA) and the corresponding drop in the number of individuals without health insurance.

Key factors that influence health spending by each type of sponsor:

- In 2014, the federal government (28%) and households (28%) each accounted for the largest shares of health care spending. This was followed by private businesses (20%) and state and local governments (17%).
- Growth in federal government spending overtook growth in expenditures for all other sponsors of health care in 2014, increasing 11.7% (compared to 3.5% in 2013). The main force for the increase in federal spending in 2014 was largely related to provisions of the ACA, such as Medicaid enrollment expansion (100% financed by the federal government) and the health insurance premium tax credits.

PUBLIC HEALTH AND WELLNESS

In 1999 the Institute of Medicine (IOM) published its landmark publication, "To Err is Human: Building a Safer Health System," reporting that at least 44,000 people—and perhaps as many as 98,000—die in hospitals each year as a result of medical errors that could have been prevented. This exceeds deaths attributed to breast cancer, motor vehicle collisions, and HIV. Approximately 1 in 10 patients entering the hospital will suffer harm from an adverse event.

Patient harm from preventable medical errors is a serious concern in health care. The impact of these errors can have dramatically negative effects on patients, their families, and the health care personnel involved. In addition to the toll on human suffering, medical errors also present a significant source of inefficiency and increased cost in the health care system.

Medical errors are the eighth leading cause of wrongful death in the United States. The problem is not limited to this country; medical errors are a global problem.

Medication errors represent one of the most common causes of preventable patient harm. An estimated 1.5 million deaths occur each year in the United States due to medication error. The IOM estimates that 1 medication error occurs per hospitalized patient each day.

Common causes of medication error:

- Poor handwriting technique on a prescription pad or order form, resulting in a pharmacist or nurse administering the wrong drug or wrong dose
- Dosing or route of administration errors
- Failure to identify that a given patient is allergic to a prescribed medication
- Look-alike or sound-alike drugs (e.g., rifampin/rifaximin)

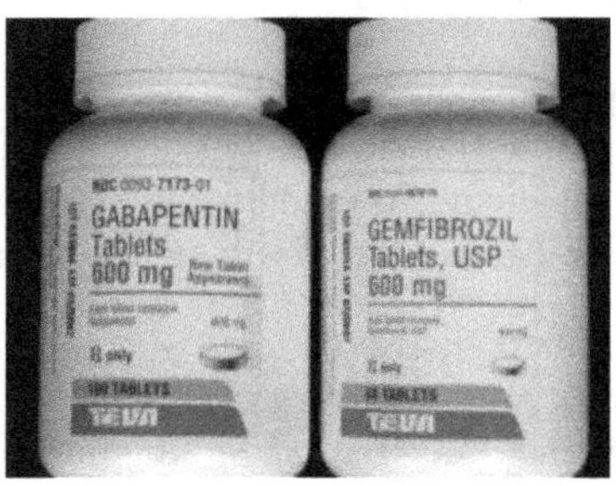

Figure 12-1. 'Look-Alike' Medications

Strategies that help to reduce or prevent medication errors:

- The **5 Rs** help to confirm several key points before the administration of any medication.
  - **R**ight drug
  - **R**ight patient
  - **R**ight dose
  - **R**ight route
  - **R**ight time
- Computerized physician order entry (CPOE) involves entering medication orders directly into a computer system rather than on paper or verbally. The computer software (i.e. electronic health record) can automatically check for prescribing errors or allergies.

Hospital-acquired infections (HAI) affect 5 to 15% of all hospitalized patients and 40% of patients in ICU. The World Health Organization (WHO) estimates that the mortality from health-care-associated infections ranges from 12 to 80%.

HAI can occur in many forms; the most common in hospitalized patients is **urinary catheter-related infection** (UCRI). UCRI accounts for 40% of all HAI; >80% of these infections are attributable to use of an indwelling urethral catheter. Adhering to strict indications for using indwelling catheters, maintaining sterile technique during catheter insertion, and exercising prompt removal of the catheter when it is no longer required can help reduce the risk of a urinary catheter-related infection.

Central line associated bloodstream infection (CLABSI) is another common HAI, and among one of the most common infections observed in patients admitted to critical care units; approximately 70% of hospital-acquired bloodstream infections occur in patients with central venous catheters. Symptoms include fever, chills, erythema at the skin surrounding the central line site, and in severe cases, hypotension secondary to sepsis. These infections can be associated with significant morbidity and mortality, increased length of hospital stay, and increased hospital cost. Checklists have been developed which provide best practices for the placement of central lines that lower the risk of infection (e.g., hand washing, gloving and gowning, sterile barriers, and early removal of central lines when possible).

Hospital-acquired pneumonia (HAP) is an infection that occurs more often in ventilated patients, typically ≥48 hours after admission to a hospital. These ventilator-associated pneumonias (VAP), a subtype of HAP, tend to be more serious because patients are often sicker and less able to mount effective immune responses. HAP is the second most common nosocomial infection. Common symptoms include coughing, fever, chills, fatigue, malaise, headache, loss of appetite, nausea and vomiting, shortness of breath, and sharp or stabbing chest pain that gets worse with deep breathing or coughing. Several methods have been undertaken to prevent HAP, including infection control (e.g. hand hygiene and proper use of gloves, gown and mask), elevation of the head of the bed in ventilated patients, and other measures to reduce the risk of aspiration.

Surgical site infections (SSI) occur following a surgical procedure in the part of the body where the surgery took place. Some SSIs are superficial and limited to the skin, while others are more serious and involve deep tissue under the skin, body cavities, internal organs, or implanted material (e.g. knee or hip replacements). Symptoms include fever, drainage of cloudy fluid from the surgical incision, or erythema and tenderness at the surgical site. Most superficial SSIs (e.g., cellulitis) can be treated with appropriate antibiotics, whereas deeper infections (i.e., abscess) require drainage. Pre-operative antibiotics have been effective in reducing the rate of SSIs.

Patient falls are a common cause of injury in hospitals and other health care settings such as nursing homes. Over $\frac{1}{3}$ of elderly people age >65 fall each year. Researchers estimate that >500,000 falls happen each year in U.S. hospitals, resulting in 150,000 injuries. Approximately 30% of inpatient falls result in injury, with 4 to 6% resulting in serious injury. Injuries can include bone fractures, head injury, bleeding, and even death. Injuries from falls also increase hospital costs.

Assessing a patient's fall risk helps to identify high-risk patients who can benefit from preventative resources. Some risk factors include advanced age (age >60), muscle weakness, taking >4 prescription medications (especially sedatives, hypnotics, antidepressants, or benzodiazepines), impaired memory, and difficulty walking (e.g. use of a cane or walker). Interventions such as increased observation, nonslip footwear, and making the environment safe all play a role in preventing injury from falls.

Unplanned readmissions occur when patients unexpectedly return to the hospital <30 days after being discharged. According to a *New England Journal of Medicine* study analyzing close to 12 million Medicare beneficiaries, nearly 20% of those discharged were readmitted within 30 days. Several factors can lead to a hospital readmission, such as poor quality of care or breakdowns in communication during a transition of care (e.g. hospital to rehabilitation center). Readmissions may also occur if patients are discharged from hospitals prematurely, discharged to inappropriate settings, or if they do not receive adequate information or resources to aid in recovery.

For example, say a 79-year-old patient treated for congestive heart failure (CHF) returns to the hospital 10 days after discharge with exacerbation of CHF. It was discovered that upon release the patient had failed to fill the prescription for the diuretic started during the initial hospitalization. Improving communication and patient education and providing appropriate support to patients at risk for readmissions are all strategies to reduce unplanned readmissions.

Causes of Medical Error

Machines break down, a team can't get moving fast enough, or a simple step is forgotten or the wrong step applied. The greater the number of steps required, the greater the risk of something going wrong. Couple that with the fact that human beings are prone to error, especially when working under less-than-ideal circumstances, and it is no wonder that medical errors pose such a threat to health care. Understanding medical error and the science of patient safety can help us design a health care system capable of getting it right every time.

Note

Errors are bound to occur due to a combination of a complex health care system and the reality of human fallibility.

The potential for human error is amplified by poor working conditions. This includes poor workplace conditions (e.g., overworked staff, time pressures, lack of safety protocols or lack of appropriate supervision), as well as poor individual conditions (e.g., fatigue, stress or illness).

The following is a mnemonic to help assess the fitness of a health care professional to attend to patient care.

IM SAFE

I: Illness (Are you suffering from an illness that is degrading your performance?)

M: Medications (Are you taking medications that may impair your judgment?)

S: Stress (Are you adequately managing the stressors in your life?)

A: Alcohol (Are you using alcohol in excess with negative consequences?)

F: Fatigue (Are you getting enough rest?)

E: Eating (Are you maintaining a healthy diet?)

For example, one study on physician performance found that being awake 24 hours was equivalent to having a blood alcohol level of .10 (legally intoxicated by most standards) (Dawson & Reid, 1997).

Communication and teamwork failures are another leading cause of adverse patient events. Lack of appropriate communication creates situations where medical errors are likely to occur. These errors have the potential to cause severe injury and unexpected patient death. Errors at the time of transitions or handoffs are among the most common communication errors in healthcare; handoffs occur frequently between nurses and between residents in teaching hospitals, but also among attending faculty (e.g., on-call physicians, hospitalists, ED staff). Using techniques of structured communication (e.g., SBAR, call-backs) can help safeguard against errors.

A growing recognition of the need for improved teamwork in health care has led to the application of teamwork training principles, originally developed in aviation, to a variety of clinical settings. Recognized barriers to effective teamwork include:

- Inconsistency in team membership
- Lack of time

- Lack of Information Sharing
- Hierarchy
- Defensiveness
- Conventional Thinking
- Complacency
- Varying Communication Styles
- Conflict
- Lack of Coordination
- Distractions
- Fatigue
- Workload
- Misinterpretation of Cues
- Lack of Role Clarity

Teamwork training attempts to reduce the potential for patient harm by developing effective communication skills, a supportive working environment, and an atmosphere in which all team members feel comfortable speaking up when they suspect a problem. Team members are trained to cross-monitor, check each other's actions, offer assistance when needed, and address errors in a nonjudgmental fashion (i.e. watch each other's backs). Huddles, briefs and debriefs are essential components of teamwork training; as is providing feedback, especially after critical incidents. Remember, a chain is only as strong as its weakest link.

Types of Medical Errors

DIAGNOSTIC

- Error or delay in diagnosis
- Failure to employ indicated tests
- Use of outmoded tests or therapy
- Failure to act on results of monitoring or testing

TREATMENT

- Error in the performance of an operation, procedure, or test
- Error in administering the treatment
- Error in the dose or method of using a drug
- Avoidable delay in treatment or in responding to an abnormal test
- Inappropriate (not indicated) care

PREVENTIVE

- Failure to provide prophylactic treatment
- Inadequate monitoring or follow-up of treatment
- Other
  - Failure of communication
  - Equipment failure
  - Other system failure

Source: Leape, Lucian; Lawthers, Ann G.; Brennan, Troyen A., et al. Preventing Medical Injury. Qual Rev Bull. 19(5): 144–149, 1993

Errors can be categorized as slips, lapses, or mistakes.

- **Slips** are actions not carried out as intended or planned: e.g. injecting a medication intravenously when you meant to give it subcutaneously. Slips are observable.
- **Lapses** are missed actions and omissions: e.g. forgetting to monitor and replace serum potassium in a patient treated with furosemide for acute congestive heart failure. Lapses are generally not observable (one cannot directly "see" a lapse of memory).

Both slips and lapses are actions that do not "go as intended."

- **Mistakes** are a specific type of error brought about by a faulty plan or incorrect intentions; the intended action is wrong (e.g. extubating a patient prematurely based on misapplication of guidelines or treating a patient for a suspected pneumonia when the patient was misdiagnosed and actually has a pulmonary embolism).

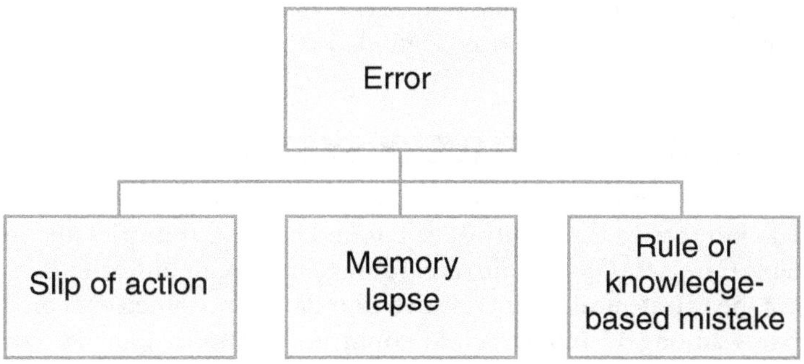

Figure 12-2. Types of Error

It is important to differentiate errors (slip, lapse, or mistake) from violations.

- **Violations** are deliberate actions, whereby someone does something and knows it to be against the rules (e.g. deliberately failing to follow proper procedures). A health care professional may consider that a violation is well-intentioned; however, it would still technically constitute a "violation" rather than an error. For example, a physician may decide to forgo entering a patient's allergies into the electronic record due to time constraints in starting treatment. If this act led to an adverse medication reaction due to a missed allergic reaction, it would technically be considered a violation and not an error.

Errors may result in adverse events or near-misses.

- **Adverse events** are harms or injuries that result directly from medical care, not from negative outcomes due to the patient's disease or medical condition.
- **Near-misses** are errors that occur but do not result in injury or harm to patients because they are caught in time or simply because of luck.

Diagnostic errors account for at least 17% of preventable errors in hospitalized patients. Diagnostic errors can be categorized as no-fault, system-related, and cognitive.

- **No-fault errors** may happen when there are masked or unusual symptoms of a disease, or when a patient has not fully cooperated in care.
- **System-related** errors include technical failure, equipment problems and organizational flaws.
- **Cognitive errors** frequently result from a diagnosis that was wrong, missed, or unintentionally delayed due to clinician error.

The following are examples of common cognitive errors.

A **wrong diagnosis** may occur when the clinician holds on to a particular diagnosis (usually the initial one, in a phenomenon called **anchoring bias**) and becomes dismissive to signs and symptoms pointing to another diagnosis. For example, a 65-year-old man presents with epigastric pain and emesis, and sits leaning forward. He has a history of alcoholism. The patient is likely to be diagnosed with pancreatitis. However, holding on to this diagnosis to the exclusion of any other diagnosis—despite the patient's denial of alcohol use for several years, normal blood levels of pancreatic enzymes, and abnormal EKG, which is ignored—would be an anchoring error.

Confirmation bias, looking for evidence to support a pre-conceived opinion rather than looking for evidence that refutes it or provides greater support to an alternative diagnosis, may accompany an anchoring error. Clinicians should regard conflicting data as evidence for the need to continue to seek the true diagnosis (e.g. in the case above; acute MI) rather than as anomalies to be disregarded.

Availability bias is the tendency to assume a diagnosis based on recent patient encounters or memorable cases (i.e., the most cognitively "available" diagnosis).

It is estimated that thousands of hospitalized patients die every year due to diagnostic errors. Missed or delayed diagnoses (particularly of cancer) are a prominent reason for malpractice claims. Poor teamwork/communication between clinicians and a lack of reliable systems for common outpatient clinical situations (e.g., triaging acutely ill patients by telephone and following-up on test results) have been identified as predisposing factors for diagnostic error.

U.S. VS WORLD HEALTH CARE DELIVERY SYSTEMS

The United States spends more money on health care per capita than all other industrialized countries in the world. However, Americans still do not receive the quality of care found in other countries *and* many still don't have access to care despite the Affordable Care Act (Obamacare) according to the Commonwealth Fund report (commonwealthfund.org). This report from the private health care research foundation examined data on expenditures, delivery, and access to health care services among 13 industrialized countries: Australia, Canada, Denmark, France, Germany, Japan, Netherlands, New Zealand, Norway, Sweden, Switzerland, the United Kingdom, and the United States.

According to this report, the United Kingdom and Switzerland ranked highest for factors that included quality, access, efficiency, and equity of health care; the United States, Canada, and France ranked lowest overall. The United States was ranked worst in areas concerning cost of care, efficiency, equity, and overall health of its citizens, despite the fact that health care expenditures were highest per capita compared with the other 12 countries in the report.

- In 2014, the United States spent $9,523 per person (per capita) in health care expenditures.
- In 2013, the United Kingdom spent $3,364 per person. They were the country with the highest ranked health care system overall.

Although the United Kingdom scored best in most categories (and has the highest ranking overall), it ranked second worst after the United States in terms of the overall health of its citizens.

- This large disparity was based on factors, such as higher rates of adult and infant mortality rates and life expectancy at age 60.
- With respect to overall health of its citizens, France, Sweden, and Switzerland were found to rank the highest.

Although the Affordable Care Act has improved patient access to medical and diagnostic services for many Americans, the global impact of this new governmental policy on the overall health of Americans has yet to be determined.

PRACTICE QUESTIONS

1. A Medicare patient has prescription coverage through which of the following?

   A. Medicare Part A
   B. Medicare Part B
   C. Medicare Part C
   D. Medicare Part D
   E. Medicare does not cover prescription medications.

2. Which of the following is a FALSE statement regarding mental illness in the United States?
   A. Advances in medication therapy have resulted in shorter hospital stays.
   B. It is estimated that 1 in 20 persons in the United States will be hospitalized for psychiatric illness at least once in their life.
   C. The number of hospital admissions has not changed over the past 30 years.
   D. The number of outpatient clinics has increased over the past 30 years.
   E. The number of patients occupying hospitals beds has been declining over the past 30 years.

3. Which of the following is the top non-genetic cause of death in the United States?
   A. Alcohol
   B. Illicit drug use
   C. Sedentary lifestyle
   D. Suicide
   E. Tobacco

4. The 5 "rights" of medication administration are which of the following?
   A. Drug, Cost, Adverse Effects, Route, Time
   B. Drug, Dose, Route, Adverse Effects, Time
   C. Drug, Patient, Cost, Route, Time
   D. Drug, Patient, Dose, Route, Time
   E. Drug, Route, Toxicity, Dose, Time

5. The most common hospital-acquired infection in the United States is which of the following?
   A. Central line associated bloodstream infection
   B. Hospital-acquired cellulitis
   C. Hospital-acquired pneumonia
   D. Urinary catheter infection
   E. Ventilator-related pneumonia

6. A patient comes to the pharmacy with a new prescription. The pharmacist explains that the prescription needs a prior authorization before filling. Who will the pharmacist likely call first?
   A. Patient's health insurance company
   B. Pharmacy consulting physician
   C. Pharmacy help desk
   D. Prescribing physician
   E. Primary insurance card holder

7. A 61-year-old uninsured male who falls below the established poverty level in the U.S. will most likely be covered under which of the following for prescription medications?

    A. Medicaid
    B. Medicare Part A
    C. Medicare Part D
    D. Out-of-pocket expense
    E. Private insurance

8. Which of the fallowing is a FALSE statement regarding HMOs and PPOs?

    A. HMOs and PPOs generally ask patients to pay for a claim and then get reimbursed.
    B. HMOs are often less expensive than PPOs.
    C. HMOs do not permit out-of-network physicians visits but PPOs do.
    D. HMOs require a designated PCP and PPOs do not.
    E. HMOs require specialist referrals and PPOs do not.

9. A patient is preapproved to see a specialist. When entering the physician's office, they are charged a $50 copay. If the cost of the service was $1250 and the patient has insurance coverage that requires a $750 deductible, what is the total cost of the service to the patient?

    A. $50
    B. $750
    C. $800
    D. $1250
    E. $1300

10. Which of the following is a FALSE statement regarding worldwide health care?

    A. France, Sweden and Switzerland rank the highest in terms of overall health of its citizens.
    B. The U.K. has the highest ranked health care system overall in the world.
    C. The U.S. Affordable Care Act has provided access to medical and diagnostic services for almost every American.
    D. The U.S. spends more money on health care per capita than all other industrialized countries in the world.
    E. All of the above are true statements.

Answers and Explanations

1. **The correct answer is D.** Medicare is a federally funded health insurance for those 65 years of age or older and those with specific disabilities <65 years. Each Medicare plan provides different benefits. Medicare Part A covers inpatient care in hospitals, skilled nursing facility and hospice. Medicare Part B covers services from physicians, hospital outpatient care, home health care, preventive services and durable medical equipment (DME). Medicare Part C includes all benefits and services covered under Part A and Part B; however, it is run by Medicare-approved private insurance companies; hence, additional benefits may also be included depending on the company. Medicare Part D helps cover the cost of outpatient prescription drug coverage for MOST medications.

2. **The correct answer is B.** Mental illness is an important public health problem since it is estimated by the Centers for Disease Control and Prevention (CDC) that approximately 25% of U.S. adults have a mental illness. It is also estimated that 1 in 10 persons in the United States will be hospitalized for psychiatric illness at least once in their life. The economic burden of mental illness in the United States is substantial due to loss of productivity, hospitalization, outpatient care and medications. It is also associated with chronic medical diseases such as cardiovascular disease, diabetes, and obesity. Answer choices A, C, D and E are all true statements.

3. **The correct answer is E.** According to the Centers for Disease Control and Prevention (CDC) the overall mortality among both male and female smokers in the United States is approximately 3 times higher than that among similar people who never smoked. The primary causes of increased mortality among smokers are diseases that are related to smoking, including cancer as well as respiratory and vascular disease. Smokeless tobacco is also a well-established cause of cancer. Tobacco usage is the number 1 non-genetic cause of death in the United States AND is the leading preventable cause of death in the United States.

4. **The correct answer is D.** One of the primary strategies to reduce or prevent medication errors is to utilize methods that confirm the "5 Rights" of a medication before it is physically administered to a patient. These "5 rights" are as follows: Right drug; Right patient; Right dose; Right route; and Right time.

5. **The correct answer is D.** Hospital-acquired infections (HAI) affect 5-15% of all hospitalized patients and 40% of patients in ICU. The World Health Organization (WHO) estimates that the mortality from health-care-associated infections ranges from 12–80%. It is currently estimated that more than 1 million HAIs occur in the U.S. health care system every year. These infections can lead to significant morbidity and mortality. HAI can occur in many forms, the most common of which in hospitalized patients is urinary catheter-related infection (UCRI). UCRI accounts for 40% of all HAI; > 80% of these infections are attributable to use of an indwelling urethral catheter. In 2011, the CDC indicated that infections associated with specific indwelling devices (urinary catheters, central-lines, and ventilators) along with surgical site infections account for approximately half of all HAIs.

6. **The correct answer is A.** Prior authorization is a well-established process used by most health insurance companies in the United States to determine if they will cover (pay for) a prescribed medication, medical procedure, imaging service and/or general service. Certain medications and medical procedures are "flagged" by insurance companies to ensure the appropriateness of the medication/procedure and that currently accepted medical guidelines are being followed. The prior authorization process is intended to act as a safety and cost-saving measure.

7. **The correct answer is A.** In the United States, Medicaid is a health care program for individuals and families with limited financial resources, old age, persons with specific disabilities and those who meet specific criteria. Medicaid is a government insurance program for persons of all ages whose income and resources are insufficient to pay for health care products and services. In the U.S., Medicaid is the largest source of health care funding for the aforementioned groups of patients. Thus, the patient described in this question would likely receive prescription coverage from Medicaid (choice A is correct) and not choices D and E. Medicare is a federally funded health insurance for those >65 years of age or older and those with specific disabilities <65 years. Each Medicare plan provides different benefits. Medicare Part A (choice B) covers inpatient care in hospitals, skilled nursing facility and hospice. Medicare Part D (choice C) helps cover the cost of outpatient prescription drug coverage for MOST medications.

8. **The correct answer is A.** Health maintenance organizations (HMOs) and preferred provider organizations (PPOs) are 2 of the most common models used by health insurance companies. Both health insurance models have some important differences. Of the answer choices, only choice A is a false statement. As a general rule, both HMOs and PPOs do not require patients to pay for claims for general procedures and services. However, PPOs may require that patients pay for physician services obtained for an out-of-network physician and then file a claim to get reimbursed.

9. **The correct answer is C.** The patient has a \$50 copay, a \$750 deductible and receives a \$1250 procedure. A co-payment (copay) is a set amount that a patient will pay when a prescription or medical service is received. This amount will be deducted by the insurance company when reimbursing the physician for services rendered and will be added to the total cost of the office visit. A deductible is a fixed payment amount that needs to be paid by the patient before an insurance company will begin to pay for health or prescription services. Thus, since \$750 < \$1250, the patient would pay \$750 PLUS the \$50 copay. This totals \$800, which is the total expense for the patient.

10. **The correct answer is C.** The United States spends more money on health care per capita than all other industrialized countries in the world. However, Americans still do not receive the quality of care found in other countries AND many still don't have access to health care despite the Affordable Care Act (Obamacare) according to the Commonwealth Fund report (Choice C is correct.). Choices A, B and D are true statements.

Pharmacoepidemiology 13

Learning Objectives

- ❑ Discuss principles of pharmacoepidemiology
- ❑ Differentiate between the different types of pharmacoepidemiologic studies
- ❑ Demonstrate proficiency in medication surveillance systems

Epidemiology is the study of the distribution and determinants of health-related conditions within a given population, which can be as large as the entire population of a country or limited to members of a small community.

Pharmacoepidemiology is a branch of epidemiology that studies the uses and effects of drugs in well-defined patient populations. As the name implies, it is based on pharmacology and epidemiology principles. Many consider pharmacoepidemiology as the bridge between these two sciences.

Pharmacoepidemiology is particularly important for the science of clinical pharmacology, since pharmacoepidemiological data will help clinical pharmacists assess the benefits and risks of a medication or class of medications in a particular patient population.

INTRODUCTION TO PHARMACOEPIDEMIOLOGY

Epidemiology is the study of the distribution and determinants of health-related states within a population.

- Epidemiology sees disease as distributed within a group, not as a property of an individual.
- The tools of epidemiology are numbers. Numbers in epidemiology are ratios converted into rates.
- The denominator is key: who is “at risk” for a particular event or disease state.
- Compare the number of actual cases with the number of potential cases to determine the rate.

$$\frac{\text{Actual cases}}{\text{Potential cases}} = \frac{\text{Numerator}}{\text{Denominator}} = \text{RATE}$$

- Rates are generally, but not always, per 100,000 persons by the Centers for Disease Control and Prevention (*CDC*), but can be per any multiplier. (Vital statistics are usually per 1,000 persons.)

Incidence and Prevalence

Incidence rate (IR): the rate at which **new events** occur in a population. The numerator is the number of NEW events that occur in a defined period; the denominator is the population at risk of experiencing this new event during the same period.

$$\text{Incidence rate} = \frac{\text{Number of new events in a specified period}}{\text{Number of persons "exposed to risk" of becoming new cases during this period}} \times 10^n$$

Remember, IR should include only **new** cases of the disease that occurred during the specified period. It should **not** include cases that occurred or were diagnosed earlier. This is especially important when working with infectious diseases such as tuberculosis and malaria.

Examples:

- Over the course of 1 year, 5 men are diagnosed with prostate cancer, out of a total male study population of 200 (who do not have prostate cancer at the beginning of the study period). We would then say the incidence of prostate cancer in this population was 0.025 (or 2,500 per 100,000 men-years of study).
- A population at risk is composed of 100 pharmacy students. Given that 25 pharmacy students develop symptoms consistent with acute infectious diarrhea and are confirmed by laboratory testing to have been infected with campylobacter, if 12 students developed campylobacter in September and 13 developed campylobacter in October, what is the incidence rate of campylobacter for those 2 months? In this case, the numerator is the 25 new cases. The denominator (person-time at risk) could be calculated by:

$$\left[\frac{(\text{100 students at risk at the beginning of Sept.} + \text{75 students at risk at the end of Oct.})}{2}\right] \times 2 \text{ months}$$

$$= \left[\left(\frac{175}{2}\right) \times 2\right] \text{months}$$

$$= 175 \text{ person-months of risk}$$

Since 25 students got campylobacter in September or October, there are 75 students remaining at risk at the end of October.

The incidence rate would then be:

$$\frac{(25 \text{ new cases})}{(175 \text{ person-months of risk})} = 14\% \text{ of the students are getting campylobacter each month}$$

It is measured from the beginning of an outbreak to the end of the outbreak. It is often referred to as an attack ratio.

For instance, if there are 70 people taken ill out of 98 in an outbreak, the attack rate is $\frac{70}{98}$ ~0.714 or about 71.4%.

Consider an outbreak of Norwalk virus in which 18 persons in 18 different households all became ill. If the population of the community was 1,000, then the overall attack rate was $\frac{18}{1{,}000} \times 100\% = 1.8\%$.

Attack rate is the cumulative incidence of infection in a group of people observed over a period of time during an epidemic, usually in relation to food borne illness. It is the number of exposed people infected with the disease divided by the total number of exposed people.

<u>Prevalence rate</u>: all persons who experience an event in a population. The numerator is ALL individuals who have an attribute or disease at a particular point in time (or during a particular period of time); the denominator is the population at risk of having the attribute or disease at this point in time or midway through the period.

$$\text{Prevalence rate} = \frac{\text{All cases of a disease at a given point/period}}{\text{Total population "at risk" for being cases at a given point/period}} \times 10^n$$

Prevalence is the proportion of people in a population who have a particular disease at a specified point in time, or over a specified period of time.

- The numerator includes not only new cases, but also old cases (people who remained ill during the specified point or period in time). A case is counted in prevalence until death or recovery occurs.

- This makes prevalence different from incidence, which includes only new cases in the numerator.
- Prevalence is most useful for measuring the burden of chronic diseases such as tuberculosis, malaria and HIV in a population.

For example, the CDC estimated the prevalence of obesity among American adults in 2001 at approximately 20%. Since the number (20%) includes ALL cases of obesity in the United States, we are talking about *prevalence.*

Prevalence is distinct from incidence. Prevalence is a measurement of *all* individuals (new and old) affected by the disease at a particular time, whereas incidence is a measurement of the number of *new* individuals who contract a disease during a particular period of time.

Point vs. Period Prevalence

The amount of disease present in a population changes over time. Sometimes, you want to know how much of a particular disease is present in a population at a single point in time, a sort of "snapshot view."

For example, you may want to find out the prevalence of TB in Community A today. To do that, you need to calculate the **point prevalence** on a given date. The numerator would include all known TB patients who live in Community A that day, and the denominator would be the population of Community A that day. Point prevalence is useful in comparing different points in time to help determine whether an outbreak is occurring.

Period prevalence is prevalence during a specified period or span of time. There is a focus on *chronic* conditions.

Prevalence = Incidence × Duration (**P = I × D**)

"Prevalence pot"

- Incident cases or new cases are monitored over time.
- New cases join pre-existing cases to make up total prevalence.
- Prevalent cases leave the prevalence pot in 1 of 2 ways: recovery or death.

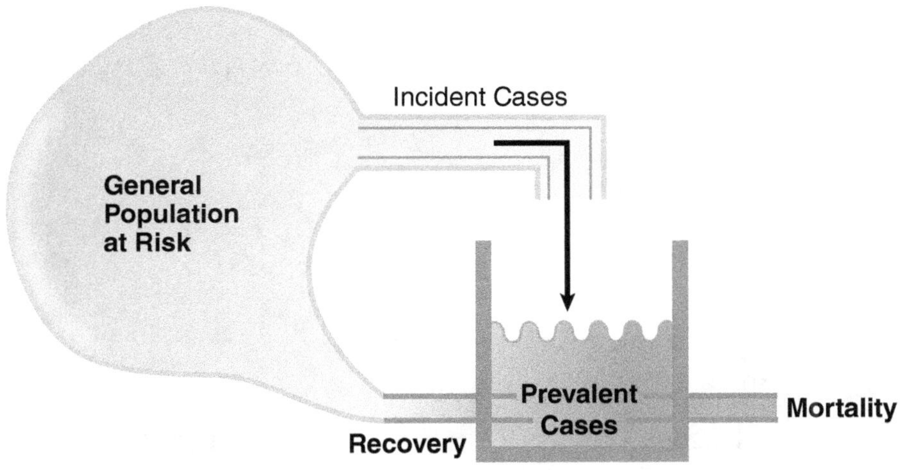

Figure 13-1. Prevalence Pot

Morbidity rate: rate of disease in a population at risk; refers to both incident and prevalent cases

Mortality rate: rate of death in a population at risk; refers to incident cases only

Table 13-1. Incidence and Prevalence

What happens to incidence and prevalence if:	Incidence	Prevalence
New effective treatment is initiated?	N	↓
New effective vaccine gains widespread use?	↓	↓
Number of persons dying from the condition increases?	N	↓
Additional Federal research dollars are targeted to a specific condition?	N	N
Behavioral risk factors are reduced in the population at large?	↓	↓
Contacts between infected persons and noninfected persons are reduced:		
For airborne infectious disease?	↓	↓
For noninfectious disease?	N	N
Recovery from the disease is more rapid than it was 1 year ago?	N	↓
Long-term survival rates for the disease are increasing?	N	↑

N = no change; ↓ = decrease; ↑ = increase

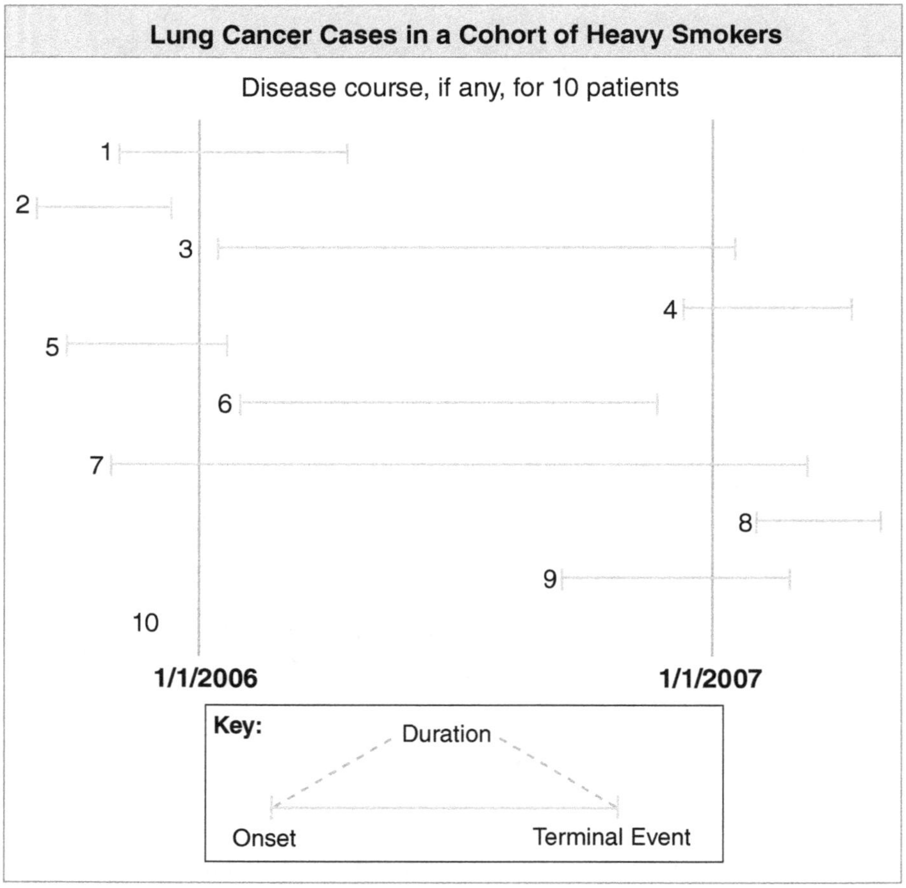

Figure 13-2. Calculating Incidence and Prevalence

Crude, Specific, and Standardized Rates

Crude rate: actual measured rate for **whole population**

Specific rate: actual measured rate for **subgroup of population**, e.g., "age-specific" or "sex-specific" rate. A crude rate can be expressed as a weighted sum of age-specific rates. Each component of that sum has the following form:

(proportion of the population in the specified age group) × (age-specific rate)

Standardized rate (or adjusted rate): adjusted to make groups equal on some factor, e.g., age; an "as if" statistic for comparing groups. The standardized rate adjusts or removes any difference between 2 populations based on the standardized variable. This allows an "uncontaminated" or unconfounded comparison.

Table 13-2. Types of Mortality Rates

Crude mortality rate	$\frac{\text{Deaths}}{\text{Population}}$
Cause-specific mortality rate	$\frac{\text{Deaths from cause}}{\text{Population}}$
Case-fatality rate	$\frac{\text{Deaths from cause}}{\text{Number of persons with the disease/cause}}$
Proportionate mortality rate (PMR)	$\frac{\text{Deaths from cause}}{\text{All deaths}}$

PHARMACOEPIDEMIOLOGICAL STUDIES

Pharmacoepidemiology is defined as the study of the uses and effects of drugs in a well-defined population. It serves as a bridge between pharmacology and epidemiology. This section reviews some of the essential screening tests used in epidemiology, certain study designs and selected types of research studies.

Pre-test Probabilities

Table 13-3. Screening Results in a 2 × 2 Table

		Disease		
		Present	**Absent**	**Totals**
Screening Test Results	Positive	TP (60)	FP (70)	TP + FP
	Negative	FN (40)	TN (30)	TN + FN
	Totals	TP + FN	TN + FP	TP + TN + FP + FN

TP = true positives; TN = true negatives; FP = false positives; FN = false negatives

Sensitivity and **specificity** are measures of the performance of different tests (and in some cases, physical findings and symptoms). Why do we need them? We can't always use the gold-standard test to diagnose or exclude a disease so we usually start off with imperfect tests that are cheaper and easier to use. Think about what would happen if you called the cardiology fellow to do a cardiac catheterization (the gold standard test to diagnose acute myocardial ischemia) on a patient without having an EKG.

But these tests have their limitations. That's what sensitivity and specificity measures: the limitations and deficiencies of our every-day tests.

Sensitivity: the probability of correctly identifying a case of disease. Sensitivity is the **proportion of truly diseased persons** in the screened population who are **identified as diseased** by the screening test. This is also known as the "true positive rate."

Sensitivity = TP/(TP + FN)
= true positives/(true positives + false negatives)

- Measures only the distribution of persons with disease
- Uses data from the left column of the 2 × 2 table (Table 13-3)
- Note: 1-sensitivity = false negative rate

If a test has a high sensitivity then a negative result would indicate the absence of the disease. Take for example temporal arteritis (TA), a large vessel vasculitis involving predominantly branches of the external carotid artery which occurs in patients age >50. TA has elevated ESR in every case. So, 100% of patients with TA have elevated ESR. The sensitivity of an abnormal ESR for TA is 100%. If a patient you suspect of having TA has a normal ESR, then the patient does not have TA.

Mnemonic for the clinical use of sensitivity: **SN-N-OUT (sensitive test-negative-rules out disease)**

Specificity: the probability of correctly identifying disease-free persons. Specificity is the **proportion of truly nondiseased persons** who are **identified as nondiseased** by the screening test. This is also known as the "true negative rate."

Specificity = TN/(TN + FP)
= true negatives/(true negatives + false positives)

- Measures only the distribution of persons who are disease-free
- Uses data from the right column of the 2 × 2 table (Table 13-3)
- Note: 1-specificity = false positive rate

If a test has a high specificity then a positive result would indicate the existence of the disease. Example: CT angiogram has a very high specificity for pulmonary embolism (97%). A CT scan read as positive for pulmonary embolism is likely true.

Mnemonic for the clinical use of specificity: **SP-I-N (specific test-positive-rules in disease)**

Remember SNOUT and SPIN!

For any test, there is usually a trade-off between the two. This trade-off can be represented graphically as the screening dimension curves (figure 13-3).

Post-test Probabilities

Positive predictive value: the probability of disease in a person who receives a positive test result. The probability that a **person with a positive test is a true positive.** (i.e., has the disease) is referred to as the "predictive value of a positive test."

Positive predictive value = TP/(TP + FP)
= true positives/(true positives + false positives)

- Measures only the distribution of persons who receive a positive test result
- Uses data from the top row of the 2 × 2 table (Table 13-3)

Negative predictive value: the probability of no disease in a person who receives a negative test result. The probability that a **person with a negative test is a true negative** (i.e., does not have the disease) is referred to as the "predictive value of a negative test."

Negative predictive value = TN/(TN + FN)
= true negatives/(true negatives + false negatives)

- Measures only the distribution of persons who receive a negative test result
- Uses data from the bottom row of the 2 × 2 table (Table 13-3)

Accuracy: total percentage correctly selected; the degree to which a measurement, or an estimate based on measurements, represents the true value of the attribute that is being measured.

Accuracy = (TP + TN)/(TP + TN + FP + FN)
= (true positives + true negatives)/total screened patients

Sample Questions

1. What is the effect of increased incidence on sensitivity? On positive predictive value?

   None; screening does not assess incidence.

2. What is the effect of increased prevalence on sensitivity? On positive predictive value?

   Sensitivity stays the same, positive predictive value increases.

3.

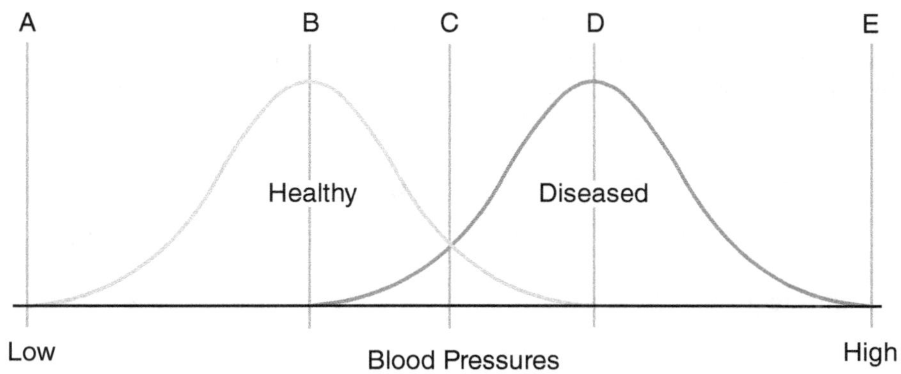

Figure 13-3. Healthy and Diseased Populations Along a Screening Dimension

1) Which cutoff point provides optimal sensitivity? (Answer = B)
2) Which cutoff point provides optimal specificity? (Answer = D)
3) Which cutoff point provides optimal accuracy? (Answer = C)
4) Which cutoff point provides optimal positive predictive value? (Answer = D)

Study Designs

Bias is one of the primary reasons why study results may not be applicable. Understanding each type of bias is essential to determine the overall validity of the study.

Bias in Research: Deviation from the Truth of Inferred Results

Reliability: ability of a test to **measure something consistently**, either across testing situations (test-retest reliability), within a test (split-half reliability), or across judges (inter-rater reliability). Think of the clustering of rifle shots at a target. (Precision)

Validity: degree to which a test **measures that which was intended**. Think of a marksman hitting the bullseye. Reliability is a necessary, but insufficient, condition for validity. (Accuracy)

Types of Bias

Selection bias (sampling bias): the **sample selected is not representative** of the population. Examples:

- Predicting rates of heart disease by gathering subjects from a local health club
- Berkson bias: using only hospital records to estimate population prevalence
- Nonrespondent bias: people included in a study are different from those who are not
- Solution: random, independent sample; weight data

Measurement bias: information is **gathered in a manner that distorts the information.** Examples:

- Measuring patients' satisfaction with their respective physicians by using leading questions, e.g., "You don't like your doctor, do you?"
- Hawthorne effect: subjects' behavior is altered because they are being studied. Only a factor when there is no control group in a prospective study
- Solution: have a control group

Experimenter expectancy (Pygmalion effect): **experimenter's expectations inadvertently communicated** to subjects, who then produce the desired effects. Solution: **double-blind design,** where neither the subject nor the investigators who have contact with them know which group receives the intervention under study and which group is the control.

Lead-time bias: gives a **false estimate of survival rates.** Example: Patients seem to live longer with the disease after it is uncovered by a screening test. Actually, there is no increased survival, but because the disease is discovered sooner, patients who are diagnosed *seem* to live longer. Solution: use life-expectancy to assess benefit

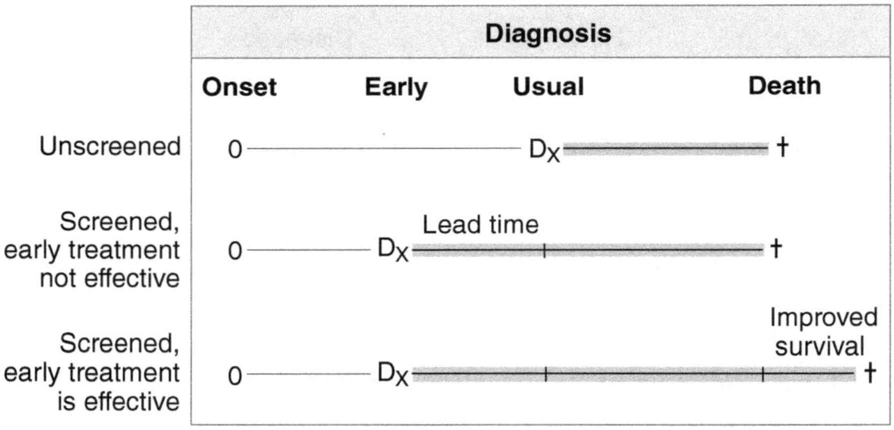

Figure 13-4. Diagnosis, Time, and Survival

Recall bias: subjects **fail to accurately recall events** in the past. Example: "How many times last year did you kiss your mother?" Likely problem in retrospective studies. Solution: confirmation

Late-look bias: **individuals with severe disease are less likely to be uncovered** in a survey **because they die first.** Example: a recent survey found that persons with AIDS reported only mild symptoms. Solution: stratify by disease severity

Confounding bias: **factor being examined is related to other factors** of less interest. Unanticipated factors obscure a relationship or make it seem like there is one when there is not. More than one explanation can be found for the presented results. Example: comparing the relationship between exercise and heart disease in two populations when one population is younger and the other is older. Are differences in heart disease due to exercise or to age? Solution: combine the results from multiple studies, meta-analysis

Design bias: **parts of the study do not fit together** to answer the question of interest. Most common issue is non-comparable control group. Example: comparing the effects of an antihypertensive drug in hypertensives versus normotensives. Solution: random assignment. Subjects assigned to treatment or control group by a random process.

Table 13-4. Type of Bias in Research and Important Associations

Type of Bias	Definition	Important Associations	Solutions
Selection	Sample not representative	Berkson's bias, nonrespondent bias	Random, independent sample
Measurement	Gathering the information distorts it	Hawthorne effect	Control group/placebo group
Experimenter expectancy	Researcher's beliefs affect outcome	Pygmalion effect	Double-blind design
Lead-time	Early detection confused with increased survival	Benefits of screening	Measure "back-end" survival
Recall	Subjects cannot remember accurately	Retrospective studies	Multiple sources to confirm information
Late-look	Severely diseased individuals are not uncovered	Early mortality	Stratify by severity
Confounding	Unanticipated factors obscure results	Hidden factors affect results	Multiple studies, good research design
Design	Parts of study do not fit together	Non-comparable control group	Random assignment

Note

- Random error is unfortunate but okay and expected (a threat to reliability).
- Systematic error is bad and biases result (a threat to validity).

Types of Research Studies: Observational Versus Clinical Trials

The 2 major types of research studies are observational and interventional (clinical trials).

Observational Studies: Nature is Allowed to Take Its Course, No Intervention

Case report: brief, objective report of a **clinical characteristic or outcome from a single clinical subject** or event, $n = 1$. E.g., 23-year-old man with treatment-resistant TB. No control group

Case series report: objective report of a **clinical characteristic or outcome from a group of clinical subjects,** $n > 1$. E.g., patients at local hospital with treatment-resistant TB. No control group

Cross-sectional study: the **presence or absence of disease and other variables** are determined in each member of the study population or in a representative sample **at a particular time**. The co-occurrence of a variable and the disease can be examined.

- Disease prevalence rather than incidence is recorded.
- The temporal sequence of cause and effect cannot usually be determined in a cross-sectional study
- Example: who in the community now has treatment-resistant TB

Case-control study: identifies **a group of people with the disease** and **compares them with a suitable comparison group without the disease.** Almost always retrospective. E.g., comparing cases of treatment-resistant TB with cases of nonresistant TB

- Cannot assess incidence or prevalence of disease
- Can help determine causal relationships
- Very useful for studying conditions with very low incidence or prevalence

Cohort study: population group of those who have been **exposed to risk factor** is identified and followed over time and **compared with a group not exposed to the risk factor.** Outcome is disease incidence in each group, e.g., following a prison inmate population and marking the development of treatment-resistant TB.

- Prospective; subjects tracked forward in time
- Can determine incidence and causal relationships
- Must follow population long enough for incidence to appear

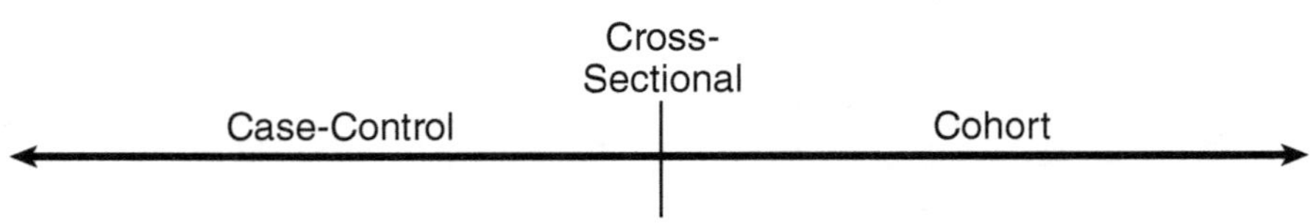

Figure 13-5. Differentiating Study Types by Time

Analyzing Observational Studies

For cross-sectional studies: use *chi*-square (x^2); for cohort studies: use relative risk and/or attributable risk.

Relative risk (RR): comparative probability asking "How much more likely?"

- Incidence rate of **exposed group divided by** the incidence rate of the **unexposed group.**
- How much greater chance does one group have of contracting the disease compared with the other group?
- E.g., if infant mortality rate in whites is 8.9 per 1,000 live births and 18.0 in blacks per 1,000 live births, then the relative risk of blacks versus whites is 18.0 divided by 8.9 = 2.02. Compared with whites, black infants are twice as likely to die in the first year of life.
- For statistical analysis, yields a *p*-value

Attributable risk (AR): comparative probability asking "How many more cases in one group?"

- Incidence rate of **exposed group minus** the incidence rate of the **unexposed group**
- Using the same example, attributable risk is equal to 18.0 minus 8.9 = 9.1. Of every 1,000 black infants, there were 9.1 more deaths than were observed in 1,000 white infants. In this case attributable risk gives the excess mortality.
- Note that both relative risk and attributable risk tell us if there are differences, but do not tell us why those differences exist.

Number Need to Treat (NNT) = Inverse of attributable risk (if looking at treatment)

- How many people do you have to perform some intervention in to prevent one case from occurring?

Note that the Number Needed to Harm (NNH) is computed the same way. For NNH, take the inverse of attributable risk, where comparison focuses on exposure.

NNH = Inverse of attributable risk (if looking at exposure)

- $\frac{18}{1{,}000} - \frac{8}{1{,}000} = \frac{10}{1{,}000} = \text{AR}$
- Inverse of $\frac{10}{1{,}000} = 100 = \text{NNT or NNH}$
- Interpretations: for every 100 people treated, 1 case will be prevented

Table 13-5. Cohort Study

	Disease	No Disease
Risk Factor	60 A	240 B
No Risk Factor	60 C	540 D

For case-control studies: use odds ratio (OR).

Odds ratio: looks at the increased odds of getting a disease with exposure to a risk factor versus nonexposure to that factor

- Odds of **exposure for cases divided by** odds of **exposure for controls**
- The odds that a person with lung cancer was a smoker versus the odds that a person without lung cancer was a smoker

Table 13-6. Case-Control Study: Lung Cancer and Smoking

	Lung Cancer	No Lung Cancer
Smokers	659 (A)	984 (B)
Nonsmokers	25 (C)	348 (D)

$$\text{Odds ratio} = \frac{A/C}{B/D} = \frac{AD}{BC}$$

Use OR = AD/BC as working formula.

For the above example:

$$\text{OR} = \frac{AD}{BC} = \frac{659 \times 348}{984 \times 25} = 9.32$$

- Interpretation: the odds of having been a smoker are more than 9 times greater for someone with lung cancer compared with someone without lung cancer.
- Odds ratio does not so much predict disease as estimate the strength of a risk factor.

Sample Question

1. How would you analyze the data from this case-control study?

Table 13-7. Case-Control Study: Colorectal Cancer and Family History Practice

	No Colorectal Cancer	Colorectal Cancer	TOTALS
Family History of Colorectal Cancer	120	60	180
No Family History of Colorectal Cancer	200	20	220
TOTALS	320	80	400

ANSWER: $= \frac{AD}{BC} = \frac{(60)(200)}{(120)(20)} \rightarrow OR = 5.0$

Interpretation: the odds of having a family history of colorectal cancer are five times greater for those who have the disease than for those who do not.

Table 13-8. Differentiating Observational Studies

Characteristic	Cross-Sectional Studies	Case-Control Studies	Cohort Studies
Time	One time point	Retrospective	Prospective
Incidence	NO	NO	YES
Prevalence	YES	NO	NO
Causality	NO	YES	YES
Role of disease	Prevalence of disease	Begin with disease	End with disease
Assesses	Association of risk factor and disease	Many risk factors for single disease	Single risk factor affecting many diseases
Data analysis	*Chi*-square to assess association	Odds ratio to estimate risk	Relative risk to estimate risk

Clinical Trials (Intervention Studies)

These are research studies that involve the administration of a test regimen to evaluate its safety and efficacy.

Control group: subjects who **do not receive the intervention under study**; used as a **source of comparison** to be certain that the experiment group is being affected by the intervention and not by other factors. In clinical trials, this is most often a placebo group. Note that control group subjects must be **as similar as possible to intervention group** subjects.

For Food and Drug Administration (FDA) approval, 3 phases of clinical trials must be passed.

- Phase I: testing **safety in healthy volunteers**
- Phase II: testing **protocol and dose levels** in a small group of **patient volunteers**
- Phase III: testing **efficacy and occurrence of side effects** in a larger group of **patient volunteers**. Phase III is considered the definitive test.
- Post-marketing Survey (Phase IV): collecting reports of drug side-effects when out in common usage (post-FDA approval)

Randomized controlled clinical trial (RCT)

- Subjects in the study are **randomly allocated** into "intervention" and "control" groups to receive or not receive an experimental preventive or therapeutic procedure or intervention.

- Generally regarded as the **most scientifically rigorous** studies available in epidemiology
- **Double-blind RCT** is the type of study **least subject to bias**, but also the **most expensive** to conduct. Double-blind means that neither subjects nor researchers who have contact with them know whether the subjects are in the treatment or comparison group.
- Two types of control group
  - Placebos: often 25–40% of patients show improvement in placebo group
  - Standard of care: current treatment versus new treatment

Community trial: experiment in which the unit of allocation to receive a preventive or therapeutic regimen is an **entire community or political subdivision.** Does the treatment work in real-world circumstances?

Cross-over study: for ethical reasons, no group involved can remain untreated. **All subjects receive intervention**, but at different times. Also makes recruitment of subjects easier.

- Example: AZT trials. Assume double-blind design. Group A receives AZT for 3 months, Group B is control. For second 3 months, Group B receives AZT and Group A is control.

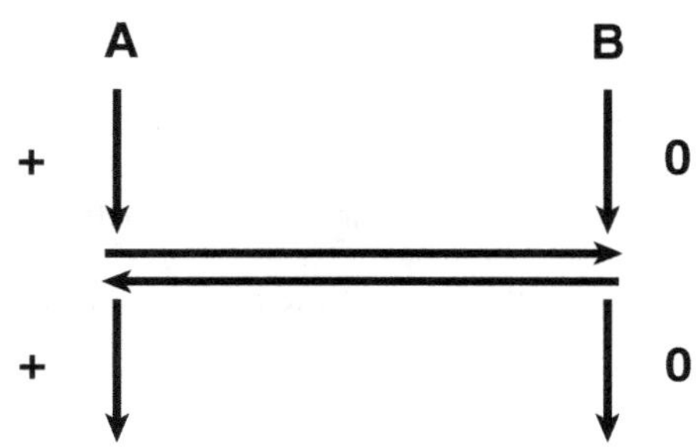

Figure 13-6. Cross-Over Study

MEDICAL AND MEDICATION SURVEILLANCE SYSTEMS

According to the World Health Organization (WHO), public health surveillance involves a continuous, systematic collection, analysis, and interpretation of health-related data needed for the planning, implementation, and evaluation of public health practice. This comprehensive type of surveillance can:

- function as an early warning system for impending public health emergencies;
- document the overall impact of an intervention;
- track progress towards a definite objective; and
- monitor and elucidate the epidemiology of health complications to ensure continual updating of health-related priorities to maintain appropriate public health policy and strategies.

There are 2 primary types of surveillance systems: passive and active. Passive surveillance depends on health care providers (or patients) reporting data to health departments (or the FDA), while active surveillance encompasses a proactive approach to collecting data from the general population or health care providers.

Passive Surveillance

A passive surveillance system relies on the collaboration of both individual clinicians and their medical institutions to report the occurrence of a medication-related adverse effect as a form of postmarketing surveillance (PMS). Once the data has been received by a responsible organization (i.e. drug manufacturer or FDA), the information must be compiled and then analyzed to determine a true "cause and effect" relationship. Passive surveillance involves the regular collection and reporting of adverse effect data and is the most common method used to detect rare or serious drug adverse events.

PMS is the practice of monitoring the safety (and efficacy) of a pharmaceutical drug or medical device after it has been released on the market (following a phase III clinical trial, for example). PMS is an essential part of the pharmacovigilance process. Drugs and medical devices are approved on the basis of clinical trial results, which generally involve small numbers of people that represent only a fraction of the general population. Thus, PMS can further validate the safety of a drug or device AFTER it has been used by larger numbers of people in the general population.

- Example: Patients (in the general population) may begin to experience a rare adverse effect after taking the medication. The reporting of these adverse effects can impact the safety warnings for the drug or change the products labeling information.

In the United States, postmarketing surveillance is overseen by the FDA, which operates a system of passive surveillance called MedWatch (www.fda.gov/Safety/MedWatch/). MedWatch is the reporting system where physicians or the general public can voluntarily report adverse drug events or adverse effects occurring following the use of a medical device. The FDA also performs active surveillance of selected regulated products.

- Example: Researchers or the FDA can monitor the safety and effectiveness of a medical device through a Postmarket Surveillance Study.

Active Surveillance

Active surveillance systems are generally very effective in identifying drug safety issues since they use a detailed process to capture data. They may also provide motivation to health care workers in the form of individual feedback or other incentives. Reporting frequency by clinicians in an active surveillance system is often monitored; hence, providers who consistently fail to report or who complete the forms incorrectly are given instructions on how to improve their performance.

Active surveillance generally requires considerably more time and resources (as compared to passive surveillance) and is therefore less commonly used in emergency situations. Examples of active surveillance include medical records and sentinel surveillance.

Sentinel Surveillance

A sentinel surveillance system randomly or intentionally selects a small group of clinicians to gather data. A sentinel surveillance system is an essential "data collection site" otherwise known as a sentinel site.

Sentinel surveillance generally requires more time and resources than most types of active surveillance. However, it can produce more detailed data on cases of illness or drug adverse events because the clinicians have agreed to participate and may also receive incentives.

A sentinel system may be the best type of surveillance if intensive investigation of each case is needed to collect the essential data. An example includes drug adverse effect surveillance (for a new medication) that can be performed in a physician's office.

Medication Safety Leaders

It is widely accepted in the United States that medication safety is an essential responsibility of every pharmacist. There are numerous types of medication safety programs, but they all have an innovative leader. Some responsibilities of the medication leader include (but are not limited to the following):

- Become an expert in all areas related to the medication safety program
- Train others on essential responsibilities
- Develop standard operating procedures, internal and external emergency-preparedness procedure and technical guidelines
- Be a resource on medication safety to all patients and other clinicians
- Investigate and act on all medication safety events or issues
- Become an expert in all patient safety methodologies, such as root cause analysis, Six Sigma and others
- Collect and analyze all medication error, adverse drug reaction, and continuous quality improvement data to identify necessary improvements and error-reduction strategies for improving patient outcomes

Systems Approach to Medical Error

Health professionals dedicate their lives to the care of patients. Most are highly trained and competent; however, the nature of health care is extremely complex, and people, despite good intentions, are still capable of making errors.

Although hospitals, clinics, and doctor's offices take many steps to keep their patients safe, medical errors can, and do, occur. Rather than penalize individuals who make honest mistakes, the goal of patient safety is to redesign systems to be more fool-proof and able to compensate for human error.

Bad Apples/Blame Culture: When a medical error occurs, the bad apple approach seeks to identify who is responsible for the error and take punitive action against that individual. However, this approach does not improve safety. It creates a culture of fear and doesn't address the root cause of the error.

Only 5% of patient harm is due directly to incompetence or poor intentions. People need to be accountable, but systems changes are needed to truly transform care. Unfortunately, health care has a long tradition of a blame culture. Blaming people who make errors does not get to underlying causes or help to prevent the error from happening to someone else in the future.

The most effective approach to reducing harm from medical error is to find out *how* the error happened, rather than who did it, and then fix the system to prevent errors from causing injury to patients. Improvements in patient safety will be hindered as long as there is a focus on blaming individuals.

Systems Approach to Failure

An understanding of medical error requires an understanding of the systems failures underlying the majority of adverse patient events. Health care is a complex system. Errors that harm patients tend to have multiple causes that are ingrained in this complex system. James Reason, a pioneer and leader in the research area of human error and organizational processes, describes the **Swiss Cheese Model** of accident causation; it is a model used in risk analysis and risk management in complex systems including health care.

The Swiss cheese model encompasses the understanding that patient harm often results from multiple, upstream or proximal errors. In the Swiss cheese model, each 'slice' represents a barrier, and each hole is a failure in the system due to either active or latent failures. Under normal circumstances, one of the barriers works to prevent patient harm (e.g. the nurse catches that the medication ordered is the wrong dose before giving it to the patient); however, occasionally the perfect storm scenario arises where the holes line up and allow an error to reach the patient resulting in harm.

For example, if the hazard were wrong-site orthopedic surgery, slices of cheese might include policies for identifying sidedness on radiology imaging, a protocol for signing the correct site when the surgeon and patient meet in the preoperative area, and a second protocol for reviewing the medical record and checking the previously marked site in the operating room. Many more layers exist but the point is that no single barrier is foolproof. They each have "holes," hence, the Swiss cheese.

Note

Approximately 80% of medical errors or adverse patient events are system-derived.

In some serious events such as wrong site surgery, even though the holes will only align infrequently, the result is still unacceptable patient injury. For instance, in an emergency situation, all 3 of the surgical identification safety checks mentioned above may fail or be bypassed, resulting in the surgeon meeting the patient for the first time in the operating room already under anesthesia. A hurried x-ray technologist might mislabel a film (or simply hang it backward and a hurried surgeon may not notice); confirming the surgical site with the patient may not take place at all (e.g. if the patient is unconscious) or, if it takes place, be rushed and offer no real protection.

Under the blame culture traditionally present in health care, a person may be reprimanded for an error but the holes in the system are not addressed; making it quite probable that the same error will be committed by someone else in the future leading to more patient harm. The goal is to examine the system and develop methods to redesign care so that the holes are removed.

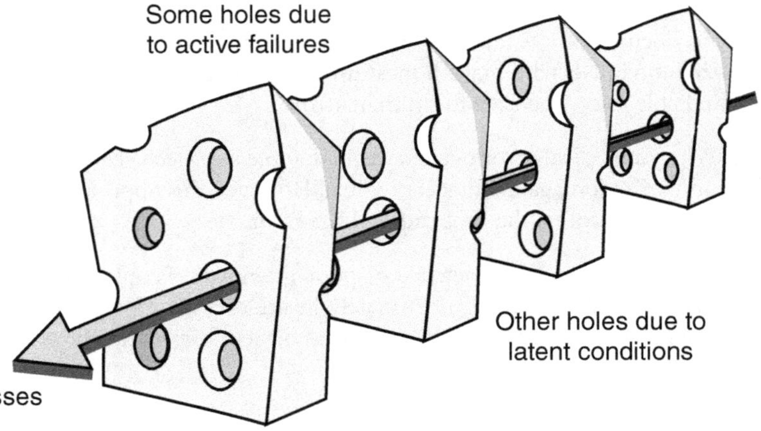

Figure 13-7. Successive Layers of Defenses, Barriers, and Safeguards

Source: James Reason

Other industries with complex systems, such as aviation and nuclear power plants, have successfully employed systems engineering to drastically improve safety and reliability. These industries have also made changes to improve communication, teamwork, and the culture of safety.

Another example of lessons learned from systems engineering is the automobile safety industry. Most motor vehicle collision (MVC) deaths are due to driver error or deliberate misbehavior (e.g. speeding, running a red light, failure to wear a seatbelt, etc.). The death toll from MVC in the past several decades has declined significantly. Drivers today are not necessarily safer drivers than before; however, design changes in cars (e.g. collapsible steering columns, air-bags) and safe highway design (e.g. improved lighting, deformable lampposts) have resulted in drastic reductions in mortality from MVCs.

Likewise, the goal in patient safety is to prevent errors from resulting in harm to patients. Health care must create safety nets that absorb mistakes before they reach patients. Some examples of system-based redesigns for patient safety include protocols to ensure proper patient identification, such as the following:

- Using at least 2 methods such as patient name and date of birth to confirm patient identity prior to the administration of medications
- Using a standardized pre-operative checklist to help operating room staff review critical information prior to surgery (e.g. pre-operative antibiotics)
- Removing look-alike drugs from the nursing unit in order to prevent medication errors

Error Disclosure and Reporting

Many victims of medical errors never learn that the mistake occurred, because the error is simply not disclosed. Healthcare professionals have traditionally shied away from discussing errors with patients, due to fear of precipitating a malpractice lawsuit, issues of professional embarrassment or discomfort with the disclosure process. It is both an ethical and professional responsibility to ensure that errors resulting in patient harm are disclosed and reported.

The first priority after an event that causes patient harm is to care for the patient's medical needs. **Disclosure** of the error is another important early action. Following an adverse event, patients and families want to hear an apology and to know what is being done to prevent the error from harming someone else in the future. They may also require emotional and social support. Honesty and transparency are essential. There is no acceptable reason for covering up an error (e.g. altering documentation to conceal the error) or withholding information from the patient or family.

Such practices are unethical and betray the professional responsibility we have to patients. Studies have demonstrated that a timely and sincere apology may actually reduce the likelihood of a lawsuit.

Often the most senior physician responsible for the patient and most familiar with the case will make the official disclosure. An error disclosure should include the following 3 elements:

- Accurate description of the events and their impact on the patient
- Sincere apology showing care and compassion
- Assurance that appropriate steps are being taken to prevent the adverse event from happening to another patient in the future

Reporting allows for errors to be studied so that system-based improvements can be made to help prevent such errors from harming patients in the future. Reporting errors is essential for error prevention and provides opportunities to improve processes of care by learning from failures of the health care system. In order to be effective, reporting must be safe. Individuals who report incidents must not be punished or suffer other ill-effects from reporting. The fear of punitive retaliation or other negative consequences will serve as an impediment to incident reporting. The identities of reporters should not normally be disclosed to third parties.

Other barriers to error reporting include the belief that no corrective action will be taken and having an overly burdensome reporting system. To overcome these barriers, reported events should be reviewed and acted upon in a timely fashion, and the system for reporting errors should be made as straightforward as possible.

One other recognized barrier to error reporting is failure to recognize that an error has occurred. For example, an interventional cardiologist accidentally orders the wrong dose of medication during a cardiac catheterization; however, the nurse who has worked with this cardiologist for years knows the correct dose intended and makes the appropriate adjustment. No harm has occurred but it would be wrong not to realize that an error did happen.

Health care professionals need to be educated about medical error identification, including the identification and importance of near-misses. Although near-misses (errors that occur but fortunately do not result in patient harm) do not generally need to be disclosed to patients, they should still be reported to the system so that they, too, can be studied. One person's near-miss may be the next person's fatal error. Estimates of the scope of medical errors likely do not reflect the numerous near-misses that do not result in patient harm.

Note

Estimates are that voluntarily reported medical errors only reflect 10–20% of actual errors.

It is important to have a culture that promotes error reporting and error analysis in order to enhance health systems. Every error represents an opportunity to improve a process; however, in order to improve, these errors must be recognized and made known so that system-wide learning and performance can take place.

Analysis of Medical Errors

A systematic approach for understanding the cause of adverse events and identifying flaws in the system, which can be corrected to prevent harm in the future, is called **root cause analysis** (RCA). RCA is *retrospective* in nature; the focus is on systems and process rather than individual blame. The question asked is, "**how did this happen?**," not "whose fault is this?" The goal is to determine why an event happened and what can be done to prevent it from happening again. RCA is not applicable to negligence or willful harm.

A classic tool used in RCA is the **Fishbone** or **Ishikawa diagram** (also known as a **Cause and Effect diagram**), which analyzes a complex system and identifies possible causes for an effect or problem. This type of diagram is used to explore and display all the possible causes of a particular error.

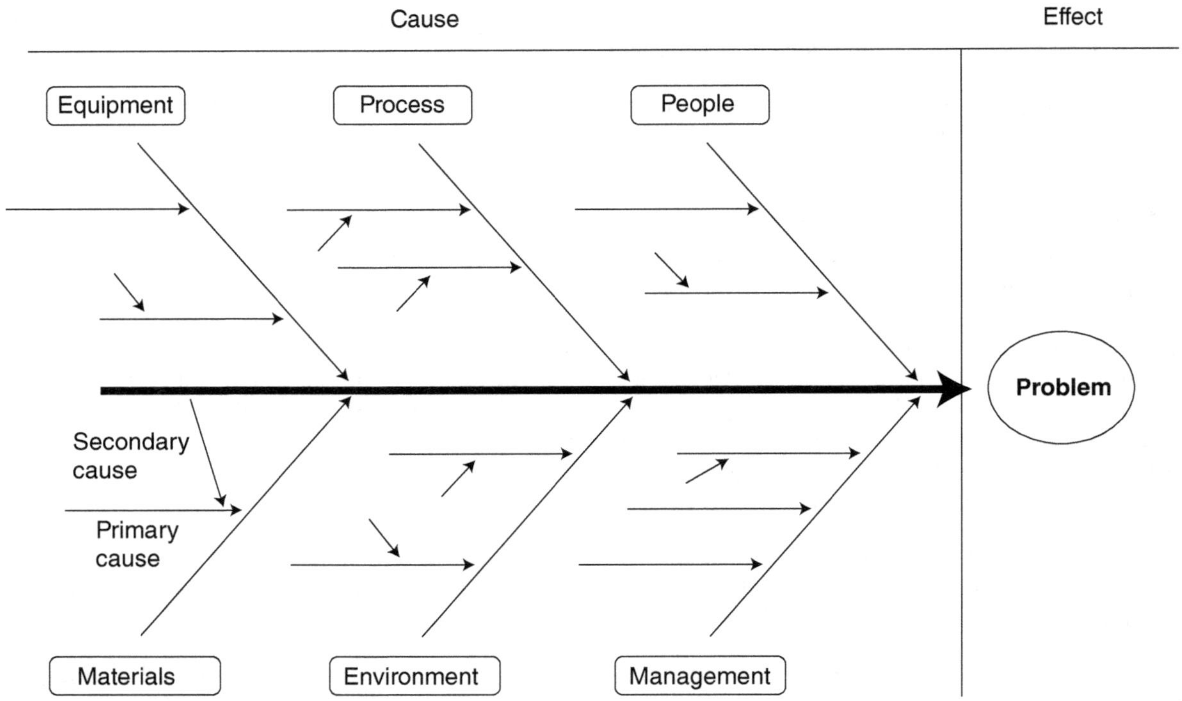

Figure 13-8. Sample Fishbone (Ishikawa) Diagram

The RCA allows the team to identify problems in the system or process of care. The end product of the RCA process is a list of recommended actions to prevent the recurrence of the adverse event in the future. Recommendations commonly consist of one or more of the following actions: standardizing equipment, using double checks or backup systems, employing forcing functions that physically prevent users from making common mistakes, making changes to the physical set-up, updating or improving technology, using cognitive aids (e.g. checklists or mnemonic devices), simplifying a process, educating staff or implementing new safety policies.

In contrast to the retrospective nature of RCA, the prospective failure mode effects analysis (FMEA) is an engineering approach which seeks to anticipate and prevent adverse events through safety design. The goal of FMEA is to prevent patient problems before they occur. FMEA is a systematic and proactive approach that seeks to identify possible failures in the system and potential weaknesses in order to develop strategies to prevent the failures from occurring.

PRACTICE QUESTIONS

1. The results of a phase III clinical trial prove that a pharmaceutical manufacturer developed a new oncology drug that cures 57% of patients with colorectal cancer (including metastatic cases) provided that they have a KRAS mutation (of any type). What impact will this drug have on the incidence and prevalence of metastatic colorectal cancer in the United States?

   A. Incidence will decrease AND prevalence will decrease
   B. Incidence will decrease AND prevalence will increase
   C. Incidence will not change AND prevalence will not change
   D. Incidence will not change AND prevalence will decrease
   E. Incidence will not change AND prevalence will increase

2. A researcher is trying to determine the incidence of undiagnosed type 2 diabetes in the general population. He offers a free screening outside of a local fast food restaurant. What type of bias is most likely to occur in his study?

   A. Design bias
   B. Lead time bias
   C. Measurement bias
   D. Recall bias
   E. Selection bias

3. Researchers developed a new hepatitis C screening test. It was initially used in 500 patients with confirmed hepatitis C and 400 patients without the disease. The test correctly identified 420 patients with hepatitis C and 360 patients without the disease. What is the sensitivity of the test?

   A. 44%
   B. 58%
   C. 68%
   D. 84%
   E. 92%

4. Researchers developed a new hepatitis C screening test. It was initially used in 500 patients with confirmed hepatitis C and 400 patients without the disease. The test correctly identified 420 patients with hepatitis C and 360 patients without the disease. What is the positive predictive value of the test?

   A. 64%
   B. 78%
   C. 88%
   D. 91%
   E. 99%

5. A researcher is trying to determine if jogging/running outside is associated with a higher risk of facial skin cancer than people who normally spend time outside (without exercising). He enrolls 200 men and women who regularly run $\frac{1}{2}$–1 hour 5 times per week and 200 men and women who eat their lunches outside daily. If he then follows them forward in time, which of the following best describes this study?

   A. Case-control study
   B. Cohort study
   C. Cross-over study
   D. Cross-sectional study
   E. Phase 1 clinical trial

6. With regards to the analysis of observational studies, which of the following is FALSE?

   A. Attributable risk is calculated as the incidence rate of the exposed group minus the incidence rate of the unexposed group.
   B. For cohort studies, use relative risk and/or attributable risk.
   C. For cross-sectional studies, use chi-square (x^2).
   D. Number Need to Treat (NNT) equals the inverse of attributable risk (if looking at treatment).
   E. Relative risk is calculated as the incidence rate of the unexposed group divided by the incidence rate of the exposed group.

7. A pharmaceutical company develops a new herpes simplex vaccine. What impact will this vaccine have on the incidence and prevalence of herpes simplex in the United States?

   A. Incidence will decrease AND prevalence will decrease
   B. Incidence will decrease AND prevalence will increase
   C. Incidence will not change AND prevalence will not change
   D. Incidence will not change AND prevalence will decrease
   E. Incidence will not change AND prevalence will increase

8. All of the following statements about the Swiss cheese model are true EXCEPT

   A. Each 'slice of cheese' represents a barrier, and each hole is a failure in the system.
   B. It is based on the premise that patient harm often results from multiple, upstream or proximal errors.
   C. The errors that occur in this model are described as being active errors.
   D. The goal of the model is to examine the entire system and develop methods to redesign care so that the "holes are removed".
   E. All of the above are true statements.

9. Which of the following is NOT an element of error disclosure?

   A. Accurate description of the events and their impact on the patient
   B. Assurance that appropriate steps are being taken to prevent the adverse event from happening to another patient in the future
   C. Complete offer on how to make things right for the patient
   D. Sincere apology showing care and compassion
   E. All of the above are error disclosure elements

10. A physician prescribed metformin for a patient with type 1 diabetes, the pharmacist does not catch the error and a nurse administers the medication to the patient resulting in harm. Which of the following is the best approach by the hospital to this handle this type of error?

    A. Perform a bad Apples/Blame Culture
    B. Perform a Drug Utilization Review (DUR)
    C. Perform a Failure Mode and Effects Analysis (FMEA)
    D. Perform a Root Cause Analysis (RCA)
    E. Suspend all parties involved until the problem is resolved

Answers and Explanations

1. **The correct answer is D.** The incidence rate refers to new cases of a disease during a given time frame and prevalence refers to ALL cases of a disease within a specific period of time. The development of a cure for colorectal cancer would not be expected to have an impact on incidence because patients would still develop the disease at the same rate; hence, incidence would not change. However, prevalence would be expected to decrease since patients would be "cured" thus there would be less people with the disease (on average) during this time frame. Choice D is correct. If the new drug (described in the question stem) had prolonged survival (as opposed to providing a cure), you would expect to see an increase in prevalence (choice E), since patients with the disease will live longer.

2. **The correct answer is E.** Selection bias occurs when the patient sample is not representative of the general population. Since patients who eat at "fast food" restaurants are more likely to be overweight (a risk factor for type 2 diabetes), the estimated incidence of undiagnosed type 2 diabetes is likely to be much

higher in this study. A classic example of selection bias is Berkson bias where a researcher uses only hospital records to estimate population prevalence in a given disease. In design bias (choice A), certain parts of the study do not fit together to answer the particular question of interest. The most common issue is a non-comparable control group. Lead-time bias (choice B) gives a false estimate of survival rates. For example, a new diagnostic test becomes available that can diagnose a disease state earlier and patients may appear to live longer when in actuality they do not. Measurement bias (choice C) is where the information is collected in a manner that distorts the meaning of the information. The classic example of measurement bias is the Hawthorne effect where a group of workers improve their productivity simply because they are being watched. In recall bias (choice D), the patients fail to precisely recall past events. Recall bias is most commonly found in retrospective studies.

3. **The correct answer is D.** Here are you given the number of patients in each test group as well as the number of "true" positives (420) and negatives (360). The "false" positives and negatives can be calculated by subtracting the true positives and negatives from the total number of patients in each group. The results of the test can be represented by the following 2 × 2 table.

	Hepatitis C Present	Hepatitis C Absent	Totals
Screening Test Results Positive for Hepatitis C	TP (420)	FP (40)	460
Screening Test Results Negative for Hepatitis C	FN (80)	TN (360)	440
Totals	500	400	900

Sensitivity = TP/TP + FN; this equals 420/420 + 80 = 84%

4. **The correct answer is D.** Here you are given the number of patients in each test group as well as the number of "true" positives (420) and negatives (360). The "false" positives and negatives can be calculated by subtracting the true positives and negatives from the total number of patients in each group. The results of the test can be represented by the following 2 × 2 table.

	Hepatitis C Present	Hepatitis C Absent	Totals
Screening Test Results Positive for Hepatitis C	TP (420)	FP (40)	460
Screening Test Results Negative for Hepatitis C	FN (80)	TN (360)	440
Totals	500	400	900

Positive Predictive Value = TP/TP + FP = 420/420 + 40 = 91%

5. **The correct answer is B.** Participants in cohort studies are followed forward in time, in contrast to case-control studies (choice A), which are retrospective. In cohort studies, the study group are the participants that have been exposed to the risk factor (in this case, running outside). This is compared to the control group, who are not exposed to the risk factor (in this case, not running outside but spending the same amount of time outside). The outcome of this observational study is the incidence of new disease (skin cancer) in each group. Cross-over studies (choice C) are interventional clinical trials where 2 comparison groups both receive the drug being tested as well as the comparative intervention but at different times. Cross-sectional studies (choice D) are observational studies that assess the prevalence of a disease in a specific population as well as the co-occurring factors. Phase 1 clinical trials (choice E) are the first stage of human testing (i.e. new drug). Phase 1 clinical trials assess the general safety and tolerability of the new drug as well as collect relevant pharmacokinetic and pharmacodynamic information.

6. **The correct answer is E.** RR is the comparative probability asking "How much more likely?" RR is calculated as follows: Incidence rate of exposed group divided by the incidence rate of the unexposed group. RR determines how much greater chance does one group have of contracting the disease compared with the other group? Choices A, B, C and D are all true statements.

7. **The correct answer is A.** The incidence rate refers to new cases of a disease during a given time frame. The numerator (of incidence rate) is the number of NEW events that occur in a defined period; the denominator is the population at risk of experiencing this new event during the same period. The prevalence rate refers to ALL cases of a disease within a specific period of time. The numerator (of prevalence) is ALL individuals who have an attribute or disease at a particular point in time (or during a particular period of time); the denominator is the population at risk of having the attribute or disease at this point in time. The development of a herpes simplex vaccine would be expected to decrease both incidence and prevalence since vaccines prevent a disease from occurring.

8. **The correct answer is C.** The Swiss cheese model analyzes how serious systems failures often reveal multiple, smaller failures that caused a hazard leading up to patient harm. It encompasses the understanding that patient harm often results from multiple, upstream or proximal errors (choice B). In the Swiss cheese model, each 'slice' represents a barrier (choice A), and each hole is a failure in the system due to either active or latent failures (choice C is a false statement and the correct answer). Under normal circumstances one of the barriers works to prevent patient harm (i.e. a pharmacist that catches a medication error); however, occasionally a number of cascading smaller events lead to a catastrophic failure resulting in an error or harm. The goal of the model is to examine the entire system and develop methods to redesign care so that the "holes are removed".

9. **The correct answer is C.** Following an error resulting in patient harm, the first priority is always to care for the patient's medical needs. Disclosure of the error is another very important early action. Patients and their families want an explanation of what happened (choice A), what actions are being done to prevent future similar errors from harming another patient (choice B) and a sincere apology (choice D). These are the only 3 essential elements for error disclosure. Depending on the severity of the error, these 3 elements are often sufficient for patients and their families. However, some may want a form of compensation for the error. Offers on compensation (free service, refunds, remuneration, etc.) may need to occur later but they are NOT part of the error disclosure process.

10. **The correct answer is D.** An RCA is a retrospective method of problem solving used for the identification of the "root causes" of faults or problems. The focus is on systems and process rather than individual blame. The question asked is, "how did this happen?," not "whose fault is this?" The goal of an RCA is to determine why an event happened and what can be done to prevent it from happening again. A DUR (choice B) is a review of prescribing patterns to identify combinations of inappropriate medication use. It is generally performed by the pharmacist before the medication is dispensed. Since the adverse event already occurred, an RCA is the next appropriate step. A FMEA (choice C) is a prospective method for evaluating a process to identify where and how it might fail. It is useful for evaluating a new hospital system prior to its implementation. A Bad Apples/Blame Culture (choice A), including employee suspension (choice E), seeks to identify who is responsible for the error and take punitive action against that individual. However, this approach does not improve safety, creates a culture of fear and doesn't address the root cause of the error.

Economic Outcomes of U.S. Health Care 14

Learning Objectives

- ❑ Differentiate between microeconomic and macroeconomic principles
- ❑ Explain pharmacoeconomics analysis and application principles
- ❑ Describe humanistic analysis and application principles

Population health management is an important strategy for improving the quality of patient outcomes, containing costs, and promoting health maintenance.

Pharmacoeconomic principles play a crucial role in population health management by helping to evaluate the monetary cost of a given drug treatment and its resultant effects (expressed in terms of monetary value, efficacy, or enhanced quality of life).

Successful population health management requires data-driven clinical decision-making, transformations in primary care leadership, meaningful use of health technology, and patient-family engagement. Accountable care involves an integrated, proactive approach to improving the quality of health in identified patient populations.

MICROECONOMIC AND MACROECONOMIC PRINCIPLES

Microeconomics focuses on the smaller business sectors and market's supply and demand factors. It also determines the economic price levels at which "something" becomes profitable or beneficial. Macroeconomics is a broader concept that encompasses an entire sector of the economy, price indices, gross domestic product (GDP) and unemployment rates.

Both microeconomics and macroeconomics are dependent on one another and together they help develop the strategy for the overall growth of an organization (i.e. a pharmacy or the pharmaceutical industry). Some key points about microeconomics and macroeconomics are:

- Microeconomics focuses on the day-to-day decisions that people and small businesses make regarding the allocation of limited resources and helps to set the prices of goods and services.
- Microeconomics concentrates on supply and demand factors within a given market.
- Macroeconomics is a broad field of study that focuses on economic growth and changes in the national income.

Both microeconomic and macroeconomic principles can be applied to the field of pharmacoeconomics.

APPLIED PHARMACOECONOMICS: HUMANISTIC ANALYSIS AND APPLICATION PRINCIPLES

Pharmacoeconomics is defined as the scientific discipline that compares the overall value of one medication (or medication therapy) to another. Pharmacoeconomics studies, for example, evaluate the "monetary" cost of the drug treatment and resultant effects, which are generally expressed in terms of monetary value, efficacy and/or enhanced quality of life. Results from these studies help to guide the allocation of limited healthcare resources in the United States.

Pharmacoeconomics is an integral part of overall health care economics. Hence, this section will focus on many different aspects of United States health care economics. It is important to remember that ALL of the concepts covered in this section can be applied to pharmacoeconomics.

Economics of Health Care in the United States

Health care in the United States has traditionally focused on the management of acute medical problems, such as trauma, myocardial infarction, and stroke. Outstanding advances have been made in these areas and outcomes from acute presentation of disease have steadily improved over the years, with outcomes among some of the best observed in any health system in the world.

However, the health care system here has lagged significantly in the area of disease prevention and health maintenance. Major disparities in access to preventative care services such as prenatal care, cancer screening, and diabetes management; together with social inequalities with respect to patient education and income; as well as persistent individual behaviors such as poor diet, lack of exercise, and cigarette smoking have contributed to the overall "poor" health status seen in many individuals in the United States.

Determinants of health in the United States can thus be summarized with the BIG GEMS mnemonic:

- **B**ehavior
- **I**ncome
- **G**enetics
- **G**eography
- **E**nvironment
- **M**edical Care
- **S**ocial-culture

Problems with patient safety and variations in care that do not follow evidence-based standards further erode the value of patient care. Ironically, the United States spends more on health care than any other nation in the world, yet ranks among the lowest in health measures, compared to other developed nations. Furthermore, the current rate of health care spending in the United States is unsustainable.

Value-Based Care

The traditional health care system operates under a fee-for-service model, where a fee is collected for each provision of health care service. For example, hospitals and physicians collect a fee each time a patient comes to the hospital for the treatment of congestive heart failure (CHF), including any diagnostic tests or procedures (e.g. chest x-ray, B-type natriuretic peptide, cardiac angiogram).

A new model of health care in the United States, supported by legislation, is accountable care. Under the Accountable Care Act (Obamacare), the fee-for-service model is being replaced with value-based care, where health care professionals are rewarded for keeping entire populations of patients healthy.

Using the CHF example, a value-based system would reward health care professionals for encouraging lifestyle changes that prevent hospital admissions for CHF, such as promoting a heart healthy diet, monitoring home fluid intake, and motivating patients to engage in regular exercise. Instead of rewarding exclusively for the treatment of acute medical problems, the new system provides incentives for the health care system to maintain healthy populations, prevent disease, and avoid acute medical problems through the active monitoring and management of chronic disease. Quality in health care is measured by outcomes achieved, rather than the volume of services delivered.

- Note: Value in patient care can be defined as quality of care divided by total cost of care.

Strategies that increase quality and reduce unnecessary costs result in improved value for patients. Unnecessary costs may be generated from the following examples:

- Duplication of services (e.g., a surgeon orders a routine pre-operative ECG for a patient undergoing elective surgery, not realizing the same test was done 1 week ago in the primary care physician's office and was normal)
- Non evidence-based care (e.g., ordering antibiotics for a viral infection)
- Avoidable inefficiencies in care (e.g., a patient returns to the hospital with acute CHF 1 week after being treated for the same condition because he was unaware that a new diuretic had been started in the hospital and was therefore never filled upon discharge)

Failures in preventive health also lead to avoidable health care spending, such as hospitalization for the treatment of acute pneumonia in a patent who did not receive an influenza vaccination. Shifting the focus from volume of care to value of care will improve the overall status of health care in the United States and help to contain the currently unsustainable costs of patient care.

It is **important not to confuse value-based care with rationing of care**, which seeks to reduce needed services in order to preserve resources. Value-based care seeks to reduce unnecessary or unwanted waste in care which increases cost without increasing quality of care to the patient.

- Studies, for instance, have shown that performing stress cardiac imaging or advanced non-invasive imaging in patients without symptoms on a serial or scheduled pattern (e.g., every 1–2 years or at a heart procedure anniversary) rarely results in any meaningful change in patient management. This practice may, in fact, lead to unnecessary invasive procedures and excess radiation exposure without any proven impact on patients' outcomes. An exception to this rule would be for patients >5 years after a bypass operation.
- Similarly, using antibiotics for a sore throat or runny nose that is due to a viral infection not only provides no immediate benefit to the patient, it may also increase harm from adverse drug reactions or development of antibiotic resistant bacterial strains.

Many health care organizations are developing guidelines and recommendations to promote value-based care. These approaches motivate patients and their clinicians to follow effective care practices and guide them away from unnecessary and ineffective care; the result is greater value and effectiveness of healthcare utilization. For example, Choosing Wisely™ (choosingwisely.org) is a national initiative of the American Board of Internal Medicine Foundation which promotes conversations between patients and physicians about unnecessary medical tests/procedures that increase cost without enhancing patient outcomes.

Population health management employs value-based care principles by promoting preventive care, encouraging care patterns that have been proven effective, and reducing waste and unnecessary care.

$$\text{Value equation in health care: } \uparrow \textit{Value} = \frac{\uparrow \textit{Quality}}{\downarrow \textit{Cost}}$$

These principles can be applied to pharmacoeconomics which focuses on the overall value of a given medication or medication regimen. Pharmacoeconomics utilizes the principles of cost-benefit analysis and/or cost-effectiveness analysis. An important measure of this analysis is the quality-adjusted life years (QALY). QALY has become one of the prevailing outcomes of interest in pharmacoeconomics evaluations.

- By definition, QALY is a measure of disease burden, including both the quality and the quantity of life lived.
- QALY is used in economic evaluation to assess the value for money of medical interventions.
- One QALY equates to one year in perfect health.

Pharmacoeconomics evaluations are generally carried out alongside randomized controlled trials and using methods of decision-analytic modelling to help determine the value and pricing structure of a drug therapy.

Implementation of Population Health Management

The goal of population health management is to keep a patient population as healthy as possible. The components required to achieve this goal include the following:

- Delivery of patient care through multidisciplinary teams
- Coordination of care across care settings
- Increased access to primary care
- Patient education in disease self-management
- Emphasis on health behaviors and lifestyle choices
- Meaningful use of health information technology for data analysis, clinical communication, and outcome measurement

This requires clinicians to identify target populations of patients who may benefit from additional services, such as patients who require reminders for preventative care appointments or patients not meeting management goals. Continual access to patient data and analysis of outcomes is the key to providing proactive, preventive care.

Steps in Population Health Management

There are 6 well-defined steps in population health management:

- Step 1: Define population
- Step 2: Identify care gaps
- Step 3: Stratify risks
- Step 4: Engage patients
- Step 5: Manage care
- Step 6: Measure outcomes

Several advances in technology are required to perform effective population health management and accomplish risk stratification; identify gaps in care; achieve patient education, compliance education, disease state monitoring; ensure general wellness; as well as to implement and assess specific interventions targeted to selected populations.

- The electronic health record can produce integrated, accessible population-wide data systems capable of generating reports that drive effective quality and care management processes.
- Web-based tools designed to educate patients about their condition, promote self-care, and encourage preventative behaviors have been used successfully to reduce hospitalization rates by enabling patients to take charge of their health.
- Telemedicine programs have been implemented to establish remote care in order to facilitate patient outreach, allow patient follow-up after discharge from the hospital, and improve health care in rural populations.
- The automation of processes and programs is essential in order to make population health management feasible, scalable, and sustainable, such as a health IT system which targets patients in greatest need of services, generates alerts to those patients seeking appropriate and timely appointments with clinicians, and alerts clinicians in real-time to patient care needs.

However, technology alone will not be sufficient for population health management; effective **teamwork** in patient care is also important. Effective population health involves establishing multidisciplinary care teams to coordinate care throughout the entire continuum of care. High-performance clinical care teams can manage a greater number of patients and more comprehensively respond to patient care needs compared with individual clinicians working in isolation. Care teams can include physicians, nurses, nurse practitioners, physician assistants, pharmacists, patient navigators, medical assistants, dieticians, physical therapists, social workers, and care managers, and others.

The **patient-centered medical home (PCMH)** is one emerging model used to deliver patient-centered, value-based care, and it plays an important role in population health management. The medical home model emphasizes care coordination and communication beyond episodic care in order to transform primary care. It stresses prevention, early intervention and close partnerships with patients to tightly manage chronic conditions and maintain health. The PCMH is not necessarily a physical place, but rather an organizational model that delivers the core functions of primary health care. Key principles in this model include:

- Access to a personal physician who leads the care team within a medical practice
- Adoption of a whole-person orientation to providing patient care
- Integrated and coordinated care
- Focus on quality and safety

The medical home is intended to result in more personalized, coordinated, effective and efficient care. Many of the goals of PCMH directly support efforts in population health.

In 2006, the Massachusetts General Hospital (MGH) worked with the U.S. Centers for Medicare and Medicaid to establish 1 of 6 population health demonstration projects nationwide. During the 3-year demonstration, the MGH implemented strategies to improve health care delivery to its most vulnerable high risk patients (those with multiple health conditions and chronic disease). The hospital system took steps to address the needs of 2,500 of their highest-risk patients.

- Each patient was assigned to a comprehensive care team consisting of a primary care physician, experienced nurse case manager, social worker, and pharmacist.
- A non-clinical community resource specialist was employed to work with the care teams in addressing non-clinical factors influencing health outcomes (for example, if the patient was not able to come to the primary care office for a scheduled visit because of transportation issues, this specialist connected the patient to local transportation resources).

This structure of care allowed clinicians to focus the majority of their time on patients' medical needs. The results revealed a decrease in hospital readmissions by 20%, and a decrease in emergency room visits by 13% for the patients enrolled in the program. Satisfaction was extremely high among both patients and caregivers, and the system was associated with significant cost savings. This is one example of using population health to increase quality while decreasing costs, thereby increasing value in patient care.

PRACTICE QUESTIONS

1. Which of the following best represents quality-adjusted life years (QALY)?

   A. A year of perfect health = 1

   B. A year of less than perfect health = < 1 but > 0

   C. Death = 0

   D. Some disease states have a QALY = < 0

   E. All of the above correctly represent QALY.

2. Determinants of health in the United States can be summarized with the BIG GEMS mnemonic. Which of the following is not listed in this mnemonic?

   A. Genetics

   B. Geography

   C. Education

   D. Medical care

   E. Social-culture

3. The value equation for health care is best represented as which of the following?

   A. Increased Value = Increased Quality / Decreased Cost
   B. Increased Value = Increased Quality × Decreased Cost
   C. Increased Value = Increased Quality × Decreased Cost × Demand
   D. Increased Value = Increased Quality – Decreased Cost
   E. Increased Value = Increased Quality + Decreased Cost

4. All of the following are true about patient-centered medical homes EXCEPT

   A. Critics cite its lack of focus on disease prevention as its primary weakness.
   B. Integrated and coordinated care is at the center of the model.
   C. The patient-centered home does not have a physical location.
   D. The patient-centered home concept directly supports efforts in population health.
   E. There is a focus on quality and patient safety.

5. Microeconomics would be most concerned with which of the following?

   A. Agricultural market
   B. Gross domestic product (GDP)
   C. Initial price for a product
   D. Price indices
   E. Unemployment rates

6. Which of the following is the first step in a population health management strategy?

   A. Define population
   B. Engage patients
   C. Identify care gaps
   D. Manage care
   E. Stratify risks

Answers and Explanations

1. **The correct answer is E.** Pharmacoeconomics utilizes the principles of cost-benefit analysis and/or cost-effectiveness analysis. An important measure of this analysis is the quality-adjusted life years (QALY). QALY has become one of the prevailing outcomes of interest in pharmacoeconomics evaluations. By definition, QALY is a measure of disease burden, including both the quality and the quantity of life lived. A QALY places a numerical weight on time in different health/disease states. For example, a year of perfect health is worth 1. However, a year of less than perfect health (emergence of type 2 diabetes, myocardial infarction, etc.) is worth less than 1 and death is equivalent to 0. There are however some disease states (i.e. ALS, advanced cancer, etc.) that may be considered worse than death (in this model) and have negative scores.

2. **The correct answer is C.** The U. S health care system is noted for its deficiencies in areas of disease prevention and health maintenance. The overall health status of a person can be determined by a number of factors. These factors can be summarized by the BIG GEMS mnemonic, which includes patient: Behavior, Income, Genetics (choice A), Geography (choice B), Environment Medical Care

(choice D) and Social-culture factors (choice E). Although education (choice C) contributes to the level of income, for example, it is not listed as a determinant in this model.

3. **The correct answer is A.** Population health management employs value-based care principles by promoting preventive care, encouraging care patterns that have been proven effective, and reducing waste and unnecessary care. These principles can be summarized in the value equation of health care, which is best represented as: Increased Value = Increased Quality/Decreased Cost.

4. **The correct answer is A.** The patient-centered medical home (PCMH) is an emerging model used to deliver patient-centered, value-based care. It plays an important role in population health management (choice D) and patient safety (choice E). The medical home model emphasizes care coordination and communication beyond episodic care in order to transform primary care. It stresses prevention (choice A is false and the correct answer), early intervention and close partnerships with patients and other health care providers to tightly manage chronic conditions and maintain health (choice D). The PCMH is not necessarily a physical place (choice C), but rather an organizational model that delivers the core functions of primary health care.

5. **The correct answer is C.** Microeconomics focuses on the smaller business sectors and market's supply and demand factors. It also determines the economic price levels (choice C) at which "something" becomes profitable or beneficial. On the other hand, macroeconomics is a broader concept that encompasses the entire sectors of the economy (choice A), price indices (choice D), gross domestic product (GDP) (choice B) and unemployment rates (choice E).

6. **The correct answer is A.** The goal of population health management is to keep a patient population as healthy as possible. This requires clinicians to identify target populations of patients who may benefit from additional services. Continual access to patient data and analysis of outcomes is the key to providing proactive, preventive care. There are 6 well-defined steps in population health management: Step 1: Define population (knowing exactly who is in need of care will be the foundation on which your care plan is designed); Step 2: Identify care gaps (what is missing, what is needed); Step 3: Stratify risks (for the existing gaps and how will the new intervention help the patient); Step 4: Engage patients (offer services to the patient); Step 5: Manage care (implement the service); Step 6: Measure outcomes (how did the service improve patient outcomes).

Pharmacy Practice Management 15

Learning Objectives

- ❑ Define introductory pharmacy practice management principles
- ❑ Discuss principles of pharmacy personnel management
- ❑ Answer questions on pharmacy business and strategic planning
- ❑ Summarize pharmacy practice marketing principles
- ❑ Explain pharmacy financial management principles
- ❑ Define pharmacy budgeting principles
- ❑ Show proficiency in pharmacy risk management

Management is described as a function in any business which coordinates the efforts of employees to accomplish an established set of goals and objectives by using available resources efficiently and effectively. Whether a pharmacy is classified as an institutional-based or retail-based operation, it is still considered to be a business.

As the leader of the business, the pharmacy manager needs to set strategic goals, manage personnel, manage finances, and budget for growth.

PRINCIPLES OF PHARMACY PRACTICE MANAGEMENT

Pharmacy is a business that needs to be effectively manged by a competent leader. In most instances, a pharmacist is the pharmacy manager.

Fayol Management Principles

Many of today's management principles were originally developed around 1900 by the French theorist Henri Fayol. Most attribute his work as a philosopher of administration to the current theories and practice of organizational management today.

In the early 20th century, Fayol developed 14 principles of management to help managers accomplish their goals and objectives more efficiently and effectively:

1. **Division of work:** Each objective is divided into smaller tasks that are accomplished by individuals with that particular skill set.
2. **Delegation of authority:** The manager assigns responsibility for each task to an individual who may also be responsible for managing a group of individuals as a department head.

3. **Discipline:** Obedience and proper conduct are an essential part of any business. Non-adherence to these principles can be enforced with disciplinary measures.
4. **Chain of command:** Each subordinate receives directions from one leader; they are accountable to this person.
5. **Scalar chains:** There is an unbroken chain of command from the lowest rank to the organizational head.
6. **Congenial workplace:** The workplace should be designed to permit productivity and individual employee growth.
7. **Interrelation between individual interests and common organizational goals:** The manager should always put the goals and objectives of the organization above their own personal interests, biases and feelings.
8. **Compensation package:** Workers should be paid appropriately for their services and receive proper incentives for increased productivity.
9. **Centralization:** The concentration of decision making authority rests with the top management but should also encourage ideas and recommendations from employees from different levels of the organization.
10. **Order:** Material order ensures safety and efficiency in the workplace with rules and regulations. Social order guarantees the fluid operation of a company/pharmacy through appropriate authoritative procedures.
11. **Equity:** All employees should be treated equally, kindly, respectfully, and fairly, irrespective of their personal beliefs.
12. **Job guarantee:** Employees should feel safe and secure in their jobs provided that they regularly meet their goals and objectives. Managers should create an appropriate work environment to prevent job turnover.
13. **Initiatives:** Employee initiatives strengthen an organization because they provide new and innovative ideas. Employees are more likely to take greater interest in the functioning of the organization if they feel that they are part of the success of the organization.
14. **Team-Spirit or Esprit de corps:** Managers need to develop proper morale in the workplace.

Within his theory, Fayol outlined 5 fundamentals (elements) of management which represent the kinds of behaviors and attitudes managers should engage in so that organizational goals and objectives are effective and effectively met. These 5 fundamentals can be DIRECTLY applied to various pharmacy practice settings and patient outcomes:

1. **Planning:** Develop goals and objectives and create a plan of action to achieve them. The planning step involves establishing these goals/objectives and arranging them in a logical order and is essential to business success. The manager essentially needs to develop an action plan that determines in advance exactly what needs to be done, the resources needed to complete the task, the timing for each step, and who should perform each action.
2. **Organizing:** Once the action plan is developed, managers need to acquire all of the resources needed to complete the plan. Resources include materials, tools, capital, and human resources. From the human resource perspective, the manager needs to assign responsibilities and timelines.
3. **Command:** Managers are responsible for implementing the action plan; however, the employees are responsible for completing the objectives. For larger organizations, the manager can assign individual project managers (department heads) to carry out the goal and objectives. Managers should understand the strengths and weaknesses of their personnel and provide an effective support system. A good manager is one that has excellent interpersonal skills and the ability to motivate people.
4. **Coordination:** Proper communication is the primary coordinating mechanism for all management activities. Business managers must strive to "harmonize" all business-related activities to ensure success of the organization. Coordination of all aspects of the business encompasses the establishment of strategic goals, management of personnel, management of company finances, and budgeting for growth (purchasing new equipment, expanding operations and marketing). There also needs to be proper delegation of authority and responsibility for the employees.
5. **Control:** The manager is responsible for comparing the actual outputs of the personnel to required outputs of the original action plan. This aspect of the management process can be considered the evaluation and adjustment component. Evaluation can be divided into smaller (day-to-day, weekly) time increments and larger (quarterly and yearly) time increments. Irrespective of the time increment, the manager will evaluate the quality and efficiency associated with each aspect to ensuring high-quality performance and satisfactory results while maintaining an orderly and problem-free environment. Corrective actions will be taken when desired outputs do not meet the goals and objectives of the action plan.

Pharmacy Practice Management

In order for a pharmacy business to prosper, a pharmacy manager must be proficient in the following 6 key areas:

- Pharmacy personnel management
- Pharmacy business and strategic planning
- Pharmacy practice marketing principles
- Pharmacy financial management principles
- Pharmacy budgeting principles
- Pharmacy risk management

Pharmacy Personnel Management

Pharmacy personnel management can be defined as organizing, compensating, and stimulating a competent work force to meet the organizational goals and objectives. A pharmacy manager is responsible for having the right workers scheduled at the proper times to maximize output and provide customer service while maintaining an acceptable budget. For example, a pharmacy manager would schedule more pharmacy technicians during peak business hours and less during non-peak hours. A competent pharmacy manager will also stimulate employee productivity, resolve employee grievances and continually strive to improve customer service.

Pharmacy Business and Strategic Planning

Pharmacy business and strategic planning is an essential skill that all good pharmacy managers must possess. It is defined as the process of defining a growth strategy and making decisions on how to allocate limited resources to attain the organizational goals and objectives.

A good strategy will outline how each goal will be achieved and what resources will be used to achieve these goals. A strategic plan may also have contingencies on how to alter the allocated resources (for example) if a given goal or objective is not met. Thus strategic planning is an evolving process with predefined inputs, activities, outputs and outcomes. As part of the strategic planning process, a pharmacy manager may perform a SWOT analysis.

SWOT analysis is an initialism for strengths, weaknesses, opportunities, and threats. It is a well-structured planning method that evaluates these 4 elements of a project or business venture. A SWOT analysis can be carried out for a product, place, industry, or person.

- **Strengths:** characteristics of the pharmacy business that give it an advantage over other pharmacies
- **Weaknesses:** characteristics that place the pharmacy business disadvantage relative to others pharmacies
- **Opportunities:** elements that the pharmacy business could exploit to its advantage to improve sales and/or service
- **Threats:** elements in the environment or from competitors that could cause concern for the pharmacy business

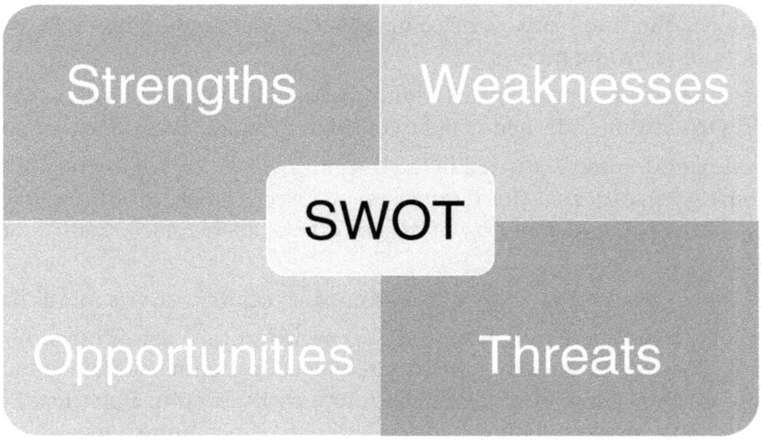

Figure 15-1. SWOT Diagram

Identification of SWOTs is essential since this data can dictate how an action plan can be written to achieve the desired objectives. When evaluating SWOTs:

- The pharmacy manager should first consider if the desired objective is attainable (based on the SWOT results).
- If the objective is unattainable, then the pharmacy manager should create a new objective and repeat the SWOT process.

Pharmacy Practice Marketing Principles

The American Marketing Association recently defined marketing as "the activity, set of institutions, and processes for creating, communicating, delivering, and exchanging offerings that have value for customers, clients, partners, and society at large." In essence, marketing seeks to identify and satisfy the needs of the consumer by creating a sense of need for a given product/service through an exchange process.

Although most pharmacists are not directly involved with marketing, they should understand the following 7 essential P's of marketing:

1. **Product:** there must be a product or service that is being promoted
2. **Price:** the amount charged for this product or service must be appropriate (supply and demand principle)
3. **Place:** the location (physical or virtual) where a consumer can purchase the product or service must be clear; for service, the same facility may be where the actual "service" is performed. For example, MTM (Chapter 22) will likely be performed in the pharmacy.
4. **Promotion:** the most effective way to inform the potential consumer about the value of the product or service
5. **People:** everyone involved in the marketing process (advertising, shipping, storing, and selling)
6. **Positioning:** the way a business differentiates itself from a competitor (could be a better price, better product, more features of the product, better customer service, etc.)
7. **Packaging:** the most effective way to physically (or visually) present the product or service to the consumer to peak and maintain his interest

An alternative to the 7 P's is Product, Price, Place, Promotion, People, **Physical Evidence** (lasting proof that the service has happened), and **Process** (set of activities that results in delivery of the product).

Pharmacy marketing thus encompasses all of the activities and communications involved in the transfer of goods (or services) from the seller to the consumer. It includes advertising, shipping, storing, and selling.

Pharmacy Financial Management and Budgeting Principles

Pharmacy is a business that requires a manager to understand basic financial accounting and reporting principles. This section briefly outlines the most important components of the accounting cycle, which includes revenue, expenses, capital, budget and reporting process.

- **Revenue**: the income that a business obtains from its normal business activities, usually from the sale of goods and services to customers; revenue can be considered the "retail" price of the goods and/or services
- **Expenses:** commitments for costs incurred in the design, development, or delivery of a product or services to another person. e.g., salaries, rent (fixed expenses) and electric bills, advertising (variable expenses); expenses can also be defined as the outflow of cash or other valuable assets from an organization to another person or company
- **Capital:** form of money or assets owed by a given company; **capital = assets minus liabilities (debt)**
- **Budget:** estimate of income and expenditures for a set period of time that is used to help an organization obtain its strategic objectives; in most organizations, budget development is a lengthy, complicated process that involves close analysis of historical trends and future projections (in a pharmacy there are various budgets, e.g., operational budgets, staffing budgets, and fixed expenditure budgets)

- **Reporting process:** process of reporting all revenue, expenses and capital to the U.S. government for tax purposes

Pharmacy Risk Management

Risk management is defined as the identification, assessment, and prioritization of risks followed by a calculated application of organizational resources to diminish, monitor, and control the probability and/or impact of disastrous events as well as capitalize on the forthcoming opportunities.

As outlined in Chapter 13 ("Medical and Medication Surveillance Systems"), there are 2 types of surveillance systems that can be used as part of a risk management strategy: passive and active. While **passive surveillance** depends on health care providers (or patients) reporting data to health departments (or the FDA), **active surveillance** proactively collects data from the general population and/or health care providers.

In addition to these surveillance systems, a risk management program will generally encompass a review of the areas of actual or potential sources of risk and/or liability involving patients, staff, visitors, and property.

- An incident reporting system collects data on adverse occurrences in all areas throughout the facility.
- A quality improvement committee, for example, may assist with the data collection in the risk management areas through the medical/pharmacy staff.

In general, risk management programs are required by insurance companies for both commercial and medical malpractice coverage. Risk management programs are generally designed to train staff in minimizing or eliminating risks or safety concerns throughout an organization.

Table 15-1. Pharmacy Risk Management Strategies and Programs

Risk Management Tool	Definition/Comments
Drug utilization review (DUR)	• Used for the review of practitioner prescribing and pharmacist dispensing of a medication. • Involves an inclusive review of patients' current prescription and medication information before, during and after the dispensing of the drug to ensure proper medication decision-making and prevent patient harm. • Attempts to identify drug-drug and drug-disease interaction as well as therapeutic duplications, improper dosage, and improper treatment durations. • DUR programs provide corrective actions and information to prompt further evaluations by the pharmacist.
Root Cause Analysis (RCA)	• Retrospective evaluation that focuses on systems and process rather than placing individual blame. • The question asked by an RCA is, "how did this happen?" not "whose fault is this?" • The goal of an RCA is to determine why an event happened and what can be done to prevent it from happening again. • RCA is used to analyze serious adverse events, including medication errors. • By definition, an individual factor is considered a "root cause" if the removal of this factor from the problem-fault-sequence consequently prevents the final undesirable event from recurring. Thus an RCA determines what is really causing this situation to occur and removing the causative factors so that incident does not repeat. • RCA is not applicable to negligence or willful harm.

(Continued)

Risk Management Tool	Definition/Comments
Failure Mode and Effects Analysis (FMEA)	• A prospective analysis that seeks to anticipate and prevent adverse events through safety design. • The goal of FMEA is to prevent patient problems before they occur. • FMEA is a systematic and proactive approach that seeks to identify possible failures in the system and potential weaknesses in order to develop strategies to prevent the failures from occurring. • FMEA evaluates 1) Steps in implementing the process, 2) Failure modes (What could go wrong with a particular solution?), 3) Failure causes (Why would a particular failure happen?) and 4) Failure effects (What would be the consequences of each type of failure?). • Useful in evaluating a new process, such as implementing a new telepharmacy solution, prior to deployment. It will also assess the impact of a proposed change to an existing process.
Swiss Cheese Model	• The Swiss cheese model encompasses the understanding that patient harm often results from multiple, upstream or proximal errors. • In this model, each 'slice' represents a barrier, and each hole is a failure in the system due to either active or latent failures. Under normal circumstances one of the barriers works to prevent patient harm (e.g. the pharmacist catches that the medication ordered is the wrong dose before giving it to the patient); however, occasionally the perfect storm scenario arises where the holes line up and allow an error to reach the patient resulting in harm. • *Please see Chapter 13 under "Medical and Medication Surveillance Systems" for additional information.*
Activity Hazard Analysis (AHA)	• Risk assessment tool used to identify and control workplace hazards. • An AHA is a second tier risk assessment tool with a goal of preventing personal injury to the worker and others coming in contact with the workplace.
Bad Apples/Blame Culture	• Not recommended. • When a medical error occurs, the bad apple approach seeks to identify who is responsible for the error and take punitive action against that individual. • This approach does not improve safety. It creates a culture of fear and doesn't address the root cause of the error.

PRACTICE QUESTIONS

1. The assets of a pharmacy equals

   A. Capital MINUS Liabilities
   B. Capital MINUS Property PLUS Liabilities
   C. Capital PLUS Property MINUS Liabilities
   D. Capital PLUS Liabilities
   E. Liabilities MINUS Capital

2. The main difference between passive and active surveillance is that passive surveillance:
   A. Depends on health care providers or patients voluntarily reporting data to health departments
   B. Encompasses a proactive approach of collecting data from patients or health care providers
   C. Is a mandatory form of reporting
   D. Is performed only by patients
   E. Is utilized only by health care providers

3. Regarding the 5 fundamentals of Faylor's management, which of the following is FALSE?
   A. Command: Employees implement the plan and complete the objectives.
   B. Control: Manager compares the actual outputs of employees to original plan, evaluates results and makes changes where necessary.
   C. Coordination: Proper communication is the primary coordinating mechanism for all management activities.
   D. Organizing: Acquire the resources needed to complete the plan.
   E. Planning: Develop an action plan that outlines the goals, objectives, resources needed to complete and timing for completion.

4. Which of the following SWOT analysis components are incorrectly matched with their definitions?
   A. Strength: Characteristics of a business that give it an advantage over the competition
   B. Weakness: Characteristics of a business that give it a disadvantage over the competition
   C. Opportunity: Exploitable elements that a business could use to improve sales and services offered
   D. Threats: Elements in the environment or from competitors that could cause concern for the business
   E. All of the above are correctly matched

5. A pharmacy manager is considering offering a new clinical service and performs a SWOT analysis. If the objective is unattainable, the pharmacy manager should do which of the following?
   A. Abandon the idea completely
   B. Develop a new objective and begin implementing the clinical service
   C. Develop a new objective and gather a focus group
   D. Develop a new objective and repeat the SWOT process
   E. Temporarily abandon the idea and perform a comprehensive market analysis

6. The original 4 essential P's of marketing are Product, Price, Place, and Promotion. This list has been expanded to include all of the following EXCEPT
   A. Packaging
   B. Partitioning
   C. People
   D. Positioning
   E. All of the above are in the expanded list

7. Which of the following is NOT an asset?
   A. Cash
   B. Land
   C. Inventory
   D. Notes receivable
   E. All of the above are assets

8. Chet's family pharmacy has a shareholder equity of $300K at the beginning of the year and earned a net income of $700K during the year. Assuming that no dividends were paid to the owner and the pharmacy has $500K of total liabilities, what is the value of Chet's assets?
   A. $500K
   B. $800K
   C. $1 million
   D. $1.5 million
   E. More information is needed to answer the question

9. A retail pharmacy chain in a large city is considering the addition of a telepharmacy solution for rural areas in another part of the country. Which of the following should be performed prior to implementing this solution?
   A. Activity Hazard Analysis (AHA)
   B. Drug Utilization Review (DUR)
   C. Failure Mode and Effects Analysis (FMEA)
   D. Root Cause Analysis (RCA)
   E. None of the above would be appropriate for this scenario

10. Chet's pharmacy has a building and land, each having an original purchase price of 1 million dollars. After 3 years of being in business, the total depreciation of both the building and land is $300K. What is the value of the land and building 3 years from the purchase date?
    A. Land = $700K; Building = $700K
    B. Land = $700K; Building = $1 million
    C. Land = $850K; Building = $850K
    D. Land = $1 million; Building = $700K
    E. Land = $1 million; Building = $1 million

Answers and Explanations

1. **The correct answer is D.** The basic accounting equation describes the relationship between the assets, liabilities, and owner's equity of a business (capital). In business, it is the foundation for the double-entry bookkeeping system. The original equation is as follows: Assets = Capital + Liabilities.

2. **The correct answer is A.** There are 2 primary types of surveillance systems that can be used as part of a risk management strategy: Passive and Active. The main difference between passive and active surveillance is that passive surveillance depends on health care providers (or patients) voluntarily

reporting data to health departments (or the FDA) while active surveillance encompasses a proactive approach to collecting data from the general population and health care providers.

3. **The correct answer is A.** Within Fayol's Principles of Management theory, he outlined 5 fundamentals (elements) of management that represent the kinds of behaviors and attitudes managers should engage in so that the organizational goals and objectives are effective and effectively met. These 5 fundamentals can be DIRECTLY applied to various pharmacy practice settings and patient outcomes. The 5 fundamentals of Fayol's management are planning, organization, command, coordination, and control. Of the answer choices, only choice A is an incorrect statement. For the Command fundamental of his theory, managers are responsible for implementing the action plan; however, the employees are responsible for completing the objectives. For larger organizations, the manager can assign individual project managers (department heads) to carry out the goal and objectives.

4. **The correct answer is E.** SWOT analysis is an initialism for strengths, weaknesses, opportunities, and threats. It is a well-structured planning method that evaluates four elements of a project or business venture. These elements are strengths, weaknesses, opportunity and threats. A SWOT analysis can be carried out for a product, place, industry, or person.

5. **The correct answer is D.** As part of the strategic planning process, a pharmacy manager may perform a SWOT analysis. SWOT analysis is an initialism for strengths, weaknesses, opportunities, and threats. Identification of SWOTs is essential since this data can dictate how an action plan can be written to achieve the desired objectives. The pharmacy manager should first consider if the desired objective is attainable (based on the SWOT results). If the objective is unattainable, then the pharmacy manager should create a new objective and repeat the SWOT process.

6. **The correct answer is B.** Marketing seeks to identify and satisfy the needs of the consumer by creating a sense of need for a given product/service through an exchange process. The original 4 essential "P's" of marketing are Product, Price, Place, Promotion. This list has been expanded to "7 P's" to include People, Positioning and Packaging. An alternative to the above mentioned "7 P's" is as follows: Product, Price, Place, Promotion, People, Physical Evidence (lasting proof that the service has happened) and Process (set of activities that results in delivery of the product).

7. **The correct answer is E.** Simply stated, an asset is an economic resource that can be converted to cash. In financial accounting, an asset is defined as anything tangible or intangible that is owned or controlled by a person (or organization) to produce value and that is seen to have positive economic value. All of the answer choices are considered assets, including notes receivable which is a long term asset.

8. **The correct answer is D.** The basic accounting equation is Assets – Liabilities = Owner's Equity (capital). This is rearranged to Assets = Liabilities + Owner's Equity (OE). At the beginning of the year, Chet has $300K in equity. He then retains $700K of net income (net income is income after taxes are paid) into the business since no dividends were paid to him. Thus you can then calculate the ending balance of OE by adding the beginning equity ($300K) + net income ($700K) to give an ending balance of $1 million. This is then added to liabilities ($500K) to give a total asset valuation of $1.5 million.

9. **The correct answer is C.** A FMEA is a prospective method for evaluating a process to identify where and how it might fail. It is useful for evaluating a new hospital system (or telepharmacy solution) prior to its implementation. The goal of FMEA is to prevent patient or organizational problems before they occur. FMEA is a systematic and proactive approach that seeks to identify possible failures in the system and potential weaknesses in order to develop strategies to prevent the failures from occurring. An AHA (choice A) is a second tier risk assessment tool with a goal of preventing personal injury to the worker and others coming in contact with the workplace. A DUR (choice B) is a review of prescribing patterns to identify combinations of inappropriate medication use. It is generally performed by the pharmacist before the medication is dispensed. An RCA (choice D) is a retrospective method of problem solving

used for the identification of the "root causes" of faults or problems. The goal of an RCA is to determine why an event happened and what can be done to prevent it from happening again.

10. **The correct answer is D.** Depreciation is essentially the allocation of the cost of assets to periods in which the assets are used. In this question, both land and a building are purchased for $1 million each. We are then told that there is a total depreciation of $300K for both the building and the land and asked to determine the value of each after 3 years. This was a bit of a trick question because land does NOT depreciate so its value is the same as the original purchase price of $1 million. Buildings do depreciate; hence, the value of the building after 3 years is calculated as follows: $1 million MINUS $300K = $700K.

U.S. Pharmacy Law and Regulations 16

Learning Objectives

- ❑ Define introductory principles of pharmacy law and regulations
- ❑ Describe pharmacy civil and criminal liability
- ❑ Show proficiency in the administration and enforcement pharmacy laws and regulations

In the United States, a combination of state and federal pharmacy laws govern the way pharmacy is practiced in each individual state. However, since pharmacy laws vary from state to state, the FPGEE will only test your knowledge of federal pharmacy law.

U.S. PHARMACY LAW, REGULATIONS, AND LEGAL LIABILITY

State pharmacy laws generally outline the scope of pharmacy practice, as well as requirements for practicing as a licensed pharmacist. State laws are enforced by state boards of pharmacy and state law enforcement agencies. Federal pharmacy laws primarily focus on the regulation of narcotics and other controlled substances and are enforced by the Food and Drug Administration.

A comprehensive review of federal pharmacy law can be obtained from the following websites: uscode.house.gov and gpo.gov.

Federal Pharmacy Law History

Today's federal pharmacy law has evolved over the past 100+ years as a result of a number of health issues and concerns at a given point in time. For example, the Pure Food and Drug Act of 1906 prohibited interstate commerce in misbranded and adulterated foods, drinks, and drugs. It became the first pharmacy law designed to promote public safety.

The cornerstone of all pharmacy law today is the Federal Food, Drug, and Cosmetic Act (FDCA) that was passed as a public safety concern when 107 individuals who consumed a drug product (Sulfanilamide Elixir) containing diethylene glycol (antifreeze) died. Numerous other laws and regulations have been enacted as a result of significant patient safety issues with national implications.

The U.S. federal government is also able to implement legislation affecting pharmacy practice throughout the country based on Medicaid participation. For example, the counseling provisions of the Omnibus Budget Reconciliation Act (OBRA) required individual state governments to establish additional "state sponsored" pharmacy practice standards. Under OBRA, states that did not comply with the specified regulations risked losing federal funding of their programs. In other words, the federal government has the ability to indirectly govern all aspects of pharmacy practice if it chooses to do so.

The FDCA and OBRA are only 2 examples of the way the federal government can impact the practice of pharmacy in each state.

The following table summarizes some of the key federal pharmacy acts and amendments affecting the practice of pharmacy today. It is essential you understand the individual summaries of each act. For example, the Durham-Humphrey Amendment described what information should appear on a prescription label and knowing this information is essential for all U.S. pharmacists.

Table 16-1. Key Federal Pharmacy Acts and Amendments

Amendment or Act	Summary of Act or Amendment
Pure Food and Drug Act of 1906	• Considered to set the framework for the Food and Drug Administration (FDA). • This act prohibited interstate commerce of misbranded (mislabeled or fraudulently labeled) and adulterated (made impure by adding improper or inferior ingredients) foods, drinks and drugs under penalty of seizure of the questionable products and/or prosecution of the responsible parties. • A later amendment to this act prohibited the labeling of drugs/foods with false therapeutic claims intended to defraud the consumer.
Harrison Narcotics Tax Act of 1914	• Federally regulated and taxed the importation, distribution, production and use of all opiates. • The act was later amended to ban the importation of heroin into the U.S. for any purpose in 1924.
Food, Drug, and Cosmetic Act (FDCA) of 1938 • The following are ALL amendments to the FDCA	Replaced the Pure Food and Drug Act of 1906. The FDCA still remains the basis of the FDA authority in the United States. The original FDCA contains the following provisions: • Requires all new drugs to be proven safe (by the manufacturer) before marketing to the general public. It is important to note that this act only requires that a drug be safe. The efficacy requirement came with the Kefauver-Harris Amendment. • Extended federal control to both cosmetics and therapeutic devices, which must also be proven to be safe before marketing. • Granted federal authority for authorizing standards of drug and food identity and quality. • Manufacturers must provide safe tolerances for unavoidable poisonous substances. • Establish and authorize federal drug/device factory inspections.
Durham-Humphrey Amendment	Commonly known as the Prescription Drug Amendment because it established 2 classes of drugs: Rx legend (prescription) and OTC (over the counter). Other requirements of this amendment include: • Granted the FDA the authority to classify prescription drugs as those that are "habit-forming and/or subject to the new drug application approval process." • Instituted the requirement that a patient can only receive an Rx legend medication with a valid prescription from a licensed practitioner. This requirement further stated that a patient must receive a written prescription from a physician or an "oral prescription" can be called into the pharmacy by that physician and the pharmacist must immediately reduce the prescription to writing. • Granted authorization of refills on prescriptions. • Drug manufacturer can switch their product from Rx to OTC by meeting certain criteria. • Provided guidance on the minimal information that must be included on the prescription label: 1) name and address of the pharmacy, 2) serial number of the prescription, 3) date of its filling, 4) the name of the prescriber, 5) the name of the patient, 6) the directions for use, and 7) applicable warning labels.

(Continued)

Amendment or Act	Summary of Act or Amendment
Kefauver-Harris Amendment	Commonly known as the Efficacy Amendment. The amendment requires: • Drug manufacturers to show the effectiveness of their products (through clinical trials with preclinical trials through phase IV trials) as well as drug safety. ***Note: Additional information on clinical trials can be found in Chapter 13.*** • Drug manufactures must report adverse events (along with incidence and severity) to the FDA. • Drug manufactures must ensure that advertisements disclose the benefits and risks of each drug. • Informed consent is also required from participants prior to starting clinical studies. • The FDA also was given jurisdiction over prescription drug advertising.
Comprehensive Drug Abuse Prevention and Control Act of 1970	Also known as the Controlled Substances Act (CSA). • The CSA provides guidance for the proper classification, purchasing, distribution and record keeping requirements of all controlled substances. • Required the registration/verification of controlled-substance prescribers. • Created the Drug Enforcement Administration (DEA), which is responsible for enforcing the laws created by the CSA. • ***An in-depth discussion of the CSA is provided later in this chapter.***
Occupational Safety and Health Act	• Resulted in the creation of both the Occupational Safety and Health Administration (OSHA) and the National Institute for Occupational Safety and Health (NIOSH). • This act was written to help prevent work-related injuries, illnesses and deaths by establishing and enforcing standards for workplace health and safety.
Poison Prevention Packaging Act	Created the Consumer Product Safety Commission (CPSC) that requires manufacturers to perform tests on household products that could be poisonous to ensure that children under 5 years of age would find the packaging expressively difficult to open. This act also applies to prescription medications. • Failure to comply with packaging requirements with the use of child resistant prescription bottles is considered a misbranding violation under the FDCA. • A pharmacist who fails to comply could be imprisoned for not more than 1 year or pay a fine of not more than $1000. According to the law, all legend drugs and controlled substances must be packaged in a child-resistant container (Rx bottle), with limited exceptions including: • Patient or physician requests non-child-resistant packaging • Topical preparations • Sublingual nitroglycerine or similar products • Various estrogens in smaller doses

(Continued)

Amendment or Act	Summary of Act or Amendment
Medical Device Amendments of 1976	Required all devices to be divided into 3 classes, with varying amounts of control required in each one. • Class I: General devices with limited human exposure (ACE bandages, tongue depressors) • Class II: Has performance standards requiring safety and efficacy (hospital beds, wheel chairs) • Class III: Device that supports or sustains human life or is of substantial importance in preventing impairment of human health or presents a potential, unreasonable risk of illness or injury. Examples include artificial heart and ventilator
Orphan Drug Act	• Established the path for development of drugs for rare diseases. • An orphan drug is defined as a medication developed specifically to treat a rare medical condition. • Drug manufacturers receive federal incentives for developing orphan drugs.
Drug Price Competition and Patent-Term Restoration Act	• Established generic drugs • Increased the length of time for a drug patent to expire from 12 years to 17 years.
Omnibus Budget Reconciliation Act of 1987	• Commonly known as OBRA and also the Federal Nursing Home Reform Act. OBRA provisions include: • Granted Centers of Medicare and Medicaid Services (CMS) authority to enact measures to decrease unnecessary costs while improving the quality of patient care in long-term facilities.
Omnibus Budget Reconciliation Act of 1990	Commonly known as OBRA. Required individual state governments to establish additional "state sponsored" pharmacy practice standards. It also established how the pharmacist should interact with the patient. Additional OBRA provisions include: • Established a prospective drug utilization review (ProDUR) where the pharmacist must screen for the following prior to filling any prescription: Therapeutic duplications, Drug–disease contraindications, Drug–drug interactions, incorrect drug dosage, incorrect duration of treatment, Drug–allergy interactions and Clinical abuse/misuse of medication. Pharmacists must also offer to discuss the following with the Medicaid recipient prior to dispensing the medication: 1. Name and description of the drug 2. Dosage form, dosage, route of administration, and duration of drug therapy. 3. Special directions and precautions for preparation, administration, and use by the patient. 4. Common severe side effects, drug interaction and contraindications 5. Refill authorization 6. Self-monitoring techniques of drug therapy. 7. Storage information 8. Special dispensing information, such as "what to do in the event of a missed dose"

(Continued)

<table>
<tr><th>Amendment or Act</th><th>Summary of Act or Amendment</th></tr>
<tr><td>Dietary Supplement Health and Education Act</td><td>Permits the FDA to regulate a dietary supplement as a drug if the supplement is proven to be harmful. The Dietary Supplement Health and Education Act of 1994 (DSHEA) defines a supplement as a product that is intended to supplement the diet and bears or contains 1 or more of the following dietary ingredients:<ul><li>vitamin</li><li>mineral</li><li>herb or other botanical (excluding tobacco)</li><li>amino acid</li><li>substance used to supplement the diet (i.e. protein powder)</li><li>A combination of any of the above</li></ul></td></tr>
<tr><td>Health Insurance Portability and Accountability Act</td><td>Commonly known as HIPAA. HIPAA is a federal regulation developed to safeguard the privacy of protected health information (PHI). All pharmacies (and medical institutions) that maintain patient information in electronic format or conduct financial and administrative transactions electronically, such as billing and fund transfers, must comply with HIPAA.<ul><li>A more detailed explanation of HIPAA is found in the Kaplan NAPLEX review text in the Health Policy chapter.</li></ul></td></tr>
<tr><td>Food and Drug Administration Modernization Act of 1997</td><td>Food and Drug Administration Modernization Act (FDAMA) mandates the following provisions:<ul><li>Abolishes the prohibition on dissemination by manufacturers of information about unapproved uses of drugs and medical devices. It permits the dissemination of peer-reviewed journal articles about an off-label indication of its product.</li><li>Ensures availability of non-commercially available compounded drug products prepared by pharmacists for individualized therapies.</li><li>Increases patient access to experimental drugs and medical devices</li><li>Accelerates review of new medications and new medication indications</li></ul></td></tr>
<tr><td>Combat Methamphetamine Epidemic Act</td><td>Regulates the over-the-counter sales of ephedrine, pseudoephedrine, and phenylpropanolamine products since these products are the precursor chemicals used in the manufacture of methamphetamine or amphetamine. The Federal statute included the following requirements for pharmacies who sell these drugs:<ul><li>A retrievable record (kept for 2 years) of all purchases identifying the name and address of each purchaser.</li><li>Verification of proof of identity of all purchasers</li><li>Disclosure and protection methods for the collection of personal information</li><li>Reports to the state Attorney General's office of any suspicious payments or disappearances of the regulated products</li><li>Tablets/Capsules containing these products may only be sold in unit dose blister packs</li><li>Restricted products are to be sold behind the pharmacy counter to restrict access</li><li>Daily sales of regulated products not to exceed 3.6 grams</li><li>A 30-day sales limit not to exceed 9 grams of pseudoephedrine</li></ul></td></tr>
</table>

(Continued)

Amendment or Act	Summary of Act or Amendment
Food and Drug Administration Amendments Act of 2007	Authorized the FDA to require risk evaluation and mitigation strategies (REMS) on certain medications if necessary to minimize the risks associated with some drugs. REMS programs are designed to restrict access to medications that carry a lot of treatment risk provided that the benefits of a medication still outweigh the potential risks of that medication. REMS programs (in addition to traditional labeling requirements) can require medication guides, implementation plans, timetables for laboratory studies, and physician certification on prescribing the medication. • Medications requiring REMS include clozapine, buprenorphine, AndroGel and Aranesp. • A complete list of medications and description of the REMS program can be found at http://www.accessdata.fda.gov/scripts/cder/rems/index.cfm
Patient Protection and Affordable Care Act of 2010	Commonly known as Obamacare. Major components include: • Guaranteed insurance issue to all applicants at the same age, sex and geographical location (at the same premium) regardless of pre-existing disease conditions • State Medicaid program eligibility will permit inclusion of all individuals with incomes up to 133% of the poverty level. Additional support in the form of a sliding scale based on income as well. • Improved benefits for Medicare prescription drug coverage • Expanded requirements for businesses to offer insurance • Requires that all persons in the United States have health insurance or will be penalized

Controlled Substances Act (CSA)

The CSA provides guidance for the proper classification, purchasing, distribution, and record keeping requirements of all controlled substances. It requires the registration/verification of controlled-substance prescribers. The CSA also created the Drug Enforcement Administration (DEA), which is responsible for enforcing the laws created by the CSA.

Controlled substances are defined as medications with abuse potential. The CSA divides them into 5 schedules based on abuse potential.

Table 16-2. Controlled Substance Schedules

Schedule	Definition	Examples
I	High potential for abuse, have no currently accepted medical use in treatment in the United States, and there is a lack of accepted safety for use of the drug or other substance under medical supervision	Heroin, LSD, PCP, 3,4-methylenedioxymethamphetamine ("ecstasy"), etc.
II	High potential for abuse which may lead to severe psychological or physical dependence.	Oxycodone (OxyContin®), fentanyl (Duragesic®), hydromorphone (Dilaudid®), methadone (Dolophine®), meperidine (Demerol®), amphetamine (Dexedrine®, Adderall®), Hydrocodone (Vicodin®), etc.
III	Have a potential for abuse less than substances in schedules I or II and abuse may lead to moderate or low physical dependence or high psychological dependence	Testosterone (AndroGel®), buprenorphine and naloxone (Suboxone®), Codeine when combined with acetaminophen or a cough suppressant in a solid dosage form (Tylenol #3®)

(Continued)

Schedule	Definition	Examples
IV	Substances that have a low potential for abuse relative to substances in schedule III	Alprazolam (Xanax®), clonazepam (Klonopin®), clorazepate (Tranxene®), diazepam (Valium®), lorazepam (Ativan®), etc.
V	Low potential for abuse relative to substances listed in schedule IV and consist primarily of preparations containing limited quantities of certain narcotics. Generally used for antitussive, antidiarrheal, and analgesic purposes	Cough preparations containing not more than 200 milligrams of codeine per 100 milliliters or per 100 grams (Robitussin AC® and Phenergan with Codeine®).

Controlled Substance Prescriptions

General controlled-substance prescription regulations include:

- A prescription for a controlled substance must be written in ink (unless it is an electronic prescription) and must include: the date; the patient's name and address; and the prescriber's name, address, and DEA number.
- Prescriptions are valid for 6 months from the date they are written; after 6 months, the prescription may not be dispensed or refilled.
- Schedule II drugs may be written for up to a 90 day supply.
- Schedule II prescriptions cannot include refills. If a patient has a 30 day limit from their insurance, for example, the physician must write 3 separate prescriptions for 30 days each to cover the 90 days.
- Pharmacies may accept phone-in orders and faxes for Schedule III–V medications. However, the pharmacist must immediately transcribe telephone order prescriptions to writing.
- Schedule II medications may not be ordered over the phone or via a fax machine under ordinary circumstances.
- Oral prescriptions for Schedule II drugs are permitted only in emergency situations and must be followed with a written prescription to the pharmacy within 72 hours; only a 72-hour supply is to be prescribed.
- As of 2010, physicians (and pharmacies) are permitted to electronically transmit prescriptions for Schedule II, III, IV, and V medications as long as they are using properly certified software.

For partial prescriptions, the following regulations apply:

- The pharmacist may dispense the medication "in portions" provided that the quantity dispensed does not exceed the total quantity prescribed (with refills) and all of the medication is not dispensed in a time period greater than 6 months for schedule III and IV and 12 months for schedule V medications.
- Note the 6 or 12 month time period begins on the date that the prescription is written (not on the date it is first dispensed).
- For a schedule II medication, the prescription may be partially dispensed if the pharmacist is not able to supply the full quantity of the prescription. The remaining portion must be supplied within 72 hours of the first partial dispensing or the remaining amount is forfeited.

Regarding the transfer of prescriptions, the following regulations apply:

- Schedule II controlled substances cannot be transferred between pharmacies if partially filled at one pharmacy.
- Hardcopy Schedules III, IV, and V controlled substances may be transferred between pharmacies on a one-time basis. However, pharmacies which electronically share a real-time, online database (such as a retail pharmacy chain) may transfer the controlled substance prescription up to the maximum number of refills on the prescription.

Purchasing and Receiving Controlled Substances by a Pharmacy

The high-yield concepts pertaining to the purchasing and receiving of controlled substances by a pharmacy include the following:

- Schedule III–V drugs may be ordered by a pharmacy in the same manner that the pharmacist orders non-scheduled medications.
- Schedule II drugs must be purchased with either a "triplicate" DEA 222 order form or an electronic 222 form through a controlled substances ordering system (CSOS). Regarding the DEA form 222, the pharmacy keeps the third sheet and sends the first and second pages to the wholesaler. The wholesaler keeps the first page and must then send the second page to the DEA.
- When the Schedule II medications arrive in the pharmacy, they should be checked in against the DEA form.
- Schedule II medications may be stocked separately in a secure place or disbursed throughout the remaining pharmacy stock of general Rx legend drugs.

Miscellaneous Controlled Substance Act Provisions

Authorized DEA registrants that comply with a series of controlled substance-related regulatory requirements are classified individuals or organizations that may receive a "DEA number." These registrants include the following:

- All health professionals permitted to prescribe, dispense, or administer a controlled substance
- All organizations that manufacture or distribute a controlled substance
- All pharmacies entitled to fill controlled substance prescriptions. Registrants must comply with a series of regulatory requirements relating to drug security, records accountability, and adherence to standards.

Each pharmacy must maintain accurate and complete controlled substance records for all controlled substances purchased, received, distributed, dispensed, and destroyed. These records must be maintained for 2 years. Inventory records for Schedule II and Schedule III, IV, and V drugs must be maintained separately from all other records in the pharmacy or are classified as being "readily retrievable."

- The DEA requires that a pharmacy take an inventory of controlled substances every 2 years.
- If controlled substances are missing or stolen, the pharmacy should contact the local police and DEA as well as fill out and file DEA form 106 within 24 hours following the incident.

PRACTICE QUESTIONS

1. A patient brings in a prescription for 60 tablets of brand name Percocet™; however, the pharmacy only has 45 tablets in stock. The remainder of this prescription must be filled in what time frame?

   A. 48 hours
   B. 72 hours
   C. 6 months
   D. 12 months
   E. Within a "reasonable" time frame

2. Which of the following established the 2 separate classes of drugs: Rx legend and Over-the-Counter?

   A. Comprehensive Drug Abuse Prevention and Control Act of 1970
   B. Durham-Humphrey Amendment
   C. Food, Drug, and Cosmetic Act
   D. Kefauver-Harris Amendment
   E. Pure Food and Drug Act

3. All of the following are Schedule II medications EXCEPT

   A. Codeine (combined with acetaminophen)
   B. Fentanyl
   C. Hydrocodone (combined with acetaminophen)
   D. Hydromorphone
   E. Meperidine

4. Which of the following statements regarding the purchasing and receiving of controlled substances are FALSE?

   A. Schedule II drugs must be purchased with either a duplicate DEA 222 order form or an electronic 222.
   B. Schedule II medications may be stocked separately in a secure place.
   C. Schedule II medications may be stocked with the general legend medications.
   D. Schedule III–V medications may be ordered with general legend medications.
   E. When the Schedule II medications arrive in the pharmacy, they should be checked in against the DEA form.

5. A patient brings in a prescription dated April 15 for alprazolam 1 mg (60 tablets) with 2 refills. If the prescription is filled on May 1, it is valid until what date?

   A. May 15
   B. September 15
   C. October 1
   D. April 15 of the following year
   E. May 1 of the following year

6. According to the Durham-Humphrey Amendment, all of the following are required to be on the prescription label EXCEPT

   A. Applicable warning labels
   B. Date of prescription filling
   C. Hours of pharmacy operation
   D. Name and address of pharmacy
   E. All of the above are required to be on a prescription label

7. Chet's Family Pharmacy performs a complete controlled substances inventory on July 7, 2016. The DEA requires that the next controlled substances inventory be performed by what date?

   A. January 7, 2017
   B. July 7, 2018
   C. January 7, 2018
   D. July 7, 2018
   E. July 7, 2019

8. A handwritten prescription for enalapril must have ALL of the following EXCEPT?
   A. Medication name
   B. Patient's name
   C. Physician's DEA number
   D. Physician's name
   E. All of the above are required on this prescription.

9. According to the Medical Device Amendments of 1976, a ventilator would be classified as which of the following?
   A. Class I medical device
   B. Class II medical device
   C. Class III medical device
   D. Class IV medical device
   E. Medical devices are not classified

10. Physicians are permitted to electronically transmit prescriptions for all of the following EXCEPT
    A. Alprazolam
    B. Enalapril
    C. Codeine (with acetaminophen)
    D. Oxycodone
    E. All of the above can be transmitted electronically from a physician to a pharmacy

Answers and Explanations

1. **The correct answer is B.** Percocet™ is the brand name product that contains the Schedule II controlled substance oxycodone plus the general legend analgesic acetaminophen. For schedule II medications, the prescription may be partially dispensed if the pharmacist is not able to supply the full quantity of the prescription. The remaining portion must be supplied within 72 hours of the first partial dispensing or the remaining amount is forfeited. Also, the pharmacist may dispense "other" controlled substances "in portions" provided that the quantity dispensed does not exceed the total quantity prescribed (with refills) and all of the medication is not dispensed in a time period greater than 6 months (choice C) for schedule III and IV and 12 months (choice D) for schedule V medications.

2. **The correct answer is B.** The Durham-Humphrey Amendment is commonly known as the Prescription Drug Amendment because it established 2 classes of drugs: Rx legend (prescription) and OTC (over the counter). This act also made a requirement that a patient can only receive an Rx legend medication with a valid prescription from a licensed practitioner. The Comprehensive Drug Abuse Prevention and Control Act of 1970 (choice A), also known as the Controlled Substances Act, provides guidance for the proper classification, purchasing, distribution and record keeping requirements of all controlled substances. The Food, Drug, and Cosmetic Act (choice C) required that all new drugs be proven safe (by the manufacturer) before marketing to the general public. It also extended federal control to both cosmetics and therapeutic devices. The Kefauver-Harris Amendment (choice D) required drug manufacturers to show the effectiveness of their products (through clinical trials with preclinical trials through phase IV trials) as well as drug safety. The Pure Food and Drug Act of 1906 (choice E)

prohibited interstate commerce of misbranded and adulterated foods, drinks and drugs under penalty of seizure of the questionable products and/or prosecution of the responsible parties. A more comprehensive overview of these and all other key pharmacy acts and amendments needed for the FPGEE is found in this chapter.

3. **The correct answer is A.** Controlled substances are defined as medications with abuse potential. The Controlled Substances Act (CSA) divides them into 5 schedules based on abuse potential. Schedule II medications are described by the CSA as those with high potential for abuse which may lead to severe psychological or physical dependence. Examples of schedule II medications include: fentanyl (Duragesic®), hydrocodone w/APAP (Vicodin®), hydromorphone (Dilaudid®), meperidine (Demerol®), methadone (Dolophine®), amphetamine (Dexedrine®, Adderall®), and oxycodone (OxyContin®). Codeine (combined with acetaminophen) is a Schedule III medication.

4. **The correct answer is A.** The DEA has strict guidelines relating to the purchasing and receiving of controlled substances by a pharmacy. For example: Schedule II medications must be purchased with either a "triplicate" DEA 222 order form or an electronic 222 form through a controlled substances ordering system (CSOS). Regarding the DEA form 222, the pharmacy keeps the third sheet and sends the first and second pages to the wholesaler. The wholesaler keeps the first page and must then send the second page to the DEA. All of the other answer choices are true statements.

5. **The correct answer is B.** A prescription for a controlled substance must be written in ink (unless it is an electronic prescription) and must include: the date; the patient's name and address; and the prescriber's name, address, and DEA number. Prescriptions are valid for 6 months from the date they are written (choice B is correct) not dispensed (choice C is incorrect); after 6 months, the prescription may not be dispensed or refilled. If the prescription was written for a general legend medication, its expiration date would be April 15 of the following year (choice D).

6. **The correct answer is C.** The Durham-Humphrey Amendment established 2 classes of drugs [Rx legend (prescription) and OTC (over the counter)], made a requirement that a patient can only receive an Rx legend medication with a valid prescription from a licensed practitioner AND provided guidance on the minimal information that must be included on the prescription label. The following must appear on the prescription label: 1) name and address of the pharmacy, 2) serial number of the prescription, 3) date of its filling, 4) the name of the prescriber, 5) the name of the patient, 6) the directions for use, and 7) applicable warning labels. The pharmacy hours of operation are not required.

7. **The correct answer is D.** Each pharmacy must maintain accurate and complete controlled substance records for all controlled substances purchased, received, distributed, dispensed, and destroyed. These records must be maintained for 2 years. Inventory records for Schedule II and Schedule III, IV, and V drugs must be maintained separately from all other records in the pharmacy or are classified as being "readily retrievable". The DEA requires that a pharmacy take an inventory of controlled substances every 2 years. Thus if the inventory is performed on July 7, 2016, the next inventory must be completed by July 7, 2018.

8. **The correct answer is C.** A prescription for a "controlled substance" must be written in ink (unless it is an electronic prescription). Prescriptions for Schedule II–V medications must include the following: the date; the patient's name and address; and the prescriber's name, address, and DEA number. However, general legend medication prescriptions, such as the ACE inhibitor enalapril, do NOT need to have the physician's DEA number on the prescription.

9. **The correct answer is C.** The Medical Device Amendments of 1976 required that all medical devices be divided into 3 classes, with varying amounts of control required in each one. Class I (choice A) devices include general devices with limited human exposure (i.e. ACE bandages, tongue depressors). Class II (choice B) devices have performance standards requiring specific safety and efficacy standards (i.e. hospital

beds, wheel chairs). Class III (choice C) devices are those that support or sustain human life or are of substantial importance in preventing impairment of human health or present a potential, unreasonable risk of illness or injury. Examples include artificial hearts and ventilators.

10. **The correct answer is E.** Electronic prescribing (or E-Prescribing) is defined as a prescriber's ability to electronically send an accurate, error-free and understandable prescription directly from the point-of-care to a pharmacy. Electronic prescribing was initially limited to general legend (i.e. enalapril) drugs. However, as of 2010, physicians (and pharmacies) are permitted to electronically transmit prescriptions for Schedule II (choice D), III (choice C), IV (choice A), and V medications as long as they are using properly certified software.

Biostatistics and Research Study Design 17

Learning Objectives

❑ Explain introductory principles of research study design

❑ Demonstrate proficiency in the application of statistical and research findings

The most appropriate study design is dependent on the type of research being performed as well as the nature of the research question(s). To fully understand the data obtained from a research study, clinicians must first have a grasp of the general and statistical principles used to evaluate the study data.

This chapter was designed to be used with the Biostatistics chapter in Kaplan's *NAPLEX Strategies, Practice, and Review* book. It starts with a basic review of biostatistics (as part of the introduction to research study design) and then discusses inferential statistics (as part of the application principles for statistics and research findings).

NAPLEX Reference

Biostatistics chapter

RESEARCH STUDY DESIGN

Clinical trials can be described as being either retrospective or prospective in nature. They can also be classified as observational or experimental studies. The most common study designs in research today include:

- Case report/case series
- Cross-sectional studies
- Case-control studies
- Cohort studies
- Randomized controlled trials
- Meta-analyses

NAPLEX Reference

Biostatistics chapter:
"Clinical Trial Design"

A comprehensive review of these types of research studies can be found in Kaplan's *NAPLEX Strategies, Practice, and Review* book.

Additional information on these research studies can be found in Chapter 13 of this text in "Pharmacoepidemiological Studies."

This section will focus on basic biostatistical principles.

Key Probability Rules

Key probability rules are based on both dependent and independent variables.

Independence: Across Multiple Events

Combine probabilities for independent events by **multiplication**.

- Events are **independent if** the **occurrence of one tells you nothing about the occurrence of another.** The issue here is the intersection of 2 sets. E.g., if the chance of having blond hair is 0.3 and the chance of having a cold is 0.2, the chance of meeting a blond-haired person with a cold is: 0.3 × 0.2 = 0.06 (or 6%).

If events are nonindependent, multiply the probability of one event by the probability of the second, assuming that the first has occurred. E.g., if a box has 5 white balls and 5 black balls, the chance of picking 2 black balls is:

$$\left(\frac{5}{10}\right) \times \left(\frac{4}{9}\right) = 0.5 \times 0.44 = 0.22 \text{ (or 22\%)}$$

Mutually Exclusive: Within a Single Event

Combine probabilities for mutually exclusive events by **addition**.

- Mutually exclusive means that the **occurrence of one event precludes the occurrence of the other.** The issue here is the union of 2 sets. E.g., if a coin lands on heads, it cannot be tails; the 2 are **mutually exclusive.** If a coin is flipped, the chance that it will be either heads or tails is: 0.5 + 0.5 = 1.0 (or 100%).

If 2 events are not mutually exclusive, the combination of probabilities is accomplished by adding the 2 together and subtracting out the multiplied probabilities. E.g., if the chance of having diabetes is 10% and the chance of being obese is 30%, the chance of meeting someone who is obese or has diabetes or both is: $0.1 + 0.3 - (0.1 \times 0.3) = 0.37$ (or 37%).

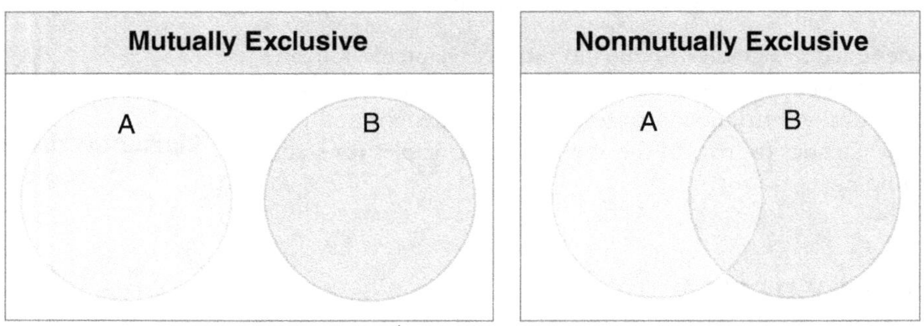

Figure 17-1. Venn Diagram Representations of Mutually Exclusive and Nonmutually Exclusive Events

Sample Questions

1. If the prevalence of diabetes is 10%, what is the chance that 3 people selected at random from the population will all have diabetes?

   Answer: 0.1 × 0.1 × 0.1 = 0.001

2. Chicago has a population of 10,000,000. If 25% of the population is Latino, 30% is African American, 5% is Arab American, and 40% is of European extraction, how many people in Chicago are classified as other than of European extraction?

   Answer: 25% + 30% + 5% = 60%. 60% × 10,000,000 = 6,000,000

3. At age 65, the probability of surviving for the next 5 years is 0.8 for a white man and 0.9 for a white woman. For a married couple who are both white and age 65, the probability that the wife will be a living widow 5 years later is:

   A. 90%
   B. 72%
   C. 18%
   D. 10%
   E. 8%

Answer: **C.** This question asks for the joint probability of independent events; therefore, the probabilities are multiplied. Chance of the wife being alive: 90%. Chance of the husband being dead: 100% – 80% = 20%. Therefore, 0.9 × 0.2 = 18%.

4. If the chance of surviving for 1 year after being diagnosed with prostate cancer is 80% and the chance of surviving for 2 years after diagnosis is 60%, what is the chance of surviving for 2 years after diagnosis, given that the patient is alive at the end of the first year?

   A. 20%
   B. 48%
   C. 60%
   D. 75%
   E. 80%

   Answer: **D.** The question tests knowledge of "conditional probability." Out of 100 patients, 80 are alive at the end of 1 year and 60 at the end of 2 years. The 60 patients alive after 2 years are a subset of those that make it to the first year. Therefore, $\frac{60}{80} = 75\%$.

Descriptive Statistics: Summarizing the Data

Statistics deals with the world as **distributions.** These distributions are summarized by a **central tendency and variation around that center.** The most important distribution is the **normal or Gaussian curve.** This "bell-shaped" curve is **symmetric,** with one side the mirror image of the other.

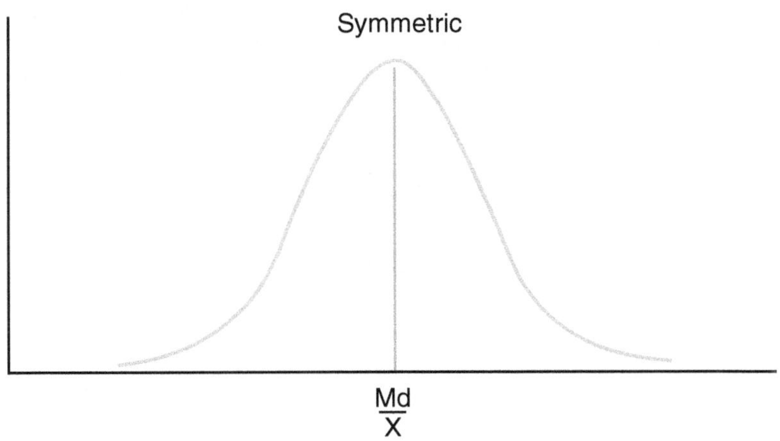

Figure 17-2. Measures of Central Tendency

Central Tendency

Central tendency is a general term for several characteristics of the distribution of a set of values or measurements around a value **at or near the middle of the set.**

- **Mean ($\bar{X}$) (a synonym for average)**: the sum of the values of the observations divided by the numbers of observations
- **Median (Md)**: the simplest division of a set of measurements is into 2 parts—the upper half and lower half. The **point on the scale that divides the group** in this way is the median. The measurement below which half the observations fall: the 50th percentile
- **Mode**: the **most frequently occurring value** in a set of observations

Given the distribution of numbers: 3, 6, 7, 7, 9, 10, 12, 15, 16, the mode is 7, the median is 9, the mean is 9.4.

Skewed curves: not all curves are normal. Sometimes the curve is skewed either positively or negatively. A **positive skew** has the tail to the right and the **mean greater than the median.** A **negative skew** has the tail to the left and the **median greater than the mean.** For skewed distributions, the median is a better representation of central tendency than is the mean.

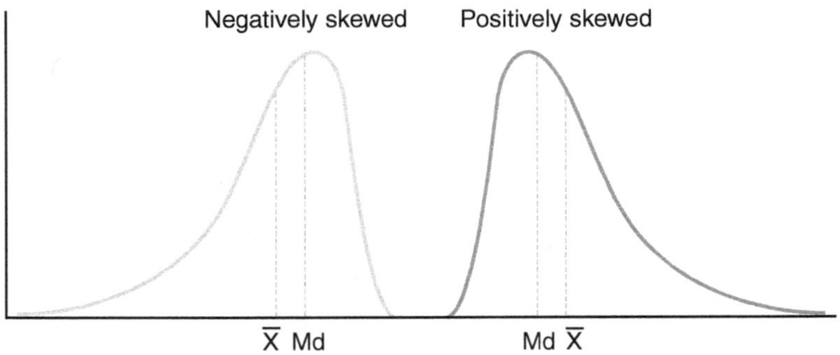

Figure 17-3. Skewed Distribution Curves

Measures of Variability

The simplest measure of variability is the **range**, the difference between the highest and the lowest score. But the range is unstable and changes easily. A more stable and more useful measure of dispersion is the **standard deviation.**

To calculate the standard deviation, first subtract the mean from each score to obtain **deviations from the mean.** This will give you both positive and negative values. But squaring the deviations, the next step, makes them all positive. The *squared* deviations are added together and *divided by the number of cases.* The square root is taken of this average, and the result is the standard deviation (S or SD).

$$s = \sqrt{\frac{\sum (X - \bar{X})^2}{n - 1}}$$

The square of the standard deviation (s^2) equals the **variance.**

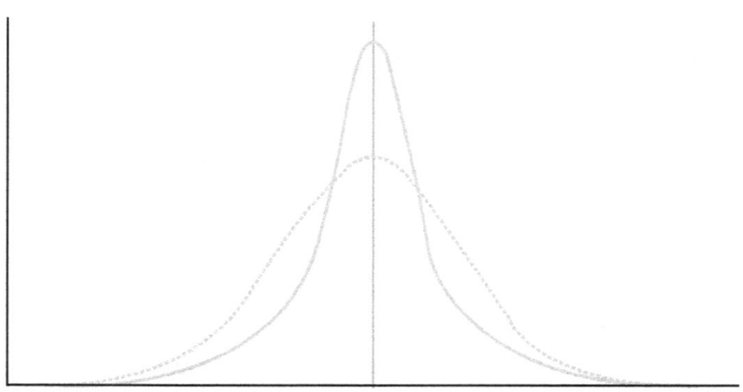

Figure 17-4. Comparison of 2 Normal Curves with the Same Means, but Different Standard Deviations

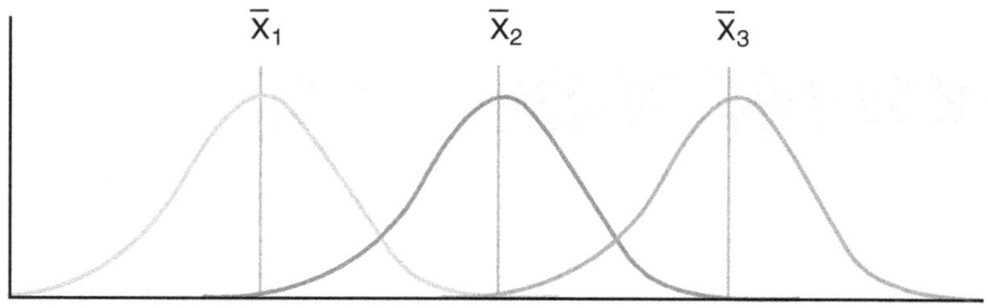

Figure 17-5. Comparison of 3 Normal Curves with the Same Standard Deviations, but Different Means

You will not be asked to calculate a standard deviation or variance on the exam, but you do need to know what they are and how they relate to the normal curve. In ANY normal curve, a constant proportion of the cases fall within 1, 2, and 3 standard deviations of the mean.

- Within 1 standard deviation: 68%
- Within 2 standard deviations: 95.5%
- Within 3 standard deviations: 99.7%

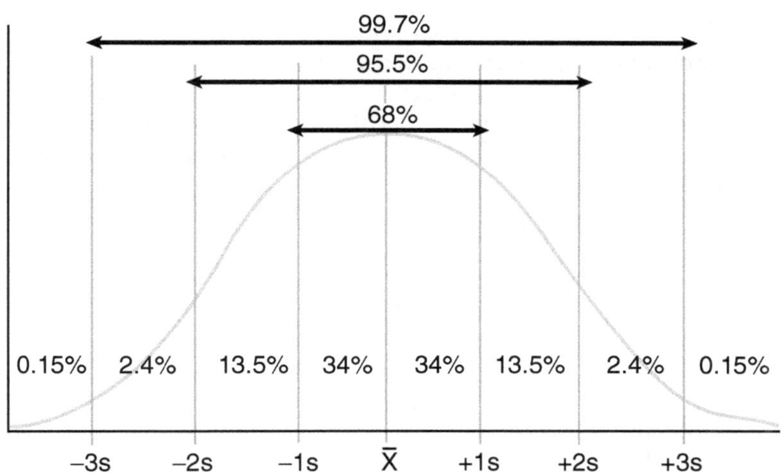

Figure 17-6. Percentage of Cases within 1, 2, and 3 Standard Deviations of the Mean in a Normal Distribution

You should know the constants presented in Figure 17-6 and be able to combine the given constants to answer simple questions.

Sample Questions

1. In a normal distribution curve, what percent of the cases are below 2 standard deviations below the mean?

   Answer: 2.5%

2. In a normal distribution curve, what percent of the cases are above 1s below the mean?

   Answer: 84%

3. A student who scores at the 97.5 percentile falls where on the curve?

   Answer: 2s above the mean

4. A student took 2 tests:

	Score	Mean	Standard Deviation
Test A	45%	30%	5%
Test B	60%	40%	10%

On which test did the student do better, relative to his classmates?

Answer: On Test A, she scored 3s above the mean versus only 2s above the mean for Test B.

APPLICATION OF STATISTICAL AND RESEARCH FINDINGS

The purpose of inferential statistics is to designate **how likely it is that a given finding is simply the result of chance.** Inferential statistics would not be necessary if investigators studied all members of a population. However, because we can rarely observe and study entire populations, we try to select samples that are representative of the entire population so that we can **generalize the results from the sample to the population.**

Confidence Intervals

Confidence intervals are a way of admitting that any measurement from a sample is only an **estimate** of the population. Although the estimate given from the sample is likely to be close, the true values for the population may be above or below the sample values. A confidence interval **specifies how far above or below a sample-based value the population value lies** within a given range, from a possible high to a possible low. Reality, therefore, is most likely to be somewhere within the specified range.

Sample Question

1. Assuming the graph (Figure 17-7) presents 95% confidence intervals, which groups, if any, are statistically different from each other?

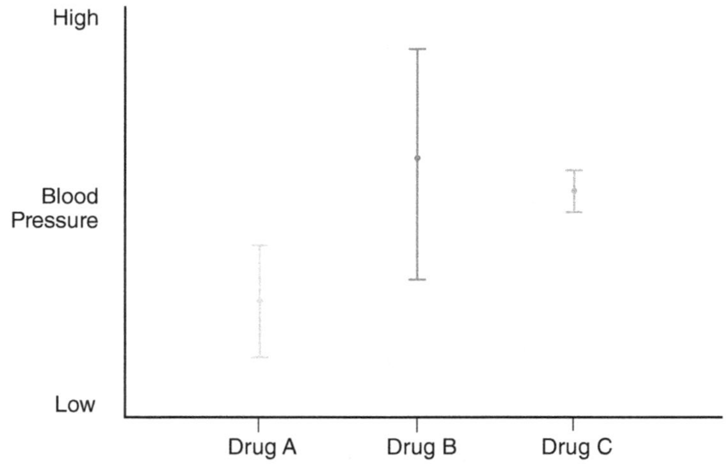

Figure 17-7. Blood Pressures at End of Clinical Trial for 3 Drugs

Answer: When comparing two groups, any overlap of confidence intervals means the groups are not significantly different. Therefore, if the graph represents 95% confidence intervals, Drugs B and C are no different in their effects; Drug B is no different from Drug A; Drug A has a better effect than Drug C.

If the given confidence interval contains 1.0, then there is no statistically significant effect of exposure.

Example:

Relative Risk	Confidence Interval	Interpretation
1.77	(1.22 – 2.45)	Statistically significant (increased risk)
1.63	(0.85 – 2.46)	NOT statistically significant (risk is the same)
0.78	(0.56 – 0.94)	Statistically significant (decreased risk)

- If RR > 1.0, then subtract 1.0 and read as percent increase. So 1.77 means one group has 77% more cases than the other.
- If RR < 1.0, then subtract from 1.0 and read as reduction in risk. So 0.78 means one group has a 22% reduction in risk.

Understanding Statistical Inference

The goal of science is to define reality. Think about statistics as the referee in the game of science. We have all agreed to play the game according to the judgment calls of the referee, even though we know the referee can and will be wrong sometimes.

Basic Steps of Statistical Inference

1. Define the research question: what are you trying to show?
2. Define the null hypothesis, *generally the opposite of what you hope to show*
   i. Null hypothesis says that the **findings are the result of chance or random factors**. If you want to show that a drug works, the null hypothesis will be that the drug does NOT work.
   ii. Alternative hypothesis says what is left after defining the null hypothesis. In this example, that the drug does actually work.

   Two types of null hypotheses:
   i. One-tailed, i.e., directional or "one-sided," such that one group is *either* greater than, or less than, the other. E.g., Group A is not < than Group B, or Group A is not > Group B
   ii. Two-tailed, i.e., nondirectional or "two-sided," such that two groups are not the same. E.g., Group A = Group B

Hypothesis Testing

At this point, data are collected and analyzed by the appropriate statistical test. How to run these tests is not tested on FPGEE, but you may need to be able to interpret results of statistical tests with which you are presented.

Note

Never accept the null hypothesis; either reject it or fail to reject it. Saying you do not have sufficient evidence to reject it is not the same as being able to affirm that it is true.

p-value: to interpret output from a statistical test, focus on the *p*-value. The term *p*-value refers to two things. In its first sense, the *p*-value is a standard against which we compare our results. In the second sense, the *p*-value is a result of computation.

- The **computed *p*-value is compared with the *p*-value criterion to test statistical significance.** If the computed value is less than the criterion, we have achieved statistical significance. In general, the smaller the *p* the better.

- The *p*-value criterion is traditionally set at $p \leq 0.05$. (Assume that these are the criteria if no other value is explicitly specified.) Using this standard:
  - If $p \leq 0.05$, reject the null hypothesis (reached statistical significance).
  - If $p > 0.05$, do not reject the null hypothesis (has not reached statistical significance).
  - If $p = 0.02$, reject the null hypothesis, i.e., decide that the drug works.
  - If $p = 0.13$, fail to reject the null hypothesis, i.e., decide that the drug does not work.

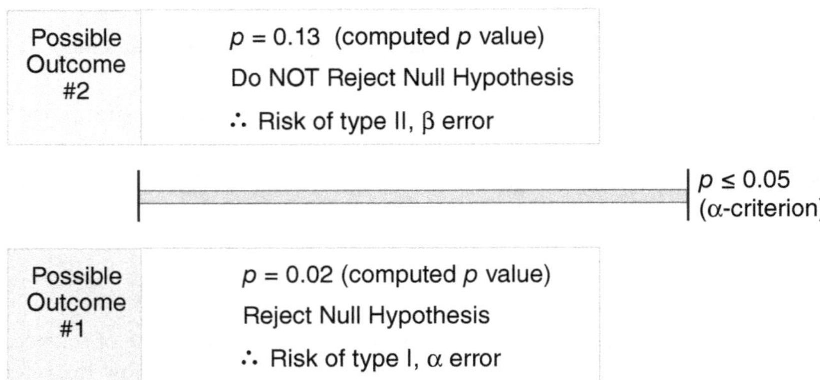

Figure 17-8. Making Decisions Using *p*-Values

Types of Errors

Note

- If the null hypothesis is rejected, there is no chance of a type II error. If the null hypothesis is not rejected, there is no chance of a type I error.
- Type I error (error of commission) is generally considered worse than type II error (error of omission).

Just because we reject the null hypothesis, we are not certain that we are correct. For some reason, the results given by the sample may be inconsistent with the full population. If this is true, any decision made on the basis of the sample could be in error. There are 2 possible types of errors:

- Type I error (α error): **rejecting the null hypothesis when it is really true**, i.e., assuming a statistically significant effect on the basis of the sample when there is none in the population, e.g., asserting that the drug works when it doesn't. The chance of type I error is given by the *p*-value. If $p = 0.05$, then the chance of a type I error is 5 in 100, or 1 in 20.
- Type II error (β error): **failing to reject the null hypothesis when it is really false**, i.e., declaring no significant effect on the basis of the sample when there really is one in the population, e.g., asserting the drug does not work when it really does. The chance of a type II error cannot be directly estimated from the *p*-value.

Meaning of the p-value

The *p*-value provides criterion for making decisions about the null hypothesis

- Quantifies the chances that a decision to reject the null hypothesis will be wrong
- Tells statistical significance, not clinical significance or likelihood of benefit
- Limits to the *p*-value: the *p*-value does NOT tell us
  - The chance that an individual patient will benefit
  - The percentage of patients who will benefit
  - The degree of benefit expected for a given patient

Statistical Power

In statistics, **power** is the capacity to detect a difference if there is one.

- Just as increasing the power of a microscope makes it easier to see what is going on in histology, increasing statistical power allows us to detect what is happening in the data.
- Power is directly related to type II error: $1 - \beta$ = Power
- There are a number of ways to increase statistical power. The most common is to increase the sample size.

		Reality	
		Drug Works	**Drug Does Not Work**
Research	Reject	Power	Type I Error
	Not Reject	Type II Error	

Nominal, Ordinal, Interval, and Ratio Scales

To convert the world into numbers, use 4 types of scales. Focus on nominal and interval scales for the exam.

Table 17-1. Types of Scales in Statistics

Type of Scale	Description	Key Words	Examples
Nominal (Categorical)	Different groups	This or that	Gender, comparing among treatment interventions
Ordinal	Groups in sequence	Comparative quality, rank order	Olympic medals, class rank in medical school
Interval	Exact differences among groups	Quantity, mean, and standard deviation	Height, weight, blood pressure, drug dosage
Ratio	Interval + true zero point	Zero means zero	Temperature measured in degrees Kelvin

Nominal or Categorical Scale

Note

The scales are hierarchically arranged from least information provided (nominal) to most information provided (ratio). Any scale can be degraded to a lower scale, e.g., interval data can be treated as ordinal.

For the FPGEE, concentrate on identifying nominal and interval scales.

A nominal scale puts people into boxes, without specifying the relationship between the boxes. Gender is a common example of a nominal scale with 2 groups, male and female. Anytime you can say, "It's either this or that," you are dealing with a nominal scale. Other examples: cities, drug versus control group.

Ordinal Scale

Numbers can also be used to express ordinal or rank order relations. For example, we say Ben is taller than Fred. Now we know more than just the category in which to place someone. We know something about the relationship between the categories (quality). What we do not know is how different the 2 categories are (quantity). Class rank in pharmacy school and medals at the Olympics are examples of ordinal scales.

Interval Scale

Uses a scale graded in equal increments. In the scale of length, we know that one inch is equal to any other inch. Interval scales allow us to say not only that 2 things are different, but also by how much. If a measurement has a mean and a standard deviation, treat it as an interval scale. It is sometimes called a "numeric scale."

Ratio Scale

The best measure is the ratio scale. This scale orders things and contains equal intervals, like the previous 2 scales. But it also has one additional quality: a **true zero point**. In a ratio scale, zero is a floor, you can't go any lower. Measuring temperature using the Kelvin scale yields ratio scale measurement.

Statistical Tests

Table 17-2. Types of Scales and Basic Statistical Tests

	Variables		
Name of Statistical Test	**Interval**	**Nominal**	**Comment**
Pearson Correlation	2	0	Is there a linear relationship?
Chi-square	0	2	Any # of groups
t-test	1	1	2 groups only
One-way ANOVA	1	1	2 or more groups
Matched pairs *t*-test	1	1	2 groups, linked data pairs, before and after
Repeated measures ANOVA	1	1	More than 2 groups, linked data

ANOVA = Analysis of Variance

Correlation Analysis (r, ranges from –1.0 to +1.0)

A **positive value** means that **2 variables go together in the same direction,** e.g., PCAT scores have a positive correlation with pharmacy school grades. A **negative value** means that the **presence of one variable is associated with the absence of another variable,** e.g., there is a negative correlation between age and quickness of reflexes.

- The further from 0, the stronger the relationship ($r = 0$)
- A **zero correlation** means that **2 variables have no linear relation to one another,** e.g., height and success in pharmacy school.
- Graphing correlations using scatterplots
  - Scatterplot will show points that approximate a line.
  - Be able to interpret scatterplots of data: positive slope, negative slope, and which of a set of scatterplots indicates a stronger correlation.

Note

Remember, your **default choices** are:

- Correlation for interval data
- *Chi*-square for nominal data
- *t*-test for a combination of nominal and interval data

Note

You will not be asked to compute any of these statistical tests. Only recognize what they are and when they should be used.

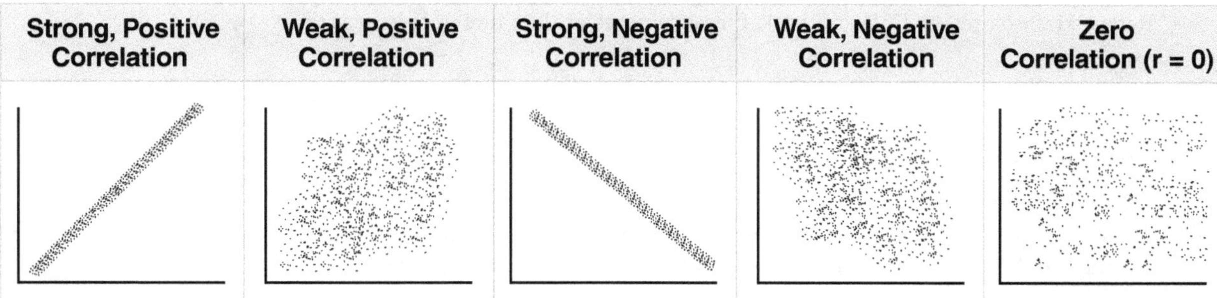

Figure 17-9. Scatterplots and Correlations

NOTE: Correlation, by itself, does not mean causation. A correlation coefficient indicates the **degree to which 2 measures are related,** not why they are related.

It does not mean that one variable necessarily causes the other. There are 2 types of correlations.

1. Pearson correlation: compares 2 interval level variables
2. Spearman correlation: compares 2 ordinal level variables

t-tests

Output of a *t*-test is a "*t*" statistic.

- **Comparing the means of 2 groups** from a single nominal variable, using means from an interval variable to see whether the groups are different.
- Used for 2 groups only, i.e., compares 2 means. E.g., do patients with MI who are in psychotherapy have a reduced length of convalescence compared with those who are not in therapy?
- "Pooled *t*-test" is a regular *t*-test, assuming the variances of the 2 groups are the same.
- Matched pairs *t*-test: each person in one group is matched with a person in the second. Applies to before and after measures and linked data.

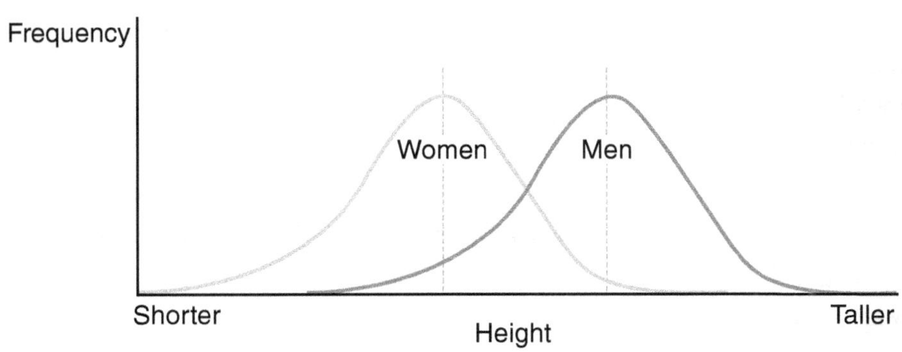

Figure 17-10. Comparison of the Distributions of Two Groups

Analysis of Variance (ANOVA)

Output from an ANOVA is 1 or more "F" statistics

- One-way: **compares means of many groups** (2 or more) **of a single nominal variable** using an interval variable. Significant p-value means that at least 2 of the tested groups are different.
- Two-way: **compares means of groups generated by 2 nominal variables** using an interval variable. Can test effects of several variables at the same time.
- Repeated measures ANOVA: multiple measurements of the same people over time.

Chi-Square

- Nominal data only
- Any number of groups (2×2, 2×3, 3×3, etc.)
- Tests to see whether 2 nominal variables are independent, e.g., testing the efficacy of a new drug by comparing the number of recovered patients given the drug with those who are not

Table 17-3. *Chi*-Square Analysis for Nominal Data

	New Drug	Placebo	Totals
Recovered	45	35	80
Not Recovered	15	25	40
Totals	60	60	120

PRACTICE QUESTIONS

1. A 62-year-old female with type 2 diabetes comes to the pharmacy for counseling. After reviewing her daily glucose log, the pharmacist notices that her morning glucose levels have been erratic for the past week. Her readings are as follows: 230 mg/dl, 126 mg/dl, 245 mg/dl, 184 mg/dl, 126 mg/dl, 188 mg/dl, and 108 mg/dl. What is the mode for these blood glucose readings?

   A. 108 mg/dl
   B. 126 mg/dl
   C. 172 mg/dl
   D. 184 mg/dl
   E. 245 mg/dl

NAPLEX Question Reference

Biostatistics chapter: End of chapter questions

2. Which of the following best characterizes the equation to calculate statistical power?

   A. $1 - \alpha = \text{Power}$
   B. $1 + \alpha = \text{Power}$
   C. $1 - \beta = \text{Power}$
   D. $1 + \beta = \text{Power}$
   E. $1 - \beta - \alpha = \text{Power}$

3. Researchers at a University hospital designed a randomized, double-blinded, controlled clinical drug trial to evaluate the safety and efficacy an experimental drug (JAK0817) verses galantamine for the treatment of Alzheimer's disease in treatment of naïve patients. Patients will be randomized to receive either the experimental agent or galantamine. What is the best way to state the study's null hypothesis?

   A. JAK0817 is less safe and less effective than galantamine for the treatment of Alzheimer's disease.

   B. JAK0817 is NOT less safe and NOT less effective than galantamine for the treatment of Alzheimer's disease.

   C. JAK0817 is safer and more effective than galantamine for the treatment of Alzheimer's disease.

   D. JAK0817 is NOT safer and NOT more effective than galantamine for the treatment of Alzheimer's disease.

   E. Cannot be determined

4. The results of a randomized, double-blinded, controlled clinical drug trial evaluating the safety and efficacy an experimental drug (JAK0817) verses galantamine for the treatment of Alzheimer's disease in treatment naïve patients are published. The results show that experimental medication was safer and more effective than galantamine for the treatment of Alzheimer's disease ($p = 0.004$). What is the chance that a type I error was committed in this study?

   A. 1/20

   B. 1/25

   C. 1/125

   D. 1/250

   E. More information is needed to calculate the chance of a type 1 error

5. Researchers are performing a study to determine if drinking hot beverages is associated with an increased risk of esophageal cancer in both men and women older than 40 years of age. He followed 2 groups of patients (those who drink coffee or tea daily vs those who do not) forward in time to determine if there was an increased risk of esophageal cancer. What type of test should be used to analyze the data?

   A. Chi-squared

   B. One-way ANOVA

   C. Pearson correlation

   D. t-test

   E. More information is needed

Answers and Explanations

1. **The correct answer is B.** The mode is the most frequently occurring value in the set of observations, which in this case is 126 mg/dl, since this value appears twice. Choice A is the lowest value. Choice B is the mean of the values. The mean defined as the sum of the values divided by the number of observations. In this case, you would add the blood glucose levels together and divide by 7 to get 172 mg/dl (choice C). Choice D is the median. The median is the simplest division of a set of measurements into 2 parts: the upper half and lower half. Hence, it is the measurement below which half of the observations fall. In this case, there are 7 blood glucose levels so the median would be the measurement that falls in the middle or 184 mg/dl. Choice E is the highest blood glucose level.

2. **The correct answer is C.** In statistics, power is the capacity to detect a difference if there is one. Just as increasing the power of a microscope makes it easier to see what is going on in histology, increasing statistical power allows us to detect what is happening in the data. Power is directly related to type II error: $1 - \beta = \text{Power}$. There are a number of ways to increase statistical power. The most common is to increase the sample size.

3. **The correct answer is D.** The null hypothesis defines the opposite of what you hope to show. The null hypothesis says that the findings are the result of chance or random factors. If you want to show that a drug works, the null hypothesis will be that the drug does NOT work. In this case, the likely hypothesis is JAK0817 is safer and more effective than galantamine for the treatment of Alzheimer's disease (choice C). Thus the null hypothesis would be JAK0817 is NOT safer and NOT more effective than galantamine for the treatment of Alzheimer's disease (choice D is correct).

4. **The correct answer is D.** The p-value is a standard against which researchers compare their results and is the result of a computation. In order to show statistical significance, the p-value criterion is generally set at $p \leq 0.05$. When $p \leq 0.05$, researchers can reject the null hypothesis since statistical significance was obtained. Conversely, if $p > 0.05$, researchers must accept the null hypothesis. With respect to type 1 error estimates, the p-value is simply a mathematical estimate of an error occurring in the study. For example, the p-value in this question is 0.004, which means that there is a 4/1000 or 1/250 chance that a type I error was committed.

5. **The correct answer is A.** In this type of question, one needs to first determine how best to categorize the 2 types of data. In this example, researchers are looking at regular hot beverage ingestion verses no regular hot beverage ingestion. The primary endpoint is esophageal cancer positive or negative. Both of these data sets are considered to be nominal data. By definition, a nominal scale puts patients, risk factors or outcomes into "boxes", without specifying the relationship between the boxes. Gender is a common example of a nominal scale with 2 groups, male and female. Anytime you can say, "It's either this or that," you are dealing with a nominal scale. Other examples: cities, drug versus control group. The following table outlines when each type of test should be used:

Name of Statistical Test	Interval	Nominal	Comments
Chi-square (choice A)	0	2	Any number of groups
One-way ANOVA (choice B)	1	1	2 or more groups
Pearson Correlation (choice C)	2	0	Is there a linear relationship?
t-test (Choice D)	1	1	2 groups only

Biomedical Ethics 18

Learning Objectives

- ❑ Define introduction principles to biomedical ethics
- ❑ Explain ethical decision making
- ❑ Demonstrate understanding of biomedical research ethics

One of the most important aspects of pharmacy practice is ethics. In fact, the pharmacist oath is centered in ethical principles.

BIOMEDICAL ETHICS AND ETHICAL DECISION MAKING

The Oath of a Pharmacist was adopted by the American Association of Colleges of Pharmacy (AACP) House of Delegates in July 2007.

"I promise to devote myself to a lifetime of service to others through the profession of pharmacy. In fulfilling this vow:

- *I will consider the welfare of humanity and relief of suffering my primary concerns.*
- *I will apply my knowledge, experience, and skills to the best of my ability to assure optimal outcomes for my patients.*
- *I will respect and protect all personal and health information entrusted to me.*
- *I will accept the lifelong obligation to improve my professional knowledge and competence.*
- *I will hold myself and my colleagues to the highest principles of our profession's moral, ethical and legal conduct.*
- *I will embrace and advocate changes that improve patient care.*
- *I will utilize my knowledge, skills, experiences, and values to prepare the next generation of pharmacists.*

I take these vows voluntarily with the full realization of the responsibility with which I am entrusted by the public."

On the FPGEE, you will likely be presented with a few ethical situations and asked to choose the best answer from what will likely be more than one "good" answer choice.

- Example: You may be given a scenario and asked to choose the most appropriate "initial response or action" by the pharmacist. There may be several answer choices relating to appropriate responses or actions to be taken by the pharmacist. However, only one of the answer choices is the "correct initial response."

Core Ethical Principles

The 4 core ethical principles that guide pharmacists and physicians alike are beneficence, nonmaleficence, justice, and patient autonomy.

Beneficence is defined as **"the state or quality of being kind, charitable or beneficial."** From a biomedical ethics point of view, beneficence simply means "Do good!" A pharmacist has an ethical (fiduciary) duty to always act in the best interest of their patients. However, beneficence may sometimes conflict with the core ethical principle of patient autonomy.

- Example: A patient who just attempted to commit suicide would be deemed incompetent and thus unable to make their own decisions. The clinician is thus obligated to impose a specified level of care on this individual in the event that they refuse it.
- As previously mentioned, this is a classic example of where 2 ethical principles oppose one another.
- Note: if the patient is competent to make an informed decision, they have the ultimate right to decide. This is the principle of patient autonomy (outlined later in this section).

Nonmaleficence is defined as **"a principle of bioethics that asserts an obligation not to inflict harm intentionally."** It is useful in dealing with difficult issues surrounding the terminally or seriously ill and injured. Some philosophers combine nonmaleficence and beneficence, but for the sake of the FPGEE, **nonmaleficence simply means "Do no harm."**

A pharmacist should never intentionally actively or passively inflict harm on a patient.

- Example 1: A pharmacist should not "actively" administer a medication that will intentionally harm the patient and provide no therapeutic benefit.
- Example 2: Passively harming a patient means that the pharmacist does not do what is necessary to properly treat the patient, such as refusing to call a patient's physician to clarify/verify an issue related to the prescription.

An important point to note about nonmaleficence is that each pharmacist needs to always weigh the risks and benefits of a treatment measure.

- Example: all medications have side effects, which could be considered harmful to the patient. However, if the likely benefit to the patient outweighs the risk of potential side effects, then the medication should be dispensed.
- If the pharmacist feels that the medication is inappropriate then they should call the prescribing physician or practitioner.

Justice is a core ethical principle that states that a pharmacist should "**treat all patients equally by providing the same, appropriate level of care, attention and resources**." This principle may seem straightforward but can sometimes be the most difficult to follow.

- Example: Imagine the scenario where a pharmacist is working in a retail pharmacy and 2 patients come to the counter indicating that they need to have their prescription filled immediately. However, one patient is dressed in a suit and the other patient is poorly dressed.
- By imagining this scenario, you may have begun to formulate an opinion of what you would do and how you would treat one patient (person in a suit) versus another patient (poorly dressed). However, always remember that the principle of justice states that all patients will be treated equally irrespective of their religious, personal, financial or political beliefs as well as past actions.

Patient autonomy is an obligation by the pharmacist to respect the wishes of an "informed and competent" patient as well as honor their individual preferences in medical care. In other words, the patient ultimately decides what treatments or procedures they will or will not receive.

- Example: The pharmacist may strongly feel that a patient should take a medication (or be treated for a condition) but the patient has the ultimate authority to make an informed decision to not be treated.

Together, these core ethical principles can be summarized as, "A pharmacist should always do what is in the best interest of the patient (which includes doing no harm), treat all patients equally, and ensure that the informed and competent patient ultimately decides what is in their best interest."

The following section will review some key court cases that helped define the way medicine (and pharmacy) are practiced today.

Selected Important Court Cases

Karen Ann Quinlan: Substituted Judgment Standard

In the Quinlan case, Karen Ann was in a persistent vegetative state, being kept alive only by life support. Karen Ann's father asked to have her life support terminated according to his understanding of what Karen Ann would want. The court found that "if Karen herself were miraculously lucid for an interval . . . and perceptive of her irreversible condition, she could effectively decide upon discontinuance of the life support apparatus, even if it meant the prospect of natural death."

The court therefore allowed termination of life support, not because the father asked, but because it held that the father's request was most likely the expression of Karen Ann's own wishes.

Substituted judgment begins with the premise that decisions belong to the competent patient by virtue of the rights of autonomy and privacy. In this case, however, the patient is unable to decide, and a decision-maker who is the best representative of the patient's wishes must be substituted. In legal terms, the patient has the right to decide but is incompetent to do so. Therefore, the decision is made for the patient on the basis of the best estimate of her subjective wishes.

Note the key here is *not* who is the closest next of kin, but who is most likely to represent the patient's own wishes.

Brother Fox *(Eichner vs Dillon)*: Best Interest Standard

The New York Court of Appeals, in its decision of *Eichner vs Dillon,* held that trying to determine what a never-competent patient would have decided is practically impossible. Obviously, it is difficult to ascertain the actual (subjective) wishes of incompetents.

Therefore, if the patient has always been incompetent, or no one knows the patient well enough to render substituted judgment, the use of substituted judgment standard is questionable, at best.

Under these circumstances, decisions are made for the patient using the **best interest standard**. The object of the standard is to decide what a hypothetical "reasonable person" would decide to do after weighing the benefits and burdens of each course of action.

Note here the issue of who makes the decision is less important. All persons applying the best-interest standard should come to the same conclusions.

Infant Doe: Foregoing Lifesaving Surgery, Parents Withholding Treatment

As a general rule, parents cannot withhold life- or limb-saving treatment from their children. Yet, in this exceptional case they did.

Baby Boy Doe was born with Down syndrome (trisomy 21) and with a tracheoesophageal fistula. The infant's parents were informed that surgery to correct his fistula would have "an even chance of success." Left untreated, the fistula would soon lead to the infant's death from starvation or pneumonia. The parents, who also had 2 healthy children, chose to withhold food and treatment and "let nature take its course."

Court action to remove the infant from his parents' custody (and permit the surgery) was sought by the county prosecutor. The court denied such action, and the Indiana Supreme Court declined to review the lower court's ruling. Infant Doe died at 6 days of age, as Indiana authorities were seeking intervention from the U.S. Supreme Court.

Note that this case is simply an application of the best-interest standard. The court agreed with the parents that the burdens of treatment far outweighed any expected benefits.

Roe vs Wade (1973): The Patient Decides

Known to most people, as the importance of this case is not limited to its impact on abortion.

Faced with a conflict between the rights of the mother versus the rights of the putative unborn child, the court held that in the first trimester, the mother's rights are certainly paramount, and that states may, if they wish, have the mother's rights remain paramount for the full term of the pregnancy.

Because the mother gets to decide, even in the face of threats to the fetus, by extension, all patients get to decide about their own bodies and the health care they receive. In the United States, the locus for decision-making about health care resides with the patient, not the physician or pharmacist.

Note that courts have held that a pregnant woman has the right to refuse care (e.g., blood transfusions) even if it places her unborn child at risk.

Tarasoff Decision: Duty to Warn and Duty to Protect

A student visiting a counselor at a counseling center in California states that he is going to kill someone. When he leaves, the counselor is concerned enough to call the police but takes no further action. The student subsequently kills the person he threatened. The court found the counselor and the center liable because they did not go far enough to warn and protect the potential victim.

The counselor should have called the police and then should also have tried in every way possible to notify the potential victim of the potential danger.

In similar situations, first try to detain the person making the threat, next call the police, and finally notify and warn the potential victim. All 3 actions should be taken, or at least attempted.

Legal Issues Related to Medical/Pharmacy Practice

This section lays out a set of rules that constitute the general consensus of legal opinion. Apply these rules to individual situations as they arise.

Note

Family matters only to the degree that reflects the patient's wishes. Family's own wishes are not relevant.

Rule #1: Competent patients have the right to refuse medical treatment.

- Incompetent patients have the same rights, but must be exercised differently (via a surrogate).
- Patients have an almost absolute right to refuse. Patients have almost absolute control over their own bodies. The sicker the patient, the lesser the chance of recovery, the greater the right to refuse treatment.

Rule #2: If patient is incompetent to make decisions, the physician may rely on advance directives.

- Advance directives can be oral.
- Living will: written document expressing wishes
  - Care facilities must provide information at time of admission
  - Responsibility of the institution, not the physician or pharmacist
  - Only applies to end-of-life care

- Health power of attorney: designating the surrogate decision-maker
  - "Speaks with the patient's voice"
  - Beats all other decision rules
- In end-of-life circumstances, if power of attorney person *directly* contradicts the living will, follow the living will.

Rule #3: Assume that the patient is competent unless clear behavioral evidence indicates otherwise.

- Competence is a legal, not a medical issue.
- A diagnosis, by itself, tells you little about a patient's competence.
- Clear behavioral evidence would be:
  - Patient is grossly psychotic and dysfunctional
  - Patient's physical or mental state prevents simple communication
- If you are unsure, assume the patient is competent. The patient does not have to prove to you that he is competent. You have to have clear evidence to assume that he is not.

Rule #4: When surrogates make decisions for a patient, they should use the following criteria and in this order:

- Subjective standard
  - Actual intent, advance directive
  - What did the patient say in the past?
- Substituted judgment
  - Who best represents the patient?
  - What would patient say if he or she could?
- Best-interest standard
  - Burdens versus benefits
  - Interests of patient, not preferences of the decision-maker

Rule #5: Feeding tube is a medical treatment and can be withdrawn at the patient's request.

- Not considered killing the patient, but stopping treatment at patient's request.
- A competent person can refuse even lifesaving hydration and nutrition.

Rule #6: Do nothing to actively assist the patient to die sooner.

- Active euthanasia and assisted suicide are on difficult ground.
  - Passive, i.e., allowing to die = OK
  - Active, i.e., killing = NOT OK
- On the other hand, do all you can to reduce the patient's suffering (e.g., giving pain medication).

Rule #7: The physician decides when the patient is dead.

- If the physician thinks continued treatment is futile (the patient has shown no improvement), but the surrogate insists on continued treatment, the treatment should continue.
- If there are no more treatment options (the patient is cortically dead), and the family insists on treatment, there is nothing the physician can do; treatment must stop.

Rule #8: Never abandon a patient.

- Lack of financial resources or lack of results are never reasons to stop treatment of a patient.
- An annoying or difficult patient is still your patient.
- You can not ever threaten abandonment.

Rule #9: Keep the physician/pharmacist–patient relationship within bounds.

- Intimate social contact with anyone who is or has been a patient is prohibited. AMA guidelines (for physicians) say, "for at least 2 years."
- Do not date parents of pediatric patients or children of geriatric patients.
- Do not treat friends or family.
- Do not prescribe for colleagues unless a physician/patient relationship exists.
- If patients are inappropriate, gently but clearly let them know what acceptable behavior would be.
- Any gift from a patient beyond a small token should be declined.

Rule #10: Stop harm from happening.

- Beyond "do no harm," you must stop anyone from hurting himself or others.
- Take whatever action is required to prevent harm.
- Harm can be spreading disease, physical assault, psychological abuse, neglect, infliction of pain or anything which produces notable distress.
- You must also protect your patient, or anyone not your patient, from being hurt by another.

Rule #11: Always obtain informed consent.

- Full, informed consent requires that the patient has received and understood 5 pieces of information:
  - Nature of procedure
  - Purpose or rationale
  - Benefits
  - Risks
  - Availability of alternatives
- Four exceptions to informed consent:
  - Emergency
  - Waiver by patient
  - Patient is incompetent
  - Therapeutic privilege (unconscious, confused, physician deprives patient of autonomy in interest of health)
- Gag clauses that prohibit a physician or pharmacist from discussing treatment options that are not approved violate informed consent and are illegal.
- Consent can be oral.
- A signed paper the patient has not read or does not understand does NOT constitute informed consent.
- Written consent can be revoked orally at any time.

Rule #12: Special rules apply with children.

- Children younger than 18 years are minors and are legally incompetent.
- Exceptions: emancipated minors
  - If older than 13 years and taking care of self, i.e., living alone, treat as an adult.
  - Marriage makes a child emancipated, as does serving in the military.
  - Pregnancy or giving birth, in most cases, does not.
- Partial emancipation
  - Many states have special ages of consent: generally age 14 and older
  - For certain issues only:
    - Substance drug treatment
    - Prenatal care

  - Sexually transmitted disease treatment
  - Birth control

Rule #13: Parents cannot withhold life- or limb-saving treatment from their children.

- If parents refuse permission to treat child:
  - If immediate emergency, go ahead and treat.
  - If not immediate, but still critical (e.g., juvenile diabetes), generally the child is declared a ward of the court and the court grants permission.
  - If not life- or limb-threatening (e.g., child needs minor stitches), listen to the parents.
- Note that the child cannot give permission. A child's refusal of treatment is irrelevant.

Rule #14: For the purposes of the FPGEE, issues governed by laws that vary widely across states cannot be tested. This includes elective abortions (minor and spousal rights differ by locality) and legal age for drinking alcohol (vary by state).

Rule #15: Good Samaritan Laws limit liability in nonmedical settings.

- Not required to stop to help
- If help offered, shielded from liability provided:
  - Actions are within physician's (or pharmacists) competence
  - Only accepted procedures are performed.
  - Health care professional remains at scene after starting therapy until relieved by competent personnel
  - No compensation changes hands

Rule #16: Confidentiality is absolute.

- Physicians and pharmacists cannot tell anyone anything about their patient without the patient's permission.
- Physician and pharmacist must strive to ensure that others *cannot* access patient information.
- Getting a consultation is permitted, as the consultant is bound by confidentiality, too. However, watch the location of the consultation. Be careful not to be overheard (e.g., not elevator or cafeteria).
- If you receive a court subpoena, show up in court but do not divulge information about your patient.
- If patient is a threat to self or other, the physician (or pharmacist) MUST break confidentiality
  - Duty to warn and duty to protect (Tarasoff case)
  - A specific threat to a specific person
  - Suicide, homicide, and abuse are obvious threats.
  - Infectious disease should generally be treated as a threat, but be careful. Here issue is usually getting the patient to work with you to tell the person who is at risk
  - In the case of an STD, the issue is not really whether to inform a sexual partner, but how they should be told. Best advice: Have patient and partner come to your office.

Rule #17: Patients should be given the chance to state DNR (Do Not Resuscitate) orders, and physicians should follow them.

- DNR refers only to cardiopulmonary resuscitation.
- Continue with ongoing treatments.
- Most physicians are unaware of DNR orders.
- DNR decisions are made by the patient or surrogate.
- Have DNR discussions as part of your first encounter with the patient.
- Do not ask the patient about "do not resuscitate" wishes. Explain details of what is entailed.

Rule #18: Committed mentally ill patients retain their rights.

- Committed mentally ill adults legally are entitled to the following:
  - They must have treatment available.
  - They can refuse treatment.
  - They can command a jury trial to determine "sanity".
- They lose only the civil liberty to come and go.
- They retain their competence for conducting business transactions, marriage, divorce, voting, driving
- The words "sanity" and "competence" are legal, not psychiatric, terms. They refer to prediction of dangerousness, and medicopsychological studies show that health care professionals cannot reliably and validly predict such dangerousness.

Rule #19: Detain patients to protect them or others.

- Emergency detention can be effected by a physician and/or a law enforcement person for 48 hours, pending a hearing.
- A physician can detain; only a judge can commit.
- With children, special rules exist. Children can be committed only if:
  - They are in imminent danger to self or others.
  - They are unable to care for their own daily needs.
  - The parents have absolutely no control over the child, and the child is in danger (e.g., fire-setter), but not because the parents are unwilling to discipline a child.

Rule #20: Remove from patient contact health care professionals who pose risk to patients.

- Types of risks
  - Infectious disease (TB)
  - Substance-related disorders
  - Depression (or other psychological issues)
  - Incompetence
- Actions
  - Insist that they take time off
  - Contact their supervisors if necessary
- The patient, not professional solidarity, comes first.

Rule #21: Focus on what is the best ethical conduct, not simply the letter of the law.

The best answers are those that are both legal and ethical.

Sample Questions

1. Should pharmacists answer questions from insurance companies or employers?

   Not without a release from the patient

2. Should pharmacists answer questions from the patient's family without the patient's explicit permission?

   No

3. What information can the pharmacist withhold from the patient?

   Nothing. If patient may react negatively, figure out how to tell patient to mitigate negative outcome

4. What if the family requests that certain information be kept from the patient?

   (Tell the patient, but first find out why they don't want the patient told)

5. Who owns the medical record?

   Health care provider, but patient must be given access or copy upon request

What should the physician (or pharmacist) do in each of these situations?

6. Patient refuses lifesaving treatment on religious grounds?

   Don't treat

7. Wife refuses to consent to emergency lifesaving treatment for unconscious husband citing religious grounds?

   Treat, no time to assess substituted judgment

8. Wife produces card stating unconscious husband's wish to not be treated on religious grounds?

   Don't treat

9. Mother refuses to consent to emergency lifesaving treatment for her daughter on religious grounds?

   Treat

10. What if the child's life is at risk, but the risk is not immediate?

    Court takes guardianship

11. From whom do you get permission to treat a girl who is 17 years old?

    Her guardian

From whom does the physician (or pharmacist) obtain consent in each case?

12. A 17-year-old girl's parents are out of the country and the girl is staying with a babysitter?

    (If a threat to health, the physician can treat under doctrine of *in locum parentis*)

13. A 17-year-old girl who has been living on her own and taking care of herself?

    The girl herself

14. A 17-year-old girl who is married?

    The girl herself

15. A 17-year-old girl who is pregnant?

    Her guardian

16. A 16-year-old daughter refuses medication but her mother consents, do you write the prescription?

    Yes

17. The 16-year-old daughter consents, but the mother refuses?

    No

18. The mother of a minor consents, but the father refuses?

    Yes, only one permission needed

19. When should the physician or pharmacist provide informed consent?

    Always

20. Must informed consent be written?

    No

21. Can written consent be revoked orally?

    Yes

22. Can a physician (or pharmacist) get informed consent from a schizophrenic man?

    Yes, unless there is clear behavioral evidence that he is incompetent

23. Must a physician get informed consent from a prisoner if the police bring in the prisoner for examination?

    Yes

BIOMEDICAL RESEARCH ETHICS

Biomedical ethics can be defined as "an area of study concerned with the ethics and philosophical implications of specific biological and medical procedures, technologies, and treatments."

As scientific discoveries are made (and/or postulated) and health care evolves, the values at stake in biomedical research and health care are continually contested and debated. However, appropriate ethical norms can be used to assess and address difficult questions about right and wrong in both medicine and biomedical research.

History

History is full of horrifying examples of where biomedical research was inappropriately performed, including the human experiments in Nazi concentration camps in World War II, the Tuskegee Syphilis Study (in which subjects with syphilis were not given treatment), and the Willowbrook hepatitis studies (in which institutionalized subjects were intentionally exposed to hepatitis).

All of these atrocities have led to the development of numerous laws and ethical guidelines.

- The Nuremburg Code and the World Declaration of Geneva are 2 key documents that establish bioethical standards for research.
- The United States National Institute of Health (NIH), National Science Foundation, and FDA were also formed to help protect the general public and develop ethical norms for practicing medicine.

Ethical Norms

The ethical norms required in today's medical research include righteousness, integrity, honor, and social responsibility.

Today's biomedical research requires:

- Thorough and uncompromising approach to research design, data collection and interpretation.
- Informed consent of the patient or parent/guardian (in the case of minors)
- Study oversight: Institutional Review Board (IRB) approval
- Patient confidentiality
- Patient Protection: Protect the subjects/patients included in the research study by minimizing risks and maximizing benefits

Institutional Review Board

An institutional review board (IRB), also known as a research ethics board (REB), is defined as a "**formal committee used in biomedical research in the United States that has been designated to approve, monitor, and review biomedical and behavioral research involving humans.**"

In the United States, IRBs are governed by Title 45 Code of Federal Regulations Part 46, which defines the rules and responsibilities for all IRBs. IRBs are regulated by the Office for Human Research Protections (OHRP) within the Department of Health and Human Services (HHS).

IRBs generally perform a "risk-benefit analysis" to help determine whether or not the proposed human research should be performed. The primary purpose of the IRB is to assure the researchers, participants and general public that appropriate processes are followed to protect the rights and welfare of all persons participating in the research study.

The primary goal of an IRB is to protect participants from physical or psychological harm as a result of participation in the clinical trial. Attainment of this goal is achieved by reviewing research protocols and related study materials.

The protocol for a study should include the following:

- **Study Synopsis:** Overview of study design and procedures; identification of experimental aspects of the trial and which aspects are considered standard of care; costs that will be incurred by the subject and any payments made during the study to both researchers and participants.
- **Background:** Discussion of previous relevant studies
- **Objectives:** Purpose and expected outcomes of the research study
- **Subject Selection:** Overview of participant selection including a list of inclusion and exclusion criteria
- **Study Procedures/Materials/Methods:** Comprehensive discussion of the study design, procedures, study treatment and explanation of how the study treatment will be administered, materials used in the study, methods used to collect and analyze data, expected duration of study, informed consent process, and other important study components.
- **Risk/Safety Information:** Description of the expected (and potential) risks of study related procedures, including those related to experimental procedures and medications. There is also a discussion of how these risks are minimized by the study design.
- **Monitoring/Reporting of Adverse Effects (minor and serious):** Discussion on who will monitor and report the adverse effects. There should also be an established plan on how to mitigate or treat participants who experience these adverse effects.
- **Study Oversight:** Discussion of the clinical setting and how the researchers are continually monitoring each aspect of the study. There should be a description of the process for prematurely terminating the study and those responsible for making this determination. There should also be a description of how all aspects of the study will be made available for monitoring, auditing, IRB review and regulatory inspection.
- **Data Management:** Discussion of how the clinical trial results will be collected, analyzed and reported.
- **Informed Consent:** The study must be conducted in accordance with the regulations of the United States Food and Drug Administration (FDA) as described in 21 CFR 50 and 56 [add 312 for IND studies or 812 for device studies], applicable laws and the IRB requirements. The researchers must document all processes of ensuring how the informed consent process will be properly conducted. Informed consent is a complete discussion of proper information related to a treatment or procedure between a researcher and their study participant where the patient voluntarily agrees to the care plan and is free of coercion. Full, informed consent requires that the patient has received and understood 5 pieces of information: 1) Nature of the treatment; 2) Purpose or rationale of the treatment; 3) Risks of the treatment regimen; 4) Benefits of the treatment regimen; and 5) Alternatives to the recommended treatment regimen.
- **Participant Confidentiality:** Detailed discussion on how patient confidentiality will be maintained throughout the clinical trial as well as following the clinical trial.
- **Intended Use of the Data:** Description of how the "de-identified" data collected from the clinical trial will be used to support or refute the stated goals and objectives of the research.

PRACTICE QUESTIONS

1. A pharmacist receives a call from each of the following persons about a patient's antihypertensive medication. The pharmacist is permitted to discuss the findings with whom?

   A. The patient's adult son
   B. The patient's physical therapist
   C. The patient's wife
   D. The prescribing physician
   E. The pharmacist is permitted to discuss the patient's antihypertensive medication will all of these people.

2. A pharmacist has an ethical duty to always act in the best interest of their patients. This statement is most closely linked to which of the following core ethical principles?

   A. Beneficence
   B. Justice
   C. Nonmaleficence
   D. Patient autonomy
   E. This is not linked to any of the core ethical principles.

3. A 14-year-old female is considered legally competent in certain medical scenarios including which of the following?

   A. Broken arm while playing with friends
   B. Prenatal care
   C. Sexual assault
   D. Type 1 diabetes
   E. All of the above

4. A United States pharmacist is expected to do which of the following?

   A. Adhere to religious and personal beliefs ahead of the patient good
   B. Discard all personal moral values when practicing pharmacy
   C. Dispense every medication requested by a physician despite moral objection
   D. Refuse to help patients who are requesting services that go against personal and religious beliefs
   E. Use ethical judgment and not personal beliefs when practicing pharmacy

5. A pharmacist who refuses to counsel certain patients is

   A. Within both ethical and legal guidelines
   B. Within ethical guidelines but not legal
   C. Within legal guidelines but not ethical
   D. Within neither legal nor ethical guidelines

6. A 78-year-old mentally competent female was given a terminal diagnosis. She has the ability to refuse all of the following EXCEPT

    A. Medications for her coexisting conditions NOT related to her terminal diagnosis
    B. Medications for terminal diagnosis
    C. Pain medication
    D. Surgical intervention
    E. The patient may refuse all of these

7. Exceptions to informed consent include ALL of the following EXCEPT

    A. Emergency
    B. Patient is incompetent
    C. Therapeutic privilege
    D. Waiver by patient
    E. All of the above are exceptions to informed consent.

Answers and Explanations

1. **The correct answer is D.** Patient confidentiality is absolute! HIPAA is a federal regulation developed to enforce this principle and safeguard the privacy of protected health information (PHI). PHI consists of any type of identifiable health information that relates to the patient's past, present, or future medical or mental health conditions as well as provisions of health care and payment of health care services. Based on HIPAA laws and biomedical ethics, pharmacists cannot tell anyone anything about their patient without the patient's permission. These laws are exempt for health care providers directly involved in the care of the patient. Thus, the only person that the pharmacist is permitted to discuss the patient's antihypertensive medication with is the prescribing physician. The pharmacist must receive direct authorization from the patient to discuss their "medication" with all of the other people listed as answer choices.

2. **The correct answer is A.** Beneficence is defined as "the state or quality of being kind, charitable or beneficial". It simply means 'Do good!' from a biomedical ethics point of view. A pharmacist has an ethical (fiduciary) duty to always act in the best interest of their patients. Justice (choice B) is a core ethical principle that states that a pharmacist should "treat all patients equally by providing the same, appropriate level of care, attention and resources." Nonmaleficence (choice C) is a principle of bioethics that asserts an "obligation not to inflict harm intentionally." With patient autonomy (choice D), a pharmacist must respect the wishes of an "informed and competent" patient as well as honor their individual preferences in medical care.

3. **The correct answer is B.** Children younger than 18 years of age are minors and are legally incompetent to make decisions for themselves. Exceptions (emancipated minors) include those who are >13 years and taking care of self (i.e. living alone), marriage, and serving in the military. For these minors, they have complete control over their medical decisions. Partial emancipation is permitted to ensure that proper care is available for certain medical conditions, such as substance drug treatment, prenatal care, sexually transmitted disease treatment and birth control. A minor may not want to involve their parents when seeking treatment for these conditions; hence, without partial emancipation, the child may not receive care. The "patient" is considered a minor in choices A, C and D.

4. **The correct answer is E.** All pharmacists in the United States take an oath (found in the beginning of this chapter) that is centered on the core ethical principles of beneficence, justice, nonmaleficence and patient autonomy. One of the verses of this oath is "I will ***embrace*** and advocate changes that improve

patient care." Part of the meaning of this statement is that pharmacists will "use ethical judgment and not personal beliefs when practicing pharmacy".

5. **The correct answer is D.** The Omnibus Budget Reconciliation Act of 1990 requires pharmacists to counsel Medicaid patients; this is now extended to all patients. Pharmacists also are ethically required to counsel all patients despite their personal or religious beliefs. Thus, patient counseling is both an ethical and legal requirement.

6. **The correct answer is E.** Patients have almost absolute control over their own bodies. Furthermore, patient autonomy is an obligation by the pharmacist to respect the wishes of an "informed and competent" patient as well as honor their individual preferences in medical care. In other words, competent patients have the right to refuse medical treatment. As a general rule, the sicker the patient, the lesser the chance of recovery and the greater the right to refuse treatment. NOTE: Incompetent patients have the same rights, but must be exercised differently (via a surrogate).

7. **The correct answer is E.** Informed consent is a complete discussion of proper information related to a treatment or procedure between a health care provider (or researcher) and their patient. Full informed consent requires that the patient has received and understood 5 pieces of information: 1) Nature of the treatment; 2) Purpose or rationale of the treatment; 3) Risks of the treatment regimen; 4) Benefits of the treatment regimen; and 5) Alternatives to the recommended treatment regimen. Exceptions to informed consent are necessary when the patient is physically and/or mentally unable to make an informed decision. The 4 primary exceptions to informed consent are emergency (life-threating) situations, patient is incompetent, therapeutic privilege or there is a waiver by the patient.

Professional Communication 19

Learning Objectives

- ❑ Describe the introductory principles of professional communication
- ❑ Explain proper communication techniques between health care providers
- ❑ Show proficiency in assertiveness and problem-solving techniques
- ❑ Summarize health literacy principles
- ❑ Demonstrate proficiency in cultural competency in pharmacy personnel

Effective communication is often considered as important to health care as the actual clinical skills of the providers themselves. To improve individual patient outcomes and assist in the building of healthy communities, pharmacists need to recognize and address the health literacy and language barriers of a diverse patient population. Pharmacists should also continually strive to improve their interpersonal communication skills with other health care providers.

PROFESSIONAL COMMUNICATION WITH HEALTH CARE PROVIDERS AND PATIENTS

The role of the pharmacist in the health care community has evolved over the years. Originally, the pharmacist was primarily concerned with medication dispensing and compounding. Today, the pharmacist has added responsibilities of providing patient information, education, and pharmaceutical care services.

With the passage of the Omnibus Budget Reconciliation Act of 1990 (requiring the offer for patient counseling) and the more recent passage of Medicare legislation permitting pharmacists to be reimbursed for providing medication therapy management (MTM) services to eligible Medicare beneficiaries, the importance of professional communication skills with both patients and other health care providers is essential.

Communication Skills

The role of the pharmacist in patient/health care provider communications involves **sharing of clinical information**, **professional behavior**, and **general interpersonal communication skills**.

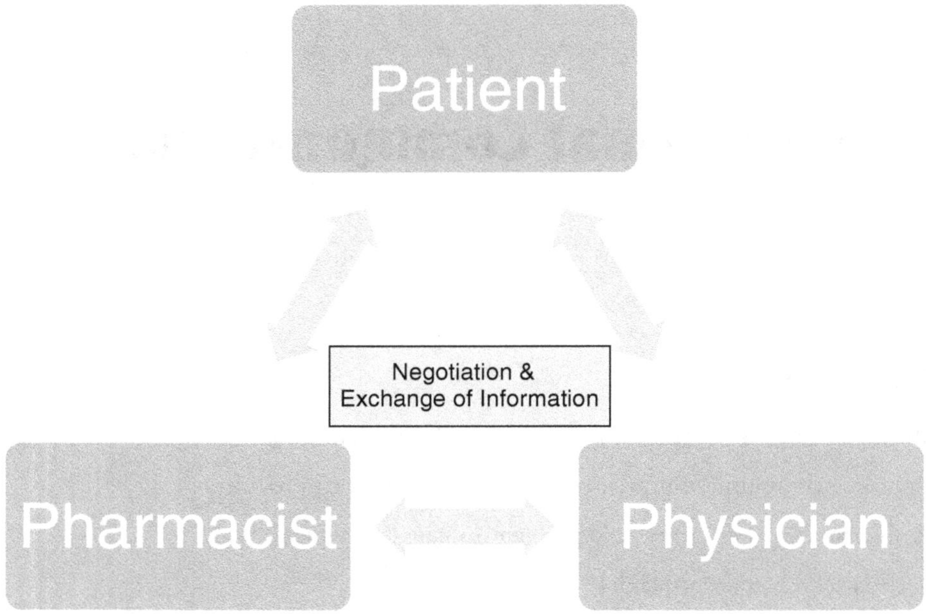

Figure 19-1. Cooperative Communication Process

The main idea with patient communication is to talk **with** the patient (and health care provider), not **to** them. Communication should be a 2-way process:

- Always be respectful
- Be empathetic
- Use appropriate language: Use words the listener will understand
- Organize your thoughts
- Focus on the primary reason for the communication (then discuss other issues when appropriate)
- Ensure your "nonverbal" and "verbal" communications match
- Strive to maintain self-confidence and self-esteem at all times
- Ask for feedback
- Minimize communication barriers (pharmacy counter, lack of privacy, cultural differences, inaccurate perceptions by the patient, lack of consultation time)

Also consider that there are different types of patient/health care provider interviewing techniques.

Table 19-1. Types of Patient/Health Care Provider Interviewing Techniques

Interview Technique	Explanation	Example Question/Comment
Open-Ended Questions	Allow the patient to speak in his own words as much as possible.	Can you tell me how the medication made you feel?
Close-Ended Questions	Ask for specific information without allowing options in answering.	Did the medication make you sick?
Facilitation	Pharmacist helps the patient continue by providing verbal and nonverbal cues.	Yes, please continue in more detail how the medication made you feel.

(Continued)

Interview Technique	Explanation	Example Question/Comment
Confrontation	Pharmacist points something out to the patient.	You seem very upset today.
Reassurance (Truthful)	Truthful communication can lead to increased medication compliance; however, dishonest communication can lead to decreased compliance.	Reassurance (truthful): Unfortunately your medication side effects are normal; Reassurance (Dishonest): Your side effects will be gone soon . . . hang in there.
Leading	The answer is suggested in the question.	Is your medication causing you to experience dizziness when you get out of a chair?
Non-verbal communication	Your body language is constantly speaking and "showing" the listener how you truly feel. ***(More information on non-verbal communication is found in the cultural competency section of this chapter.)***	Facial expressions, eye contact, posture, tone of voice, gestures with extremities are continually revealing one's true attitude (positive or negative)

Development of effective communication skills and interviewing techniques will aid in the establishment of a productive relationship with other health care providers. These skills are essential to appropriately engage in population health management.

Population Health Management

The goal of population health management (PHM) is to keep a patient population as healthy as possible, and one essential component of that is proper communication between health care providers. Requirements for this to succeed are:

- Delivery of patient care through multidisciplinary teams
- Coordination of care across care settings
- Increased access to primary care
- Patient education in disease self-management
- Emphasis on health behaviors and lifestyle choices
- Meaningful use of health information technology for data analysis, clinical communication, and outcome measurement

PHM requires clinicians to identify target patient populations who may benefit from additional services. This includes patients who require reminders for preventative care appointments or those not meeting pre-established management goals. According to PHM principles, continual access to patient data, communication between health care providers and analysis of outcomes is the key to providing proactive, preventive care.

Steps in population health management:

- **Step 1: Define population**
- **Step 2: Identify care gaps**
- **Step 3: Stratify risks**
- **Step 4: Engage patients**
- **Step 5: Manage care**
- **Step 6: Measure outcomes**

Several advances in technology have made it possible to perform effective PHM by identifying gaps in health care and accomplishing risk stratification. With these technological advances, clinicians are also able to provide comprehensive patient education, compliance education, disease state monitoring, and ensure general wellness.

Strategies and processes used to implement and assess specific PHM interventions in selected populations include:

- Electronic health records, which can produce integrated, accessible population-wide data systems capable of generating reports that drive effective quality and care management processes.
- Web-based tools that are designed to educate patients about their condition, promote self-care, and encourage preventative behaviors. These tools have been used successfully to reduce hospitalization rates by enabling patients to take charge of their health.
- Telemedicine programs that establish remote care in order to facilitate patient outreach, allow patient follow-up after discharge from the hospital, and improve health care in rural populations.
- Automation of processes and programs to make PMH feasible, scalable, and sustainable; for example, a health IT system which targets patients in greatest need of services, generates alerts to those patients seeking appropriate and timely appointments with clinicians, and alerts clinicians in real-time to patient care needs.

However, technology alone will not be sufficient for PHM; effective teamwork in patient care is also important. Effective population health involves establishing multidisciplinary care teams to coordinate care throughout the entire continuum of care. High-performance clinical care teams can manage a greater number of patients and more comprehensively respond to patient care needs compared with individual clinicians working in isolation. Care teams can include physicians, nurses, nurse practitioners, physician assistants, pharmacists, patient navigators, medical assistants, dieticians, physical therapists, social workers, care managers, and others.

Patient-Centered Medical Home

The patient-centered medical home (PCMH) is one emerging model used to deliver patient-centered, value-based care, and it plays an important role in PHM. The medical home model emphasizes care coordination and communication beyond episodic care in order to transform primary care. It stresses prevention, early intervention and close partnerships with patients to tightly manage chronic conditions and maintain health.

The PCMH is not necessarily a physical place, but rather an organizational model that delivers the core functions of primary health care. Key principles in this model include:

- Access to a personal physician who leads the care team within a medical practice
- Adoption of a whole-person orientation to providing patient care
- Integrated and coordinated care
- Focus on quality and safety

The medical home is intended to result in more personalized, coordinated, effective and efficient care. Many of the goals of PCMH directly support efforts in population health.

In 2006, the Massachusetts General Hospital (MGH) worked with the U.S. Centers for Medicare and Medicaid to establish 1 of 6 population health demonstration projects nationwide. During the 3-year demonstration, the MGH implemented strategies to improve health care delivery to its most vulnerable high risk patients (those with multiple health conditions and chronic disease). The hospital system took steps to address the needs of 2,500 of their highest-risk patients.

- Each patient was assigned to a comprehensive care team consisting of a primary care physician, experienced nurse case manager, social worker, and pharmacist.
- A non-clinical community resource specialist was employed to work with the care teams in addressing non-clinical factors influencing health outcomes (for example, if the patient was not able to come to the primary care office for a scheduled visit because of transportation issues, this specialist connected the patient to local transportation resources).

This structure of care allowed clinicians to focus the majority of their time on patients' medical needs. The results revealed a decrease in hospital readmissions by 20% and a decrease in emergency room visits by 13% for the patients enrolled in the program.

Satisfaction was extremely high among both patients and caregivers, and the system was associated with significant cost-savings. This is one example of using population health (with exemplary inter-profession communication) to increase quality while decreasing costs, thereby increasing value in patient care.

ASSERTIVENESS AND PROBLEM SOLVING TECHNIQUES

Assertiveness can be defined as a confident declaration in behavior or style without being aggressive or threatening the rights of others. Assertive people generally express their thoughts and feeling without pressuring others to conform to their views. Furthermore, assertive people are able to control their anger and are often willing to compromise.

The pharmacist will interact (on a daily basis) with a variety of patients, clinicians, employees, and administrators about a number of different issues. Assertive communication assumes a cooperative interest of all parties in fulfilling the medical needs of the patient. Hence, this type of communication is essential in the pharmacy setting to help ensure the best outcome for each issue.

Assertive behavior is also essential in problem solving. If you ask any pharmacist, it is likely that they could not recall a day without some type of patient insurance company, medication regimen or medication prescriber problem.

Problem Solving Techniques

It is well known that different problems require different solutions; however, the key aspects of successful problem solving are being able to:

1. clearly identify the problem,
2. collect all of the information (data) about the problem,
3. analyze the information as a basis for developing a solution,
4. generate a solution,
5. plan for an implementation of the solution by setting up a system of strategies and objectives to solve the problem, and
6. implement the solution and evaluate the results for future problems.

The following figure outlines these steps with a patient-centered focus of continued improvement.

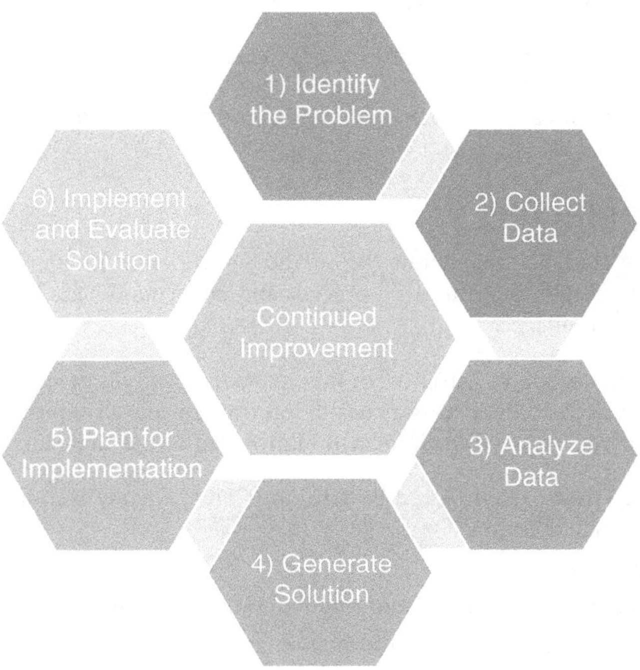

Figure 19-2. Patient-centered focus steps to continued improvement.

Problem solving generally becomes easier and less intimidating when a person takes an assertive, proactive approach toward solving the problem. However, there are some barriers to effective problem solving.

Recognition of these barriers is the first step to overcoming them.

Table 19-2. Problem Solving Barriers

Barrier	Definition/Comments
Functional fixedness	A type of cognitive bias that limits a person to using an object (or following a process) only in the way it was traditionally meant to be used (or followed). Applied to problem solving, the problem solver is hindered in reaching the solution to a problem by their own knowledge of an object's conventional function. Common sense is a plausible solution to this barrier provided that the problem solver can consider another use for the object (or process).
Unnecessary constraints	Generally occurs when the problem solver places subconscious boundaries on resolving the problem. They are unable to become more innovative in their thinking and become fixated on only one way to solve the problem at hand. It becomes progressively more difficult for them to see anything other than the problem solving method they have chosen.
Confirmation bias	A type of cognitive bias where the problem solver has a tendency to collect and interpret data in a way that confirms the person's pre-conceived opinion or hypotheses about a situation, while giving disproportionately less consideration to alternative possibilities. In other words, the problem solver is looking for evidence to support a pre-conceived opinion, rather than looking for evidence that refutes it or provides greater support to an alternative diagnosis; this may accompany an anchoring error. Clinicians should regard conflicting data as evidence for the need to continue to seek the truth rather than as anomalies to be disregarded.
Irrelevant information	Information presented within a problem that is unrelated or irrelevant to the defined problem. This type of information is often detrimental to the problem solving process.
Mental Set	A tendency to only see the problem or potential solution that has worked for "similar" problems in the past. This type of thinking can make it difficult to formulate an effective solution to the "similar" problem.

HEALTH LITERACY PRINCIPLES

The Patient Protection and Affordable Care Act of 2010 (Title V) defines health literacy as "the degree to which an individual has the capacity to obtain, communicate, process, and understand basic health information and services to make appropriate health decisions."

One of the key words in this definition is "capacity." In this context, capacity is defined as the potential a patient has to successfully perform an act, such as find necessary health information as well as properly communicate their needs to a clinician and subsequently understand the information provided by the clinician.

According to the Centers for Disease Control and Prevention (CDC), **anyone who needs health information and services** also needs health literacy skills to:

- find information and services;
- communicate their needs and preferences and respond to information and services;
- process the meaning and usefulness of the information and services;
- understand the choices, consequences and context of the information and services; and
- decide which information and services match their needs and preferences so they can act.

The CDC further states that **anyone who provides health information and services to others,** such as a doctor, nurse, dentist, pharmacist, or public health worker, also **needs health literacy skills** to:

- help people find information and services;
- communicate about health and healthcare;
- process what people are explicitly and implicitly asking for;
- understand how to provide useful information and services; and
- decide which information and services work best for different situations and people so they can act.

Based on these 2 skill sets defined by the CDC, the competent pharmacist is thus responsible for the facilitation of information exchange as well as directing the patient to the proper medical service.

In addition to the efforts of the CDC, the National Action Plan to Improve Health Literacy (https://www.healthypeople.gov/) sponsored by the U.S. Department of Health and Human Services works with health care professionals, patients, and organizations to improve health literacy. The founding principles of this plan are that all patients have the right to health information to assist them in making informed decisions AND health services offered in the United States should be delivered in a manner that is both understandable and beneficial to the individual patient ultimately resulting in improved health outcomes.

The vision of the National Action Plan to Improve Health Literacy is the creation of a society that:

- Provides everyone with access to accurate and actionable health information;
- Delivers person-centered health information and services; and
- Supports lifelong learning and skills to promote good health.

To bring all of the concepts together, the practicing pharmacist should provide all patients with information in a manner that they understand so that they can make informed health decisions that will ultimately maximize their health outcomes. The pharmacist should also facilitate patient health by directing them to the best health care provider or service provider when appropriate.

CULTURAL COMPETENCY IN PHARMACY PERSONNEL

The U.S. Department of Health and Human Services established the Office of Minority Health (OMH). OMH has a goal of "Improving the health of racial and ethnic minority populations through the development of health policies and programs that will help eliminate health disparities."

As part of the effort to attain this goal, the OMH has established the Center for Linguistic and Cultural Competency in Health Care (CLCCHC) to address the health needs of individuals with a limited understanding of English and/or those with differing cultural backgrounds. The CLCCHC's mission is to "Collaborate with federal agencies and other public and private entities to enhance the ability of the health care system to effectively deliver linguistically appropriate and culturally competent health care to limited English-speaking populations."

Cultural competence in health care can be defined as the ability of a provider (pharmacist) to effectively communicate and interact with patients who have diverse values, beliefs, and behaviors. Cultural competence also includes an appropriate consideration and respect for the patient's unique social, cultural, and linguistic limitations.

The first step in demonstrating cultural competence is understanding the importance of both verbal and non-verbal communication. When dealing with some culturally diverse patients, non-verbal communication may assume more significance than verbal communication.

- Example: Imagine a scenario where there is a patient with a very limited understanding of English. If the pharmacist is rolling her eyes, showing frustration or continually looking at her watch, the patient will sense that the pharmacist is not interested in providing care to them. As a result, the patient will either seek care elsewhere OR will not seek care at all.

The following figure provides a high-level overview of culturally appropriate communication.

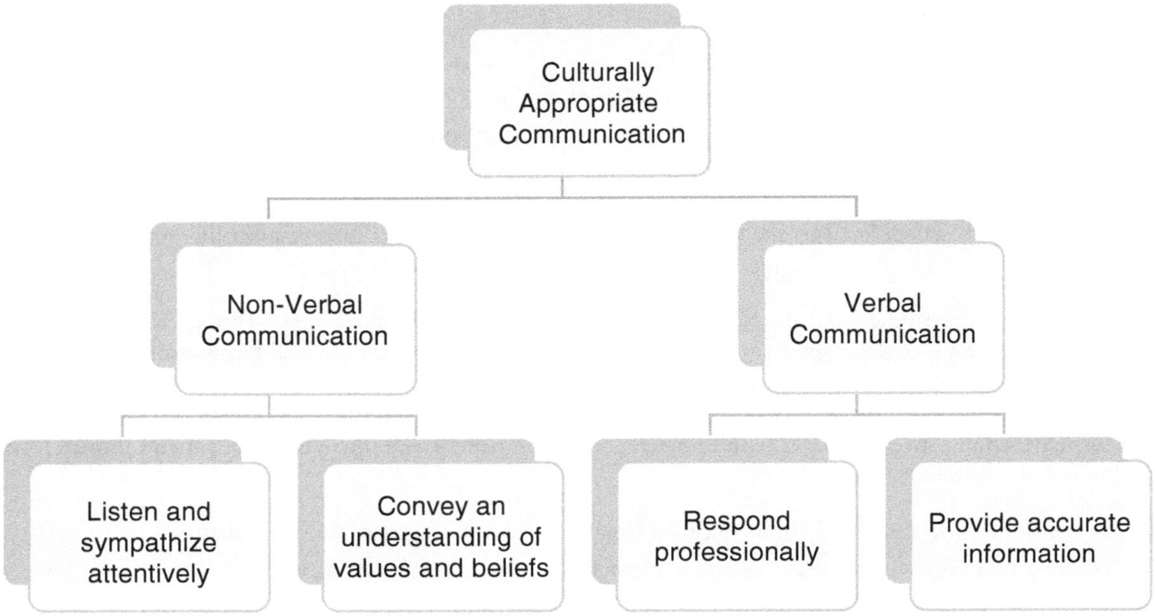

Figure 19-3. Cultural appropriate communication.

Nonverbal communication involves both the conscious and unconscious processes of programming and deciphering. Nonverbal programming is the act of generating the information such as facial expressions, gestures, and postures. Decrypting is the interpretation of information from received sensations from previous experiences.

Table 19-3. Nonverbal Communication

Type of Nonverbal communication	Definition/Comments
Eye contact	Speaking while looking directly at a patient. It is often used to evaluate one's trustworthiness.
Posturing	A set of personal signals that communicate how an individual is experiencing the interaction. For example, a person who sits with his/her arms folded and legs crossed is in a defensive or resistant posture.
Ambulation	The way a person walks. If a person is stomping their feet, for example, the patient on the receiving end will likely interpret anger or disgust.
Touching	Often considered the most powerful form of nonverbal communication. Touching can convey compassion, trust and other positive feelings. Note: People differ in their willingness to touch or be touched.
Vocalization	The way the message is presented in both words and tone.
Gesturing	The movement of parts of the body to emphasize a point. For example, throwing up the hands in the air while speaking is a sign of frustration and/or anger.
Distancing	Maintaining a proper space between the patient and health care provider. Too close is considered an invasion of "personal space" and too far away is considered to convey mistrust. A distance of approximately 3 feet is generally considered by most to be an acceptable distance/space between a patient and provider.

A culturally-competent health care provider (pharmacist) recognizes and accepts the importance of cultural diversity and language barriers as well as understands the importance of:

- **Sociocultural barriers:** Some patients may feel that they cannot ask for assistance since it is a sign of weakness or that only certain family members can ask for advice (about an issue from someone not in their immediate family).
- **Attitudes towards health care:** The importance of and emphasis on health care may be different than that of United States citizens.
- **Beliefs in the diagnosis or treatment:** Some patients may not want to receive blood products or "non-essential" medications.

Pharmacists need to provide culturally sensitive patient-centered care. This can be accomplished by treating each patient as an individual and identifying and respecting their personal beliefs and values.

PRACTICE QUESTIONS

1. A patient asks to speak with the pharmacist. When the pharmacist comes to the counter they have their arms crossed. This is an example of what type of nonverbal communication?

   A. Ambulation
   B. Gesturing
   C. Distancing
   D. Posturing
   E. Vocalization

2. A patient is diagnosed with polycystic ovary syndrome and prescribed spironolactone. However, the patient is worried about the side effects and asks for an alternative medication. The pharmacist calls the physician, presents clinical research and subsequently recommends metformin. The physician replies "metformin is a diabetes drug and I will not prescribe a diabetes drug for a patient that does not have diabetes". This is an example of which of the following problem solving barriers?

   A. Confirmation bias
   B. Functional fixedness
   C. Irrelevant information
   D. Mental set
   E. Unnecessary constraints

3. Which of the following patient health literacy skills are the most important?

   A. Communicating their needs to health care providers
   B. Determining what information matches their needs
   C. Finding the information
   D. Processing the meaning and usefulness of the information
   E. All are equally important

4. Which of the following is an open-ended question?
    A. Do you take the medication each day with food, on an empty stomach or both?
    B. How are you taking the medication each day?
    C. What time do you take the medication, each morning?
    D. When you took the medication, did it make you sick?
    E. All of the above are open-ended questions

5. Which of the following is the most appropriate question to ask a patient when obtaining a medication list?
    A. Do you take any medications?
    B. Do you take any prescription, over-the-counter or natural product medications?
    C. What is your past drug history?
    D. What prescription, over-the-counter or natural product medications do you take?
    E. All of the above are equally appropriate.

6. Cultural competence is best defined as which of the following?
    A. Effectively communicating and interacting with patients who have diverse values, beliefs, and behaviors.
    B. Finding a health care provider that has the same values, beliefs and behaviors of the patient to improve medical care.
    C. Obtaining the knowledge necessary to speak with the patient in their "primary" language.
    D. Temporarily adopting the values, beliefs and behaviors of the patient to improve medical care.
    E. Understanding the values, beliefs and behaviors of the patient and conveying them to the rest of the health care team.

7. The CDC states that, when dealing with patients from different backgrounds, healthcare providers need health literacy skills to:
    A. Assist others in finding appropriate health services
    B. Determine what information and services are most appropriate for a patient
    C. Properly communicate health information
    D. Understand how to provide information and services
    E. All of the above

8. Which of the following is the most appropriate question to ask a patient when beginning the counseling session?
    A. Can you pay for your medication first and then I will counsel you if you like?
    B. Do you have any questions?
    C. Have you ever taken this medication before?
    D. What can you tell me about your medication's adverse effects, proper usage, storage and other important facts?
    E. Would you like to be counseled on your medication's adverse effects, proper usage, storage and other important facts?

Answers and Explanations

1. **The correct answer is D.** Nonverbal communication involves both the conscious and unconscious processes of programming and deciphering. Posturing (choice D) is defined as a set of personal signals that communicate how an individual is experiencing the interaction. For example, a person who sits with his/her arms folded and legs crossed is in a defensive or resistant posture. Ambulation (choice A) is related to the way a person walks. Gesturing (choice B) is the moving of body parts to emphasize a point. Distancing (choice C) is the proper or improper amount of space between the healthcare provider and the patient. Vocalization (choice E) is the choice of words and the tone in which they are presented.

2. **The correct answer is B.** Functional fixedness is a type of cognitive bias that limits a person to using an object (or following a process) only in the way it was traditionally meant to be used (or followed). In this case, metformin is the drug of choice for type 2 diabetes. Applied to problem solving, the problem solver is hindered in reaching the solution to a problem by their own knowledge of an object's conventional function. In other words, the physician has a mental block against using the drug in a new way that is required to solve a problem. All of the other answer choices are discussed in the problem solving barriers table in this chapter.

3. **The correct answer is E.** Health literacy is the degree to which an individual has the capacity to obtain, communicate, process, and understand basic health information and services to make appropriate health decisions. Without one of these components, the patient's opportunity to receive appropriate health care greatly diminishes.

4. **The correct answer is B.** There are 2 general types of questions: Open-ended and close (or closed)-ended questions. When interviewing patients, open-ended questions are generally considered to be more effective since they cannot be answered with a simple "yes" or "no", or with a specific piece of information. Open-ended questions often start with "How" or "Can you describe, explain, outline, etc". These types of questions prompt the patient to "explain" a process or series of symptoms. All of the answer choices are close-ended questions since they can be answered with a Yes/No answer OR a single word/phrase answer.

5. **The correct answer is D.** When obtaining a medication list, the pharmacist should ask open-ended questions that are very specific. For example, do you take any medications (choice A) would likely be a good question for a health care provider to ask, since the patient would provide information on every prescription, over-the-counter and natural product that they consume. However, many patients do not consider "natural supplements" and/or over-the-counter products as mediations. Hence, asking an open-ended question about prescription, over-the-counter or natural product medications is most appropriate (choice D is correct). Choice B is incorrect since it is a closed-ended question. Choice C may be misinterpreted by the patient. They may think that you are implying that they use "illicit drugs". Furthermore, it is not a specific question.

6. **The correct answer is A.** Cultural competence is defined as the ability of a health care provider (pharmacist) to effectively communicate and interact with patients who have diverse values, beliefs, and behaviors. Cultural competence also includes an appropriate consideration and respect for the patient's unique social, cultural, and linguistic limitations. The pharmacist does not need to learn the patient's language (choice C); however, they should find a way to communicate with the patient. Furthermore, the pharmacist does not need to find another healthcare provider for the patient (choice B), adopt their values (choice D) or convey patient beliefs to the healthcare team (choice E).

7. **The correct answer is E.** The CDC states that anyone who provides health information and services to others, such as a doctor, nurse, dentist, pharmacist, or public health worker, also needs health literacy skills to assist others in finding appropriate health services (choice A), determine what information and services are most appropriate for a patient (choice B), properly communicate health information (choice C), process what people are explicitly and implicitly asking for, and understand how to provide information and services (choice D).

8. **The correct answer is E.** With the passage of the Omnibus Budget Reconciliation Act of 1990, pharmacists must offer to discuss a series of medication-related issues prior to dispensing the medication. These issues include the name and description of the drug, dosage form, dosage, route of administration, and duration of drug therapy, special directions and precautions for preparation, administration, and use by the patient as well as other issues. Thus the pharmacist should "appropriately" offer to counsel the patient. Choice E outlines possible topics for the patient counseling. After hearing this question, the patient can decide if they want to be counseled or not. Choice A is inappropriate because it gives the impression that the pharmacist is "hurrying" them out of the pharmacy and is only concerned with collecting payment. Choice B is not specific to what the question is pertaining. Choice C does not address counseling at all. In choice D, the pharmacist is not offering to counsel the patient but is testing their knowledge. Some patients may feel foolish if they cannot answer and this could be a barrier to communication.

Social and Behavioral Aspects of Pharmacy Practice 20

Learning Objectives

- ❑ Explain medically-related behaviors of patients
- ❑ Define behavior modification principles
- ❑ Discuss principles of medication adherence
- ❑ Answer questions on medical and pharmacy caregiving
- ❑ Demonstrate understanding of death and dying

Although 2 patients may have a similar disease, the way in which they deal with the disease may be completely different. While patient behaviors do not typically influence treatment results, at times they can negatively affect a desired therapeutic outcome.

As the most accessible health care provider, the pharmacist is generally in a position to identify patients who are not properly managing their condition. Furthermore, the pharmacist can help the patient better understand their medical condition, adhere to the prescribed regimen, and make better health-related decisions.

MEDICALLY-RELATED BEHAVIORS OF PATIENTS

The illness experience, originally defined by Edward Suchman in 1965, occurs in stages that can explain the behaviors of most patients receiving medical care. According to Suchman's model, there are 5 key stages of the illness experience:

1. Symptom-experience
2. Assumption of the sick role
3. Medical care contact
4. Dependent-patient role
5. Recovery or rehabilitation

Each stage may present new challenges (for the health care provider) that require different kinds of decisions and medical action. Furthermore, it is believed that the behavior of the sick individual is influenced by a number of social and medical factors.

In the illness experience, each stage involves a decision by the patient that determines whether they will progress to the next stage, remain in the existing stage or abandon the illness experience.

- To help understand each stage, we have **applied Suchman's principles to a new onset of angina symptoms** in a patient.

Symptom-Experience

The illness experience (as outlined in Suchman's model) is initiated when a patient first notices that something is wrong. There may be pain, discomfort, dizziness, disruption of normal body function, or just a general sense that "something is wrong."

If Suchman's model were applied to angina symptoms, there would be 3 distinct processes that occur at the beginning of angina symptoms: (1) the physical chest pain or discomfort, (2) cognitive recognition that the physical symptoms of an abnormal symptom/illness is present, and (3) an emotional response of concern in the patient about the social implications of the chest pain, such as an inability to play with grandchildren, mow the lawn or effectively perform their duties at work.

Although the illness experience was originally defined by Edward Suchman, David Mechanic (1968) later developed a theory of help-seeking behaviors used by patients when assessing "potential illness" symptoms. Mechanic's theory helps promote an understanding of the symptom assessment process. It also helps explain how different patients interpret symptom severity and either move on to step 2 of Suchman's theory or dismiss the symptom all together.

Table 20-1. Mechanic's Theory: Patient Response to Illness

Factors Determining Individual's Response	Definition
Perceived seriousness of symptoms	Varies from person to person; if the symptom has occurred before without perceived negative consequences then it is unlikely that the patient will seek medical care.
Recognizability or perceptual importance of symptoms	Varies from disease state to disease state; an acute onset of chest pain is likely recognizable by a patient; however, early stages of colorectal cancer are not noticeable.
Extent to which symptoms disrupt daily life	Varies from person to person; lower back pain may not be perceived as being as serious for a person who works in an office; however, a construction worker is likely to place more emphasis on this symptom since it will impact their ability to function at their job.
Frequency of symptom appearance	Varies from disease state to disease state; the more frequent the symptom, the more likely the patient is to seek care.
Individual tolerance threshold	Varies from person to person; some patients are able to tolerate pain better than others.
Needs competing with illness treatment	Varies from person to person; the patient may know they are "sick"; however, they are unable to seek medical care because of financial or other personal obligations.
Personal and cultural understanding of the illness evaluator	Varies from person to person; an individual's knowledge of the illness or cultural beliefs can dramatically impact whether or not a patient will seek medical attention.
Perceptual needs related to anxiety and fear	Varies from person to person; the more fearful the patient becomes about the symptom, the more likely they are to seek care.
Competing interpretations of a symptom	Varies from person to person; a symptom that commonly occurs may not be interpreted as being serious. For example, a construction worker who begins experiencing muscle pain and generalized fatigue following the institution of an HMG-CoA reductase inhibitor may be less likely to seek care than an office worker.
Availability of treatment and psychological and monetary costs of taking action	Varies from person to person; what is the overall cost of the treatment for the patient? Can they monetarily and psychologically afford the treatment?

Assumption of the Sick Role

The patient "accepts" that the symptoms (i.e. chest pain) are a sign of illness and are sufficiently troublesome. Once this occurs, the patient has essentially transitioned to the sick role, thus the patient begins to relinquish some or all normal social roles. Examples of components of the sick role include:

- Exempt from normal responsibilities,
- Patient is not to blame for illness, and
- Patient is obligated to get well and seek competent help.

Medical Care Contact/Self-Care

The patient makes a decision to seek care either professionally, institute a method of self-care or a combination of both. For example, if the patient is shoveling snow and begins to experience shortness of breath and chest pain, they may quickly progress through the first 2 steps and determine that they are going to sit down and rest for a few moments. If the pain subsides, they may not seek medical care immediately. However, if the pain continues then they may dial 911 or head to the emergency department.

Dependent-Patient Role

In this stage, the patient is expected to make every effort to get well. For example, the angina patient will undergo appropriate diagnostic tests (EKG, imaging studies, etc), non-pharmacological therapy (diet, mild exercise), pharmacological therapy (aspirin, beta-blockers, nitrates as needed, etc). However, some patients enjoy the benefits of this role (i.e. increased attention, decreased work responsibilities) and attempt to malinger. This model does not apply to malingering.

The severity and longevity (acute vs chronic) of the illness, personal coping skills, culturally-influenced reactions to illness, spiritual beliefs and the amount of social support all contribute to the overall impact of the illness on the "dependent patient". Studies have shown that the following are the primary concerns for patients in stage 4:

- Impairments of personal cognitive functioning
- Loss of personal independence
- Changes in body image
- Withdrawal from their primary social roles
- Their "new" future as a result of the illness

Recovery or Rehabilitation

Once in stage 4, the acute patient will either clinically improve and move on to this stage (Stage 5) or terminate the treatment (and possibly seek alternative treatment).

The path taken by the patient will vary depending on the nature of the illness:

- **Acute patients**: There is a relinquishing of the sick role and movement back to normal role obligations. For example, the patient had a minor myocardial infarction and was told that with proper diet, exercise, and medication, they can live a normal life.
- **Chronic patients**: The degree of the sick role will vary based on the severity of the chronic illness, personal coping skills, culturally-influenced reactions to illness, spiritual beliefs and the amount of social support. The extent to which prior role obligations (Stage 4 for example) may be resumed ranges from those who forsake the sick role to those who will never be able to leave it.

BEHAVIOR MODIFICATION PRINCIPLES

Behavior modification can be applied to many different aspects of medicine today. The clinical pharmacist should understand these principles.

Learning and Behavior

In the behaviorist model of learning and behavior modification, internal states, subjective impressions, and unconscious processes are not relevant. All that matters is the objective data (i.e. only what can be seen, observed, and measured). The behaviorist definition of learning is as follows: a relatively permanent change in behavior, not due to fatigue, drugs, or maturation.

The main types of learning paradigms are classical (elicited) conditioning and operant (emitted) conditioning.

Classical Conditioning

The conditioned response is elicited by the conditioned stimulus after repeated pairings of the unconditioned stimulus (UCS) and conditioned stimulus (CS).

- **Example**: In the Pavlovian experiment, the ringing of a bell was paired with the bringing of food, so that eventually, the sound of the bell (conditioned stimulus) elicited the salivatory response in the dog (conditioned response - [CR]), which previously occurred only with the sight of the food.
- **Example**: A patient receives chemotherapy (UCS), which induces nausea (UCR). Eventually, the sights and sounds of the hospital alone (CS) elicit nausea (now a CR).

Stimulus Generalization

Stimulus generalization is the tendency for the conditioned stimulus to evoke similar responses after the response has been conditioned.

- **Example**: Generalization will have occurred if any hospital, or even meeting a physician, comes to elicit nausea from the patient.

Extinction

After learning has occurred, removal of the pairing between the UCS and the CS results in a decreased probability that the conditioned response will be made.

- **Example**: Breaking the pairing between chemotherapy and the medical setting by giving chemotherapy at home. The nausea-eliciting properties of hospitals will be extinguished.

Table 20-2. Types of Reinforcement

Type	Definition/Comments
Positive reinforcer	Stimulus that, when applied following an operant response, strengthens the probability of that response occurring. For example, increased complaining leads to increased attention from the pharmacy staff.
Negative reinforcer	Stimulus that, when removed following an operant response, strengthens the probability of that response occurring. For example, a child learns that he can stop his parents' nagging by cleaning up his room.
Punishment	Like negative conditioning, usually uses a noxious stimulus. However, this stimulus is imposed to weaken response. Thus, punishment should be paired with positive reinforcement for alternative behaviors.
Extinction	Refers to the disappearance of a response when it is no longer being reinforced. For example, a pharmacist who is bombarded by constant complaints of one of their technicians stops paying attention to them whenever they complain.

Operant or Instrumental Conditioning

In operant conditioning, a new response is emitted, perhaps randomly at first, which results in a consequence. The consequence acts as reinforcement and changes the probability of the response's future occurrence.

- **Example**: In the Skinner experiment, pressing a lever (by the animal) resulting in the delivery of food. After receiving food, the bar-pressing behavior increased. Because it changed behavior, the food is a reinforcing event.

Reinforcement is delivery of a consequence that increases the likelihood that a response will occur. A reinforcer is defined by its effects; any stimulus is a reinforcer if it increases the probability of a response.

Behavior Therapy and Behavior Modification

Behavior therapy and behavior modification based on classical conditioning involves 3 main types of therapy:

1. Systematic desensitization
2. Exposure
3. Aversion conditioning

Systematic Desensitization

Systematic desensitization usually begins with imagining oneself in a progression of fearful situations and using relaxation strategies that compete with anxiety. It is most commonly used to treat anxiety and phobias and is based on the counterconditioning or reciprocal inhibition of anxiety responses.

There are 3 steps of systematic desensitization:

1. Hierarchy of fear-eliciting stimuli is created, building from least to most stressful
2. Therapist teaches the technique of muscle relaxation, a response that is incompatible with anxiety
3. Patient is taught to relax in the presence, real or imagined, of each stimulus on the hierarchy from least to most stressful

When the person is relaxed in the presence of the feared stimulus, objectively, there is no more phobia. It essentially works by replacing anxiety with relaxation, an incompatible response.

Exposure

Simple phobias can sometimes be treated by forced exposure to the feared object. In this type of therapy, the exposure is maintained until the fear response is extinguished.

- Example: Fear of heights treated by having the patient ride in an elevator to the top floor. The next step is looking out a window from a distance, followed by moving over to the window and looking down.

Aversion Conditioning

Aversion conditioning occurs when a stimulus that produces deviant behavior is paired with an aversive stimulus. Here, the key properties of the original stimulus are changed.

- **Example**: Pavlov's dog is presented with spoiled meat upon ringing bell. The dog does not salivate, but instead recoils as the spoiled meat is presented.

Aversion conditioning can be used in the treatment of alcoholism where the alcoholic is given a nausea-inducing drug (disulfiram) whenever he drinks so that drinking eventually comes to elicit unpleasant rather than pleasant events.

Behavior Therapy and Behavior Modification Based on Operant Conditioning

Therapy/modification based on classical conditioning involves 5 types of therapy:

- Shaping
- Extinction

- Stimulus control
- Biofeedback
- Fading

Shaping

Shaping (or successive approximations) achieves final target behavior by reinforcing successive approximations of the desired response. The reinforcement is gradually modified to move behaviors from the more general to the specific responses desired.

- **Example**: A child with autism spectrum disorder who won't speak is first reinforced, perhaps with candy, for any utterance. From those utterances, the appropriate phonemes are selected and reinforced until the child utters the sought-after sounds. Eventually, reinforcement is contingent on his using speech correctly in the proper context.

Extinction

Extinction involves discontinuing the reinforcement that is maintaining an undesired behavior.

- **Example**: If complaining results in a patient receiving a lot of attention, stopping the attention will eventually stop the undesired behavior.

Stimulus Control

Sometimes stimuli inadvertently acquire control over behavior. When this is true, removal of that stimulus can extinguish the response.

- **Example**: An insomniac is permitted in his bed only when he is so tired that he falls asleep almost at once.

Biofeedback

Biofeedback (neurofeedback) uses external feedback to modify internal physiologic states. It used to be thought that certain functions of the autonomic nervous system (heart rate, blood pressure, body temperature) were beyond the deliberate control of a person. We now know both animals and humans can attain a measure of control over some of their own bodily functions through the technique of biofeedback. Biofeedback often uses electronic devices to present physiologic information, e.g., heart monitor to show heart rate. It involves providing the person with information about his internal responses to stimuli and methods to control or modify them.

Biofeedback works by means of trial-and-error learning and requires repeated practice to be effective. It can be used for the treatment of hypertension, migraine and muscle contraction headaches, Raynaud syndrome, torticollis, cardiac arrhythmia, and anxiety. It should be noted that most biofeedback treatment measures affect the parasympathetic system.

Fading

Fading gradually removes the reinforcement without the subject discerning the difference.

- **Example**: Gradually replacing postoperative painkiller with a placebo.

MEDICATION ADHERENCE PRINCIPLES

Research has shown that physicians (and pharmacists) cannot tell which of their patients do and do not adhere to prescribed treatment regimens. In fact, most probably assume that more of their patients are adhering than actually are.

A number of factors can increase or decrease medication adherence throughout the life cycle of the patient. The human life cycle begins at the time of conception (prenatal care for the mother), then infancy, childhood, adulthood, and finally old age. Illness with accompanying treatment measures (and associated treatment adherence) can occur at any stage. Thus, a basic understanding of how to interact with a patient at each stage is essential for promoting medication adherence. A high-level overview of the dynamics surrounding medication adherence can be explained by the Health Belief Model.

Health Belief Model

The Health Belief Model (HBM), originally developed in the 1950's by the U.S. Public Health Service, is a health behavior change model that may be able to predict health-related behaviors. This model postulates that an individual's beliefs about health issues, perceived benefits of action, necessity for treatment, and barriers to health care all impact their adherence to a prescribed treatment regimen. The model also suggests that a "stimulus" is generally needed to trigger a health-promoting behavior.

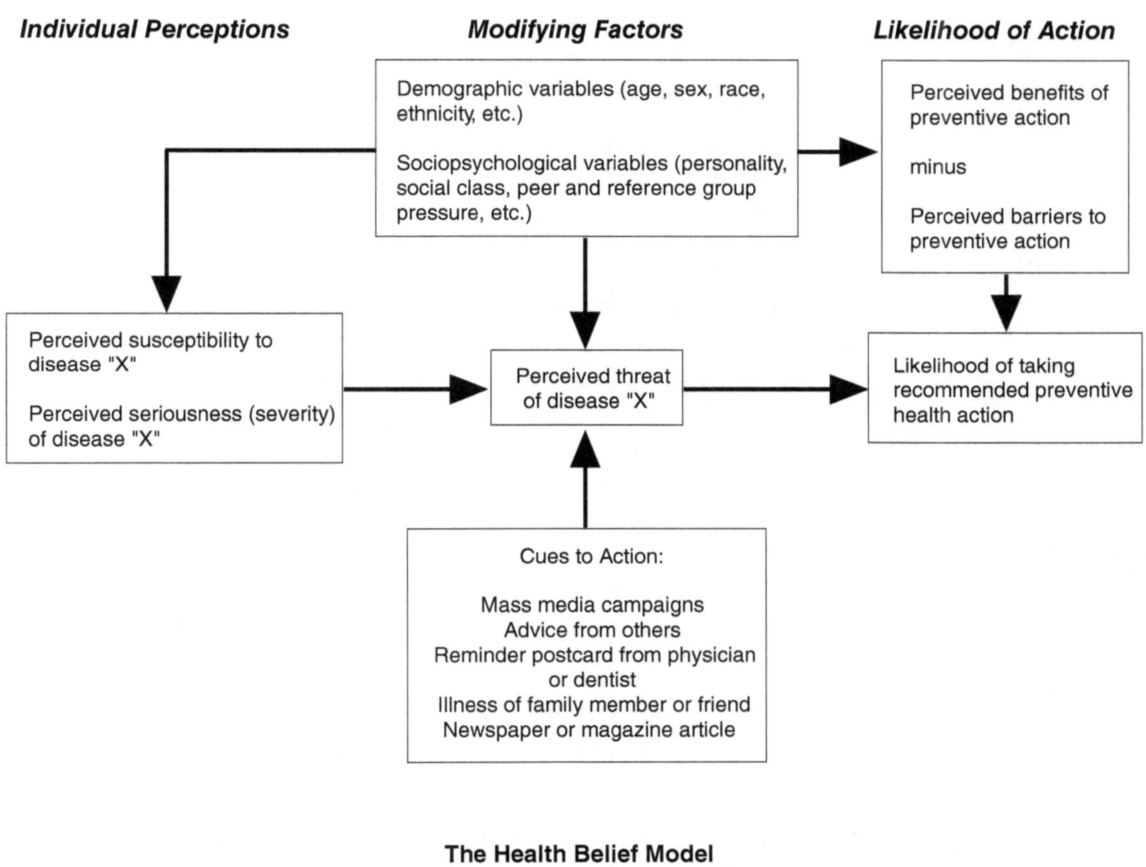

Figure 20-1. Health Belief Model

When a patient fails to adhere to a prescribed therapeutic regimen, the physician/pharmacist often blames the patient. However, as depicted in the HBM, there are numerous factors that can promote nonadherence. For example, nonadherence may occur as a result of 1) patient dissatisfaction with physician or pharmacist, 2) inability to understand medication instructions, 3) interference by family and/or inability to afford medications.

Conversely, therapeutic adherence increases if the physician/pharmacist is familiar with the patient's cultural beliefs and health beliefs, even if they are different from the physician's/pharmacist's.

The following table outlines the most common factors contributing to treatment nonadherence. As a general rule, when these factors are present, adherence to therapy may be decreased. Hence, it is the responsibility of the pharmacist to not only identify these factors but also lessen their negative impact at each stage of the patient life cycle when possible.

Table 20-3. Factors Contributing to Treatment Nonadherence

Factor	Comments

Patient variables	Type and severity of psychiatric diagnosis and changing stage of the patient lifecycle. Illness or increasing age can impact the following:
	• Sensory disabilities
	• Forgetfulness
	• Lack of understanding
	• Inappropriate or conflicting health benefits
	• Competing sociocultural and ethnic folk concepts of disease and treatment
	  ◦ Implicit model of illness
	  ◦ Apathy and pessimism
	  ◦ Failure to recognize that one is ill or in need of medication
	  ◦ Previous or present history of nonadherence with other regimens
	  ◦ Health beliefs (e.g., misconceptions about disorder, no understanding of prophylaxis, belief that medicine is necessary only in acute illness)
	  ◦ Dissatisfaction with practitioner or treatment

Characteristics of individual's social situation	• Family instability or disharmony • Parent's expectations and attitudes toward treatment • Residential instability • Environment that supports nonadherent behavior • Competing or conflicting demands or other pressing demands (poverty, unemployment) • Lack of resources (transportation, money, time)
Disease or disorder variables	• Chronic condition with lack of overt symptomatology • Stability of symptoms • Disorder-related characteristics (e.g., confusion, visual distortion, psychological reactions)
Treatment variables	• Characteristics of treatment setting • Absence of continuity of care • Long waiting time • Long elapsed time between referral and actual appointment (more than 8 days) • Timing of referral • Absence of individual appointment times • Lack of cohesiveness of treatment delivery system • Inconvenience associated with operation of clinics (e.g., inefficiency, unfriendly personnel) • Poor reputation of treatment facility • Inadequate supervision by professionals • Characteristics of treatment recommendations • Complexity of treatment regimen (e.g., multiple medications) • Long duration of treatment regimen

(Continued)

Factor	Comments

Treatment variables (cont.)	• Degree of behavioral change (e.g., interferes with personal behavior and depends upon alteration of one's lifestyle)
	  ◦ Inconvenience (e.g., location of clinic, poor transportation)
	  ◦ Excessive expense
	  ◦ Characteristics of medicine (e.g., color of pill, drug size, preparation form—i.e., capsule or tablet)
	  ◦ Inadequate labels
	  ◦ Awkward container design
	  ◦ Failure of parents to supervise drug administration
	  ◦ Medication side effects or side effects associated with altered behavior (e.g., sedation, extrapyramidal involvement)

Relationship variables: Patient-health care provider (PCP) interaction	• Inadequate communication with health care provider (pharmacist/physician) • Poor rapport with health care provider • Attitudinal and behavioral (verbal and nonverbal) faults on the part of either HCP or patient • Failure of HCP to elicit negative feedback about problems stemming from treatment regimen • Patient's dissatisfaction • Inadequate supervision

Finally, it is not enough for a pharmacist to provide information about a treatment and leave adherence to the patient; the pharmacist must present information in ways that will optimize patient adherence:

- Attending to the amount of information and its complexity
- Detailing the patient's changing affective state throughout the life cycle
- Explaining why the particular treatment is being recommended
- Stressing the threat that nonadherence poses to patient's health
- Stressing the effectiveness of the prescribed regimen

DEATH AND DYING

The care of the dying often encompasses a multidisciplinary approach from the patient's health care provider team. This may involve multiple clinical approaches to end-of-life care, which often must be adapted to meet the needs of the patient and their family.

Depending on the nature of the illness, the pharmacist may not have direct contact with the patient; at the very least, he/she will likely interact with the patient's family.

This section will address numerous aspects of death and dying, including decision-making capacity, surrogate decisions, and palliative care. There is also a reference to the Pain Management chapter in Kaplan's *NAPLEX Strategies, Practice, and Review* book, since many of the principles in this chapter are applicable to both hospice and palliative care.

NAPLEX Reference

Pain Management chapter

Kübler-Ross Model

The Kübler-Ross model suggests a series of feelings or emotions experienced by the dying patient. This model is based on the stages identified by Elisabeth Kübler-Ross in her 1969 book, *On Death and Dying*. She believed most individuals experience stages that are common reactions to death. The dying patient commonly moves back and forth through the stages. She also noted that not everyone passes through all stages or reaches adequate adjustment.

- **Stage 1: Shock and denial.** Patient is often surprised by diagnosis; may also believe diagnosis is somehow mistaken and may request a "second opinion"
- **Stage 2: Anger.** After moving past denial stage, patient may become angry and blame herself or others for diagnosis
- **Stage 3: Bargaining.** Patient negotiates with physician and/or "God" for a longer life in exchange for a reformed lifestyle, i.e., "I want to watch my grandson graduate" or "I want to celebrate the New Year one more time."
- **Stage 4: Depression.** Patient becomes dysthymic/depressed about prognosis; may refuse to go out or see family/friends and instead focus on everything wrong with life and what she will be missing out on
- **Stage 5: Acceptance.** Patient embraces her mortality and may become calm/stable or react in a manner consistent with original personality

From a pharmacist's perspective, follow these rules when treating the dying patient:

- Tell the patient everything.
- Do not give false hope.
- Allow the person to talk about feelings.
- Encourage the patient to keep involved in activities.
- Encourage the patient to avoid social isolation.

Decision-Making Capacity

The concept of decision-making capacity relates back to the ethical core principle of patient autonomy. Remember, patient autonomy is an obligation by the physician/pharmacist to respect the wishes of an "informed and competent" patient as well as honor their individual preferences in medical care. In other words, the patient ultimately decides what treatments or procedures they will or will not receive.

- **Example**: A dying patient may prefer to stop chemotherapy so that they can spend their remaining time with their loved ones without the unpleasant side effects associated with chemotherapy. Other patients may ask for higher doses of pain medication since they do not want to spend their remaining days in agony.

A physician (or provider) MUST first determine if the patient is legally and psychologically competent to make healthcare-related decisions, such as stopping their chemotherapy or requesting more pain medications. The essential components of competent decision making are as follows:

- The patient initially makes and communicates a healthcare-related choice.
- The patient knows and understands what is about to happen if that action is performed (Patient is informed).
- The decision remains stable over time.
- The decision is consistent with the patient's normal core values and goals (Not affected by a mood disorder).
- The decision is not occurring as a result of a psychiatric disorder (delusion, hallucination, etc).

Bringing these concepts together, the patient must be fully "informed" about all issues related to a treatment regimen and their decision-making capacity cannot be impaired. Another important point to remember is that a family member cannot require the physician to withhold information from the patient. The classic example for this last point is an elderly person who does not want their spouse to be upset about a "terminal" diagnosis of cancer. Remember that all patients have a right to know all information pertaining to their personal health.

Surrogate Decisions

Surrogate decisions can be considered an extension of the patient's decision-making authority. When the patient is unable to make a medical decision for themselves, someone needs to make a decision for them. The person making decisions for the patient is termed a surrogate decision maker.

In order for a surrogate to make a decision for the patient, 3 things must occur:

1. Patient is incapacitated
2. Patient has not made an advance directive.
3. Identification of an individual (surrogate) who knows what the patient would truly want if competent

- **Example**: A severe accident results in a woman becoming unconscious. The surrogate will be asked by the physician, "What do you think she would want if she were conscious?" Based on the surrogate's response, the patient will be appropriately treated or treatment measures will be withdrawn.

If an advance directive is not made by the patient designating a surrogate, the priority of surrogates is as follows:

1. Spouse
2. Adult children
3. Parents
4. Adult siblings
5. Other relatives

Advance Directives

An advance directive is a set of instructions given by a patient in anticipation of the need for a medical decision in the event that they become incompetent. The primary forms of advance directive are oral advance directive, living will, and medical power of attorney.

Oral Advance Directive

Oral advance directives include statements made by a patient prior to incapacitation. One of the major issues with an oral advance directive is that problems can arise from variance and interpretation.

- **Example**: Was the patient properly informed about the ramifications of the action before they were incapacitated? How specific was the directive or did the person to whom the directive was made fully understand the patient's wishes?

A good rule to follow: the more people who heard the oral directive, the more valid the directive.

Living Will

A living will is a "written advance directive" that fully outlines the treatment measures that the patient wants to receive or not receive if they lose decision-making capacity. Here, the patient provides written instructions for the physician in case of incapacitation. A family member cannot override the patient's wishes (even if they have power of attorney), and the physician must follow the directive irrespective of a family member's wishes.

- **Example**: If the patient indicates that they do not want to be intubated in the event that they become incapacitated and the patient's family wants them to be intubated, the physician cannot intubate the patient.

Medical Power of Attorney

A medical power of attorney (or healthcare power of attorney) is a designated agent assigned by the patient to make medical decisions in the event that he loses decision-making capacity. It is assumed that the person designated as "power of attorney" fully understands and will convey the wishes of the patient. When making a medical decision, the physician (and other health care providers) must follow the directives of this individual irrespective of other family member's wishes.

Advance directives are in place so the patient's wishes are fulfilled in the event of incapacitation.

Hospice and Palliative Care Principles

Patient care is the primary focus for both hospice care and palliative care in the dying patient. Hospice can be defined as supportive care for patients in the final phase of a terminal illness with a focus on personal comfort and quality of life, rather than cure for the disease.

The World Health Organization defines palliative care as "*An approach that improves the quality of life of patients and their families facing the problem associated with life-threatening illness, through the prevention and relief of suffering by means of early identification and impeccable assessment and treatment of pain and other problems, physical, psychosocial and spiritual.*" It is essential that the candidate understand the characteristics and differences between hospice and palliative care.

Table 20-4. Hospice vs Palliative Care

Feature	Hospice	Palliative Care
Primary Objective	Patient care combined with pain and symptom relief	Patient care combined with pain and symptom relief
Goals	Comfort care ***without*** curative intent	Comfort care ***with or without*** curative intent
Patient eligibility	Two physicians certify that the patient has <6 months to live if the disease follows its usual course	Can be started at the discretion of the physician & patient at any time, at any stage of illness, with or without a terminal prognosis
Location	Generally in the patient's home and often relies on the "family caregiver" as well as a visiting hospice nurse	Can be administered in the patient's home. It is most common to receive palliative care in an institution (hospital, nursing home, etc) with a palliative care team.
Timing of Care	Terminal illness or within 6 months of death to be eligible	There are no time restrictions.
Treatment	Treatment plans are designed so that patients can achieve a level of comfort that allows them to concentrate on the emotional and practical issues of dying. Pain management is commonly a large component of hospice care.	Treatment plans are designed to provide comfort and treatment (behavioral +/– curative) at any stage of any disease, whether terminal or chronic. Note: There is no expectation that life-prolonging therapies will be avoided like hospice. Pain management is commonly a large component of palliative care.
Payment	Hospice is paid 100% by Medicare, Medicaid and private insurance companies. Hospice is the only Medicare benefit that includes medications, medical equipment, and 24/7 access to care (nursing, social services, group support).	Patient office visits, medical equipment and prescription charges are "partially" paid for by insurance and the patient. There may also be some assistance from a charity.

PRACTICE QUESTIONS

1. After witnessing an inappropriate interaction between a technician and a customer, the pharmacy manager says to the technician "You are suspended until you apologize to the customer. I suggest you catch up to them now!" The pharmacist's comments are best defined as which of the following?

    A. Biofeedback
    B. Extinction
    C. Negative reinforcement
    D. Positive reinforcement
    E. Punishment

NAPLEX Question Reference

Pain Management chapter: end of chapter questions

2. Which of the following is NOT part of Suchman's illness experience model?

    A. Assumption of the sick role
    B. Dependent-patient role
    C. Medical care contact
    D. Recovery or rehabilitation
    E. Relapse into the sick role

3. A patient comes to the pharmacy complaining of continual "chest burning" especially after large meals and at bedtime when they lay on their back. According to Suchman's illness experience model, the patient is in which of the following stages?

    A. Assumption of the sick role
    B. Dependent-patient role
    C. Medical care contact
    D. Recovery or rehabilitation
    E. Symptom-experience

4. According to the Kübler-Ross model, after a patient is given a terminal diagnosis, he/she will experience which of the following first?

    A. Acceptance
    B. Anger
    C. Bargaining
    D. Denial
    E. Depression

5. A 44-year-old man is in a serious car accident. If he/she does not have an advanced directive, who will have the first right to make to medical decisions for the patient?

   A. Adult children
   B. Adult siblings
   C. Favorite aunt
   D. Parents
   E. Spouse

6. All of the following are true with respect to hospice and palliative care EXCEPT

   A. One physician must certify that the patient has <6 months to live for hospice
   B. Palliative care has a goal of comfort care with or without curative intent
   C. Hospice is paid 100% by Medicare, Medicaid and private insurance companies
   D. Hospice is permitted when the patient has a terminal illness or has <6 months to live
   E. There are no time restrictions for palliative care

7. Which of the following is considered a patient variable factor that contributes to treatment nonadherence?

   A. Characteristics of treatment recommendations
   B. Inappropriate or conflicting health benefits
   C. Long duration of treatment regimen
   D. Poor rapport with health care provider
   E. Unemployment

8. A patient tells the pharmacist that they have been given a terminal diagnosis. After acknowledging empathy for the patient, which of the following is an inappropriate question or comment to the patient?

   A. "Do you have any questions about your diagnosis or medication therapy?"
   B. "I am sure there is an experimental therapy available."
   C. "Please let me know if I can be of any assistance to you or your family."
   D. "Would you like to review your medications so that you know what to expect?"
   E. All of the above are appropriate questions or comments.

9. With a focus on the patient lifecycle, which of the following is the most important factor for medication adherence?

   A. Delivery route of medication
   B. Medications administered
   C. Patient's age
   D. Patient's disease
   E. Patient's socioeconomic status

10. A patient with advanced esophageal cancer indicates that he/she wants to discontinue chemotherapy. All of the following are needed to justify this as being a "competent" decision EXCEPT

    A. An understanding of consequences
    B. The decision remains stable over time
    C. The patient's family approves of the decision
    D. There is no evidence of a mood or psychiatric disorder
    E. All of the above are needed

Answers and Explanations

1. **The correct answer is C.** The pharmacy technician has a choice; apologize or be suspended (punishment). A punishment (choice E) uses a noxious stimulus, such as suspension, following an incident. A negative reinforcement (as in choice C) has a stimulus that, when removed following an operant response, strengthens the probability of that response occurring. In this case, the technician avoids an official suspension after they apologize to the patient. Biofeedback (choice A) is the use of external feedback (i.e. heart monitor) to modify internal physiologic states. Extinction (choice B) is the discontinuation of the reinforcement that is maintaining the undesired behavior (i.e. cessation of attention to a continually complaining patient). A positive reinforcement (choice D) is where the stimulus when applied following an operant response, strengthens the probability of that response occurring.

2. **The correct answer is E.** Suchman's illness experience occurs in 5 stages that can be explained by common patient behaviors: symptom-experience; assumption of the sick role; medical care contact; dependent-patient role; and recovery or rehabilitation. Relapse into the sick role is NOT part of this model. In this question, the first stage (symptom-experience) was missing. This is the stage where the patient first notices or senses that something is wrong. Without this stage, the patient will not seek medical attention.

3. **The correct answer is C.** To apply Suchman's model to this scenario, the patient first notices that his "chest burning" is abnormal (choice E) and then accepts that these symptoms are abnormal (choice A). When he comes to the pharmacy to seek care, he is in the medical care contact stage (choice C). Once he/she begins taking the medication and making lifestyle changes to prevent the reoccurrence of likely esophageal reflux symptoms, he is in the dependent-patient role (choice B). He/She will then progress to the recovery/rehabilitation (choice D) stage provided that he maintains this current course of therapy.

4. **The correct answer is D.** The Kübler-Ross model suggests an ordered series of feelings or emotions experienced by the dying patient. The model also suggests that the dying patient often traverses back and forth through the stages. The first stage is generally shock and denial where the patient is surprised by the diagnosis and may believe that the diagnosis is mistaken. The second stage is anger (choice B) surrounding the diagnosis. Stage 3 is bargaining where the patient often negotiates with the physician and/or their "God" for a longer life. Stages 4 and 5 are depression and acceptance, respectively.

5. **The correct answer is E.** If an advance directive is not made by the patient designating a surrogate prior to an event that incapacitates the patient, the priority of surrogates is spouse, adult children, parents, adult siblings, and then other relatives.

6. **The correct answer is A.** Hospice is a type of supportive care for patients in the final phase of a terminal illness with a focus on personal comfort and quality of life, rather than cure for the disease. In order to be eligible for hospice care, 2 physicians must certify that the patient has <6 months to live if the disease follows its usual course. All of the other answer choices are correct.

7. **The correct answer is B.** There are numerous reasons why patients do not adhere to a prescribed regimen. Factors that contribute to nonadherence include patient variables (i.e. choice B); treatment variables (i.e. choices A and C); relationship variables with health care provider (i.e. choice D);

characteristics of the individual's social situation (i.e. choice E) and disease/disorder variables (i.e. type of condition, stability of symptoms).

8. **The correct answer is B.** When given a terminal diagnosis, patients will be flooded with emotions and feelings. Depending on the nature of the illness, the pharmacist may or may not have direct contact with the patient; however, they will likely interact with the patient's family. In this case, the patient comes to the pharmacist with the information on their terminal diagnosis. From a pharmacist perspective, one should follow these rules when treating the dying patient: Tell the patient everything (choices A, D); Do not give false hope (see choice B); allow person to talk about feelings (choice C); keep them involved in activities and help them avoid social isolation.

9. **The correct answer is C.** There are a number of factors that can increase or decrease medication adherence throughout the life cycle of the patient. The human lifecycle begins at the time of conception (prenatal care for the mother), then infancy, childhood, adulthood and finally old age. Illness with accompanying treatment measures (and associated treatment adherence) can occur at any stage. Thus a basic understanding of how to interact with a patient at each stage is essential for promoting medication adherence.

10. **The correct answer is C.** A patient's decision-making capacity is directly related to the ethical core principle of patient autonomy; the patient has the right to make their own medical decisions. The physician and pharmacist must respect the wishes of an "informed and competent" patient. Choices A, B and D are all requirements of competence; however, the patient's family does NOT need to approve a decision. Once competence is proven (in this case), the physician will discontinue the chemotherapy irrespective of the patient's family's wishes.

Medication Dispensing and Distribution Systems 21

Learning Objectives

- ❑ Discuss the proper preparation and dispensing of medications
- ❑ Demonstrate understanding in pharmacy automation and informatics
- ❑ Show proficiency in continuous quality improvement programs or protocols

The responsibilities of a given pharmacist today will vary depending on whether it is an institutional or retail setting; however, most are responsible for dispensing medications, providing (and interpreting) drug information, and monitoring patient responses to their prescribed drug regimen.

PREPARATION AND DISPENSING OF MEDICATIONS

The goal of each practicing pharmacist is to improve patient outcomes by providing drug information, monitoring therapeutic responses, and dispensing medications. However, several steps occur prior to the pharmacist dispensing a medication.

Understanding the pathway between a physician's decision to prescribe a medication and the patient receiving the medication is essential.

Table 21-1. Pathway Leading to Medication Administration

Step	Description/Comments
Patient evaluation	• Physician (or other prescriber) obtains patient history and performs a physical examination and laboratory evaluation. • A thorough patient evaluation is needed for a correct diagnosis and subsequent ordering of an appropriate therapy.
Ordering	• Physician (or other prescriber) selects the most appropriate medication based on the diagnosis and individual patient factors. • The pharmacist may be consulted at this step.
Transcribing	• This step is an intermediary step where a pharmacist interprets the "hand written" prescription written by a physician and correctly enters information into the computer system. • ePrescribing will soon make this step obsolete.

(Continued)

Step	Description/Comments
Dispensing	• Pharmacist reviews the prescription (***more information in the "components of a prescription" table***) and then checks for drug–drug interactions, drug-disease interactions, proper route and dosing of the medication and performs other revaluations. • Pharmacist fills the prescription. • Pharmacist dispenses the medication to the patient (retail) or nurse (hospital).
Administration	• Patient (or nurse) will administer the medication. • Nurse is responsible for administering the medication that has already been approved by both the physician and the pharmacist.
Evaluation	• Pharmacist continually monitors for the appearance of adverse events and other necessary findings.

Medication Prescription

A "classic" prescription is defined as a written order from a physician (or other prescriber) for the preparation and administration of a medication or other treatment measure. There are 4 parts to a drug prescription, plus a 5th part for special instruction, if needed.

- **Superscription:** symbol ℞ from the Latin recipe, meaning "take."
- **Inscription:** Specifies the ingredients and their quantities.
- **Subscription:** Directions on how to compound the medication and designation of the form (pill, powder, solution, etc.)
- **Signature (or sig):** Defines what instructions are to be placed on the prescription label. Indicates when and how to take the medication and in what quantities.
- **Special Instructions:** Below the signature line is where the prescriber can place special instructions as well as well as warnings and precautions.

A prescription must be written or printed on a tamper-resistant form consistent with federal requirements for Medicaid. This requirement applies to all written prescriptions for drugs in federal Schedules II-V as well as Schedule VI (general legend) medications.

Table 21-2. Components of a Prescription

Category of Information on Prescription	Specific Prescription Components	Comments
Patient	Name (unless veterinary prescription or prescription for expedited partner therapy)	
	Address (unless prescription for expedited partner therapy)	
	Date of Birth	State requirement varies
	Other: Height, Weight, Sex, Drug Allergies	State requirement varies

(Continued)

Category of Information on Prescription	Specific Prescription Components	Comments
Prescriber	Name	Institution forms must contain the name of the facility and a line directly below the signature line for the prescriber to print or type their name
	Prescriber address and phone number	Institution forms must contain the address of the facility
	DEA number for Schedules II – V	
	Line for Signature on lower portion of form	Physician signature is required for Schedule II-V
	Unique identification number (for institutional use)	Requirement varies
Supervising Physician	For mid-level prescribers (such as physician assistants), the name of the supervising physician must be clearly indicated.	There may also be a requirement for a co-signature by the supervising physician
Prescription	Date Written	
	Date to be Dispensed *(In accordance with DEA Rule)*	
	Time the order was written (for institutional orders)	Requirement varies
General legend (Schedule VI) or Controlled Substance (Schedule II – V)	Name	
	Dosage Unit	
	Strength per Unit	
	Quantity of Dosage Units to be Dispensed	
	Directions for Use	
	Cautionary Statements if Required	
	Number of Times to be Refilled	
Brand/Generic Interchange	Below the signature line there shall be a space in which the prescriber may manually indicate "no substitution" OR "no substitution" may be preprinted on the prescription.	

Preparation of Prescription Medication

Accurate prescription preparation is consistently achieved through strict adherence to a series of steps. Remember that medication errors may occur at any step in this process. Although the precise order of steps may vary from pharmacy to pharmacy, all of the steps should be followed.

1. Verify the validity and completeness of all prescription elements.
2. Review the interpretation (translation) of the prescription.
3. Enter the prescription into a pharmacy computer system. (Steps 2 and 3 do NOT apply for electronic prescriptions).
4. Perform a drug utilization review (DUR) and take appropriate corrective action if necessary.
5. Verify the "5 rights" of a prescription: Right Medication, in the Right Dose, at the Right Time, by the Right Route, to the Right Patient.
6. Perform calculations of measurable quantities of all components (if needed).
7. Accurately weigh/measure all components (if needed).
8. Use proper compounding techniques to convert separate components into a completed drug product OR place the proper number/amount of pre-formulated dosage forms (tablets, capsules) into an approved prescription container.
9. Ensure proper packaging of the drug product.
10. Ensure proper labeling of the product. The pharmacy label must contain the following (Name and address of the pharmacy, patient's name, prescription date, prescription's unique identification number, drug's name, drug strength, quantity dispensed, directions for use, prescriber's name, drug expiration date, pharmacist initials and appropriate auxiliary labels.
11. Verification of correctness for steps 1–10.
12. Patient counseling
13. Dispense the drug/product to the patient.
14. Evaluate the patient for desired and undesired medication effects.

After a "handwritten" prescription is received by the pharmacist, the review, interpretation, and subsequent labeling may be contingent upon proper interpretation of common medical abbreviations.

In medicine today, there are thousands of these abbreviations; however, we have compiled the most commonly used pharmacy abbreviations. It should be noted that the use of abbreviations is on the decline with electronic prescribing; however, you should still know the most common medical abbreviations.

Table 21-3. Essential Prescription Abbreviations

Abbreviation	Meaning	Abbreviation	Meaning
aa, āā, ĀĀ	of each	mL	Milliliter
AAA	apply to affected area	N.M.T.	not more than
a.c.	before meals	NPO	nothing by mouth
a.d.	right ear	NS	Normal saline (0.9%)
agit	stir/shake	1/2NS	Half strength normal saline
alt. h.	every other hour	N.T.E.	not to exceed
a.m.	morning, before noon	o_2	both eyes, sometimes written as o_2
amt	Amount	od	right eye

(Continued)

Abbreviation	Meaning	Abbreviation	Meaning
aq	Water	o.s.	left eye
a.l., a.s.	left ear	o.u.	both eyes
A.T.C.	around the clock	oz	Ounce
a.u.	both ears	p.c.	after meals
b.i.d./b.d.	twice daily	p.m.	evening or afternoon
B.M.	bowel movement	p.o.	by mouth *or* orally
B.S.	blood sugar	p.r. or PR	by rectum
B.S.A	body surface areas	PRN, prn	as needed
BUCC	inside cheek	pulv.	Powder
cap., caps.	Capsule	PV	via the vagina
cf	with food; also cf. means confer=compare	q	every, per
comp.	compound	q.a.m.	every day before noon
cr., crm	Cream	q.d./q.1.d.	every day
CST	Continue same treatment	q.p.m.	every day after noon or every evening
D or d	days or doses	q.h.	every hour
D5W	Dextrose 5% solution (sometimes written as D_5W)	q.h.s.	every night at bedtime
D5NS	Dextrose 5% in normal saline (0.9%)	q.i.d.	4 times a day
D.A.W.	dispense as written (i.e., no generic substitution)	q.o.d.	every other day
dc, D/C, disc	discontinue or discharge	qqh	every 4 hours
dil.	Dilute	q.s.	a sufficient quantity
disp.	dispersible or dispense	QWK	every week
div.	Divide	rep., rept.	Repeats
dL	Deciliter	SC, subc, subcut, subq, SQ	subcutaneous
D.W.	distilled water	s.i.d/SID	once a day
elix.	Elixir	sig	write on label
et	And	SL	sublingually, under the tongue

(Continued)

Abbreviation	Meaning	Abbreviation	Meaning
eod	every other day	S.O.B, SOB	shortness of breath
ex aq	in water	sol	Solution
fl., fld.	Fluid	s.o.s., si op. sit	if there is a need
ft.	make; let it be made	ss	$\frac{1}{2}$ or sliding scale
g	Gram	stat	immediately
gr	Grain	SubQ	subcutaneously
gtt(s)	drop(s)	supp	Suppository
h, hr	Hour	susp	suspension
h.s.	at bedtime **or** half-strength	syr	Syrup
ID	intradermal	tab	Tablet
IJ, inj	Injection	tal., t	Such
IM	intramuscular	tbsp	Tablespoon
IN	intranasal	t.i.d.	3 times a day
IP	intraperitoneal	t.i.w.	3 times a week
IT	Intrathecal	top.	topical
IU	international unit	T.P.N.	Total parenteral nutrition
IV	Intravenous	tr, tinc., tinct.	tincture
IVP	intravenous push	troche	lozenge
IVPB	intravenous piggyback	tsp	Teaspoon
kg	Kilogram	U	Unit
LCD	Liquid coal tar solution	u.d., ut. dict.	as directed
liq	Solution	ung.	ointment
lot.	Lotion	vag	vaginally
mcg	Microgram	w	With
mEq	milliequivalent	w/a	while awake
mg	Milligram	w/o, s	without
mg/dL	milligrams per deciliter	X	times

"Do Not Use" Abbreviation List

The Joint Commission has devised a "Do Not Use" abbreviation list as part of their Information Management Standards guidelines. This requirement does not currently apply to preprogrammed health information technology systems (i.e. electronic medical records, CPOE or electronic prescribing systems).

Table 21-4. Joint Commission "Do Not Use" Abbreviation List

Do Not Use	Potential Problem	Use Instead
U, u (unit)	Mistaken for "0" (zero), the number "4" (four) or "cc"	Write "unit"
IU (International Unit)	Mistaken for IV (intravenous) or the number 10 (ten)	Write "International Unit
Q.D., QD, q.d., qd (daily)	These are mistaken for each other.	Write "daily"
Q.O.D., QOD, q.o.d, qod (every other day)	Period after the Q mistaken for "I" and the "O" mistaken for "I"	Write "every other day"
Trailing zero (X.0 mg)	Decimal point is missed	Write X mg
Lack of leading zero (.X mg)	Decimal point is missed	Write 0.X mg
MS	These are mistaken for each other.	Write "morphine sulfate"
MSO_4 and $MgSO_4$	Can mean morphine sulfate or magnesium sulfate	Write "magnesium sulfate"

PHARMACY AUTOMATION AND INFORMATICS

Pharmacy automation includes the mechanical and informational processes of managing and distributing medications. It includes point-of-care automation processes as well as preparation and packaging automation processes. Medication order, ordering and receiving, pharmacy robots, bar-code medication dispensing, and medication dispensing devices may also be automated.

All of these automated processes are designed to enhance workflow and improve patient safety.

Table 21-5. Pharmacy Automation

Type of Pharmacy Automation	Comments
Computerized prescriber order entry (CPOE)	• Touted as one of the first major improvements in patient safety. • Physicians are able to electronically transmit physician orders from one department to another (pharmacy, laboratory, radiology, etc). • CPOEs decrease the time for order completion and distribution as well as patient resource allocation. • CPOEs have resulted in decreased transcription errors and duplicate ordering as well as provide error reducing measures (drug interactions, incorrect dosing, etc). • Disadvantages include slower communication in emergency situations (the receiver needs to be alerted to an order) and false sense of security.
Electronic Health Record (EHR) systems	• Allow health-care providers to record patient information electronically as well as the capability to perform various tasks that can assist in health-care delivery (ePrescribing, clinical decision support, drug-interaction checker, billing options, ICD-10/CPT code assignment, development of treatment templates). • Disadvantages include: Time required to enter "very granular patient information" and the physician may be required to "check" all normal values which adds to the time needed to enter patient data. There can also be identity theft as well as data loss in the event of a computer crash.

(Continued)

Type of Pharmacy Automation	Comments
Bar code medication administration	• The primary goals of bar code medication administration are to assure the "5 rights" (patient, medication, dose, route, time) by improving medication administration accuracy, preventing drug errors, and generating online records of medication administration. • Components include barcode reader, a computer with wireless connection, a computer server, and medication management software. • Disadvantages include more reliance on technology and less on professional judgment.
Smart medication infusion pumps	• The first programmable IV infusion pumps came into use over 40 years ago but were causes of numerous errors related to improper programming (i.e. programming 61 "units/time" instead of 6.1 "units/time", etc) • Compared to medications delivered via other routes, IV medication errors are twice as likely to result in patient harm. • Today's smart IV pumps have drug dose limits, have wireless capabilities, standardized concentration and dosing units, provide all types of infusion data and document "good catches" and prevent programming errors. • Disadvantages include alarm fatigue; user competency and programming errors still persist.
Automated dispensing units/ cabinets	• Computerized drug storage devices designed for hospitals that allow "commonly used" medications to be stored and dispensed at the point of care while controlling and tracking drug distribution. • Designed to replace non-automated drug cart or hospital floor stock storage as well as improve control over medication inventory. • Disadvantages include lack of pharmacy screening of medication orders prior to availability for administration, excessive use of system overrides in cabinets with patient profiling, placing the patient at risk of drug interactions, etc., and failure of user to recognize look-alike names.
Robotic devices	• Automated dispensing systems that can fill a prescription (and place medication in a prescription bottle with a label) as well as ensure no cross-contamination of medications and will track all "will call", partial fill, and out of stock prescriptions. • Disadvantages include required manual filling of each medication dispensing unit.

Pharmacy Informatics

Healthcare informatics uses health information technology (HIT) to improve patient care by disseminating critical information that can improve patient outcomes. This multidisciplinary field incorporates computer, social, and behavioral sciences as well as business management principles. HIT integrates all of these sciences to augment the procurement, storage, and subsequent usage of health information to improve biomedical processes and ultimately patient outcomes.

The National Library of Medicine defines health informatics as "*the interdisciplinary study of the design, development, adoption and application of information technology-based innovations in healthcare services delivery, management and planning.*" HIT incorporates all medical professions, including pharmacy.

Pharmacy informatics is defined as the scientific field that focuses on medication-related data and knowledge within the continuum of the U. S. healthcare system. This field of science can provide valuable insights and opportunities to improve numerous elements of existing pharmaceutical care processes and treatment guidelines.

There are 7 elements of a pharmacy informatics system.

Table 21-6. Elements of a Pharmacy Informatics System

Pharmacy Informatics Element	Comments
System design and/or System implementation	• Identifies information and sources that best address a process or guideline objective. • Identifies who will access, collect, analyze, interpret and disseminate the data findings. • Identifies the methods and under what conditions the data will be collected, managed, analyzed and interpreted. • Identifies how best to implement the pharmacy informatics system.
Data collection	• Collects required data according to protocol. • Identifies potential bias with different collection methods. • Identifies proper use of structured data and data standards as well as more efficient and effective ways to collect the data.
Data Management	• Identifies ways to share data across different computing/technology platforms. • Continually identifies better ways to improve data collection and organization while ensuring data privacy and security.
Data Analysis	• Identifies appropriate statistical tests and applications. • Generates algorithms and/or processes to inform members of the health community of irregularities in health events. • Analyzes the data using predetermined processes and protocols.
Data Interpretation	• Determines the usefulness of comparing the data collected with other pharmacy processes or treatment guidelines (related by time, place, person, medication, process, protocol or other element) for new health care perspectives.
Data Dissemination	• Outlines the most appropriate way to disseminate the findings to the "right" members of the healthcare community. • Outlines the best methods to reproduce the findings. • Identifies the benefits (and risks) for the clinical utilization of the data.
Application to existing pharmacy processes or guidelines	• Applies the findings to improve existing processes or guidelines. • Improves access to and use of information produced by the pharmacy informatics system.

CONTINUOUS QUALITY IMPROVEMENT PROGRAMS AND PROTOCOLS

"Every system is perfectly designed to get the results it gets."

—*Source: Don Berwick, M.D.*

Continuous quality improvement (CQI) consists of incessant and methodical actions that result in a "sustained" quantifiable improvement in health care services as well as the health status of specific groups of patients.

The Institute of Medicine (IOM) defines quality in health care as "*a direct correlation between the level of improved health services and the desired health outcomes of individuals and populations.*"

The previous section of this chapter outlined steps that occur prior to the pharmacist dispensing a medication. It is essential to understand these steps, as well as examples of various patient safety and CQI strategies to help prevent medication adverse events and medication errors.

- Additional information on causes and types of medical errors can be found in the "Medication Surveillance Systems" section in Chapter 13.

Table 21-7. Required Steps for a Patient to Receive a Medication with CQI Strategies

Step	Description/Comments	Identification and Prevention of Medication Errors with Patient Safety and CQI Strategies
Patient evaluation	• Physician (or other prescriber) obtains patient history and performs a physical examination and laboratory evaluation. • A thorough patient evaluation is needed for a correct diagnosis and subsequent ordering of an appropriate therapy.	• Computerized physician diagnosis combined with clinical decision support systems to choose the most appropriate medication. • Newer electronic health record systems help to assign diagnosis based on patient history and laboratory findings.
Ordering	• Physician (or other prescriber) selects the most appropriate medication based on the diagnosis and individual patient factors. • The pharmacist may be consulted at this step.	• Computerized physician order entry (CPOE) combined with clinical decision support systems • Medication reconciliation especially during times of transitions in patient care • Evaluate for unnecessary polypharmacy • Consult with a clinical pharmacist
Transcribing	• This step is an intermediary step where a pharmacist interprets the "hand-written" prescription written by a physician and correctly enters information into the computer system. • ePrescribing will soon make this step obsolete.	• Computerized provider order entry (ePrescribing) to eliminate handwriting errors
Dispensing	• The pharmacist reviews the prescription (***more information in the "components of a prescription" table***) and the checks for drug–drug interactions, drug-disease interactions, proper route and dosing of the medication and performs other revaluations. • The pharmacist fills the prescription. • The pharmacist dispenses the medication to the patient (retail) or nurse (hospital).	• Pharmacist performs an automated drug utilization review (DUR) • Consults with clinical pharmacist when appropriate • Use "tall man" lettering to minimize patient confusion between look-alike, sound-alike medications. • Strict adherence to the "Five Rights" of medication dispensing (the Right Medication, at the Right Dose, at the Right Time, by the Right Route, to the Right Patient)

(Continued)

Step	Description/Comments	Identification and Prevention of Medication Errors with Patient Safety and CQI Strategies
Administration	• The patient (or nurse) will administer the medication. • The nurse is responsible for administering the medication that has already been approved by both the physician and the pharmacist.	• Medication counseling techniques to improve patient comprehension of drug administration instructions as well as patient adherence to the prescribed therapeutic regimen • Barcode medication administration in the hospital setting to ensure adherence to the "5 Rights" of medication dispensing • Smart infusion pumps for IV infusions
Evaluation	• The pharmacist continually monitors for the appearance of adverse events and other necessary findings.	• Strict adherence to all medication safety strategies • Root Cause Analysis (RCA) can be performed to determine how a medical error occurred. • The PDSA model, Six Sigma model, Run charts and Pareto charts can be used for CQI purposes once the RCA determines how the medical error occurred.

Principles of Continuous Quality Improvement

One principle of quality improvement is to design systems capable of identifying, preventing, absorbing, and mitigating errors. Some everyday examples of safety design outside of health care are seatbelt alarms in cars, heat-sensitive fire sprinkler systems, and tip-over switches which automatically turn off space heaters that have accidentally fallen over.

In 2001, the IOM published the report "Crossing the Quality Chasm," which aimed at promoting fundamental changes in health care in order to close the quality gap. The report recommended a redesign of the American health care system and provided principles for guiding quality improvement. Specifically, the report defined 6 aims of health care (STEEEP):

1. **Safe**: avoidance of injuries to patients from the care that is intended to help them
2. **Timely**: reduce waits and harmful delays in care
3. **Effective**: provide care based on scientific knowledge likely to benefit patients
4. **Efficient**: avoid waste in equipment, supplies, ideas, and energy
5. **Equitable**: provide care that does not vary in quality because of personal characteristics such as gender, ethnicity, geographic location, and socioeconomic status
6. **Patient-centered**: provide care that is respectful of and responsive to individual patient preferences, needs, and values

Another significant initiative in quality improvement is the Institute for Health Care Improvements (IHI) Triple Aim that describes an approach to optimizing health system performance using new designs to pursue 3 dimensions (i.e. "Triple Aim"):

- Improve the patient experience of care (including quality and satisfaction)
- Improve the health of populations
- Reduce per capita cost of health care

Measures of Quality

There are 3 traditional categories of measures used in quality improvement: structure, process, and outcomes.

- **Structure** relates to the physical equipment, resources, or facilities (e.g., number of ICU beds in a hospital).
- **Process** relates to how the system works (e.g. how often nurses use bar coding to identify patients prior to administering medication).
- **Outcomes** represent the final product or end result in patient care (e.g. infection rate in pediatric hematology patients admitted to the hospital). Outcomes are often difficult to assess in quality improvement, and many people often use process measures as a surrogate for outcomes. For example, it may be difficult to accurately track all HAI (*outcomes measure*), so rates of compliance with hand washing are monitored instead (*process measure*).

A fourth type of measure introduced to quality improvement is the concept of a balancing measure. **Balancing measures** ask whether changes made to improve one part of the system cause an unanticipated decrease in performance in another part of the system (e.g. did an initiative aimed at increasing the efficiency of discharging patients from the hospital lead to more patients being sent home without appropriate follow-up instructions).

Models of Quality Improvement

One example of a common quality improvement model is a combination of building and applying knowledge to make an improvement by asking 3 questions and using the **PDSA** (**P**lan, **D**o, **S**tudy, **A**ct) cycle developed by W. Edwards Deming, a pioneer and influential leader in quality control.

1. What are we trying to accomplish?
2. How will we know whether a change is an improvement?
3. What changes can we make that will result in an improvement?

This model takes the simple concept of "trial and error" and transforms it into the PDSA model that can be used to make improvements in health care.

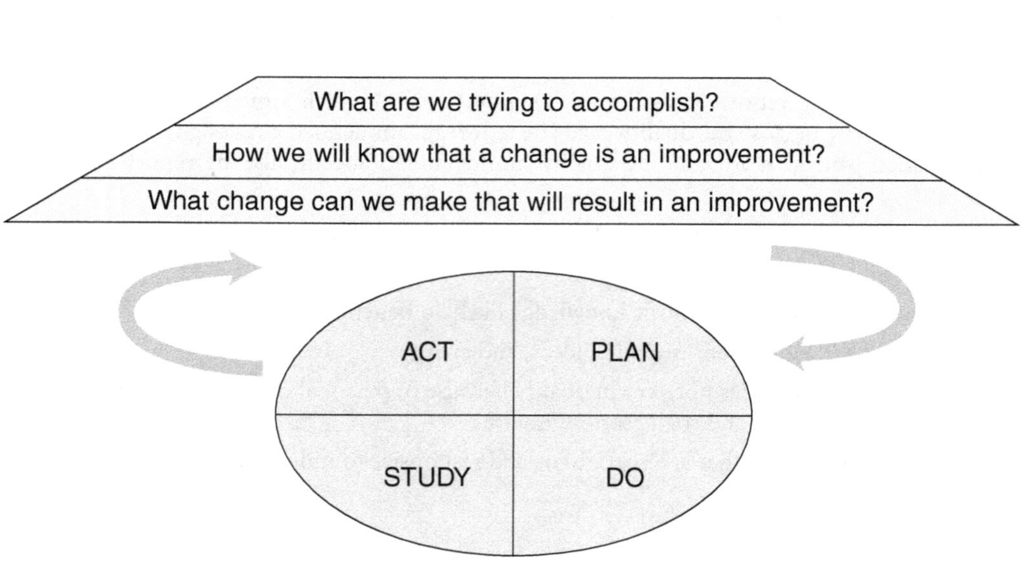

Figure 21-1. The Model for Improvement
Source: Langley, Nolan, Nolan & Provost 1999

- **Plan**: plan a change or a pilot test of a new intervention or innovation
- **Do**: carry out the plan
- **Study**: evaluate the results
- **Act**: decide what actions should be taken to improve (i.e. implement the new intervention or start over with a new plan based on the prior results)

Six Sigma is another model for quality improvement with origins from the manufacturing industry. The term comes from the use in statistics of the Greek Letter (sigma) to denote Standard Deviation from the mean. Six Sigma is equivalent to 3.4 defects (or errors) per million. This system uses specific steps to reduce variation and improve performance.

- DMAIC (define – measure – analyze – improve – control): an improvement system for **existing processes** falling below specification
  - **Define**: Define the problem in detail.
  - **Measure**: Measure defects (in terms of "defects per million," or Sigma level).
  - **Analyze**: Do in-depth analysis using process measures, flow charts and defect analysis to determine the conditions under which defects occur.
  - **Improve**: Define and test changes aimed at reducing defects.
  - **Control**: What steps will you take to maintain performance?

Lean (also called Lean Enterprise or Toyota Production System) is an improvement process that seeks to improve value from the patient's perspective by reducing waste in time and resources that do not enhance patient outcomes. This includes certain lab tests, imaging studies, or care services that may be commonly performed but in reality do not actually help the patient. For example, a pre-operative EKG obtained on a healthy 21 year-old with no cardiac symptoms undergoing a small outpatient procedure can be considered a wasteful test that does not help the patient.

Flowcharts allow health care teams to understand the steps involved in the delivery of patient care service. A flowchart is a visual illustration of all the steps or parts of a process in patient care. There are 2 types of flowcharts: **high-level flowcharts** (more conceptually focused, 'big picture') and **detailed flowcharts** (more focused on specific, fine points).

Flowcharts are more accurate and effective when all representative members of a health care team actively participate in their design. They help health-care providers achieve a shared understanding of a clinical process and use that knowledge as the basis for designing new ways to improve services. Specifically, they can help to identify steps that do not add value to the process (e.g. unnecessary duplication of services), to determine areas of delay in care, and to discover failure points in the system.

Pareto charts are used to describe a large proportion of quality problems being caused by a small number of causes. It is based on the classic $\frac{80}{20}$ rule from economics, where 80% of the world's wealth is described to be in the hands of an elite 20% of the population.

The Pareto principle applied to health care states that the **majority of patient safety errors stem from only a few recurring contributing factors**, which should serve as the focus of the problem-solving efforts. In essence, it is a method of prioritizing problems, highlighting the fact that most problems are affected by a few factors and indicating which problems to solve and in what order. A Pareto chart includes the multiple factors that contribute to an effect arranged in descending order (according to the magnitude of their effect). The ordering is an important step because it helps the team concentrate efforts on those factors that have the greatest impact.

Run charts (or time plots) are graphs of data collected over time which can help determine whether an intervention or enhancement in the patient care process has resulted in true improvement over time or rather if it simply represents a random fluctuation (that might be incorrectly interpreted as a significant improvement). Run charts are created by plotting time along the X axis (e.g. minutes, hours, days, months) and the quality measure on the Y axis (e.g. number of infections, wait times, falls). The median (or 50th percentile) is measured using baseline historical data and then compared to outcomes measured following the quality improvement intervention.

Run charts help identify whether there is a true trend vs. a random-pattern. A shift in the process signaling a significant change in quality can be identified, for example, by observing ≥6 consecutive points above or below the median, or by ≥5 consecutive points all increasing or decreasing.

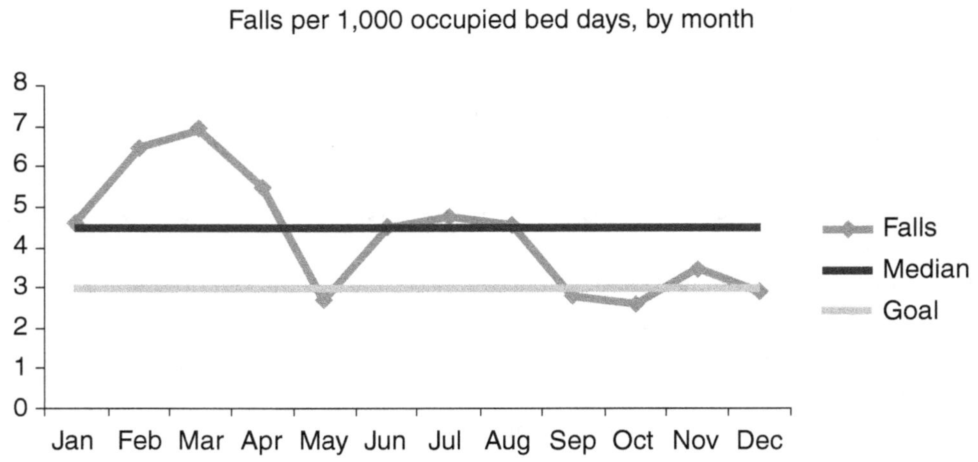

Figure 21-2. Sample Run Chart Plotting Patient Falls (ahrq.gov)

A Shewhart (or control chart) applies formal statistical calculations (statistical process control) to determine whether the observed rise and fall of a quality measured over time is within a predictable range of variation or is an indication of a significant change in the system. Control charts use upper and lower control limits (sometimes called "natural process limits") which indicate the threshold at which the process output is considered statistically 'unlikely,' and are drawn typically at 3 standard errors from the center line.

A **convenience sample** is the study group or population used in the test of a quality improvement initiative. Using convenience sampling is an efficient and simple method to test an intervention. This is not the same process often used in randomized controlled trials, and thus may not be an accurate reflection of the larger group. Ideally, however, the sample will have approximately similar characteristics to the larger population.

Leading Change in Patient Safety

Patient safety is the professional responsibility of everyone on the patient care team. In order to effect change in the quality of health care, health care professionals must utilize leadership principles. Changing behavior is difficult, and there are always multiple barriers to change efforts. To be effective in leading transformation, change efforts need to create a sense of urgency, be data-driven, team-based, specific, and measurable.

Successful leadership can be achieved even without a formal position of authority. Strategies for effectively influencing change include the following:

- Gathering compelling data
- Adopting a "systems" view of the problem
- Getting buy-in from administrative leadership or a powerful clinical ally
- Developing ideas to solve the problem
- Formulating an action plan

Goals should be SMART (**S**pecific, **M**easurable, **A**chievable, **R**ealistic, and **T**ime-sensitive). Good leaders are able to organize a team, articulate clear goals, manage conflict resolution, and make decisions based on the input of team members. Good leaders also lead by example and model good patient safety behavior.

Key Patient Safety and CQI Definitions

Adverse event: any injury caused by medical care

- An adverse event results in unintended harm to a patient by an act of commission or omission, rather than by the underlying disease or condition of the patient. Identifying something as an adverse event does not imply error, negligence, or poor quality care. It simply indicates that an undesirable clinical outcome resulted from some aspect of diagnosis or therapy, not an underlying disease process.

Adverse reaction: occurs when unexpected harm results from a justified action

- An adverse drug reaction occurs when the correct process was followed for the context in which the medication was used.

Authority gradient: command hierarchy of power or balance of power, measured in terms of steepness

- First used in aviation to describe the phenomenon where pilots and copilots failed to communicate effectively in stressful situations due to the significant difference in their perceived expertise or authority. Hierarchies which exist in medicine are also subject to causing errors. Most health care teams require some degree of authority gradient; otherwise roles are blurred and decisions cannot be made in a timely fashion. However, within a hierarchy, tools of effective clinical communication and teamwork can overcome risks to patient safety.

Brief: short planning session prior to the start of a clinical activity, in order to achieve team orientation, establish expectations, anticipate problems, and plan for contingencies

Checklist: algorithmic listing of actions to be performed in a given clinical setting, with the goal of ensuring that no critical step will be forgotten

- Though a seemingly simple intervention, checklists have played a leading role in the most significant successes of the patient safety movement, including the near-elimination of central line–associated bloodstream infections in many intensive care units. Checklists have also been used in the operating room to ensure that OR teams are well-oriented and that evidence-based standards known to reduce complications are followed (e.g. use of pre-operative antibiotics).

Closed-loop communication: a type of communication whereby, when a request is made of team members, someone specifically affirms out loud that he will complete the task and states out loud when the task has been completed.

- **Example**: During a cardiac resuscitation a physician orders a medication to be given intravenously and the nurse verbally confirms receipt of the order and verbally confirms when the medication has been administered as requested.

Debrief: information exchange process designed to improve team performance and effectiveness, held after a clinical event in order to review and learn

Error: failure of a planned action to be completed as intended or the use of a wrong plan to achieve an aim (i.e. an act of commission or doing something wrong); also includes failure of an unplanned action that should have been completed (i.e. an act of omission, or failing to do the right thing)

- **Example**: Ordering a medication for a patient with a documented allergy to that medication is an error of commission. Failing to prescribe a proven medication with major benefits for an eligible patient (e.g. low-dose unfractionated heparin for venous thromboembolism prophylaxis for a patient after hip replacement surgery) is an **error of omission.** Errors of omission are more difficult to recognize than errors of commission but are thought to represent a larger scope of the problem in patient safety.

  Errors can also be defined in terms of active or latent as coined by Professor James Reason, one of the founders in the field of safety science. According to Professor Reason, **active errors** occur at the point of contact between a human and some aspect of a larger system (e.g., a human–machine interface). They are generally readily apparent (e.g., pushing an incorrect button, ignoring a warning light) and almost always involve someone at the frontline. Active errors or active failures are sometimes referred to as errors at the 'sharp end,' figuratively referring to a scalpel. In other words, errors at the sharp end are noticed first because they are committed by the person closest to the patient. This person may literally be holding a scalpel (e.g., an orthopedist operating on the wrong leg) or figuratively be administering any kind of therapy (e.g., a nurse programming an intravenous pump with the wrong medication dose) or performing any aspect of care.

Latent errors (or latent conditions), in contrast, refer to less apparent failures of organization or design that contribute to the occurrence of errors or allow them to cause harm to patients. To complete the metaphor, latent errors are those at the other end of the scalpel—the "blunt end"—referring to the many layers of the health care system that affect the person "holding" the scalpel. For example, policies that allow a patient to enter an operating room and start an operation before confirming the patient's identify, intended procedure and site of surgery are considered latent errors that can result in wrong patient or wrong site surgery.

Forcing function: aspect of a design which prevents a specific action from being performed or allows its performance only if another specific action is performed first.

- **Example**: Automobiles are now designed so that the driver cannot shift into reverse without first putting a foot on the brake pedal. One of the first forcing functions identified in health care was the removal of concentrated potassium from general hospital wards. This action is intended to prevent the inadvertent preparation of intravenous solutions with concentrated potassium, an error that had produced small but consistent numbers of deaths for many years.

Handoffs: the process whereby one health care professional updates another on the status of ≥1 patients for the purpose of taking over their care

- **Example**: A resident physician who has been on call overnight tells an incoming resident about the patients admitted who require ongoing management. Nurses commonly conduct a handover at the end of their shift, updating the oncoming nurse about the status of the patients and tasks that need to be performed. Handoffs are a potential source of patient safety failure from the lack of important information being conveyed or misinformation being conveyed.

Harm/hazard: harm is the impairment or any negative effect on the structure of function of the body (e.g., disease, injury, suffering, disability, death); hazard is a circumstance, agent or action with the potential to cause harm

Huddle: an often impromptu problem-solving meeting conducted in order to assess a critical situation, reestablish situation awareness, reinforce plans already in place, and determine the need to adjust the plan

Iatrogenic: an adverse effect of medical care, rather than of the underlying disease (literally "brought forth by healer," from Greek *iatros*, for healer, and *gennan*, to bring forth)

Incident reporting: collecting and analyzing information about an event which could have harmed (near-miss) or did harm (adverse event) a patient in a health care setting

Medication error: any preventable event which may cause or lead to unintended and incorrect medication use or patient harm, while the medication is in the control of the health care professional or patient

- Medication error occurs when a patient receives (a) the wrong medication, or (b) the right medication but in the wrong dosage or manner (e.g. given orally instead of IV, correct medication given at the wrong time).

Medication reconciliation: process of avoiding unintended inconsistencies in medication regimens which can occur with any transition in care (e.g. hospital admission, transfer to ICU, discharge to rehab center) by reviewing the patient's current medication regimen and comparing it with the regimen being considered for the new setting of care

- Medical reconciliation helps to ensure that the intended medications are continued, and that medications that are supposed to be discontinued are not inadvertently continued. For example, medical reconciliation performed prior to discharging a patient from the hospital can detect if medication changes were made during the hospital stay that need to be continued once the patent is home (e.g. intravenous antibiotics started in the hospital during the treatment of pneumonia which are intended to be continued orally at home).

Near-miss (or close call): error or other incident which does not produce patient injury, but only because of intervening factors or pure chance

- This good fortune might reflect robustness of the patient (e.g., a patient with penicillin allergy receives penicillin, but has no reaction) or a fortuitous, timely intervention (e.g., a nurse happens to realize that a physician wrote an order in the wrong chart).

Patient safety: The WHO defines patient safety as 'the reduction of risk of unnecessary harm associated with health care to an acceptable minimum' (2009)

- The Agency for Healthcare Research and Quality uses the definition that "patient safety is a discipline in the health care sector that applies safety science methods toward the goal of achieving a trustworthy system of health care delivery." Patient safety is also an attribute of health care systems; it minimizes the incidence and impact of, and maximizes recovery from, adverse events.

Quality assurance (QA): an older term, not likely to be used today; QA was reactive, retrospective, policing, and in many ways punitive; often involved determining who was at fault after something went wrong

Quality improvement (QI): involves both prospective and retrospective reviews; is aimed at improvement—measuring where you are and figuring out ways to make things better; specifically attempts to avoid attributing blame and to create systems to prevent errors from happening

Read backs (or call-backs): when a listener repeats key information so that the transmitter can confirm its correctness

- To address the possibility of miscommunication when information is conveyed verbally, many high-risk industries use protocols for mandatory read-backs. For example, a laboratory technician calling a physician with a critical lab value may request that the physician read back the critical lab value to ensure it was received correctly.

Root cause analysis (RCA): structured process for identifying the causal or contributing factors underlying adverse events or other critical incidents

- Initially developed to analyze industrial accidents, RCA is now widely employed in error analysis within health care. A central tenet of RCA is to identify underlying problems that increase the likelihood of errors, while avoiding the trap of focusing on mistakes by individuals. RCA seeks to explore all the possible factors associated with an incident by asking what happened, why it happened, and what can be done to prevent it from happening again.

SBAR: a form of structured communication first developed for use in naval military procedures; it stands for situation (what is going on with the patient?), background (what is the clinical background or context?), assessment (what do I think the problem is?), recommendation/request (what would I do to correct it?)

- It has been adapted for health care as a helpful technique for communicating critical information that requires immediate attention and action concerning a patient's condition. It promotes patient safety by helping individuals communicate with shared expectations in a concise and structured format which improves efficiency and accuracy.

Sentinel event: adverse event in which death or serious harm to a patient has occurred; used to refer primarily to events that were not at all expected or acceptable (e.g., an operation on the wrong patient or body part)

Violation: intentional or deliberate deviation from safe operating procedures, standards, or policies

- A violation is different from an error, which is an unintentional action. Unlike errors, which are honest mistakes due to human nature, intentional violations are behaviors for which individuals need to be held accountable.

Wrong-site procedure: operation or procedure done on the wrong part of the body or on the wrong person; it can also mean the wrong surgery or procedure was performed

- Wrong-site procedures are rare and preventable, though they do still occur. A standard system to confirm the patient, site, and intended procedure with the medical team and patient before starting the procedure is a widely employed method of reducing or eliminating wrong-site procedures.

PRACTICE QUESTIONS

1. A CPOE system has made which of the following "Steps for a Patient to Receive a Medication" obsolete?

   A. Administration
   B. Dispensing
   C. Ordering
   D. Patient evaluation
   E. Transcribing

2. A pharmacy informatics system is designed around which of the following?

   A. Medication–related costs
   B. Medication–related data
   C. Medication usage
   D. Medication formulary
   E. Patient preferences

3. A physician's handwritten signature is required for all of the following EXCEPT

   A. Delsym®
   B. Percocet®
   C. Robitussin AC®
   D. Ultram®
   E. All of the above

4. Disadvantages of automated dispensing cabinets include all of the following EXCEPT?

   A. Lacks inventory control
   B. Inconvenient locations
   C. Pharmacist oversight
   D. Prolonged times to receive medication
   E. All of the above are disadvantages

5. Based on the Joint Commission's Do NOT Use abbreviation list, how many violations are found in the following "hand-written" prescription? "Warfarin 1.0 mg Q.D"

   A. 0
   B. 1
   C. 2
   D. 3
   E. 4

6. The part of the prescription that specifics the ingredients (or medication) and their quantities is which of the following?

   A. Inscription
   B. Sig
   C. Special instruction
   D. Subscription
   E. Superscription

7. A child receives a prescription with the following directions. “2 gtts a.u. bid”. Which of the following should appear on the prescription label?

   A. 2 gtts a.u. bid
   B. Instill 2 drops in each ear twice daily
   C. Instill 2 drops in the left ear twice daily
   D. Instill 2 drops in each eye twice daily
   E. Instill 2 drops in the left eye twice daily

8. The primary question answered by a Root Cause Analysis is which of the following?

   A. How did this happen?
   B. Is this medication appropriate for this patient?
   C. What potential problems will occur with this new system?
   D. When did this happen?
   E. Who caused this to happen?

9. Which of the following would invalidate a prescription for enalapril?

   A. No DEA number
   B. No handwritten signature
   C. Photocopy of prescription
   D. Preprinted prescription with only the number of tablets and drug strength left blank
   E. All of the above will invalidate a prescription for enalapril

10. Which of the following medication and dispensing system technologies are INCORRECTLY matched?

    A. Automated dispensing cabinets : Administration
    B. Bar coding at point of care : Dispensing and Administration
    C. CPOE : Patient evaluation and medication prescribing
    D. Smart infusion pumps : Administration
    E. All of the above are correct

Answers and Explanations

1. **The correct answer is E.** A number of steps must occur from the time a patient enters the hospital to the time he/she receives a medication. First, he/she is evaluated (choice D) by a physician, who makes a diagnosis. The physician (or other provider) prescribes a medication (choice C) using a computerized

physician order entry (CPOE) combined with clinical decision support systems. This order is then sent directly to the pharmacy. One of the advantages of a CPOE (ePrescribing) system is that it eliminates handwriting errors; hence, there is no transcribing by the pharmacist. In the dispensing step (choice B), the pharmacist evaluates the appropriateness of the prescription and "dispenses" it to a nurse (hospital) or patient (retail). The medication is then administered (by a nurse) to the patient.

2. **The correct answer is B.** Pharmacy informatics is a scientific field that concentrates on medication-related data and knowledge within the continuum of the United States healthcare system. This field of science can provide valuable insights and opportunities to improve various elements of existing pharmaceutical care processes and treatment guidelines. All of the 7 general elements of a pharmacy informatics system are designed to "handle" data, which includes data on medication cost (choice A), usage (choice C), formulary issues (choice D) and even patient and physician preferences (choice E).

3. **The correct answer is A.** A prescription is an instruction written by a medical practitioner that authorizes a patient to be provided a medication, medical device, laboratory test or a specific medical treatment. A physician's handwritten signature MUST appear on prescriptions for Schedule II–V medications (choices B, C and D). However, a "stamp" of the physician's signature can be used for general legend drugs. No prescription is needed for the over-the-counter cough suppressant Delsym®. On the FPGEE, the candidate should know both brand and generic names for both prescription and non-prescription medications.

4. **The correct answer is C.** Automated dispensing cabinets are computerized drug storage devices used in hospitals at the point of care (choice B) to permit rapid access (choice D) to the most commonly used medications. These cabinets are designed to replace non-automated drug carts to improve medication inventory control (choice A). Disadvantages include lack of pharmacy screening of medication orders (choice B) prior to availability for administration; excessive use of system overrides; and failure of user to recognize look-alike names.

5. **The correct answer C.** The Joint Commission devised a "Do Not Use" abbreviation list as part of its Information Management Standards guidelines, and applies to hand-written prescriptions. This requirement does not currently apply to preprogrammed health information technology systems (i.e. electronic medical records, CPOE or electronic prescribing systems). Based on the guidelines, there should NOT be a trailing "0" after the 1 mg dose, since it could be mistaken for 10 mg. Also, the abbreviations Q.D. and Q.I.D. should not be used since they can easily be mistaken for one another if the physician inadvertently alters the height of the period or I in Q.D. and Q.I.D, respectively. Thus there are "2" violations to the Joint Commission's abbreviation guidelines.

6. **The correct answer is A.** There are four parts to a drug prescription plus a fifth part for special instruction if needed. The inscription (choice A) specifies the ingredients (or medication) and their quantities. The signature (or sig – choice B) defines what instructions are to be placed on the prescription label. The sig indicates when and how to take the medication and in what quantities. The special instructions (choice C) are found below the signature line, where the prescriber can place special instructions as well as warnings and precautions. The subscription (choice D) specifies directions on how to compound the medication and designation of the form (pill, powder, solution, etc.). Superscription (choice E) is the symbol ℞ from the Latin recipe, meaning "take."

7. **The correct answer is B.** Although the use of abbreviations is on the decline with electronic prescribing, the pharmacist should still know the most common medical abbreviations. Choice A is incorrect because the patient is not likely to understand the directions. Choice B is correct. Choice C would be "2 gtts a.s. bid". Choice D would be "2 gtts o.u. bid". Choice E would be "2 gtts a.d. bid".

8. **The correct answer is A.** An RCA (Root Cause Analysis) is a retrospective method of problem solving used for the identification of the "root causes" of faults or problems. It is generally performed AFTER an adverse event or issue occurs. An RCA focuses on systems and processes rather than individual blame.

The question asked is, "how did this happen? (choice A is correct)," not "whose fault is this? (choice E)" The goal of an RCA is to determine why an event happened and what can be done to prevent it from happening again. A drug utilization review (DUR) is a review of prescribing patterns to identify combinations of inappropriate medication use (choice B). A failure mode analysis (FMEA) is a prospective method for evaluating a process to identify where and how it might fail. FMEA answers the question posed in choice C. Clinicians do not need to perform an analysis of "when" an incident occurs (choice D). It would be in the patient chart, for example.

9. **The correct answer is C.** In order to be valid, a prescription must be written or printed (choice D) on a tamper-resistant form consistent with federal requirements for Medicaid. Photocopies using plain paper are NOT considered valid. This requirement applies to all written prescriptions for drugs in federal Schedules II – V as well as Schedule VI (general legend) medications. The DEA number (choice A) and handwritten signature (choice B) are required for all controlled substance prescriptions.

10. **The correct answer is A.** Pharmacy automation includes the mechanical and informational processes of managing and distributing medications. It includes point-of-care automation processes as well as preparation and packaging automation processes. Medication order, ordering and receiving, pharmacy robots, bar-code medication dispensing, and medication dispensing devices may also be automated. Choice A is incorrect because automated dispensing cabinets are computerized drug storage devices designed for use by hospital staff (i.e. nurses, physicians). The physician or nurses will initially perform the dispensing step (normally performed by the pharmacist first) and then remove the medication from the dispensing cabinets, NOT the patient. The nurse will then administer the medication to the patient.

Evidence-Based Pharmacy Practice 22

Learning Objectives

- ❑ Show proficiency in the interpretation and evaluation of drug information
- ❑ Discuss medication therapy management
- ❑ Explain how to properly evaluate medical information and the medical literature
- ❑ Demonstrate understanding of the clinical interpretation and application of medical guidelines
- ❑ Answer questions on the clinical application of scientific and systems-based knowledge
- ❑ Summarize principles on the development and implementation of drug treatment protocols
- ❑ Demonstrate proficiency in the evaluation and application of clinical trial results

Evidence-based medicine (EBM) has been defined by the National Library of Medicine (NLM) as *An approach of practicing medicine with the goal to improve and evaluate patient care. It requires the judicious integration of best research evidence with the patient's values to make decisions about medical care. This method is to help physicians make proper diagnosis, devise best testing plan, choose best treatment and methods of disease prevention, as well as develop guidelines for large groups of patients with the same disease.*

Although the NLM definition specifies "physicians," each practicing pharmacist should understand and be able to apply the principles of EBM to each clinical recommendation. With a solid understanding of EBM, the pharmacist can provide more clinically relevant information, devise better treatment plans, scrutinize physician orders, and select the most cost-effective medication. The ultimate goal of EBM is to optimize decision-making and improve patient outcomes by accentuating evidence from well-designed, peer-reviewed research.

INTERPRETATION AND EVALUATION OF DRUG INFORMATION

Proficient drug information (DI) skills are essential for all practicing clinicians, especially pharmacists. These skills can enhance the pharmacist's ability to efficiently and effectively answer detailed medication-related questions that require research and/or medical literature evaluations.

An ability to effectively obtain necessary DI is also essential for other pharmacy-related areas such as formulary management, pharmacoeconomics, pharmacogenomics, and assessment and use of practice guidelines.

Once the desired information from the appropriate source is obtained, the pharmacist must communicate these findings to both patients and other members of the health care team (See Chapter 19 of this guide for more information on professional communication principles).

NAPLEX Reference

Drug Information chapter

Providing Accurate and Complete Medical Information

On a daily basis, most clinical pharmacists will receive a variety of medication and non-medication related questions which will often require a review of the medical literature. When responding to these questions, the pharmacist needs to provide healthcare practitioners with timely, evidence-based drug information. This information will promote the safe, rational use of medications and ultimately improve patient outcomes.

The process of providing accurate and complete information generally follows a series of steps.

Table 22-1. Steps to Providing Accurate and Complete Medication (and Non-Medication) Information

Step	Action Performed in Step	Comments
1	Clarify the question being asked	Clarification will help ensure that the information provided fulfills the needs of the practitioner, the pharmacist understands what is being asked AND facilitates a timely response.
2	Obtain accurate and thorough background information on the request	The pharmacist must understand the context of the question being asked; this is necessary to accurately and thoroughly respond to the drug information question.
3	Systematically search appropriate drug information sources	A literature search may be required for more complex questions and will help ensure the accuracy and completeness of the response. See NAPLEX Reference: Drug Information chapter on the information provided in each major drug information source.
4	Utilize appropriate primary, secondary or tertiary reference sources.	A primary, secondary or tertiary reference source will be more appropriate depending on the nature of the clinical question being asked. ***See "Primary, Secondary and Tertiary Literature" table for more information.***
5	Critically analyze and synthesize information derived from each literature source	The information from the primary, secondary or tertiary sources should be evaluated for relevance to the question being asked, the date of the reference, accuracy of information and level of evidence provided.
6	Formulate a clinically relevant response	The response will include information/recommendations from all relevant sources. Note: The accuracy and completeness of the response will ultimately affect patient care and outcomes.
7	Document the formulated response and include all references used	The documented response should be in an understandable format and easily retrievable.
8	Communicate the response to the healthcare provider in the format requested	The response will be documented by the pharmacist electronically; however, the practitioner may want a verbal, paper or electronic version of the response.
9	Provide contact information	Information generally includes a phone number and email address.

Primary, Secondary, and Tertiary Literature

Drug information resources are classified as primary, secondary, and tertiary sources. As described in steps 5 and 6 of the previous table, pharmacists will often use a combination of each type of literature source when formulating a response to a question posed by a healthcare provider or patient.

Table 22-2. Primary, Secondary, and Tertiary Literature

Type of Literature	Comments	Examples
Primary	• Authored by original researcher. • The original research results are published in peer-reviewed journals, dissertations and conference proceedings. • May include conference papers and preliminary reports.	Nature, NEJM, JAMA
Secondary	• Interpretations and evaluations derived "directly" from or refer to the primary literature source. • Consists of abstracting and indexing services, review of a primary journal article, systematic reviews, meta-analysis, and clinical practice guidelines. • Experts within each discipline use primary literature sources and synthesize, simplify, and integrate new research into a secondary source.	PubMed, Cochrane library, MyCancerGenome, PharmGKB, UpToDate
Tertiary	• Collection of primary and secondary sources. • Consists of medical text books, encyclopedias, handbooks, medical newspapers. • Purpose is to provide an overview of key research findings as well as introduce principles and practices within the discipline.	Harrison's principles of internal medicine; Pharmacotherapy: A Pathophysiologic Approach by. Joseph T. DiPiro, et al; Goodman & Gilman's

MEDICATION THERAPY MANAGEMENT

Medication therapy management (MTM) is defined as a service or group of services generally provided by a pharmacist to optimize therapeutic outcomes for an individual patient. MTM services include medication therapy reviews, pharmacotherapy consults, health and wellness programs, and other clinical services. The primary goal of MTM is to help patients achieve the best outcomes by managing their drug therapies and preventing and resolving drug-related issues.

> **NAPLEX Reference**
>
> **Health Policy chapter:**
> "Medication Therapy Management"

A more detailed review of MTM is found in Kaplan's *NAPLEX Strategies, Practice, and Review* book.

EVALUATION OF MEDICAL INFORMATION AND LITERATURE

Health care professionals commonly encounter journal articles on the efficacy of a "revolutionary" new medication or the "ground-breaking" results of a medical research study. However, clinicians have a responsibility to appropriately evaluate the information provided and choose or not choose to integrate their findings into clinical practice.

- Question: Should the clinical trial results be considered part of your "evidence-based" clinical recommendation?

Components of a Clinical Trial

The most commonly encountered types of research study found in the medical literature are randomized clinical trials, case-control (retrospective studies), and cohort (prospective studies) studies. In each of these studies, there are 5 components:

- **Assignment:** Selection of individuals for study and control groups based on the study hypothesis and objectives
- **Assessment:** Determination of the results of the study and the control groups
- **Analysis:** Comparison of the results of the study and the control groups using well-designed methods with appropriate study materials (such as evaluation tools, medications, etc.)
- **Interpretation:** Drawing conclusions about the meaning of the differences found between the study and control groups for those in the study
- **Extrapolation:** Drawing conclusions about the meaning of the study for individuals or situations not included in the study

These 5 general components need to be considered by the reader when answering the following questions:

- Are the study population and results applicable to the clinical question being researched by the pharmacist?
- Was the study designed properly?
- Were the results appropriately extrapolated to the general population?

The PP-ICONS method can help to answer these questions.

PP-ICONS Method

When a pharmacist, for example, finds a journal article about a meta-analysis or randomized controlled trial while researching a clinical question, the first thing that they should do is determine the validity and clinical relevance of the clinical study.

There are numerous ways to scrutinize an abstract or journal article. One of the most efficient ways to evaluate an article (on treatment, prevention, or patient screening) is to use the PP-ICONS method to accept or discard the conclusions of the study.

Table 22-3. PP-ICONS Method

Acronym	Acronym Word	Definition/Comments
P	Problem	• Clinical condition or treatment measure that was evaluated. • Does the clinical problem studied (in the journal article), parallel the clinical question being researched? • If the problem studied is not significantly similar to the clinical problem being researched, then the results are irreverent.
P	Patient/ Population	• Is the study group (in the clinical trial) similar to the patient in the question being researched by the pharmacist? • Did the study author accurately extrapolate the results of the study to patients in the general population (with similar characteristics)? • Questions include: Are they of a similar age and gender? Do they have any concomitant disease states? Do they have any abnormal laboratory findings? Are they receiving any medications?

(Continued)

Acronym	Acronym Word	Definition/Comments
	Patient/ Population (cont.)	• If the study population (in the clinical trial) are sicker, older, different gender or more clinically complicated, than the patient (in the question being researched by the pharmacist), then the study results might not be relevant. • Note: The more similar the patients in the clinical trial are to the patient for which the research is being performed, the more applicable the results.
I	Intervention	• What intervention, diagnostic tool, prognostic factor, or exposure is being evaluated in the clinical trial? • Are the interventions the same in the clinical trial as in the patient?
C	Comparison	• The comparison is what the intervention is tested against. For example, the medication (being researched) could have been tested against a placebo in the clinical trial. However, the pharmacist is researching the efficacy of the same medication in a patient receiving a comparable therapy. Thus, this particular study may not be valid. • Ensure that the comparison therapy fits the question being researched.
O	Outcome	• What is the desired outcome of the study? • Differentiate between disease-oriented evidence (DOEs) and patient-oriented evidence (POEs). • DOEs usually reflect changes in physiologic parameters (i.e. blood pressure) but may not impact patient outcomes. Conversely, POEs focus on overall clinical improvement, morbidity, mortality and cost. • Note: DOEs are interesting but of questionable clinical significance, whereas POEs are very interesting and clinically significant. • DOEs show only statistical significance and POEs show both statistical and clinical significance.
N	Number of Subjects	• The number of patients enrolled and who complete the clinical trial. • A study with less than 100 subjects is usually inadequate to provide reliable statistics. A good study generally has >300 participants.
S	Statistics and biases	• Were the proper statistical tests used in the trial? • Are there any major biases that could invalidate the results?

Another well-known (but less comprehensive) model than PP-CONS is PICO (P = Patient or population; I = Intervention; C = Comparison; and O = Outcome).

PP-ICONS Key Points

- The PP-ICONS approach is a rapid method to screen an article for both validity and clinical relevance.
- The article abstract generally contains all of the information needed for the PP-ICONS model. However, if the article abstract "passes" the PP-ICONS screen, do not immediately accept the abstract's conclusion.
- The reader must always evaluate the article in its entirety (using the PP-ICONS model) before it can be used as a reference source when answering a clinical question.

Levels of Evidence

When choosing a journal article as a potential source for a clinical question, use the articles with the highest evidence to help identify the most suitable medication for a patient. Study designs are listed in order of importance and strength of the evidence:

- Meta-analysis
- Systematic review
- Randomized controlled trials
- Cohort studies
- Case-control studies
- Case series and case reports
- Editorials and expert opinions
- Animal research/laboratory studies

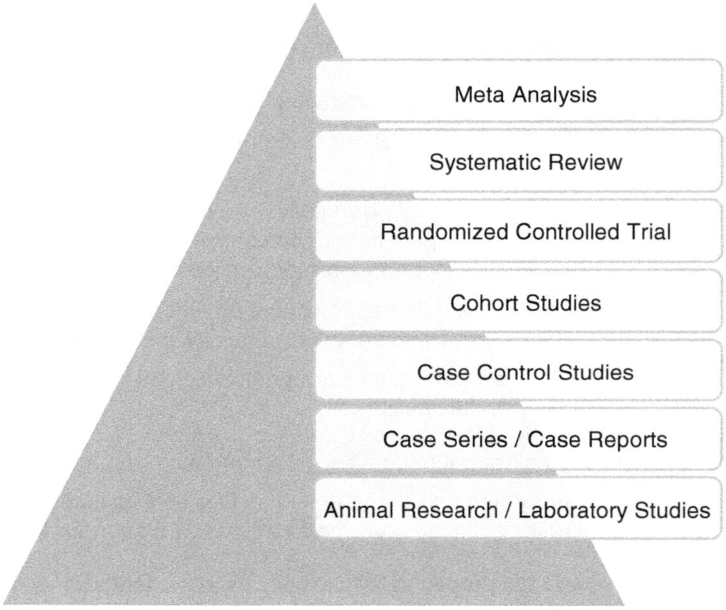

Figure 22-1. Levels of Evidence Pyramid

Systematic Review

Randomized controlled trials are performed to further test the efficacy of a single drug or procedure. A systematic review is a comprehensive approach to a question and combines clinical information (usually obtained from randomized clinical trial results).

A systematic review generally involves a series of steps:

1. Asks a clinical question
2. Identifies one or more sources of information or databases to search
3. Develops a comprehensive search strategy based on predetermined inclusion and exclusion criteria
4. Critically analyzes numerous clinical trials, research studies and research papers
5. Abstracts the data in a standardized manner

Systematic reviews are considered to have higher levels of evidence than randomized controlled trials.

Meta-Analysis

A meta-analysis is a statistical approach to combine the information and abstracted data derived from a systematic review. A meta-analysis is based on the results of a systematic review. In other words, a meta-analysis will critically and comprehensively examine the numerous randomized controlled clinical trials (derived from a systematic review), on a particular treatment regimen or disease state and then combine the results using accepted statistical methodology as if they were from one large study.

NAPLEX Reference

Biostatistics chapter: "Clinical Trial Design"

A comprehensive review of meta-analyses, randomized controlled trials, cohort studies, and other types of study designs can be found in the Biostatistics chapter of Kaplan's *NAPLEX Strategies, Practice, and Review* book in the "Clinical Trial Design" section.

Choosing the Right Type of Clinical Study

The clinical pharmacist will likely be performing research on clinical questions concerning a medication or therapeutic regimen. However, there may be instances where another health care provider, such as a physician, nurse, or hospital administrator, asks questions from another field of medicine. Thus, an understanding of what clinical concepts are best evaluated by each type of study is essential.

Table 22-4. Preferred Studies to Address the Clinical Concepts

Clinical Concept	Preferred Study to Address the Clinical Concept
Medication Therapy	Meta-analysis and controlled clinical trial (preferred); cohort, case-control, case series
Non-Medication Therapy	Meta-analysis and controlled clinical trial (preferred); cohort, case-control, case series
Surgical Procedure	Meta-analysis and controlled clinical trial (preferred); cohort, case-control, case series
Diagnosis/Diagnostic Test/ Clinical Examination	Prospective, blind comparison to reference test (Gold Standard)
Disease Prevention	Meta-analysis, controlled clinical trial, cohort, case-control, case series
Disease Etiology	Meta-analysis and controlled clinical trial (preferred); cohort, case-control, case series
Disease Prognosis	Cohort, case-control, case series

CLINICAL INTERPRETATION AND APPLICATION OF MEDICAL GUIDELINES

According to the United States Institute of Medicine, "*Clinical practice guidelines are systematically developed statements to assist practitioner and patient decisions about appropriate health care for specific clinical circumstances.*"

Clinical practice guidelines (CPGs) are often developed by specialized medical societies such as the American Heart Association and American Diabetes Association. Medical society guidelines often define the role of specific measures used for the diagnosis and management of a given disease. CPGs also commonly address the treatment of disease states when concomitant conditions occur.

- **Example**: A patient with type 2 diabetes is diagnosed with hypertension. The American Diabetes Association (ADA) treatment guideline (Standards of Medical Care in Diabetes) provides recommendations on how to treat type 2 diabetes alone as well as when hypertension or other medical conditions are present.

Most societies will indicate that their clinical guidelines contain recommendations based on evidence from a rigorous systematic review and synthesis of the published medical literature.

Interpretation and Application of Clinical Practice Guidelines

CPGs are one of the most effective ways to disseminate evidence-based recommendations for the diagnosis, treatment, and prevention of disease. These guidelines are updated as new and emerging clinical concepts are discovered (through clinical trials).

Disadvantages of CPGs

- Clinicians may not be aware of CPG recommendations or rely solely on the individual clinical protocols adopted by a medical institution (hospital, consortium, etc), which may not reflect the most current CPG recommendations.
- Accuracy and recency of CPG information may be questionable for less commonly occurring disease states. For example, CPGs for psoriasis, prostatic hypertrophy and pneumonia are updated less frequently than CPGs for diabetes, hypertension, and asthma.

The clinical pharmacist needs to understand the strengths and weaknesses of each CPG and thus be able to interpret and apply ONLY the high-quality, clinically relevant recommendations for the individual patient being diagnosed or treated.

CPG Sponsors

There are a variety of professional medical associations, prominent institutions, medical insurance companies, and government task forces that develop CPGs. Thus these guidelines can vary based on the intended audience, clinical trials used, and resources available for patients, including drug formularies.

CPGs can be directly obtained by accessing the website of each individual medical association (or other organization) or by accessing the National Guideline Clearinghouse (www.guideline.gov).

Guideline.gov is an online database of evidence-based guidelines in the United States.

- The National Guideline Clearinghouse (NGC) is an initiative of the Agency for Healthcare Research and Quality (AHRQ) of the U.S. Department of Health and Human Services.
- One of the primary benefits of this resource is that it permits a side-by-side comparison of CPGs and also indicates where there are areas of agreement and disagreement between the guidelines.
- Note: Clinicians are encouraged to evaluate each guideline and determine relevance for each clinical case to which it is being applied.

Evaluating a CPG

Due to the well-known variability of CPG content and quality, standardized quality assessment criteria have been developed. The Conference on Guideline Standardization (COGS), supported by a grant from the Agency for Healthcare Research and Quality (AHRQ), developed a checklist to assess the quality of each guideline.

- Some high-quality guidelines may not contain all 18 items in the checklist, since some of these criteria are not applicable to a particular clinical guideline.
- The 18-item checklist should still be referenced prior to using a CPG for the treatment of a patient, especially for less common disease states or CPGs that have not been recently updated.

Table 22-5. COGS Checklist for Reporting Clinical Practice Guidelines

Topic	Description
Overview material	Provides a structured abstract that includes the target population, goals and objectives, guideline's release date, status (original, revised, updated), and print and electronic sources.
Focus	Describes the primary disease/condition and intervention/service/technology that the guideline addresses. Indicates any alternative preventive, diagnostic or therapeutic interventions that were considered during guideline development.
Goal	Describes (in detail) the goals that the guideline is expected to achieve, including the rationale for development of a guideline on this topic.
Users/Setting	Describes the intended users of the guideline (i.e. provider types, patients) and the settings in which the guideline is intended to be used.
Target population	Describes the patient population eligible for guideline recommendations and lists any exclusion criteria. Should also include relevance to patients with concomitant disease states.
Developer	Identifies the organization(s) responsible for guideline development and the names/credentials/potential conflicts of interest of individuals involved in the guideline's development.
Funding source/sponsor	Identifies the funding source/sponsor and describes its role in developing, or reporting the guideline. Discloses potential conflict of interest.
Evidence collection	Describes (in detail) the methods used to search the scientific literature, including the range of dates and databases searched, and criteria applied to filter the retrieved evidence. May also include rationale for NOT including certain clinical trial results.
Recommendation grading criteria	Describes the criteria used to rate the quality of evidence that supports the recommendations and the system for describing the strength of the recommendations. Recommendation strength communicates the importance of adherence to a recommendation and is based on both the quality of the evidence and the magnitude of anticipated benefits or harms.
Method for synthesizing evidence	Describes how evidence was used to create recommendations, i.e. evidence tables, meta-analysis, decision analysis.
Pre-release review	Describes how the guideline developer reviewed and tested the guidelines prior to release.
Update plan	States whether or not there is a plan to update the guideline and, if applicable, an expiration date for this version of the guideline.
Definitions	Defines unfamiliar terms and those critical to correct application of the guideline that might be subject to misinterpretation.
Recommendations and rationale	States the recommended action precisely and the specific circumstances under which to perform it. Justifies each recommendation by describing the linkage between the recommendation and its supporting evidence. Indicates the quality of evidence and the recommendation strength, based on the criteria described in topic 9 (Recommendation grading criteria).

(Continued)

Topic	Description
Potential benefits and harms	Describes anticipated benefits and potential risks associated with implementation of guideline recommendations. May also include relevance to patients with concomitant disease states.
Patient preferences	Describes the role of patient preferences when a recommendation involves a substantial element of personal choice or values.
Algorithm	Provides (when appropriate) a graphical description of the stages and decisions in clinical care described by the guideline.
Implementation considerations	Describes anticipated barriers to application of the recommendations. Provides reference to any auxiliary documents for providers or patients that are intended to facilitate implementation. Suggests review criteria for measuring changes in care when the guideline is implemented.

Adapted from: Standardized Reporting of Clinical Practice Guidelines: A Proposal from the Conference on Guideline Standardization; Ann Intern Med. 2003;139(6):493-498. doi:10.7326/0003-4819-139-6-200309160-00013

LEVELS OF EVIDENCE

Levels of Evidence

Clinical practice guidelines provide evidence-based recommendations on how to diagnose, treat, and prevent a disease state in a specific patient population. Since the quality of evidence supporting each "individual" recommendation may vary, grading systems are employed to inform the reader about the level of evidence assigned to each recommendation.

- **Example**: The ADA provides treatment recommendations based on the level of evidence.

Table 22-6. Levels of Evidence

ADA Recommendation	Level of Evidence	Interpretation by the Pharmacist
Metformin, if not contraindicated and if tolerated, is the preferred initial pharmacological agent for type 2 diabetes.	A	This recommendation was made as the result of a randomized controlled clinical trial or evidence from a meta-analysis.
Consider initiating insulin therapy (with or without additional agents) in patients with newly diagnosed type 2 diabetes and markedly symptomatic or elevated blood glucose levels or A1c.	E	This recommendation was made as the result of an expert consensus or clinical experience; however, there has not been a randomized controlled clinical trial to support this recommendation.

Taken from Standards of Medical Care in Diabetes (http://professional.diabetes.org/content/clinical-practice-recommendations)

Assignment of Evidence Level

There is a well-established process of assigning an evidence level.

- Higher levels of evidence (Level 1 or Level A) are assigned to recommendations based on meta-analysis, systematic reviews or randomized clinical reviews.
- Low levels of evidence (Level 5 or Level E) are assigned to case series reports and expert opinions.
- Endpoints (i.e. survival, quality of life, cure) seen at the cessation of the clinical trial or case series report are also measured and affect the strength of the evidence.

There are a number of different levels of evidence grading systems.

- The American Diabetes Association (ADA) uses the "A–E" grading systems
- Other organizations use a "1–5" grading system
- Note: 1 and A are equivalent and 5 and E are equivalent.

The most comprehensive evidence grading system was developed by the Oxford (UK) Centre for Evidence-based Medicine (CEBM). The Oxford CEBM Levels of Evidence addresses this issue and provides "levels" of evidence for claims about prognosis, diagnosis, treatment benefits, treatment harms, and screening.

Table 22-7. Oxford Centre for Evidence-based Medicine – Levels of Evidence (March 2009)

Level	Therapy/Prevention, Etiology/Harm
1a	Systematic reviews (with homogeneity) of randomized controlled trials
1b	Individual randomized controlled trials (with narrow confidence interval)
1c	All or none randomized controlled trials
2a	Systematic reviews (with homogeneity) of cohort studies
2b	Individual cohort study or low quality randomized controlled trials (e.g. <80% follow-up)
2c	"Outcomes" Research; ecological studies
3a	Systematic review (with homogeneity) of case-control studies
3b	Individual Case-Control Study
4	Case-series (and poor quality cohort and case-control studies)
5	Expert opinion without explicit critical appraisal, or based on physiology, bench research or "first principles"

Comments

- Homogeneity means that a systematic review is free of worrisome variations (heterogeneity) in the directions and degrees of results between individual studies. Not all systematic reviews with statistically significant heterogeneity need be worrisome, and not all worrisome heterogeneity need be statistically significant.
- Systematic review provides a higher level of evidence than a single randomized controlled clinical trial.

Derived from Oxford Centre for Evidence-based Medicine – Levels of Evidence (March 2009)". http://www.cebm.net/oxford-centre-evidence-based-medicine-levels-evidence-march-2009/ Centre for Evidence-Based Medicine. Retrieved 22 May 2016.

Table 22-8. Recommendation Grading System

Letter	Number	Recommendation Strength	Comments
A	1	Recommend implementing	Consistent with findings from Level 1 Evidence; benefit is clearly > risk
B	2	Consider implementing when "1 or A" level therapy is not recommended	Consistent with findings from level 2 or 3 evidence or extrapolated information from level 1 evidence; benefit appears to be > risk
C	3	Consider not implementing; Consider implementing when "2 or B" level therapy is not recommended	Consistent with findings from level 4 evidence or extrapolated information from level 2 or 3 evidence; benefit ≤ risk
D	4	Generally not recommended	Consistent with findings from level 5 evidence or inconsistent/inconclusive information from any level; benefit < risk

Grading the Recommendation

Most evidenced-based treatment guidelines not only grade the level of supporting evidence but also grade the strength of the recommendation. The recommendation "strength" is generally based on both the level of supporting evidence as well as a risk-benefit analysis.

CLINICAL PRACTICE GUIDELINES AND TREATMENT PROTOCOLS

Clinical practice guidelines (CPGs) generally address clinical and practical issues for a given disease state and include treatment plans and summarized consensus statements. CPGs often form the foundation on which treatment protocols are built.

Like CPGs, treatment protocols also guide clinical decisions and provide criteria regarding diagnosis, management, and treatment of a given disease state. However, treatment protocols are often summarized versions of the CPG that provide a step-by-step treatment process. Most treatment protocols also provide visual interpretations of their guidance in the form of a treatment algorithm.

Treatment Algorithm

Medical algorithms are designed to help promote medical decision making. These decisions occur in almost every area of medicine, including medical test selection, diagnosis, therapy, and prognosis. The primary purpose of a medical algorithm is to standardize medical decisions, reduce the potential for errors, and improve patient outcomes.

Medical algorithms include a decision tree approach to medical treatment (i.e., if symptoms X, Y, and Z are present, then use treatment A; however, if symptoms X, Y, and Z are present AND disease states 1 and 2 are also present then use treatment B).

- Example: If a patient has symptoms X, Y, and Z and is diagnosed with type 2 diabetes, then metformin therapy should be instituted. However, if the same symptoms are present and the patient also has severe renal dysfunction, then metformin is contraindicated and an alternative therapy should be chosen.

A treatment algorithm can be divided into 3 general components (steps in a process):

- Step 1: Assessment
- Step 2: Management
- Step 3: Reassessment & Adjustment

The goals and objectives for each of these components are different.

Step 1: Assessment

Prior to the institution of any treatment, the patient must be assessed for:

- Disease severity
- Underlying causes of disease
- Comorbidities (that could impact treatment)
- Current medications
- Other factors that could increase or decrease the success of a given treatment regimen

Based on the patient assessment, the physician (or other health care provider) will decide to treat the patient or refer them to a specialist.

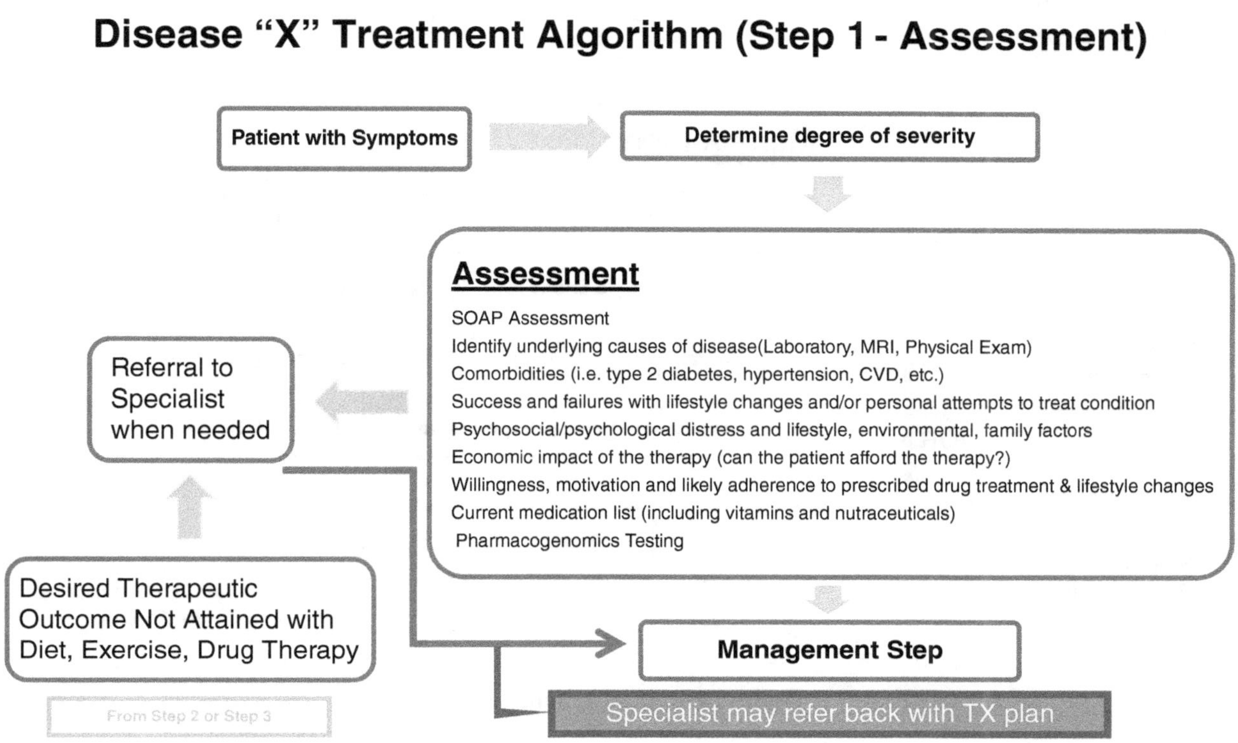

Figure 22-2. Step 1 Assessment

Step 2: Management

Once the patient has been properly assessed and the decision to treat has been made (in Step 1), the physician (or other provider) will institute an individualized, evidence-based treatment plan (based on a specific treatment protocol, clinical practice guideline or clinical trial).

The individualized treatment plan will take into account all of the patient factors (defined in the assessment step) and clinical recommendations.

- Note: Initial treatment measures may be employed until the patient can be seen by a specialist.
- **Example treatment measures include lifestyle changes, behavioral therapy, medication therapy and non-traditional therapies.**

Shortly after the initial treatment measure(s) is employed, the desired therapeutic effect will be assessed. If the desired patient outcomes are achieved, then the current therapy will be continued and assessed again at a later date. However, if the desired patient outcomes are NOT achieved, the provider will progress on to step 3.

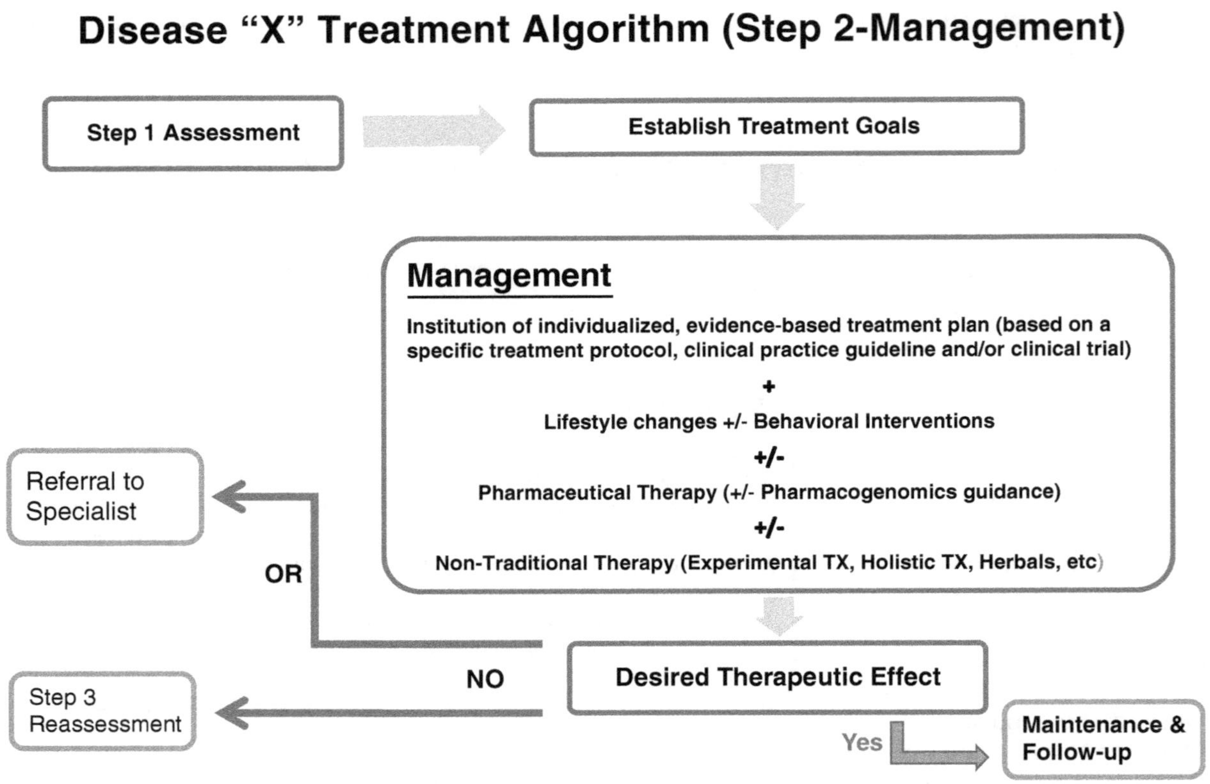

Figure 22-3. Step 2 Management

Step 3: Reassessment & Adjustment

The reassessment and adjustment step is needed to optimize therapeutic outcomes. Hence, when desired outcomes are not met, the clinician should determine reasons for successes and failures of initial therapy. A treatment failure could, for example, be related to the actual treatment algorithm itself. Remember, treatment algorithms are developed using clinical trial results and clinical practice guidelines.

When a treatment failure occurs, the physician should ask the following questions:

- Was the treatment protocol/algorithm properly designed?
- Were the proper clinical trials selected in designing the protocol? (A review of meta-analyses, randomized controlled trials and other types of study designs can be found in Kaplan's NAPLEX Review text in the "Clinical Trial Design" section of the Biostatistics chapter.)
- Does the patient meet the inclusion and exclusion criteria defined by the treatment protocol/treatment algorithm?

If the answer to any of these questions is "NO," then a different treatment protocol/treatment algorithm should be chosen. If the answer to all 3 of these questions is "YES," then the physician/pharmacist should determine other potential reasons for successes and failures of the initial therapy, including the patient's willingness to adhere to the prescribed regimen.

Other reasons for therapeutic failure include:

- The original therapeutic goals and objectives of the patient are different than those of the physician/pharmacist. The original regimen may have a diet and exercise component that is unacceptable for the patient.
- The prescribed regimen may be too expensive.

- There may be unacceptable side effects or may not meet other patient expectations. For example, the medication may treat the patient's major depressive disorder, but cause sexual dysfunction or severe CNS side effects. Hence, the patient is unwilling to adhere to the treatment regimen.

Thus the provider should work with the patient to choose the regimen that "works" best for them.

The reassessment and adjustment step may or may not occur for acute conditions and less complicated chronic conditions. However, this step is essential for managing patients with chronic, progressive conditions such as heart failure and Parkinson's disease.

- Example: For a patient with Parkinson's disease, the initial treatment regimen may only be effective for a limited amount of time and will need to be continually adjusted as the disease progresses.

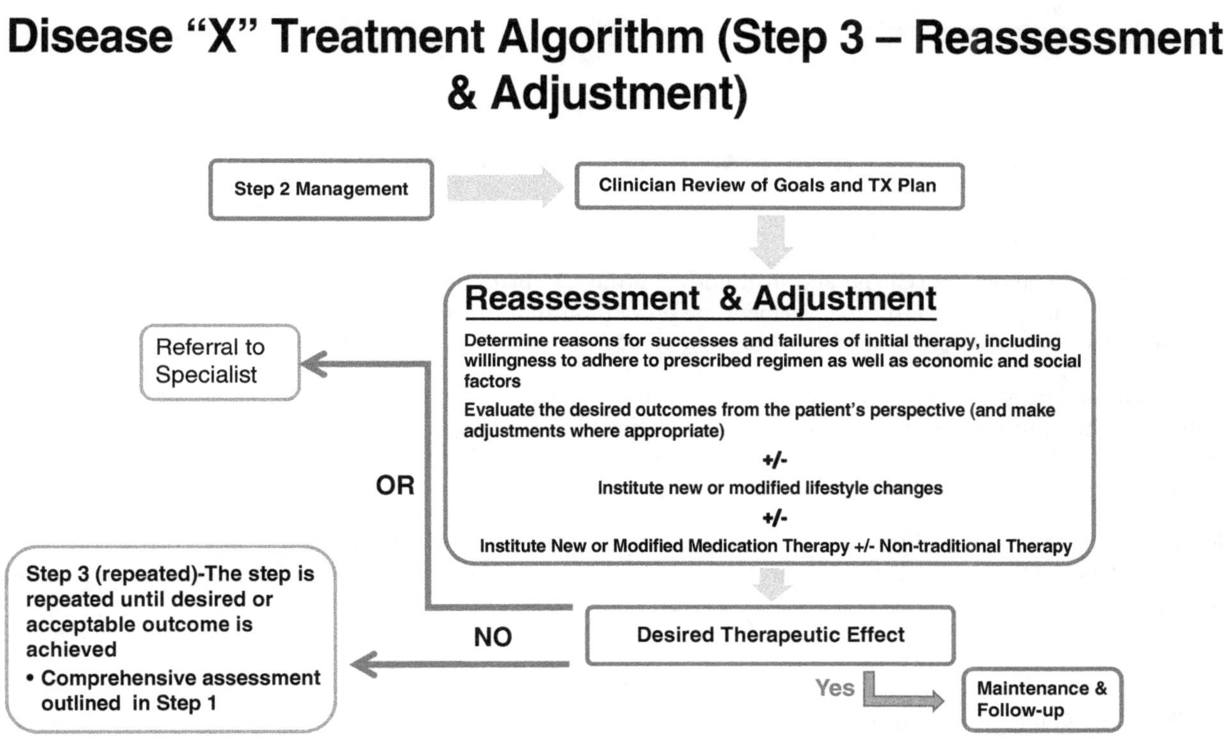

Figure 22-4. Step 3 Reassessment & Adjustment

Treatment Algorithm Summary

The purpose of a treatment algorithm is to improve and standardize the delivery of medical care. These algorithms can assist in standardizing the selection and application of a treatment regimen in a specific type of patient (with individual characteristics, concomitant disease states or receiving potentially interacting medications).

Thus, a treatment algorithm can help clinicians choose the best medication to treat a condition in a specific patient. As outlined, most treatment algorithms follow a series of basic steps.

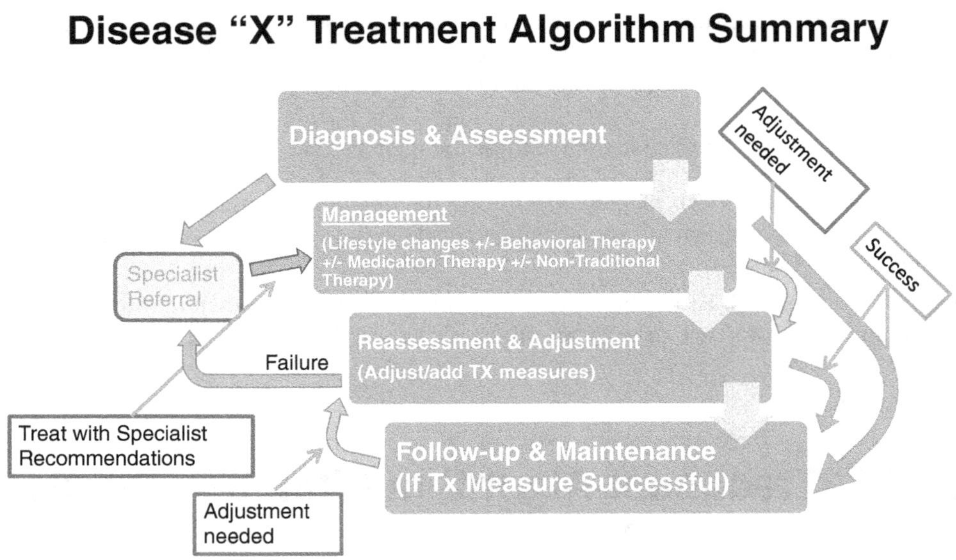

Figure 22-5. Treatment Algorithm Summary

Integrating New Scientific Knowledge into Existing Treatment Protocols

Clinical practice guidelines (CPGs) and institutional protocols incorporate the best available evidence "at a given point in time" for the diagnosis, management, or prevention of a disease into a single document for health care providers. However, these guidelines may lose their clinical relevance as they age or newer research emerges.

The quality and relevance of each practice guideline is improved by adopting standard approaches for developing the initial guideline/protocol as well as reviewing and updating them on a regular basis. Implementing new and updating existing CPGs can improve quality and efficiency of patient care. The development and updating CPG process generally requires a multidisciplinary, multifaceted approach.

Each medical society has their own process for integrating new scientific knowledge into existing treatment protocols/CPGs. These same principles can also be applied by a general practitioner to the evaluation and application of study results into clinical practice.

Table 22-9. Integrating New Scientific Knowledge into Clinical Practice and Clinical Practice Guidelines

Step Number	Step	Comments
1	New evidence is Introduced	A clinical trial (or other study) provides evidence of a promising new treatment or new use for an existing treatment.
2	Evaluation of new evidence	The clinical pharmacist (for example) reviews and analyzes the clinical trial (***See the "Evaluation of Medical Information and Literature" section of this chapter for more information***).
3	Systematic literature review	A review of the existing medical literature is performed to determine if there are any additional studies that will confirm or refute the findings of the "new evidence" presented in the original clinical trial.

(Continued)

Step Number	Step	Comments
4	Formulate guideline recommendations	The clinician will formulate new guideline recommendations with both evidence-based and consensus-based evidence. Using this approach, systematic reviews serve as the evidentiary basis for drafting new clinical care principles. However, few guideline questions can be directly or completely altered by only considering the evidence presented by the systematic review. Interpretation and extrapolation of evidence is generally necessary. Thus, new guideline recommendations necessitate consensus among guideline panel members or peers.
5	Evaluating study quality and summarizing the strength of evidence and strength of recommendations	The clinician will evaluate the study quality (using pre-determined criteria), summarizing the strength of evidence and strength of recommendations (***concepts covered earlier in this chapter***).
6	Cost considerations	The clinician will assess the overall cost-effectiveness and cost-benefit of the new treatment measure.
7	Review process and Dissemination	After the newly drafted changes have been developed, they will be submitted for external review by experts (in that particular area of medicine) as well as submitted for peer review.
8	Acceptance	The guideline committee, pharmacy and therapeutics committee or group of professionals agree that the new treatment measure should be incorporated into the existing treatment guideline or treatment algorithm.
9	Development of quality measures	Processes will be developed to evaluate the impact of the new treatment measure.
10	Implementation of updated guideline or treatment algorithm	The existing clinical practice guideline or treatment algorithm will be updated. Other potential items to update include internet materials, treatment algorithms, summary guides, patient materials, etc.
11	Continued assessment and validation of the new treatment recommendation	The processes developed in the "Development of quality measures" step will be implemented and continually evaluated to assess the impact of the new guideline statement/treatment algorithm recommendation. Furthermore, the "new" treatment measure should be validated on a patient by patient basis since each patient may have unique characteristics (concomitant disease states, interacting medications) that can impact the success or failure of therapy.

PRACTICE QUESTIONS

1. A physician calls the pharmacy and asks about an experimental treatment for a patient; however, needs more information before prescribing the treatment. The physician also provides information regarding the patient. Which of the following should be the first action by the pharmacist?

   A. Clarify the question being asked
   B. Critically analyze information
   C. Formulate a clinically relevant response
   D. Search through primary reference sources
   E. Search through tertiary references sources

NAPLEX Question Reference

Drug Information chapter: end of chapter questions

NAPLEX Question Reference

Health Policy chapter: end of chapter questions

2. An example of secondary medical literature is which of the following?

   A. Goodman & Gilman's
   B. Harrison's principles of internal medicine
   C. JAMA
   D. Nature
   E. PubMed

3. Using the PP-ICONS method for evaluating a journal article, in which of the following would a diagnostic tool being evaluated be characterized?

   A. Comparison
   B. Intervention
   C. Population
   D. Problem
   E. Statistics

4. Which of the following has the highest level of evidence?

   A. Case-control study
   B. Case series
   C. Meta-analysis
   D. Randomized, controlled clinical trials
   E. Systematic review

5. A meta-analysis is the preferred study to address the clinical concepts for all of the following EXCEPT

   A. Clinical examination
   B. Disease Prevention
   C. Disease Prognosis
   D. Medication therapy
   E. Surgical Intervention

6. When evaluating a treatment guideline, a pharmacist notices that a medication has an evidence strength rating of 3. For the treatment of the disease state in question, the medication is best described as which of the following?

   A. Benefit >> risk
   B. Benefit > risk
   C. Benefit ≤ risk
   D. Benefit << risk
   E. Benefit and risk is not assessed in strength rating scales

7. All of the following are true with respect to medication therapy management (MTM) EXCEPT

   A. MTM can be performed via telemedicine technologies.
   B. MTM is a comprehensive medication review.
   C. MTM is a covered benefit of Medicare Part B.
   D. MTM often results in therapeutic adjustments being made.
   E. MTM will assess the patient's overall health status.

8. An individual cohort study would have a level of evidence of which of the following?

   A. 1a
   B. 1c
   C. 2a
   D. 2b
   E. 3b

9. A treatment algorithm is best described as which of the following?

   A. A cost analysis tool
   B. A clinical decision tree
   C. A drug management tool
   D. A patient preference tool
   E. An assessment tool

10. A clinical pharmacist reads an article on a phase III clinical trial evaluating a new use for an existing medication. Assuming the trial was performed correctly, which of the following article components is most important when determining if the medication should be used in his patient?

   A. Analysis
   B. Assessment
   C. Assignment
   D. Extrapolation
   E. Interpretation

Answers and Explanations

1. **The correct answer is A.** Pharmacists commonly receive clinical questions that require a review of the medical literature. There is a series of steps that are needed to ensure that the most accurate and complete information is provided. These steps are as follows: Clarify the question being asked (choice A) so that the information provided accurately matches the request. Without clarification, it is possible that misinformation will be provided. The pharmacist will then obtain background information, perform an appropriate search of the medication literature (choices D and E) and then analyze the information (choice B). Finally the pharmacist will formulate a response (choice C), document the findings and then communicate the response to the clinician.

2. **The correct answer is E.** Drug information resources are classified as primary, secondary and tertiary sources. Primary sources (choices C and D) are authored by the original researcher and published in peer-reviewed journals, dissertations and conference proceedings. Secondary sources (choice E) are interpretations and evaluations derived "directly" from or referring to the primary source literature source. Secondary sources consist of abstracting and indexing services, review of a primary journal article, systematic reviews, meta-analysis, and clinical practice guidelines. Tertiary sources consist of both primary and secondary sources. Common examples include medical text books (choices A and B) and medical newspapers.

3. **The correct answer is B.** The PP-ICONS approach is a rapid method to screen an article for both validity and clinical relevance. The intervention includes the diagnostic tool, prognostic factor, or exposure that is being evaluated in the clinical trial. The comparison (choice A) is what the intervention is measured against. Population (choice C) is the study and control group in the study. The problem (choice D) is the clinical condition or treatment measure being evaluated. Statistics (choice E) are the tools used to calculate the findings.

4. **The correct answer is C.** A meta-analysis critically and comprehensively examines numerous randomized controlled clinical trials (derived from a systematic review) on a particular treatment regimen or disease state and then combines the results using accepted statistical methodology as if they were from one large study. It is considered to have the highest level of evidence. Study designs are listed in order of importance and strength of the evidence: meta-analysis (choice C), systematic reviews (choice E), randomized controlled trials (choice D), cohort studies, case-control studies (choice A), case series (choice B) and case reports, editorials and expert opinions and animal research/laboratory studies.

5. **The correct answer is C.** A meta-analysis examines numerous randomized controlled clinical trials (RCT) on a particular treatment regimen or disease state and then combines the results using accepted statistical methodology as if they were from one large study. Meta-analyses are the best source of clinical information for ALL studies involving treatment measures, diagnostic tests, disease prevention and clinical examination techniques. However, an RCT would not be performed to assess the prognosis of a given disease. Thus a meta-analysis would not be applicable. In this case, a cohort study, which is an observational trial that follows patients forward in time, would be the best study type to evaluate this data.

6. **The correct answer is C.** Most evidenced-based treatment guidelines not only grade the level of supporting evidence but also grade the strength of the recommendation. The recommendation "strength" is generally based on both the level of supporting evidence as well as a risk-benefit analysis. Choice A has a strength rating of "A" or "1". Choice B has a strength rating of "B" or "2". Choice C has a strength rating of "C" or "3". Choice D has a strength rating of "D" or "4".

7. **The correct answer is choice C.** Medication therapy management (MTM) is defined as a service or group of services generally provided by a pharmacist to optimize therapeutic outcomes for an individual patient. MTM services include medication therapy reviews, pharmacotherapy consults, health and wellness programs as well as other clinical services. All of the answer choices are true statements EXCEPT choice C. MTM is a covered benefit of Medicare part D.

8. **The correct answer is D.** The most comprehensive evidence grading system is the Oxford (UK) Centre for Evidence-based Medicine (CEBM). It provides 'Levels' of evidence for claims about prognosis, diagnosis, treatment benefits, treatment harms, and screening. In order of appearance in the answer choices: 1a = Systematic reviews (with homogeneity) of randomized controlled trials; 1c = All or none randomized controlled trials; 2a = Systematic reviews (with homogeneity) of cohort studies; 2b = Individual cohort study or low quality randomized controlled trials (e.g. <80% follow-up) and 3b = Individual Case-Control Study.

9. **The correct answer is B.** Medical algorithms are designed to help promote medical decision making. These decisions occur in almost every area of medicine, including medical test selection, diagnosis (choice E), therapy (choice C), and prognosis. Additional factors to include are drug cost (choice A) and patient preference (choice D). Incorporating all of these factors and concepts together, medical algorithms are essentially clinical decision tree (choice B) approaches to medical treatment. Thus the primary purpose of a medical algorithm is to standardize medical decisions, reduce the potential for errors and improve patient outcomes.

10. **The correct answer is D.** There are 5 general components of a clinical trial. Of these components, extrapolation (final portion of the conclusion) is the part of the study needed to determine if the information provided is applicable to their patient. In other words, the extrapolation section draws conclusions about the meaning of the study for individuals or situations NOT included in the study. Analysis (choice A) includes the study evaluation tools, materials and methods. Assessment (choice B) is where the results of the study and the control groups are calculated. Assignment (choice C) is responsible for selecting individuals for study and control groups based on the study hypothesis and objectives. Interpretation (choice E) is the first part of the conclusion. Here the authors will draw conclusions about the meaning of the differences found between the study and control groups for those in the study.

Clinical Pathophysiology 23

Learning Objectives

- ❑ Show proficiency in the clinical application of pathophysiological principles

Dispensing medications to treat a disease is one of the primary responsibilities of a pharmacist. Each human disease is associated with some type of functional change resulting from a pathophysiological abnormality.

Although most pharmacists are not going to diagnose a disease, they should have an understanding of the basic and clinical pathophysiological characteristics of the most commonly encountered diseases in the pharmacy setting and be able to identify the impact of drug therapy on various disease states.

This chapter will focus on basic pathophysiological principles. Kaplan's *NAPLEX Strategies, Practice, and Review* book provides a good high-yield overview of the pathophysiological characteristics of diseases most commonly encountered by pharmacists.

CLINICAL APPLICATION OF PATHOPHYSIOLOGICAL PRINCIPLES

Pharmacists should have an understanding of basic pathophysiological principles, including causes of cellular injury, cellular adaptive responses to injury, and cellular alterations of injury. Furthermore, the clinical pharmacist should recognize the general pathological principles related to medical conditions commonly requiring pharmacist intervention, such as hypertension, dyslipidemia, asthma, and diabetes mellitus. Each of these disease states can be found in the Kaplan's NAPLEX Review book.

- Additional information on the pathological principles for common medical conditions can be found throughout the NAPLEX text.
- The "Review of Therapeutics" section of Kaplan's NAPLEX Review book covers each of the major body systems, as well as major disease processes. Within each body system/disease process are commonly encountered disease states. In cardiovascular disorders, for example, hypertension, dyslipidemia, and heart failure are discussed. Disease state definitions (including pathological principles), diagnostic characteristics, and disease state signs and symptoms are covered first (prior to a discussion on clinical practice guidelines and the individual pharmacological agents used in each of these conditions).

> **NAPLEX Reference**
>
> **Cardiovascular, Endocrine, and Respiratory chapters:**
>
> "Hypertension"
> "Dyslipidemia"
> "Heart Failure"
> "Diabetes"
> "Asthma"

Overview of Pathology

Pathology is the study of the essential nature of disease, including symptoms/signs, pathogenesis, complications, and morphologic consequences including structural and functional alterations in cells, tissues, and organs. It is also the study of all aspects of the disease process focusing on the pathogenesis leading to classical structural changes (gross and histopathology) and molecular alterations.

The **etiology** (cause) of a disease may be genetic or environmental. The **pathogenesis** of a disease defines the temporal sequence and the patterns of cellular injury that lead to disease. **Morphologic** changes of the disease process include both gross changes and microscopic changes. The **clinical significance** of a disease relates to its signs and symptoms, disease course including complications, and prognosis.

Methods Used

Gross examination of organs on exam questions has 2 major components: identifying the organ and identifying the pathology. Useful gross features include consideration of size, shape, consistency, and color.

In light **microscopic examination of tissue, hematoxylin and eosin (H&E)** is considered the gold standard stain and is used routinely in the initial microscopic examination of pathologic specimens.

Table 23-1. Structures Stained by Hematoxylin and Eosin

Hematoxylin	Eosin
Stains blue to purple	Stains pink to red
• Nuclei	• Cytoplasm
• Nucleoli	• Collagen
• Bacteria	• Fibrin
• Calcium	• RBCs
	• Thyroid colloid

The common denominator of the features shown is that hematoxylin binds nucleic acids and calcium salts, while eosin stains the majority of proteins (both extracellular and intracellular).

Other histochemical stains (chemical reactions): Prussian blue (stains iron), Congo red (stains amyloid), acid-fast (Ziehl-Neelsen, Fite; stains acid-fast bacilli), periodic acid-Schiff (PAS, stains high carbohydrate content molecules), Gram stain (stains bacteria), trichrome (stains cells and connective tissue), and reticulin (stains collagen type III molecules).

Immunohistochemical (antibody) stains include cytokeratin (stains epithelial cells), vimentin (stains cells of mesenchymal origin except the 3 muscle types; stains many sarcomas), desmin (stains smooth, cardiac, and skeletal myosin), prostate specific antigen, and many others.

Ancillary techniques include **immunofluorescence microscopy (IFM)**, typically used for renal and autoimmune disease, and **transmission electron microscopy (EM)**, used for renal disease, neoplasms, infections, and genetic disorders.

Molecular techniques include protein electrophoresis, Southern and Western blots, polymerase chain reaction (PCR), and cytogenetic analysis (karyotyping, in situ hybridization studies).

Cellular Injury and Adaptation

Hypoxia is the most common cause of injury; it occurs when lack of oxygen prevents the cell from synthesizing sufficient ATP by aerobic oxidation. Major mechanisms leading to hypoxia are ischemia, cardiopulmonary failure, and decreased oxygen-carrying capacity of the blood (e.g., anemia). **Ischemia**, due to a loss of blood supply, is the most common cause of hypoxia and is typically related to decreased arterial flow or decreased venous outflow (e.g., atherosclerosis, thrombus, thromboembolus).

Pathogens (viruses, bacteria, parasites, fungi, and prions) can injure the body by direct infection of cells, production of toxins, or host inflammatory response.

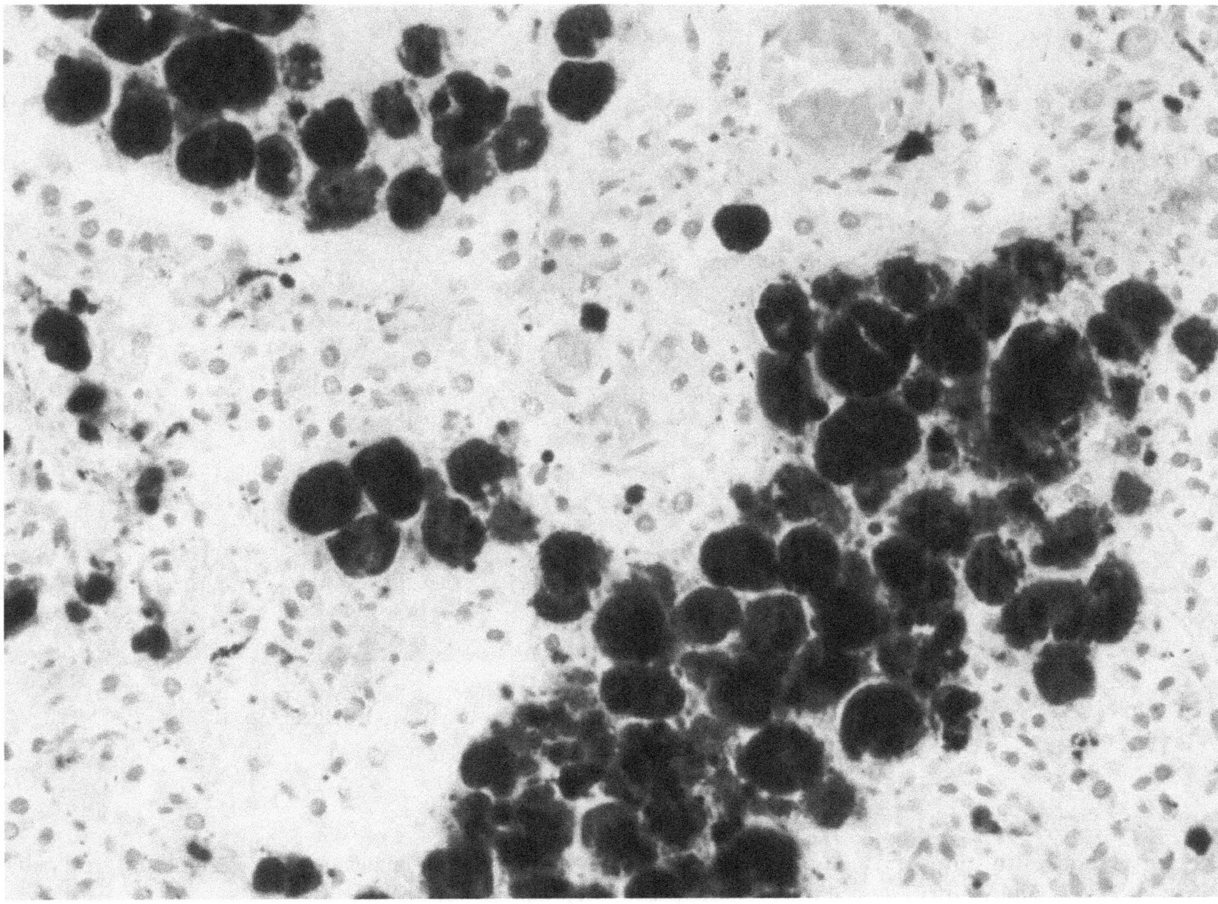

Figure 23-1. Prussian Blue Stain Showing Hemosiderin, Which Results from RBC Breakdown Within Macrophages

Immunologic dysfunction includes hypersensitivity reactions and autoimmune diseases.

Congenital disorders are inherited genetic mutations (e.g., inborn errors of metabolism).

Chemical injury can occur with drugs, poisons (cyanide, arsenic, mercury, etc.), pollution, occupational exposure (CCl_4, asbestos, carbon monoxide, etc.), and social/lifestyle choices (alcohol, smoking, IV drug abuse, etc.)

Physical forms of injury include trauma (blunt/penetrating/crush injuries, gunshot wounds, etc.), burns, frostbite, radiation, and pressure changes.

Nutritional or Vitamin Imbalance

- **Inadequate calorie/protein intake** can cause marasmus (decrease in total caloric intake), and kwashiorkor (decrease in total protein intake).
- **Excess caloric intake** can cause obesity (second leading cause of premature preventable death in the United States) and atherosclerosis.
- **Vitamin deficiencies** can be seen with vitamin A (night blindness, squamous metaplasia, immune deficiency), vitamin C (scurvy), vitamin D (rickets and osteomalacia), vitamin K (bleeding diathesis), vitamin B12 (megaloblastic anemia, neuropathy, and spinal cord degeneration), folate (megaloblastic anemia and neural tube defects), and niacin (pellagra [diarrhea, dermatitis, and dementia]).
- **Hypervitaminosis** is less commonly a problem but can result in tissue specific abnormalities.

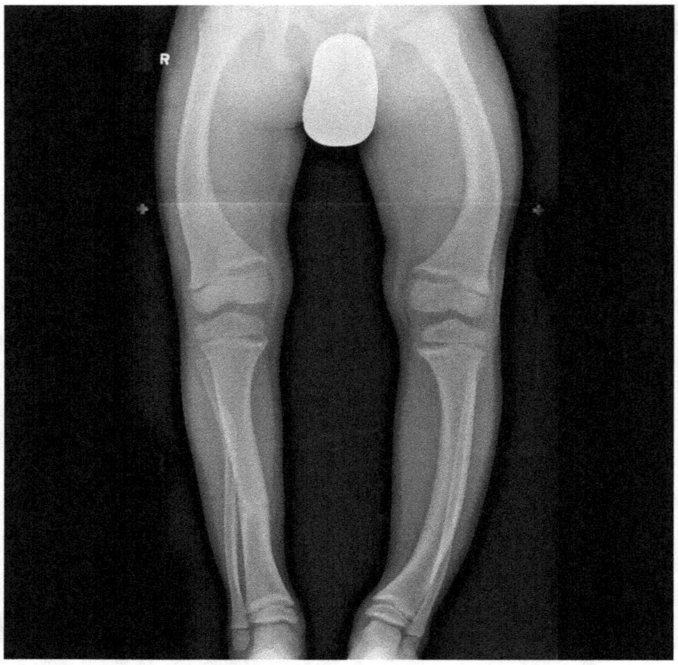

Figure 23-2. Radiograph of a Child with Rickets Shows Bowed Legs

Cellular Changes During Injury

Cellular responses to injury include adaptation (hypertrophy or atrophy, hyperplasia or metaplasia), reversible injury, and irreversible injury and cell death (necrosis, apoptosis, or necroptosis).

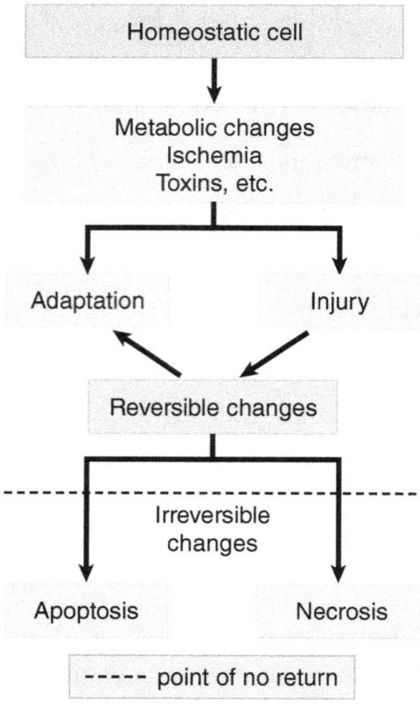

Figure 23-3. Cellular Response to Stress and Injurious Stimuli

The **cellular response to injury depends on several important factors**, including the type of injury, duration (including pattern) of injury, severity and intensity of injury, type of cell injured, the cell's metabolic state, and the cell's ability to adapt.

Note

Protective factors against free radicals include:

- Antioxidants
- Vitamins A, E, and C
- Superoxide dismutase
- Superoxide ⟶ hydrogen peroxide
- Glutathione peroxidase
- Hydroxyl ions or hydrogen peroxide ⟶ water
- Catalase

The **critical intracellular targets that are susceptible to injury** are DNA, production of ATP via aerobic respiration, cell membranes, and protein synthesis.

Important mechanisms of cell injury are as follows:

- Damage to DNA, proteins, lipid membranes, and circulating lipids (LDL) can be caused by oxygen-derived free radicals, including superoxide anion ($O_2^{\bullet-}$), hydroxyl radical ($OH^{\bullet}$), and hydrogen peroxide (H_2O_2).
- ATP depletion: Several key biochemical pathways are dependent on ATP. Disruption of Na^+/K^+ or Ca^{++} pumps cause imbalances in solute concentrations. Additionally, ATP depletion increases anaerobic glycolysis that leads to a decrease in cellular pH. Chronic ATP depletion causes morphological and functional changes to the ER and ribosomes.
- Increased cell membrane permeability: Several defects can lead to movement of fluids into the cell, including formation of the membrane attack complex via complement, breakdown of Na^+/K^+ gradients (i.e., causing sodium to enter or potassium to leave the cell), etc.

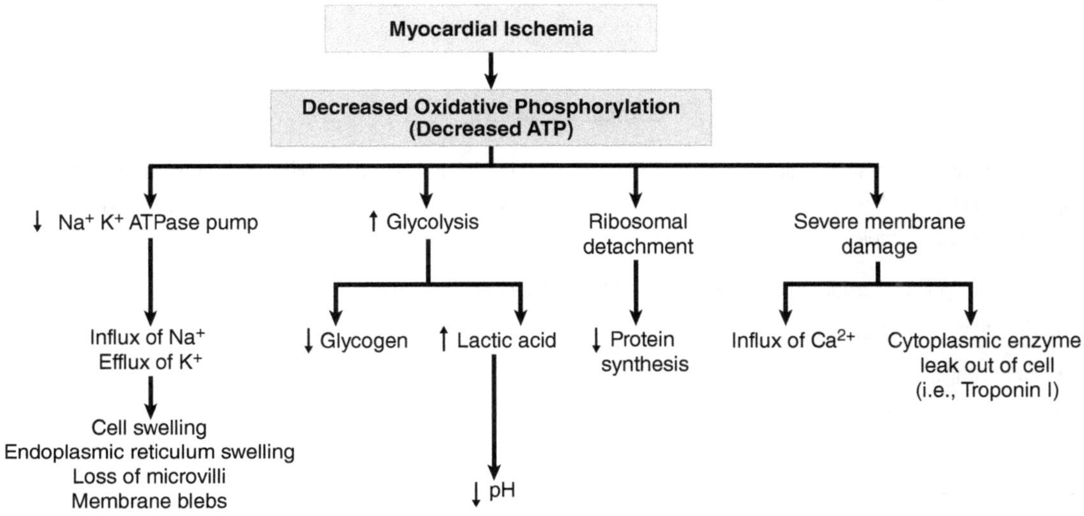

Figure 23-4. Classic Example of Cellular Injury Caused by Hypoxia

- Influx of calcium can cause problems because calcium is a second messenger, which can activate a wide spectrum of enzymes. These enzymes include proteases (protein breakdown), ATPases (contributes to ATP depletion), phospholipases (cell membrane injury), and endonucleases (DNA damage).
- Mitochondrial dysfunction causes decreased oxidative phosphorylation and ATP production, formation of mitochondrial permeability transition (MPT) channels, and release of cytochrome c (a trigger for apoptosis).

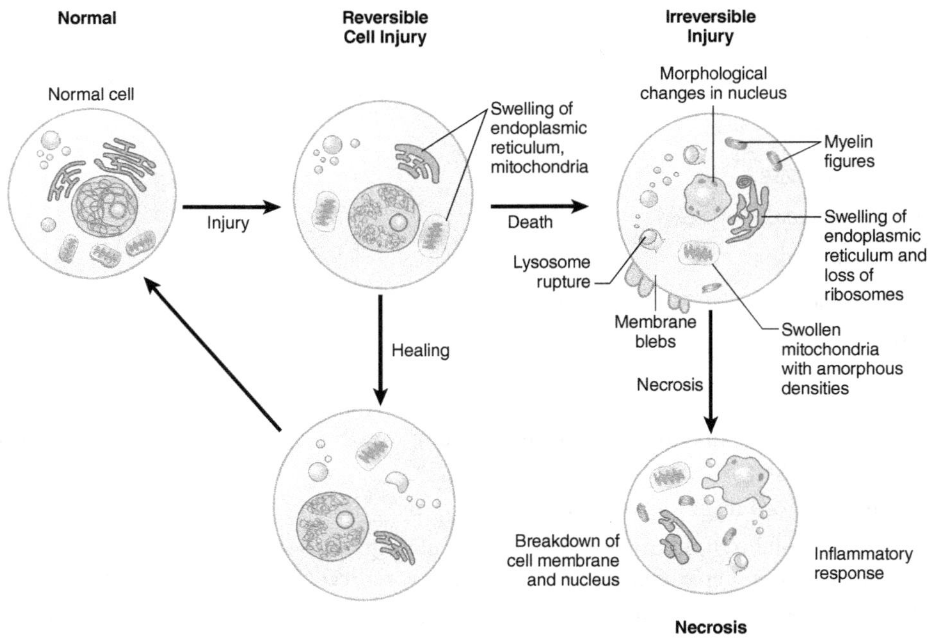

Figure 23-5. Cell Injury

Note

Reversible and irreversible changes represent a spectrum. Keep in mind that any of the reversible changes can become irreversible.

Clinical Correlate

The loss of membrane integrity (cell death) allows intracellular enzymes to leak out, which can then be measured in the blood. Detection of these proteins in the circulation serves as a clinical marker of cell death and organ injury. Clinically important examples:

- Myocardial injury: troponin (most specific), CPK-MB, lactate dehydrogenase (LDH)
- Hepatitis: transaminases
- Pancreatitis: amylase and lipase
- Biliary tract obstruction: alkaline phosphatase

Reversible cell injury:

- **Decreased synthesis of ATP** by oxidative phosphorylation.
- **Decreased function of Na^+/K^+ ATPase membrane pumps**, which in turn causes influx of Na^+ and water, efflux of K^+, cellular swelling (hydropic swelling), and swelling of the endoplasmic reticulum.

- The **switch to anaerobic glycolysis** results in depletion of cytoplasmic glycogen, increased lactic acid production, and decreased intracellular pH.
- **Decreased protein synthesis** leads to detachment of ribosomes from the rough endoplasmic reticulum.
- **Plasma-membrane blebs and myelin figures** may be seen.

Irreversible cell injury:

- **Severe membrane damage** plays a critical role in irreversible injury, allows a massive influx of calcium into the cell, and allows efflux of intracellular enzymes and proteins into the circulation.
- **Marked mitochondrial dysfunction** produces mitochondrial swelling, large densities seen within the mitochondrial matrix, irreparable damage of the oxidative phosphorylation pathway, and an inability to produce ATP.
- **Rupture of the lysosomes** causes release of lysosomal digestive enzymes into the cytosol and activation of acid hydrolases followed by autolysis.
- **Nuclear changes** can include pyknosis (degeneration and condensation of nuclear chromatin), karyorrhexis (nuclear fragmentation), and karyolysis (dissolution of the nucleus).

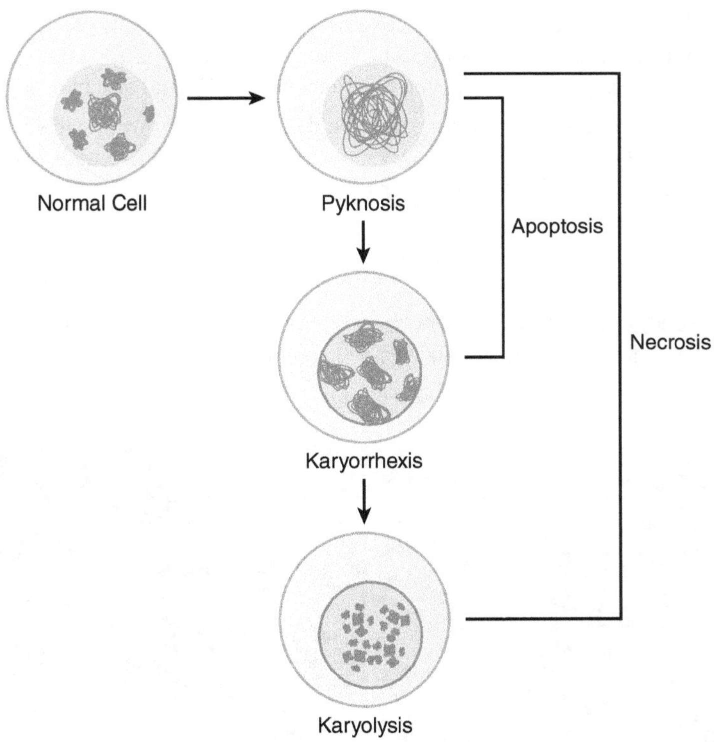

Figure 23-6. Nuclear Changes in Irreversible Cell Injury

Cell Death

Morphologic types of necrosis (cell death in living tissue, often with an inflammatory response) are as follows:

> **Note**
>
> Liquefaction by leukocyte enzymes is called suppuration, and the resultant fluid is called pus.

Bridge to Biochemistry

Damage to fat cells releases triglycerides. The triglycerides are broken down by the action of lipases to fatty acids. The fatty acids may associate with calcium and form calcium soaps (saponification).

- **Coagulative necrosis**, the most common form of necrosis, is most often due to ischemic injury (infarct). It is caused by the denaturing of proteins within the cytoplasm. Microscopic examination shows loss of the nucleus but preservation of cellular shape. Coagulative necrosis is common in most organs, including the heart, liver, and kidney, but not the brain.
- **Liquefaction necrosis** results from cellular destruction by hydrolytic enzymes, leading to autolysis (release of proteolytic enzymes from injured cells) and heterolysis (release of proteolytic enzymes from inflammatory cells). Liquefaction necrosis occurs in abscesses, brain infarcts, and pancreatic necrosis.
- **Caseous necrosis** is a combination of coagulation and liquefaction necrosis. The gross appearance is soft, friable, and "cheese-like." Caseous necrosis is characteristic of granulomatous diseases, including tuberculosis.
- **Fat necrosis** is caused by the action of lipases on adipocytes and is characteristic of acute pancreatitis. On gross examination fat necrosis has a chalky white appearance.
- **Fibrinoid necrosis** is a form of necrotic connective tissue that histologically resembles fibrin. On microscopic examination fibrinoid necrosis has an eosinophilic (pink) homogeneous appearance. It is often due to acute immunologic injury (e.g., hypersensitivity type reactions II and III) and vascular hypertensive damage.
- **Gangrenous necrosis** is a gross term used to describe dead tissue. Common sites of involvement include lower limbs, gallbladder, GI tract, and testes. Dry gangrene has coagulative necrosis for the microscopic pattern, while wet gangrene has liquefactive necrosis.

Note

Necrotic tissue within the body evokes an inflammatory response that removes the dead tissue and is followed by healing and tissue repair. Necrotic debris may also undergo dystrophic calcification.

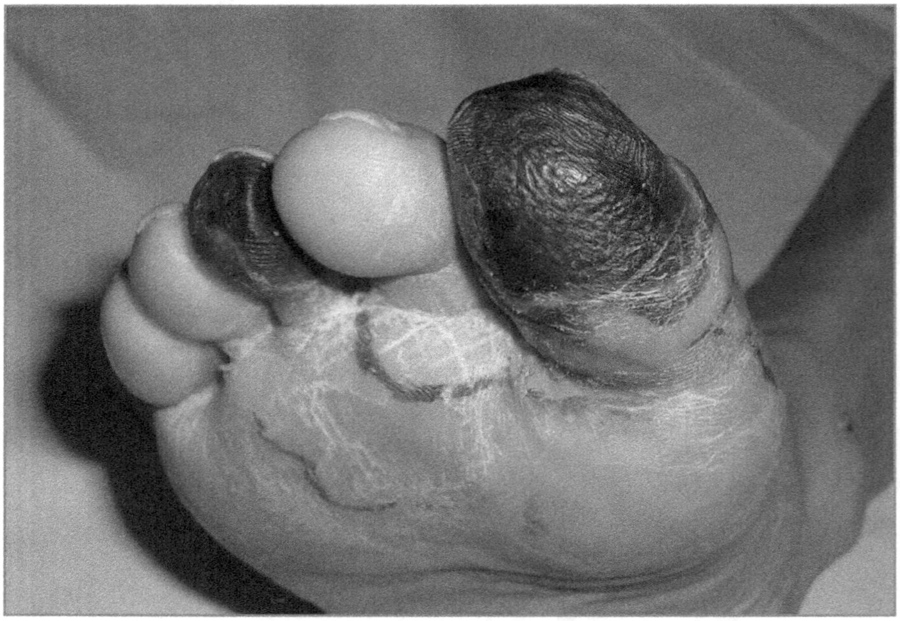

Figure 23-7. Gangrenous Necrosis Affects the First and Third Toes of a Diabetic Foot

Clinical Correlate

- If the cells in the interdigital space fail to undergo apoptosis, the fetus will be born with webbed hands or webbed feet, a condition known as *syndactyly*.
- Another example is the hormone-dependent apoptosis prior to menstruation; programmed cell death plays a role in endometrial gland morphological changes.

Apoptosis is a specialized form of programmed cell death without an inflammatory response. It is an active process regulated by proteins that often affects only single cells or small groups of cells.

- In **morphologic appearance,** the cell shrinks in size and has dense eosinophilic cytoplasm. Next, nuclear chromatin condensation (pyknosis) is seen that is followed by fragmentation of the nucleus (karyorrhexis).Cytoplasmic membrane blebs form next, leading eventually to a breakdown of the cell into fragments (apoptotic bodies). Phagocytosis of apoptotic bodies is by adjacent cells or macrophages.
- **Stimuli for apoptosis** include cell injury and DNA damage, lack of hormones, cytokines, or growth factors, and receptor-ligand signals such as Fas binding to the Fas ligand and tumor necrosis factor (TNF) binding to TNF receptor 1 (TNFR1).
- **Apoptosis is regulated by proteins.** The protein bcl-2 (which inhibits apoptosis) prevents release of cytochrome c from mitochondria and binds pro-apoptotic protease activating factor (Apaf-1). The protein p53 (which stimulates apoptosis) is elevated by DNA injury and arrests the cell cycle. If DNA repair is impossible, p53 stimulates apoptosis.
- **Execution of apoptosis** is mediated by a cascade of caspases (cysteine aspartic acid proteases). The caspases digest nuclear and cytoskeletal proteins and also activate endonucleases.
- **Physiologic examples of apoptosis** include embryogenesis (organogenesis and development), hormone-dependent apoptosis (menstrual cycle), thymus (selective death of lymphocytes).
- **Pathologic examples of apoptosis** include viral diseases (viral hepatitis [Councilman body]), graft-versus-host disease, and cystic fibrosis (duct obstruction and pancreatic atrophy).

Serum enzyme markers of cell damage include aspartate aminotransferase (AST) (liver injury), alanine aminotransferase (ALT) (liver injury), creatine kinase (CK-MB) (heart injury), and amylase and lipase (pancreatic injury; amylase also rises with salivary gland injury).

Clinical Correlate

Graft-versus-host disease (GVHD) is an example of apoptosis which occurs in allogeneic hematopoietic stem cell transplant recipients. The transplanted marrow has cytotoxic T-cells which recognize the new host proteins (usually HLA) as foreign. Organs typically involved include the skin, mucosa, liver, and GI tract. The histologic hallmark of GVHD is apoptosis.

Cellular Adaptive Responses to Injury

In general, cellular adaptation is a potentially reversible change in response to the environment.

Atrophy is a decrease in cell/organ size and functional ability. Causes of atrophy include decreased workload/disuse (immobilization); ischemia (atherosclerosis); lack of hormonal or neural stimulation, malnutrition, and aging.

Light microscopic examination shows small shrunken cells with lipofuscin granules. Electron microscopy shows decreased intracellular components and autophagosomes.

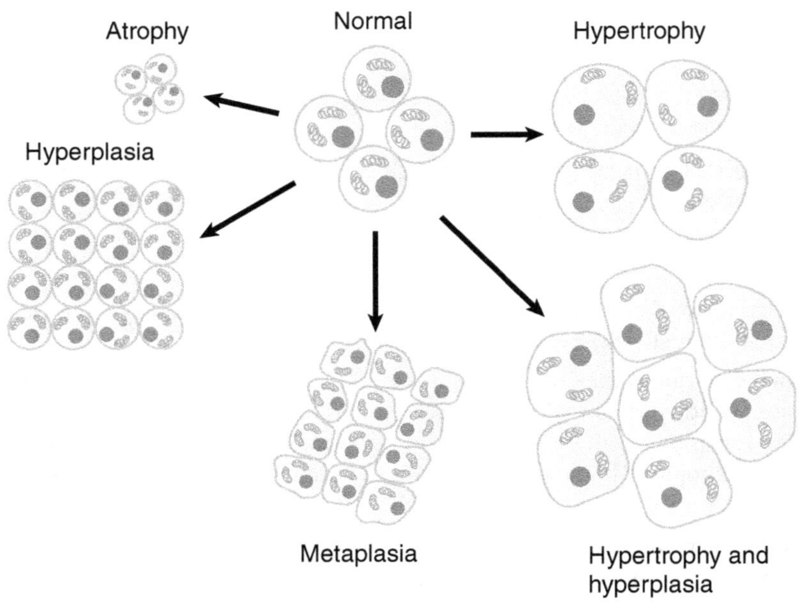

Figure 23-8. Cellular Adaptive Responses to Cell Injury

Hypertrophy is an increase in cell size and functional ability due to increased synthesis of intracellular components.

Causes of hypertrophy include:

- Increased mechanical demand can be physiologic (striated muscle of weight lifters) or pathologic (cardiac muscle in hypertension).
- Increased endocrine stimulation plays a role in puberty (growth hormone, androgens/estrogens, etc.), gravid uterus (estrogen), and lactating breast (prolactin and estrogen).

Hypertrophy is mediated by growth factors, cytokines, and other trophic stimuli and leads to increased expression of genes and increased protein synthesis.

Hypertrophy and hyperplasia often occur together.

Clinical Correlate

Residence at high altitude, where oxygen content of air is relatively low, leads to compensatory hyperplasia of red blood cell precursors in the bone marrow and an increase in the number of circulating red blood cells (secondary polycythemia).

Hyperplasia is an increase in the number of cells in a tissue or organ. Some cell types are unable to exhibit hyperplasia (e.g., nerve, cardiac, skeletal muscle cells).

- Physiologic causes of hyperplasia include compensatory mechanisms (e.g., after partial hepatectomy), hormonal stimulation (e.g., breast development at puberty), and antigenic stimulation (e.g., lymphoid hyperplasia).
- Pathologic causes of hyperplasia include endometrial hyperplasia and prostatic hyperplasia of aging.

Hyperplasia is mediated by growth factors, cytokines, and other trophic stimuli; increased expression of growth-promoting genes (proto-oncogenes); and increased DNA synthesis and cell division.

Clinical Correlate

Barrett's esophagus is a classic example of metaplasia. The esophageal epithelium is normally squamous, but it undergoes a change to intestinal epithelium (columnar) when it is under constant contact with gastric acid.

Metaplasia is a reversible change of one fully differentiated cell type to another, usually in response to irritation. It has been suggested that the replacement cell is better able to tolerate the environmental stresses. For example, bronchial epithelium undergoes squamous metaplasia in response to the chronic irritation of tobacco smoke.

The proposed mechanism is that the reserve cells (or stem cells) of the irritated tissue differentiate into a more protective cell type due to the influence of growth factors, cytokines, and matrix components.

Other Cellular Alterations During Injury

Pathologic Accumulations

- **Lipids** that can accumulate intracellularly include triglycerides (e.g., fatty change in liver cells), cholesterol (e.g., atherosclerosis, xanthomas), and complex lipids (e.g., sphingolipid accumulation).
- **Proteins** can accumulate in proximal renal tubules in proteinuria and can form Russell bodies (intracytoplasmic accumulation of immunoglobulins) in plasma cells.
- **Glycogen storage diseases**
- **Exogenous pigments** include anthracotic pigmentation of the lung (secondary to the inhalation of carbon dust), tattoos, and lead that has been ingested (e.g., gingival lead line, renal tubular lead deposits).

Endogenous Pigments

- **Lipofuscin** is a wear-and-tear pigment that is seen as perinuclear yellow-brown pigment. It is due to indigestible material within lysosomes and is common in the liver and heart.
- **Melanin** is a black-brown pigment derived from tyrosine found in melanocytes and substantia nigra.
- **Hemosiderin** is a golden yellow-brown granular pigment found in areas of hemorrhage or bruises. Systemic iron overload can lead to hemosiderosis (increase in total body iron stores without tissue injury) or hemochromatosis (increase in total body iron stores with tissue injury). Prussian blue stain can identify the iron in the hemosiderin.
- **Bilirubin** accumulates in newborns in the basal ganglia, causing permanent damage (kernicterus).

Hyaline change is a nonspecific term used to describe any intracellular or extracellular alteration that has a pink homogenous appearance (proteins) on H&E stains.

- Examples of **intracellular hyaline** include renal proximal tubule protein reabsorption droplets, Russell bodies, and alcoholic hyaline.
- Examples of **extracellular hyaline** include hyaline arteriolosclerosis, amyloid, and hyaline membrane disease of the newborn.

Pathologic Forms of Calcification

- **Dystrophic calcification** is the precipitation of calcium phosphate in dying or necrotic tissues. Examples include fat necrosis (saponification), psammoma bodies (laminated calcifications that occur in meningiomas and papillary carcinomas of the thyroid and ovary), Mönckeberg medial calcific sclerosis in arterial walls, and atherosclerotic plaques.
- **Metastatic calcification** is the precipitation of calcium phosphate in normal tissue due to hypercalcemia (supersaturated solution). The many causes include hyperparathyroidism, parathyroid adenomas, renal failure, paraneoplastic syndrome, vitamin D intoxication, milk-alkali syndrome, sarcoidosis, Paget disease, multiple myeloma, metastatic cancer to the bone. The calcifications are located in the interstitial tissues of the stomach, kidneys, lungs, and blood vessels.

Inflammation

Acute inflammation is an immediate response to injury or infection, which is part of innate immunity.

- Short duration in normal host
- Cardinal signs of inflammation include rubor (redness); calor (heat); tumor (swelling); dolor (pain); functio laesa (loss of function).

The important components of acute inflammation are hemodynamic changes, **neutrophils**, and chemical mediators.

Hemodynamic Changes

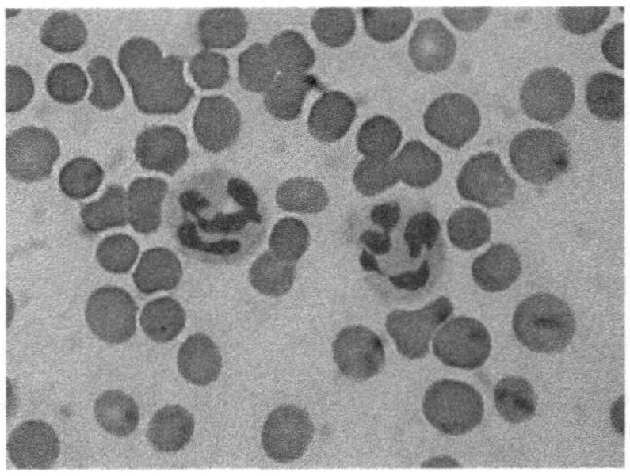

Lobed nucleus, small granules Neutrophil
Source: commons.wikimedia.org (Mgiganteus)

- Initial transient vasoconstriction
- Massive vasodilatation mediated by histamine, bradykinin, and prostaglandins
- Increased vascular permeability
  - Chemical mediators of increased permeability include vasoactive amines (histamine and serotonin), bradykinin (an end-product of the kinin cascade), leukotrienes (e.g., LTC4, LTD4, LTE4).
  - The mechanism of increased vascular permeability involves endothelial cell and pericyte contraction; direct endothelial cell injury; and leukocyte injury of endothelium.
- Blood flow slows (stasis) due to increased viscosity, allows neutrophils to marginate

Neutrophils

Clinical Correlate

- A normal mature neutrophil has a segmented nucleus (3–4 segments).
- Hypersegmented neutrophils (>5 segments) are thought to be pathognomonic of the class of anemias called megaloblastic anemias (vitamin B12 or folate deficiencies).

- Life span in tissue 1–2 days
- Synonyms: segmented neutrophils, polymorphonuclear leukocytes (PMN)
- Primary (azurophilic) granules contain myeloperoxidase, phospholipase A2, lysozyme (damages bacterial cell walls by catalyzing hydrolysis of 1,4-beta-linkages), and acid hydrolases. Also present are elastase, defensins (microbicidal peptides active against many gram-negative and gram-positive bacteria, fungi, and enveloped viruses), and bactericidal permeability increasing protein (BPI).
- Secondary (specific) granules contain phospholipase A2, lysozyme, leukocyte alkaline phosphatase (LAP), collagenase, lactoferrin (chelates iron), and vitamin B12-binding proteins.
- **Macrophages** (life span in tissue compartment is 60–120 days) have acid hydrolases, elastase, and collagenase.

Neutrophil margination and adhesion. Adhesion is mediated by complementary molecules on the surface of neutrophils and endothelium.

Note

Selectins: weak binding; initiate rolling

Integrins: stable binding and adhesion

- In **step 1**, the endothelial cells at sites of inflammation have increased expression of *E-selectin* and *P-selectin.*
- In **step 2**, neutrophils weakly bind to the endothelial selectins and roll along the surface.
- In **step 3**, neutrophils are stimulated by chemokines to express their integrins.
- In **step 4**, binding of the integrins to cellular adhesion molecules (ICAM-1 and VCAM-1) allows the neutrophils to firmly adhere to the endothelial cell.

Table 23-2. Selectin and Integrin Distribution in the Endothelium and Leukocyte

	Endothelium	Leukocyte
Selectins	P-Selectin	Sialyl-Lewis X & PSGL-1
	E-Selectin	Sialyl-Lewis X & PSGL-1
	GlyCam-1/CD34	L-Selectin
Integrins	ICAM-1	LFA-1 & MAC-1
	VCAM-1	VLA-4

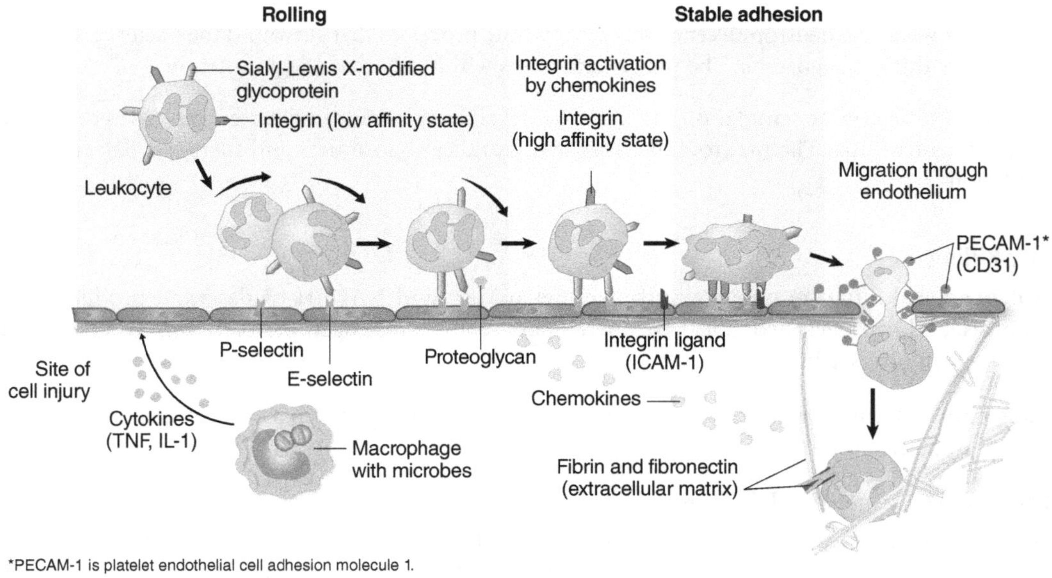

Figure 23-9. Adhesion and Migration

Clinical Correlate

Leukocyte Adhesion Deficiency Type I

- Autosomal recessive
- Deficiency of β2 integrin subunit (CD18)
- Recurrent bacterial infection
- Delay in umbilical cord sloughing

Modulation of adhesion molecules in inflammation occurs as follows. The fastest step involves redistribution of adhesion molecules to the surface; for example, P-selectin is normally present in the Weibel-Palade bodies of endothelial cells and can be mobilized to the cell surface by exposure to inflammatory mediators such as histamine and thrombin.

- Additionally, synthesis of adhesion molecules occurs. For example, proinflammatory cytokines IL-1 and TNF induce production of E-selectin, ICAM-1, and VCAM-1 in endothelial cells.
- There can also be increased binding affinity, as when chemotactic agents cause a conformational change in the leukocyte integrin LFA-1, which is converted to a high-affinity binding state.

Defects in adhesion can be seen in diabetes mellitus, corticosteroid use, acute alcohol intoxication, and leukocyte adhesion deficiency (autosomal recessive condition with recurrent bacterial infections).

In **emigration (diapedesis),** leukocytes emigrate from the vasculature (postcapillary venule) by extending pseudopods between the endothelial cells. They then move between the endothelial cells, migrating through the basement membrane toward the inflammatory stimulus.

Chemotaxis is the attraction of cells toward a chemical mediator that is released in the area of inflammation. Important chemotactic factors for neutrophils include bacterial products such as *N*-formyl-methionine and host derived molecules such as leukotriene B4 (LTB4), complement system product C5a, and α-chemokines (IL-8).

Phagocytosis and degranulation. Opsonins coat microbes to enhance their detection and phagocytosis. Important opsonins include the Fc portion of IgG isotypes, complement system product C3b, and plasma proteins such as collectins (which bind to bacterial cell walls).

Engulfment occurs when the neutrophil sends out cytoplasmic processes that surround the bacteria. The bacteria are then internalized within a phagosome. The phagosome fuses with lysosomes (degranulation).

Defects in phagocytosis and degranulation include Chédiak-Higashi syndrome, an autosomal recessive condition characterized by neutropenia. The neutrophils have giant granules (lysosomes) and there is a defect in chemotaxis and degranulation.

Intracellular Killing

In oxygen-dependent killing, respiratory burst requires oxygen and NADPH oxidase and produces superoxide, hydroxyl radicals, and hydrogen peroxide. Myeloperoxidase requires hydrogen peroxide and halide (Cl–) and produces HOCl (hypochlorous acid).

Oxygen-independent killing involves lysozyme, lactoferrin, acid hydrolases, bactericidal permeability increasing protein (BPI), and defensins.

Deficiencies of oxygen-dependent killing include:

- Chronic granulomatous disease of childhood can be X-linked or autosomal recessive. It is characterized by a deficiency of NADPH oxidase, lack of superoxide and hydrogen peroxide, and recurrent bacterial infections with catalase-positive organisms (*S. aureus*). The nitroblue tetrazolium test will be negative.
- Myeloperoxidase deficiency is an autosomal recessive condition characterized by infections with *Candida*. In contrast to chronic granulomatous disease, the nitroblue tetrazolium test will be positive.

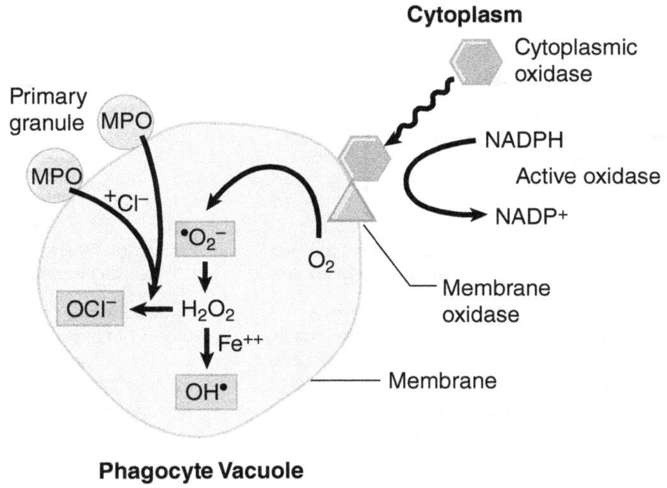

Figure 23-10. Oxygen-Dependent Killing

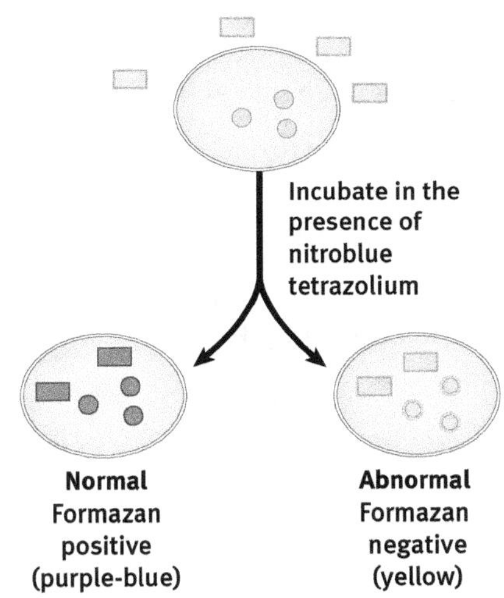

Figure 23-11. Nitroblue Tetrazolium Reduction

Chemical Mediators of Inflammation

Vasoactive Amines

- **Histamine** is produced by basophils, platelets, and mast cells. It causes vasodilation and increased vascular permeability. Triggers for release include IgE-mediated mast cell reactions, physical injury, anaphylatoxins (C3a and C5a), and cytokines (IL-1).
- **Serotonin** is produced by platelets and causes vasodilation and increased vascular permeability.

Kinin System

- Activated Hageman factor (factor XII) converts prekallikrein → kallikrein
- Kallikrein cleaves high molecular weight kininogen (HMWK) → bradykinin
- Effects of bradykinin include increased vascular permeability, pain, vasodilation, bronchoconstriction, and pain

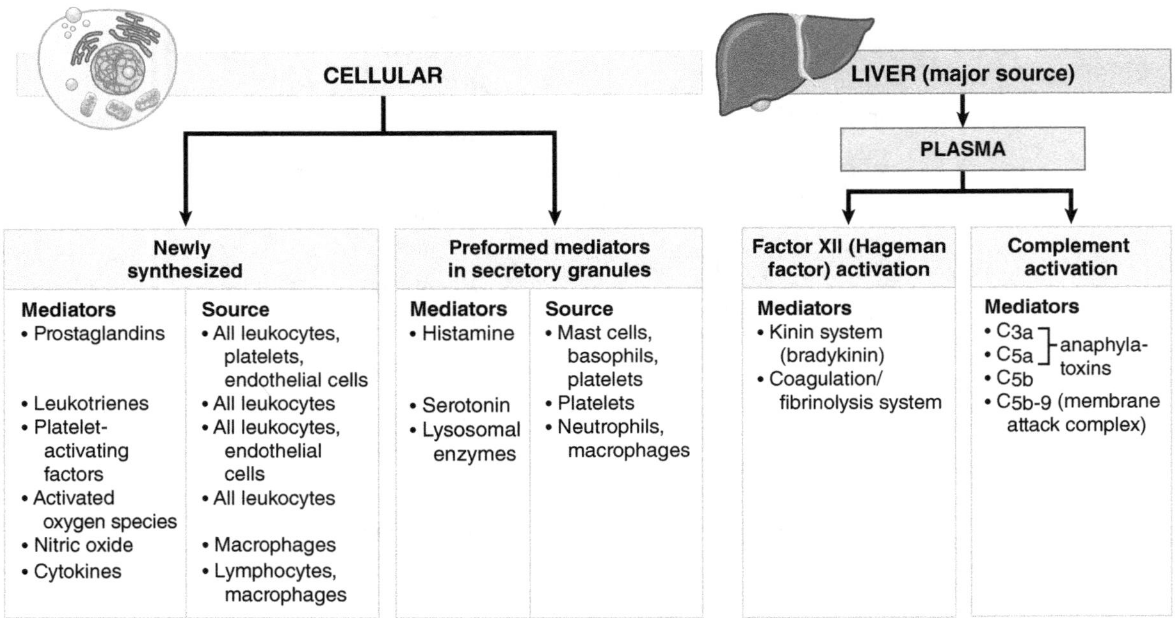

Figure 23-12. Sources of Chemical Mediators of Inflammation

Arachidonic Acid Products

> **In a Nutshell**
>
> **Mediators of Pain**
>
> - Bradykinin
> - Prostaglandins (E_2)

- **Cyclooxygenase pathway**
  - Thromboxane A2 is produced by platelets and causes vasoconstriction and platelet aggregation.
  - Prostacyclin (PGI2) is produced by vascular endothelium and causes vasodilation and inhibition of platelet aggregation.
  - Prostaglandin E_2 causes pain.
  - Prostaglandins PGE2, PGD2, and PGF2 cause vasodilatation.
- **Lipoxygenase pathway**

  Leukotriene B4 (LTB4) causes neutrophil chemotaxis, while leukotriene C4, D4, E4 cause vasoconstriction. Lipoxins are antiinflammatory products which inhibit neutrophil chemotaxis.

> **In a Nutshell**
>
> **Mediators of Fever**
>
> - Cytokines IL-1, IL-6, and TNF-α
> - Prostaglandins

Important products in the complement cascade include C5b-C9 (membrane attack complex), C3a,C5a (anaphylatoxins stimulate the release of histamine), C5a (leukocyte chemotactic factor), and C3b (opsonin for phagocytosis).

Cytokines

- IL-1 and TNF cause fever and induce acute phase reactants; enhance adhesion molecules; and stimulate and activate fibroblasts, endothelial cells, and neutrophils.
- IL-8 is a neutrophil chemoattractant produced by macrophages.

Four Outcomes of Acute Inflammation

- Complete resolution with regeneration
- Complete resolution with scarring
- Abscess formation
- Transition to chronic inflammation

Chronic Inflammation

Causes of chronic inflammation include the following:

- Following a bout of acute inflammation
- Persistent infections
- Infections with certain organisms, including viral infections, mycobacteria, parasitic infections, and fungal infections
- Autoimmune diseases
- Response to foreign material
- Response to malignant tumors

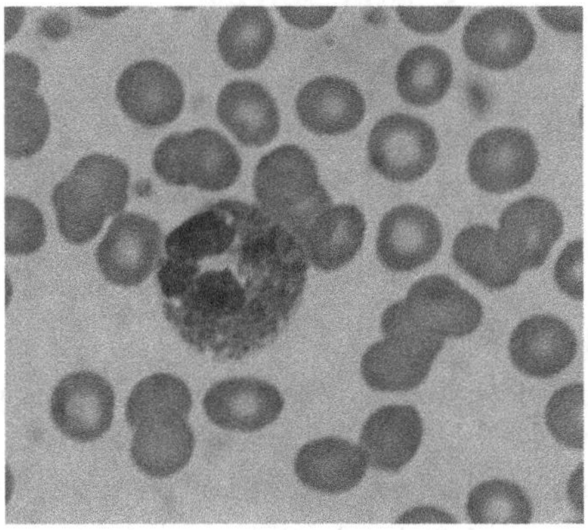

Figure 23-13. Bilobed nucleus, large granules (pink) Eosinophil
Source: commons.wikimedia.org (Bobjgalindo)

There are several **important cells** in chronic inflammation.

- **Macrophages** are derived from blood monocytes. Tissue-based macrophages (life span in connective tissue compartment is 60–120 days) are found in connective tissue (histiocyte), lung (pulmonary alveolar macrophages), liver (Kupffer cells), bone (osteoclasts), and brain (microglia). During

inflammation, circulating monocytes emigrate from the blood to the periphery and differentiate into macrophages.
  - Respond to chemotactic factors: C5a, MCP-1, MIP-1α, PDGF, TGF-β
  - Secrete a wide variety of active products (monokines)
  - May be modified into epithelioid cells in granulomatous processes
- **Lymphocytes** include B cells and plasma cells, as well as T cells. Lymphotaxin is the lymphocyte chemokine.
- **Eosinophils** play an important role in parasitic infections and IgE-mediated allergic reactions. The eosinophilic chemokine is eotaxin. Eosinophil granules contain major basic protein, which is toxic to parasites.
- **Basophils** contain similar chemical mediators as mast cells in their granules. Mast cells are present in high numbers in the lung and skin. Both basophils and mast cells play an important role in IgE-mediated reactions (allergies and anaphylaxis) and can release histamine.

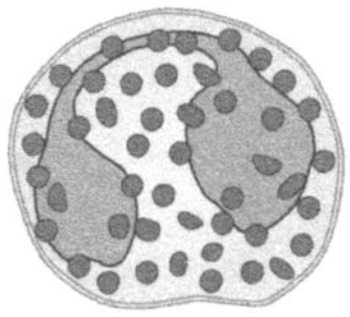

Figure 23-14. Bilobed nucleus, large granules (blue) Basophil

Chronic granulomatous inflammation is a specialized form of chronic inflammation characterized by small aggregates of modified macrophages (epithelioid cells and multinucleated giant cells) usually populated by CD4+ Th1 lymphocytes.

Clinical Correlate

Patients who are to be placed on tumor necrosis factor (TNF) inhibitors such as infliximab must undergo a PPD test before starting therapy. The PPD checks for latent tuberculosis infection, which can be reactivated by the TNF alpha inhibitor.

Composition of a granuloma is as follows:

- Epithelioid cells, located centrally, form when IFN-γ transforms macrophages to epithelioid cells. They are enlarged cells with abundant pink cytoplasm.
- Multinucleated giant cells, located centrally, are formed by the fusion of epithelioid cells. Types include Langhans-type giant cell (peripheral arrangement of nuclei) and foreign body type giant cell (haphazard arrangement of nuclei).
- Lymphocytes and plasma cells are present at the periphery.
- Central necrosis occurs in granulomata due to excessive enzymatic breakdown and is commonly seen in *Mycobacterium tuberculosis* infection as well as fungal infections and a few bacterial infections. Because of the public health risk of tuberculosis, necrotizing granulomas should be considered tuberculosis until proven otherwise.

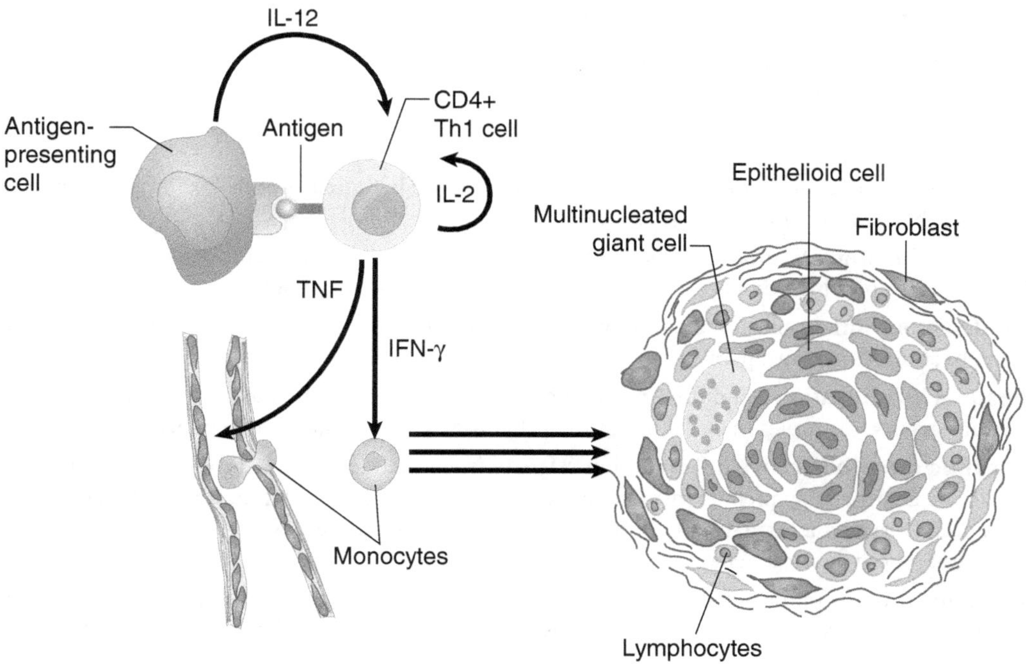

Figure 23-15. Granuloma Formation

Granulomatous diseases include tuberculosis (caseating granulomas), cat-scratch fever, syphilis, leprosy, fungal infections (e.g., coccidioidomycosis), parasitic infections (e.g., schistosomiasis), foreign bodies, beryllium, and sarcoidosis.

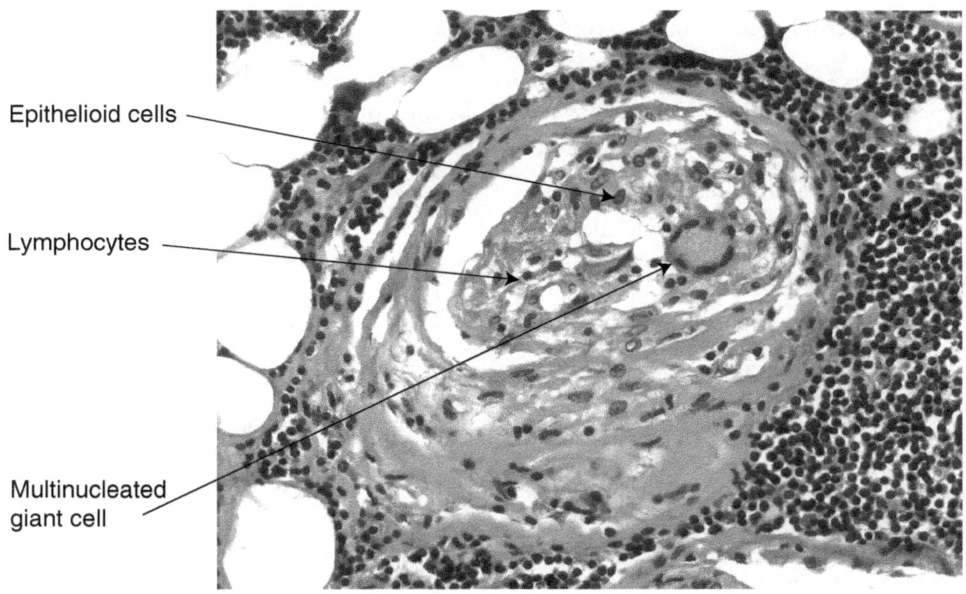

Figure 23-16. A Granuloma Is Seen in the Large, Poorly Circumscribed Nodule in the Center of the Field

Tissue Responses to Infectious Agents

Infectious diseases are very prevalent worldwide and are a major cause of morbidity and mortality. Infectious agents tend to have **tropism** for specific tissues and organs.

There are **6 major histologic patterns:**

- **Exudative inflammation** is an acute inflammatory response with neutrophils. Examples include bacterial meningitis, bronchopneumonia, and abscess.
- **Necrotizing inflammation** occurs when a virulent organism produces severe tissue damage and extensive cell death. Examples include necrotizing fasciitis and necrotizing pharyngitis.
- **Granulomatous inflammation.** Granulomatous response predominates with slow-growing organisms such as mycobacteria, fungi, and parasites.
- **Interstitial inflammation** is a diffuse mononuclear interstitial infiltrate that is a common response to viral infectious agents. Examples include myocarditis (Coxsackie virus) and viral hepatitis.
- **Cytopathic/cytoproliferative** inflammation refers to inflammation in which the infected/injured cell is altered. The changes may include intranuclear/cytoplasmic inclusions (cytomegalic inclusion disease, rabies [Negri body]); syncytia formation (respiratory syncytial virus and herpes virus); and apoptosis (Councilman body in viral hepatitis).
- **No inflammation.** An inflammatory response to microbes cannot occur in severely immunosuppressed individuals due to primary immunodeficiencies or acquired immunodeficient states (e.g., AIDS).

Tissue Repair

Regeneration and healing of damaged cells and tissues starts almost as soon as the inflammatory process begins. Tissue repair involves 5 overlapping processes:

- Hemostasis (coagulation, platelets)
- Inflammation (neutrophils, macrophages, lymphocytes, mast cells)
- Regeneration (stem cells and differentiated cells)
- Fibrosis (macrophages, granulation tissue [fibroblasts, angiogenesis], type III collagen)
- Remodeling (macrophages, fibroblasts, converting collagen III to I)

The extracellular matrix (ECM) is an important tissue scaffold with 2 forms, the interstitial matrix and the basement membrane (type IV collagen and laminin). There are 3 ECM components:

- Collagens and elastins
- Gels (proteoglycans and hyaluronan)
- Glycoproteins and cell adhesion molecules

Different tissues have different **regenerative** capacities.

- **Labile cells** (primarily stem cells) regenerate throughout life. Examples include surface epithelial cells (skin and mucosal lining cells), hematopoietic cells, stem cells, etc.
- **Stable cells** (stem cells and differentiated cells) replicate at a low level throughout life and have the capacity to divide if stimulated by some initiating event. Examples include hepatocytes, proximal tubule cells, endothelium, etc.
- **Permanent cells** (few stem cells and/or differentiated cells with the capacity to replicate) have a very low level of replicative capacity. Examples include neurons and cardiac muscle.

Scar formation occurs in a series of steps when repair cannot be effected by regeneration.

- Angiogenesis is promoted by vascular endothelial growth factor (VEGF) and the fibroblast growth factor (FGF) family of growth factors
- Platelet-derived growth factor (PDGF), fibroblast growth factor 2 (FGF-2), and transforming growth factor β (TGF-β) drive fibroblast activation
- TGF-β, PDGF, and FGF drive ECM deposition. Cytokines IL-1 and IL-13 stimulate collagen production.

Types of Wound Healing

Primary union (healing by first intention) occurs when wounds are closed physically with sutures, metal staples, dermal adhesive, etc.

Secondary union (healing by secondary intention) occurs when wounds are allowed to heal by wound contraction and is mediated by myofibroblasts at the edge of the wound.

> **Note**
>
> Clinicians make decisions about wound healing techniques based on clinical information and the size of the tissue defect.

Repair in specific organs occurs as follows:

- **Liver:** Mild injury is repaired by regeneration of hepatocytes, sometimes with restoration to normal pathology. Severe or persistent injury causes formation of regenerative nodules that may be surrounded by fibrosis, leading to hepatic cirrhosis.
- In the **brain**, neurons do not regenerate, but microglia remove debris and astrocytes proliferate, causing gliosis.
- Damaged **heart muscle** cannot regenerate, so the heart heals by fibrosis.
- In the **lung**, type II pneumocytes replace type I pneumocytes after injury.
- In **peripheral nerves**, the distal part of the axon degenerates while the proximal part regrows slowly, using axonal sprouts to follow Schwann cells to the muscle.

Aberrations in Wound Healing

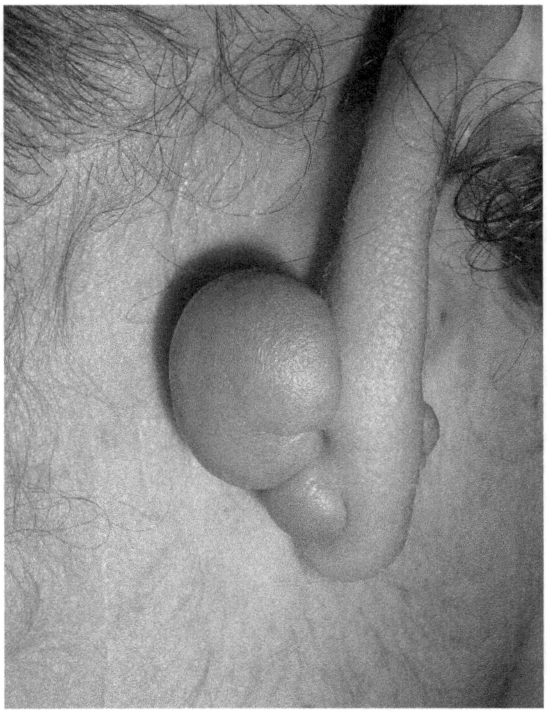

Figure 23-17. Keloid on Posterior Surface of Ear (Auricle)

- **Delayed wound healing** may be seen in wounds complicated by foreign bodies, infection, ischemia, diabetes, malnutrition, scurvy, etc.

- **Hypertrophic scar** results in a prominent scar that is localized to the wound, due to excess production of granulation tissue and collagen. It is common in burn patients.
- **Keloid formation** is a genetic predisposition that is common in African Americans. It tends to affect the earlobes, face, neck, sternum, and forearms, and it may produce large tumor-like scars extending beyond the injury site. There is excess production of collagen that is predominantly type III.

PRACTICE QUESTIONS

1. The parents of an 11-year-old boy come to the pharmacy stating that their son has not been feeling well is somewhat nauseated and has been eating a lot more for the past couple of days. Which of the following is the most appropriate next question?

   A. Has your son been drinking and urinating more frequently?
   B. Has your son broken out in a rash as well?
   C. How much weight has your son gained?
   D. Would you like me to recommend a cough and cold preparation?
   E. Would you like something for nausea?

2. The most common cause of cellular injury is which of the following?

   A. Bacteria
   B. Hypoxia
   C. Ionizing radiation
   D. Trauma
   E. Viruses

3. The morphological changes associated with a myocardial infarction are best described as which of the following?

   A. Caseous necrosis
   B. Coagulative necrosis
   C. Fibrinoid necrosis
   D. Gangrenous necrosis
   E. Liquefaction necrosis

4. A patient is diagnosed with a condition that was caused when there was a change of one fully differentiated cell type to another. This process can best be described as which of the following?

   A. Apoptosis
   B. Atrophy
   C. Hyperplasia
   D. Hypertrophy
   E. Metaplasia

5. All of the following are affected by a medication that inhibits the activity of the cyclooxygenase pathway EXCEPT

   A. Prostaglandin E2
   B. Prostaglandin F2
   C. Prostacyclin
   D. Thromboxane A2
   E. All of the above are affected

6. A patient is diagnosed with bleeding diathesis. They are most likely deficient in which of the following?

   A. Vitamin A
   B. Vitamin B12
   C. Vitamin C
   D. Vitamin D
   E. Vitamin K

7. Myocardial ischemia leads to decreased oxidative phosphorylation which ultimately leads to each of the answer choices. Which of these answer choices is the result of anaerobic glycolysis?

   A. Cytoplasmic enzymes leaking out of the cell
   B. Decreased pH
   C. Decreased protein synthesis
   D. Influx of calcium in to the cell
   E. Swelling of the cell

Answers and Explanations

1. **The correct answer is A.** Based on the patient's age and the appearance of 2 symptoms (malaise and polyphagia), there is a good possibility that the child has type 1 diabetes. Hence, the best initial question would be related to other common type 1 diabetes presenting symptoms such as polydipsia (excessive thirst) and polyuria (excessive urination). Without asking more questions, the administration of an antinausea medication (choice E) could delay an emergency room visit that could be detrimental to the patient. Choices B and C are inappropriate. For choice D, a patient that does not "feel well" is not necessarily related to "cough and cold symptoms".

2. **The correct answer is B.** Hypoxia is the most common cause of injury. Hypoxia occurs when lack of oxygen prevents the cell from synthesizing sufficient ATP by aerobic oxidation. Major mechanisms leading to hypoxia are ischemia, cardiopulmonary failure, and decreased oxygen-carrying capacity of the blood (e.g., anemia).

3. **The correct answer is B.** Morphologic types of necrosis are as follows: Coagulative necrosis (most common form of necrosis) generally caused by ischemic injury (i.e. myocardia infarction). It is caused by the denaturing of proteins within the cytoplasm. Coagulative necrosis is common in most organs, but not the brain. Caseous necrosis (choice A) is a combination of coagulation and liquefaction necrosis (i.e. tuberculosus). Fibrinoid necrosis (choice C) is a form of necrotic connective tissue that histologically resembles fibrin (i.e. hypersensitivity type reactions II and III). Gangrenous necrosis (choice D) describes completely dead tissue. Liquefaction necrosis (choice E) results from cellular destruction by hydrolytic enzymes, leading to autolysis and heterolysis (i.e. brain infarcts).

4. **The correct answer is E.** Metaplasia is a reversible change of one fully differentiated cell type to another, usually in response to irritation. It has been suggested that the replacement cell is better able to tolerate the environmental stresses. The classic example of metaplasia is seen in Barrett's esophagus. Apoptosis (choice A) is a specialized form of programmed cell death without an inflammatory response. Atrophy (choice B) is a decrease in cell/organ size and functional ability. Hyperplasia (choice C) is an increase in the number of cells in a tissue or organ. Hypertrophy (choice D) is an increase in cell size and functional ability due to increased synthesis of intracellular components.

5. **The correct answer is E.** The nonsteroidal antiinflammatory drugs and corticosteroids inhibit the activity of the cyclooxygenase pathway. Thus, all of the answer choices would be affected. Prostaglandin E2 causes pain. Prostaglandins PGE2, PGD2, and PGF2 cause vasodilatation. Prostacyclin (PGI2) is produced by vascular endothelium and causes vasodilation and inhibition of platelet aggregation. Thromboxane A2 is produced by platelets and causes vasoconstriction and platelet aggregation.

6. **The correct answer is E.** Vitamin deficiencies can be seen with vitamin K (bleeding diathesis), vitamin A (night blindness, squamous metaplasia, immune deficiency), vitamin B12 (megaloblastic anemia, neuropathy, and spinal cord degeneration), vitamin C (scurvy), vitamin D (rickets and osteomalacia), folate (megaloblastic anemia and neural tube defects), and niacin (pellagra [diarrhea, dermatitis, and dementia]).

7. **The correct answer is B.** The cellular response to injury depends on several important factors, including the type of injury, duration (including pattern) of injury, severity and intensity of injury, type of cell injured, the cell's metabolic state, and the cell's ability to adapt. When ATP is depleted as a result of decreased oxidative phosphorylation, there are numerous key biochemical pathways dependent on ATP that become disrupted. For example, ATP depletion increases anaerobic glycolysis that leads to an increased production of lactic acid and ultimately a decrease in cellular pH. Decreased ATP leads to severe membrane damage that results in choices A and D. Chronic ATP depletion causes morphological and functional changes to the ER and ribosomes leading to decreased protein synthesis (choice C). Disruption of Na^+/K^+ or Ca^{2+} pumps cause imbalances in solute concentrations leading to swelling of the cell (choice E).

Clinical Pharmacokinetics 24

Learning Objectives

- ❏ Show proficiency in the application of pharmacokinetic data to drug therapy
- ❏ Explain the importance of pharmacokinetics with low-therapeutic-index drugs

Drug pharmacokinetics is concerned with the processes of absorption, distribution, metabolism, and excretion (ADME). Clinical pharmacokinetics applies ADME concepts to the facilitation of individualized drug therapies along with therapeutic drug monitoring.

An overview of clinical pharmacokinetics can be found in Kaplan's *NAPLEX Strategies, Practice, and Review.* Additional information on basic principles of pharmacokinetics can be found in Chapter 9 of this FPGEE text.

CLINICAL APPLICATION OF PHARMACOKINETIC DATA

When a medical provider makes a diagnosis, the clinical pharmacist may be asked to choose an appropriate medication or recommend a medication dosing schedule based on individual patient factors (renal function, hepatic function, weight, etc.).

NAPLEX Reference

Pharmacokinetics chapter

Determination of the desired therapeutic effect is the first step in choosing a medication. The next step is to decide how the "standard" dose should be manipulated (based on individual patient factors) to achieve its desired outcome with minimal adverse effects.

The initial dose of the medication can then be titrated until the preferred effect is achieved. Medication titration is dependent on the following:

- Ease at which the therapeutic effect is evident (see Chapter 28)
- Time frame in which the therapeutic effect is evident (see Chapter 28)
- Changes in condition requiring dosage change (see Chapter 28)
- Drug's therapeutic index

Therapeutic Index

The main goal of drug therapy is to obtain the desired therapeutic outcome while experiencing minimal adverse effects. This goal can generally be achieved (for many medications) by obtaining a specific plasma concentration (Cp) range within the preferred therapeutic index, otherwise known as the therapeutic window.

In this theoretical window, the medication (at ideal dosing) is prescribed above the minimal effective concentration (MEC), but below the minimal toxic concentration (MTC).

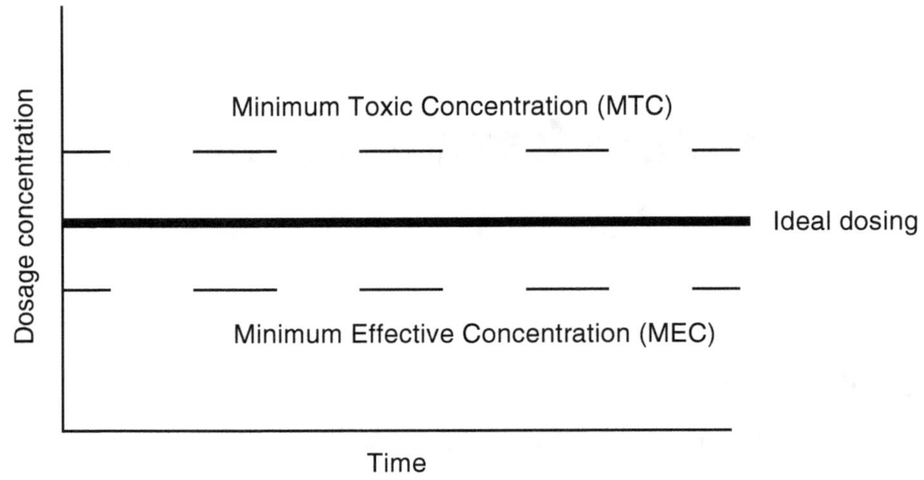

Figure 24-1. Ideal Drug Dosing

High Drug Dose

If the medication dose (or dosing regimen) is too high or the patient has impaired hepatic and/or renal function, the resultant effect will be a drug concentration above the MTC. The net effects would be:

- Excessive therapeutic effect
- Increased frequency and/or severity of adverse effects

Low Drug Dose

If the medication dose (or dosing regimen) is too low or the patient has enhanced hepatic or renal function, the resultant effect will be a drug concentration below the MTC. The net effects would be:

- Insufficient therapeutic effect
- Decreased frequency and/or severity of adverse effects

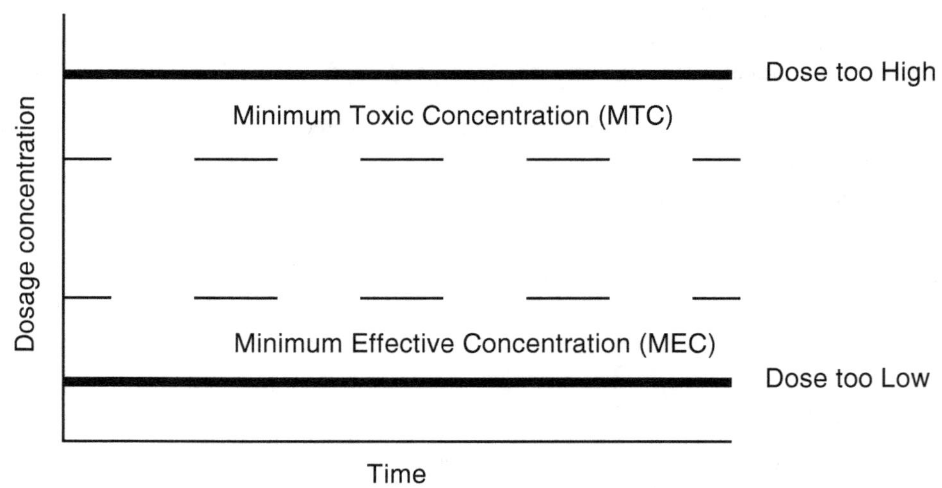

Figure 24-2. High and Low Drug Dosing

Therapeutic Index and Toxicity Measurement

The therapeutic index can also be defined as the ratio of the drug dose that results in toxicity in 50% of subjects (TD50) divided by the dose that results in the desired (effective) pharmacological effect in 50% of subjects (ED50).

- Another therapeutic index calculation involves comparison of the lethal dose in 50% of patients (LD50) divided by the ED50.

Comparisons between ED50 and TD50 values permit evaluation of the relative safety of a drug (the therapeutic index), as would comparison between ED50 and the lethal median dose (LD50) if the latter is known. When the ratio of the toxic dose to the effective dose is small (i.e. 2 to 1 for digoxin), the medication is considered to have a low therapeutic index (TI) and thus the potential for toxicity is high.

$$TI = \frac{TD50}{ED50} \text{ or } \frac{LD50}{ED50}$$

It is important to remember that **there is an indirect correlation between therapeutic index and toxicity**. As the therapeutic index increases, the risk for toxicity decreases.

A dose-response (D-R) curve can also be used to show the relationship between dose and toxic effects of a drug. Remember the median toxic dose of a drug (TD50) is the dose that causes toxicity in 50% of a population.

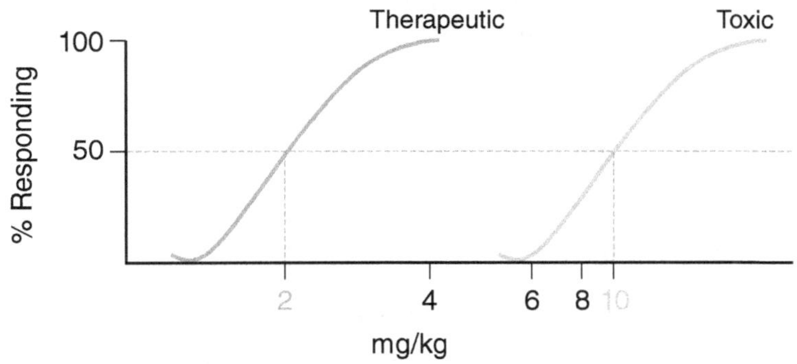

Figure 24-3. Quantal D-R Curves of Therapeutic and Toxic Effects of a Drug

Use of Low-Therapeutic Index Drugs

Clinical pharmacokinetics considers all of the factors (patient, drug, disease, etc) that can impact the variability in the drug's plasma concentrations over time. Therapeutic drug monitoring is one of the tools used in this area of medicine to help achieve the desired therapeutic effect and minimize toxicity, especially with narrow low therapeutic index drugs.

Table 24-1. Accepted Drug Levels for Narrow Therapeutic Index Drugs (in Alphabetical Order)

Drug	Usual Therapeutic Range
Amikacin	Peak: 25–40 trough: 4–8 mcg/mL (Please level based on severity)
Aminophylline	10 to 20 mcg/mL
Amitriptyline	120 to 150 ng/mL
Carbamazepine	4 to 12 mcg/mL
Desipramine	150 to 300 ng/mL

(Continued)

Drug	Usual Therapeutic Range
Digoxin	0.5–1.5 ng/mL (inotropic effects) 0.8–2.0 ng/mL (chronotropic effects) >2 ng/mL (toxicity)
Disopyramide	2 to 5 mcg/mL
Ethosuximide	40 to 100 mcg/mL
Gentamicin	Conventional dosing: Peak: 4–10 mcg/mL Trough: <0.5–2 mcg/mL – safety, for serious infections Trough <1 mcg/mL – safety, for hospital-acquired pneumonia
Lidocaine	1.5 to 5.0 mcg/mL
Lithium	0.5 to 1.3 mEq/L (Some references are 0.6 to 1.2 mEq/L)
Phenobarbital	10 to 40 mcg/mL
Phenytoin	10 to 20 mcg/mL (Note: Must be corrected for hypoalbuminemia – Corrected phenytoin concentration = measured total concentration/[0.2*albumin] + 0.1)
Primidone	5 to 12 mcg/mL
Procainamide	4 to 10 mcg/mL
Quinidine	2 to 5 mcg/mL
Theophylline	10 to 20 mcg/mL
Tobramycin	Conventional dosing: Peak: 4–10 mcg/mL Trough: <0.5–2 mcg/mL – safety, for serious infections Trough <1 mcg/mL – safety, for hospital-acquired pneumonia
Valproic acid	40 to 100 mcg/mL
Vancomycin	Peak: 20–40 mcg/mL Trough: 10–20 mcg/mL

Strategies to Minimize Toxicity Associated with Narrow Therapeutic Index Drugs

Physiological changes that occur with disease and aging may change the pharmacokinetics and pharmacodynamics of both narrow therapeutic index and wide therapeutic index drugs. The net effect is most commonly an increased incidence of adverse drug effects attributed to an extension of the pharmacological effects of the drug.

Practical strategies to prevent toxicity when prescribing to patients at risk for toxicity include:

- Use nonpharmacological approaches (when appropriate)
- Use the lowest possible dose and the smallest dose incremental increases ("start low, go slow")
- Use the smallest number of medications (i.e. eliminate polypharmacy whenever possible)
- Continually review medication regimens for adverse effects and drug interactions. Make drug dosage adjustments when appropriate.
- Continually review changes in disease state and make drug dosage adjustments when appropriate.

PRACTICE QUESTIONS

1. In order for a medication to be effective at a therapeutic target (i.e. receptor, enzyme) in the body it must reach which of the following?

   A. ED50
   B. MEC
   C. MTC
   D. TD50
   E. Tmax

NAPLEX Question Reference

Pharmacokinetics chapter: end of chapter questions

2. Which of the following has the lowest therapeutic index?

   A. Alprazolam
   B. Amoxicillin
   C. Fluoxetine
   D. Ibuprofen
   E. Warfarin

3. A physician prescribes a medication that has a volume of distribution of approximately 45 L. What is the dose (mg) that is needed to obtain an initial plasma level of 6 mg/L if the patient weighs 82 kg?

   A. 195 mg
   B. 270 mg
   C. 380 mg
   D. 540 mg
   E. 775 mg

4. A medication reaches steady state in 48 hours. A reasonable estimation of this drug's elimination half-life is which of the following?

   A. 6 hours
   B. 10 hours
   C. 18 hours
   D. 24 hours
   E. Cannot be determined

5. A patient previously diagnosed with heart failure and currently receiving digoxin is brought to the emergency department. Laboratory studies show a digoxin level of 2.4 ng/mL. Which of the following would be expected to be seen in this patient?

   A. Hypertension
   B. Nephrotoxicity
   C. Peripheral edema
   D. Yellow halos around lights
   E. No symptoms related to the digoxin level since it is normal

Answers and Explanations

1. **The correct answer is B.** In this theoretical window, the medication (at ideal dosing) is prescribed above the minimal effective concentration (MEC) (choice B), but below the minimal toxic concentration (MTC)(choice C). The MEC is the minimum concentration that is needed at a therapeutic target (i.e. receptor, enzyme) to obtain a desired therapeutic effect. The ED50 (choice A) is the dose that results in the desired (effective) pharmacological outcome in 50% of subjects and the TD50 (choice D) is the drug dose that results in toxicity in 50% of patients. The Tmax (choice E) is the time to reach the maximum concentration in the blood.

2. **The correct answer is E.** The therapeutic index or therapeutic window can be defined as the ratio of the drug dose that results in toxicity in 50% of subjects (TD50) divided by the dose that results in the desired (effective) pharmacological effect in 50% of subjects (ED50). Thus medications more likely to cause toxicity are assigned a "lower" therapeutic index. Of the medications listed, warfarin (choice E) would be considered to have the lowest therapeutic index and amoxicillin (choice B) would have the highest therapeutic index.

3. **The correct answer is B.** This question is asking for the loading dose. The loading dose equation is as follows: (LD = Vd × Cp). In the question stem we are told that the drug's Vd is 45 L and the initial plasma level is 6 mg/L. Hence LD = 45 L × 6 mg/L = 270 mg. Thus the initial dose is 270 mg.

4. **The correct answer is B.** By definition, it takes 4-5 half-lives for a drug to reach steady state. Since 48 hours/4 = 12 hours and 48 hours/5 = 9.6 hours, a reasonable estimation of this drug's elimination half-life is 10 hours since it falls between these 12 hours and 9.6 hours.

5. **The correct answer is D.** This is a 2-step question where the reader has to assess the appropriateness of the digoxin level and then determine its impact. A therapeutic blood level for digoxin in heart failure is 0.5–1.5 ng/mL (inotropic effects); toxicity is seen when the level is >2 ng/mL. Digoxin toxicity is associated with confusion, drowsiness, yellow halos around lights (xanthopsia), photophobia, nausea, hypotension (choice A). Nephrotoxicity (choice B) is seen with gentamicin toxicity. Peripheral edema (choice C) is a symptom of heart failure.

Clinical Pharmacogenomics 25

Learning Objectives

- ❑ Show proficiency in the application of pharmacogenomics data to drug therapy

Pharmacogenomics testing, along with clinical knowledge and expertise, can help to ensure that patients are treated with the most appropriate medications based on their unique genotypes.

Pharmacogenomics is an emerging and evolving science. Although the benefits are widely known and well accepted, there is still much to be learned.

APPLICATION OF PHARMACOGENOMIC DATA TO DRUG THERAPY

According to the National Institute of Health (NIH) genetics home reference, pharmacogenomics (PGx) is defined as the study of how genes affect a person's response to drugs.

> **NAPLEX Reference**
>
> **Pharmacogenomics chapter**
> **Biopharmaceutics and Drug Disposition chapter:** Focus on "Drug Metabolism"

Most oral medications today are available in a limited number of dosage forms, such as 10, 20, and 40 mg capsules/tablets. Although these limited number of "dosage strengths" are appropriate to treat the majority of patients with a given disease state, they may be inappropriate for some. In other words, most medications available today are designed as a "few sizes fits all." However, they don't initially produce the desired therapeutic effect for everyone using these dosage sizes (strengths) since the clinician often does not know *exactly* "what size to choose first." Hence, it can be difficult to predict:

- who will benefit from a medication;
- who will not respond at all; and
- who will experience adverse effects.

With the knowledge gained from the Human Genome Project, researchers and clinicians now have an understanding of how inherited differences in genes affect a person's response to certain medications. Clinicians now have the ability to predict the effectiveness, ineffectiveness, or likelihood for toxicity for some medications when they have information on the patient's genetic makeup.

Most human drug-metabolizing enzymes exhibiting genetic polymorphisms with clinical relevance are those responsible for modification of functional groups (phase I reactions) or for conjugation of endogenous substituents (phase II reactions). There is also wide variation in the types of genetic polymorphisms found in Americans.

- Example: It is estimated that 30% of Americans have a genetic variation of the cytochrome P450 3A4/5 system and another 20% have a genetic variation of the cytochrome P450 2D6 system.

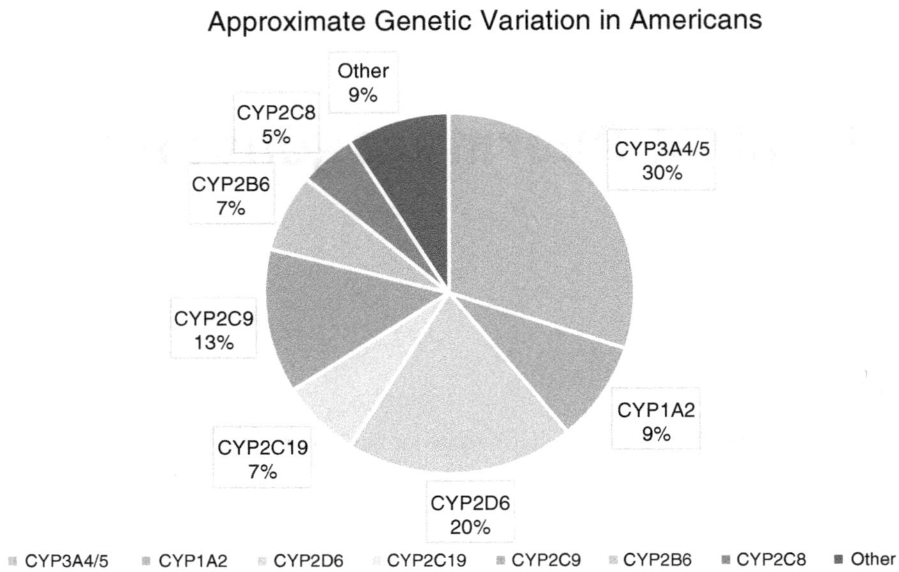

Figure 25-1. Approximate Genetic Variation in Americans

The Approximate Genetic Variation in Americans chart only represents the estimated percentage of the Americans with an abnormality of each phase I system; however, it does NOT represent the type of genetic polymorphism.

Patients categorized as having a genetic polymorphism may be further classified as:

- Ultrarapid metabolizer (UM)
- Extensive (Normal) metabolizer (EM)
- Intermediate metabolizer (IM)
- Poor metabolizer (PM)

With respect to this information, it is more correct to state that it is estimated that 30% of Americans have a genetic variation of the Cytochrome P450 3A4/5 system (UM, IM or PM) and another 20% have a genetic variation of the Cytochrome P450 2D6 system (UM, IM, PM).

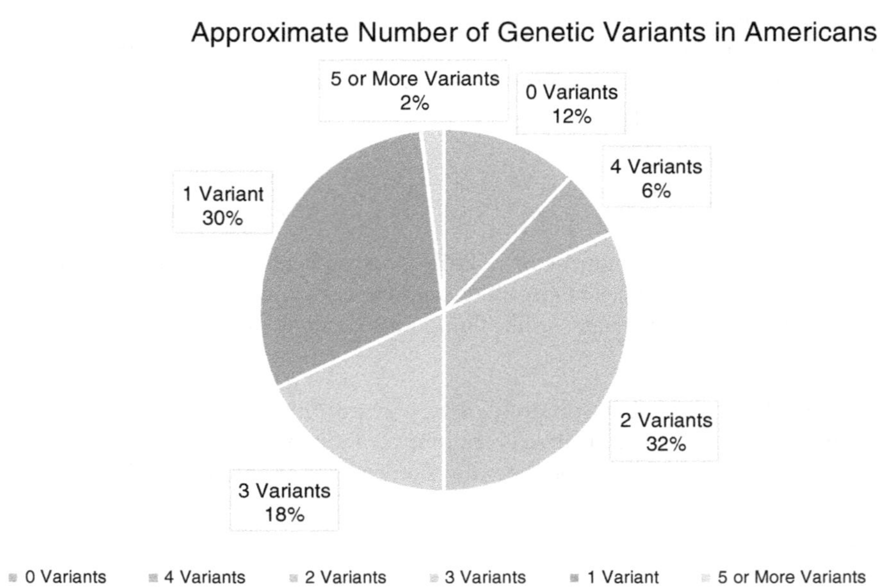

Figure 25-2. Approximate Number of Genetic Variations in Americans

The number of genetic polymorphisms present in a single American also varies.

As depicted in both graphs, there is wide disparity in the number and type of genetic polymorphisms in United States citizens.

- The number and type of genetic variations in an individual patient is variable.
- Different medications used in the treatment of a given disease state (depression, hypertension, diabetes, etc.) are often metabolized through different cytochrome pathways.
- **Correlating the patient's unique genetic variations with the medications metabolized through (or outside) these affected pathways is the fundamental premise of clinical pharmacogenomics.**
- Pharmacogenomic information may help clinicians predict the therapeutic impact or appearance of adverse effects prior to the patient taking the medication.

Incorporating Pharmacogenomic Information into Clinical Practice

The following cytochrome enzymes are responsible for the metabolism of most medications metabolized through Phase I processes in the liver: CYP2D6, CYP2C9, CYP2C19, CYP2B6, CYP1A2, and CYP3A4/5.

- Example: CYP2D6 metabolizes approximately 25% of clinically relevant medications and affects the pharmacokinetics of approximately 50% of drugs currently in clinical use.
- A working knowledge of the cytochrome substrate type for each of the most commonly prescribed medications is essential.
- A Phase I processes in common drugs metabolized by pathway is found in the Biopharmaceutics and Drug Disposition chapter of the NAPLEX text.

Pharmacogenomic analysis of these cytochrome enzymes is generally considered sufficient to assess a person's genetic impact on drug metabolism and can subsequently be used to evaluate the initial choice and/or dose of a medication.

CLINICAL EXAMPLE

If a patient with hypertension and major depressive disorder is classified as a CYP2D6 poor metabolizer, then the prescriber has the following options:

- Start the patient on "lower" doses of venlafaxine and metoprolol since these medications are CYP2D6 substrates; or
- Prescribe medications that are NOT CYP2D6 substrates, such as citalopram and losartan.

An understanding of the impact of genetic variation on drug metabolism is essential; however, pharmacogenomics has clinical relevance in many other areas. Pharmacogenomics is therefore best defined as a discipline that uses genome technology to study the relationship between drug effects and all relevant genes.

Table 25-1. Clinical Application of Pharmacogenomics

Gene Variant	Clinical Utility and Implications
Cytochrome P450 (CYP) Enzymes	• CYP2D6, CYP2C9, CYP2C19, CYP2B6, CYP1A2, and CYP3A4/5 account for the metabolism of most hepatically metabolized enzymes. • Identification of ultrarapid, intermediate and poor metabolizers can help prescribers choose an appropriate dose or alternative medication (metabolized through an alternate pathway) • PGx data on each of the cytochrome enzymes can help prescribers obtain their desired therapeutic outcome while minimizing side effects.

(Continued)

Gene Variant	Clinical Utility and Implications
ABCB1	• ABCB1 is a transporter protein that has a key role in the CNS bioavailability of several psychotropics, antiepileptics and various other medications entering the CNS. • ABCB1 polymorphisms help identify nonresponders of selected CNS medications.
ADRA2A	• Adrenoceptor alpha 2A (ADRA2A) has a critical role in regulating neurotransmitter release from sympathetic nerves and from CNS adrenergic neurons. • ADRA2A polymorphisms are associated with the degree of severity of attention-deficit/hyperactivity disorder (ADHD) symptoms as well as a favorable response to methylphenidate. • Genotyping ADHD patients for the ADRA2A polymorphism can help identify those more likely to benefit the most from methylphenidate therapy.
Apolipoprotein E	• Apolipoprotein E (APOE) is responsible for transporting cholesterol from the cells in the blood vessel wall to the liver for excretion. • Defects in APOE can lead to dyslipidemia and subsequently atherosclerosis and cardiovascular disease (CVD). • Early identification can help formulate preventative medicine strategies.
SLCO1B1	• SLCO1B1 encodes a hepatic-specific transporter responsible for the removal of bile acids and medications, such as statins from the blood to the liver. • All statins are substrates of SLCO1B1 with a varying degree of effects of the SLCO1B1 genetic polymorphism (simvastatin > pitavastatin > atorvastatin > pravastatin > rosuvastatin) • SLCO1B1 genetic polymorphism are associated with statin-induced myopathy (and potentially rhabdomyolysis). • Identification could dictate therapy with another class OR show indication for fluvastatin which is NOT affected by the SLCO1B1 polymorphism.
UGT2B15	• Uridine diphosphate glucuronosyl transferases (UGT) are "phase II" enzymes that catalyze the addition of glucuronic acid to various substrates, including drugs. • UGT polymorphisms are associated with decreased elimination of oxazepam and lorazepam. • Other essential phase II polymorphisms include UGT1A1 (associated with decreased elimination and toxicity of irinotecan) AND TPMT (associated with severe 6-mercaptopurine toxicity).
VKORC1	• Vitamin K epoxide reductase complex, subunit 1 (VKORC1) is the target of coumarin anticoagulants. • VKORC1 polymorphisms are associated with varying levels of warfarin sensitivity. • VKORC1 variant testing is commonly used in conjunction with CYP2C9 variant testing to optimize warfarin dosing and minimize the risks of bleeding or thrombotic complications.

PRACTICE QUESTIONS

> **NAPLEX Question Reference**
>
> **Pharmacogenomics chapter and Biopharmaceutics and Drug Disposition chapter:** end of chapter questions

1. A patient with atrial fibrillation is currently receiving digoxin. The patient's physician is considering switching them to warfarin but wants to know about its pharmacogenomics. In addition to CYP2C9, genotyping for which of the following is most recommended prior to receiving warfarin therapy?

   A. CYP1A2
   B. CYP2C19
   C. CYP3A4/5
   D. HLA-B*5701
   E. VKORC1

2. In addition to CYP2D6, CYP2C9, CYP2B6, CYP1A2 and CYP3A4/5, which of the following are responsible for the metabolism of the majority of medications available today?

   A. CYP1B1
   B. CYP2C8
   C. CYP2C19
   D. CYP2J2
   E. CYP11A1

3. Prior to receiving clopidogrel, a patient receives a pharmacogenomics test. The results show that the patient is a poor metabolizer at CYP2C19. Which of the following recommendations should be made by the pharmacist to the patient's physician?

   A. An alternative medication should be selected.
   B. The dose of clopidogrel will need to be decreased.
   C. The dose of clopidogrel will need to be increased.
   D. The medication is not impacted by a CYP2D6 polymorphism.
   E. This patient cannot receive antiplatelet therapy.

4. Following a pharmacogenomics test, a patient is noted as being a normal metabolizer at CYP2D6. Thus they would be classified as which of the following?

   A. Extensive metabolizer (EM)
   B. Intermediate metabolizer (IM)
   C. Poor metabolizer (PM)
   D. Ultrarapid metabolizer (UM)
   E. None of the above

5. A patient experiences life-threatening azathioprine-associated myelosuppression. This is most likely related to a genetic polymorphism of which of the following?

   A. ABCB1
   B. Apolipoprotein E
   C. ADRA2A
   D. TPMT
   E. VKORC1

Answers and Explanations

1. **The correct answer is E.** Genotyping for VKORC1 and CYP2C9 polymorphisms has also been widely used to determine whether or not to choose warfarin or an alternative anticoagulant. Warfarin is unique in that it is recommended to test for 2 independent genetic variants (in the CYP2C9 and VKORC1 genes). CYP2C9 is the primary enzyme involved in warfarin's metabolism AND polymorphisms within the VKORC1 gene appear to dictate the daily dose of warfarin needed to achieve the desired level of anticoagulation. CYP1A2 (choice A) is involved in the metabolism of fluvoxamine and caffeine. CYP2C19 (choice B) is involved in the metabolism of clopidogrel, cimetidine, omeprazole and many others. CYP3A4/5 (choice C) is involved in the metabolism of indinavir, itraconazole and nefazodone, and many others. HLA-B*5701 (choice D) is important for determining hypersensitivity reaction to abacavir.

2. **The correct answer is C.** The following cytochrome enzymes are responsible for the metabolism of most medications metabolized through Phase I processes in the liver: CYP2D6, CYP2C9, CYP2C19, CYP2B6, CYP1A2, and CYP3A4/5. For example, CYP2D6 metabolizes approximately 25% of clinically relevant medications and affects the pharmacokinetics of approximately 50% of drugs currently in clinical use.

3. **The correct answer is A.** Clopidogrel is an antiplatelet medication that acts by irreversibly binding to P2Y12 adenosine diphosphate receptors and ultimately reducing platelet activation and aggregation. Clopidogrel is a prodrug and a CYP2D6 substrate. Therefore, a patient that is classified as a poor metabolizer (PM) will not convert the drug to its active metabolite. Also, the drug's package insert lists a "contraindication" for CYP2D6 PM's. Hence, the best recommendation would be to choose an alternative medication, such as prasugrel or ticagrelor. Choices B and C will not provide therapeutic benefit.

4. **The correct answer is A.** This question is essentially asking "which of the following is classified as a normal metabolizer?" Extensive metabolizers are classified as being normal metabolizers. EM's have 2 normally functioning alleles, thus have "normal" enzyme activity. IM's have 1 non-functional allele and 1 normally functioning allele; hence, have decreased enzyme activity. PM's have 2 non-functional alleles and thus have little enzyme activity. UM's have 1 or more alleles duplicated or amplified alleles compared to EM; hence, will metabolize drugs more rapidly.

5. **The correct answer is D.** TPMT is responsible for the metabolism of azathioprine and mercaptopurine (6-MP). Genetic variations of the TPMT gene can result in functional inactivation of the enzyme leading to a significantly increased risk of life-threatening myelosuppression. ABCB1 (choice A) is a transporter protein for several psychotropics, antiepileptics and various other medications entering the CNS. Defects in Apolipoprotein E (choice B) can lead to dyslipidemia. ADRA2A polymorphisms (choice C) are associated with the degree of severity of ADHD symptoms as well as response to methylphenidate. VKORC1 polymorphisms (choice E) are associated with varying levels of warfarin sensitivity.

Disease Prevention and U.S. Population Health 26

Learning Objectives

- ❑ Describe the proper use of nonpharmacologic therapies
- ❑ Show proficiency in health, wellness, and disease prevention
- ❑ Answer questions on immunizations

The primary focus of medical and pharmacy education is based on the diagnosis and treatment of disease. Although this focus is necessary, equal emphasis (at least clinically) should be placed on the preservation and enhancement of "current" health with preventative medicine practices.

HEALTH, WELLNESS, AND DISEASE PREVENTION WITH PHARMACOLOGICAL AND NONPHARMACOLOGIC THERAPIES

Preventive medicine focuses on the health of individuals, entire communities, and well-defined populations. According to the American College of Preventative Medicine, its primary goal is to *protect, promote, and maintain health and well-being and to prevent disease, disability, and death.*

There are 4 main types of disease prevention.

NAPLEX Reference

Preventative Medicine chapter:
"Weight Loss"
"Smoking Cessation"

Over-the-Counter Medications chapter

Table 26-1. Types of Prevention

Prevention Type	Definition and Comments
Primary	• Main goal is to prevent disease or injury before it occurs. • Actions: Preventing exposures to diseases/dangers that result in disease or injury, changing unhealthy behaviors, and increasing resistance to disease. • Primary prevention will decrease both the incidence and prevalence of disease. • Examples: Condoms, immunizations, patient education, diet and exercise (before obesity or disease occurs).
Secondary	• Main goal is to reduce the impact of a disease or injury that has already occurred. • Actions: Identification of people who have already developed a disease, at an early stage in the disease's natural history, through screening or early intervention thus slowing the disease progress.

(Continued)

Prevention Type	Definition and Comments
Secondary (cont.)	• Secondary prevention has no impact on incidence but will decrease disease prevalence (because patients have a greater potential to be cured). • Examples: Screening exams and tests, low-dose aspirin or diet and exercise programs to prevent future heart attacks or strokes, encouraging personal strategies to prevent reinjury or recurrence.
Tertiary	• Main goal is to mitigate the impact of a chronic illness in a patient that already has symptoms of the disease. • Actions: Minimize future pathological changes and complications of the disease; slow disease progression AND increase the quality of life for those with the disease. • Tertiary prevention has no impact on incidence but will INCREASE disease prevalence (because patients live longer with the disease). • Examples: Antiretrovirals in HIV, chronic disease management programs/medications (diabetes, hypertension, heart failure), cardiac or stroke rehabilitation programs, including diet and exercise programs.
Quaternary	• Main goal is to avoid or mitigate unnecessary or excessive health care interventions. • Actions include physician and patient education and insurance company payment restrictions. • Quaternary prevention has no impact on incidence or prevalence (assuming that the excessive intervention did impact the course of the disease). • Examples: Prescribing antibiotics for a viral infection, overprescribing pain medications and overuse of diagnostic tests.

Diet, Exercise, and Nonpharmacological Therapies

Although practicing pharmacists most commonly deal with medication-related therapies, you should demonstrate proficiency in implementing diet, exercise, and nonpharmacological therapies, including complementary and alternative medicines.

- A comprehensive review of both non-prescription and natural products is found in Kaplan's NAPLEX Review.
- Additional information on the use of nonprescription and natural products can be found in this guide in Chapter 28 ("Promotion of Nonprescription and Natural Products"), Chapter 2 ("Vitamins and Enzymes") and Chapter 7 ("Pharmacognosy and Dietary Supplements").

Diet and exercise are often considered the "nonpharmacological cornerstones" by which many preventative medicine (and treatment) strategies are based.

- Example: Primary, secondary, and tertiary preventative measures for cardiovascular disease (and many other diseases) all involve diet and exercise programs.

The differentiating factors on whether intervention (i.e. exercise) is classified as primary, secondary, or tertiary is how and when the preventative measure is employed:

- **Primary:** Healthy diet and regular exercise program is started by a person with a family history of cardiovascular disease in their early 30's (long before any disease is present). The goal is to prevent the onset of cardiovascular disease.
- **Secondary:** A low fat diet and regular exercise program is instituted by a person who had a minor myocardial infarction (with no apparent long-term consequences). The goal is to prevent disease reoccurrence.
- **Tertiary:** A restrictive diet and restrictive exercise program is instituted by a person who had a major myocardial infarction (with decreased left ventricular function). The goal is to mitigate the long-term impact of the MI.

Patient motivation is a prerequisite for achieving an effective diet or exercise program. Motivation can be increased when a practitioner thoroughly describes the benefits of a healthy diet and exercise program. Additional motivation can occur when the health risks of obesity and a sedentary lifestyle are also outlined.

Before recommending a diet or exercise program, the following should be considered by the clinical pharmacist:

- How determined is the patient to institute and maintain a healthy lifestyle?
- How well does the patient understand the benefits of diet and exercise?
- How well does the patient understand the risks of obesity or a sedentary lifestyle?
- Does the patient have a support system to help with the diet or exercise program?
- Are there any barriers to the patient starting a diet and exercise program?
- Does the patient have sufficient time to spend on diet and exercise therapy?

Diet

Diet is a key component of healthy living and weight reduction. Most American diets consist of approximately 15% protein, 35% fat, and 50% carbohydrates.

The Food and Drug Administration (FDA) has established a recommended Food Labeling Guide to serve as the average daily values for all major food components based on a caloric intake of 2,000 calories, for adults and children (>4 years old). Each of the individual recommended daily values can vary depending on a person's age, height, weight, and presence of disease.

Table 26-2. FDA Food Labeling Guide

Food Component	DV	Comments
Total Fat	65 grams (g)	Recommended as 20–30% of total daily calories; Total fat should not exceed 30% of daily calories.
Saturated Fat	20 g	Less than 10% of total daily calories should come from saturated fat
Cholesterol	300 milligrams (mg)	
Sodium	2,400 mg	
Potassium	3,500 mg	
Total Carbohydrate	300 g	Recommended as 45–65% of total daily calories
Dietary Fiber	25 g	
Protein	50 g	Recommended as 10–35% of total daily calories; the intake of protein should be at a level of 1.0 to 1.5 g/kg of ideal body weight.
Vitamin A	5,000 International Units (IU)	
Vitamin C	60 mg	
Calcium	1,000 mg	
Iron	18 mg	
Vitamin D	400 IU	

(Continued)

Food Component	DV	Comments
Vitamin E	30 IU	
Vitamin K	80 micrograms µg	
Thiamin	1.5 mg	
Riboflavin	1.7 mg	
Niacin	20 mg	
Vitamin B6	2 mg	
Folate	400 µg	
Vitamin B12	6 µg	
Biotin	300 µg	
Pantothenic acid	10 mg	
Phosphorus	1,000 mg	
Iodine	150 µg	
Magnesium	400 mg	
Zinc	15 mg	
Selenium	70 µg	
Copper	2 mg	
Manganese	2 mg	
Chromium	120 µg	
Molybdenum	75 µg	
Chloride	3,400 mg	

Additional dietary considerations include:

- High-fiber foods, such as fruits and vegetables, should be encouraged.
- Although weight loss is discussed in Kaplan's NAPLEX Review book (in the "Preventative Medicine" chapter), the goals of obesity treatment are to stop weight gain, decrease overall body weight, maintain long-term weight loss, and decrease the risk for obesity-related complications.
- When weight loss is desired, the NHLBI Guidelines recommend starting dietary therapy with a calorie deficit of 500 to 1000 kcal/day. This equates to a diet containing 1000 to 1200 kcal/day for most women and between 1200 and 1600 kcal/day for men.

Exercise

According to the Centers for Disease Control and Prevention (CDC), regular physical activity is one of the most important preventative health measures that a person can do.

Table 26-3. Benefits of Exercise

Exercise Benefit	Comments
Control body weight	• The CDC recommends that a person work up to 150 minutes of moderate-intensity aerobic activity or 75 minutes of vigorous-intensity aerobic activity, or an equivalent mix of the 2 each week. • Strong scientific evidence shows that physical activity can help a person maintain their weight over time.
Reduce the risk of cardiovascular disease, type 2 diabetes and metabolic syndrome	• Following the recommendation of at least 150 minutes per week of moderate-intensity aerobic activity can lower the risk of cardiovascular disease, for example. • Exercise can decrease blood pressure, improve glycemic control and lower cholesterol.
Reduce the risk of some cancers	• Studies suggest that exercise can decrease the risk of colon cancer in men and women as well as decrease the risk of breast cancer in women.
Strengthen a person's bones and muscles	• Regular exercise (150 minutes/week) can slow bone density loss, lower the risk of hip fracture and increase muscle mass (at any age).
Improve mental health and mood	• Regular exercise (150 minutes/week) can improve cognition and reduce the risk of major depressive disorder.
Improve one's ability to do daily activities and prevent falls (for the elderly)	• Regular exercise (150 minutes/week) can improve/maintain coordination and balance.
Increase the chances of living longer	• According to the CDC, people who are physically active for about 7 hours a week have a 40 percent lower risk of dying early than those who are active for less than 30 minutes a week. • The risk of early death decreases with regular exercise (150 minutes/week).

The number of calories burned increases as the intensity of the exercise increases.

Table 26-4. Estimated Calories Burned While Performing Specific Exercises

	Weight of Person and Calories Burned	
Activity (1-Hour Duration)	**160 Pounds (73 Kilograms)**	**200 Pounds (91 Kilograms)**
Aerobics, high impact	530	660
Aerobics, low impact	370	460
Bicycling, <10 mph	290	360
Elliptical trainer (moderate effort)	370	460
Hiking	440	550
Racquetball	510	640

(Continued)

	Weight of Person and Calories Burned	
Activity (1-Hour Duration)	**160 Pounds (73 Kilograms)**	**200 Pounds (91 Kilograms)**
Weight training/Weight lifting	370	460
Running, 5 mph	610	760
Running, 8 mph	860	1,100
Skiing, cross-country	500	620
Stair treadmill	660	820
Swimming laps, light or moderate	420	530
Swimming laps, vigorous	720	900
Walking, 2 mph	200	260
Walking, 3.5 mph	310	400
Weight (resistant) training	370	460
Weight lifting	610	760

The remaining topics in this section of the chapter are additional strategies for health, wellness and disease prevention.

Cancer Prevention

A 39-year-old woman comes to the clinic very concerned about her risk of developing cancer. Her father was diagnosed with colon cancer at age 43, and her mother was diagnosed with breast cancer at age 52. She is sexually active with multiple partners and has not seen a physician since a motor vehicle accident 15 years ago. She denies any symptoms at this time, and her physical examination is normal. She asks what is recommended for a woman her age.

Cancer screening tests are done on seemingly healthy people to identify those at increased risk of disease. However even if a diagnostic test is available, that does not necessarily mean it should be used to screen for a particular disease.

- Several harmful effects may potentially result from screening tests.
- Any adverse outcome that occurs (large bowel perforation secondary to a colonoscopy) is iatrogenic.
- Screening may be expensive, unpleasant, or inconvenient.
- Screening may also lead to harmful treatment.

Finally, there may be a stigma associated with incorrectly labeling a patient as "sick."

For all diseases for which screening is recommended, effective intervention must exist, and the course of events after a positive test result must be acceptable to the patient. Most importantly, the screening test must be valid, i.e., it must have been shown in trials to decrease overall mortality in the screened population. For a screening test to be recommended for regular use, it has to be extensively studied to ensure that all of the above requirements are met.

The 3 malignancies for which regular screening is recommended are **cancers of the colon, breast**, and **cervix.**

Colon Cancer

In the patient with no significant family history of colon cancer, screening should begin at age 50. The preferred screening modality for colon cancer is colonoscopy every 10 years. Other choices include annual fecal occult blood testing and sigmoidoscopy with barium enema every 5 years.

In the patient with a single first-degree relative diagnosed with colorectal cancer before age 60 or multiple first-degree relatives with colon cancer at any age, colonoscopy should begin at age 40 or 10 years before the age at which the youngest affected relative was diagnosed, *whichever age occurs earlier*. In these high-risk patients, colonoscopy should be repeated every 5 years. The U.S. Preventive Services Task Force (USPSTF) does not recommend routine screening in patients age >75.

Note

Tamoxifen prevents cancer by 50% in those with >1 family member with breast cancer.

Note

Prostate Screening

USPSTF concludes that the current evidence is insufficient to assess the balance of benefits/risks of prostate cancer screening in men age <75. It recommends against screening in men age >75.

For FPGEE, do not screen for prostate cancer.

Breast Cancer

The tests used to screen for breast cancer are mammography and manual breast exam. Mammography with or without clinical breast exam is recommended every 1–2 years from age 50–74. The American Cancer Society no longer recommends monthly self breast examination alone as a screening tool. Patients with very strong family histories of breast cancer (defined as multiple first-degree relatives) should consider prophylactic tamoxifen, discussing risks and benefits with a physician. Tamoxifen prevents breast cancer in high-risk individuals.

Cervical Cancer

The screening test of choice for the early detection of cervical cancer is the Papanicolaou smear (the "Pap" test). In average risk women, screening with Pap smear should be started at age 21, **regardless of onset of sexual activity**. It should be performed every 3 years until age 65. As an alternative, women age 30–65 who wish to lengthen the screening interval can do co-testing with Pap and HPV testing every 5 years. In higher risk women, e.g., HIV, more frequent screening or screening beyond age 65 may be required.

Travel Medicine

A 44-year-old executive comes to the clinic before traveling to Thailand for business. He has no significant past medical history and is here only because his company will not let him travel until he is seen by a physician. The patient appears agitated and demands the physician's recommendation immediately.

It is important to set up a pre-travel counseling session approximately 4 to 6 weeks before the patient's departure.

Hepatitis A infection is travelers' most common vaccine-preventable disease. Hepatitis A infection is possible wherever fecal contamination of food or drinking water may occur. Infection rates are particularly high in nonindustrial countries. If a patient is leaving within 2 weeks of being seen, both the vaccine and immune serum globulin are recommended. A booster shot given 6 months after the initial vaccination confers immunity for approximately 10 years.

All travelers to less-developed countries should get hep A vaccine.

Hepatitis B vaccination is recommended for patients who work closely with indigenous populations. Additionally, patients who plan to engage in sexual intercourse with the local populace, to receive medical or dental care, or to remain abroad for >6 months should be vaccinated.

Malaria: Mefloquine is the agent of choice for malaria prophylaxis. It is given once per week; it may cause adverse neuropsychiatric effects such as hallucinations, depression, suicidal ideations, and unusual behavior. Doxycycline is an acceptable alternative to mefloquine, although photosensitivity can be problematic. For pregnant patients requiring chemoprophylaxis for malaria, chloroquine is the preferred regimen.

Rabies vaccination is recommended for patients traveling to areas where rabies is common among domesticated animals (India, Asia, Mexico). Chloroquine can blunt the response to the *intradermal* form of rabies vaccine. Therefore, in patients who require malaria prophylaxis, in addition to rabies prophylaxis the *intramuscular* form of the vaccine should be administered. Rabies vaccination is not considered a routine vaccination for most travelers.

Typhoid vaccination is recommended for patients who are traveling to developing countries and will have prolonged exposure to contaminated food and water. Typhoid vaccination comes in 2 forms: an oral live attenuated form and a capsular polysaccharide vaccine given parenterally. The live attenuated form needs to be refrigerated and is contraindicated in patients who are HIV positive. The polysaccharide vaccine is given intramuscularly as a single injection. Side effects include irritation at the injection site. Fever and headache are rare adverse reactions to the vaccine. The polysaccharide vaccine is the preferred form for almost all subjects as it is well-tolerated and convenient (no need for refrigeration). It is safe for HIV patients.

Polio: Adults who are traveling to developing countries and have never received a polio vaccine should receive 3 doses of the inactivated polio vaccine. Patients who have been previously immunized should receive a one-time booster. The live attenuated polio vaccine is no longer recommended because of the risk of vaccine-associated disease.

Patients traveling to areas where **meningococcal meningitis** is endemic or epidemic (Nepal, sub-Saharan Africa, northern India) should be immunized with the polysaccharide vaccine. Additionally, Saudi Arabia requires immunization for pilgrims to Mecca. Patients with functional or actual asplenia and patients with terminal complement deficiencies should also receive the vaccine. Meningococcal vaccine is now routinely administered at age 11.

To prevent **traveler's diarrhea**, patients should be advised to avoid raw and street vendor salads, unwashed fruit, and tap/ice water. Patients who experience mild loose stools without fever or blood can safely take loperamide. Treatment with a fluoroquinolone or azithromycin is reserved for patients with moderate to severe symptoms.

Smoking Cessation

> A 25-year-old man comes to the clinic for evaluation of a stuffy nose and fever. Over the course of the interview the patient states that he smokes 3 packs of cigarettes per day and has been doing so for the last 7 years.

Smoking is responsible for 1 in every 5 deaths in the United States. Smoking cessation is the most preventable cause of disease. Physicians and pharmacists can take the following steps to assist:

ASK about smoking at every visit.

ADVISE all smokers to quit at every visit.

ATTEMPT to identify those smokers willing to quit.

ASSIST the patient by setting a quit date (usually within 2 weeks) and using nicotine patches/ gum, the oral antidepressant bupropion or varenicline as supportive therapy. Varenicline and bupropion are more effective than patches.

ARRANGE follow-up. Provide positive reinforcement if the quit attempt was successful. If the quit attempt was not successful, then determine why the patient smoked and elicit a recommitment to smoking cessation. Most patients will require several attempts before being successful.

Note

Varenicline should not be used in patients with a history of psychiatric disease.

Monotherapy treatment for smoking cessation includes nicotine replacement therapy (trans-dermal nicotine patches, gum, lozenges, inhalers), bupropion, and varenicline. Bupropion lowers the seizure threshold so do not use in cases of alcohol abuse. With varenicline, screen first for depression since it causes increased rate of suicidal thoughts.

Place a follow-up call 1–2 weeks after quit date. The use of pharmacotherapy doubles the effect of any tobacco cessation intervention.

Osteoporosis Prevention

All women age >65 should be given a DEXA bone density scan. Screening should begin at age 60 if there is low body weight or increased risk of fractures. A bone density test uses x-rays to measure how many grams of calcium and other bone minerals are packed into a segment of bone. The bones that are tested are in the spine, hip and forearm. Bone density test results are reported in 2 numbers: T-score and Z-score.

The **T-score** is the bone density compared with what is normally expected in a healthy young adult of the same sex. The T-score is the number of units—standard deviations—that bone density is above or below the average. T-score >2.5 SD indicates the likelihood of osteoporosis and increased risk of fracture. The diagnosis of osteoporosis by DEXA scan also means that treatment should be initiated with bisphosponates, oral daily calcium supplementation, and vitamin D.

The **Z-score** is the number of standard deviations above or below what is normally expected for someone of the same age, sex, weight, and ethnic or racial origin. Z-score ≤–2 may suggest that something other than aging is causing abnormal bone loss (consider drugs causing osteoporosis such as corticosteroids). The goal in this case is to identify the underlying problem.

Abdominal Aortic Aneurysm Prevention

U/S should be done once in men age >65 who have ever smoked. There are no screening recommendations for male nonsmokers and women, regardless of smoking history.

Hypertension, Diabetes Mellitus, and Hypercholesterolemia Prevention

A 45-year-old man comes to the physician anxious about his health. Five years ago his mother was diagnosed with diabetes and high cholesterol. He is worried about his health and risk for heart disease. Physical examination is within normal limits.

Cholesterol screening should commence at age 35 in men who have no risk factors. In both men and women with risk factors for coronary artery disease, screening should be done routinely after age 20. Management should not be determined by an isolated reading because cholesterol levels may fluctuate between measurements. Repeat in 5 years in low-risk individuals.

Screening for diabetes mellitus should be considered only for patients with hypertension (>135/80 mm Hg). Diabetes mellitus is diagnosed when:

- 2 fasting glucose measurements are >125 mg/dL, HbA1c > 6.5%, or
- random glucose >200 mg/dL accompanied by symptoms

There is insufficient evidence for or against routine screening. The strongest indication is for those with hypertension and hyperlipidemia.

Screening is recommended for elevated blood pressure in those age >18, at every visit. Screening is not recommended for carotid artery stenosis with duplex.

Alcohol Abuse (Alcohol Use Disorder)

A 55-year-old man comes to a physician's office for evaluation of a sore throat. The patient admits that he was recently fired from his job and is having marital problems at home. The patient has no significant past medical history, and physical examination is within normal limits. He attests to drinking 3 shots of whiskey every day after work (prior to loosing his job).

Physicians (and pharmacists) should screen for alcohol abuse (Alcohol Use Disorder) by using the CAGE questionnaire:

Have you ever felt the need to:	**C**ut down on your drinking?
Have you ever felt:	**A**nnoyed by criticism of your drinking?
Have you ever felt:	**G**uilty about your drinking?
Have you ever taken a morning:	**E**ye opener?

A positive screen is 2 "yes" answers. One "yes" should raise the possibility of alcohol abuse.

Prevention of Violence and Injury

A 27-year-old woman presents to the emergency department complaining of right-arm pain. When asked how she sustained the injury, she states that she fell down the steps in front of her house. The patient appears anxious and nervous. On physical examination there are various 2 cm wide lacerations on her buttocks.

Injuries are the most common cause of death in those age <65. The role of the physician is to advise patients about safety practices that can prevent injury, e.g., using seat belts, wearing bicycle helmets, and not driving after drinking alcohol.

Identifying women who are at increased risk of physical or sexual abuse is an essential role for physicians. Simply asking women if they have been hit, kicked, or physically hurt can increase identification by >10%.

IMMUNIZATIONS

Note

Patients must get pneumovax, meningococcal, and Haemophilus vaccines 2 weeks before a splenectomy.

Immunization is the best method available to prevent serious infectious disease. Between 50,000 and 70,000 adults die every year from preventable infectious diseases (influenza, invasive pneumococcal disease, and hepatitis B). Surveys have shown that among patients who have an indication for any vaccination, very few actually receive it (pneumococcal vaccination 20%, influenza 40%, hepatitis B 10%). It is for this reason that the American College of Physicians recommends that every patient's immunization status should be reviewed at age 50. Risk factors that would indicate specific vaccinations should be evaluated at that time.

NAPLEX Reference

Preventative Medicine chapter:

"Immunizations"

Most patients received a primary immunization against tetanus and diphtheria as children. Adults who were never vaccinated should receive a total of 3 doses, the first 2 of which are given 1 to 2 months apart, with the third dose given 6 to 12 months later. The principle is that adults require a total of 3 vaccinations against tetanus and diphtheria. A booster vaccination should be given every 10 years for life. One of the boosters should use Tdap instead of Td booster. If the wound is dirty, revaccinate after 5 years.

- Additional immunization information as well as live and inactivated vaccine tables are found in the Preventative Medicine chapter of the NAPLEX text.

Influenza Vaccine

Recommended annually for all adults regardless of age. Patients who have a history of cardiopulmonary disease, diabetes mellitus, or hemoglobinopathy, or are age 50+ residents of chronic care facilities derive the greatest benefit from an annual influenza vaccination. Pregnant women who will be in their second or third trimester during the influenza season should also receive the vaccine.

Pneumococcal Vaccine

Indicated for all adults age ≥65. Additionally, patients with a history of sickle-cell disease or splenectomy, those who have a history of cardiopulmonary disease, alcoholism, or cirrhosis, and Alaskan natives and certain Native American populations should receive the vaccine regardless of age. Immunocompromised patients (patients with hematologic malignancies, chronic renal failure, or nephrotic syndrome; HIV-positive patients; or patients receiving immunosuppressive medications) should also receive the vaccine at any age. Revaccination should be performed in healthy patients who received their initial vaccination age <65 and were age <60 at the time of primary vaccination. Patients with a high risk of fatal infection (CKD, asplenic patients, immunocompromised patients) should be revaccinated once after 5 years. No one gets >1 booster shot per lifetime.

Hepatitis B Vaccine

Recommended when there is a history of IV drug abuse, male homosexuality, household or sexual contact with hepatitis B carriers, or frequent exposure to blood or blood products. Additionally, patients with a history of chronic liver disease should receive the vaccine. Immunity is confirmed serologically. Also recommended for all children through age 18, those with STIs, those who are sexually active but not monogamous, workers with occupational exposure to blood, and prison inmates.

Hepatitis A Vaccine

The vaccine against hepatitis A protects against the virus in >95% of cases. There are 2 types of vaccine; both types stimulate active immunity against a future infection.

- One contains inactivated hepatitis A virus
- One contains a live but attenuated virus

For the best protection, the vaccine should be given in 2 doses; a booster should follow up the initial dose 6–12 months later. Protection against hepatitis A begins approximately 2–4 weeks after the initial vaccination. Those who miss the follow-up booster dose should receive only the remaining booster dose.

In the United States, the vaccine is strongly recommended for all children age 12–23 months in an attempt to eradicate the virus nationwide. There are also recommendations that the following populations should be vaccinated:

- All children age >1 year
- People whose sexual activity puts them at risk
- People with chronic liver disease
- People who are being treated with clotting factor concentrates
- People who are living in communities where an outbreak is present

Hepatitis A is the most common vaccine-preventable virus acquired during travel, so people traveling to places where the virus is common (Indian subcontinent, Africa, Central America, South America, the far East, and Eastern Europe) should be vaccinated.

Varicella Vaccine

A live attenuated vaccine recommended for use in all adults who lack a history of childhood infection with varicella virus. Being a live attenuated vaccine, varicella vaccine should not be given to immunocompromised patients, HIV-positive patients when symptomatic or <200 CD4 cells, or pregnant women.

Patients age ≥60 are recommended to receive the varicella zoster (shingles) vaccine, which has been shown to reduce the risk of zoster and its associated pain (post-herpetic neuralgia). It is indicated regardless of whether there is a history of shingles, as it is possible to have a second herpes zoster infection.

Measles, Mumps, Rubella (MMR) Vaccine

A live attenuated vaccine usually given in childhood. Healthy adults born after 1956 should receive 1 dose of the vaccine. Pregnant women and immunocompromised patients should not be vaccinated. HIV-positive patients who are asymptomatic may receive the vaccine.

Meningococcal Vaccine

Recommended for everyone at age 11 visit. Also recommended for young adults living in dormitories or barracks, people exposed to outbreaks, those with asplenia or terminal complement deficiencies, those who travel to endemic regions (traveling to Mecca), and those exposed to *Neisseria menigitidis.*

Human Papillomavirus (HPV) Vaccine

Recommended for women age 9–26, regardless of sexual activity. Do not use in pregnancy. Regimen is in 3 doses: 0, 2, and 6 months.

Herpes Zoster Vaccine

The zoster vaccine is a live vaccine that has been shown to reduce the incidence of shingles by 50%. It has also been shown to reduce the number of cases of post-herpetic neuralgia, as well as the severity and duration of pain/discomfort associated with shingles. The vaccine is, basically, a larger-than-normal dose of the chicken pox vaccine, as both shingles and chickenpox are caused by the same virus, varicella zoster (VZV).

The shingles vaccine (Zostavax) is recommended for adults age ≥60, whether they have already had shingles or not. The shingles vaccine is a live vaccine given as a single injection. Some people report a chickenpox-like rash after receiving it. The vaccine should NOT be given to:

- Those with a weakened immune system due to HIV/AIDS or another disease that affects the immune system
- Those who are receiving immune system-suppressing drugs or treatments, such as steroids, adalimumab (Humira), infliximab (Remicade), etanercept (Enbrel), radiation or chemotherapy
- Those who have neoplasia, which affects the bone marrow or lymphatic system, such as leukemia or lymphoma

PRACTICE QUESTIONS

1. A patient with type 2 diabetes takes a new medication for treatment of their disease. This is an example of what kind of prevention?

   A. Primary prevention
   B. Secondary prevention
   C. Tertiary prevention
   D. Quaternary prevention
   E. Treatment measures cannot be considered preventative

NAPLEX Question Reference

Preventative Medicine end of chapter questions

2. Screening for colorectal cancer should begin at what age for a male with no significant family history?

    A. 40
    B. 50
    C. 55
    D. 60
    E. 65

3. A female in her first trimester of pregnancy is traveling to an area of Africa with a high incidence of malaria. Which of the following is the preferred treatment of choice for this woman?

    A. Azithromycin
    B. Ciprofloxacin
    C. Chloroquine
    D. Doxycycline
    E. None of the above

4. According to the FDA, the recommended percentage of calories derived from fat is which of the following?

    A. <10%
    B. 10–35%
    C. 20–30%
    D. 30–40%
    E. 45–65%

5. The vaccine for *Streptococcus Pneumoniae* is recommended for which of the following age groups by the CDC?

    A. Persons >10 years
    B. Persons >40 years
    C. Persons >50 years
    D. Persons >65 years
    E. There is no specific recommendation for this vaccine

6. According to the Centers for Disease Control and Prevention (CDC), regular physical activity is defined as which of the following?

    A. 15 minutes of moderate-intensity aerobic activity per day
    B. 15 minutes of moderate-intensity aerobic activity per week
    C. 75 minutes of moderate-intensity aerobic activity per day
    D. 75 minutes of moderate-intensity aerobic activity per week
    E. 150 minutes of moderate-intensity aerobic activity per week

7. A 53-year-old female has a breast exam and mammography on July 9, 2016. Which of the following is the most recommended date of her next breast exam and mammography?

   A. October 8, 2016
   B. January 8, 2017
   C. January 8, 2018
   D. July 8, 2019
   E. July 8, 2021

Answers and Explanations

1. **The correct answer is C.** A patient with type 2 diabetes is taking a new medication to prevent disease complications in an incurable disease. According to the CDC, tertiary prevention is used in a patient who has symptoms of a disease to slow progression, prevent complications and increase the quality of life for a patient with the disease. Primary prevention (choice A) employs the use of preventative measures so that a person does not get the disease. Examples include condoms and sunscreen. Secondary prevention (choice B) is a form of prevention that is used after the disease has occurred but before the person notices that anything is wrong. For example, screening tests. Quaternary prevention (choice D) is the use of methods to mitigate or avoid consequences of unnecessary or excessive interventions in the health system. For example, prevent overuse of antibiotics.

2. **The correct answer is B.** In the patient with no significant family history of colon cancer, screening for colorectal cancer should begin at age 50. The preferred screening modality for colon cancer is colonoscopy every 10 years. Other choices include annual fecal occult blood testing and sigmoidoscopy with barium enema every 5 years.

3. **The correct answer is C.** Mefloquine is the agent of choice for malaria prophylaxis; however, it should not be given in the first trimester of pregnancy. Doxycycline (choice D) is an acceptable alternative to mefloquine, although it is contraindicated in pregnancy. For pregnant patients requiring chemoprophylaxis for malaria, chloroquine (choice C) is the preferred regimen. Azithromycin (choice A) and ciprofloxacin (choice B) can be used to prevent travelers' diarrhea.

4. **The correct answer is C.** Daily values for all major food components are based on a caloric intake of 2,000 calories, for adults and children (>4 years old). Each of the individual recommended daily values can vary depending on a person's age, height, weight and presence of disease. It is recommended that the total fat intake be 20-30% of total daily calories. Choice A (<10%) represents the total daily calories derived from saturated fat. Choice B (10–35%) is the recommended number of daily calories derived from protein. Choice E (10–35%) is the recommended number of daily calories derived from carbohydrates.

5. **The correct answer is D.** Pneumococcal vaccines are licensed by the FDA for individuals aged ≥50 years (choice D); however, the Advisory Committee on Immunization Practices (ACIP) for the CDC recommends routine vaccination with both pneumococcal vaccines PCV13 and PPSV23 for individuals aged ≥65 years.

6. **The correct answer is E.** According to the Centers for Disease Control and Prevention (CDC), regular physical activity is one of the most important preventative health measures that a person can do. Regular exercise can help control body weight; reduce the risk of cardiovascular disease, type 2 diabetes and metabolic syndrome; reduce the risk of some cancers; strengthen a person's bones and muscles as well as numerous other benefits. The CDC recommends that a person work up to 150 minutes of moderate-intensity aerobic activity or 75 minutes of vigorous-intensity aerobic activity, or an equivalent mix of the 2 each week.

7. **The correct answer is C.** The tests used to screen for breast cancer are mammography and manual breast exam. Mammography with or without clinical breast exam is recommended every 1–2 years from age 50–74. Thus, choice C is the best answer since it is 18 months after the "current" breast exam and mammography.

Patient Assessment 27

Learning Objectives

- ❑ Explain how to obtain a comprehensive patient history
- ❑ Show proficiency in the physical assessment of the patient
- ❑ Describe application principles of physical assessment findings
- ❑ Demonstrate an understanding of clinical laboratory and diagnostic tests
- ❑ Solve clinical calculation problems
- ❑ Answer questions on OTC testing devices

Pharmacists consistently rank as one of the most trusted health care professionals in the United States. As a result, patients commonly seek medical advice from "their pharmacist" prior to contacting a physician.

The pharmacist's assessment of a patient's history, chief complaint, laboratory reports or physical assessment findings will determine if their condition can be treated by over-the-counter products purchased at the pharmacy OR if a referral to a physician is necessary. Thus pharmacists should have a strong understanding of common physical assessment techniques and procedures.

THE COMPREHENSIVE PATIENT HISTORY

Patient Interview

Obtaining a complete and accurate history is the first step in determining the etiology and severity of a patient's condition. Most of the time, an experienced pharmacist will be able to make a presumptive diagnosis and recommend treatment (or refer the patient to a physician) based on their history alone.

- The value of the history report will depend on the pharmacist's ability to verbally elicit pertinent information from the patient.
- Note: professional communication principles are discussed in Chapter 19.

In the pharmacy setting, the process for obtaining a comprehensive patient history generally begins by initiating a professional conversation with the patient with a primary goal of improving patient outcomes. Whereas a patient will speak with a nurse or fill out a questionnaire at a physician's office, the history taking process at most pharmacies generally begins with an oral patient interview.

Table 27-1. Conducting a Successful Patient Interview

Step	Steps in the Interview	Comments
1	Initial greeting	• The initial encounter will set the tone for the forthcoming interview. • Examples: Say hello, introduce yourself, shake hands, maintain eye contact, etc.
2	Establish rapport	• Defined as a state of harmonious understanding with another individual (or group) that enables better and more productive communication. • Ensure proper verbal and nonverbal communication forms (See Chapter 19), including active listening and proper body language.
3	Elicit the chief complaint	• Determine why the patient is seeking medical advice using both open and closed-ended questions. • Listen to the patient's explanation without interrupting. • Ask for more information if appropriate. • Never make assumptions; the patient's health is contingent on the establishing the correct diagnosis.
4	Establishing the agenda and expected outcomes	• Establish the patient's and pharmacist's goals from the interview. • The pharmacist may notice some additional issues that need to be addressed based on the information obtained in the chief complaint.
5	Expand and clarify the chief complaint	• Clarify the patient's chief complaint and include additional comments or concerns. • Whenever possible, use the patient's words, making sure to clarify their meaning. • Ask questions if something is not clear. • Follow: **OLD CARTS** (**O**nset, **L**ocation, **D**uration, **C**haracter, **A**ggravating/**A**lleviating Factors, **R**adiation, and **T**iming) and **OPQRST** (**O**nset, **P**alliating/**P**rovoking Factors, **Q**uality, **R**adiation, **S**ite, and **T**iming). ***See Table 27.2*** • A thorough examination is critical. For example, if the patient has a complaint of heartburn but the pharmacist fails to question about onset, aggravating factors and timing, they may miss a myocardial infarction diagnosis.
6	Obtain other pertinent information	• This is the step where the pharmacist determines if additional information should be obtained (i.e. family history, social history, past medical history, current medications, allergies, etc.) • For example, a diagnosis of tinea pedis would not require this information. However, some of this information should be obtained before recommending a medication with numerous drug-drug or drug-disease interactions (i.e. omeprazole, pseudoephedrine, diphenhydramine, antacids, etc.)
7	Generate diagnostic hypotheses (and refer for testing if condition is not treatable by pharmacist)	• After listening to the patient and following the OLD CARTS (or similar) process, the pharmacist will formulate a hypothesis as to the possible diagnosis. • Based on this hypothesis, a presumptive diagnosis will be made and the pharmacist will recommend the next course of action.

(Continued)

Step	Steps in the Interview	Comments
8	Outline a mutual understanding of the presumptive diagnosis	• Present information on the disease (clinical diagnosis) and be empathetic to the patient's view of the illness (diagnosis + personal feelings/impact of the illness). • For example, an elderly patient presents with polyuria, polydipsia and polyphagia. The pharmacist should be empathetic to the fact that a presumptive diagnosis of diabetes mellitus will dramatically impact the patient's life.
9	Negotiate a treatment (or referral) plan	• Once the presumptive diagnosis is made, the pharmacist should discuss the goals, expectations, risk/benefits and costs of therapy. • The pharmacist can make recommendations but the patient ultimately decides if they will accept the treatment recommendations, make lifestyle changes or be referred to a physician.
10	Follow-up plan	• Clarify the recommendations and next steps with the patient. • Provide contact information for the pharmacist or physician referral.
11	Close the interview process	• Express genuine concern for the patient and emphasize that they may contact the pharmacist again if they have further questions.

OLD CARTS Mnemonic

The OLD CARTS (Onset, Location, Duration, Character, Aggravating/Alleviating Factors, Radiation, and Timing) AND OPQRST (Onset, Palliating/Provoking Factors, Quality, Radiation, Site, and Timing) methods for evaluating the patient's chief complaint symptoms should be conducted with open-ended questions.

Table 27-2. Symptom Attributes – OLD CARTS Mnemonic (With OPQRST Included)

Attribute	Questions to Ask the Patient
Onset (Onset)	When did the "current" symptoms onset?
Location (Site)	Where exactly are the symptoms located?
Duration (Timing)	How long do the symptoms last?
Character (Quality)	What exactly does it feel like? For pain, ask for a rating on a scale of 1–10.
Aggravating/***A***lleviating factors (Palliating/Provoking Factors)	What makes the symptoms better or worse?
Radiation (Radiation)	When the symptom occurred, did it spread to other areas of the body? Have you noticed anything else that accompanies the symptoms?
Timing (Timing)	Have these symptoms occurred before? If yes, then when did they last occur? Is there a particular setting in which these symptoms occur? If yes, how long while in this situation before the symptoms begin to appear?

SOAP Notes

When documentation is required, the information obtained from the patient interview should be well organized and readily retrievable. A SOAP note is a documentation method commonly used by health care providers to create a patient's chart.

There are 4 parts of a SOAP note: Subjective, Objective, Assessment, and Plan.

Table 27-3. Components of a SOAP Note

Components	Definition	Examples
Subjective	• Subjective observations • Primarily contains information given by the patient to the provider • Includes notes/comments provided by previous caregivers	**OLD CARTS** (**O**nset, **L**ocation, **D**uration, **C**haracter, **A**ggravating/**A**lleviating Factors, **R**adiation, and **T**iming)
Objective	• Objective observations that are repeatable and traceable facts about the patient's status • Includes vital signs, physical exam findings, laboratory tests and personal measurements	Vital signs (heart rate, blood pressure, etc); physical exam findings (abnormal breathing, arrhythmia, bruising, etc); laboratory findings (CBC, Chem-18, etc); personal measurements (height, weight, age, etc.)
Assessment	• Subjective and objective observations are analyzed and used to formulate a differential diagnosis • Diagnoses are listed from most likely to least likely • Ensure that all health care providers are on the same page (if applicable)	Patient presents with continual "heartburn" and no other symptoms. • GERD • Gastric ulcer • Myocardial infarction
Plan	• All actions to be performed by the health care provider • Includes goals of therapy and individualized drug and disease-state monitoring parameters	Ordering labs, referrals, procedures performed, medications prescribed, patient education, etc.

PHYSICAL ASSESSMENT AND APPLICATION OF FINDINGS

Although most pharmacists are not likely to perform a physical examination, the FPGEE exam makers feel that foreign pharmacists should understand and be able to apply the principles of a physical examination.

Physical Assessment Overview

A physical assessment (PA) is performed to examine a patient's current health status with a focus on the information obtained in the patient interview (PI).

The collective goals of the PA and PI are to:

- Collect patient data (subjective and objective information as well as psychological and sociocultural information)
- Formulate a list of differential diagnoses and a presumptive diagnosis
- Establish the provider-patient relationship

During the evaluation, the patient history is obtained first; then a physical examination is performed with a focus on information obtained from the history. A complete physical assessment is not necessary for all patients. The provider will generally assess only the parts of the body involved in the chief complaint. However, the clinician should still observe some type of systematic process to avoid excluding essential assessment areas.

Prior to the physical examination, the provider should:

- quickly review the patient history, making note of the patient's name, age, occupation, race and religion to help ensure a proper culturally-centered examination (see Chapter 19 for cultural considerations);
- establish rapport (discussed in the comprehensive patient history section of this chapter);
- ensure proper physical examination environment (privacy, temperature, colleagues present);
- properly position the patient for the physical examination;
- tell the patient that you will explain what you are doing throughout the physical examination process;
- ask permission to examine the patient immediately prior to the examination; and
- begin the examination.

Physical Assessment Techniques and Possible Abnormal Findings

Objective data, obtained from the physical assessment, are obtained through the use of 4 diagnostic techniques:

- Inspection
- Palpation
- Percussion
- Auscultation

These assessment techniques are generally performed in this order (by a physician) when body systems are assessed with the exception of the abdomen (auscultation is performed prior to percussion and palpation, as the latter two can alter bowel sounds). However, the pharmacist should have an understanding of these physical assessment techniques.

- When differentiating between abnormal physical assessment findings caused by a medication or a disease state, the pharmacist should first reference the "current" medication list.
- See the Therapeutics chapters in Kaplan's *NAPLEX Strategies, Practice, and Review* book for high-yield medication side effects.

Inspection

Inspection can be done alone or in combination with other assessment techniques. It is defined as a method of systematic observation that begins with a series of broad observations progressing to specific areas of the body.

Inspection involves use of the following senses: Eyes (what do you see?); Ears (what do you hear?) and Nose (what do you smell?)

Common examples include:

- Skin color: cyanosis (bluish tint- decreased oxygenation); jaundice (yellow-brown due to increased bilirubin; hepatic or drug hepatotoxicity); erythematous (inflammation or rashes; disease or drug allergy)
- Moisture: Excessive sweating (diaphoresis); excessive dryness (elderly or anticholinergic side effects)
- Breath: Sweet smell (diabetes mellitus)
- Breathing: Cheyne-Stokes (crescendo-decrescendo-apnea; drugs or CNS damage); bradypnea (opioid toxicity)

Palpation

Palpitation is the act of touching a patient in a therapeutic manner to elicit specific information.

Table 27-4. Types of Palpitation

Type	Depth	Comments
Light	1 – 2 cm (½ – 1 inch)	• Press gently with the tips of 2 or 3 fingers held close together on the affected area. • Used to detect pulse rate, tenderness, warmth, texture, vibration (joints) or size and position of physiological structures or pathological masses. • Examples: Skin lesions (pathological or drug related), inconsistency of tissue directly or indirectly with finger pads, presence of thrills, misalignment of body structures and asymmetry of body parts.
Deep	5 – 8 cm (2 – 3 inches)	• Place one hand on top of the other, then press down with the fingertips of both hands. • A deep palpation can be used to estimate the size of the liver (right upper quadrant). • Examples: Hepatomegaly

Percussion

Examination of specific parts of the body by "tapping it" with the fingers is called percussion. With the percussion technique, there is a tapping of the fingers placed on the body part lightly but sharply enough to determine the consistency of tissues or organs through vibration and areas of tenderness.

Percussion involves placing the middle finger of the nondominant hand on an area of the patient's body and then tapping it briskly with the middle finger of the dominant hand making a sound loud enough to be heard by the examiner.

Table 27-5. Normal and Abnormal Percussion Sounds

Percussion Sound	Comments	Examples
Resonance	Low-pitched sound heard over hollow structures (lungs and abdomen)	Normal lung
Hyperresonance	Loud, very long sound, lower pitched than resonance	Normal when percussing the chests of children and very thin adults; abnormal lungs hyperinflated with air (COPD, Acute asthma)
Flat	Soft, high-pitched, short sound heard over solid areas	Normal muscle or bone
Dull	Medium-pitched, slightly louder than a flat sound normally heard over dense areas; Dullness replaces resonance when fluid or solid tissue replaces air-containing lung tissues	Normal heart or liver sound; abnormal lung (pneumonia, pleural effusions, or tumors)
Tympany	High-pitched, "drum-like" sound of medium duration heard over the stomach or gastric bubble; Tympanic sounds heard over the chest indicate excessive air in the chest	Normal stomach sound; abnormal chest sound (pneumothorax)

Auscultation

Auscultation is defined as the process of listening for normal and abnormal sounds over body cavities. The aim of auscultation is to determine presence and quality of lung, heart, and bowel sounds.

Auscultation is usually performed last in the physical assessment with a stethoscope in direct contact with the skin.

Table 27-6. Normal and Abnormal Breath Sounds

Breath Sound	Comments
Vesicular	• Heard over most of lung and described as low pitch, soft.
Bronchovesicular	• Heard over main bronchus, described as having a medium pitch. Note this sound is considered abnormal if heart at periphery.
Bronchial	• Heard over the trachea, described as loud, high pitch. Note this sound is considered abnormal if heart at periphery.
Wheeze	• Whistling-like sound heard during expiration (and sometimes inspiration) when air is forced through narrow airways. • Caused by bronchoconstriction, secretions, mucosal edema, other. • Most commonly caused by asthma and emphysema and potentially pneumonia and tumor.
Rales (Crackles)	• Scratchy sounds that occur secondary to conditions causing fluid to accumulate within the alveolar and interstitial spaces. • Pulmonary edema (secondary to heart failure) is the most common cause. May also be seen in pneumonia.
Rhonchi	• Gurgling-type noise caused by accumulation of secretions in the larger airways. • May be seen in bronchitis or other mucous creating process.

LABORATORY AND DIAGNOSTIC TESTS

Interpretation of clinical laboratory values and diagnostic tests is an essential part of being a pharmacist. These test results are commonly used in drug dosage calculations and to measure the safety and efficacy of medications. Thus it is essential that all pharmacists have a strong understanding of how to interpret and incorporate these findings clinically.

NAPLEX Reference

Calculations chapter
Renal chapter

Creatine clearance and body mass index are 2 common calculations used by pharmacists.

- Additional clinical calculations can be found in Kaplan's *NAPLEX Strategies, Practice, and Review* book.

Creatinine Clearance

In the body, the metabolism of creatine from skeletal muscle and dietary meat products results in a somewhat constant rate of release into the circulation resulting in a stable plasma concentration. Thus, the creatinine clearance (CrCl) is most commonly used to estimate the glomerular filtration rate (GFR).

The creatinine clearance is usually determined from a 24-hour urine collection.

- Creatinine clearance (mL/minute) = urine creatinine concentration (mL/dL) × volume of urine (mL/24 hour) ÷ plasma creatinine concentration (mg/dL) × 1440 minute/24 hour.
- The normal value for the creatinine clearance is 95 ± 20 mL/min per 1.73 m^2 in women and 120 ± 25 mL/min per 1.73 m^2 in men.

Major errors that can limit the accuracy of the CrCl as an estimate of GFR include errors in urine collection (incomplete collection), increase in creatinine secretion and increase in extrarenal creatinine degradation as the GFR falls. Due to these limits, many clinicians will estimate the GFR from the serum creatinine (SrCr) concentration using the Cockcroft-Gault equation instead of a timed urine collection.

The Cockcroft-Gault (C-G) equation (for men) allows the creatinine clearance to be estimated from the serum creatinine in a patient with a stable serum creatinine:

$$CCr\,(\mathrm{mL/min}) = \frac{(140\text{-}age) \times \textit{lean body weight}\ [\mathrm{kg}]}{Cr[\mathrm{mg/dL}] \times 72}$$

- For women, the equation requires multiplication by 0.85 to account for smaller muscle mass compared to men.
- Assumptions: creatinine production decreases with advancing age and is greater in individuals with greater weight. The equation is not adjusted for body surface area; hence, the result should be adjusted for body surface area to compare with normal values.
- The C-G equation was developed prior to the development of standardized creatinine assays; hence using the equation with creatinine values measured in most laboratories will result in a 10 to 40 percent overestimate of creatinine clearance. However, this equation can still be used clinically as a rapid method to estimate GFR provided the limitations are considered.

Body Mass Index

Obesity is a considerable public health issue in the United States and in other industrialized countries. It is classified as a chronic disease that is increasing in prevalence in adults, adolescents, and children.

NAPLEX Reference

Preventative Medicine chapter:
"Weight Loss"

Many clinicians consider obesity as part of a global epidemic associated with a significant increase in mortality. It is also a risk factor for many disorders, including diabetes mellitus, hypertension, heart disease, stroke, cancer, and many others.

- A more comprehensive review of obesity and its treatment is found in the Weight Loss section of the Preventative Medicine chapter in Kaplan's *NAPLEX Strategies, Practice, and Review* book.

Body mass index (BMI) is the most rational first step for evaluating the degree of obesity. It is calculated from the weight and square of the height as follows:

$$BMI = \frac{\text{weight (kg)}}{[\text{height (m)}]^2}$$

The recommended classifications for BMI adopted by NIH and WHO are found below.

Table 27-7. NIH and WHO BMI Classifications

Classification	BMI	Comments
Underweight	<18.5 kg/m^2	
Normal weight	≥18.5 to 24.9 kg/m^2	
Overweight	≥25.0 to 29.9 kg/m^2	
Obesity	≥30 kg/m^2	
Obesity class I	30.0 to 34.9 kg/m^2	
Obesity class II	35.0 to 39.9 kg/m^2	
Obesity class III	≥40 kg/m^2	Referred to as severe, extreme, or massive obesity

In addition to measuring BMI, a waist circumference in overweight and obese adults is used to assess abdominal obesity.

- A waist circumference of ≥40 in. (102 cm) for men and ≥35 in. (88 cm) for women is considered high and suggestive of an increased cardiometabolic risk.

A comprehensive review on the interpretation of common clinical laboratory test results is found in Kaplan's *NAPLEX Strategies, Practice, and Review* book.

- The remaining sections of this chapter will focus on cardiovascular and emergency medicine clinical evaluation tools and principles.

NAPLEX Reference

Clinical Lab Tests chapter

Cardiac Action Potential

The cardiac action potential is a transmembrane potential in the heart consisting of 5 phases. Cardiac abnormalities can alter the action potential and lead to the development of cardiac arrhythmias.

Fast-Response Fibers: Cardiac Muscle, His-Purkinje System

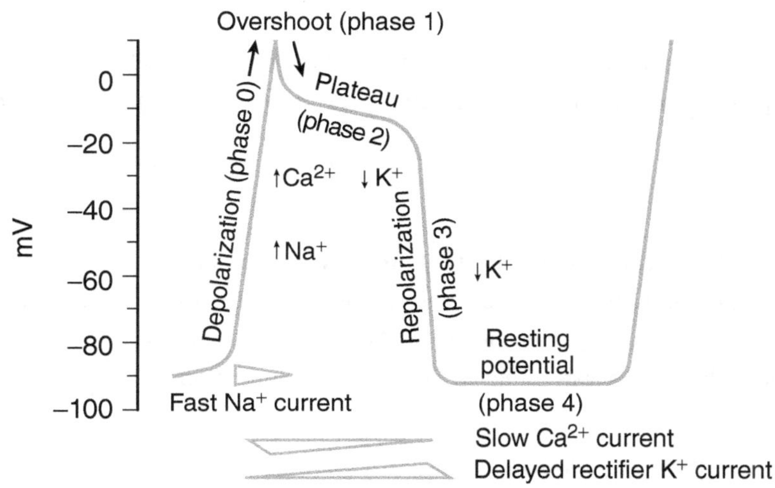

Figure 27-1. Cardiac Action Potentials in Fast-Response Fibers

Phase 0

- Na^+ channels open—sodium enters the cell down its concentration gradient (fast I_{Na}), causing membrane depolarization.
- Rate of depolarization depends on the number of Na^+ channels open, which in turn depends on resting membrane potential of the cell.
- Class I antiarrhythmic drugs can slow or block phase 0 in fast-response fibers.

Phase 1

- Na^+ channels are inactivated.
- In some His-Purkinje cells, transient outward K^+ currents and inward Cl^- currents contribute to the "notch"and overshoot.
- Antiarrhythmic drugs have no significant effects on these transient currents.

Phase 2

- Plateau phase in which a slow influx of Ca^{2+} (I_{Ca-L}) is "balanced" by a late-appearing outward K^+ current (the delayed rectifier current I_K).
- Antiarrhythmic drugs have no significant effects on these currents during this phase of the action potential (AP).

Phase 3

- Repolarization phase in which the delayed rectifier K^+ current rapidly increases as the Ca^{2+} current dies out because of time-dependent channel inactivation.
- Class III antiarrhythmic drugs slow this repolarization phase.
- Note that during phases 0 through 3, a slow Na^+ current ("window current") occurs, which can help prolong the duration of the action potential.

Phase 4

- Return of membrane to resting potential—maintained by activity of the Na^+/K^+-ATPase.

Responsiveness

- Capacity of a cell to depolarize, associated with the number of Na^+ channels in a ready state.
- This in turn depends on resting membrane potential: the more negative the resting potential (RP), the faster the response.

Conductance

Rate of spread of an impulse, or conduction velocity—3 major determinants:

- Rate of phase 0 depolarization—as V_{max} decreases, conduction velocity decreases and vice versa.
- Threshold potential—the less negative, the slower the conduction velocity.
- Resting potential—the more negative the RP, the faster the conduction.

Slow-Response Fibers (SA and AV Nodes, Specialized Cells)

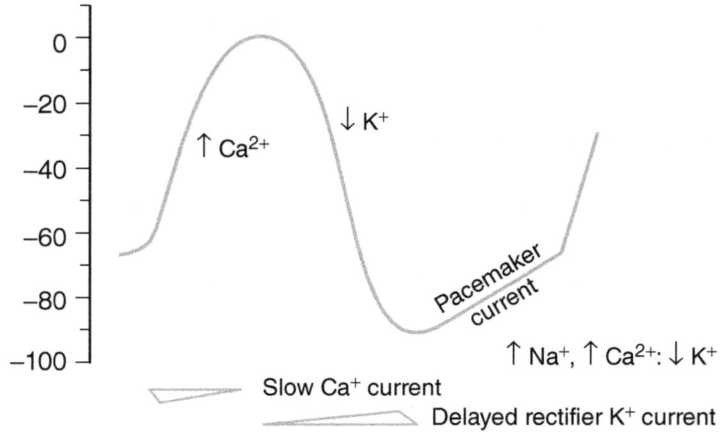

Figure 27-2. Cardiac Action Potentials in Slow-Response Fibers

- No appreciable Na^+ current during phase 0 in these cells because the Na channels are either absent or in an inactive form because of the existing voltage.
- Depolarization depends on activation of Ca^{2+} channels ($I_{Ca\text{-}L}$ and $I_{Ca\text{-}T}$).
- Class IV antiarrhythmic drugs can slow or block phase 0 in slow-response fibers.
- During repolarization, the Ca^{2+} currents are opposed and overcome by the delayed rectifier K^+ current. The relative magnitudes of these opposing currents determine the "shape" of the action potential.
- The major distinctive feature of slow fibers is their spontaneous depolarization, shown by the rising slope of phase 4 of the AP, referred to as the pacemaker potential or "pacemaker current." Although not completely understood, pacemaker potential is a composite of inward Na^+ (I_f) and Ca^{2+} ($I_{Ca\text{-}T}$) currents and outward K^+ currents (I_K).
- Class II and IV antiarrhythmic drugs can slow phase 4 in pacemaker fibers.

Automaticity

- The ability to depolarize spontaneously confers automaticity on a tissue.
- The fastest phase 4 slope will determine the pacemaker of the heart, which is normally the SA node.

Refractoriness

- The inability to respond to a stimulus—property of all cardiac cells.

Effective Refractory Period (ERP)

- No stimulus, of any magnitude, can elicit a response.
- Lasts into late stage 3 of the AP because Na^+ channels are effectively inactivated and not in the "ready" state.
- Blockers of K^+ channels prolong the ERP.

Relative Refractory Period (RRP)

- A strong stimulus can elicit a response, but the timing will be out of sync with the rest of the heart and arrhythmias may occur.
- Ratio of ERP to the action potential duration (APD) is a measure of refractoriness. Decreases in ERP favor the formation and propagation of premature impulses.

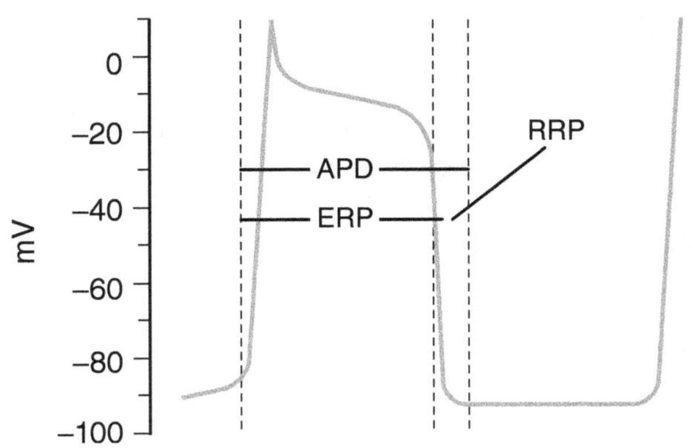

Figure 27-3. Relationship of ERP to APD

Na^+ Channels

Activation

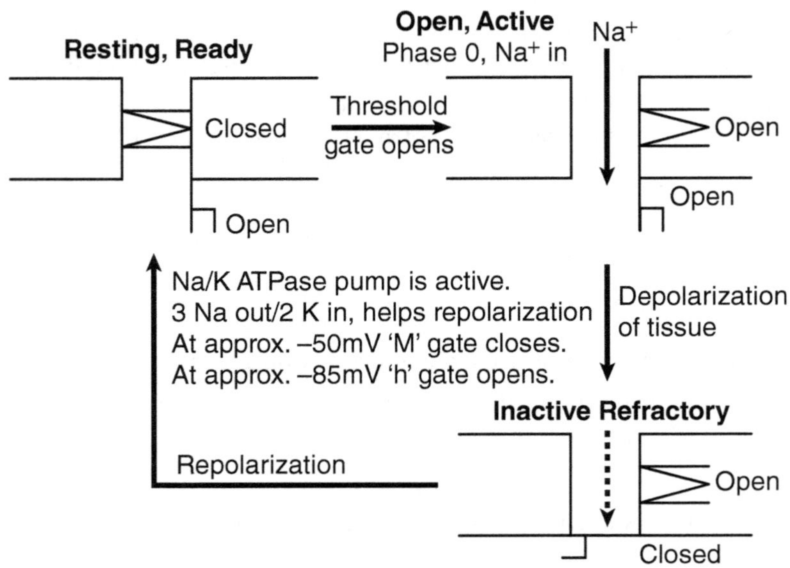

Figure 27-4. Mechanism of Action of Voltage-Gated Na^+ Channels

- This voltage-gated channel, which is responsible for the fast Na^+ current (I_{Na}), exists in 3 conformations:
  - Resting or ready state
  - Open or active state
  - Inactivated or refractory state
- The channel has 2 gates: M (activating) and h (inactivating), both of which are sensitive to voltage changes.
- Inactivation of the h gate is slower; therefore, it stays open longer and the Na^+ channel is active.

Recovery

- Rate of recovery of the Na^+ channel is dependent on resting potential (RP).
- Fastest rate of recovery occurs at normal RP, and recovery slows as membrane voltage increases.
- Rate of recovery is slower in ischemic tissue because cells may be partly depolarized at rest. This reduces the number of channels able to participate in the next depolarization, which leads to a decrease in conduction rate in ischemic tissue.
- Na^+ channel blockers also slow the rate of recovery in such tissues.

Emergency Medicine

Basic Life Support (Cardiopulmonary Resuscitation)

A 54-year-old man is at the opera when he suddenly jumps up and clutches his chest. He falls to his side into the lap of the woman sitting next to him.

Definition. The initial management algorithm of any patient who seems to have become unresponsive.

Etiology. A cardiac, neurologic, or toxicologic event leading to markedly diminished responsiveness or loss of pulse. Most causes of cardiac arrest are related to ventricular rhythm disturbance. The most common etiology of serious cardiac dysrhythmia is ischemia-related, particularly with coronary artery disease or another cardiac anatomic abnormality (especially cardiomyopathy).

Clinical Presentation. Any patient with diminished responsiveness that is usually sudden in onset.

Diagnosis. This is a clinically determined diagnosis at first. The initial step is, in fact, to assess the responsiveness of the patient to make sure that he is truly unresponsive and not just asleep. This is accomplished by calling to or gently shaking the patient. Be careful about shaking a patient who might have serious traumatic injury, particularly of the cervical spine.

Treatment. After determining that the patient is truly unresponsive, the next step is to call for help (dial 911). Although it is natural to reach down to check a pulse, this is not the action that the FPGEE or the American Heart Association (AHA) wants you to build as a reflex. Without the EKG, defibrillator, and cardiac medications you need, there is very little that 1 or even 2 rescuers can do for a patient with a serious dysrhythmia beyond chest compressions and opening the airway.

If a patient has a serious dysrhythmia such as asystole or ventricular fibrillation, there is virtually no survival if the heart has not been restarted within 10 minutes. Chest compressions just perfuse vital organs; they will not convert the arrhythmia back to normal sinus.

AHA guidelines emphasize the following:

- High-quality CPR with uninterrupted chest compressions of adequate depth (5 cm, 2 in.) at a rate of 100/min
- Decreased intervals between stopping the chest compression and shock delivery

Avoid excessive ventilation because it can be detrimental. ABC, according to new guidelines is now **CAB** (excluding newborns). Removing the 2 rescue breaths allows chest compressions to be delivered sooner. Earlier chest compressions and defibrillation are critical elements of CPR.

- Do look, listen, feel for breathing.
- Do check for pulse (for 10 seconds); if you establish that there is no pulse, start chest compressions (after calling 911).
- Do not give rescue breaths first, as that has been shown to delay vital chest compressions, which leads to an increase in mortality.
- Do not perform jaw thrust, which just delays chest compression.

After calling for help, position the patient on a firm, flat surface, and roll the patient so that she is face up. Check to see if there is a pulse by feeling for at least 5–10 seconds at the carotid artery. If there is no pulse, perform chest compressions at a rate of 100 per minute, "push hard and push fast." In adults, provide 30 compressions and then 2 ventilations, regardless of whether 1 or 2 rescuers is present. In children, perform 30 compressions and 2 ventilations if 1 rescuer is present, and give 15 compressions and 2 ventilations if 2 rescuers are present. Depth of chest compression: 2 in. or 5 cm.

Advanced Cardiac Life Support Algorithms

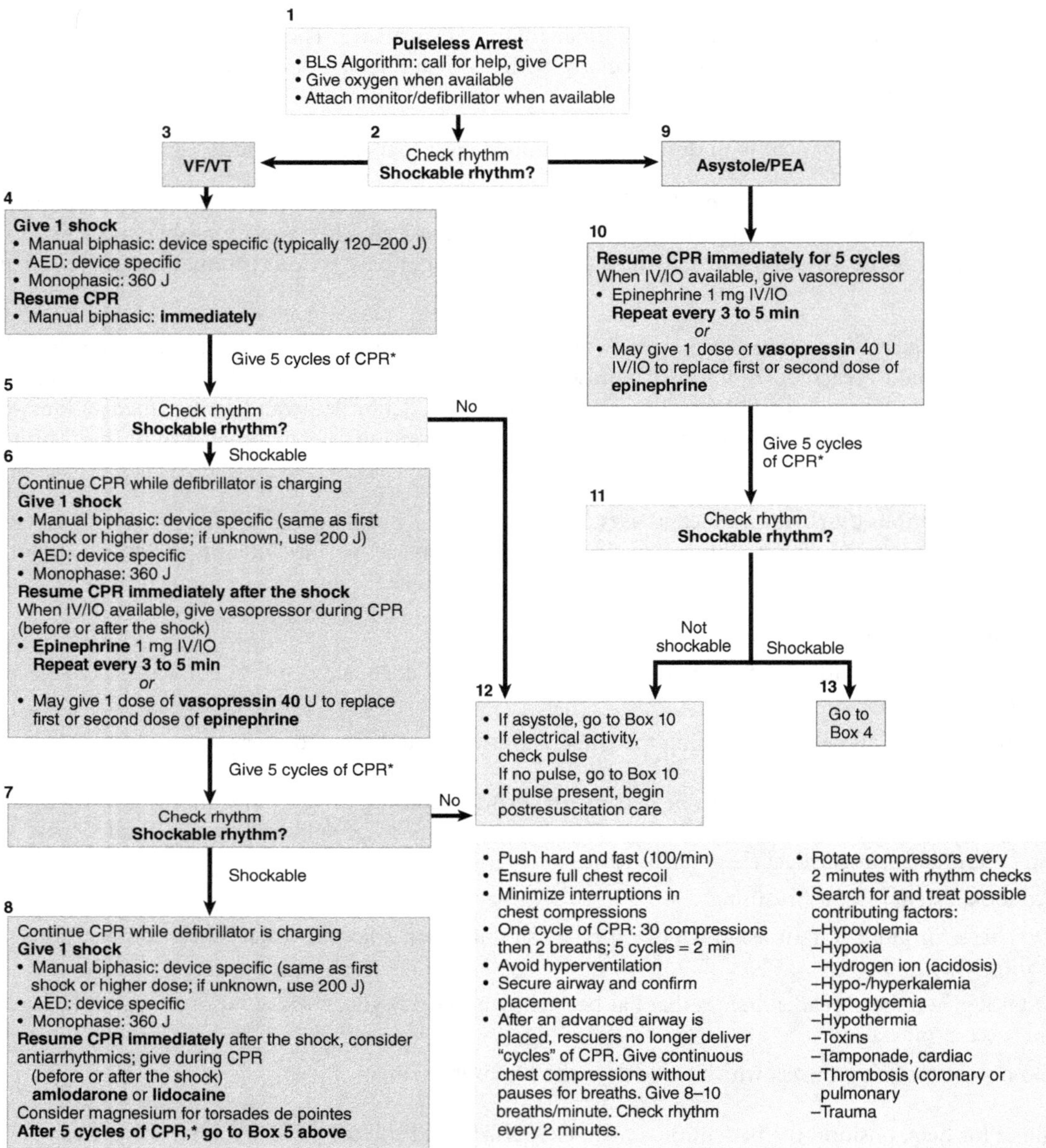

Figure 27-5. ACLS Pulseless Arrest Algorithm (For Reference ONLY—Do NOT Memorize)

CARDIAC DYSRHYTHMIAS

The 4 main types of cardiac arrhythmias are extra beats, supraventricular tachycardias, ventricular arrhythmias, and bradyarrhythmias.

Management of Specific Cardiac Dysrhythmias

The clinical pharmacist should know how to treat each of the major cardiac arrthythmias.

Asystole

A 54-year-old man is at the opera when he suddenly jumps up and clutches his chest. He falls to his side into the lap of the woman sitting next to him. After confirming that he is unresponsive, a nearby physician performs chest compressions and ventilations. An EKG is done and reveals no evidence of electrical activity.

Definition. The complete absence of electrical activity in the heart. This does not necessarily mean a completely flat line on an EKG because there may be slight variability on the rhythm strip.

Etiology. Ischemia and severe underlying cardiac disease most commonly underlie asystole. Other possible etiologies include metabolic derangements, drug overdose, trauma, and others.

Clinical Presentation. An unresponsive person with asystole on EKG; person has no pulse.

Note

For asystole and other arrhythmias in this chapter, remember the "Hs and Ts":

Hypoxia

Hyper/Hypokalemia

Hypothermia

Hypoglycemia

Hypovolemia

Trauma

Toxins (including overdose)

Tamponade

Tension pneumothorax

Thrombosis (coronary and pulmonary)

Diagnosis. Asystole should always be confirmed by observing the rhythm in more than one lead on the EKG.

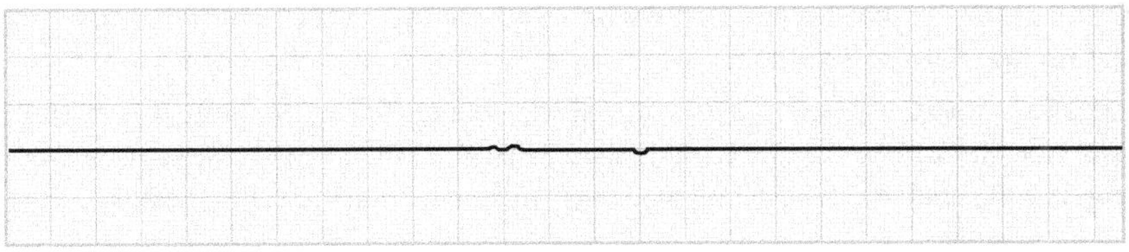

Figure 27-6. Asystole

Treatment. As you continue cardiopulmonary resuscitation (CPR), obtain IV access and prepare the patient for intubation.

1. Transcutaneous pacing should be considered and performed only for very slow bradycardia. Perform it as early as possible. Pacing is not for asystole.
2. Next, administer 1 mg epinephrine via IV push every 3–5 minutes. **(Atropine is no longer recommended for asystole.)**
3. If asystole persists, withhold resuscitative efforts in order to evaluate the presence of atypical clinical features or cease-effort protocol.

Note

Atropine is no longer indicated in asystole.

When you see asystole on the monitor, make sure of the following:

1. There are no loose or disconnected leads
2. The power to EKG machine and monitor is on
3. There is not a low signal gain on the monitor

Note

Transcutaneous pacemaker is not useful for asystole.

Note: Bicarbonate is useful if the cause of asystole is attributed to a preexisting acidosis (except hypercarbic acidosis), tricyclic antidepressant overdose, aspirin overdose, hyperkalemia, or diabetic ketoacidosis.

Ventricular Fibrillation

A 54-year-old man is at the opera when he suddenly jumps up and clutches his chest. He falls to his side into the lap of the woman sitting next to him. He is not breathing. After confirming that he is unresponsive, a nearby physician performs chest compressions and ventilations. An EKG is done and reveals ventricular fibrillation. He has no spontaneous respirations.

Definition. Significant electrical activity on EKG with no signs of an organized pattern.

Etiology. Ischemia, myocardial infarction, cardiomyopathy, and severe underlying cardiac disease most commonly underlie ventricular fibrillation. Remember the "Hs and Ts."

Clinical Presentation. A dead person with ventricular fibrillation on EKG.

Diagnosis. Entirely based on the EKG.

Treatment. The differences between defibrillation and cardioversion are very important.

- **Defibrillation** is a nonsynchronized delivery of shock at any phase of cardiac cycle. It is used in VF and pulseless VT. During defibrillation you depolarize all of the myocytes simultaneously, hoping that the SA node will start up normal sinus rhythm.
- **Cardioversion** means that the shock is synchronized with the QRS complex. When performing cardioversion, the defibrillator will not shock until the QRS complex appears. You will be able to see spikes over the QRS complexes on the monitor. If you shock on the T wave, when ventricular repolarization is taking place, you may induce VF.

Make sure that the SYN button is pushed when performing cardioversion. Use UNsynchronized shock (defibrillation) for VF or pulseless VT only.

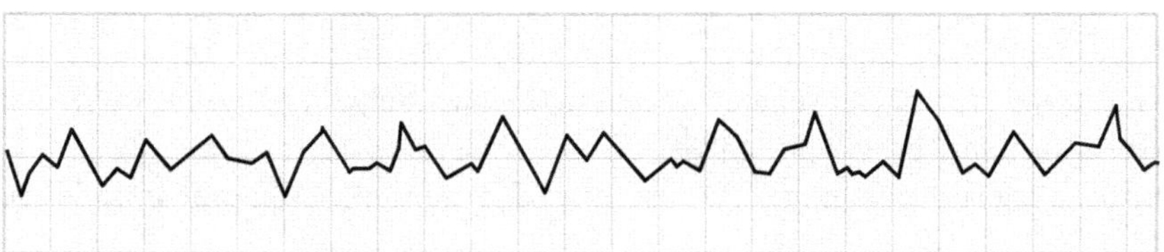

Figure 27-7. Ventricular Fibrillation

Post-Resuscitation Care. Most patients who survive resuscitation have anoxic brain injury. Hypothermia protocol reduces the risk of this type of severe neurologic injury. If a patient is not following commands or showing purposeful movements, the hypothermia protocol should be used. The goal of protocol is to reach core temperature 32–34°C (90–93°F) within 6 hours and maintain for 12–24 hours. Absolute contraindications for induced hypothermia are active bleeding and do-not-resuscitate order.

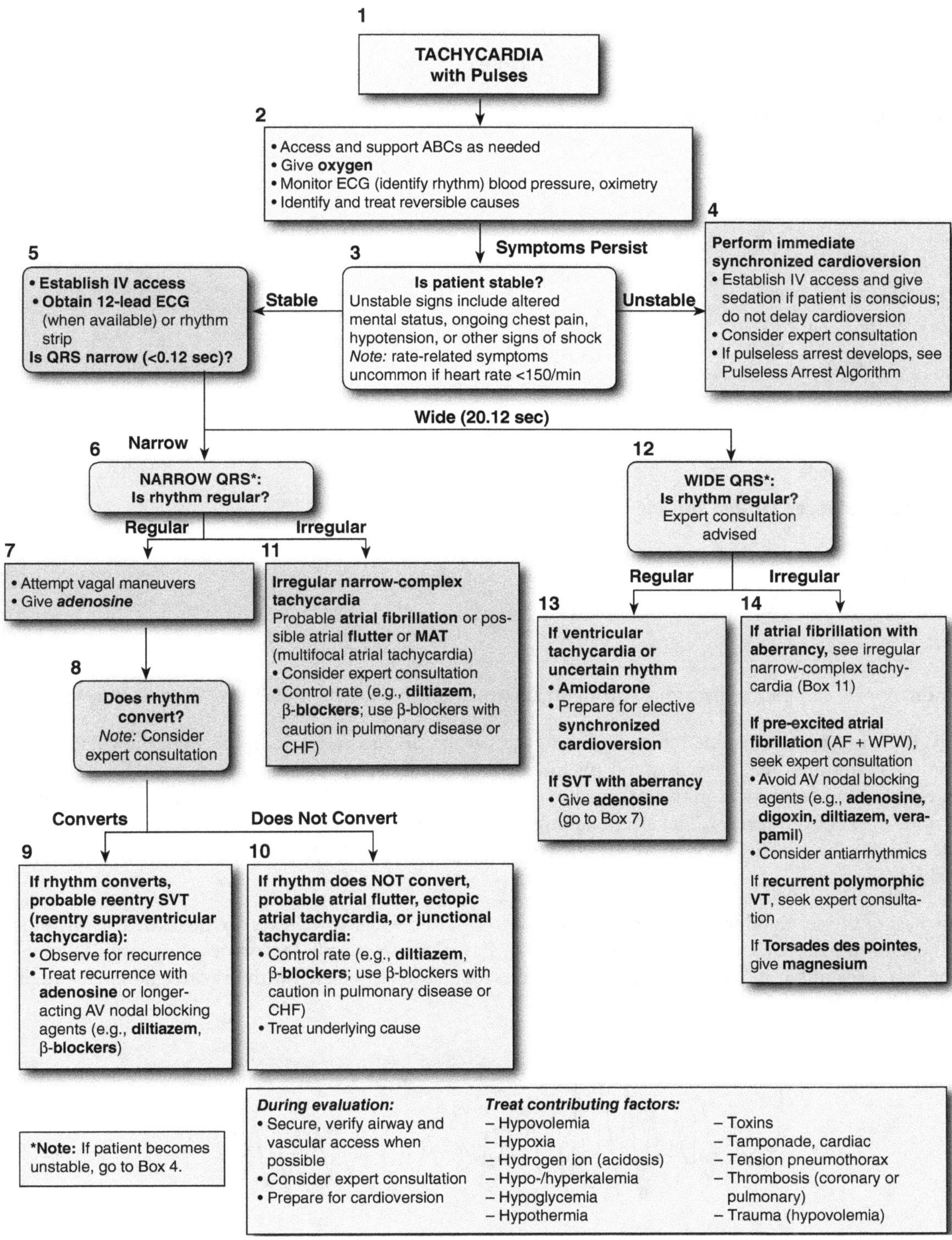

Figure 27-8. Algorithm for Tachycardia with Pulses (For Reference ONLY—Do NOT Memorize)

Ventricular Tachycardia

A 54-year-old man is at the opera when he suddenly jumps up and clutches his chest. He falls to his side into the lap of the woman sitting next to him. He is awake but disoriented and confused. He is complaining of dyspnea and lightheadedness. His exam reveals jugulovenous distention and a blood pressure of 114/80. The EKG shows ventricular tachycardia at a rate of 180.

Note

Medications that Prolong QT Interval

- TCAs
- Antipsychotics
- Erythromycin
- Methadone
- Fluoroquinolones
- Amiodarone
- Quinidine
- Sotalol
- Flecainide
- Procainamide

Causes of Prolonged QT and Torsade

- Mg
- K
- Ca

Definition. A wide complex tachycardia with an organized, uniform pattern on the EKG. There are no P-waves visible.

Etiology. Ischemia, myocardial infarction, and anatomic cardiac disease most commonly underlie VT. Other possible etiologies include quinidine, tricyclics, and phenothiazines. Long QT syndromes also cause VT. The dysrhythmia originates from an ectopic focus in the myocardium or from the AV node. When the impulse originates from around the AV node, this is from reentry. The electrical impulses must travel throughout the myocardium from myocyte to myocyte without the benefit of the more rapidly conducting normal pathways, such as the bundle branches or the His-Purkinje fibers.

The slowness of the conduction produces the slower and therefore wider complexes on the EKG. The rate most often varies 160–240/min. Torsade de pointes is a form of VT in which the morphology varies with an undulating amplitude, making it seem that it "twists around a point." Torsade may be associated with hypomagnesemia and preceded by long QT interval.

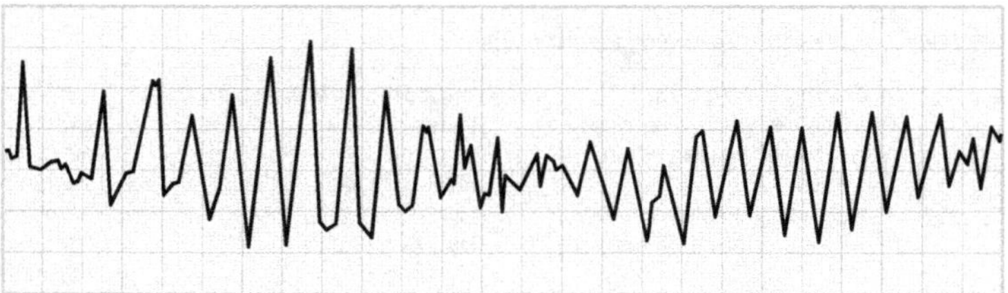

Figure 27-9. Torsade

Note

Amiodarone is superior to lidocaine for VF/VT.

Clinical Presentation. Symptoms are often related to duration of the dysrhythmia. Short bursts of a few seconds may produce no symptoms at all. VT lasting >30 seconds is referred to as sustained VT. Symptoms include lightheadedness, hypotension, CHF, syncope, and death.

Diagnosis. The EKG shows the VT. For those patients presenting with syncope suspected to be of cardiac origin and in whom an arrhythmia is not visible on the initial EKG, an electrophysiologic study can be done to try to elicit the VT.

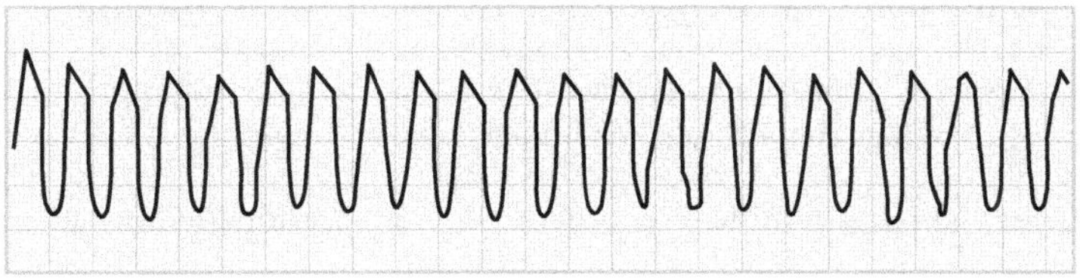

Figure 27-10. Ventricular Tachycardia

Note

Management of VT Without Hemodynamic Instability

1. Amiodarone
2. Lidocaine
3. Cardioversion

Treatment. For those with sustained VT and a pulse who are hemodynamically unstable, immediate synchronized cardioversion is required. Signs of hemodynamic instability requiring cardioversion include hypotension, chest pain, altered mental status, and CHF. A lower dose of electricity, starting at 100 J, can be used at first for monomorphic VT. The cardioversion should be synchronized. Conscious patients should be sedated with midazolam, fentanyl, or morphine before cardioversion.

VT in those patients without a pulse should be managed in the same way as ventricular fibrillation (unsynchronized shock). Stable VT (wide, monomorphic, regular) without serious hemodynamic compromise can be treated medically with adenosine initially and then with antiarrhythmics if no response. In stable patients with pulse, procainamide and sotalol are preferred drugs. If there is no response to procainamide, then amiodarone may be tried, followed by lidocaine and finally electrical cardioversion.

Note

For systolic dysfunction, the only antiarrhythmics that are safe are amiodarone, lidocaine, and dofetilide.

Magnesium may be useful in general but it is most useful for Torsade de pointes. If magnesium fails to treat Torsade, then isoproterenol or lidocaine can be attempted. Overdrive pacing can be used if pharmacologic treatment fails. Patients undergoing cardioversion should be sedated first with midazolam, fentanyl, or morphine. Long-term therapy is most effective with beta-blockers. VT that produces sudden death or VT that is sustained through initial drug therapy may require the placement of an implantable cardiac defibrillator (ICD). All patients with ejection fraction <35% should have ICD, due to increased risk of VT and VF.

Pulseless Electrical Activity

Definition. Hypotension to the point of losing one's pulse; there is still some type of electrical activity on the EKG that may even be normal or a simple tachycardia.

Etiology. More than the other dysrhythmias, knowing the etiology of pulseless electrical activity (PEA) is the key to the therapy because the specific therapies are so divergent. Essentially, the heart may still be beating, but there is no blood in the heart, and therefore there is no cardiac output. Examples of this type of PEA are severe hypovolemia, cardiac tamponade, tension pneumothorax, massive pulmonary embolism, and a massive myocardial infarction. Other types of PEA in which there may not be actual muscular contraction are hypoxia, hypothermia, potassium disorders, acidosis, and drug overdoses with tricyclics, digoxin, beta-blockers, or calcium channel blockers.

Clinical Presentation. The patient appears to be dead with no pulse. Other symptoms are based on the specific nature of what led to the PEA, such as those described above.

Diagnosis. A pulseless patient who has significantly organized, and occasionally normal, activity on the EKG.

Treatment. The most important action is to maintain CPR while determining the specific origin of the PEA. General therapy includes CPR, IV access, intubation, and epinephrine. Do not shock PEA arrest. The most important therapy is repair of the cause (possibilities described above). Bicarbonate is useful if a known acidosis has caused the arrest; it can also be used in a prolonged resuscitation if severe lactic acidosis develops and causes the refractory state of arrest. Pericardiocentesis may be attempted if all else fails.

Atrial Dysrhythmias

> A 24-year-old pharmacy student is brought to the emergency department because of palpitations. He has been studying vigorously for the FPGEE exam and has been up for the last 24 hours. He has had 5 cups of coffee, 4 beers, 3 stimulant tablets, 2 cheeseburgers, and 1 Viagra. An electrocardiogram reveals an atrial dysrhythmia.

Definition. A-fib, atrial flutter, and SVT are all characterized by either an ectopic focus in the atrium or re-entry at the AV node. All have normal conduction in the ventricular myocardium once the impulse successfully passes the AV node and travels down the normal ventricular conduction system. They all have a normal or narrow QRS complex and the absence of a normal P-wave.

Etiology. A-fib is most commonly caused by chronic hypertension, but it can also be caused by valvular heart disease (most often mitral valve pathology), left ventricular hypertrophy, cardiomyopathy, atrial fibrosis, atrial dilation, CAD, and CHF. Another cause is toxicity causing overstimulation of the heart, i.e., hyperthyroidism, pheochromocytoma, caffeine, theophylline, alcohol, and cocaine. Drug toxicity (such as digoxin), pericarditis, pulmonary embolism, surgery, chest wall trauma, or ischemia can also cause atrial dysrhythmias.

SVT is caused by a re-entrant mechanism around or within the AV node.

Clinical Presentation. Symptoms vary on the basis of the duration of the disorder, the ventricular rate, and the underlying health of the heart. With a normal heart, only 10–20% of cardiac output is directly derived from the contribution of atrial systole. With a dilated or postinfarction heart, or with significant valvular disease, this contribution may rise to 30–40%, in which case more severe symptoms arise. Symptoms range from complete absence to palpitations to lightheadedness, hypotension, disorientation, CHF, and syncope. Rate-related symptoms are unlikely in those with heart rate <150 per minute in atrial dysrhythmias.

Narrow complex tachycardia is always atrial in origin (QRS <0.12). Wide complex tachycardia can be atrial or ventricular. For example, it is very difficult to distinguish A-fib in the presence of LBBB and VT. The key is that in A-fib with LBBB, the rate is irregular on EKG, whereas in VT it is regular. If in doubt, treat as VT.

Diagnosis. Initially, the diagnosis is based entirely on the EKG. Other patients may need a 24–72 hour Holter monitor to detect brief paroxysms of the dysrhythmia not seen on the initial brief EKG.

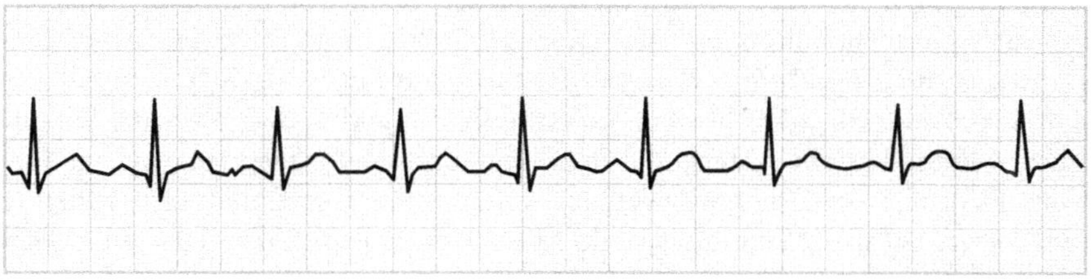

Figure 27-11. Normal Sinus Rhythm

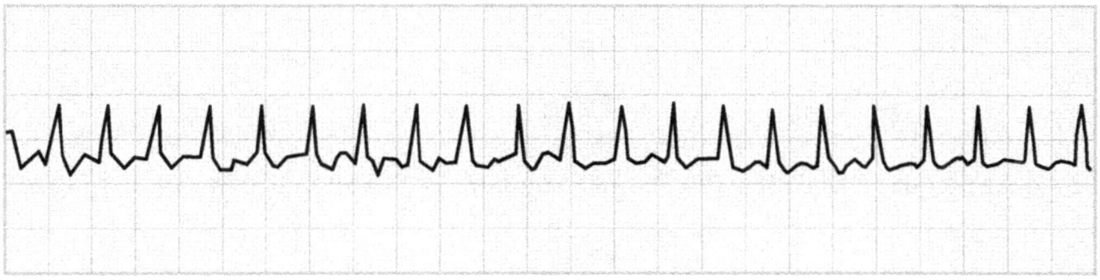

Figure 27-12. Atrial Tachycardia

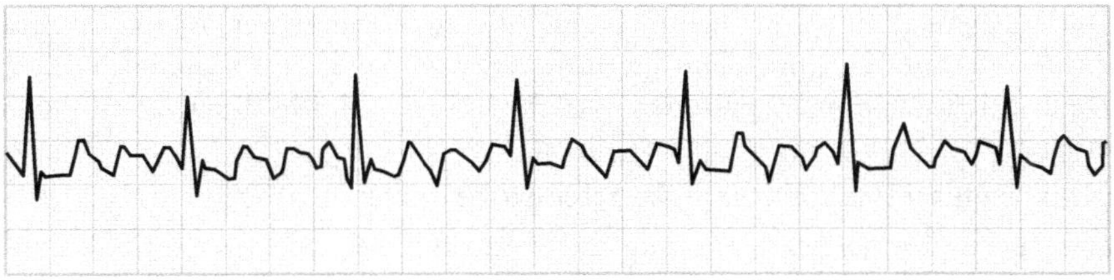

Figure 27-13. Atrial Flutter

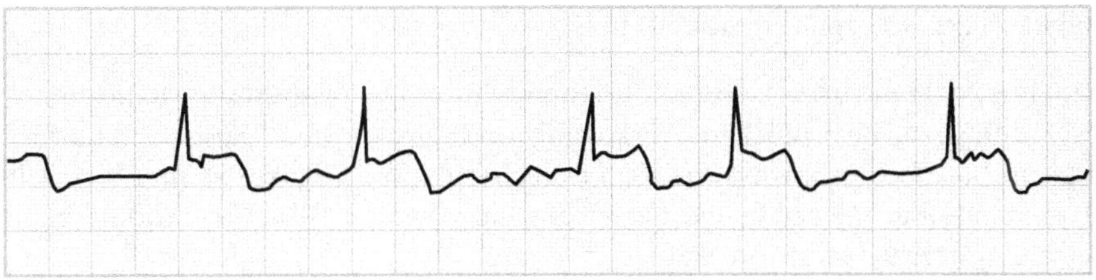

Figure 27-14. Atrial Fibrillation

Note

- Narrow complex tachycardia is *always* atrial in origin (QRS <0.12).
- Wide complex tachycardia can be atrial or ventricular in origin.

Treatment. Initial therapy is based on whether there are signs or symptoms of severe hemodynamic compromise, such as hypotension, confusion, CHF, or chest pain. If these are present, then immediate synchronized cardioversion is performed. Palpitations and lightheadedness are not signs of hemodynamic compromise. If the patient is hemodynamically stable, then the first step is to control the ventricular rate. Vagal maneuvers such as carotid sinus massage, Valsalva, or ice water immersion are most effective in SVT. Do not do carotid sinus massage bilaterally. Avoid carotid massage in those with carotid bruits. If vagal maneuvers do not work, SVT is initially treated with several rapid IV infusions of adenosine. For atrial fibrillation, atrial flutter, and in SVT after the failure of adenosine, several therapies are available to slow the heart rate. These include calcium channel blockers (such as diltiazem or verapamil), beta-blockers, or digoxin. Do not use verapamil in those with severe left ventricular dysfunction and low ejection fractions, and beware of using beta-blockers in those with a history of reactive airway disease.

After the rate has been lowered to <110 beats/min, conversion of the rhythm to normal sinus does not need to be routinely done. Chronic rate control with anticoagulation with warfarin to an INR of 2–3 is superior to converting the patient into sinus rhythm. Returning the patient to a normal sinus rhythm is preferable because chronic atrial fibrillation can result in embolic stroke in 5–7% of patients per year.

Note

Atrial fibrillation and flutter are routinely rate-controlled with anticoagulation with aspirin, warfarin, dabigatran, or rivaroxaban.

Amiodarone, ibutilide, propafenone, and dofetilide can all convert a minority of patients to sinus rhythm.

Rate Control vs. Rhythm Control. When patients present in A-fib with rapid ventricular response, hemodynamic stability must first be determined. If they are hemodynamically stable, they should be rate-controlled with AV nodal blocking agents. If they are unstable, immediate synchronized cardioversion is required. With long-term management, rate control and anticoagulation are preferred over rhythm control. **Rhythm control** should be considered in the following situations:

1. Symptomatic patients on rate control (poor exercise tolerance)
2. Younger patients with normal heart structure and function
3. Patients that are unable to be rate controlled with AV nodal blocking agents

It is very difficult to keep patients with structural heart disease in normal sinus rhythm. Several studies have shown an increase in overall mortality with rhythm control. Catheter-directed ablation of the AV node or accessory pathway may also be used when pharmacological treatment fails to control rate.

The rate control goal is 60–80 bpm at rest and 90–115 bpm with moderate exercise. Medications that might be used for **rate control** are diltiazem, beta-blockers, verapamil, or digoxin. Most patients require combined therapy. B-blockers with digoxin have been shown to be the best combination. Digoxin should be used for rate control in patients with CHF first; amiodarone can be used as second-line therapy. B-blockers should be started with caution in CHF patients once they are euvolemic on exam.

Note

$CHADS_2$ RISKS:

- **C**HF
- **H**TN
- **A**ge >75
- **D**iabetes mellitus
- **S**troke (gives 2 points)

Agents for chemical cardioversion in A-fib: amiodarone, dofetilide, flecainide, ibutilide, propafenone. In CHF patients, use amiodarone and dofetelide.

Agents for maintaining sinus rhythm: flecainide, propafenone, sotalol, dofetilide, and amiodarone. To maintain normal sinus rhythm in CHF patients, use only amiodarone or dofetilide. In patients with coronary artery disease, dofetilide and sotalol are superior to amiodarone.

- The $CHADS_2$ score is used to determine if a patient with non-valvular A-fib needs anticoagulation.

$CHADS_2$ Score	Treatment
0	Give aspirin
1	Give aspirin or anticoagulation
≥2	Give anticoagulation

Dabigatran is an oral direct thrombin inhibitor that has been shown to reduce the incidence of ischemic stroke compared to warfarin, with similar rates of bleeding. Rivaroxaban is an oral factor Xa inhibitor. For anticoagulation, you can use coumadin, dabigatran, or rivaroxaban. Apixaban, another oral factor Xa inhibitor, may be used instead of coumadin for stroke prophalaxis in patients with atrial fibrillation and a high risk of stroke ($CHADS_2$ score of 2 or higher). All 3 drugs—dabigatran, rivaroxaban, and apixaban—lead to similar or lower rates both of ischemic stroke and major bleeding compared to coumadin; there is no need for monitoring INR.

Important additional advantages of these newer agents include convenience (no requirement for routine testing of the international normalized ratio), a small reduction in the risk of intracranial hemorrhage, and less susceptibility to dietary and drug interactions.

Disadvantages include lack of an antidote and the potential that new side effects may be seen over time.

Note

Patients with A-fib and thyrotoxicosis always get anticoagulation until euthyroid and back in NSR.

For patients undergoing elective cardioversion, first determine if they have been in A-fib for >48 hours. If they have, there are 2 options:

- Transesophageal echo can be done to exclude a clot; then, cardioversion (electrical or chemical). Cardioversion should be followed by 6 weeks of coumadin.
- Coumadin can be administered for 3 weeks before electrical or chemical cardioversion. Cardioversion should be followed by another 6 weeks of coumadin.

It is very difficult to maintain patients with structural heart disease in NSR, and most convert back into atrial fibrillation. Atrial flutter is managed the same way as atrial fibrillation.

For patients in A-fib with Wolff-Parkinson-White syndrome, administration of drugs which slow AV node conduction (Ca-channel blockers, digoxin) is strongly contraindicated as they can induce VT. Procainamide, ibutilide, flecainide, or amiodarone can be used in such cases.

If none of the medications described above can successfully convert the patient to a normal sinus rhythm, then elective electrical cardioversion can be attempted. This too must be preceded and followed by several weeks of anticoagulation if the A-fib has been present for >48 hours. Transesophageal echo can be done to exclude a clot and allow the cardioversion without preconversion anticoagulation. Neither medical nor electrical cardioversion can permanently maintain the majority of patients on sinus rhythm. Most convert back into atrial fibrillation.

Bradycardia

A 48-year-old manager comes for advice about vaccinations and travel medicine before traveling to a far-off land. He feels well and has no symptoms. He takes no medications. On examination you find a blood pressure 118/76 mm Hg and pulse 40/min.

Definition. A slow heart with a rate <60 beats/min.

Etiology. Sinus bradycardia can be a normal phenomenon, particularly in trained athletes. Medications such as beta-blockers can also give a sinus bradycardia without serious sequelae. Symptomatic sinus bradycardia from sinus node disease can be from degeneration of the node or from ischemia. More serious types of bradycardia can be from Mobitz type II second-degree heart block and third-degree (complete) heart block. These can occur secondary to ischemic damage of the AV node. Other causes are myocarditis, infiltrative disease, such as amyloidosis or sarcoidosis, or neoplasms.

Clinical Presentation. This can range from the lifelong absence of symptoms to severe symptoms of hypotension and decreased cardiac output.

Diagnosis. EKG

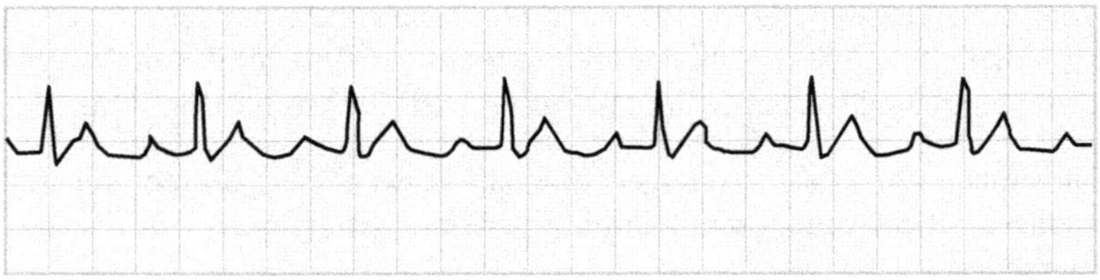

Figure 27-15. First-Degree Heart Block

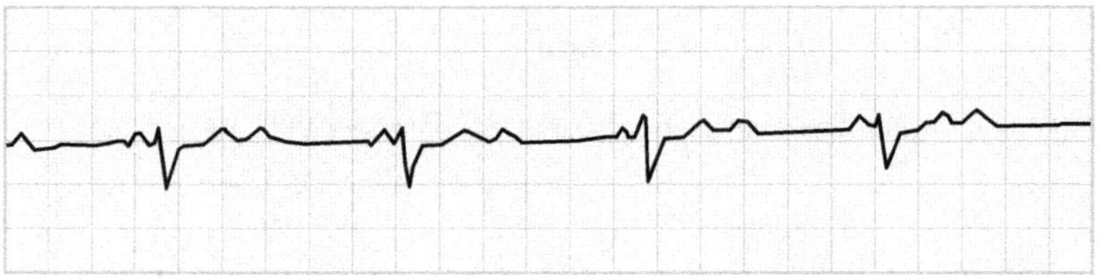

Figure 27-16. Second-Degree Heart Block

Note

Mobitz type I second-degree block is characterized by *progressive* P-R lengthening, whereas in Mobitz-type II, the P-R interval remains constant.

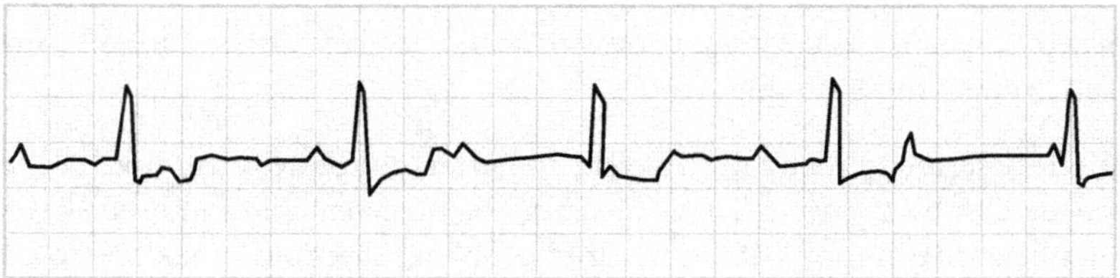

Figure 27-17. Complete Heart Block

Note

Transcutaneous pacing is always preferred over transvenous pacing in the acute setting.

Note

- If the patient is on a beta-blocker, give glucagon.
- If the patient is on a calcium channel blocker, give calcium.

Treatment. Asymptomatic sinus bradycardia, first-degree AV block, and Mobitz type I (Wenckebach) second-degree AV block often need no specific therapy. Any form of severe symptomatic bradycardia is treated initially with atropine and then a pacemaker, if there is no improvement in symptoms.

Mobitz type II second-degree block and third-degree block require the placement of a pacemaker, even in the absence of symptoms. Dopamine or epinephrine is used to improve blood pressure if there is still hypotension after the use of atropine.

For symptomatic sinus bradycardia, treatment is atropine. If atropine fails, then use transcutaneous pacing.

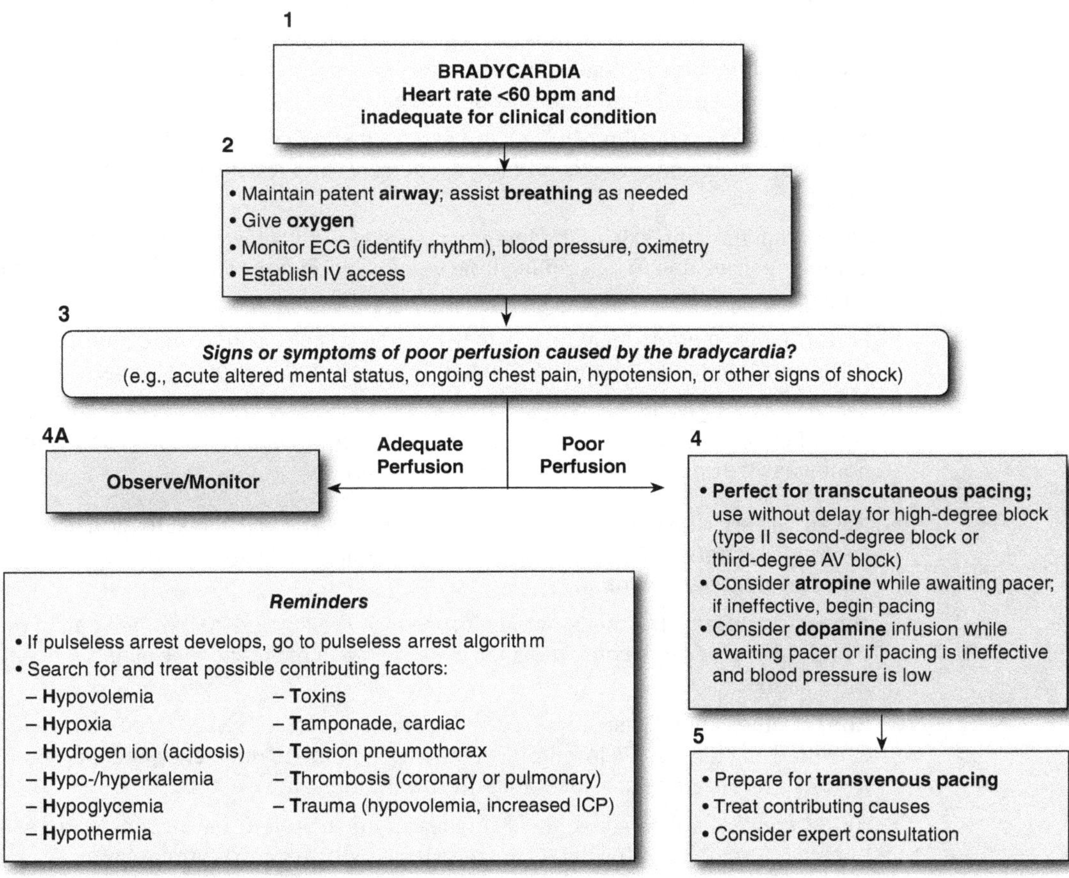

Figure 27-18. Algorithm for Bradycardia (For Reference ONLY—Do NOT Memorize)

OTC TESTING DEVICES

Point of care (POC) diagnostic devices or methods are used to obtain diagnostic results in a patient where the operator of the devices is either a trained clinician or an untrained user/patient. These devices can be used in hospitals, doctors' offices, and in patient homes.

There are numerous advantages to using point of care testing devices, including more rapid results and ability to implement or modify existing treatment regimens.

POC devices are designed to provide rapid diagnostic or clinical feedback on a variety of medical conditions.

Table 27-8. Point of Care Testing Devices and Methods

Device or Method	Comments
Glucose Monitoring	• All patients with diabetes mellitus (type 1 and type 2) who take medications to lower blood glucose should measure their blood glucose concentrations to help obtain and maintain safe, target-driven glucose control. • Self-monitoring of blood glucose (SMBG) utilizes capillary blood sampling for the testing strips and a glucose meter to analyze and provide information on the "current" blood glucose level. • The American Diabetes Association (ADA) recommends that patients with type 1 diabetes using multiple-dose insulin or insulin pump therapy monitor blood glucose "at least" prior to meals, snacks and at bedtime. They should occasionally monitor post-prandially, prior to exercise, when hypoglycemia is suspected and after treating hypoglycemia. Recommended monitoring for type 2 patients is variable and patient specific. • Procedures for operating an individual glucose monitor differ since each monitor utilizes different technologies, has variable features, methods for calibration accessories, storage capacity and recording software. • Many blood glucose meters permit the use of sites other than the finger to obtain blood samples, are reasonably accurate (+/−10 percent) and require only a very small drop of blood. • Monitoring from the skin of the forearm may give slightly lower results than those taken at the fingertips due to a sampling from venous blood rather than capillary blood in the fingers. • Factors causing errors include: use of the wrong test strips for a meter, meter calibration errors, inadequate hand washing, dirty meters and improper storage of the test strips (exposure to humidity, moisture or heat). • Other POC glucose monitoring systems include continuous glucose sensors and noninvasive devices (not requiring blood sample).
HbA1c	• Next to SMBG, HBA1c (or A1c) is the most widely used clinical test to assess glucose control in diabetes; SMBG and HbA1c are generally used together to design and modify diabetes treatment plans. • The HbA1c reflects the mean blood glucose over the entire 120 day life span of the red blood cell; however, it correlates best with the mean blood glucose over the previous 8 to 12 weeks. • HbA1c values are influenced by red cell survival; hence, the HbA1c can be falsely high when red cell turnover is low (iron, vitamin B12, or folate deficiency anemia). Conversely HbA1c levels are falsely low when these conditions are treated. • HbA1c concentrations are generally higher in African American, Hispanics and Asians than in Caucasians with similar average plasma glucose concentrations. • Available as a clinical laboratory test and POC test.

(Continued)

Device or Method	Comments
Pregnancy Test	• Detection of human chorionic gonadotropin (hCG) in blood or urine is the basis of all pregnancy tests. • hCG is secreted into maternal circulation shortly after implantation, which occurs 6–12 days after ovulation. • Types of pregnancy tests include clinical serum, clinical urine and home screening pregnancy tests. The clinical tests have a higher degree of sensitivity and specificity. • Positive "home pregnancy" test results should always be confirmed with a clinical (office-based) hCG test or other definitive test (i.e. Doppler confirmation of fetal cardiac activity or sonographic visualization of the pregnancy). • The accuracy of a home pregnancy test is affected by user technique and ability to interpret the results. For example, most use an array of colored bands/lines/symbols/words in the window of the device a few minutes after it is exposed to urine. • The most common reason for a false negative reading is because the test was performed too soon after the expected onset of menses. • Reasons for false positives include operator error, pregnancy loss shortly after implantation, pituitary hCG secretion in perimenopausal women and hCG secreting tumor.
Drug Screening	• The most common drug of abuse (DOA) screens used in the United States test for amphetamines, cocaine, opioids, marijuana (THC) and phencyclidine (PCP); benzodiazepines and alcohol may also be added. All of these compounds are all present in the body for at least 1–3 days following ingestion. • Screens for individual drugs and more comprehensive tests are also available. • These tests are available over the counter and through laboratories. • DOA screens are most commonly used as part of the preemployment process; random DOA screens during employment and sobriety verification. • The most common use for the OTC DOA test is for personal use (i.e. parent testing a teen, spouse testing a spouse, etc). • Urine specimens are the most common POC method for DOA; however, blood or hair can also be used clinically. • In forensic toxicology, a DOA screen is generally performed on blood, urine or vitreous fluid.
Paternity/ Pharmacogenomics	• Genetic samples can be obtained by using buccal swabs. • In the case of paternity testing, buccal swabs should be taken from both the presumptive father and the child. • Once the DNA is collected on the buccal swabs, they are sent to a laboratory for analysis. A paternity or pharmacogenomics test report is then sent to the patient and/or patient's physician.
HIV	• Enzyme-linked immunosorbent assays (ELISAs) that detect antibody to HIV are most commonly used as the initial test to screen for HIV infection. • ELISA tests detect the presence of HIV-1 and HIV-2 antibody as early as 3 weeks after exposure to the virus. • The sensitivity and specificity of laboratory-based tests approach 100% for diagnosing chronic infection. • Rapid screening tests are designed to provide results in <20 minutes and have similar sensitivity and specificity as the laboratory-based tests. • The "at home" HIV screening test uses oral secretions (instead of blood) and has a sensitivity of approximately 92%, which means that 1 in 12 patients with HIV will test false negative.

PRACTICE QUESTIONS

NAPLEX Question Reference

Clinical Lab Tests chapter: end of chapter questions

1. One of the steps for conducting a successful patient interview is to "negotiate a treatment plan". Which of the following best characterizes this "negotiating"?
   A. Determine a price that is fair for the medication dispensed
   B. Determine a price that is fair for the medication dispensed and services provided
   C. Determine if the medication selected by the patient satisfies the pharmacist's goals, expectations and risk/benefits of therapy
   D. Determine the treatment measure that best satisfies the patient's goals, expectations, risk/benefits and costs of therapy
   E. Determine the treatment measure that best satisfies the pharmacist's goals, expectations, risk/benefits and costs of therapy

2. A pharmacist is obtaining a pulse rate from a patient. How deep should he/she palpate the patient?
   A. 1/2 cm
   B. 1–2 cm
   C. 2–3 cm
   D. 3–4 cm
   E. 5–8 cm

3. A chief complaint is best described as which of the following?
   A. The most serious condition a patient currently has
   B. The most serious condition a patient has ever had
   C. The patient's medical diagnosis
   D. The statement describing the patient's medical diagnosis
   E. The statement describing the symptoms that caused the patient to seek care

4. Which of the following is the best estimate for a patient's average blood glucose level if their A1c value is 8%?
   A. 100 mg/dL
   B. 125 mg/dL
   C. 155 mg/dL
   D. 180 mg/dL
   E. 210 mg/dL

5. All of the following are accurate patient counseling statements EXCEPT
   A. A drug of abuse urine screen for amphetamines, cocaine, opioids, marijuana (THC) and phencyclidine (PCP) will produce positive results for at least 1–3 days following last ingestion.
   B. HIV screening tests using oral secretions have a sensitivity of >90%.
   C. Paternity genetic samples can be obtained using buccal swabs.
   D. Perimenopausal women may test falsely positive on a pregnancy test.
   E. When obtaining a SMBG blood sample from the skin of the forearm, it may give slightly higher results than those taken at the fingertips.

6. In the OLD CARTs mnemonic, the "R" is which of the following?
   A. Radical findings
   B. Radiation
   C. Reverberation
   D. Right diagnosis
   E. Right side of the body

7. A patient comes to the pharmacy complaining of a "burning sensation" following large meals and at bedtime. This information would be included in what component of a SOAP note?
   A. Subjective
   B. Objective
   C. Assessment
   D. Plan
   E. The information presented is NOT part of a SOAP note

Answers and Explanations

1. **The correct answer is D.** Once the presumptive diagnosis is made, the pharmacist should discuss the goals, expectations, risk/benefits and costs of therapy with the patient. The pharmacist will then make recommendations, but the patient ultimately decides if they will accept the treatment recommendations, make lifestyle changes and/or be referred to a physician.

2. **The correct answer is B.** Palpitation is the act of touching a patient in a therapeutic manner to elicit specific information. Light palpation (1–2 cm or ½–1 inch) is used to detect pulse rate, tenderness, warmth, texture, vibration (joints) and/or size and position of physiological structures or pathological masses. Deep palpation (5–8 cm or 2–3 inches) is used to estimate the size of the liver.

3. **The correct answer is E.** The chief complaint is a subjective statement given by the patient to the physician (or pharmacist) describing the most noteworthy or serious symptoms, illness, or dysfunction that caused them to seek care.

4. **The correct answer is D.** The A1c represents a patient's average blood glucose level over an approximate 90-day time period. It is the most common laboratory test used by clinicians to monitor glycemic control in patients with diabetes. Although 4–6% is a normal range; <6.5–7% is generally the goal for most patients. In order of appearance, an A1c of 5% approximates 100 mg/dL (choice A); an A1c of 6% approximates 125 mg/dL (choice B); an A1c of 7% approximates 155 mg/dL (choice C); an A1c of 8% approximates 180 mg/dL (choice D) and an A1c of 9% approximates 210 mg/dL (choice E).

5. **The correct answer is E.** Point of care (POC) diagnostic devices are used by trained clinicians or untrained users/patients. Hence, pharmacists should be proficient in counseling patients on the most commonly used POC devices and methods. All of the answer choices are true statements except choice E. When obtaining a SMBG blood sample from the skin of the forearm, it may give slightly LOWER (not higher) results than those taken at the fingertips due to a sampling from venous blood rather than capillary blood in the fingers.

6. **The correct answer is B.** When expanding and clarifying the chief complaint, the health care provider should follow the OLD CARTS mnemonic: **O**nset, **L**ocation, **D**uration, **C**haracter, **A**ggravating/**A**lleviating Factors, **R**adiation, and **T**iming. Another mnemonic is OPQRST: **O**nset, **P**alliating/**P**rovoking Factors, **Q**uality, **R**adiation, **S**ite, and **T**iming.

7. **The correct answer is A.** When documentation of a patient encounter is required, the information obtained from the patient interview should be well organized and readily retrievable. A SOAP note is a documentation method commonly used by health care providers to create a patient's chart. Subjective information (choice A) contains the patient's observations and descriptions. Objective observations (choice B) are repeatable and traceable facts about the patient's status. They include vital signs, physical exam findings, laboratory tests and personal measurements. Assessment (choice C) is the clinician's analysis of the subjective and objective data. The plan (choice D) includes the goals of therapy and individualized drug and disease-state monitoring parameters.

Therapeutic Decision Making 28

Learning Objectives

- ❑ Discuss introductory principles to therapeutic decision-making
- ❑ Answer questions on therapeutic drug concentrations
- ❑ Describe the individualized assessment of pharmacotherapeutic drug regimens
- ❑ Summarize triage and patient referral principles
- ❑ Design patient-centered, culturally relevant treatment plans
- ❑ Express proficiency in the application of evidence-based medicine
- ❑ Summarize principles of the promotion of nonprescription and natural products
- ❑ Solve problems in the management of drug toxicity and drug-induced diseases
- ❑ Demonstrate an understanding of misuse, abuse, or therapy non-adherence

Today's clinical pharmacist must be proficient in strategic clinical decision making, using an evidenced-based, culturally-centered approach to working through each clinical scenario. The main goal of the clinical pharmacist is to design, monitor and adjust (if necessary) a therapeutic regimen with the highest probability of safely and effectively improving patient outcomes.

The objectives for this clinical pharmacology and therapeutics chapter include all of the concepts and principles covered in the previous chapters of this book, as well as those found in Kaplan's *NAPLEX Strategies, Practice, and Review* book.

You should be able to:

- Answer questions on the basic biomedical sciences (Chapters 1–4);
- Demonstrate proficiency in pharmaceutical sciences (Chapters 5–11);
- Demonstrate an understanding of the social, behavioral and administrative sciences (Chapters 12–21);
- Utilize evidence-based pharmacy practice principles to develop and implement treatment plans and protocols (Chapter 22);
- Appropriately apply the principles of clinical pathophysiology, clinical pharmacokinetics, clinical pharmacogenetics, disease prevention and patient assessment to clinical pharmacy and therapeutics (Chapters 23–27); and
- Show proficiency in clinical pharmacology and therapeutics (Chapter 28).

INTRODUCTION TO THERAPEUTIC DECISION MAKING

While treating patients, healthcare providers commonly face instances where a clinical decision needs to be made. These "decision points" include multiple scenarios where clinical issues need to be addressed, including:

- a specific therapeutic intervention not accomplishing its desired effect;
- adverse events occurring;
- an insurance company not paying for a particular medication and a change needs to be made;
- the patient not understanding or accepting the rationale for the treatment;
- a secondary condition developing that necessitates multiple therapeutic interchanges be made; or
- a medical emergency arising that requires a shift in the treatment focus.

These clinical issues contribute to the dynamic and evolving nature of personalized medicine. Thus today's clinical pharmacist must dispel the myth that there is a single "right" therapeutic intervention that must be delivered to all patients with a given disease state and a few unique characteristics (age, sex, weight, etc).

With effective communication skills and proficiency in designing evidence-based, culturally-centered treatment plans, a clinical pharmacist should be able to make therapy recommendations based on:

- individual clinical and disease-specific characteristics–see Chapter 23 of this book and Kaplan's *NAPLEX Strategies, Practice, and Review* book; Cardiovascular, Endocrine, and Respiratory chapters: "Hypertension," "Dyslipidemia," "Heart Failure," "Diabetes," and "Asthma";
- evidence-based medicine and treatment protocols–see Chapter 22 of this book and Kaplan's *NAPLEX Strategies, Practice, and Review* book: Drug Information chapter;
- dosage calculations–see Chapter 11 of this book and Kaplan's *NAPLEX Strategies, Practice, and Review* book; Calculations chapter: "Problem-Solving Techniques";
- dosage in special populations–see Kaplan's *NAPLEX Strategies, Practice, and Review* book: Renal Disorders;
- nutritional and support therapy–see Kaplan's *NAPLEX Strategies, Practice, and Review* book: Calculations chapter; and
- specific uses and indications of drugs–see Kaplan's *NAPLEX Strategies, Practice, and Review* book: Therapeutics chapters, where you should pay close attention to the top 200 drugs (denoted by *) in the drug tables.

NAPLEX Reference

Cardiovascular, Endocrine, and Respiratory chapters: "Hypertension," "Dyslipidemia," "Heart failure," "Diabetes," and "Asthma"

Drug Information chapter

Calculations chapter: "Problem-Solving Techniques

Renal Disorders chapter

Calculations chapter: "Nutrition"

Therapeutics chapters

NOTE: The tables in the Independent FPGEE-focused review of Kaplan's *NAPLEX Strategies, Practice, and Review* book should be reviewed prior to studying this content. These tables (in Unit II of this text) outline the highest yield concepts for the FPGEE.

Thus, there are numerous clinical and professional considerations that need to be incorporated into a therapeutic decision.

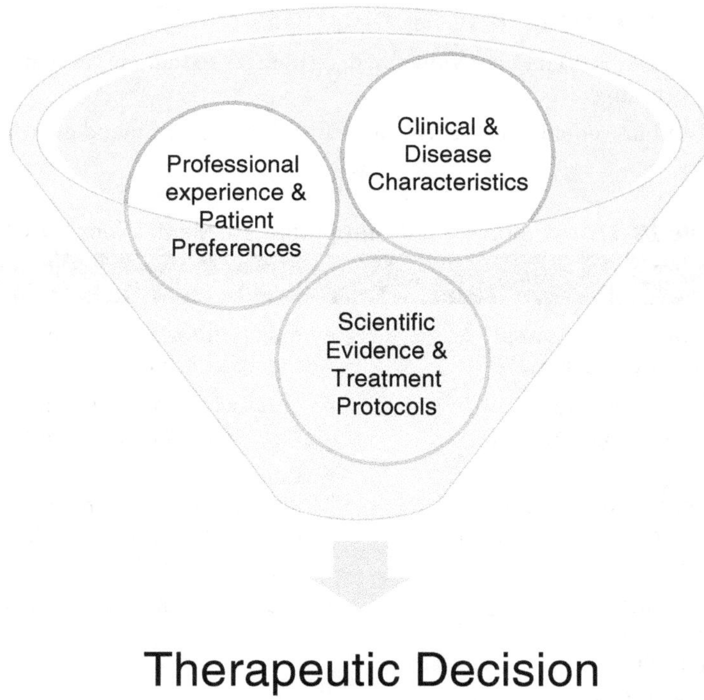

Figure 28-1. Therapeutic Decision Making Process

THERAPEUTIC DRUG CONCENTRATIONS

Therapeutic drug monitoring (TDM) involves measuring drug concentrations in plasma, serum, or blood as well as the clinical interpretation of the result.

TDM requires extensive knowledge of:

- the drug's pharmacokinetics,
- individual patient factors that may impact the drugs pharmacokinetics or pharmacodynamics,
- the sampling time,
- patient drug history and
- the patient's clinical condition.

The basic assumptions underlying TDM are:

- drug metabolism and renal elimination of metabolites varies from patient to patient AND
- plasma levels of a drug are more closely related to the drug's therapeutic effect and/or toxicity than is the actual medication dosage.

When TDM is ordered, the following should be documented to ensure proper interpretation of the data:

- Indication for TDM
- Time of the sample collection
- Time of the last drug dose
- Prescribed drug regimen

Appropriate and Non-Appropriate Medications for TDM

Information obtained from TDM is used to individualize drug dosages so that the resultant drug concentrations will be maintained within a target range.

- Note: Both desired and unwanted effects correlate well with plasma or blood concentrations for **many (but not all)** medications.

Table 28-1. Appropriate and Non-Appropriate Medications for TDM

Appropriate Medications for TDM	Non-Appropriate Medications for TDM
• drugs with narrow therapeutic windows (NTW) (i.e. lithium, phenytoin, digoxin) • drugs with concentration-dependent pharmacokinetics (i.e. aminoglycosides, antineoplastics) • Patients with impaired renal or clearance of a drug with an NTW (i.e. renal dysfunction and digoxin) • drugs whose toxicity is difficult to distinguish from a patient's underlying disease (i.e. theophylline and COPD) • drugs whose efficacy is difficult to establish clinically (i.e. phenytoin, carbamazepine, ethosuximide, etc.) • A table of the most commonly monitored medications is found the Clinical Lab Tests Chapter of the NAPLEX text.	• drugs with wide therapeutic windows/wide therapeutic indexes (i.e. amoxicillin) • drugs with a better means of assessing effects and toxicity (i.e. warfarin is monitored by INR) • Drug concentrations are expected to be within normal therapeutic range but other variables impact drug toxicity (i.e. hypokalemia precipitates digoxin toxicity). • Drugs without established therapeutic drug levels

Rationale for TDM

With the cost of healthcare continually increasing, it is essential that costly laboratory tests be used appropriately and only when necessary. (See Kaplan's *NAPLEX Strategies, Practice, and Review* book; "Therapeutic Drug Levels" and "Appropriate and Non-Appropriate Medications for TDM" table).

NAPLEX Reference

Clinical Lab Tests chapter:
"Therapeutic Drug Levels"

- Example: Only certain medications necessitate TDM. Furthermore, when a medication is chosen, the blood levels (for example) MUST be taken at an appropriate time or the resultant information will be worthless.

TDM–Sample Collection Timing

Appropriate sample timing for TDM is often considered as important as the actual drug concentration obtained from the sample. Important sample timing considerations include:

- Drug **trough levels** should be taken approximately **30 minutes BEFORE** the administration of the **next dose.**
- Drug **peak levels** should be taken approximately **½ to 2 hours following** the **administration of a medication** (actual time will vary depending on route and type of medication administered).
- Medications with long half-lives can have blood levels taken anytime during the dosing interval (i.e. amiodarone)
- Drug levels taken at times of disease symptom appearance or toxic symptoms may reveal subtherapeutic and or toxic peak concentrations, respectively.

TDM Indications and General Considerations

Table 28-2. Indications for TDM

Indication	Comments
Monitoring Effectiveness	• Correlating patient response with drug levels and assessment of drug effectiveness (i.e. prophylactic anticonvulsants) • Diagnosing reason for failed therapy (i.e. If drug level is therapeutic and patient has seizure then medication is ineffective; however, if drug level is subtherapeutic then the patient may have a genetic polymorphism causing increased drug metabolism, a drug interaction leading to increased metabolism OR the patient is not compliant with prescribed drug regimen) • Assessment of patient compliance (i.e. opioids where drug levels are taken to ensure that the patient is not "selling" their opioids on the black market)
Monitoring for Toxicity	• Used to evaluate drug levels commonly associated with toxicity (i.e. lithium, aminoglycosides, cyclosporine) • Diagnose toxicity (i.e. nephrotoxicity secondary to aminoglycosides)
Drug Dosing	• Assessment of the appropriateness of a loading dose • Assessment of a dosing change (i.e. impact on drug steady state or peak/trough concentrations) • Assessment of dose and subsequent dose requirements
Target Concentration	• Assessment of target concentration for a drug with different indications (i.e. digoxin for heart failure and atrial fibrillation) • Suspiciously low or high drug concentrations may indicate altered drug metabolism

General considerations for interpreting TDM results include:

- Ensure that the TDM results are received within a clinically useful timeframe.
- Drug concentrations should be interpreted on an individual basis using clinical judgment. For example, a patient experiencing symptoms of toxicity from a medication that is within the recommended therapeutic drug level would necessitate a decrease in drug dose. Conversely, a patient that has a subtherapeutic drug level and is experiencing the desired therapeutic effect would NOT require a dosage increase.
- If an increased or decreased drug level is believed to be caused by a drug-drug interaction, the clinician needs to determine if a therapeutic interchange should be made to remove the interacting drug.
- Before making a dosage adjustment, ensure that the data is accurate (sample collection time is correct, no drug interactions, etc.).
- If a medication has active metabolites, such as carbamazepine, factor this into future dosage changes. TDM is only effective for a few selected medications. It is not indicated for most drugs.
- Although many medications are not recommended for TDM, the clinical pharmacist should understand the impact of renal and hepatic dysfunction on drug dosing. See Renal Disorders Chapter of the Kaplan NAPLEX review text for more information.
- TDM is not a substitute for clinical judgment; however, it can be used as a tool to help optimize therapeutic drug levels and patient outcomes.

PERSONALIZED TREATMENT PLANS: FROM DIAGNOSIS TO FOLLOW-UP

The practice of pharmacy has dramatically evolved over the past 10 years. Following a decision to treat the patient, the pharmacist has **traditionally been tasked** with:

- Dispensing the medication according to the "5 rights" (patient, drug, dose, route, time);
- Counseling the patient (or other health care providers) on medication adverse reactions, warnings and precautions; and
- Providing an avenue for follow-up.

Today's clinical pharmacist is more involved with the overall care and monitoring of the patient. In addition to their "traditional" responsibilities, pharmacists also provide a number of clinical services, such as developing individualized drug regimens and treatment plans.

Pharmacist's Role in Developing Individualized Drug Regimens and Treatment Plans

Once a therapeutic decision has been made, a clinical pharmacist may be involved in each of the following steps to develop an individualized drug regimen or treatment plan:

- **Step 1:** Assist in the design of an action plan (after a diagnosis has been made)
- **Step 2:** Determine the most appropriate prescription (Rx) and nonprescription (non-Rx) therapies
- **Step 3:** Reassessment and therapeutic adjustment based on patient response and outcomes
- **Step 4:** Continued patient evaluation and follow-up

While the clinical pharmacist plays an integral role in the development of an individualized drug regimen or treatment plan, they must remember that they are a part of a clinical care team. Thus when appropriate, the pharmacist (or physician) may refer the patient to a specialist.

Step 1: Assist in the Design of an Action Plan

Once a presumptive diagnosis is made by the patient's physician (or other provider), the first step for a pharmacist is to assist in the design of an action plan.

When designing an action plan, a clinical pharmacist may need to address one or more clinical questions based on the complexity of the patient's condition:

Table 28-3. Questions for Consideration in the Initial Action Plan

Description	Comments
Complexity of condition	• The more complex the condition, the more comprehensive the treatment plan that is needed. • Example: a patient with athlete's foot may require a few questions and visual inspection; however a patient with hypertension and type 2 diabetes who is diagnosed with heart failure will need a comprehensive treatment plan with extensive monitoring.
Need for more diagnostic tests	• Are more diagnostic tests needed to confirm the diagnosis (i.e. Gold standard test)? • Will additional tests be needed to help determine the appropriateness of a likely therapeutic intervention (i.e. assessment of renal/hepatic function; potassium level for patients receiving a diuretic, digoxin, etc)?
Triage and identify when to refer patients to other health professionals or specialist	• After the initial diagnosis and assessment, the physician or pharmacist will use professional judgment to determine if the patient should be referred to a specialist or another health care professional for further assessment or treatment (specialized drug dosing, surgery, behavioral health, counseling) • ***See "Triage and Patient Referral" in this section for more information***.

(*Continued*)

Description	Comments
Decision to treat	• What are the necessary components of treatment? • Use of common prescription and non-prescription medications as well as non-pharmacological therapies
Patient-centered, culturally-relevant treatment	• A review of cultural competency is discussed in Chapter 19. • The pharmacist should understand how to work within certain cultural parameters. ***See "Culturally-Relevant Treatment Plans" (in this section) for more information.***
Review of proposed actions with patient	• Patient informed consent (verbal or written) is needed prior to instituting any treatment option. • Example items to discuss with the patient include (but are not limited to) indications for therapy; goals for therapy; side effects of various options; treatment options; likely treatment monitoring plan
Development OR utilization of preexisting treatment algorithm	• Treatment algorithm complexity will be based on disease complexity (i.e. treatment of athlete's foot vs heart failure in a patient with comorbidities) • ***Treatment algorithms are discussed in Chapter 22*** • The selection of medication or therapy (based on the algorithm) will be chosen based on individual drug and patient characteristics (***outlined in Step 2***).

Culturally-Relevant Treatment Plans

Development of culturally-relevant treatment plans begins with a health care provider that understands the relevance of cultural diversity and ethnic health disparities in the United States.

In order to optimize patient outcomes (for all patients), the clinical pharmacist must show proficiency in developing culturally-relevant treatment plans that incorporate:

- **Educational background:** When patients do not understand what clinicians are telling them, compliance and patient outcomes are both likely to be lower. Information should be presented in a manner that the patient understands. Open-ended questions are encouraged. See Chapter 19 for more information.
- **Solutions to language barriers:** If the patient and clinician do not speak the same language, the clinician should make every effort to find an interpreter or interpreting device.
- **Solutions to sociocultural barriers:** Some patients may not feel that they can ask for assistance since it is a sign of weakness. Also, with some patients, only certain family members can ask for advice (about an issue from someone not in their immediate family). Thus, the pharmacist should work within the cultural dynamic.
- **Facilitating the change in a negative attitude towards healthcare:** The importance or emphasis on health care may be different than that of the pharmacist. Thus, patient education and counseling can help change the negative attitude. The importance or emphasis on health care may be different than that of the pharmacists. Thus patient education and counseling can help change the negative attitude.
- **Patient beliefs about the diagnosis or treatment:** Some patients may not want to receive blood products or "non-essential" medications. Respect of personal and religious beliefs is paramount. The pharmacist should always work within the parameters set by the patient.
- **Set aside personal racial and cultural beliefs:** The pharmacist may not have the same beliefs (cultural, religious, etc.) as the patient; however, all patients should be treated equally and without judgment.

In summary, pharmacists need to develop culturally sensitive patient-centered treatment care plans. This can be accomplished by treating each patient as an individual and identifying and respecting their personal beliefs and values.

Table 28-4. Common Medical Conditions Treated by Pharmacists

Medical Condition	Comments	When to Refer
Cold symptoms	• One of the most common reasons why patients seek pharmacist's advice. • Hydration and rest are often considered first line treatment. • Common medications include decongestants and analgesics. Consider all drug-drug and drug-disease interactions.	• Sometimes difficult to differentiate between bacterial and viral; when in doubt, refer to physician. • Refer if symptoms are worsening over past couple of days. • Refer if patients have certain underlying medical conditions (Asthma, heart failure, diabetes, etc.)
Cough	• Common medications include cough suppressant, expectorants and analgesics (for sore throat). Consider all drug-drug and drug-disease interactions. • Can be the result of numerous etiologies (Bacterial infection, ACE Inhibitors, asthma, etc.)	• Refer if patients have certain underlying medical conditions (Asthma, heart failure, diabetes, etc.) • Refer for prolonged cough symptoms (>5 days). • Refer if sputum is thick, colored (green, yellow, gray) or blood tinged.
Headache	• Very common complaint with patients • Can be treated with a variety of OTC medications (NSAIDS, APAP, aspirin) • Consider age (No ASA children <15), current conditions renal dysfunction (No ASA, NSAIDs), hepatic (no APAP). • Other drug-disease interactions; no NSAIDs/aspirin with coagulation disorders, asthma, GI ulcers, heart failure, allergies.	• Refer for severe acute onset, extended duration (>2 days). • Refer if any of the conditions listed in the comments section are present. • Use professional judgment if suggesting a medication to treat one of these referral patients.
Muscle aches	• Can be treated with a variety of OTC medications (NSAIDS, APAP, aspirin) • Same warning as for headache	• Refer if there is muscle weakness or a broken bone is suspected. • For elderly, refer if patient is on a statin.
Diarrhea, constipation, athlete's foot, GERD	• ***See NAPLEX text Over-the-Counter Medications chapter***	• ***See NAPLEX text Over-the-Counter Medications chapter***
Conditions that normally require a prescription medication	• Patients may want to treat a medical condition/disease state that normally requires a prescription from a provider themselves. • The pharmacist may be able to provide some information on lifestyle changes but should advise the patient to seek medical advice from a physician.	• Refer to physician or other health care provider. • ***See NAPLEX text Therapeutics chapters for general information on disease states and drug information.***

Triage and Patient Referral

The retail pharmacist is often the first health care professional contacted when patients need medical advice. Reasons for this preference include:

- **Ease of access:** Patients can call or stop in at a pharmacy to ask questions AND receive immediate answers. When they call a physician's office, for example, they often leave a message for a nurse who calls them back at a later time.

- **Knowledge of medicine:** Since most conditions are treated medically, patients often consult the medical experts first.
- **Ability to recommend OTC products:** For common conditions (headache, muscle aches, GERD, etc.) patients can receive rapid treatment.
- **Ability to differentiate between less serious and more serious conditions:** Pharmacists are generally able to rapidly triage the patient or recommend the next best course of action. Example, a patient with "heartburn" could have acid reflux or be experiencing a myocardial infarction.

Other conditions where pharmacists commonly recommend treatment include cold sores, dandruff, minor diaper rash, eczema, minor topical fungal infections (nails, genital), hemorrhoids, lice, minor cuts, poison ivy and sunburn.

Before recommending any medications for a condition, the pharmacist should ALWAYS consider ALL treatment options and ask about current medical conditions or medications that could interact with the proposed therapy.

Step 2: Determine the Most Appropriate Prescription (Rx) and Nonprescription (non-Rx) Therapies

Once a patient is being treated, the clinical pharmacist may be asked to select the most appropriate medication (Rx and/or non-Rx). The pharmacist's medication of choice should be based on individual drug and patient characteristics as well as evidence-based medicine principles.

Drug characteristics (pharmacokinetic, pharmacodynamic, etc) are summarized in a drug monograph (package insert) that accompanies each medication. There are also electronic versions of drug monograph databases.

- Drug monographs are available for all FDA-approved prescription medications as well as some over-the-counter (OTC) and investigational medications as well as selected nutritional and herbal drug products.
- Databases are also available to provide information on other medications with accepted medical/therapeutic utility. DEA Schedule I substances (i.e. heroin, methamphetamine) are generally not covered in drug monographs; however, they are generally discussed in toxicology databases.
- The Therapeutics chapters in Kaplan's NAPLEX Review book provide a series of drug tables (Rx and non-Rx) that highlight the most high-yield concepts found in drug monographs. Furthermore, the top 200 drugs in the United States are denoted with a "*" in each of these drug tables. These same chapters also provide evidence based recommendations for the clinical use of these medications. **See "Complete NAPLEX Review Book Test User's Guide" for more information.**

NAPLEX Reference

Therapeutics chapters

See the Complete NAPLEX Review Book User's Guide for more information

The information contained within a drug monograph is generally presented in a standardized format to help clinicians rapidly assess the appropriateness of a given medication as well as its benefits and risks.

Table 28-5. Components of a Drug Monograph

Component	Description/Comments
Description/ Classification	• Provides an overview of the drug product, place in therapy, and potentially regulatory information. • Therapeutic classifications (i.e. beta-blocker, ACE inhibitor) and image of the chemical structures.
Mechanism of action	• Outlines the drug mechanism of action and necessary pharmacodynamic information.

(Continued)

Component	Description/Comments
Pharmacokinetics	• Summary of the drug's pharmacokinetic profile • Pharmacokinetic information is based on the method of drug administration and dosage form. • Different pharmacokinetics information would be provided for each dosage form (IV, Tablet, Oral Liquid, etc.) • Absorption, distribution, metabolism, and excretion (ADME) information unique to each dosage form will be provided. • Special pharmacokinetic considerations are generally provided for special populations (i.e. pediatrics, elderly, hepatic dysfunction, renal dysfunction, etc).
Indications/ Dosage	• This section can be quite comprehensive and outlines all conditions "approved for use by the FDA" as well as the dosing information in each of these conditions. If more than one route of administration is available, then the preferred route of administration will be provided. • Precise diagnostic terms are used (i.e. type 2 diabetes mellitus NOT diabetes mellitus, torsades de pointes NOT cardiac dysrhythmia) • Many drug databases will also provide indications/dosing information on non-FDA approved uses for the drug (provided that there is evidence that proves clinical utility of the medication for this particular use). • Information on age restrictions will be provided as well according to the following age groups: – Elderly: 65 years of age and above – Adults: 18 years of age and older – Adolescents: 13–18 years of age – Children: 1–12 years of age – Infants: 1 month to 1 year of age – Neonates: Full-term newborn 0–4 weeks of age – Premature neonates: Neonates born at <38 weeks gestation. • Additional information provided includes dosing information for hepatic or renal insufficiency and maximum dosage limits by patient population.
Drug interactions	• Common information includes ***drug-drug or drug-class interactions*** which are ***essential when prescribing medication for a patient with concomitant conditions***. • Additional information may include drug-food and drug-herbal/nutritional supplement interactions. • Drug databases will provide information based on clinical data as well as those outlined in the manufacturer's product labeling (i.e. package insert) • Both pharmacokinetic (impact on ADME) and pharmacodynamic interactions are generally provided. Assessment of pharmacodynamic interactions can help prevent drug-drug interactions as well as therapeutic duplication. • Pharmacogenomics-related information may also be provided (i.e. codeine should not be used in CYP2D6 poor metabolizers)
Contraindications/ Precautions	• Contraindications are defined as conditions where a drug should absolutely not be used. • Precautions are defined as conditions where a drug can be used with caution. • Information will be provided on use in allergies, pregnancy, breastfeeding, renal/ hepatic dysfunction, concomitant diseases, etc

(Continued)

Component	Description/Comments
Adverse reactions	• Adverse reaction (ADR) data is most commonly obtained from pre-approval clinical trials; however, some information may be provided from post-marketing surveillance. • ADR incidence rate may be provided • A severity rating may also be provided
Administration	• Provide drug administration instructions (i.e. take by mouth, inject subcutaneously) and common warnings for all available dosage forms (i.e. take on empty stomach) • May also include information on product preparation information (i.e. reconstitution instructions for amoxicillin suspension)
Monitoring parameters	• Provide information on unique monitoring parameters for the medication and generally includes adverse effects related to the medication itself. • There will also be information on how to monitor patients with a specific disease state (i.e. renal dysfunction) • Monitoring parameters include physical (i.e. ophthalmologic exam, osteoporosis), laboratory (i.e. blood glucose, potassium level) and other specific examinations that the provider should perform prior to and during drug therapy. • Monitoring perimeters can generally be derived from the information contained in the contraindications, precautions, and adverse reaction sections of the drug monograph.
Patient counseling information	• Information for the patient that includes storage information, drug-food interactions, major warnings (i.e. if you experience muscle pain, contact your physician or pharmacist.)
How supplied	• Summarizes the dosage forms and strengths of the medications available on the US market. • Products are generally grouped by ingredient, strength, and dosage form. • Contains information on the distributor and manufacturer of the product.

Evidence-Based Medicine

The drug monograph provides all of the information needed to "match" a drug to an individual patient's disease. However, choosing the best medication (or medication combination) to "treat" their condition is primarily based on evidence-based medicine (EBM). Thus, incorporating EBM is an indispensable component of the drug selection process.

There are a number of key principles that the clinical pharmacist must remember when applying evidence-based decision making to patient care.

- Example: Simply matching a drug's indication, side effect profile, and contraindications to a patient condition without proper use of EBM can produce insufficient or unwanted therapeutic outcomes.
- A comprehensive discussion of evidence-based medicine is in Chapter 22.

The drug and patient characteristics, along with evidence-based medicine principles, are the foundation on which a good therapeutic regimen is built. However, the clinician must also evaluate the overall medication cost and patient preferences before prescribing a medication.

Thus, selection of the most appropriate medication involves consideration of:

- Individual drug characteristics (outlined in the drug monograph); see drug tables in Kaplan's *NAPLEX Strategies, Practice, and Review* book, Therapeutics chapters (Additional information in "Complete NAPLEX Review Book User's Guide");
- Evidence-based medicine principles and treatment guidelines (See FPGEE Chapter 22 for more information);
- Cost-effectiveness of the therapy (see FPGEE Chapter 14 for more information); and
- Culturally-centered patient preferences (See FPGEE Chapter 19 for more information).

Table 28-6. Key Principles of Evidence-Based Medicine (EBM)

Principle	Comments
Primary goals are to improve and evaluate patient care	• Each goal is achieved by integrating and applying the best research evidence into the decision making process on the care of the patient while being mindful of their values.
EBM can be applied throughout the continuum of patient care	• Clinicians can use EBM to make a correct diagnosis, devise the best evaluation plan, choose the most appropriate treatment and methods of disease prevention, design a follow-up and evaluation plan, make therapeutic adjustments where appropriate as well as develop treatment algorithms and guidelines for large groups of patients with the same disease.
EBM requires proficient drug information skills	• Evidence-based medicine can only be applied if the clinician is able to appropriately locate, interpret and then evaluate the medical literature.
EBM requires good communication skills	• As part of the patient care team, a pharmacist must be able to effectively communicate with other members of the clinical care team (***See Chapter 19***).
Understanding the benefits and limitations of each reference source is essential	• Drug information resources are classified as primary, secondary and tertiary sources with the primary medical literature generally providing the highest level of evidence and most current information. • The clinician must be able to answer the following question: Does the information provided in the reference source apply to "my" patient?
Understand the characteristics, benefits and limitations of each type of clinical study.	• The most commonly encountered types of research studies found in the medical literature are randomized clinical trials, case-control and cohort studies. Each of these are beneficial to determine a specific type of information. • A meta-analysis will critically and comprehensively examine the numerous randomized controlled clinical trials (derived from a systematic review) on a particular treatment regimen or disease state and then combine the results using accepted statistical methodology as if they were from one large study.
EBM requires proper evaluation of the medical literature	• Not all studies are properly designed or properly extrapolate the findings. • One of the most efficient ways to evaluate an article (on treatment, prevention, or patient screening) is to use the PP-ICONS method to accept or discard the conclusions of the study. PP-ICONS = Patient/Population; Intervention; Comparison; Outcome; Number of Subjects and Statistics and biases. • ***The Drug Information chapter in the NAPLEX text provides a list of well known, peer-reviewed medical references commonly used by US pharmacists.***
Proper application of the levels of evidence is essential.	• The clinical value of a study depends on the study design. For example, the results of a controlled clinical trial will provide a much higher level of evidence than a case report that has similar results.

(*Continued*)

Principle	Comments
Clinical practice guidelines (CPG) and treatment algorithms are based on EBM	• CPGs are systematically developed clinical statements designed to assist the practitioner and patient in making decisions about appropriate health care for specific clinical circumstances. • Medical algorithms are designed to help promote medical decision making and are often derived from CPGs. The primary purpose of a medical algorithm is to standardize medical decisions, reduce the potential for errors and improve patient outcomes. • Understand that unique patient characteristics (concomitant disease states, existing drug therapy, etc) can impact CPG recommendations. For example, metformin is the initial drug of choice for type 2 diabetes; however, if the patient has renal dysfunction, another medication should be chosen. • The clinician must be able to answer the following question: Does the information provided in the CPG (or treatment algorithm) apply to "my" patient? • Guidelines between different medical associations may differ and it is up to the clinician to decide what guideline is more appropriate based on professional evaluation of each guideline.
EBM requires the continual integration of new scientific knowledge into existing treatment protocols	EBM is continually evolving. The drug of choice for a condition today may be different in the near future as clinical trials provide new information or new medications or procedures are developed. Understanding how to properly evaluate and apply new information is critical to the proper integration of new clinical information (***See Chapter 22 for more information***).
EBM facilitates the integration of new and emerging treatment measures into patient care	The primary goals of EBM are to improve and evaluate patient care by making therapeutic decisions based on the most current and accurate information available. Proper application of all of the principles in this table are required for the appropriate integration of new and emerging treatment measures into patient care (***See Chapter 22 for more information***).

In step 2, the pharmacist is providing evidence-based, guideline-driven care while considering the financial needs/limitations and personal preferences of the patients.

Patient Counseling

Prior to dispensing the medication, the pharmacist should provide appropriate drug information to the patient, such as:

- Indications for therapy
- Goals of therapy
- Treatment monitoring plan

Also remember that the counseling provisions of the Omnibus Budget Reconciliation Act (Chapter 16) require individual state governments to establish additional state sponsored pharmacy practice standards. Thus, **pharmacists must also offer to discuss** the following with the recipient prior to dispensing a medication:

- Name and description of the drug
- Dosage form, dosage, route of administration, and duration of drug therapy

- Special directions and precautions for preparation, administration, and use by the patient
- Common severe side effects, drug interactions and contraindications
- Refill authorization
- Self-monitoring techniques of drug therapy
- Drug storage information
- Special dispensing information, such as "what to do in the event of a missed dose?"

Note: Although this counseling requirement is for Medicaid recipients, most pharmacies will offer to provide this information to all patients.

Step 3: Reassessment and Therapeutic Adjustment Based on Patient Response and Outcomes

The **first 2 steps** in the development of individualized drug regimens and treatment plans involve the **diagnosis of the patient** and choice of what is believed to be the **best treatment option** based on individual patient and drug factors. However, many patients require therapeutic adjustments following the initial patient reassessment, due to inappropriate dosing, unacceptable adverse effects and other issues.

After drug therapy has been instituted, a pharmacist is in a unique position to identify and help resolve clinical issues that may negatively impact the desired outcome.

Table 28-7. Reasons for Inadequate Therapeutic Response, Therapeutic Failure or Appearance of Unwanted Adverse Effects

Reason for Unsatisfactory Effect	Clinical Resolution and General Comments
Inappropriate medication(s) for the disease	• Most common reason for an inappropriate medication is a misdiagnosis. • Continued monitoring and reassessment of the patient will help determine the correct diagnosis and thus an appropriate therapeutic interchange can be made.
Appearance of unwanted or unanticipated adverse effects	• Adverse effects are the #1 reason for patient noncompliance and therapeutic interchange. • Adverse effects also account for 5% of all hospital admissions. • All medications are associated with adverse effects that may be more or less severe in an individual patient. • Some adverse effects are situationally beneficial (drowsiness in diphenhydramine for a patient wanting to rest) or situationally non-beneficial (drowsiness in diphenhydramine for a patient operating heavy machinery). • Dosage decreases or therapeutic interchanges are the most common resolutions.
Inappropriate route of administration	• The route of administration may be essential for therapeutic success. For example, oral dosing would not be recommended for a condition requiring immediate attention. • A noncompliant patient may require once daily dosing or an IM injection. • ***See the Pharmaceutics chapter (Pharmaceutical Dosage Forms) in the NAPLEX text for more information.***
Underdosing/overdosing	• The initial dose is generally based on a "one size fits all" dosing schedule or a dosing algorithm. • Underdosing generally results in subtherapeutic effects and minimal side effects. • Overdosing generally results in supra-therapeutic effects and more extreme side effects.

(Continued)

Reason for Unsatisfactory Effect	Clinical Resolution and General Comments
Therapeutic duplication	• Occurs when a patient takes more than one medication with the same therapeutic effect resulting in an extension of the desired therapeutic effect or appearance of unwanted side effects. • Resolution involves decreasing the dose of one or both medications or discontinuation of one of the medications.
Drug interactions (drug-drug and drug-disease)	• Very common cause of adverse effects • May be pharmacokinetic (affects ADME of a drug) or pharmacodynamic (impacts the therapeutic effect) • Especially important with low therapeutic index drugs • Resolution includes therapeutic adjustment of the original or new medication, dosage change and/or alteration of dosing schedule
Patient tolerance to certain drugs	• The 2 main issues are disease progression (requiring an increased dose) or actual tolerance to the medication itself (commonly seen with opioid analgesics).
Poor patient compliance	• Determining the reason for noncompliance is essential. • Is the noncompliance related to drug cost, side effects, dosing schedule, or other? • Once the reason for the noncompliance is identified then the pharmacist can recommended a therapeutic change.
Expired medicines	• Unless otherwise stated, most medications have an average expiration date of 1 year (eyedrops, insulin, etc are different). • Medication should NOT be used past the expiration date.
Improper storage conditions	• Medications should be stored at room temperature (approximately 65–75°F) in a space with no more than 60% relative humidity and away from direct sunlight. • Medications should NOT be stored in a bathroom medicine cabinet.
Manufacturing errors (rare but can be seen)	• Major errors are widely publicized.
Substandard medicines	• Seen more commonly with herbal/natural products and medications imported from other countries. • Recommend only using FDA approved medications for major conditions. • Natural/herbal products should only be purchased from quality manufacturers.

One or more of the above may be present.

Step 4: Continued Patient Evaluation and Follow-up

Evaluation, monitoring, and follow-up occur in the final stage of most pharmacotherapeutic drug regimens and treatment plans. Clinicians understand the saying "**What works well today may not work well tomorrow.**" Thus, patients with chronic conditions need to be continually evaluated and monitored to ensure that their previously prescribed therapeutic regimen is "still" facilitating optimal clinical outcomes.

The frequency of monitoring is dependent on:

- The disease state
- The severity of the disease state
- Presence of contributing factors (concomitant disease states, medications, process of aging)

When the patient evaluation identifies an inadequate or inappropriate therapeutic effect ultimately impacting patient outcomes, a therapeutic adjustment occurs by the prescribing clinician or from a specialist referral.

- There is continual "back and forth" movement between steps 3 and 4.
- Remember, there is an evolving "process" for developing individualized drug regimens and treatment plans.

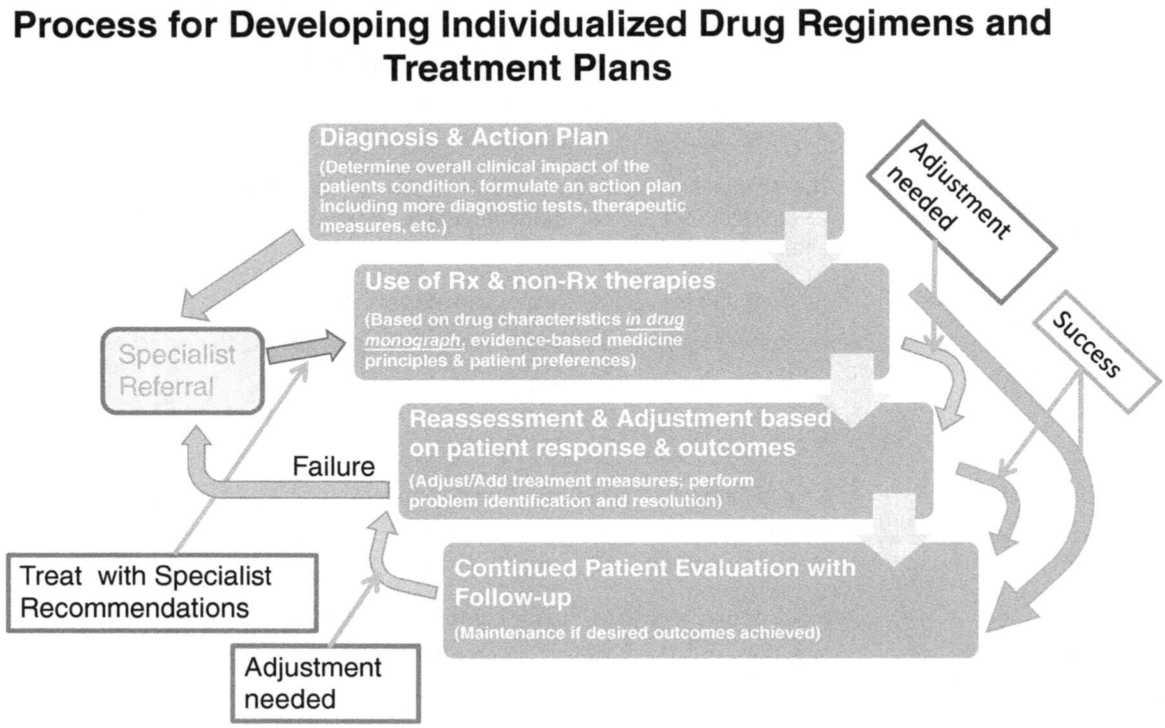

Figure 28-2. Process for Developing Individualized Drug Regimens and Treatment Plans

PROMOTION OF NONPRESCRIPTION AND NATURAL PRODUCTS

Advising patients on nonprescription (over-the-counter or OTC) and natural products is an integral part of providing patient care for many pharmacists. Although pharmacists have very limited "prescribing" privileges, these types of medicinal products can be recommended by pharmacists.

- A comprehensive review of both nonprescription and natural products is found in the Over-the-Counter Medications chapter in Kaplan's *NAPLEX Strategies, Practice, and Review* book.
- Additional information on the use of nonprescription and natural products can be found in this text in Chapter 28 ("Promotion on Nonprescription and Natural Products"), Chapter 2 ("Enzymology and Coenzymes and Kinetics"), and Chapter 7 ("Pharmacognosy and Dietary Supplements").

NAPLEX Reference

Over-the-Counter Medications chapter

OTC (nonprescription) and natural drug products play an increasingly vital role in America's health care system. OTC drugs are defined by the FDA as drugs that are safe and effective for use by the general public without seeking treatment by a health professional.

- Patients are able to obtain OTC products without seeking medical advice; however, many patients prefer to consult their pharmacist prior to the purchase of an OTC product.
- Before recommending any OTC medication for a medical condition, the clinical pharmacist should consider all treatment options AND ask about ALL current medical conditions or medications that could interact with the proposed therapy.

Dietary Supplements

Dietary supplements, such as natural and herbal products, are also available without a prescription; however, the FDA does not have the authority to review dietary supplement products for safety effectiveness before they are marketed.

The following statements are made by the FDA regarding dietary supplements:

- It is recommend that "**Before making decisions about whether to take a supplement or natural product, a person should talk to their healthcare provider.**"
- **Unlike all FDA approved prescription and nonprescription drugs, supplements and natural products are NOT intended to treat, diagnose, prevent, or cure diseases.** That means supplements should not make claims, such as "reduces pain" or "treats heart disease." Claims like these can only legitimately be made for FDA approved drugs, not dietary supplements. However, this does NOT mean that these products lack pharmacological effects.
- Dietary supplements include ingredients such as vitamins, minerals, herbs, amino acids, and enzymes.
- Dietary supplements are marketed in forms such as tablets, capsules, softgels, gelcaps, powders, and liquids.
- If a dietary supplement (or herbal product) contains a NEW ingredient, manufacturers must notify the FDA about that ingredient prior to marketing. However, the notification will only be reviewed (not approved) by the FDA.
- Dietary supplement labels must contain the following statement: **This statement has not been evaluated by the Food and Drug Administration. This product is not intended to diagnose, treat, cure, or prevent any disease.**

Risks associated with dietary (and herbal) supplements include the following:

- Dietary supplement products are NOT evaluated by the FDA for safety and effectiveness before they are marketed.
- Many supplements contain active ingredients that have strong pharmacological effects.
- When used without medical supervision, dietary (and herbal) supplements can result in sometimes severe drug-drug or drug-disease interactions causing significant negative health consequences.
- Long-term effects are unknown.
- Dietary supplement manufacturers do not always follow some rules regarding labeling and the claims made about their products.

Despite the aforementioned risks, most dietary supplements are safe provided the labeled instructions are followed. However, the pharmacist should be aware of the benefits and risks for each natural (herbal) product.

MANAGEMENT OF DRUG TOXICITY AND DRUG-INDUCED DISEASES

The clinical approach to the diagnosis and initial management of a patient who is suspected of ingesting a toxic substance OR a toxic dose of a medication (i.e. opioid, digoxin, amitriptyline) varies for each toxic exposure.

The clinical presentation of a toxic exposure (ingestion, inhalation, etc) varies widely depending upon:

- Drug characteristics (pharmacology, presence of excipients, etc.)
- Amount ingested
- Timing of last ingestion

- Current level of drug in the body
- Presence of existing comorbidities or interacting medications
- Other patient unique characteristics (pharmacogenomics, acute reactions, etc.)

Key factors to consider:

- The severity can range from asymptomatic to critically ill.
- The "current condition" of the patient can rapidly deteriorate.
- Acute toxicity should be considered for both children and adults with an acute onset of altered mental status, multiorgan system dysfunction, acute CNS, respiratory or cardiac complications.

Table 28-8. Goals and Objectives of Toxicology Case Management

Goal/Objective	Comments
Recognition of toxicity	• The first step is recognizing that the patient's symptoms are related to a poison or toxic amount of a medication.
Provide initial evaluation and stabilization	• ABC (Airway, Breathing, Circulation) • Vital signs, mental status, and pupil size • Pulse oximetry, cardiac monitoring, ECG • Protect airway • Obtain IV access • Rule out hypoglycaemia • Naloxone for suspected opiate poisoning • Rapid toxicology screen • Gastrointestinal decontamination (orally administered medications within the past hour) • Cervical immobilization if trauma is suspected
Identify the agent(s) involved	• Evaluate results of a drug screen, patient history, prescription bottles, items found at scene of initial toxicity, suicide note, etc. • Recognize the clinical characteristics of each toxic agent ***(See "Common Toxic Syndromes" in this section as well as the "Adverse Effects" sections of the high-yield drug tables in the Therapeutics chapters of the NAPLEX text)***
Administer antidote	• Administer antidote if available or enhance elimination of toxic substance (if appropriate). • ***See Antidotes chapter of the NAPLEX text***
Assess the severity of toxicity (short-term and long term effects)	• Comprehensive physical and mental status examination as well as laboratory findings should be considered.
Prevention of future toxicity	• Depends on the nature of the toxicity. • If the toxicity occurred as a result of a drug overdose, assist patient in getting substance use disorder treatment (rehabilitation, counseling, 12 Step Program). • If the toxicity occurred as a result of accidental medication toxicity, determine the source of the toxicity and make therapeutic adjustments to prevent future toxicity.

The following 3 tables provide high-yield information on the characteristics of common toxic syndromes and heavy metal poisoning, as well as commonly used antidotes.

Common Toxic Syndromes

Table 28-9. Signs, Symptoms, and Interventions or Antidotes for Common Toxic Syndromes

Compound(s)	Signs and Symptoms	Interventions and Antidotes
AChE inhibitors	Miosis, salivation, sweats, GI cramps, diarrhea, muscle twitches → seizures, coma, respiration failure	Respiratory support; atropine + pralidoxime (for irreversible AChE inhibitors)
Atropine and muscarinic blockers	↑ HR, ↑ BP, hyperthermia (hot, dry skin), delirium, hallucinations, mydriasis	Control cardiovascular symptoms and hyperthermia + physostigmine (crosses blood–brain barrier)
Carbon monoxide (>10% carboxyHb)	Nausea and vomiting, dyspnea with hyperventilation, mydriasis, vertigo; cardiovascular signs prominent, ↓ BP, syncope, ↑ HR, arrhythmias	Hyperbaric O_2 and decontamination (humidified 100% O_2 okay in mild overdose)
CNS stimulants	Anxiety/agitation, hyperthermia (warm, sweaty skin), mydriasis, ↑ HR, ↑ BP, psychosis, seizures	Control cardiovascular symptoms, hyperthermia, and seizures— +/– BZs or antipsychotics
Opioid analgesics	Lethargy, sedation, ↓ HR, ↓ BP, hypoventilation, miosis, coma, respiration failure	Ventilatory support; naloxone at frequent intervals
Salicylates (ASA)	Confusion, lethargy, hyperventilation, hyperthermia, dehydration, hypokalemia, acidosis, seizures, coma	Correct acidosis and electrolytes—urinary alkalinization, possible hemodialysis
Sedative-hypnotics and ethanol	Disinhibition (initial), lethargy, ataxia, nystagmus, stupor, coma, hypothermia, respiratory failure	Ventilatory support—flumazenil if BZs implicated
SSRIs	Agitation, confusion, hallucination, muscle rigidity, hyperthermia, ↑ HR, ↑ BP, seizures	Control hyperthermia and seizures—possible use of cyproheptadine, antipsychotics, and BZs
Tricyclic antidepressants	Mydriasis, hyperthermia (hot, dry skin), 3Cs (convulsions, coma, and cardiotoxicity) → arrhythmias	Control seizures and hyperthermia, correct acidosis and possible arrhythmias

Heavy Metal Poisoning

Signs and symptoms are distinctive but usually result from inhibition of –SH groups on enzymes and regulatory proteins.

Table 28-10. Signs, Symptoms, and Interventions or Antidotes for Heavy Metal Poisoning

Metals and Source	Signs and Symptoms	Interventions and Antidotes
Arsenic (wood preservatives, pesticides, ant poisons)	*Acute:* gastroenteritis, hypotension, metabolic acidosis, garlic breath, "rice water" stools, torsades, seizures *Chronic:* pallor, skin pigmentation (raindrop pattern), alopecia, stocking glove neuropathy, myelosuppression	Activated charcoal, **dimercaprol** **Penicillamine** or succimer
Iron (medicinal for anemias and prenatal supplements)	*Acute* (mainly children): severe GI distress → necrotizing gastroenteritis with hematemesis and bloody diarrhea, dyspnea, shock, coma	Gastric aspiration + carbonate lavage, **deferoxamine** IV
Lead (tap water, leaded paint chips, herbal remedies, gas sniffing, glazed kitchenware, etc.)	*Acute:* nausea and vomiting, GI distress and pain, malaise, tremor, tinnitus, paresthesias, encephalopathy (red or black feces) *Chronic:* multisystem effects—anemia (↓ heme synthesis), neuropathy (wrist drop), nephropathy (proteinuria, failure), hepatitis, mental retardation (from pica), ↓ fertility and ↑ stillbirths	Decontamination—gastric lavage + **dimercaprol** (severe) or EDTA or succimer (penicillamine if unable to use dimercaprol or succimer) Children: **succimer** PO
Mercury (elemental in instruments); salts used in amalgams, batteries, dyes, electroplating, fireworks, photography	*Acute:* vapor inhalation—chest pain, dyspnea, pneumonitis; *Acute:* inorganic salt ingestion—hemorrhagic gastroenteritis, acute tubular necrosis, shock; *Chronic:* organic Hg—CNS effects, ataxia, paresthesias, auditory and visual loss, loosening of teeth	**Succimer** PO or **dimercaprol (IM)** Activated charcoal for oral ingestion, then support with succimer PO or dimercaprol (*not* IV)→ causes redistribution of Hg to the CNS →↑neurotoxicity

Antidotes

Table 28-11. Summary of Antidotes

Antidote	Type of Poisoning
Acetylcysteine	Acetaminophen
Atropine + pralidoxime (for irreversible AChE inhibitors)	AChE inhibitors—physostigmine, neostigmine, and pyridostigmine; organophosphates, including insecticides, such as malathion and parathion
Deferoxamine	Iron and iron salts
Digoxin immune F(ab)	Digoxin
Dimercaprol (BAL)	Arsenic, gold, mercury, lead; oral succimer for milder lead and mercury toxicity
EDTA	Backup in lead poisoning, then for rarer toxicities (Cd, Cr, Co, Mn, Zn)
Esmolol	Theophylline, beta agonists
Ethanol, fomepizole	Methanol or ethylene glycol
Flumazenil	Benzodiazepines, zolpidem, zaleplon

(Continued)

Antidote (cont.)	Type of Poisoning (cont.)
Naloxone	Opioid analgesics
Oxygen	Carbon monoxide
Penicillamine	Copper (e.g., Wilson's disease), iron, lead, mercury
Physostigmine	Anticholinergics: atropine, antihistamine, antiparkinsonian—*not* tricyclics
Protamine	Heparins
Vitamin K	Warfarin and coumarin anticoagulants
Activated charcoal	Nonspecific: all oral poisonings except Fe, CN, Li, solvents, mineral acids, or corrosives

MISUSE, ABUSE, OR THERAPY NON-ADHERENCE

Opioids, stimulants, and sedative-hypnotics are the most commonly misused and abused classes of prescription medications. You should be able to differentiate between misuse, abuse, and non-adherence for these medications, as well as recognize the symptoms of a substance use disorder caused by these and illicit substances.

- **Medication misuse**: improper use of a medication for the wrong purpose
- **Medication abuse**: overindulgence in or dependence on an addictive substance, such as alcohol, prescription medication, or illicit substance
- **Medication nonadherence**: deviation from prescribed dosing schedule for any reason (i.e. overuse, underuse, cost-prohibitive, etc.)
- **Medication risky use**: consumption of drug/alcohol amounts that increase the likelihood of health consequences (i.e. injury, DUI, interpersonal problems); may include characteristics of misuse, abuse or nonadherence)
- **Substance use disorder**: DSM-IV criteria of substance abuse and substance dependence were combined into single substance-use disorders (in DSM-5) specific to each substance of abuse within a new "addictions and related disorders" category; each disorder is characterized as having a mild, moderate, or severe subtype.

Substance Use Disorders (DSM-5)

Substance use disorders (for alcohol, prescription medication, and illicit substances) are comprised of 11 different criteria/symptoms. The use of one of these substances leads to clinically significant impairment or distress as manifested by 2 or more of the following occurring within a 12-month period (Derived from Diagnostic and Statistical Manual of Mental Disorder, Fifth Edition. Arlington, VA, American Psychiatric Association, 2013):

- Taking the substance in larger quantities or for longer than intended
- Wanting to decrease the amount or stop using the substance but unable
- Spending a lot of time getting, using, or recovering from use of the substance
- Cravings and urges to use the substance
- Not managing to do what you should at work, home or school, because of substance use
- Continuing to use, even when it causes problems in social or interpersonal relationships
- Reduction in or completely giving up important social, occupational or other activities because of use

NAPLEX Reference

Pain Management chapter:
"Opioids"

Psychiatric Disorders chapter:
"Stimulants"
"Sedative-hypnotics"
"Non-benzodiazepine sedative hypnotics"

- Continually using the substance despite danger or negative consequences
- Continuing to use, even when aware that a physical or psychological problem could have been caused or made worse by the substance
- Continually needing more of the substance to attain desired effect (development of tolerance)
- Development of withdrawal symptoms that can be reversed by taking the substance

Severity of Disorder

- 2 or 3 symptoms = mild substance use disorder
- 4 or 5 symptoms = moderate substance use disorder
- ≥ 6 symptoms = severe substance use disorder

Substance Use Disorders General Comments

- The addiction pathway in the brain is primarily a dopamine pathway.
- Activation of this pathway accounts for the "positive reinforcement" feeling and makes us want to repeat the action that triggered that feeling.
- Pharmacological properties of the opioids, stimulants, and sedative-hypnotics can be found in Kaplan's NAPLEX Review book in the Pain Management and Psychiatric chapters.

Alcohol Use Disorder

Table 28-12. Alcohol Use Disorder

Intoxication	Withdrawal	Treatment	Comments
• Impaired judgment, slurred speech, uncoordination, unsteady gait, stupor, coma, confusion, falls, memory problems	• General: Nausea and vomiting; Diaphoresis; Agitation and anxiety; Headache; Tremor; Visual and auditory hallucinations • Delirium tremens: General + tachycardia, hypertension, hyperthermia, seizures	• Disulfiram (Inhibits alcohol dehydrogenase) • Acamprosate • Benzodiazepines (Prevent seizures) • Naltrexone (decreases alcohol craving) • Supportive care • Alcoholics Anonymous	• Defined as a chronic, relapsing disorder that results from a variety of genetic, psychosocial, and environmental factors • Characterized by physiologic/physical dependence & tolerance as well as symptoms of withdrawal when consumption is interrupted
Complications • Hepatic: Liver disease, hepatic steatosis, cirrhosis, hepatic failure, hepatic encephalopathy • Wernicke-Korsakoff syndrome associated with a triad of symptoms (ophthalmoplegia, confusion, ataxia) and can be treated with thiamine • Mallory Weiss syndrome (results in lacerations at the gastroesophageal junction caused by excessive vomiting) • Delirium Tremens (life-threatening withdrawal) • Other complications include acute/chronic pancreatitis, Wernicke encephalopathy, alcoholic ketoacidosis, seizures			

Opioid Use Disorder

Table 28-13. Opiate Use Disorder

• Examples include heroin, oxycodone, morphine			
Intoxication	**Withdrawal**	**Treatment**	**Comments**
• Euphoria, pupillary constriction, constipation, drowsiness, slurred speech, respiratory depression, bradycardia, coma, death	• "Flu-like" muscle aches, nausea or vomiting, yawning, piloerection, lacrimation, rhinorrhea, fever, insomnia, pupillary dilation (7–10 days)	• For intoxication naloxone (short half-life); • Clonidine, methadone, buprenorphine for withdrawal • Supportive care • Alcoholics Anonymous	• Mechanism of Action: Stimulate μ, κ, δ receptors; μ receptors are most important in a substance use disorder

Stimulant Use Disorder

Table 28-14. Stimulant Use Disorder

• Examples include amphetamines, cocaine, methamphetamine			
Intoxication	**Withdrawal**	**Treatment**	**Comments**
• Euphoria, hypervigilance, anxiety, stereotyped behavior, grandiosity, paranoia, tachycardia, pupillary dilation	• Depression, fatigue, increased appetite unpleasant dreams, suicide	• Antipsychotics or benzodiazepines for intoxication; • Bromocriptine, amantadine, bupropion for withdrawal	• Amphetamines MOA (enhance release DA, NE) • Cocaine MOA (prevents re-uptake of DA, NE)

Sedative, Hypnotic, or Anxiolytic Use Disorder

Table 28-15. Sedative, Hypnotic, or Anxiolytic Use Disorder

• Benzodiazepines: Alprazolam, Lorazepam, Temazepam, Diazepam • Barbiturates: Phenobarbital, Pentobarbital			
Intoxication	**Withdrawal**	**Treatment**	**Comments**
Impaired judgment, slurred speech, uncoordination, unsteady gait, stupor, confusion, falls, coma, death	Autonomic hyperactivity tremors, hyperactivity; hallucinations, anxiety, grand mal seizures, death	Mechanical ventilation in overdose; sodium bicarbonate to alkalize urine in barbiturate overdose	• Benzo MOA: ↑ ***frequency*** of $GABA_A$ channel opening • Barbs MOA: ↑ duration of $GABA_A$ channel opening

Other Common Substances of Abuse

Table 28-16. Other Substances of Abuse

Substance	Intoxication	Withdrawal	Treatment
Cannabis (e.g., marijuana, hashish)	Impaired motor coordination, anxiety, slowed reaction time, impaired judgment, conjunctival injection, dry mouth, increased appetite, psychosis	None	Abstinence and support
Hallucinogens (e.g., LSD, mescaline, ketamine)	Hallucinations, illusions, anxiety, ideas of reference, depersonalization, pupillary dilation, tremors, uncoordination	None	Supportive counseling, talking down, antipsychotics or benzodiazepines for intoxication
Phencyclidine (PCP, angel dust)	Assaultive, combative, impulsive, agitated, nystagmus, ataxia, hypersalivation, muscle rigidity, decreased response to pain, hyperacusis, paranoia, unpredictable violence, psychosis	None	Nonstimulating environment, restraints, vitamin C, benzodiazepines, or antipsychotics for intoxication
Caffeine	Restlessness, agitation, insomnia, diuresis, GI disturbances, excitement	Headache, fatigue, drowsiness, nausea or vomiting (1–4 days)	Analgesics for withdrawal
Nicotine	None in usual doses but more depression (2×), impotency, traffic accidents, and more days lost from work	Irritability, depressed mood and heart rate, increased appetite, insomnia, anxiety	Nicotine patch, education, bupropion, varenicline, bromocriptine

Co-Occurring Mental Health Disorders

The Substance Abuse and Mental Health Services Administration (SAMHSA) is a branch of the U.S. Department of Health and Human Services tasked with improving the quality and availability of prevention, treatment, and rehabilitative services in order to reduce illness, death, disability, and cost to society resulting from substance abuse and mental illnesses.

- SAMSHA reports that up to 50 percent of individuals in mental health treatment also have a substance use disorder.
- Similarly, up to 70 percent of patients in substance use disorder treatment programs have a mental health condition.

Based on these statistics, pharmacists should monitor for symptoms of a substance use disorder in patients receiving psychotropics and provide information on recommended treatment options.

Table 28-17. Stages of Change in Overcoming A Substance Use Disorder

Stage	Comments
Pre-contemplation	• Substance user does not realize that there is a problem
Contemplation	• Substance user realizes there is a problem but is unwilling to take steps necessary to correct the problem
Determination	• Substance user is prepared to take necessary action to treat their disease but has not yet made corrective actions.
Action	• Act of taking necessary steps to change the behavior • May include attending a drug/alcohol rehabilitation center +/– psychotherapy • Introduction to 12-step programs • Taking 'condition specific' medication to treat withdrawal and/or prevent recurrence
Maintenance	• Maintaining the changed behavior • Take medication to prevent recurrence (condition specific) • May include psychotherapy, drug counseling, 12-step program
Relapse	• There is a return to previous behaviors and abandonment of changes made; the patient returns to 'active addiction' • After relapse occurs, the patient would then be considered in the pre-contemplation stage. • Although listed as a stage in the process, **relapse does NOT have to occur**

PRACTICE QUESTIONS

1. A 57-year-old male calls the pharmacist asking about a good medication for "muscle aches" that have been progressively getting worse over the past few days. Which of the following medications are likely causing this symptom?

   A. Amiodarone
   B. Atorvastatin
   C. Digoxin
   D. Metoprolol
   E. Sertraline

NAPLEX Question Reference

Therapeutics chapters: all end of chapter questions

2. Monitoring of therapeutic blood levels is inappropriate for all of the following EXCEPT

   A. Azithromycin
   B. Fluoxetine
   C. Simvastatin
   D. Warfarin
   E. All of the above should not have their blood levels monitored

3. The number 1 reason for patient noncompliance is which of the following?

   A. Adverse reactions
   B. Convenience of administration
   C. Cost
   D. Ease of administration
   E. Route of administration

4. If a patient is prescribed enalapril, they should be monitored for which of the following?

   A. Gingival hyperplasia
   B. Hypercalcemia
   C. Hyperkalemia
   D. Hypokalemia
   E. Thyroid function abnormalities

5. A patient receiving gentamicin should have trough levels taken:

   A. 10 minutes after the next dose is given
   B. 30 minutes before the next dose is administered
   C. 30–60 minutes after the next dose is administered
   D. Gentamicin has a long half-life so trough levels can be taken anytime in the dosing interval.
   E. It is not recommended to obtain drug levels for gentamicin.

6. A patient comes to the pharmacy with cough and cold symptoms and requests an over-the-counter medication to help treat their symptoms. The pharmacist should refer the patient to the physician if they have which of the following conditions?

   A. Hyperlipidemia
   B. Psoriasis
   C. Reflux esophagitis
   D. Type 2 diabetes
   E. The pharmacist should not refer patients with any of the above conditions

7. Dietary supplements include which of the following?

   A. Amino acids
   B. Enzymes
   C. Herbal products
   D. Vitamins
   E. All of the above are classified as dietary supplements

8. A hospitalized patient is administered protamine because which of the following was likely dosed too high?

   A. Digoxin
   B. Heparin
   C. Midazolam
   D. Morphine
   E. Warfarin

9. A patient diagnosed with a substance use disorder is noted to have miosis and respiratory depression during abuse and mydriasis during withdrawal. The most likely diagnosis is which of the following?

   A. Alcohol use disorder
   B. Hallucinogen use disorder
   C. Opioid use disorder
   D. Sedative, hypnotic, or anxiolytic use disorder
   E. Stimulant use disorder

10. Which of the following is NOT a required stage in overcoming a substance use disorder?

   A. Action
   B. Determination
   C. Contemplation
   D. Maintenance
   E. Relapse

Answers and Explanations

1. **The correct answer is B.** Knowledge of a drug's mechanism of action, indications, primary adverse effects, major drug interactions and special considerations is required for the FPGEE. Atorvastatin (choice B) is used for the treatment of hypercholesteremia and is associated with myopathy, tendon rupture, rhabdomyolysis, acute renal failure and hepatotoxicity. Amiodarone (choice A) causes hypo- or hyperthyroidism, blue-gray skin discoloration (long-term use), corneal deposits, pulmonary toxicity and cardiac arrhythmias. Digoxin (choice C) causes nausea, visual disturbances, AV block and severe bradycardia. Metoprolol (choice D) causes bradycardia, sexual dysfunction, heart failure symptoms (at higher doses). Sertraline (choice E) causes serotonin syndrome and sexual dysfunction.

2. **The correct answer is E.** Information obtained from therapeutic drug levels (TDL) is used to individualize drug dosages so that the resultant drug concentrations will be maintained within a target range. However, obtaining a TDL is not appropriate for most medications. Examples include: drugs with wide therapeutic windows/wide therapeutic indexes (i.e. azithromycin – choice A); drugs with a better means of assessing effects and toxicity (i.e. simvastatin is monitored by cholesterol level – choice C; warfarin is monitored by INR – choice E); drug concentrations are expected to be within normal therapeutic range but other variables impact drug toxicity (i.e. hypokalemia precipitates digoxin toxicity) AND drugs without established therapeutic drug levels (i.e. fluoxetine – choice B).

3. **The correct answer is A.** Once drug therapy has been instituted, a pharmacist is in a unique position to identify and help resolve clinical issues that may negatively impact the desired outcome. There are numerous reasons for patient noncompliance; however, adverse effects are the number 1 reason for noncompliance and therapeutic interchange. All medications are associated with adverse effects that may be more or less severe in an individual patient. Also, adverse effects account for 5% of hospital admissions.

4. **The correct answer is C.** On the FPGEE, candidates should know the major adverse effects for the most commonly prescribed medications. Knowledge of these adverse effects can help the pharmacist formulate a better monitoring plan. For example, enalapril (and other ACE inhibitors) are associated with the development of hyperkalemia, angioedema, chronic cough, and hypotension. Gingival hyperplasia (choice A) is seen with phenytoin, cyclosporine, phenobarbital and calcium antagonists. Hypercalcemia (choice B) is seen with thiazide diuretics, Vitamin D, estrogens, antiestrogens, androgens and lithium. Hypokalemia (choice D) is seen with most diuretics except spironolactone, eplerenone and triamterene. Thyroid function abnormalities (choice E) are seen with amiodarone, lithium and interferon-alpha.

5. **The correct answer is B.** Appropriate sample timing for therapeutic drug monitoring (TDM) is generally considered as important as the actual drug concentration obtained. Important sample timing considerations include: Drug trough levels should be taken approximately 30 minutes BEFORE the administration of the next dose (choice B); Drug peak levels should be taken approximately 30–120 minutes following the administration of a medication (choice C). Medications with long half-lives can be taken anytime during the dosing interval (i.e. amiodarone; not gentamicin – choice D).

6. **The correct answer is D.** Cold symptoms are one of the most common reasons why patients seek a pharmacist's advice. Common "cough and cold" medications include decongestants, cough suppressants, mucolytics and analgesics. Before recommending a medication, pharmacists must consider all drug-drug and drug-disease interactions. Patients should be referred to a physician when they have serious underlying medical conditions (i.e. asthma, heart failure, diabetes) that could be negatively impacted with decongestants, for example. Although all diseases and medications should be considered, choices A, B and C should not be impacted by the use of cough and cold medications.

7. **The correct answer is E.** Dietary supplements are also available without a prescription and they do not fall under the jurisdiction of the FDA's regulatory process. Hence these "natural products" are NOT evaluated for safety and effectiveness before they are marketed. Dietary supplements include ingredients, such as vitamins, minerals, herbs, amino acids, and enzymes. Dietary supplement labels must contain the following statement: This statement has not been evaluated by the Food and Drug Administration. This product is not intended to diagnose, treat, cure, or prevent any disease.

8. **The correct answer is B.** This question could have been rewritten as "Protamine is the antidote for an overdose of which of the following?" Protamine is the antidote for heparin overdose. Digoxin immune F(ab) is the antidote for digoxin (choice A) overdose. Flumazenil is the antidote for benzodiazepine (i.e. midazolam – choice C) overdose. Naloxone is the antidote for opioid (i.e. morphine – choice D) overdose. Vitamin K is the antidote for warfarin (choice E) overdose.

9. **The correct answer is C.** The FPGEE candidate should know the characteristics of each substance use disorder. With respect to this question, opioids cause miosis and respiratory depression during abuse and mydriasis during withdrawal. A complete list of all of the symptoms of intoxication and withdrawal are found in the tables of the "Misuse, Abuse, or Therapy Nonadherence" section of this chapter.

10. **The correct answer is E.** For substance use disorders, change is not an event that occurs suddenly; it is a process that gradually unfolds over time. As this process begins to unfold, a patient's motivation also changes. The most popular framework for discussing motivation to change is the Stages of Change Model. According to the model, the 6 stages are as follows: Pre-contemplation (user does not realize that there is a problem); Contemplation (user realizes there is a problem but is unwilling to take steps necessary to correct the problem); Determination (user is prepared to take necessary action); Action (act of taking steps to change the behavior); Maintenance (maintaining the changed behavior) and Relapse (return to previous behavior). Of these stages, relapse is NOT a required stage. Patients with a past medical history of a substance use disorder can successfully remain in the maintenance stage.

Index

Q

R

S

T

U

V

W

Y

Z

www.ingramcontent.com/pod-product-compliance
Lightning Source LLC
LaVergne TN
LVHW082021200926
848481LV00010B/2901